THE LETTERS
OF
KING GEORGE IV
1812–1830

IN THREE VOLUMES

VOLUME I

LONDON
Cambridge University Press
BENTLEY HOUSE

NEW YORK · TORONTO
BOMBAY · CALCUTTA · MADRAS
Macmillan

TOKYO
Maruzen Company Ltd

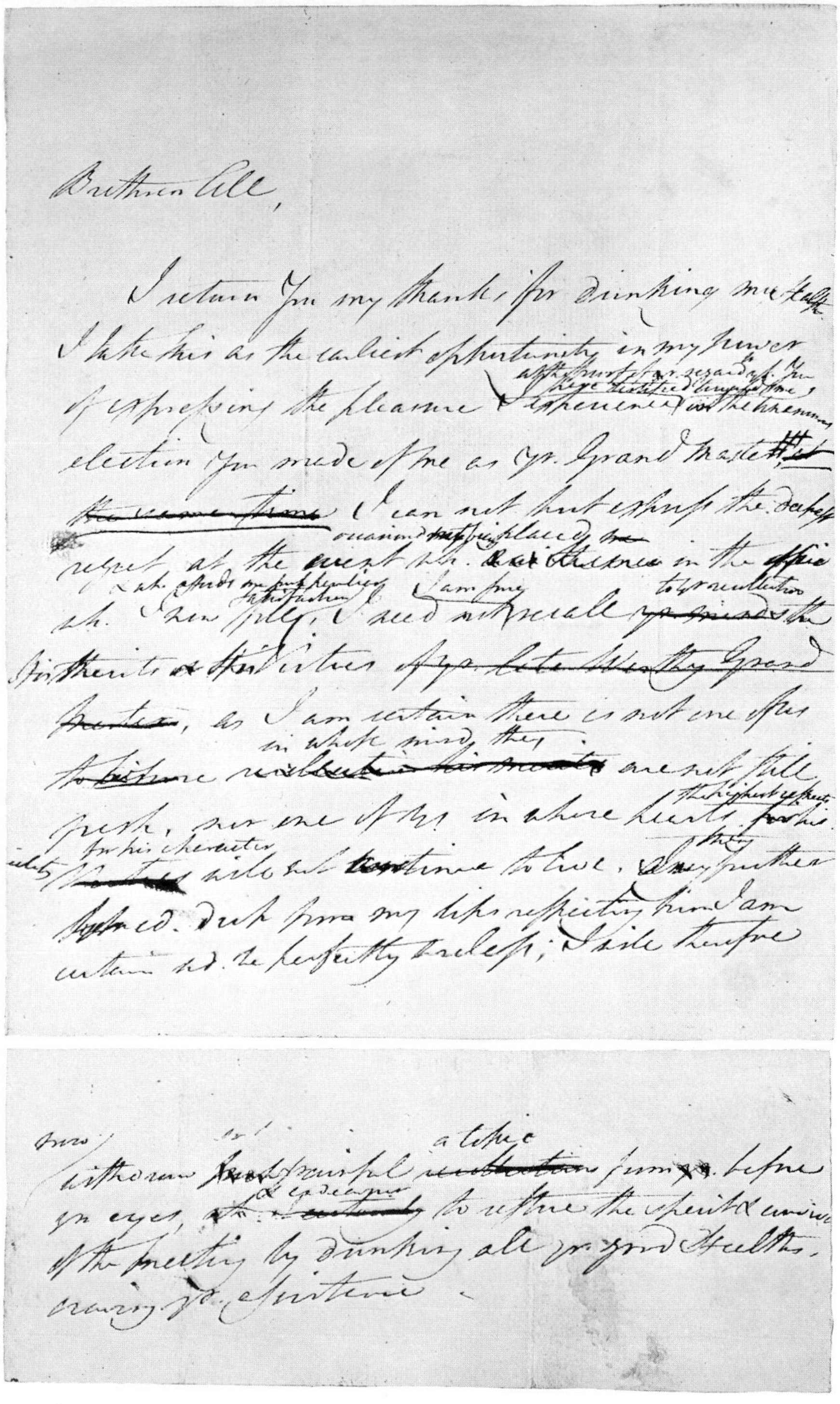

Brethren All,

I return you my thanks for drinking my health. I take this as the earliest opportunity in my power of expressing the pleasure & [illegible] at the election you made of me as yr. Grand Master [illegible] I can not but express the deepest regret at the occasion which placed me [illegible] in the office [illegible] I am sure I need not recall to your recollection the virtues of [illegible], as I am certain there is not one of us in whose mind they are not still fresh, nor one of us in whose hearts the highest respect for his character will not continue to live. Any further [illegible] from my lips respecting him I am certain wd. be perfectly useless; I will therefore

now withdraw so painful a topic from your [illegible] before your eyes, & endeavour to restore the spirits & [illegible] of the meeting by drinking all yr. good Healths, craving yr. [illegible]

The Prince Regent's draft of his speech to the Masons, 1812.

THE LETTERS
OF
KING GEORGE IV
1812–1830

Published by authority of
HIS LATE MAJESTY KING GEORGE V

Edited by

A. ASPINALL
M.A., Ph.D.
Lecturer in Modern History,
University of Reading

With an Introduction by

PROFESSOR C. K. WEBSTER
M.A., Litt.D., F.B.A.
Stevenson Professor of International History,
London School of Economics, University of London

IN THREE VOLUMES

VOLUME I

February 1812—January 1815

CAMBRIDGE
AT THE UNIVERSITY PRESS
1938

*The frontispiece is a reproduction
of the Prince Regent's Draft of
his Speech to the Masons, 1812*

CONTENTS

VOLUME I

1812

February

March

May

June

July

August

September

October

CONTENTS

1813

January

February

March

April

May

June

July

August

September

October

November

December

1814

January

April

May

June

1814   CONTENTS

CONTENTS

VOLUME II

1815

January

February

March

April

June

July

March

April

July

August

September

October

November

December

1817

January

February

March

May

July

August

September

October

November

December

1818

January

February

March

July

August

September

October

November

December

1819

January

February

March

April

May

July

November

December

1820

January

February

March

April

May

June

1820 CONTENTS

[xxxi]

November

December

1821

January

1822

1823

January

CONTENTS

VOLUME III

1823

October

November

December

1824

January

February

March

November

1825

January

February

March

June

July

[xliii]

August

September

October

December

1826

January

February

March

November

December

1827

January

February

March

[xlix]

October

November

December

[1]

1828

January

July

August

September

October

November

December

1829

November

December

1830

January

February

March

April

May

September

November

1831

April

CORRIGENDA

No. 67   Date should be "Tuesday morning, 5th May 1812."

  ,, 129   ,,   ,,   "Thursday July 15th [16th] 1812."

  ,, 372   ,,   ,,   "Sunday [19th Dec. 1813]."

  ,, 536   ,,   ,,   "8th [? 7th] March 1815."

  ,, 537   ,,   ,,   "Tuesd^y March 8th [7th] 1815."

PREFACE

THE GEORGE IV PAPERS, from which a selection has been made for publication with the gracious permission of his late Majesty King George V, may be conveniently referred to under five headings.

First, the main body of papers, which, until recent times, were housed at Apsley House. After the King's death (26 June 1830) his papers were disposed of in accordance with the terms of his Will, which was signed on 30 June 1824 in the presence of four Cabinet Ministers: Lords Eldon, Westmorland and Bathurst, and Peel. The three Executors, Lord Gifford, Chief Justice of the Common Pleas, the Duke of Wellington, and Sir William Knighton, Keeper of the Privy Purse and the King's confidential adviser, were instructed to examine the Royal Papers carefully, and to destroy or preserve such as should seem to them proper.[1] In August 1833 the Duke destroyed the Fitzherbert letters, in circumstances detailed in Wilkins' *Mrs Fitzherbert and George IV*; and much private correspondence of a similar nature was burned during the King's lifetime.[2] Lord Gifford died in 1826 and Knighton ten years later, Wellington being thereafter the sole surviving Executor. The George IV papers therefore remained at Apsley House until 1912, when, at the suggestion of the late Duke of Wellington, they were added to the Royal Archives at Windsor. By some mischance, however, a small quantity of letters had been left behind after the King's death, and was all but lost in 1835 when an old iron box, containing four smaller boxes, was sold by public auction at Buckingham House to a man

[1] Sir William Knighton wrote to the Duke of Wellington on 9 March 1832: "...I can assure his present Majesty when the late King made his Will, it was not done without the deepest consideration, in reference to those in whom His Majesty should commit the sacred trust connected with his private papers. Lord Gifford, who was Attorney General [*sic*] at the time, was joined with your Grace and myself, because His Majesty had a high opinion of him as a man and a lawyer, and, to use His Majesty's own words when speaking to me on the subject, 'I will add this gentleman's name, because, should the Duke and yourself require law, in the arrangement of my affairs, you should not have to seek it from a stranger'. But had Lord Gifford lived, he was to have had nothing to do with the examination of the King's private papers. I mention this to show that the sole confidence was placed in your Grace and myself. No man, as a man, independent of every other consideration, was ever more sincerely attached to another, than was George the fourth to your Grace. His Majesty's affection and confidence in myself were unbounded, and although it may not be very pleasant to speak of oneself, yet I am satisfied that I hold the language of truth, whatever his present Majesty may be pleased to think of me, that the late King was fully justified in adopting the confidence he was graciously pleased to place in me, because His Majesty found that my integrity, judgement and sincerity were invaluable to him!..." (*Windsor Archives.*)

[2] King George V decided in January 1913 that the letters of Georgiana, Duchess of Devonshire, should be burnt. (Lord Esher, *Journals and Letters*, iii. 117.)

named Jackson who lived in Shoe Lane. When opened, one of these boxes was found to contain some of George IV's letters, but Jackson was an honourable man and made no attempt to use them improperly. Hearing of this, Lord Duncannon, the Lord Privy Seal, suggested to Wellington that the man Jackson should be given a present of fifty pounds for the papers, which should then be sealed up and sent to Apsley House. This was presumably done.

The George IV papers also include a large quantity of family letters addressed to or written by his mother, his wife, his daughter, his brothers and sisters, various European Sovereigns and Princes connected with the Royal Family by marriage, and also from Sir William Knighton. Much of this private correspondence is of no historical importance, and I have selected from it only such letters as throw light on public events or on the characters of the writers. Amongst the Knighton papers is a portion of his manuscript Diary, parts of which were published by his widow in 1838. Whether the Windsor manuscript is merely a first draft which Knighton himself revised so as to make it more suitable for publication, or whether Lady Knighton herself touched up the manuscript, I do not at present know. It is to be assumed that these papers fell into Wellington's possession after Knighton's death.

Second, by some curious accident a number of other letters, 89 in all, including copies of some of the King's letters to Lord Liverpool, Lord Castlereagh, and Canning, were never handed over to Wellington. Lord Esher, who as Deputy-Constable and Lieutenant-Governor of Windsor Castle, had control of the Royal Archives during the reign of King Edward VII, wrote on the fly-leaf of the volume in which these letters are now bound (22 June 1913): "This correspondence was found at Windsor and did not form part of the papers brought from Apsley House in 1912." On 21 August 1905 he had written: "Princess Henry has just sent me a book full of letters from George IV's Ministers to him, about 1822–1827—found by her among some of the Queen's things. It has always been a mystery where the letters of George III and George IV and William IV disappeared to, but it is possible that as these have turned up, others may follow."[1]

Third, in 1935 a considerable quantity of documents relating to the Delicate Investigation, the Milan Commission and the Queen's Trial, was transferred to Windsor from the Public Record Office.

Fourth, at the same time a large quantity of Queen Caroline's papers, which had been in the possession of her solicitors in London (the firm is now Messrs Leman, Chapman and Harrison) since her death, was

[1] Lord Esher, *Journals and Letters*, II, 100.

handed over to the Royal Archives. These two collections of documents throw much light on the activities of the Milan Commission and its agents on the one hand, and of the Queen's legal advisers and their agents both in England and on the Continent, on the other hand. The sordid story of Queen Caroline's relations with George IV is already sufficiently familiar, and it behoves the editor of the King's papers to select for publication only such documents as are of especial interest and importance.

Finally, letters written by George IV and other contemporary members of the Royal Family have very occasionally either been presented to, or purchased by, the Royal Archives.

Andrew Dickie, confidential clerk and afterwards partner in the banking house of Messrs Coutts and Co., claimed that no accounts were ever more carefully or more scrupulously kept than those of George IV's Privy Purse. From these accounts, which are also preserved in the Royal Archives, I have selected items which illustrate George IV's patronage of the arts, and also his generosity. A number of letters from Sir Thomas Lawrence, Sir Richard Westmacott and others, which have been discovered in these boxes of Accounts, are also reproduced.

George IV was the first British Sovereign to employ a private secretary.[1] The appointment of Colonel McMahon, to whom so many of the letters printed in Volume I are addressed, on 17 March 1812 as Private Secretary to the Prince Regent, at a salary of £2000 a year, was at once challenged as unconstitutional by the Whig Opposition in the House of Commons. The Grenvillite Charles Wynn explained the Whig view of the constitutional position. The Home Secretary was the Sovereign's Private Secretary, and it was that Secretary of State's business to wait upon the King and to take the King's pleasure with regard to the business laid before him. Since the Prince Regent resided in London, Ministers had an opportunity of daily consultation with him, so that there was no need for a Private Secretary to communicate the result of their deliberations and advice. If the Private Secretary was not a Privy Councillor, it was a most unconstitutional proceeding to impart to him the secrets of the Cabinet. If he was a Privy Councillor he was bound by his oath to give his own advice: and it was improper that the Cabinet's advice to the Sovereign should be subject to the revision of his Private Secretary. In his reply the Prime Minister (Perceval) denied that Colonel McMahon would be competent to communicate the pleasure of the Prince Regent in any way that could authorise any one to act upon

---

[1] Leaving out of account, that is, the appointment of Colonel Taylor in 1805. The circumstances were unprecedented: George III was then nearly blind.

it with official responsibility; and Castlereagh pointed out that McMahon would have no legal responsibility and that it would be unreasonable to expect future Sovereigns to possess George III's exceptional habits of business. This public discussion had the effect of inducing the Prince Regent to charge his Private Secretary's salary to the Privy Purse rather than to public funds. The Ministers loyally defended an appointment which it is clear they secretly disliked, and the new office was abolished in 1822.

The correspondence now published covers only the period of the unrestricted Regency and the Reign, but one may express a hope that the early correspondence of George IV, and, too, the later correspondence of George III, will ultimately be published.

Historians and the wider reading public have reason to be grateful to his late Majesty King George V for his generosity in sanctioning the publication of these letters. I owe and have great pleasure in expressing my thanks to Mr O. F. Morshead, His Majesty's Librarian and Assistant-Keeper of the Royal Archives, Miss Mackenzie, the Registrar of the Archives, and Prof. C. K. Webster, for the valuable assistance and advice which they have generously given me in every stage in the preparation of these volumes. All students of the period will be grateful to Prof. Webster, who made use of a considerable portion of the George IV papers when writing his *Foreign Policy of Castlereagh*, 1812–15, for contributing an Introduction which sums up the historical value of this correspondence. I am greatly indebted to the Duke of Wellington, the Marquis of Londonderry, Lord Harewood, Viscount Sidmouth, the late Lord Hatherton, Sir Ernest Scott, Mr R. Bagot and Mr E. P. Stapleton for permission to quote from their private MSS. I have drawn extensively for illustrative material from the Auckland, Huskisson, Liverpool, Peel, Ripon, Sir Robert Wilson, and Vansittart MSS. in the British Museum, and the Granville MSS. in the Public Record Office.

The text of the letters has been interfered with as little as possible. The original spelling but not the capitalisation has been retained. Punctuation and paragraphing have been occasionally modified. Skeleton names and other abbreviations have been expanded where necessary, the missing letters being enclosed within square brackets. Unless it is otherwise stated, the letters are holograph letters. Important letters already in print are briefly referred to in the text. In deference to a desire expressed by his late Majesty King George V, such injunctions as "secret", "confidential", etc. have been omitted.

A. A.

January 1938

NOTE ON THE SYSTEM OF REFERENCES

Add. MSS.	British Museum Additional Manuscripts.
Ann. Reg.	The Annual Register.
Bagot	George Canning and his Friends. Ed. by Capt. Bagot. 2 vols. London, 1909.
Bathurst	Historical Manuscripts Commission Report on the MSS. of Earl Bathurst. London, 1923.
Brougham	The Life and Times of Henry, Lord Brougham, written by himself. 3 vols. London, 1871.
Cast. Corr.	Memoirs and Correspondence of Viscount Castlereagh. Ed. by the third Marquis of Londonderry. 12 vols. London, 1848–53.
Colchester	The Diary and Correspondence of Lord Colchester. Ed. by his son, Lord Colchester. 3 vols. London, 1861.
Croker	The Correspondence and Diaries of John Wilson Croker. Ed. by L. J. Jennings. 3 vols. London, 1884.
Dropmore MSS.	Historical Manuscripts Commission Report on the MSS. of J. B. Fortescue. Vol. x. London, 1927.
Ellenborough Diary	Lord Ellenborough's Political Diary, 1828–30. Ed. by Lord Colchester. 2 vols. London, 1881.
Further Memoirs	Further Memoirs of the Whig Party. By the third Lord Holland. Ed. by Lord Stavordale. London, 1905.
Gent. Mag.	The Gentleman's Magazine.
Hardcastle	Life of John, Lord Campbell. Ed. by the Hon. Mrs Hardcastle. 2 vols. London, 1881.
Hastings MSS.	Historical Manuscripts Commission Report on the MSS. of Reginald Rawdon Hastings. London, 1934.
Herries	E. Herries, Memoir of J. C. Herries. 2 vols. London, 1880.
Huskisson Papers	The Huskisson Papers. Ed. by Lewis Melville. London, 1931.
Knighton	Memoirs of Sir William Knighton, by Lady Knighton. 2 vols. London, 1838.
Life & Opinions of Earl Grey	Some Account of the Life and Opinions of the second Earl Grey. By Lieut.-Gen. Hon. C. Grey. London, 1861.
Memoir of Sydney Smith	A Memoir of the Rev. Sydney Smith, by his daughter, Lady Holland. 2 vols. London, 1855.
Miss Knight	Autobiography of Miss Cornelia Knight. 2 vols. London, 1861.
New, *Durham*	Lord Durham, by Chester W. New. Oxford, 1929.

Parker — Sir Robert Peel, from his Private Papers. Ed. by C. S. Parker. 3 vols. London, 1891–99.

Parl. Deb. — Hansard's Parliamentary Debates.

Pellew — The Life and Correspondence of Viscount Sidmouth. By G. Pellew. 3 vols. London, 1847.

Plumer Ward — E. Phipps, Memoirs of Robert Plumer Ward. 2 vols. London, 1850.

Regency Memoirs — Duke of Buckingham and Chandos, Memoirs of the Regency. 2 vols. London, 1856.

Reid, *Durham* — S. J. Reid, Life and Letters of the Earl of Durham. 2 vols. London, 1906.

Romilly — Memoirs of the Life of Sir Samuel Romilly, written by himself. Ed. by his sons. 3 vols. London, 1840.

Stapleton — A. G. Stapleton, George Canning and his Times. London, 1859; E. J. Stapleton, Some Official Correspondence of George Canning. 2 vols. London, 1887. (The reference is to the earlier work when the number of the volume is not given.)

Taylor Papers — The Papers of Lieut.-Gen. Sir Herbert Taylor. Arranged by Ernest Taylor. London, 1913.

Twiss — H. Twiss, Life and Correspondence of Lord Eldon. 3 vols. London, 1844.

Walpole, *Perceval* — Spencer Walpole, Life of Spencer Perceval. 2 vols. London, 1874.

Wellington Desp. — Despatches of the Duke of Wellington, 1799–1818. Compiled by Lieut.-Col. Gurwood. 12 vols. London, 1837–8.

W.N.D. — Despatches, Correspondence and Memoranda of the Duke of Wellington. Ed. by his son. 8 vols. London, 1867–80.

W.S.D. — Supplementary Despatches, Correspondence and Memoranda of the Duke of Wellington. Ed. by his son. 12 vols. London, 1858–72.

Wellesley Papers — The Wellesley Papers. Ed. by the editor of the Windham Papers. 2 vols. London, 1914.

Wilkins — W. H. Wilkins, Mrs Fitzherbert and George IV. 2 vols. London, 1905.

Williams — The Life and Correspondence of Sir Thomas Lawrence. By D. E. Williams. 2 vols. London, 1831.

Yonge — C. D. Yonge, The Life and Administration of the second Earl of Liverpool. 3 vols. London, 1868.

INTRODUCTION

THE PAPERS OF GEORGE IV are as unsatisfactory as the life which they portray. What proportion has survived the curious treatment meted out to the correspondence of a King, we do not know. Whatever the merits possessed by the secretaries of George IV, the systematic arrangement of his papers was not one of them. Some were destroyed by Knighton immediately before, or soon after, the King's death. Others must have been lost in changes of residence. Others were taken away by McMahon and Bloomfield. That there should be many more we know from other collections and by references in the letters themselves. But George IV did not write very much himself. Sometimes, indeed, gout in his hands or other ailments made it physically impossible for him to do so. He needed an emotional stimulus, and, perhaps, at times other stimulants as well. He preferred, as he says, *tête-a-tête* 1432 conversations to the more laborious, and, as he sometimes found, more dangerous written communications. But he wrote many more letters than are given here, and some of them survive elsewhere. His secretaries also must have written much more on his affairs than appears amongst his papers. But the whole system of correspondence was obviously a loose one. And without an ordered system all collections of correspondence tend to lose many important documents, and especially the drafts of letters despatched and copies of letters between other correspondents necessary to the understanding of the whole.

Dr Aspinall has had, therefore, an especially difficult task in editing this correspondence, where there are so many gaps and where the reference to persons is often allusive. His exceptional knowledge of the unpublished as well as printed papers of the other important actors in the Georgian scene has enabled him to elucidate much that would otherwise be obscure. Only those who have worked on these papers in their original setting at Windsor can appreciate the labour, thought and intimate acquaintance with other archives that were necessary to render them intelligible to the reader.

That so much has survived we may be grateful, when we remember that practically the whole of the correspondence of William IV has been destroyed, though he wrote much more as a King than George IV did, and had a most capable private secretary. It was only because Prince Albert taught Queen Victoria the value of a systematic record of the personal correspondence and interviews of the Sovereign that there came into existence at Windsor the magnificent collection of letters and memoranda that illustrates her reign.

When George IV did compose his own letters, they show the exuberance and vitality characteristic of the family. Clearly his thoughts went faster than his pen, yet he generally found it necessary to clothe them in so many periphrases and circumlocutions that the total effect is often confused and nebulous. Some of those which are copies, and even some which are in his own hand, are altogether different, and show that they have been drafted by others. But when he writes to his mother or his daughter or to Knighton, there is much repetition and looseness of construction. The same thing is apparent in the letters of the Duke of Cumberland, and William IV's letters to Grey and Palmerston show the same lack of conciseness and sometimes of point. But these intimate letters of a son, father or brother reveal a good deal of the character of George IV, and are more satisfactory sources than the gossip and diaries of an age that was too brilliant to possess a very strict regard for the truth.

Many of them are also of great value for the understanding of public affairs. For the monarch was still the real head of the State, and if the power of George IV was less in many respects than that of his father, it was greater than that of any of his successors. In the unreformed House of Commons the patronage of the Crown was still a powerful instrument, and the King's relations to individuals still affected all the operations of government. He was the centre of a small and intimate society which shared amongst its members the offices of the State and the perquisites of power. Though it was ultimately responsible to the rather wider body which composed Parliament, and to public opinion, already served by a free Press, the initiation and conduct of policy was in its hands, and but little of this could be carried out efficiently except with the cordial co-operation of the King. The members of this closed circle knew one another from childhood, and their private relations had a good deal of influence on their public relations. They intermarried, and the ramifications of their families were always cropping up when appointments to public office were in question. The affairs of State were, indeed, to a certain extent handled like those of a large family. Everyone knew about the incomes and the domestic circumstances of all the rest. The relations of wife and husband and father and son, the difficulties as to marriage and less respectable alliances, the pressure of debts and the possibilities of inheritance were daily canvassed in frank and familiar conversations and letters.

In this intimacy George IV had fully shared as a young Prince, and if as Regent and King he was shut off from some of it, he always retained his immense interest in the private lives of the individuals with whom he had to deal. His own misfortunes had made him on the whole sensitive to those of others. The correspondence is full of his acts of kindness towards old friends and dependents, and the testimony of his own papers is amply confirmed by evidence from other sources. Other monarchs have had the same princely generosity which George IV could display, but few could show, as he sometimes did, so much spontaneous and warm understanding of the difficulties of others, or judge less severely the frailties of friends and companions. On the other hand, at times George IV treated his dependents with an unnecessary harshness, which was, perhaps, due as much to his sensibility as to his selfishness.

George IV had a very vulnerable past which often appears in these pages. The boon companions, the mistresses, the debts, and above all the wife of his youth, were constantly menacing his peace of mind. He paid heavily for past follies, and for conduct that was sometimes worse than folly. He had shown himself at times not only vicious, but selfish and reckless of the happiness of others. He had made enemies as well as many friends. Moreover, his assumption of royal power necessarily turned some of his friends into enemies when it was realised that the Regent had a different conception of his duties than had seemed likely when he was Prince. The Whigs never forgave him for what they considered to be a betrayal. Yet, after the death of Fox, the Prince of Wales had really had no political party, and there can be no question as to where the political duty of the Regent lay in 1812. The worst charge that can be made against him in this period is, indeed, that he coquetted in 1820 with the idea of bringing in the Whigs to obtain his personal ends. But the fact that circumstances made it imperative for him to entrust the Government to the Tories, when he at last wielded the power of the Crown, was an additional embarrassment to a Prince who had once been regarded as a member of the Whig party and had taken part in the councils of its camarilla.

George IV had also inherited the most inconvenient and expensive homes in Europe, over which he had, while he was still only Regent, imperfect control. George III seems to have revelled in personal discomfort. At any rate, though Windsor Castle was partly rebuilt, he had no sense of creating a physical background worthy of the Crown of England. The palaces in London were small and badly placed, and Windsor was as bleak as a barracks. George IV on the other hand had as Prince of Wales built at Brighton the luxurious Pavilion, an absurd folly from which his finances never recovered. Though, as we are now beginning to realise, it had more beauty than the Victorian age admitted, it was never worth the large sums devoted to it. His Ministers 647 tried to insist in 1816 that he should reduce this expenditure. Yet 1541, George IV also created for himself in the Royal Lodge a private home 1542 of some comfort, at any rate as a summer residence, and some artistic beauty. Later he saw that what was really needed was a Windsor made 1502, habitable and splendid, but there is only small reference to the financial 1583 difficulties which were caused by this most justifiable expenditure. Of the failure of both the King and his Ministers to plan for an appropriate royal residence in London we are still painfully conscious, for it led to Buckingham Palace replacing Carlton House. By 1828 "poor little Nash", its architect, was being hard pressed, and had not much chance 1563 of obtaining the Baronetcy which the King in vain urged Wellington to confer on him.

There are many references to the King's love of the arts, and the large sums of money that he spent in gratifying his taste. There is not much of interest in the official correspondence with the President of the 1591 Royal Academy, Sir Benjamin West. But the list of the Lawrence pictures with the sums of money which he obtained for each is a valuable contribution to one side of artistic history. The origin of the plan of painting all the prominent personages of the Great Alliance which 438 overthrew Napoleon is seen in the rather extravagant letter of Lady 451 Anne Barnard, though it does not seem that Lawrence accepted her suggestion of introducing himself into the gallery, if only in celestial 1210 guise. George IV's support of Canova, "the Phidias of modern times", is shown in another letter. If a full list of all such sums could be obtained, the amount would be a great one. All artists competed for the royal favour, and sometimes obtained from royal good nature a sitting which 290 they endeavoured later to convert into an order for the portrait. There 1058, is only a passing reference to the surrender of the library of George III 1059 to the nation, one of the most important acts of George IV.

The most intimate of these papers are those which George IV addressed to and received from the members of his own family. In his youth he had had many passages of arms with his much tried if rather severe mother. The memoirs of Sir Herbert Taylor, the Queen's Secretary, had already revealed a few letters of this later correspondence, but those given in this collection add a good deal to our knowledge. There is much warmth in them, as much at any rate as Queen Charlotte's 314, stiffness and aridity would allow. They reveal also how George IV 319 wished his own position as the head of a victorious nation to be regarded,

and if he exaggerated the importance of the rôle he had played, it must 340,
be remembered that without his countenance and support the Tory 420
Ministry would have found it difficult to carry out the inflexible and
well-sustained effort of 1812–14. These informal letters also allude to 393
some of the family jokes, and one or two perhaps give the impression
that they have been written after dinner. They show amongst other 185
things the Regent's care for the happiness of his sisters, whose spirit
had been broken and health undermined by the tyranny exercised over 411
them at Windsor. No doubt one of his reasons for trying to obtain for
them more access to London was that they might assist him with the
introduction of Princess Charlotte into social life. But it is clear he had
real affection for "the dear sisterhood", and discounting all conven-
tionalities of language, they certainly regarded him as a splendid brother.
One of them, the Queen of Wurtemberg, had been absent from England 362–
since 1791, and one of the amusing episodes of these volumes is her 364
attempt to exploit her connection with her brother for financial purposes 385,
and to protect the position of her Consort, who had been one of the most 579
slavish of Napoleon's vassals and even as late as December 1813, after
he had changed sides, was suspected of treachery to his new allies. She
got little by this, but the invitation to visit England, leading to the
mission of little Sir Thomas Tyrwhitt, can only have been inspired by 422,
brotherly duty, for there was no public advantage to be gained from it. 424

The relations of George IV to his extraordinary brothers also do him
credit. With all except the Duke of Sussex he remained in cordial
relations, and it must be admitted that they all presented difficult
problems to their brother. The intelligence and energy of these men
have been underrated because of the peculiar life they led. George III
had no idea how to bring up a royal family, and in any case he began to
develop insanity while his sons were still young men. They were never
given a suitable education or suitable duties to absorb their energies. It
was inevitable under these circumstances, and in that age, that they
should entangle themselves with undesirable characters, especially as
they were as passionate and self-willed as their brother. They had all,
however, a surprising vitality which enabled them to survive the most
extravagant mistakes and misdemeanours without lack of self-confidence
or ambition. All of them, too, were able, like George IV himself, to
inspire real affection in women as well as much self-seeking and mer-
cenary devotion, and several at long last obtained wives who gave them
a family life, which, if experienced earlier, might have saved them from
immense harm and satisfied their dominant and passionate natures. The
Dukes of York and Cambridge showed themselves to be capable ad-

ministrators when they were given positions of trust and responsibility, and if the Duke of Cumberland had a despot's nature, his later rule over Hanover was far more successful than anyone had considered possible and survived the great upheaval of 1848.

The correspondence with the Duke of York is meagre. There must have been a good deal more on official or semi-official business, though the two brothers often saw one another. The Duke of York's private life was as lamentable as his public duty was well performed. He was an excellent Commander-in-Chief with a practically insane wife and a private menage that was as ludicrous as it was degrading. He abandoned himself in his declining years to the lowest creatures, yet George IV, who had on one or two occasions in their youth vexatious disputes with his brother, treated him with great kindness. Not many brothers would 1122 have gone into debt with the Rothschilds to the tune of £50,000 to come to the assistance of a man like the Duke of York. Yet George IV seems to have done so spontaneously and cheerfully, no doubt partly to save family disgrace, though the financial difficulties of the family had been a public scandal for years, but also from genuine kindness of heart. It has been customary to explain this kindness, as well as that to the Duke of Cumberland, as due to fears that otherwise the King's own dark secrets might be exposed. But there is no evidence for this charge, and the generosity of George IV is attested by many similar acts.

The long series of letters from the Duke of Cumberland is full of items of interest. For the most part these long epistles seem to have 440 been left without answers, though it is clear that some were sent which have been lost. George IV could do little to satisfy his brother's main ambitions, legitimate enough, for military command or the government of Hanover. For the first the Duke had, perhaps, already shown himself unfit. But he was made of tougher stuff than the Duke of Cambridge, and it would probably have been better for Britain if he had been allowed to employ his energy in Hanover during the period 1814–37. In his quarrel with the Queen over his marriage, the Duke cuts by no means a bad figure. The Queen's refusal to recognise the Duchess after first warmly approving of the marriage is due to some cause not entirely explained, for the reasons she herself gives are hardly sufficient for so 603 drastic an action. The Regent did his best to help his brother, and if he failed to produce any effect on his inflexible mother, he won the thanks of the Duke and Duchess and an affection which he retained to his death. It may of course be explained on the thesis that the Duke of Cumberland simply wished to get all he could out of his fraternal connection. But the letters seem too artless and revealing for such an explanation. Both brothers were aware of their unpopularity, though of course the hatred of Cumberland was far more deep-seated, since he had none of the tact and bonhomie that George IV could display on occasion. Both were subjected to merciless attacks by the pamphleteer and the caricaturist, which at that time were peculiarly savage. Even worse, both were ridiculed in the cruellest fashion. And it was perhaps this mutual misfortune that drew them together. At any rate at one time the Duke avowed that his brother was his only friend in the royal family, 747 and the judgment is confirmed by all the other evidence of the period, while Wellington describes the Duke as the favourite brother of the King. 1561 Even during the terrible scandal concerning Lady Graves, it was only Knighton's insistence that prevented the King from receiving the Duke 1577 as usual. The Duke certainly knew the kind of gossip that would interest his brother. The wealth of information that he sent him on the military uniforms of the Continent must have given much pleasure, for on such matters the Regent considered himself the first authority of his time— as, perhaps, he was. The comments on foreign royalties and especially 348 the criticisms of Alexander, who showed so little tact in his treatment of the Duke, are also of some importance. For they prepared the mind of the Regent for that dislike of the Tsar and his sister which was the consequence of the visit of 1814, and had some effect on the diplomacy of that important period.

There are also some small additions to our information on the Duke of Cumberland's activities in England during the crisis of Catholic Emancipation. It is at this period that the hostility against him is at its highest, for he was virtually chief of the ultra-Tory party, and the moderate Tories joined the Whigs in the outcry against him. Wellington 1557 did his best to get rid of him, and the King was also anxious for him to leave England. But this seems to have been due to the fact that Lady 1561 Conyngham disliked him and was afraid of his influence with his brother. Cumberland's actions have always been attributed to the lowest motives, and there can be no doubt of his violence and rudeness. But he had genuine convictions of the dangers of Catholic Emancipation, and in a sense was the most consistent politician of his time. It appears probable also that the private scandals that collected round his name were partly due to the hatred he had aroused by his political tactics.

The other brothers are less in evidence. The Duke of Clarence shows 730, his instability of character by the proposal to marry a commoner, and 739 his curious conduct as Lord High Admiral. His eccentricity was nearer 1525 madness than that of any of his brothers, but he fortunately found at last a wife who was able to moderate it and at the same time to allow him

to demonstrate the attachment which he undoubtedly felt for his
778 children by Mrs Jordan. The Duke of Kent only appears in his unfortunate attempt to cope with his financial difficulties by obtaining
permission from Parliament to raise money by means of a lottery
790 on an unsaleable house. His unexpected death produces a rather
critical estimate of him by the Duke of Cumberland. The Duke of
Cambridge's sensible letters from Hanover are a contrast to those of
the rest of the family. But he was really a weaker character, and later
fell a victim to Metternich's wiles, of which his brother Cumberland
was always conscious. The Duke of Sussex was the one brother who
remained a Whig. This was one reason for his bad relations with the
Regent. His attitude towards the Princess of Wales was, however, the
chief reason why the quarrel became permanent. George IV seems
675, to have made no response to the letters which his brother wrote to him
756 on escaping an assault and on the death of his mother, but they shook
hands in 1820. The return of the Queen, however, again made the Duke
an enemy—this time for life.

The relations of George IV to his wife have been the theme of innumerable writers, most of them concerned to emphasise the sensational,
ludicrous and humiliating aspects of this extraordinary marriage. There
can be no doubt that George IV had towards his wife a fierce, vindictive
hatred which her misfortunes and humiliations did nothing to assuage.
The more generous side of his character was completely submerged in
all his dealings with her. He seemed to be able to forgive false and
unworthy conduct in nearly everybody else, and to take his full share of
blame for a breach of friendship or a betrayal of trust. But for his wife,
in spite of his own conduct towards her, he had no forbearance. Such
an attitude can never be justified, but these letters reveal once more the
complete degradation of her character. Few will now dispute that she
767 was guilty of adultery, as Brougham's brother testifies in a notable
letter. But for such conduct her husband had given her every excuse.
Far worse is her attempt to corrupt, or at least compromise, her own
daughter. I confess that I could not bring myself to believe this charge
when I first learnt of it from the memoirs of the time and the reports
508, of the Ambassadors. But the additional evidence furnished in these
509 papers, in the testimony of Princess Charlotte to her Aunt and in the
547A admissions of Captain Hesse himself, leave little room for doubt. Whatever the motive and whether all the possible consequences were realised
or not, Caroline is revealed as unfit for decent human relations. A recent
biography of George IV, one of the most impartial and restrained that
has been written, calls her "irresponsible, unattractive and scatter-

[lxx]

brained", and adds that "her mind, always limited, delighted in what was vulgar and trivial". She was, indeed, not so much immoral as incapable of understanding in what morality consists. It is hard to imagine anyone less suited to be a Queen. Had not George's own conduct in regard to her been so inexcusable, neither then nor later would she have obtained so many defenders, of whom some at least were respectable and disinterested, though like all such characters she was scandalously exploited by those who served her. The worst about her husband's conduct to her, and about hers towards him and her daughter, seems now to be known. The degradation of her character was no doubt partly due to the treatment which she received. But the King's hatred, disgust and determination to be free of her can be understood, whatever view be held of the methods which he employed or of his disregard of the injury which he inflicted on his Throne and country in order to obtain his ends.

Towards his daughter George IV showed himself in a better light. Her upbringing gave him great anxiety of which these letters give many proofs. In view of all the facts he can hardly be blamed for wishing to keep her away from her mother, or desiring that she should be married as soon as possible. The Princess was saved by a streak of common sense from misfortunes which might have rivalled those of her own mother and done incalculable harm to her country. Nor was her conduct towards the Prince of Orange as capricious and selfish as some writers have suggested. The evidence of these papers goes to show that she broke off the match for very good reasons, and that outside influence, whether foreign or domestic, only played a subordinate part in bringing about her courageous and determined stand against her father. The Princess plainly says so herself, and her words imply that it was the 528, unbecoming conduct of the Prince in her presence which caused her to 531 have so invincible a repugnance to becoming his wife. We know that he committed this indiscretion, and there is other evidence of his 457 unpleasant habits at this time. Thus the intrigues of the Tatischeffs and 415 the Grand Duchess Catharine probably had little to do with the matter, while, though Brougham's support may have increased Charlotte's courage, it is not likely, in spite of his boasts, that it was a principal cause of her decision. Girl though she was, she was high spirited and determined, and found nothing that she wanted in the Prince of Orange. "The fact is," wrote Hobhouse in his Diary, "she despised him."

Prince Leopold became her husband as the result of one of Castle-reagh's discerning actions, for the King never liked him. He had been warned off the forbidden ground in 1814, as his tactful letter shows. 463

621 But he had made a good impression on Castlereagh and others at the Congress of Vienna, and steps were taken to bring these good opinions to the Prince Regent's notice. Princess Charlotte responded admirably to the tender and tactful treatment of her husband. Her attitude towards
548 her mother is more difficult to understand. Her consent to the cessation of all correspondence between them may have been due to the necessity of pleasing the Regent, but one would imagine it to be a natural emotion when she realised the dangers to which she had been exposed. It is
694 harder to account for her last pitiful letter to her mother, but it may perhaps be explained by the circumstances under which it was written.

The mistresses of George IV's youth do not appear much in these
16 papers since their letters were for the most part destroyed. There is a
504 reference to Lady Melbourne in a letter from her husband. Lady Jersey,
232, "that infernal Jezebel", as George IV calls her, was at one time driven
307, to begging for a pension. She tried to pay off old scores by making
359 mischief in the Orange marriage, but it does not seem that her influence
486 on Princess Charlotte was considerable. The refusal of George IV to
1588 recognise the marriage to Mrs Fitzherbert is stated once more in Knighton's Diary with some curious reflections that are not very convincing, but otherwise she only appears in connection with the Prince's
345, daughter, Minney Seymour, a tie that still connected them when all
1202–3 others had been severed. Neither Lady Hertford nor Lady Conyngham leaves any impress on these pages except through their families. Both these liaisons show that what George most desired after he had reached middle age was a domestic circle in which he could feel at ease rather than any very passionate attachment. Lord Yarmouth, Lady Hertford's
525 son, was of some importance in the early years of the Regency, but his influence soon waned. Lady Conyngham and her family were shrewd and hard-headed, but on the whole content with minor perquisites and much wealth. The main importance of the change of mistresses was that it made Castlereagh's position more difficult during the critical years 1820–21, for he was a connection of the Hertfords and his wife would not recognise Lady Conyngham, while Liverpool was involved in an open quarrel through his refusal to make Lord Conyngham Lord Chamberlain, and the tutor of his sons Canon of Windsor. But both these difficulties were overcome, and the King was reconciled to his Prime Minister before Castlereagh's death, largely by the latter's unceasing efforts, which may well have contributed to his final breakdown.
1432 Though early connections occasionally reappeared, as in the case of Harriette Wilson, or in the more artless appeal of Anna Crewe, "the

Queen of Bath", there is not much trace of the King's passionate youth 1434
in these pages.

Besides a substitute for a family, the King loved to have an intimate
circle in which he could be himself without too much of the apparatus of
a Court. To win his heart it was necessary to be able to show deference
without stiffness. His oldest friends now alive were Moira, Sheridan
and Erskine. Of these Moira was hopelessly compromised after the
failure to make a coalition ministry in 1812. He wisely refused the
Garter offered him by the Regent. He had, as he more than once points
out, sacrificed to his friendship with the Prince all other avenues to 139
fame and office. Moreover, the way of life thus forced on him had left
him hopelessly in debt, though that was common enough in other
circles. The way out of this situation was found in the Governor-
Generalship of Bengal, and it must have been an immense relief to the
Regent to be able to provide for Moira in so splendid a fashion, and at
the same time keep him at a safe distance. Like nearly all the most
intimate friends of George IV, he was a man of capacity, and he governed
with great success, as his letters show. His gifts to the Regent, his table 343,
on board ship, and his delight in his princely munificence in contrast to 405
his predecessor's meanness are amongst the most human touches in the 352
correspondence. The pain and suspicion that he felt in 1812 never completely wore off in spite of his success in his new position, and though 408
he avers that he could never believe that George IV would speak ill of
him, the mere mention of the subject shows the scars of the past. This is,
perhaps, also the explanation of his belief that Canning was plotting to
take his place. For though Canning certainly wanted to go to India,
there can be little doubt that this charge was entirely unfounded.

Sheridan was a hopeless case. He also was discredited in 1812, if he
had by then any credit to lose. The Prince has often been accused of
ingratitude for not rescuing him from the degradation into which he
sank, but he was an impossible person to help. The Prince did offer him 378
asylum in a royal palace so as to save him from arrest for debt and the
kind of royal services rendered to Sheridan in the past is seen in Sir 601
William Manners' claim to a peerage. Of other friends it must have
given the King pleasure to make Erskine a Knight of the Thistle in spite
of Erskine's attitude in 1820. But there were few of his old intimates
left, and as King he found his associates in the Conyngham family and
in the diplomatic circle. Noblemen like the second Duke of Northumberland, whose many letters of exhortation and advice survive, had no
influence on the King personally, but were tolerated because of their
political importance.

For his business a private secretary was indispensable to the monarch. It seems curious that any other view could have been held, but these papers, which throw much light on the method by which the royal power and influence were used, show how much the Ministers resented any intermediary between them and their Master. The exact position of such an official took more than a generation to work out. Sir Herbert Taylor had been regarded as an amanuensis for a blind Sovereign rather 993 than a private secretary. Dr Aspinall has alluded in his preface to the 31 constitutional objection. Thus not only was McMahon's salary refused 991, by Parliament, but on Bloomfield's retirement the Ministers protested 1017– against the appointment even as a private one. This was in accordance 18 with the King's mood at the time, and Knighton was never given the 1020– title of private secretary. No wonder Liverpool called the post an 21, "ambiguous situation". After Queen Charlotte's death the Regent 992 intended to appoint Sir Herbert Taylor to this position, but again the Ministers refused to allow it even if Taylor would have accepted so difficult a task. Taylor's integrity was never suspect, though both to Queen Charlotte and later to William IV he acted as adviser as well as secretary. His "situation is unknown to the Constitution", said a friend of Taylor's in 1830, "and in other hands would not be borne by the country".

Taylor came from a well-connected family. But McMahon, Bloomfield and Knighton, who, whatever the titles given to them, were private secretaries, had no such advantage and all were regarded with suspicion and dislike by the politicians. Bloomfield, who is alleged to have obtained his position by his musical talent, was in a sense the least 1017 successful of the three, for his temper seems to have failed to withstand 1007, the strain put upon it by the King's demands. His excessive estimate of 1008 his own merits is sufficiently proved by the letters of Liverpool and the King. McMahon was the least aristocratic, but he was honest and faithful, if not very competent. At first he was able to accommodate himself to the moods of his master, but he seems to have found the duties for which he had had little training much too exacting. His consolation was, as his patron the Duke of Northumberland pointed out, 141 that his position might be considered as "nearly a permanent" one in contrast to political office, and that it gave him constant access to the 1588 favours of the Crown. Knighton's account of his end, written long afterwards, is probably highly coloured.

1073 Knighton stands in a class by himself. Though refused both the title of secretary and the honour of being made a Privy Councillor, he held 1127 the key of the King's official papers and soon of every other royal activity. It is clear that in his last years George IV depended upon him to an extraordinary degree. His own memoirs had been edited with discretion, but the letters in this book reveal the intimacy with which he was treated. It must be remembered in reading the later ones that in the last three years of his life, the physical and mental condition of the King greatly deteriorated. But throughout their relations there is evidence that Knighton was a principal factor not only in the King's delicate private affairs, but also in his public duties. The success of Canning with the King was undoubtedly largely due to Knighton's assistance, and like Canning he seems to have been glad to break down the power of the aristocratic clique which dominated public life. This is no doubt one of the reasons why he is made to be a peculiarly sinister figure in the memoirs of the time. Motives of the lowest kind have been attributed to him, and he was even accused of appropriating the King's private fortune to himself.

In fact Knighton seems to have served the King with a rare fidelity. The delicate errands abroad were due in part to the King's fears for *Ap-* others, Lady Conyngham and the Duke of York, in part to a rash method *pendix* of raising money used in his youth. Knighton restored some order to the King's finances, checked his extravagances, mediated between him and his Ministers, and immensely increased his efficiency as a monarch. So far from Knighton abusing his trust, the evidence goes to show that without him the King might possibly have suffered the fate of his father, or at least had to relinquish control of public affairs. The King's pitiful appeals to him in the last three years of his reign are those of a diseased mind. The King's body also was enfeebled by the life which he had led and the remedies, including much laudanum, which his doctors prescribed. 1555 Few men had the combination of qualities necessary to deal with a situation so pregnant with danger to the State. The years 1827–30 were some of the most critical in English history. Catholic emancipation not only rent the dominant party in two, but raised exceptionally difficult personal problems for the Sovereign. If Wellington and Peel made great sacrifices in serving their distracted and diseased master at such a time, Knighton must also be given some credit for the eventual result. "Our friend the Premier", wrote Charles Arbuthnot, "relies on you. 1537 When you were absent some affairs went on not pleasantly, and he said to me it is all owing to *your* being away."

The King, had, of course, other important personal servants many of whom make an occasional appearance in these pages. The Officers of the Household were political appointments, but George IV made some attempt to make them personal ones also. The Whigs were able to use

946 this as an excuse in 1821. In 1812 Liverpool refused to make Lord
958 Conyngham Lord Chamberlain in spite of the earnestly pressed demands
966 of the King, though he was eventually made Lord Steward. Generally
the King was able to secure that congenial friends were given such posts,
1471 and he attached much importance to so staffing his Household ("my
family", as he called it).

A continual source of annoyance was the insistence of older men that
promises of honours in return for political or personal services made as
a young man by George IV, or even by his father, should be carried out
now that he had inherited the royal power. In this matter the King
could shelter himself to some extent behind his Government. As
Liverpool pointed out, such promises could not "be regarded as neces-
989 sarily binding on succeeding Kings, or on successive Administrations".
449 But the persistency of such claimants is shown in the correspondence
581 with the Earl of Carhampton and Sir William Manners. Importunity,
710 indeed, had no limits. The Marquis of Anglesey asked for the Garter in
a letter of condolence on the death of Princess Charlotte. Sir Henry
1125 Bate Dudley relied on a royal promise made through Moira more than
1505 thirty years previously. Lord Torrington claimed reward for services
1175 rendered by his ancestors one hundred years before. Hussey Vivian was
most candid of all in his request for a comfortable billet. He was in
need, and he had "daily opportunities of seeing that unless a man makes
known his wishes (even when the kindest intentions are entertained
towards him), he is constantly passed over".

There is a good deal of interesting information on the King's share
in the formation of Cabinets. Of these the most important of all was that
of 1812, when the Regent first wielded the full power of the Crown.
Much of the correspondence connected with these negotiations was
published at the time, an innovation which much shocked Queen Charlotte, but the letters in this collection add many new details. The Regent
had a difficult problem, since his previous history had made it necessary
for him to offer the Whigs a share of power, though he was well aware
of the dangers of a change of government at such a time. Moira thought
that a species of coalition or national Government, in which the King's
personal Whig friends would play a great part, could be produced by a
manipulation of the differences between Wellesley, Canning, the Grenvilles and the rest of the Tories. He was deeply disappointed at his own
failure to obtain office, nor was he satisfied that the Regent had done
sufficient to show that he remembered his old associations. But the
latter was undoubtedly mainly concerned to obtain a ministry pledged
to maintain the war in the Peninsula and to defeat Napoleon, and he was

only doing his duty in placing these objects before the satisfaction of his personal connections. It is clear also that he was not sorry to escape in this way from the party ties which he had espoused as Prince. He had, indeed, already taken steps to loosen them. Looking back in 1824, he could describe the Whigs, who certainly asked for more from the Crown than any Government since the Fox-North Coalition, as animated by "liberal & anti-Monarchical sentiments". The negotiations on behalf 1187 of the Crown were conducted with great skill. The real weakness of the Opposition was exposed, and the country realised that something far more important than the Household Appointments or even Catholic Emancipation was at stake. At any rate the rank and file of the Whigs raised loud cries at the failure to obtain office, and they had to admit that the Regent had come off remarkably well in the open debate which was carried on in the first few months of his reign.

All Cabinets were then regarded as the Crown's personal choice. But George, because of the circumstances of its origin, had a special connection with the one thus formed. Except during the period of the divorce, he was always ready to come to its support, and his attitude as a Cabinet chief is well illustrated by his advice and support in the crisis of 1819. 773 In November 1820 he seriously considered for purely personal reasons 876– the construction of a Whig or Coalition Cabinet, until it became clear 881 that he would gain little by the change. But always the constitution of the Cabinet was in his opinion as much his affair as that of his Ministers, and after 1820 it was long before he was satisfied with it. He at first flatly refused to allow the resignations and accessions which the Cabinet thought were necessary to its existence. There was, however, no congenial substitute, since Castlereagh would not, as the King desired, become Prime Minister, and eventually the King acquiesced in the necessary changes. Even in 1821 he agreed that Canning should if 958, necessary re-enter the Ministry, though he had considered Liverpool's 959 method of pressing his claims as unconstitutional. Liverpool spared him this sacrifice for a time, but in 1822 the King had to allow Canning to succeed to the whole of Castlereagh's heritage. For nearly three years he was profoundly dissatisfied with the situation, for as he had foreseen, the readmission of Canning destroyed the remarkable unity which had existed in the Cabinet since 1812. "The misfortune of this Government 1110 is that it is a Government of departments", was his comment in 1823. Eventually under Knighton's influence he sided with Canning and on Liverpool's retirement in 1827 used him to construct a Coalition Cabinet. There is little in these papers on that event, but it is clear that on Canning's death it was the King rather than the weak and unintelligent 1381

1400 Goderich who planned the new Cabinet. The King's letter on the necessity of making Herries Chancellor of the Exchequer shows how much he had imbibed of the doctrine of his late Minister: "The office requires ability & not aristocracy.... The King will have those that are proper for their business & if there be room after this—the Cabinet may if they please look out for ornaments." Possibly this phrasing was inspired by Knighton, but later letters demonstrate that the King was as 1445, determined as his father not to be the prisoner of a small group of 1454 aristocrats. He had only partial success. The Coalition Ministry that he patched up by combining the Duke of Wellington and the Canningites was a jerry-built structure from the outset. By now the King was visibly failing, and he could not supply the tact and skill, necessary to broaden the foundations of the Government, which Wellington himself lacked.

Nevertheless, the reality of the King's power is apparent through all these complicated negotiations, and this collection of papers adds new evidence for the use of those who are now engaged in giving us a clearer view of the relations of the Crown and the Cabinet in the first quarter of the nineteenth century.

The main source of power was still patronage, and the principles and precedents by which it was administered are abundantly illustrated in the King's papers. The complicated question of the King's rights over his Household appointments has already been mentioned. Other important patronage was shared between the Crown and the Prime Minister. The Government could, indeed, only go on efficiently when the two were working cordially together, as the breach with Liverpool showed. How the system of honours could be used to strengthen the 1361 Government's hands is well displayed in Canning's letter insisting that they should be conferred on "persons who are zealous in supporting 1359 your Majesty's Government". The ecclesiastical establishment was part of the same system, as the Dean of Canterbury admitted, and the 1427 question of Catholic Emancipation, therefore, added a great deal to the complications of a procedure already intricate enough.

If patronage was the main instrument of power, the importance of public opinion was also recognised, and with it that of the Press, which was already becoming independent. Through the Treasury the Government endeavoured to exert some control, but George IV himself, largely no doubt because he was often personally attacked, seems to have been more interested in the subject than his Ministers. Of this we 152 get some glimpses in the papers. The notorious Lewis Goldsmith's proposition to the Duke of Cumberland to set up a Press bureau, or even an official paper, was aimed at foreign rather than domestic enemies. The long memorial on the British Press directed to the same 148 end was also almost certainly composed by him. Nothing seems to have come of this, but the negotiations between Charles Arbuthnot, Secretary 208 of the Treasury, with Street show the Regent's activity in propaganda. This was meant to secure that the *Courier*, the Government paper, should handle the case against the Princess with discretion. Two other 187, letters reveal negotiations on the same subject with Perry, the incor- 204 ruptible editor of the *Morning Chronicle*. The long memoir on Ireland discloses some rather futile attempts to influence the Press in that 1407 country.

With the exception of Canning, not very much new light is thrown on the principal statesmen of the reign. There are only two or three formal reports from Spencer Perceval. Liverpool's smoothness of manner and steadiness of purpose are seen in the series of letters which he wrote to the King, but little of great interest is revealed. In the quarrel of 1821 over Sumner Liverpool comes out with credit, for the principles for which he contested were public as well as personal. He had been so severely tried that he lost for a time that adroit touch which had so often served him with the King, and was only rescued from a difficult position by the loyalty of Castlereagh. But generally Liverpool was at his best in the minor arts of a Prime Minister, as is often shown in his handling of patronage questions, both lay and ecclesiastical. Only a small number of letters from Castlereagh are extant and few of these are important. He seems to have written but little to George IV except the official reports as Leader of the House of Commons. The few of these which survive, as well as those of Canning, whet the appetite for more, for they sometimes add valuable details not in Hansard and give a personal point of view. The testimony of Lord Strangford as to the 145 immense increase in the efficiency of the Foreign Office when Castlereagh succeeded the wayward and inactive Wellesley is confirmed from many other sources. Without that change, indeed, the progress of events in 1813–14 would have been very different.

Wellesley himself keeps appearing throughout the period in charac- teristic fashion. On Wellington's career as Prime Minister there are some new details, but it had already been fully displayed in the *Wellington Despatches*. There is an interesting criticism of him by the man who had 1577 had him under close inspection, and, indeed, had given him invaluable help in managing the King. "There is much to admire in him", wrote Knighton in his Diary, "but a good deal to wish different. I mean as a Governor of a Kingdom. He has no humanity—no knowledge or power of judging that a man should be rewarded for civil service." A few glimpses are given of the position Eldon ("Old Bags") held in the royal counsels, and the personal trust of the King in men of the Old Guard like Sidmouth and Buckinghamshire.

On Canning there is information of some importance. The belief of 862, Hastings that Canning was endeavouring to oust him from the Governor-893, Generalship to obtain it for himself is almost certainly untrue, but it 897 shows once more the almost universal distrust that was felt for him 968 except amongst his own personal friends. When Hastings writes: "The 930 natives are extraordinarily well informed respecting all the characters that appear on the political stage in England, and they would hold him as not of a caste fitted to preside over this empire", we realise once more the prejudices against which he had to contend before he reached 875, the highest position in the King's service. It is clear also that George IV 935 believed, as many others did, that Canning had had criminal intimacy 1044 with the Princess of Wales. The King might well write, as he did to Eldon, that he had made "the greatest personal sacrifice that a Sovereign ever made to a subject, or indeed, taking *all the circumstances*, that man ever made to man". Yet in less than three years Canning had won the King entirely to his side, and with his aid had triumphed over the aristocratic clique which disliked and distrusted him. It does not seem that such petty acts as the appointment of Lord Francis Conyngham as Under-Secretary of State, or the despatch of Lord Ponsonby to Buenos 1053 Aires had much to do with the winning of the King. The first, as is here shown, was suggested by the King and not by Canning, who had approached three other persons in vain. The second occurred months after the King's favour had been won. Canning's victory was no doubt in large measure due to the commanding position which he had obtained in Parliament and public opinion. But the evidence of these papers enhances the importance of the part that Knighton played in bringing it about. For, as has been seen, Knighton also was a *novus homo* with the same dislike for the oligarchy which controlled politics, and it was undoubtedly Knighton's influence which led the King to give Canning his full confidence and use him to increase the royal control over govern-1374 ment. Brougham, who in his own party had a position not altogether unlike that of Canning's, made a similar appeal when he offered to save the Crown from the "odious thraldom preparing for it".

Still when, as the King said, "all the circumstances" are taken into account, the confidence established between Canning and the King is one of the most remarkable personal episodes in the history of the 1400 Crown. "Mr Canning never kept any thing back from the King", was

the royal testimony after Canning's death, while in 1827 Canning could 1305
send his "affectionate" duty to his Sovereign. One cannot help wonder-
ing whether this peculiar intimacy would have survived the Emancipation
crisis even with Knighton's assistance.

There are some interesting documents on foreign affairs, though unfortunately only a few. It will be noted that there are no important letters
to or from foreign Sovereigns such as illuminate the correspondence of
Queen Victoria. George IV knew few monarchs personally. Louis XVIII
did not show his gratitude in correspondence. Two others visited London
in 1814, but the Tsar quarrelled with the Regent, and the King of Prussia
was one of the most reserved men in Europe. Of the interest of George IV
in foreign affairs, however, there can be no doubt. He had throughout
his reign very definite views on British policy, and his interest in and
knowledge of Europe was greater than that of any of his Ministers save
Wellington outside the Foreign Office itself. He was, as has been noted,
proud of the part England had played in the overthrow of Napoleon and
exaggerated his own contribution to that event. But he did not, so far
as can be ascertained, scrutinise the details of foreign policy with the
same care as William IV or as Queen Victoria after Prince Albert had
taken his place at her side. The important despatches only rarely bear
the signature of royal approval which is a matter of routine in the time
of William IV. On the other hand, George IV established specially
intimate connections with the foreign Ambassadors, two of whom,
Lieven and Esterhazy, had in the early part of Canning's tenure of office
the confidence of the King to a greater degree than the Foreign Secretary
himself. Princess Lieven first won the heart of the King by her music,
and if we are to believe the lady herself, he displayed on one occasion at
least a passion for her. She was the real chief of the Russian mission.
But Esterhazy had more of the King's confidence than Prince Lieven,
and through him George IV often expressed his admiration of Metternich
and his veneration for the Emperor of Austria. Esterhazy had, however,
family troubles which repeatedly threatened to cause his resignation,
and a wife who was no great asset and whom the King did not like. These
two Ambassadors shared the intimacy of the "Cottage", and when
Canning was received into royal favour, the Lievens at least hastened
to make their peace with the Foreign Secretary.

There is hardly anything on the Congress of Vienna. Castlereagh's 494
one letter adds his testimony to that of others that Metternich was a 500
poor man of business during that period. The Duke of Cumberland's 514,
gossip on the same subject is mainly concerned with Mecklenburg and 533
Hanover, though he adds the important remark that "Castlereagh is 491

795 very difficult to get to". There is one other letter of Castlereagh in 1820 which shows how critical he could be of Metternich's conduct on
787 occasion, and one from Lord Stewart on Metternich's projected visit to England in 1820 which no one but Metternich himself thought would do much good.

1170,   In Canning's period there is more of interest. The Cabinet Minutes
1171, on sending Hanoverian troops to Portugal and the King's Minute on
1187 the proposed recognition of Buenos Aires fill up some of the gaps at a period when the dispute as to the direction of British foreign policy came to a head. The triumph of recognition meant Canning's triumph,
1252– and there soon follow papers of quite a different character—Canning's
1260 intimate reports to the King of his visit to Paris in 1826. These are the most important documents on foreign affairs in the collection. They supplement those already published which Canning wrote to Liverpool. They throw light on the relations of Villèle to Charles X and on Villèle's policy towards Spain during the Congress of Verona and in 1826. The omission of the reference to the Spanish Colonies in the King of France's letter to the King of Spain is also amusingly explained. There is not much else. Two later documents which deal with the creation of Greece
1559 are of some importance. Aberdeen was really more liberal than his letter to the King would seem to show, but he was carrying out the
1575 wishes of the Duke. The latter's attitude towards Greece is illustrated by the extract from Knighton's Diary on the candidature of Leopold for its throne.

  George IV was of course also ruler of Hanover, and in Count Münster he had an able, if somewhat narrow-minded and ultra-conservative, Minister to advise him. Münster's position grew precarious towards the close of the reign for he offended the Duke of Cambridge, but of this we learn nothing from the Windsor Archives. The Cabinet refused
553 to permit the Regent to visit Hanover in 1815 and there is nothing about his stay there in 1821, which he did not much enjoy. Only a few of Münster's letters from Vienna and Paris in 1814–15 are at Windsor, and these have already been published. There are others in the British Foreign Office records, at Hanover, and in Münster's private papers. The Hanoverian papers do not seem to have been kept with the rest of the correspondence of George IV, and the meagre information about that country in this collection comes from the letters of the Duke of Cumber-
356, land and the Duke of Cambridge. The former's attempt to become its
357 Governor in 1814 was tactfully handled by the Regent, though the refusal reduced his brother to tears. The Duke was also, like his brother,
546 the Duke of Cambridge, much perturbed at the loss of Lauenburg to the

Crown of Hanover. The revenue that George IV derived from his German Kingdom was of some importance, and he was able to raise on it the 1118, loan of £115,000 from the Rothschilds, £50,000 of which he im- 1121 mediately gave to the Duke of York, while he either gave or lent another £15,000 to Charles Arbuthnot.

George IV also became responsible in 1814 for the Duchy of Bruns- wick as guardian for the infant ruler Duke Charles. He does not seem to have devoted much attention to this duty, which Münster managed for him well enough. But it was later to cause him much trouble, for when the young Prince came to the throne he heaped abuse and insults on those who had conducted its government, not sparing George IV himself. The Duke of Cumberland was much moved by this incident and 1336, he exposed in his letters the conduct of Metternich, who thought he 1409 might gain some influence in central Germany from the quarrel. The 1417 young Prince was in fact a profligate rascal whom even Metternich failed to save in 1830, when he lost his throne.

In home affairs the great question of Catholic Emancipation was constantly recurring until the Wellington Ministry finally carried it in the face of the ultra-Tories headed by the Duke of Cumberland. All Cabinets were divided on the subject, but until 1827 the fact that the Prime Minister was a "Protestant" assured the dwindling minority of stalwarts, of whom Peel was the most prominent, that a decision against them was still far distant. Neither Castlereagh nor Canning, though "Catholics", showed any eagerness to press their views. But some saw the danger in delay. Moira urged in 1812 that the thing 130 should be done at once if the loyalty of the Irish was to be preserved. Grenville in 1821 warned the King that delay would lose all the 903 advantages to be gained from yielding. But after the King had taken his Coronation Oath he regarded himself, as his father had done, bound to refuse compliance. Eldon's Minute, supporting the King in that 1209 conclusion with much casuistry, is at the same time a valuable survey of the position of the Crown and the responsibility of Ministers. The long review of Lord Wellesley's administration in Ireland shows how that 1407 inconsistent genius tackled the Catholic question in Ireland itself and the straits to which he was put by the Catholic Association. O'Connell had begun his violent denunciations, though he did not, as the writer of the memoir seems to believe, express a hope "that a Bolivar would arise to avenge the wrongs of the Irish people". The King's interpretation of 1375 Canning's position on this question is somewhat different from that taken in the Minute which Canning himself dictated, but it was under- stood at any rate that the Prime Minister was if possible to avoid

1378 pressing the question. The Goderich Cabinet accepted the same terms.
1510 The Duke of Wellington, though a strong opponent of Emancipation, insisted that the doctrine of neutrality on the subject should be applied to ecclesiastical as well as to lay patronage, and eventually was forced to prepare the King and his own party for the inevitable. The Duke of
1535 Cumberland's response to this challenge is shown in a number of violent letters. Though George IV did not want him, he insisted on coming to England to fight a battle for his principles, on which, he told his brother,
1552 "the security of your Crown depends". Wellington's anger at this move, which is well known, is further illustrated in this collection. The
1558 Bishop of Winchester's explanatory epistle shows the kind of problem raised for those whom the King's patronage had placed in high estate.

The common people are hardly mentioned. We catch a glimpse of the unrest that lay below the surface in Queen Charlotte's exhortation to
536 her son when the Corn Law proposal produced serious disturbances in
537 London. George IV promised to follow the good example his father had shown during the Lord George Gordon riots and, indeed, he often faced the London mob with courage at this period. It was only after the divorce controversy that he sought the seclusion of the "Cottage" and even then his splendid Coronation, of which some piquant details are given, won universal applause and admiration. We have Sir Walter Scott's
1046 interesting evidence that he was able to make himself into a fine figure of a man when he made his royal tours in 1822, and that the caricatures, which were all that many of his subjects saw of him, did him monstrous injustice. During the later part of his reign his desire for privacy returned and in his last years his bodily ailments prevented him from
1097 showing himself to his people. It is not surprising that he resented the curious claim of the Dean and Chapter to have the use of his private terrace at Windsor.

But if we do not learn much of Britain beyond the circle of Court and Cabinet, we are admitted to the most intimate association with those in high places; even a recipe for easing the wearing of false teeth by the
1136 great is included. It must be remembered, however, that we see both George IV and Georgian Society in decline. Many of the characters depicted are already clearly out of place. The pressure of the rising middle classes can be felt even if it has as yet hardly penetrated into the highest circles. Some of the men and women of whom we read had passed through a generation of revolution and war. They had seen an overwhelming triumph of British arms at the end of it. But a new Britain was already in existence. It was time that they retired from the scene.

1812

THE REGENCY ACT of 1811, necessitated by George III's mental derangement, had appointed the Prince of Wales Regent, but with restricted powers for twelve months. He could not grant peerages, and his right to bestow pensions and places of profit was limited. In February 1811 he had informed his Tory Ministers that feelings of delicacy alone prevented him from removing them from office so long as any hope remained of his father's early recovery, and his Whig friends confidently expected a speedy invitation to form a Government. But on 13 February 1812, five days before the restrictions expired, the Regent informed Lords Grey and Grenville, through his brother the Duke of York, that Perceval was to remain Prime Minister, but he invited them to join the existing Cabinet. This overture was rejected, on the ground that the Whigs differed on too many points with the Ministers. Their refusal to take office, and the Regent's decision to keep the Tories in power, resulted in an open breach between him and his former friends, and a mere handful of Whigs, such as the Duke of Northumberland, Lord Cholmondeley, Lord Headfort, the few members of the House of Commons whose votes they influenced, and Sheridan, remained faithful to the Prince. Grey and most of his friends had become convinced of the hopelessness of carrying on the struggle against Napoleon, and Grey was prepared to recommend a peace which would have left the French undisputed masters of the continent. Grenville, it is true, was absolutely opposed to the idea of a negotiated peace, but he too was in favour of withdrawing the British army from the Peninsula, where Wellington was already steadily draining away Napoleon's military strength. Moreover, the Whigs were not prepared to take office except with the assurance that the Catholics should be emancipated: a policy to which the Prince Regent in spite of former pledges was no longer favourably inclined, and which was still unacceptable to the nation at large. His virtual abandonment of his old Whig friends in February 1812 was therefore in the best interests of the nation.

1 THE PRINCE REGENT *to the* DUKE OF YORK[1]

[February 1812.][2]

ALTHO I consider myself as under no obligation to explain to any persons the reasons which may, at any time, induce me to arrange, as I may think best, for the public service, the administration of the Government, yet the peculiar circumstances in which I have been placed, make me very anxious, as well from considerations of [high] personal regard, as from a desire to avoid any possibility of misinterpretation of my conduct, that the grounds of it, on the present occasion, should be communicated to the Lords Grey[3] & Grenville.[4]

I wish you therefore to see those noble Lords, for the purpose of making that communication. Possibly the most convenient & satisfactory way to yourself of making it, will be by reading to them this letter—and you will accordingly feel yourself authorised so to read it.

I am aware that such a communication as an official & formal act, exactly[5] would be open to some objection, as not according with the proper dignity of my present situation; and that however private in its nature it may be, it may not altogether escape the same objection. But I trust in the considerations of private feeling to which I have referred that I shall find sufficient justification for it.[6]

Their Lordships are sufficiently acquainted with the motives which determined me at the commencement of the Regency to continue in office the persons who had been selected by the King.[7] It was my sense

1 Frederick Augustus, Duke of York and Albany (1763–1827), second son of George III and Queen Charlotte.

2 This draft was the basis of the Prince Regent's famous letter of 13 February to his brother, and, with the exception of one paragraph, is in Perceval's handwriting. Not later than Friday, the 7th, the Prince Regent prepared a letter inviting Lords Grey and Grenville to coalesce with the existing Tory Ministers, and showed it to Perceval that day. They were both confident that the Opposition would reject the overture, and Perceval advised the Prince not to make it, saying that it would expose him to the charge of insincerity, and that it would be much better to inform the Whig leaders frankly that he could not apply to them for their services. The Prince accepted this advice; Perceval drafted the letter here printed and the Prince agreed to it on Tuesday the 11th. Next morning he characteristically changed his mind and told Eldon, the Lord Chancellor, that he had decided to send a letter inviting some of his former Whig friends to take office. Eldon and Perceval remonstrated with him, but without effect, and the letter, which had already been drafted, was despatched two days later.

The words in square brackets were added in pencil by the Duke of York.

There is a copy of the letter actually sent to the Duke of York in the Windsor archives. (See *Parl. Deb.* XXII, 39.)

3 Charles, second Earl Grey (1764–1845), the leader of the Foxite Whigs in the House of Lords. Prime Minister, 1830–34.

4 William Wyndham Grenville, Baron Grenville (1759–1834), the leader of the Grenville group. Prime Minister, 1806–7.

5 The Duke of York's marginal comment, in pencil.

6 This paragraph is in the Prince Regent's handwriting.

7 See the Prince Regent's letter to Perceval, 4 February 1811. (*Annual Register*, 1811, p. 334*.)

of duty to my Royal father which [solely] decided me in that determination. My private feelings & most valued connexions necessarily gave way to considerations which admitted of no doubt or hesitation in my mind. I trust I acted, in that respect, as the genuine representative of the august person, whose functions I was called upon to discharge: and I have the satisfaction of knowing, that such was the opinion of [many] persons, for whose judgements and honorable principles, I entertain the highest regard. I have continued to be influenced by the same motives. In various instances where the Law of the last Session left me at full liberty, I have waived ~~my~~ [every] [*sic*] personal gratification [of my own], in order that His Majesty might resume, on his restoration to health, [all the] ~~every~~ power and prerogative[s] belonging to the Crown unimpaired by my use of them. I [then] felt and ~~I still~~ [ever must] feel, that I am the last person in the Kingdom, to whom it can be permitted to despair of my Royal father's recovery.

A new era is now arrived. It is impossible for me not to reflect with satisfaction on many of the events which have distinguished the intermediate period: And I have been so well satisfied with the principles upon which my present servants have acted, and with the success which has attended their measures, as to have seen reason to depart [so far] from my former opinion that a total change of the Administration would be desireable. Such a [total] change, while it implied at least, my disapprobation of conduct which I cannot but approve, would endanger the cause of our Allies, by shaking their confidence in my determination to support them. I have no resentments to gratify; I must not suffer myself to indulge any personal predilections [however great] nor to pursue any objects but such as are common to the whole nation.

I have been desirous with a view to the national interests, to strengthen my government by the union of parties; and I had entertained strong hopes that under the peculiar circumstances in which the country and myself were placed, such an union might, by my endeavours have been effected, without any sacrifice of principle in any party. It had been my wish and my intention to have proposed such an union as soon as the termination of all restrictions on the Regency should naturally have opened a new era. I am sorry to say, that wish has been unfortunately disappointed.[1] Whether under any circumstances it could have been

---

1 This sentence is scored out, in pencil, and the following substituted by the Duke of York: "It is with great regret that I have to remark that I see but little prospect now to further encourage so favourite a hope."

[3]

I-2

effected, it is impossible for me to feel any certainty; But, when I was
preparing to have acted upon it, events occurred, which neither I [could
foresee] nor my Ministers could avoid, which have brought the different
parties into recent, & I fear [almost] irreconcileable conflict upon certain
more important points of foreign & domestic policy. It is impossible for
me to disguise from myself, that those points must now instantly recur
      [imperious]
as subjects of ~~practical~~ & immediate consideration to any Government, which I could form, and the differences so recently manifested on
them, discourage [therefore] the hope I had entertained of the possible
co-operation of the different parties. There [seems therefore to] remains
[little or] no chance at present of my being able to prevail upon them to
modify *some* of their opinions, or to view the present state of things as
furnishing the reasons for removing for a time at least the necessity of
determining upon *others*. I am therefore precluded from making with
          [that]
any propriety ~~the~~ proposal [which] I had intended. I cannot make a
proposal to either party, at a time when I feel conscious that neither
could accept it with a due regard to their own honor and consistency.[1]
[For under such circumstances] such a proposal could not but be subjected to the suspicion of insincerity on my part towards one, or other,
if not towards both parties, and I need not say how necessary it is that
I should guard myself against the possibility of incurring so unworthy
a suspicion.
          [Thus situated]
~~Under these circumstances~~ therefore I have thought it became me
                                        [shall ever]
rather to sacrifice those considerations of personal regard, which I ~~still~~
entertain, & which might otherwise have influenced my conduct, than
to abandon, as I must necessarily have done, by a total change of the
Administration, those principles & measures of policy, which, whatever
might be the case in any other situation of affairs, appear to me, under
all the circumstances of the present moment, most conducive and essential
to the welfare of the country.

1 This sentence is scored out, in pencil, by the Duke of York.

[4]

[13 February 1812.]

As the restrictions on the exercise of the Royal authority will shortly expire, the Prince Regt thinks it right to communicate to his Majestys confidential servants, those sentiments which he was withheld from expressing to them at an earlier period of the Session, by his earnest desire that the expected motion on the affairs of Ireland, might undergo the deliberate discussion of Parlt unmixed with any other consideration.[2]

The Prince Regent thinks it hardly necessary to discribe the recent circumstances under which he assumed the office of Regent; At a moment of unexampled difficulty & danger, he was called upon to make an option of persons to whom he should entrust the functions of executive Government; his sense of duty to his Royal father decided that choice; his private feelings, & most valued connections gave way to considerations which admitted of no doubt or hesitation; he trusts he acted in that respect as the genuine representative of the august person whose functions he was called on to discharge, & he has the satisfaction of knowing that such was the opinion of persons for whose judgement & honorable principles he entertains the highest respect. In various instances where the Act of last Session left him at liberty, he waived his personal gratification in order that his Majesty might resume on his restoration to health, every power and prerogative belonging to the Crown. The Prince Regent is the last person in the Kingdom to whom it can be permitted to dispair of his Royal fathers recovery.

A new era is now arrived & the Prince Regt cannot but reflect with satisfaction on the events which have distinguished his short administration; instead of suffering in the loss of any of its possessions by the gigantic force which has been employed against them, Gt. Britain has added most important acquisitions to her Empire; the national faith has been preserved inviolate towards our Allies, & if character is strength as applied to a nation, the encreased & encreasing reputation of his Majestys Arms will shew to the nations of the Continent how much they may still atchieve by inferior numbers when animated by a glorious spirit of resistance to a foreign yoke. In the critical situations of the war in the Peninsula, the Pe Regt will be most anxious to avoid every measure which can lead his Allies to suppose that he means to depart from the

1 At the conclusion of his letter to the Duke of York, the Prince Regent said that he should send a copy to Perceval. But he drafted a separate letter to the Cabinet which differs to some extent from the letter to his brother.

2 The Carlton House members, such as McMahon and Tyrwhitt in the Commons, and Lord Lake, in the House of Lords, had, as the Grenvilles now recalled, been instructed to vote against the Catholic question on 4 February and 31 January respectively.

present system; perseverance alone can atchieve the great object in question, & he cannot mark with disapprobation those who have honorably distinguished themselves in support of it. The Prince Regt has no predilections to indulge, no resentment to gratify, no objects to attain but such as are common to the whole nation. If such is the leading principle of his conduct, & he appeals to the past as evidence of what the future will be, he flatters himself he will meet with the support of the Parliament, & of a brave & generous people.

If his endeavours cannot ensure success he flatters himself they will at least prove that he is not undeserving of it.

Having made this communication of his sentiments on the new & extraordinary crisis of our affairs, the Prince Regent cannot conclude without expressing the gratification he shall feel if those persons with whom the early habits of his public life were formed[1] will strengthen his hands & constitute a part of his Administration. With such support, & such a vigorous & united Government he will never dispair of a fortunate issue to the most arduous contest in which Great Britain was ever engaged.

3 THE DUKE OF YORK *to the* PRINCE REGENT

Stable Yard, February 13, 1812.

As I did not find Lord Grey at home when I called upon him this afternoon I left the note I had written to him and just as I was getting into my carriage to go to dinner at the City of London Tavern Lord Grey called at my door to enquire at what time he could see me in the evening.

I however thought it advisable not to delay the communication and therefore took him into my room and began by informing him that the object of my visit was to communicate to him a letter which I had received from you. He immediately stopped me, and asked me if I was aware that the last communication that you had made was to Lord Grenville and him conjointly. I answered him that I was, but that the reason you had directed me to make this communication to him was out of delicacy to me, knowing as you did that I was was [*sic*] upon a much more friendly and intimate footing with him, than with Lord Grenville,

---

1 Lord Bathurst was probably not alone in thinking that by these words the Prince Regent intended to exclude Lord Grenville, who thus referred to the letter: "There is evidently an attempt in it to create disunion among ourselves. This has entirely failed. The rest is all written for popular effect—how successfully time alone can show."

but that if he wished it I could have no objection to go with him and make the communication myself to Lord Grenville.

Lord Grey however continued still to hesitate and expressed a certain degree of embarrassment at receiving the communication alone, when I told him that if he felt the least delicacy on that score I would take upon myself to delay reading the paper to him till I could do it in the presence of Lord Grenville, for which he expressed himself much gratified, and it was settled that Lord Grenville and he are to call upon me here at eleven o'clock tomorrow.

I hope that you will approve of that I have done but I thought that it was not my business to raise difficulties or make any cavil that might look like a desire to prevent the proposed arrangement if it can be effected.

As soon as the interview is over you may depend upon seeing me.

4 *Memorandum of conversation between the* DUKE OF YORK, LORDS GREY AND GRENVILLE

Memorandum of what passed at an interview between Lord Grey, Lord Grenville and myself on Friday the 14th of February 1812.

AFTER the first compliments were over, I addressed myself to Lord Grenville and told him that though I supposed that Lord Grey had informed his Lordship of the reason which had induced the Prince Regent to direct me to communicate his letter to me to Lord Grey, instead of to his Lordship and Lord Grey conjointly; yet I begged leave to repeat it to him myself, and which arose not from any disinclination or want of confidence in his Lordship, but from a delicacy on the part of my brother to me, who, knowing that I was more in the habits of intimacy and communication with Lord Grey than with his Lordship, had thought that it would be more pleasant to me to communicate with Lord Grey alone in the first instance—a proof of which his Lordship would find by the last paragraph of the letter, in which the Prince expressed his conviction that Lord Grey would communicate the contents of it to him; and that if any further corroboration was wanting to prove that there was no want of confidence on the part of the Prince to his Lordship, or any wish to exclude him, it was to be found in the readiness with which I had offered, in the first instance, to accompany Lord Grey to his Lordship, in order to communicate the Prince's letter to him myself; and afterwards upon remarking Lord Grey's hesitation, when I wished to read the letter to him, my taking upon myself to postpone the communication to him till it could be made conjointly with his Lordship.

I then turned to both their Lordships and said, that, before I communicated the letter, I begged to explain further to them the reason that had induced me to call upon Lord Grey the evening before at half past three o'clock, an hour at which there was little probability of finding his Lordship at home, which was, that the Prince had only delivered to me his letter at a quarter before three o'clock, and as he mentioned in it his intention of sending a copy of it to Mr. Percival,[1] I had thought it my duty to ride up to Lord Grey's without loss of time, in order to endeavour to communicate it to him personally before it was possible for the copy to reach Mr. Percival.

Having finished reading the letter, I gave the paper to Lord Grenville, expressing at the same time the Prince's sincere wish, and my anxious desire, for the success of the negotiation, to which Lord Grenville answered, that as it was a paper of that consequence that it required a certain time for consideration before it was answered, he thought it would be more advisable not to enter at all upon it at that moment, and hoped that the Prince did not require an immediate answer, to which I assented, and begged that their Lordships would take their own time. They then proposed the next day (Saturday) and desired me to fix the hour, which I declined, saying that I should make their time mine, when they appointed one o'clock, to which I agreed, and added, that if there was any part of the paper which they might think required explanation, I should be happy to give it to them, or if they wished to make any communication to the Prince, I should be equally ready to lay it before him; and if they should prefer a personal interview with him, that I was sure that he would be perfectly ready at any time to see them.

Minute of the Duke of York's conversation with Lords Grey and Grenville, 15 February 1812. (*Dropmore MSS.* x, 217.)
Earl Grey and Lord Grenville to the Duke of York, 15 February 1812.[2] (*Dropmore MSS.* x, 213.)

1 Spencer Perceval (1762–1812). Prime Minister since 1809.
2 Their answer contained a positive refusal to join the existing Government because of their differences on many political questions. The Prince Regent at once sent for Perceval and confirmed him in the Premiership.

5 THE MARQUIS WELLESLEY[1] *to the* PRINCE REGENT

Foreign Office, 17th Febry 1812.

½ p SIX P.M.

LORD WELLESLEY has the honor to acquaint your Royal Highness, that, in obedience to your Royal Highness's gracious commands, he saw the Lord Chancellor[2] this day at the House of Lords, according to his Lordship's appointment.

He stated to the Lord Chancellor the whole of the communication, humbly submitted to your Royal Highness yesterday.

The Lord Chancellor confirmed every part of the statement, as coinciding precisely with what he had learnt this morning from your Royal Highness, with one most important variation.

The Lord Chancellor positively declared, that he understood from your Royal Highness, that you did on Saturday last actually appoint Mr. Perceval to be permanently your Royal Highness's First Minister;[3] and that the Government was now formed under that appointment.

This statement is certainly very different from Lord Wellesley's interpretation of your Royal Highness's declarations of yesterday, nor would Lord Wellesley have presumed to offer any advice on the subject of forming an Administration, adapted to the present crisis, if he had understood that your Royal Highness had already fixed Mr. Perceval in his seat, and had formed your Government on that basis.

The Lord Chancellor will, under your Royal Highness's commands, communicate to Mr. Perceval the conversation with Lord Wellesley.[4]

1 Richard Colley Wellesley, Marquis Wellesley (1760–1842). Governor-General of Bengal, 1798–1805; Foreign Secretary, 1809–12. He had tendered his resignation of the Foreign Secretaryship on 16 January, on the ground of the Cabinet's inadequate support of the war in the Peninsula, and Perceval's unfitness for the premiership; but the Regent, wishing to postpone ministerial changes until the restrictions should have expired, persuaded him to remain for the time being. After Perceval had been confirmed in the premiership, however (15 February), Wellesley declared that he could not continue to serve under him, and urged the Regent to place his friend Lord Moira at the head of a new Government which should not be opposed to Catholic emancipation, and which should include both Castlereagh and Canning. The Prince communicated this advice to Perceval, through the Lord Chancellor, Eldon. On the night of the 17th the Cabinet unanimously decided to resign unless Wellesley's resignation was accepted, and on the 19th Wellesley delivered up the seals. His son Richard, a Junior Lord of the Treasury, resigned only at the end of the month, withholding his vote during this interval, whilst his father's other representatives in the Commons voted with the Opposition.

2 John Scott, first Earl of Eldon (1751–1838). Lord Chancellor, 1801–06; 1807–27. Barony, 1799; earldom, 1821.

3 This is confirmed in *Twiss*, II, 189; Spencer Walpole's *Perceval*, II, 269; Plumer Ward's *Diary*, I, 416; and *Bathurst Papers*, p. 166. See also Buckingham's *Regency Memoirs*, I, 252–62.

4 Wellesley's *Memorandum* (really written by one of his friends, Thomas Sydenham), explaining the grounds of his resignation, is in *Parl. Deb.* XXIII, 367. (Copy at Windsor.)

[February 1812.]

AN anxious desire not to be misunderstood by your Royal Highness, in the sentiments which the Duke of Bedford thinks it his duty to lay before your Royal Highness, has induced him to commit them to writing, and to solicit your Royal Highness's permission to leave the paper in your hands.

In the present awful situation of publick affairs, when the anxiety of every man alive to the welfare of his country is excited in a more than ordinary degree, by the recent communication which it has pleased your Royal Highness to make to the Lords Grey and Grenville, through His Royal Highness the Duke of York, on the subject of the future government of the country, the Duke of Bedford feels it to be his duty humbly to approach your Royal Highness with the expression of those apprehensions which weigh so heavily upon his mind, in the crisis in which we are placed—a crisis of almost unexampled danger to the dearest and most essential interests of the State.

The Duke of Bedford feels himself more imperatively called upon to exercise this painful duty, from a consideration of the alarming situation in which Ireland is placed, by the conduct of the Government of that country during the period of the last six months, and the little prospect which appears now to be held out of a better and a wiser policy prevailing there; and he cannot but combine his consideration of these circumstances, with the gracious and consolatory assurance, which your Royal Highness authorized him to make to the leading Catholicks of Ireland, when in the year 1806 he was entrusted by His Majesty with the government of that country; an assurance which gave the most cordial satisfaction to those to whom it was made, and enabled them successfully to repress every impatient solicitude on the part of that numerous and increasing portion of the population of Ireland. Deeply impressed with a sense of the unhappy consequences that may result from a disappointment, which must in the nature of it be severe in the extreme, the Duke of Bedford cannot but respectfully, yet earnestly implore your Royal Highness to turn your attention to that part of the United Kingdom; to relieve the anxieties and heal the wounds of four millions of His Majesty's subjects, labouring under disabilities and deprivations of the most galling and mortifying description, but which the confident hope of your Royal Highness' just sense of their wrongs, and the ultimate expectation of redress from the hands of your Royal Highness, have hitherto taught them to support with feelings of diminished irritation and impatience.

The Duke of Bedford must repeat to your Royal Highness (because

1 John Russell, sixth Duke of Bedford (1766–1839). Lord-Lieutenant of Ireland, 1806–7.

he is persuaded that it will gratify that spirit of benevolence which he has uniformly witnessed through all your actions,) that the assurance which your Royal Highness enabled him to give to the Roman Catholicks of Ireland, through the leading members of their body, that you acknowledged the full justice of their claims, and should not fail to redress the grievances of which they complained, whenever your Royal Highness felt yourself authorized to do so, produced the most heartfelt and unqualified satisfaction. Your Royal Highness may rest assured that the disappointment which they must now feel, if they find that the prayer of the petitions they have so frequently, but respectfully submitted to the Legislature is not to be sanctioned and conceded by your Royal Highness's Government, will be proportioned to the gratification they then experienced.

Not only the Catholicks of Ireland, but every part of the population of that truly interesting portion of the British Empire, have long and habitually looked to your Royal Highness as their peculiar, and almost their exclusive friend. They have uniformly considered your Royal Highness, as the avowed protector of their rights, and the natural guardian of their happiness. They have looked forward with an anxious solicitude to the period of your Royal Highness exercising the government of the united realm, as that of closing for ever the mutual animosities of Protestant and Catholick, and the various afflicting evils under which the people of Ireland have so long suffered; and your Royal Highness is further entreated to believe, from the purest and most unquestionable source of information which has reached the Duke of Bedford, that "the Viceroy who may be empowered by your Royal Highness to offer the olive branch to the two conflicting sects, would be hailed almost with one voice, as the benefactor, or rather as the saviour of the country".

If on the contrary Sir, the same system is still to be pursued towards that ill fated people; if the same ill founded jealousies are still to prevail, if the same errors are still to be acted upon; if the same unjust, unwise, and impolitick restrictions, penalties, and disabilities, are to continue to operate against the Roman Catholick body, the Duke of Bedford is under the painful necessity of repeating to your Royal Highness, what he humbly stated to the King, when he was honoured with an audience on his return from Ireland in 1807, namely, his firm and conscientious belief that Ireland must inevitably be lost to the British Empire. This strong and decided conviction of his mind, is unfortunately strengthened and confirmed by all that has happened in that country from the period alluded to, to the present hour.

[11]

The Duke of Bedford feels that it would be superfluous in him to offer any argument to convince your Royal Highness of the policy of conceding to the Catholicks what they claim from the justice of Parliament. He has had the happiness of hearing from your Royal Highness, on a former occasion, that you completely concurred in the view he has formed of this important measure. Having been honoured by the kind and partial regard of your Royal Highness for two and twenty years, he has had frequent opportunities of witnessing your Royal Highness's zeal and anxiety for the welfare of the dominions you were born to govern; he has listened with a pleasure he can but ill describe to the doctrines he has heard from your Royal Highness's mouth, on civil and religious liberty, and on the constitutional rights of the subject; he has heard your Royal Highness speak in cloquent praise of that great and virtuous statesman Mr. Fox,[1] and the Duke of Bedford can never forget the manner in which your Royal Highness was pleased to express yourself, when you condescended to write to him in Dublin on the death of that incomparable man. He has also had the melancholy gratification of hearing your Royal Highness speak in almost the same terms of one who was endeared to him by ties of consanguinity, and the warmest veneration and affection, and whose loss he has more than ever to deplore at this moment.[2]

With all these powerful feelings and gratifying reflections deeply engraven on his mind, and with a knowledge of the avowed sentiment of the two great men he has alluded to, on this important point, he cannot bring himself to doubt your Royal Highness's just and unaltered sense on the policy of the momentous question which he has ventured to submit to your Royal Highness's view; and he entreats of your Royal Highness's justice to acquit him of any thing like personal disrespect to your Royal Highness. If he has delivered himself with too much freedom, it is only because he feels warmly for the interests of the country, and that he considers the question of the Catholick claims to be of vital importance to the happiness and security of the Empire.

Upon all other questions of national policy, though of great moment, the Duke of Bedford has purposely abstained from touching. To every thing which relates to Ireland, he has long given the most deliberate and anxious consideration, and from the high and responsible station which he had the honor to fill in that country, he has thought it his bounden duty to deliver his sentiments to your Royal Highness upon what most

---

1 Charles James Fox (1749–1806). Foreign Secretary in the Grenville Ministry, 1806.
2 Francis Russell, fifth Duke of Bedford (1765–1802), Fox's devoted friend and a friend of the Prince of Wales. He died unmarried and was succeeded by his brother.

materially relates to the policy which in his humble opinion ought to govern the councils of Ireland.

Descended from a line of ancestors who for upwards of 300 years have uniformly devoted themselves to the active service of their country, & of the Sovereigns of these Realms, under whom they lived, the Duke of Bedford would have thought himself unworthy of the blood which flows in his veins, and of the hereditary honors which have descended to him, if in a moment like this, he should have neglected to open his mind freely, but dutifully and respectfully to your Royal Highness.

He has stated the serious and solemn conviction of his honest and unbiassed, but imperfect judgment, and the matters which he has presumed to lay before your Royal Highness, he thinks of the highest importance to the publick weal.

7 THE DUKE OF NORFOLK[1] *to the* PRINCE REGENT

Norfolk House, Feb. 17th, 1812

PERMIT me, Sir, with humble duty & respect to express how highly gratifying I feel your R. Highness' condescension in directing Col. Macmahon[2] to communicate to me what had passed with Lords Gray & Grenville, in imparting your sentiments to them through the medium of his R. Highness the Duke of York—and deeply to regret that your R. Highness' wishes to form a vigourous Government on a broad & liberal basis, should (at least for the present moment) be checkd & frustrated.

I should be wanting in sincerity, if I did not say I concurred in their opinion on on [*sic*] the question of concession to the Catholicks of Ireland & the danger of delay.

Engrafting in the oath of allegiance, a test of security to the Established Church; I hold it a measure of justice, of right & even of safety to the Empire.

In this opinion I have thought myself sanction'd by that of yr R. Highness, & am sure of that of Lord Moira,[3] to whom I have invariably

1 Charles Howard, eleventh Duke of Norfolk (1746–1815). He had renounced Roman Catholicism on coming of age. He now refused to countenance the Prince Regent's decision to retain his Tory Ministers by accepting the Garter. Lady Holland thought him "a chicken-hearted, trimming sort of politician".

2 The Prince Regent's Private Secretary and Keeper of the Privy Purse. Created a baronet in 1817. (d. 1817.)

3 Francis Rawdon-Hastings, first Marquis of Hastings and second Earl of Moira (1754–1826). He was one of the Prince Regent's earliest and most intimate friends, and romantically

look'd since the death of Mr. Fox, as a man of the most elevated sentiments of virtue & of honour & possessing a heart of the warmest attachment to yʳ R. Highness.

Permit me to call your attention to the feeling of the Irish Catholicks, who to a man beleive they have your friendship to their claims, & in the eagerness of their hopes, beleive they have your assured protection.

Should the inveterate enemy of this country be able to incite a commotion in the moment of dissapointment, I have no doubt but the loyalty of the more enligthend [*sic*], wuld [*sic*] be exerted against those who are less so; I pray heaven their influence might be succesfull.

Yʳ R Highness states the question has had the deliberate disscussion of Parliament unmixed with any other consideration.

Some persons of weight spoke in favour of the measure & voted against it on account of the moment. A beleived [*sic*] influence (which perhaps at the moment could not be avoided) guided the votes of others.¹

Another Parliament may determine otherwise. His Majesty's natural life may last many years, his other life I consider as closed for ever.

I fear I am going to[o] far—I write in the anxiety of the moment, without consulting or communicating with any one.

Should yr R. Highness determine otherwise I shall less regret my advanced period of life in withdrawing from poli[ti]cks, which I never can pursue with satisfaction but in support of your measures.

Earnestly hoping I do not incur yʳ R. Highness' displeasure, permit me to assure you I shall retain to the end of it, a gratefull sense of kindness shewn, & particularly for the protection experienced some years past on a trying occasion.²

attached to him. He had dissociated himself from the Whig party in 1807, and had then told Lord Holland that he wished to attach himself completely to the Prince. His devotion to the Prince now came into conflict with his fidelity to Whig principles. Like the Duke of Norfolk he declined the Garter, and announced his intention of retiring from public life; and he and the Prince Regent were estranged until the end of May, when his services were again required.

1 Lord Fitzwilliam's motion respecting the state of Ireland (31 January 1812) was defeated by 162 to 79. In the Commons, Lord Morpeth's motion was lost by 229 to 135 (4 February).

2 Grey has an interesting reference to this letter, in *Dropmore MSS.* x, 224.

Pall Mall, 17 Feb. 1812.

If I were not to avail myself of the opening you have been pleased to give me, after the explanation you have kindly received, and of the confirmation of it by my worthy relative Mr. Ward,[2] to speak to you with confidence & freedom respecting myself, I should be undeserving of the favour bestowed upon me. Your Lordship's magnanimity in permitting your ancient good will towards to [*sic*] me to prevail over an occurence, which I am sensible must have deeply wounded your feelings, and which, I beg to repeat was no less hurtful to my own, was a favour rooted in my heart.

From a few words which dropt from me, at the end of a conversation you permitted me to hold with you, as well as from what I understand Mr. Ward said to you, your Lordship will not be entirely unprepared for the object of this letter.

I have been upwards of forty years a banker, and am not conscious that I have done any thing, which would sully the character of a person in that confidential line of business. Early in my career, I became connected with a branch of the Royal family who honord me with his friendship for a course of many years, and which ended only in his death; and my attachment to him was such as to induce me to write him a letter, the answer to which, now in my possession, was, I beleive, his very last writing.

About six & twenty years ago, the late Lord Lake,[3] first made me known to the Prince of Wales, which introduction was most graciously improved by H.R.H's uncle, the Duke of Cumberland,[4] & which in a very short time procured me the honor of being upon such confidential terms with the Prince, as to raise my hopes that the whole world was successfully before me. A happy & flattering intercourse subsisted for several years, during which time I received many marks of favour & confidence, and was entrusted with the arrangement of some not trifling matters. I do not include the loans which were attempted, for the explanation of even what came to my knowledge, would require long &

1 The banker, of Pall Mall (? 1747–1812). Originally he was a clerk in the banking house of Herries & Co. Later, he entered into co-partnership with Messrs Morland and Ransom. After some years the partnership was dissolved, and Hammersley formed a co-partnership under the firm of Hammersley, Montelieu, Greenwood, Brooksbank and Drewe.

2 Hammersley's son-in-law.

3 Gerard Lake, first Viscount Lake (1744–1808). One of the Prince Regent's early friends, his gentleman-attendant for many years, and Receiver-General of the Revenues of the Duchy of Cornwall, 1807–8.

4 Henry Frederick, Duke of Cumberland (1745–1790), fourth son of Frederick, Prince of Wales, the father of George III.

ample detail.[1] The manner in which H.R.H. appointed me his banker, I believe was an occurrence as uncommon as it was flattering to me.

Towards the end of my partnership with Lord Kinnaird[2] & Mr. Morland,[3] & which as your Lordship knows, from the part you kindly took in my favour, finished not amicably, the Prince had cause of displeasure with Lord Kinnaird and withdrew his business; this was extremely mortifying to me, not only from the loss of H.R.H[s] business but from the circumstance of H.R.H. having condescended, at my request some years before, to give Lord Kinnaird his proxy & interest at an election for Scotch peers.

Notwithstanding this seperation in business, H.R.H. permitted me to have personal intercourse with him, & some few personal transactions afterwards took place—even the day before H.R.H. marriage I received a message with an assurance of his regard for me.

Some little time after this, I must confess I fell into a great error, which I sincerely deplored, but which, though under the mortification of a deservedly sharp reproof from H.R.H. served only to confirm me in the hope that I still retained a place in H.R.H. favour. The case was this. When H.R.H. removed his account from Coutt's,[4] (whither he had retaken it, after he withdrew it from us,) to Drummonds,[5] I presumed to write him a letter, expressive of my unhappiness, upon which H.R.H. immediately sent for me, & told me how extremely wrong I had acted; but still, after this rebuke, with his wonted graciousness, he did not send me cheerlessly away, but added "you ought to have known me better, Hammersley, I could *not* come to you", and gave me to understand that it was at the K[ing']s desire he removed his account from Coutts' to Drummonds.

H.R.H. however did open an account with us, & upon which there is a small balance remaining at this time; and there are besides some of the small matters of the Prince's expenditure which still pass thro' our hands. For many years however, nothing has occurrd, but my unceasing love & devotion to H.R.H. person; for so deep was the impression made

1 When, in 1788, the Prince of Wales tried to raise a loan of £300,000 upon the security of the Bishopric of Osnaburg, he placed the matter in Hammersley's hands.

2 George Kinnaird, seventh Baron Kinnaird, in the peerage of Scotland. [1754–1805.] One of the representative peers in 1787.

3 William Morland (1739–1815), head partner in the banking house of Morland, Ransom & Co., and M.P. for Taunton, 1796–1806. For many years he was Chairman of the British Fire Office, and of the Westminster Life Office. His only daughter married Scrope Bernard, M.P., who assumed the additional surname of Morland, and succeeded as head partner in the firm.

4 The banking house of Coutts & Co. in the Strand, founded by Thomas Coutts (1735–1822) and his brother James. (d. 1778.)

5 Henry Drummond, the banker of Charing Cross, died in 1794; his son Henry (1786–1860) also became a partner in the bank.

upon me, still a young man when introduced to him, that no time nor circumstance can efface.

Now, my Lord, I beg you will beleive, that I do not in any way presume upon what I have related to you—I mean only to put you in possession of my situation & feelings. If they should be sufficient to incline you to act upon them, I know it will be in my favour; if not, or any circumstances which I cannot know, prevent y^r Lordship from even thinking upon my situation, I shall know that it does not arise from the want of good will, & that the communication will be safe in your own breast.

This then, my dear Lord, is my situation.

From the fortunes of the partners in my house, & the prudence of the managers of it, there is ample security for all the customers of it. So, I can say, of both my former connections, that no person, who entrusted his money with me, was ever in danger of loosing one shilling.

I had a gentlemans education, but a small fortune, which, though not diminished, is not increased as might have been expected from my public course of 40 years. I have had a family of 16 children. I trust I have never fallen into any vicious courses; and I never had a gambling transaction in my life, in the Stocks or otherwise; but I never had what is called, a stroke of good fortune.

I have been pulled to pieces in two fabricks that I had raised, and in my present house I have had to contend with great & constantly perplexing opposition. The times also have been such as greatly to shake confidence in all bankers, hardly excepting half a dozen of the oldest houses; since I have been a banker, the number of banking houses is more than doubled, & of nearly 500 individuals who compose our body, I am the oldest banker excepting 3 persons.

I am, my Lord, rapidly advancing towards the age of man, my health is not so good as could be wished, and although I am not incapable of exertion, I cannot encounter difficulties and vanquish them, with the same courage and vigour I have done on many occasions in my life.

I now come, my Lord, to the important part of the disclosure of my situation. Some further change is become necessary in the firm of my house. Family concerns in one partner & public considerations in another, induce me to think that a change is necessary. I have already mentioned to y^r Lordship that my own fortune is not sufficient for the support of the fabrick I have reared for the benefit of my family, & my customers must not remain an instant without seeing that stability which must place them perfectly at ease; I must therefore admit into my partnership some person or persons of known property & prudence.

Had I not sustained considerable losses, not I trust from improper proceedings on my part, but from those calamities which often happen and without reproach, I might have had a sufficient fortune to have kept the whole business in my own family; the chief of which, arises from my connection with a person, & in consequence of his misfortunes, who stands deservedly high in the Prince's favour and confidence. As this is a sacrifice which cannot be avoided, the higher ground I can place myself upon, in the eyes of such new connections, the better terms, therefore, I shall be able to make for my own family.

I now come, my Lord, lastly to express my wishes, at this most important crisis of my advanced life; they naturally lead to the restoration to the confidential situation I once held of being H.R.H⁵ banker, and that he would be pleased to transfer his condescending friendship to me, to my two sons, Hugh[1] & George, who will be my successors; my second son Charles, is already in possession of a portion of H.R.H⁵ favour, by being in partnership with his uncle Greenwood & his friend & cotemporary, Henry Cox.[2]

But, my Lord, I am neither so arrogant as to suppose that I deserve this restoration; nor so unreasonable as to think that, during a lapse of 14 or 15 years, there may not have arisen persons better entitled to H.R.H⁵. favour; as to that object, I am perfectly & *cheerfully* submissive to whatever may be H.R.H⁵. good pleasure.

I am sincerely grateful for the road you have opened to me, to an object which may lead to some advantage to me, upon another important event taking place, & for which, if the occasion presented itself, I could officially apply; for there has always been some money on H.R.H⁵ account, and consequently I have never ceased to be, though partially, H.R.H⁵ banker. My wishes, therefore are that H.R.H. would be graciously pleased to re-animate this account in any small way he may think proper; the very circumstance of reviving H.R.H⁵. name in our books, & his Treasurer sending for his book of Account would lift me up in the eyes of my partners, & my clerks, seeing the circumstance, would also assist my consequence in my own profession.

This I hope is not an unpracticable wish; nor the further desire that some little mark of notice might pass, that I was not altogether discarded from H.R.H⁵ recollection. All ideas of ambition or personal advancement have long since subsided, & which would now be no gratifica-

---

1 [? 1775–1840.] He was the sole surviving partner of Hammersley's Bank, and the business therefore came to an end when he died. His wife was the eldest daughter of Lewis Montelieu, the banker.

2 The banking house of Cox, Greenwood & Cox. Greenwood was described as "the leading army agent and the confidential friend of the Horse Guards".

tion to me, as I wish to pass quietly the remainder of my life; still, as long as that life lasts, I shall preserve the gratifying feeling of attachment, & my great reward would be that he was pleased with it.

At this important crisis, it would be highly unreasonable in me to suppose that your Lordship can attend to any concern of mine; but as it is the moment when y^r Lordship should know my exact sentiments, I hope you will pardon the trouble of reading the letter, which may occupy less of your Lordship's time than granting me a personal interview.

9 SPENCER PERCEVAL *to the* PRINCE REGENT

House of Lords, Feb. 18, 1812.

MR. PERCEVAL presents his humble duty to your Royal Highness, & has the honor of forwarding for your R. Highness's signature the paper of communication to be made to Lord Wellesley, and if your Royal Highness will be so good as to direct it to be returned when so signed by the messenger who brings it, to the Lord Chancellor at the House of Lords, his Lordship will send it to Lord Wellesley with his private letter.[1]

Mr. Perceval omitted to state to your Royal Highness, that the business of Lord Wellesley's office will not experience any delay in the interval between his Lordships delivering up of the Seals and the appointment of his successor, as Lord Liverpool[2] will undertake in the interim to discharge the duties of it.[3]

The Marquis Wellesley to the Prince Regent, 18 February 1812. (*Wellesley Papers*, II, 73.)

1 Letters from Eldon and the Prince Regent, dated the 18th, informing Wellesley that his resignation would now be accepted. (*Wellesley Papers*, II, 71–2.)

2 Robert Banks Jenkinson, second Earl of Liverpool (1770–1828). At this time Secretary for War and the Colonies. Prime Minister, June 1812 to February 1827.

3 Castlereagh succeeded Wellesley as Foreign Secretary. He would have preferred to return to the War Office, but Liverpool refused to move. (Spencer Walpole's *Perceval*, II, 266.)

Downing St., Feb. 18, 1812.

UNDERSTANDING that H.R.H. has commanded the Lord Chancellor to wait upon him at 12 this day, I am aware I cannot see H.R.H. at that time. But I beg you will lay my duty before H.R.H. and and [*sic*] request that I may be permitted to wait upon him at his *earliest convenience* this day; as it humbly appears to me to be essentially necessary that I should see his R. Highness before the Ho. of Co. meets this day.

[P.S.] I should be glad if you could get the warrant for Lord Wellingtons pension and the message to the Ho of Lords and Commons this day. His R.H. having expressed the wish that this should have the grace of being the first act of his unrestricted regency.[1]

Pray be so good as to remember that the message must be signed

George P.R. at the top, & *G.P.R.* at *the bottom* of the message.[2]

11 THE DUKE OF NORTHUMBERLAND[3] *to* COLONEL McMAHON

Alnwick Castle, 18th Febry. 1812.

MAY I beg of you to deliver the accompanying letter[4] to the Prince Regent.

I was in hopes of receiving a letter from you, by the last night's post; but as that has not happened, I must now wait till tomorrow for that pleasure, as we have no post that comes in to night.

As the time is now arrived for H:R:H: to act entirely from [*sic*] himself, I trust most sincerely, that all his measures, and conduct, will be marked by that decision, & firmness, which are absolutely necessary for every Prince placed in his most exalted situation. Half measures, I flatter myself, nay indeed I am almost certain, he will never suffer to be even proposed to him. They are only the resources of weak minds.

1 After the capture of the fortress of Ciudad Rodrigo, Viscount Wellington was given an earldom and an annuity of £2000.
2 See *Parl. Deb.* XXI, 842.
3 Hugh Percy, second Duke of Northumberland (1742–1817). Served in the Army during the Seven Years' War and the American War. At first supported the younger Pitt, but after 1788 joined the Prince's party. His political influence at Carlton House was negligible. His members in the Commons voted for the Government, for the first time, on 24 February.
4 An unimportant letter of congratulation on the expiration of the Regency restrictions.

I honour his determination to preserve the utmost fidelity towards our Allies, & to persevere in the defence of the Peninsula. Of the Catholick question, I hope we shall hear no more; at least in the manner, & to the extent, to which the Irish Catholicks have been encouraged to demand it. I must own, shoud I be disappointed in this hope, H:R:H:'s situation, considering the sentiments expressed by the King on this subject, woud be truly distressing. Shoud H:R:H: be induced to accede to it, & the K:[ing] recover, it woud infallibly occasion his highest, & most marked displeasure; & probably be the means of flinging him back again into his present melancholy state. During H:M:'s lifetime therefore I hope the question will be no more agitated; & indeed I cannot say, that those who have chosen to bring it forward just at this time, have either shown their patriotism, or much consideration for the Regent's private feelings. But they laid their real caracters pretty open to H:R:H:, at the time, when H:M: was first declared incapable of carrying on the business of the State. Above all, my dear Colonel, I hope H:R:H: will never be induced, either by persuasion, or otherwise, to do anything which he does not fully approve, or desist from what he thinks proper, & necessary, from the desire of gaining, or the fear of losing a little temporary popularity; but that he will always act, in conformity to a sentiment, I remember to have heard the late Lord Chatham (then Mr. Pitt) deliver in the House of Commons, on the late Mr. Geo: Grenville[1] saying, that the measure Mr. Pitt proposed, woud not, he fancied, gain his Right Honourable relation much popularity— Mr Pitt, rose, & said "I assure the R:H: gentleman, I shall never abstain from what I think necessary, from the fear of incurring a little temporary & transient displeasure from the people—I never *courted* popularity—No, Sir, I hope I have taken a nobler line—I have always endeavoured, by my conduct, *to deserve* it."

This is a sentiment highly becoming a great statesman, and in my humble opinion, not unworthy of a Sovereign. I confess, it struck me at the time, & I have never forgot it.

I think, my dear Colonel, I cannot finish better than with this sentiment, & shall therefore conclude, with desiring you to present the compliments & best wishes of the Duchess,[2] my daughters, & myself, to Mrs. Mac-Mahon, & desiring you to accept the same yourself. I hope you are now perfectly recovered?

1 Prime Minister, 1763–65. [1712–1770.]
2 Frances Julia, daughter of Peter Burrell. She died in 1820.

Alnwick Castle, 21st Febry. 1812.

MANY thanks for your letter of the 17th, as well as for the very interesting paper accompanying it; and I feel most highly honoured by the Prince Regent, in having permitted me to peruse it.

I cannot say I am surprised, altho' not a little shocked, at the conduct of those two personages.[1] Their behaviour, just before H:R:H: was appointed Regent, afforded very little hopes that they woud act otherwise than as they have done. I trust however H:R:H:'s firmness & resolution, (which are by no means inconsistent with moderation & prudence,) will make them repent of their inconsiderate conduct.

In a former letter, long ago, I told you, my dear Colonel, that the commencement of a reign, or government, was always attended by a struggle for power & pre-eminence. The Prince Regent has now found, by experience, that my observation was correct. If however H:R:H: shall on this occasion show a necessary degree of *firmness*, & convince these gentlemen that he is not to be alarmed, & that he will never submit to be dictated to, the struggle will be a very transient one; & the rest of the time of his government, or reign, will pass off with advantage to the Kingdom, & with ease & comfort to himself. But if he suffers himself to be over-persuaded, to give way, we shall again hear the arrogance of disappointment talk of "storming the Closet". Taking places at once by storm is never seriously thought of but when it is well known that the garrison within is weak or the Gov^t is supposed to be timid. With a good garrison, & a wise, determined governor, such attempts are never made. I am therefore convinced that H:R:H:'s good understanding, & decisive character, will frustrate every attempt which arrogance, ambition, or folly may make to take him prisoner & bind him in fetters. The goodness of H:R:H:'s head & heart will make him always listen, with patience, to the advice of whoever may be his Ministers; but the ultimate decision must be his. On this I hope he will ever insist. The late Lord Chatham's sentiment, with respect to popularity, is excellent.[2] A little transient unpopularity, if the measure is a right one, ought to give a wise man very little uneasiness. By continuing to act properly, popularity soon returns again. Not the ephemeral popularity of the wicked, artfull demagogue; but a firm & stable popularity, accompanied with reverence & admiration. H:R:H: is very popular now; the two noble Lords think they are the same; but they will, on trial, find they are very much mistaken.

1 Lords Grey and Grenville.
2 See No. 11.

Adieu my dear Colonel, I fear I shall have tired you with these sentiments of mine. The Duchess, & my family, unite with me in compliments to you, & Mrs. Mac'Mahon. Of course you will be good enough to say every thing proper for me to the Prince Regent.

13 THE EARL OF DARLINGTON[1] *to the* PRINCE REGENT

Raby Castle, Feby 21st 1812.

PRESUMPTUOUS as it may appear in me to address your Royal Highness, I shall venture to rely upon your well known goodness so often experienced by myself to forgive this intrusion, & as I am by this means discharging a bounden duty that I owe to your Royal Highness I entertain a more confident hope of receiving your pardon.

As the restrictions upon the exercise of the Royal authority by your Royal Highness have now ceased, from which you are enabled to form such an Administration as you conceive to be best calculated for conducting the affairs of the Empire at this great & eventfull epoch of our history, the present period of Parliament must be consider'd as the commencement of your Royal Highness's reign.

Before I allow myself to give any vote in Parliament or to recommend any line of conduct for my friends to pursue, I must consider it my indispensable duty to communicate most humbly & respectfully to your Royal Highness such ideas as I conceive ought to govern my political conduct, least [*sic*] it might appear to be a want of respect & duty or of gratitude for the many signal marks of favor with which I have been honor'd for a long series of years, or least there might appear any inconsistency in my parliamentary conduct.

It has long been my glory & pride to be consider'd as an attached friend to your Royal Highness in my publick as well as private life, & in both I have never scrupled to avow that my obligations were such from an early period as to bind me to support your political opinions & more especially your individual interest whenever it was concern'd, in order to do which I have never ceased to endeavour to increase my parliamentary influence at considerable expence & formerly at some personal inconvenience, in which I felt myself most amply repaid by the

1 William Harry Vane, first Duke of Cleveland and third Earl of Darlington (1766–1842). Succeeded to earldom, 1792; created Marquis, 1827; Duke, 1833. Though he had long been closely connected with Carlton House he did not abandon the Whigs when they were deserted by the Prince Regent. It was said in 1815 that having been refused a great Household appointment, he had purchased seven seats, for which he meant to return seven patriots "to vex his ungrateful master". He turned Tory in January 1830.

satisfaction I experienced of evincing in that manner my sense of gratitude with the dutifull recollection of your Royal Highness's unmerited
favors bestow'd upon me. It has also been a matter of much heartfelt
gratification, that the very last time that I was honor'd with a private
Audience of your Royal Highness, you still continued to repose that
confidence in me, as to inform me & shew me a list of those whom you
consider'd your private friends in Parliament, attached to yourself, independent of those great political characters who might be expected to
fill the first offices of the State, in which list, most flattering to my feelings I had the honor of being included.

It is now necessary, Sir, to come to the most distressing & painfull
part of my duty.

Both publick & private reports agree in stating that Mr. Percival &
the principal members of his Administration still continue to enjoy your
Royal Highness's confidence & that you have allow'd him to use his
discretion in strengthening the hands of Government.

If such a report is correct I must bow with submission to your Royal
Highness's choice of servants & to your enlightend and superior
judgment; but from having opposed in most instances those measures,
which the Administration I have alluded to have for some years thought
proper to adopt, & condemning as I must conscientiously do, the avowed
determination of Mr. Percival & his friends, to persist in those principles,
which I conceive to be most injurious to the dearest interests of the
country & equally liable to censure & as repugnant to my own feelings
as those measures adopted by the same men, who deprived your Royal
Highness of your constitutional right, & who proposed & carried the
restrictions, I can not with that consistency so necessary for my own
honor & credit, support such Ministers, & abandon those opinions that
I have long formed & some political characters whom I have long respected & supported, in which I had the great happiness to believe that
I was acting in strict unison with your Royal Highness's wishes.

Thus circumstanced I feel peculiar & distressing difficulty, & shall
suspend my trifling parliamentary support to *any Party*, until I know
whether it is your Royal Highness's fixed determination that the same
men with a trifling variation are to be continued to rule the affairs of the
State, & to persevere in the same system of conduct.

If your Royal Highness should condescend to notice this humble &
respectfull Address, & should intimate any wish for me to explain more
particularly any part of my conduct or the motives which have actuated
me to presume to take this great liberty of humbly addressing you, I shall
most readily & dutifully obey your commands.

Blenheim, Feb^ry 23rd 1812.

I HAVE the honor to submit a personal request to your Royal Highness, in the earnest and humble hope that what I ask may obtain your Royal favor and sanction.

Some years ago I made a family arrangement, such as to secure an ample property to my successor for the due support of the Dukedom, and at the same time, to give to my second son estates which would be fully adequate to the dignity of the Peerage. In pursuing this line, from motives of well-founded affection to those who have so long devoted their whole existence to my happiness, and now to my comfort, I had formed a wish, at the time, to obtain the title of Viscount Churchill to accompany the estates so set apart. I will not now urge that wish, but will only solicit the grant of a Barony to my second son, Francis Almaric Spencer, by the title of Baron Churchill of Sandridge.

If however, from any consideration of which I am not aware, your Royal Highness should not be now disposed to make this grant, I then revert to what has been done in similar instances, I mean in the families of the Dukes of Northumberland and Montague,[2] and I throw myself on your Royal Highness's gracious regard and favor, to grant to me a new Patent of the dignity of Baron Churchill of Sandridge, with remainder to my said second son Francis Almaric Spencer.

I entreat your Royal Highness's kind attention to this statement, and shall receive the result as a very high personal obligation.[3]

1 George Spencer, fourth Duke of Marlborough (1739–1817).
2 After the death of his only son (1770), George Brudenell Montagu, Duke of Montagu and fourth Earl of Cardigan (1712–1790), obtained a revival of the Barony of Montagu in 1786, with remainder to his second grandson, who succeeded him as second Baron.
3 The Prime Minister wrote to the Prince two days later: "Mr. Perceval feels great regret at being obliged to suggest any difficulties in the way of accomplishing his Grace's wishes, which have been so favourably entertained by your Royal Highness, but he feels it his duty to remind your Royal Highness of the numerous claims for peerages which it will be necessary that Mr. Perceval should bring before your Royal Highness in the event of any new Peers being made, and of the consequent determination of your Royal Highness not to attend at present to any such applications. And Mr. Perceval feels satisfied that your Royal Highness will perceive that, whether the peerage be given directly to Lord Francis, or only in remainder after his father's death, it would equally, in both cases, be the grant of a new peerage, and open the question respecting peerages to the same extent. And Mr. Perceval humbly hopes, as your Royal Highness is sensible of the great embarrassments which are occasioned by any prospective engagements for the creation of peers, that your Royal Highness will avoid increasing the number of such engagements." Perceval sent the Duke a copy of this letter, by the Prince's order. Add. MSS. 38191, fo. 214. Lord Francis was created Baron Churchill in 1815. [1779–1845.]

London, Feb 23, 1812.

I am convinced that it is not without some degree of regret that your Royal Highness must reflect on the hardship of the situation in which I was last night placed at Carlton House.[2]

On recollection I can not accuse myself of being deficient either in that decorum and respect which I feel due to your Royal Highness, or in a becoming firmness in asserting my adherence to opinions in which my regard for your Royal Highness and for the welfare of my country had led me to concur.

If in the first respect I could imagine that I had been at all wanting, a consciousness of it would hurt me most seriously—but I am sure your Royal Highness if it had been so would have had the goodness to attribute it to the surprise I must have felt at such an attack, in the place and on the occasion in which of all others it was least to be expected.

In stating my own opinions with becoming firmness I know I was not deficient, but I am not so certain that your Royal Highness permitted yourself to hear me; I think it therefore right to take this mode of most respectfully communicating to your Royal Highness that I completely agreed in opinion with Lord Grey and Lord Grenville concerning the purport of the letter to the Duke of York, and that I do not believe that there are many individuals in His Majesty's dominions who do not concur in the sense they attributed to it, and in which Mr. Perceval understood it when he exultingly announced the disapointment of those dreams to which he supposed your Royal Highnesses former marked partiality had given rise.

Indeed I must fairly say both that the language used by your Royal Highness in the communication is incapable of recieveing any other interpretation—and that the tenor of the letter must convince the world that this was the sentiment intended to be conveyed, by those who ad-

1 James Maitland, eighth Earl of Lauderdale (1759–1839). One of the leading Foxite Peers, and Keeper of the Great Seal of Scotland in the Grenville Ministry, 1806–7. Turned Tory in 1820, taking a prominent part in the King's favour at the Trial of Queen Caroline. Later, a strenuous opponent of the Reform Bill.

2 At a banquet at Carlton House the Prince Regent began "a furious and unmeasured attack" on his old political friends; the Princess Charlotte, who was present, was reduced to tears—tears made memorable by Lord Byron's verses ("Weep, daughter of a Royal line" etc.). Lord Lauderdale, "with great respect but with great earnestness and propriety, addressed the Prince upon the abuse of his friends, vindicated the letters in the strongest terms, declared his adherence to every word and sentiment in them, and, having spoken very strongly but very respectfully, got up to make his bow". And, said Lord Holland, he made it clear that the decision of Lords Grey and Grenville not to join the Tory Government was approved by the rank-and-file of the Party. (*Regency Memoirs*, I, 250; *Further Memoirs*, p. 122.)

vised your Royal Highness in framing it: for it is not possible that they would regard a panegyrick in the conduct of Administration as a proper prelude to announcing their dismissal.

I agreed also with Lords Grey and Grenville in every sentiment expressed in the answer delivered to your Royal Highness. I thought there was the greatest propriety in their declaiming against all personal exclusion, feeling at the present moment an anxious desire to see a strong and extended Government formed on the most liberal basis, by those who could honourably concur in public measures. But I certainly saw no feature in the present times which rendered their junction with Mr. Perceval more consistant with that regard for their country which I trust will always distinguish their conduct, than it was last year or in 1809 on which occasions I had the honor of concuring with your Royal Highness in expressing the strongest approbation of their resolution to decline the connection.

Haveing thus put into your Royal Highnesses hands a distinct record of the opinions I last night presumed more shortly to state—and which in any other situation I should have thought it my duty to have explained much more at length, I should feel myself in the wrong if I presumed to take this opportunity of further intruding on your Royal Highness.

I must therefore suppress the moving, melancholy reflections which occur on the disagreeable scenes I hope I am wrong in anticipating, and confine myself to the more pleasing duty of assuring your Royal Highness that I can with truth say that on this occasion I have acted, as I always must act, in the manner that appeared to me to be most consistent with the regard I have long professed and sincerely feel for your Royal Highness.

16 VISCOUNT MELBOURNE[1] *to the* PRINCE REGENT

Whitehall, Feb[y] 26, 1812.

I TOOK an early opportunity of communicating to William,[2] the very gracious offer your Royal Highness had intrusted me to make to him.[3]

1 Peniston Lamb, first Viscount Melbourne (1748–1828). Created an Irish Baron, 1770; Viscount Melbourne, 1781; British peerage (Baron Melbourne), 1815. For his politics see No. 167.

2 Afterwards Prime Minister. Succeeded his father as second Viscount Melbourne, 1828. At this time, Whig M.P. for Portarlington, but already half a Canningite. (1779–1848.)

3 The offer of a seat at the Treasury Board. William Lamb's letter of the 25th to his father is in Lady Airlie, *In Whig Society*, pp. 106–7. (Copy at Windsor.)

And I humbly take the liberty of inclosing to your Royal Highness, his letter to me, by which your Royal Highness will be more acquainted with his sentiments, than by any report I could make. It gives me great satisfaction to be certain of his sincere attachment to your Royal Highness person, and of his gratitude for the constant kindness he has experienced from your Royal Highness.

And I very much lament that he is so involved at present, by the line of politicks he has followed for so many years.

I was unable on Monday, and ever shall be, Sir, to express my feelings for your Royal Highness's great kindness, by the distinguished honour you intend me.[1]

The pride of my life has been the friendship and unbounded goodness you have shown to me and Lady Melbourne[2] for so many years. Our attachment and fervent wishes for your Royal Highness's health, and happiness and prosperity in every thing, that you can desire, can only cease with our lives.

17 LORD PERCY[3] *to* COLONEL MCMAHON

North House, 27th Feby. 1812.

As I find that my being called up to the House of Peers is likely to be the cause of much observation I shall feel much obliged by your informing me whether I am correct in my ideas, by understanding it as the gracious act of the Prince Regent *alone*, without owing any particular obligation to any Minister, for I feel any [*sic*] anxious wish not to belong to any Party,[4] & believe me, [etc.].

1 His appointment as a Lord of the Bedchamber was gazetted on 10 March. It placed his Whig sons "in an uncomfortable situation". George Eden wrote to his father, Lord Auckland: "George Lamb told me of the appointment with much regret this morning, and at the same time let me know (in confidence) that he had written the fable of the 'Hare who abandoned his friends'", which was published in *The Morning Chronicle*. (Add. MSS. 34458, fo. 355.)

2 Elizabeth, daughter of Sir Ralph Milbanke. (1752–1818.)

3 He succeeded his father as third Duke of Northumberland in 1817, and was Lord-Lieutenant of Ireland, 1829–30. He represented Northumberland in the 1807–12 Parliament. [1785–1847.]

4 Perceval's letter to the Duke of Northumberland, 20 February, shows that Lord Percy owed his peerage to the Prince alone. "I have the satisfaction to acquaint your Grace that I have received His Royal Highness the Prince Regent's commands to give directions for a writ to issue under the Great Seal for calling Lord Percy up to the House of Peers. I hope your Grace will believe that I shall have great pleasure in obeying these commands, but I feel myself obliged to withhold the issuing of them till I have the honour of hearing from your Grace, whether, with a view to any arrangements respecting the County of Northumberland, it would be convenient that the writ should issue immediately...." (Add. MSS. 38191, f. 211.)

18 THE EARL OF MOIRA *to* COLONEL MCMAHON

Thursday Night, Feby 27th [1812.]

WHEN I came home yesterday, I found that Lady Loudoun[1] had had an alarming attack of illness, literally brought on by her anxiety lest the Prince might have forced me to accept the Garter.[2] Judge, therefore, how deep & general the sentiment must be relative to the lamentable circumstances in which we are placed. You will not wonder, from this knowledge of her way of thinking, at the anguish with which I expressed myself to you after we came down from the Prince. Pray take care that he shall see Adam[3] tomorrow as he promised.

19 LORD ERSKINE[4] *to the* EARL OF MOIRA

Feby 27th 1812.

KNOWING as I do the Princes affectionate temper & character, I have no doubt that H:R:H: must be greatly distressed on the subject which I *have privately heard* of; but it appears to me that there is a clear road out of exposing you even to the misconstruction of a moment, as you are too high a man to lose a moment's estimation even on mistaken grounds. The Prince has a noble opportunity of shewing a firm & constant mind towards you by locking up the ribbon in his drawer for *the present*, "*The longest day will have an end*".

I do not mean by this to offer you any advice—Nobody can judge for you.

You know how much I love both the Prince & yourself.

1 The Countess of Moira (d. 1840) was Countess of Loudoun in her own right.
2 See Nos. 7 n., 22, 23.
3 William Adam (1751–1839). Chancellor of the Duchy of Cornwall since February 1806.
4 Thomas Erskine, first Baron Erskine (1750–1823). Lord Chancellor in the Whig Ministry of 1806–7. He was still one of the Prince Regent's friends, but his speeches on behalf of Queen Caroline in 1820 estranged him from George IV.

Norland House, Kensington Gravel Pits,
Feby 28, 1812.

I HAVE to apologise for troubling you with this letter, which under any other circumstances I would not have ventured to have done.

Among my late father's property I find seven portraits on horseback painted by the same artist and of the same sizes as those H.R.H. the Prince Regent has hanging up in the Armory at Carleton House. They are portraits of his present Majesty, his late Majesty, the Duke of Cumberland,[3] uncle to his present Majesty, the late King of Denmark,[4] Marshal Saxe,[5] the Marquis of Granby[6] and the late Earl of Pembroke.[7] They are not pictures of any value. Mr. Christie[8] who I employed to value part of the property valued them at forty guineas, viz two at seven guineas, one at six guineas and four at five guineas ea[ch], but having been informed that H.R.H. collects portraits of this description I should feel exceedingly obliged if you would take an opportunity of mentioning them to H.R.H. to whose collection of equestrian portraits they would certainly be an acquisition.

The price I fix on them is Mr. Christie's valuation as I would on no account ask H.R.H. one shilling more for them than I would any other person.

21 SPENCER PERCEVAL *to the* PRINCE REGENT

Down[in]g S[tree]t, Feb. 28, 1812.

MR. PERCEVAL presents his humble duty to your Royal Highness, & humbly acquaints your Royal Highness, that Sir Thos. Turton[9] brought forward his motion for a Comm^ee on the State of the Nation

1 The clockmaker (1780–1854). The family had held the appointment of Clockmakers to the Crown since 1742.

2 Sir Tomkyns Hilgrove Turner (? 1766–1843). Served in the Netherlands and Egypt. Assistant Private Secretary to the Prince, February 1811; Groom of the Bedchamber, August 1812. Knighted, 1814. "His father", said Farington, the diarist, "was an apothecary who resided at Hillingdon near Uxbridge, but General Turner was by some means educated at Eaton."

3 William Augustus, Duke of Cumberland (1721–1765), third son of George II.

4 Christian VII (d. 1808), the father of Frederick VI.

5 The French Marshal who defeated the British army at Fontenoy in 1745. (1696–1750.)

6 John Manners, Marquis of Granby (1721–1770).

7 Henry Herbert, tenth Earl of Pembroke (1734–1794).

8 James Christie, the younger (1773–1831), antiquary and auctioneer.

9 M.P. for Southwark. [1764–1844.] Created a Baronet, 1796. "He has nothing to do with, and is not owned by, the other side", said Plumer Ward, a ministerialist.

yesterday even^g. He entered much at large into almost all the topics that were connected with the public events of the last five years. He was followed by Mr. Tighe[1] who seconded his motion and the debate proceeded in the following order

For the motion.	Against it.
	Mr. Robinson[2]
Mr. Lamb[3]	
	Mr. Herbert[4]
	Mr. Montagu[5]
Mr. Whitbread[6]	
	Ld. Castlereagh[7]
Mr. Tierney.[8]	
	Mr. Perceval
Mr. Canning.	
Sir. Thos. Turton.	

The House divided between two & three o'clock.

For the motion	136
Against it	209

Mr. Whitbread gave Lord Castlereagh and Mr. Perceval an opportunity of setting right the mistaken reports which had been circulated upon the subject of the surrender of the Ro[man] Ca.[tholic] question as a measure on which it was supposed Government had no feeling and were to have no interference hereafter, & explained the true state on which that question has been explained to stand.[9]

Lord Castlereagh will wait upon your Royal Highness tomorrow, at two o'clock, according to your Royal Highness's appointment, and will state to your Royal Highness that that explanation was quite satisfactory according to his view of it.

1 M.P. for Wicklow County. [d. 1816.]

2 Frederick John Robinson, Viscount Goderich, afterwards first Earl of Ripon (1782–1859). At this time M.P. for Ripon, and a Junior Lord of the Admiralty. Chancellor of the Exchequer, 1823–27; Prime Minister, 1827–28. After 1830 in office under Grey and Peel.

3 William Lamb.   4 Tory M.P. for Kerry County.

5 Tory M.P. for St Germans. (1762–1831.) Succeeded his brother as fourth Baron Rokeby in 1829.

6 Samuel Whitbread (1758–1815), Lord Grey's brother-in-law and leader of the Whig-Radicals and of the peace party in the House of Commons.

7 Robert Stewart, second Marquis of Londonderry (1769–1822). Foreign Secretary, 1812–22. Succeeded his father as second Marquis of Londonderry in 1821.

8 George Tierney (1761–1830), Whig M.P. for Bandon Bridge and one of the Opposition Whigs. Leader of the Opposition in the Commons, 1818–21.

9 Castlereagh joined the anti-Catholic Perceval Ministry on the understanding that he was at liberty to vote, in his individual capacity, for the Catholic question; but at this time he was convinced of the inexpediency of conceding the Catholic claims.

Feby 29th 1812.

HAVE the kindness to deliver the enclosed to our beloved Prince. I trust it will satisfy him; first, of it's being essential for his welfare that I should not now be distinguished by his favors; secondly of my affection's having known no wane or becoming ever capable of it.

23 The Earl of Moira *to the* Prince Regent

Feby 28th 1812.

WITH all humility I entreat your Royal Highness's patient perusal of this letter; which, tho' it may be very tedious, will contain matter deserving your Royal Highness immediate contemplation.

The discussion which I have this day had with Mr. Adam imposes upon me the deeply painful necessity of an explanation hitherto studiously avoided by me. Your Royal Highness is utterly unapprized of the state of the public mind at present; for, it has been too ungracious an office for any body willingly to obtrude the subject upon you. Hopeless of remedying the mischief, I would fain have won you to yield to my reluctance by partial excuses, repressing what could not but give mortification. But I must now either speak without disguise or bear the imputation of an ungenerous procedure towards your Royal Highness.

It grieves me to the soul to tell you, Sir, that the general astonishment at the step which you have taken is only equalled by a dreadful augury for your future security. It is not the dissatisfaction of disappointed expectants to which I allude. A disinterested public views with wonder your unqualified & unexplained departure from all those principles which you have so long professed. It observes with a still more uneasy sensation your abandonment of all those persons for whom you had hitherto proclaimed esteem, whose adherence you had spontaneously solicited, & of whose services (rendered at the expense of foregoing their private advantages) you had for years availed yourself. I do not class myself in this list. My attachment has been repaid by your confidence till within a short time; and both the honor & gratification of that distinction over-balanced any duties I could fulfill. Were I, however, to discriminate myself from the rest by accepting a peculiar mark of your favor, it would be universally construed as a concurrence on my part in the calamitous measures into which you have been betrayed; and from that hour I should be useless to you, when your occasion for the services of even an individual so humble as myself is becoming too probable.[1] Let me implore you Sir, not to treat as impertinent the freedom of these expressions. God knows there is not at this instant a sentiment so foreign to my heart as one that could bear the slightest tinge of disrespect. I do not address your Royal Highness but from severe constraint of circumstances, & I should not meet the necessity if I did not fairly display the case. No one knows of my writing on this subject. Further, I give your Royal Highness my honor that no copy is kept of this letter.

I had weighed, even before your Royal Highness stated it so strongly yesterday, the misrepresentation to which my non-acceptance of your proffered boon was liable; but I had satisfied myself, & I think I must satisfy you, that my disadvantage in that way is far short of the evil inseparable from my being marked as acquiescing in present arrangements. Were I to receive the Garter, it would convince everybody that your aberration was systematic. The unfortunate letter to the Duke of York is already adduced as a proof of a deliberate plan to rid yourself of your old supporters while a consciousness of the real quality of that procedure necessitated a recurrence to some excuse.

Alas, Sir, I must not conceal from you that in the eyes of the country excuse is not furnished either by that letter or by the answer to it. My intimate knowledge of your heart makes me give entire & implicit credit to the sincerity with which your Royal Highness made the overture & to the disappointment you felt at it's not being fully met. Persons who have not been equally happy in the opportunity of appreciating your Royal Highness's frank disposition can only judge from the tenor of the whole letter, which seems calculated expressly to overthrow the ostensible purpose of it. But supposing that Lord Grey & Lord Grenville were not agreeable to your Royal Highness, or admitting that they intemperately declined your overtures, the alternative was not that the existing Administration should be confirmed. With the Duke of Bedford, for instance, your Royal Highness had ancient habits; while his exalted personal character & public principles commanded the confidence of the nation. On each ground, Lord Holland[2] stood similarly recommended to your Royal Highness advertence. Of Lord Wellesley's talents your Royal Highness had recent experience; & he was believed to be personally

---

1 According to Lord Holland Moira drafted an answer to the Prince Regent's letter to the Duke of York, and it insisted, "even in a more authoritative tone than the paper" which Grey and Grenville actually sent, on the impossibility of their joining a Cabinet whose measures they had uniformly reprobated. (*Further Memoirs*, p. 124.)

2 Henry Richard Vassall Fox, third Baron Holland (1773–1840). Nephew of Charles James Fox, and one of the Whig leaders in the House of Lords.

acceptable. Let me not be misconceived by your Royal Highness as stating this from any motive but that of indicating what did unavoidably present itself to every mind on the occasion & what is continually insisted upon by those who wish to give a perverse interpretation to the transaction. The only apology which friendship or candor makes is one which without reservation I believe to be strictly true; namely, that your Royal Highness (unsuspicious from your own consciousness of rectitude) did not scrupulously weigh the terms of a letter insidiously recommended to your adoption. Allow me then, Sir, to revert to the expediency of your not proving, thro' my acceptance of the Garter, your cognizance of the bearing of this procedure. Suffer me to remain the means for your getting back into the path of safety; which you may so without humiliation effect in some future day thro' my being then supposed to have opened your eyes to circumstances before with-held from them. In no other manner can you recede from the course into which you have been plunged, & which I fear leads to fatal issues. The peril is not indistinct or remote. England is from internal distress (a distress augmenting rapidly) on the eve of dangerous ferments. The state of Ireland wants no exposition. In that alarming state of it, Mr. Perceval (I know not how he reconciles it with what he held forth to me thro' your Royal Highness) declares in Parliament the Cabinet to be unanimous against a consideration of the claims of the Irish Catholics. The latter necessarily receive this as the language of your Royal Highness. The conclusion is, that you do not deign even to temporize with their feelings, but that without reason assigned you trample on the hopes which you had encouraged, & bind yourself to a perpetual obstruction of the redress they seek. Pardon me, Sir, for adding that this conclusion is strengthened by the indiscretion of persons admitted to the high honor of your society who have circulated the notion of such being really your disposition.

Amid these mischiefs, Sir, if any one so insignificant as I am can be of use to your Royal Highness it must be by the testimony I can bear to your heart in contradiction to appearances. But that testimony will be invalid if it be not unbought. I have trusted that the sedulity of my attentions would prove to the world that nothing had happened which could interfere with the devotion of my attachment to you; & the observation of the public on that point would lead people to a more just construction of late transactions. Were I to receive the Garter, those attentions would be ascribed to mean-ness & lose their effect with the world; nay, the consciousness of their being open to that imputation would shackle me in paying them. Leave to me Sir, I supplicate you, the freedom of mani-

festing my unaltered & unalterable devotion in the manner most gratifying to my own spirit & most efficacious for your service. My life will
give the lie to all the misconstructions which you apprehend.

Deign, Sir, to believe that the affection which you have authorised me
without presumption to express was never more earnest or more sincere
to you than at this moment. With that assertion & with an attachment
no less perfect than my respect, I remain, Sir, [etc.].

24 EDWARD BOUVERIE[1] *to the* PRINCE REGENT

Somerset Place, March 8th 1812.

UNDERSTANDING that my not having the power of a vote in Parliament is an objection to my being again received in your Royal Highness's Household, I humbly presume to suggest to your Royal Highness,
that there are numerous instances of people without seats in the House,
who have places of double the emolument of what mine would be were
I honoured with your Royal Highness's appointment, such as Mr.
George Villiers[2] in his Majesty's Household, and Ld. George Seymour[3]
in the Excise with other lucrative situations; I put it therefore as a
point of feeling to your Royal Highness, whether you will so far depart
from the inherent goodnature of your disposition, as to hold me up a
marked object to the world of having apparently incurred your displeasure, who was once honoured with your partiality, and who is not
conscious of having intentionally at any time done any thing to forfeit it.

I beg pardon for again intruding upon your Royal Highness, but I
trust my anxiety upon the foregoing subject will plead my excuse.

1 Third son of the second Viscount Folkestone and first Earl of Radnor. Appointed Groom
of the Bedchamber in the Prince's household, 1787. [1760–1824.]

2 The third son of the first Earl of Clarendon, and the father of the fourth Earl (the Foreign
Secretary). [1759–1827.] See Sir Herbert Maxwell's *Life of the Fourth Earl of Clarendon*, I, 8.

3 The seventh son of the first Marquis of Hertford. [1763–1848.]

Apsley House, March 8th 1812.
Sunday night.

LORD WELLESLEY presents his humble duty to your Royal Highness and submits to your gracious consideration whether, under his situation with respect to your Royal Highness's present servants, it would not be indelicate in Lord Wellesley to originate any communication with Lord Castlereagh relating to the proposed return of Mr. Thornton[1] to Sweden.

Lord Wellesley therefore earnestly solicits your Royal Highness to dispense with his interference in this question.

Sir Philip Francis' Memorandum. (Parkes and Merivale, *Memoirs of Sir Philip Francis*, II, 373; there dated 10 March 1812. The Windsor copy is undated.)

26 COLONEL WILSON BRADDYLL[2] *to* COLONEL MCMAHON

Hampton Court, 10th March 1812.

YOU will have no difficulty in believing with what gratitude and sensibility, I have rec? the gracious communication contained in your letter of yesterday.

To you, who have always known the sincerity of my devotion and attachment to the Prince Regent, it is not necessary for me now to enlarge—but certainly if those feelings admitted of increase, they must receive it, from the spontaneous and highly flattering manner, in which he has been pleased to confer upon me this distinguished mark of his Royal favor.

To yourself, my dear Mc.Mahon, every acknowledgment from me, is due, for the very warm and friendly terms in which you have been so good as [to] notify to me, my appointment as Groom of the Bed Chamber to His Royal Highness.

P.S. In any future communications you may have to favor me with— be so good as direct to me Hampton Court, *Green*—& not *Palace*, as this latter is my sons residence.

1 Sir Edward Thornton (1766–1852). In October 1811 Wellesley had sent him to negotiate a peace treaty with Sweden, but the overture was rejected on 19 November and Thornton returned home. Castlereagh now sent him back to Stockholm, where he remained as Minister Plenipotentiary until 1817, and negotiated an alliance against Napoleon (1813).

2 Colonel of the 3rd (Prince of Wales' Own) Royal Lancashire Militia; M.P. for Lancaster, 1780–4. (1755–1818.)

Stephens Green, 10th March 1812.

I TAKE the liberty which your most kind and polite communication has given me in acknowledging its receipt, which could not fail to afford me the highest gratification. The very kind terms in which you mention the merit & celebrity of the Freemans Journal administer not a little to my vanity, as I have been its conductor for the last ten years. With regard however to the publication to which you allude I had little desert: I merely stated your merits & claims. You are therefore under no obligation to me on that head—but I freely confess, that I would be ungrateful indeed, should I not hereafter eagerly seize every opportunity of serving a person by whom I consider myself highly honored & obliged.

I feel a conscious pride that my diurnal political effusions have at all times manifested, that the first wish of my heart has been, and I trust will continue to be, to convince the people of Ireland that the illustrious personage who truly appreciates your merits, was justly entitled to their unbounded respect & confidence. In thus following the unbiassed dictates of my mind, I had a very pleasing task to perform, and succeeded in the most rancorous days of his enemies, in rendering the people of Ireland firmly devoted to His Royal Highness.

It is well known to the Prince Regent, that in 1789 this country gave him an unequivocal proof of the personal attachment of all ranks and descriptions of Irishmen to His Royal Highness;[1] that my humble and assiduous efforts to contribute to the gratification of His Royal Highness, as you have had the goodness to mention, has impressed on my mind sentiments of gratitude which my pen is unequal to describe. To be enabled to indulge the pleasing expectation that His Royal Highness will continue to estimate the merits & claims of the Irish people, in consonance to His Royal Highnesses former gracious declaration—& thereby ensure the happiness of the whole Empire, would afford me the highest gratification that a human breast could be capable of feeling. *Be assured that the situation of Ireland is critical in the extreme.*

My every effort shall be to advance, through the means of my widely circulated popular Journal, the character of my Prince, whom I have personally known for more than sixteen years—and to secure the peace & prosperity of the country. I shall continue my labours to cherish in the virtuous hearts of the people of Ireland the same attachment which they

1 On 27 February 1789 delegates from both Houses of the Irish Parliament presented an Address to the Prince of Wales, requesting him to assume the government of Ireland during the King's illness, with the title of Prince Regent of Ireland.

have hitherto felt towards His Royal Highness. They will yet prove themselves the steadfast friends of his Throne, and if it should ever be assailed its best pillars.

I shall be most anxious to possess a circumstance that will unequivocally prove with what truth I have the honor to subscribe myself [etc.].

28 VISCOUNT CASTLEREAGH *to* COLONEL MCMAHON

St James's Square, March 10, 1812.

MY brother's dutiful attachment to the Prince Regent will I am sure make the gracious mark of favor and recollection which His R.H. has been pleased to shew him, particularly consoling to his feelings at the present moment under the very heavy affliction in which the knowledge of this circumstance will find him. I shall lose no time in apprizing him of the indulgence H.R.H. has shewn for his parliamentary situation which cannot be affected, where an acceptance, *in the legal sense*, cannot be alledged to have taken place.[1]

29 VISCOUNT CASTLEREAGH *to* COLONEL MCMAHON

St James's Sq., 10 March [1812]

IF H.R.H. has done with two boxes (one *red* with Despatches from America, and a communication from the Duke del Infantado,[2] the other *blue* with secret papers) I shall be obliged to you to return them to me, as the Cabinet have not seen them.

1 Major-General the Hon. Charles William Stewart (1778–1854), who succeeded Castlereagh as third Marquis of Londonderry, was appointed a Groom of the Bedchamber in 1812 (gazetted, 18 August). M.P. for Londonderry, 1800–14; Baron Stewart, 1814; Ambassador at Vienna, 1814–22. His first wife died in February 1812.

2 Spanish Ambassador in London.

March 14th 1812.

UNGRACIOUS as is the office of ushering disagreeable information to a reluctant ear, I meant to have imposed upon you the task of representing to the Prince the importance of his conversing with the Knight of Kerry.[1] The latter, just arrived from Ireland, came to me yesterday. The details which he gave of matters brought within his knowledge by his confidential intercourse with the Catholics made me think it essential for him to offer a similar statement to the Prince: because, altho' I had pourtrayed dangers to His Royal Highness, I found I had not sufficiently rated either their magnitude or their proximity. I, therefore, told Mr. Fitz-Gerald that I should solicit you to bring about an audience for him. His answer to a note of mine will show the objections which have since occurred to him. I feel their force: yet I cannot reconcile it to myself to forbear imparting to you the quality of that which he is competent to communicate. Perhaps your best procedure will be to mention before the Prince that the Knight of Kerry is arrived & that he contemplates the state of affairs in Ireland as more immediately formidable than I had considered it. Should the observation excite the curiosity of the Prince he would probably demand the attendance of Mr. Fitz-Gerald & might give the subject more serious attention than if it were in a manner forced upon him.

I also enclose to you, in perfect confidence, a letter from Ld Forbes.[2] Fearing that his father, out of an erroneous notion of attention to me, might advise him to quit his station in the Prince's Household, I wrote most anxiously to beg that he would consider his situation as purely military & not take a step which gave the presumption of any change in our devotion to the Prince. I shall write again to-day to combat his resolution; & I entreat you to keep back his resignation in case he may have sent it to you. I trouble you with his letter merely that you may see there was no spleen in his meditated procedure.

1 Maurice Fitzgerald, Knight of Kerry (1774–1849), Whig M.P. for Kerry County for many years, but joined Wellington's Ministry in 1830 as Vice-Treasurer of Ireland.

2 George John, Viscount Forbes (1785–1836), the eldest son of the sixth Earl of Granard by a daughter of the first Earl of Moira. He was an intimate friend of Thomas Moore, the poet. "Besides being Moira's nephew", wrote Creevey on 1 June, "he is an aide-de-camp to the Regent, and he has received such usage from his Master, either on his uncle's account or his own voting in Parliament, that he won't go near him, and... he came to dine yesterday with the yellow lining and the Prince's buttons taken away from his coat. He said never again would he carry about him so degrading a badge of servitude to such a master."

Alnwick Castle, 14th March 1812.

IT is impossible for me to express the pleasure I felt at the receipt of your last letter. The Prince Regent has in the most magnificent as well as gracious manner, relieved you from any disappointment you might feel in consequence of the late decision of the House of Commons,[1] and the continuance of £800 per annum of your intended pension to Mrs. MacMahon, shoud she survive you, at the same time that it marks H.R.H's generous attention to the feelings of an old and *most faithfull* servant, removes from your mind every uneasy thought with respect to her in future, and will render the remainder of your days tranquil and happy. If I might presume to suggest anything to you, my dear Colonel, on this occasion, it woud be, as the two appointments the P.R. means to confer upon you will bring you £3,000 pr. Ann. and as this income is nearly secured to you by the pension which is to take place shoud you lose either of these places, for you to request the P.R. to permit you, *for the present*, to decline the honour he intends you of naming you one of the Privy Council, and rather to keep this in reserve as a further mark of his approbation of your services upon some future occasion. Everybody I am sure must highly approve of the rewards which H.R.H. is granting to your long, tried, and faithfull services; but I fear this last intended honour, *added to the rest*, will raise you up many enemies; and, as it is a mere feather, I should be sorry if it occasioned the smallest risk of adding any alloy to the universal satisfaction which the other parts of H.R.H's goodness to you cannot fail to occasion.

I am perfectly convinced that the office of Private Secretary to the Sovereign cannot be held with a seat in Parliament and that on your accepting it you must give up your seat.[2] But I am certain that you know my regard for you too well to imagine that I woud allow such a personal consideration to myself to stand in the way of H.R.H's intended rewards for your services. I have never allowed such considerations to interfere with your elections and re-elections when they coud be beneficial to you. From Mr. Crespigny's[3] letter, which I return you herewith,

1 On 9 January Creevey complained of the practice of increasing the number of placemen in the House of Commons, and criticised McMahon's appointment as Paymaster of Widows' Pensions, a sinecure worth about £2700 a year. On 24 February, by a majority of three, the House refused to vote McMahon's salary. Three weeks later, however, the *London Gazette* announced his appointment as Keeper of the Privy Purse and Private Secretary to the Prince Regent. See Preface.

2 McMahon vacated his seat upon being appointed Paymaster of Widows' Pensions, and was re-elected on 15 January 1812. He finally retired from Parliament when he became Keeper of the Privy Purse.

3 The Crespigny family were at this time the patrons of Aldborough, McMahon's seat. See No. 43.

I think he clearly consents to re-elect you again. How far he may consent to take Mr. Garrow[1] in your place I cannot tell, for this Parliament, when the agreement ceases. The arrangement of this however I must leave to you and Mr. Crespigny to settle. I beg H.R.H. to be assured, at all events, that I shall have great pleasure in Mr. Garrow occupying your seat if Mr. Crespigny will consent to it; and this must be as a *personal* compliment to the Prince; as otherwise Mr. Raine,[2] for whom I have been endeavouring to procure a seat, during the whole of this Parliament, might pretend to be disappointed. This being a *personal* compliment to the Prince will remove the difficulty.

I shall be very anxious till I hear from you how this matter is settled, and whether Mr. Garrow is accepted. And I hope likewise to receive from you, my dear Colonel, some information relative to the question I asked you in my last[3] about a certain Noble Lord[4] abroad. Present my duty to the P.R. and assure H.R.H. that I shall feel a singular satisfaction in gratifying his wishes by the introduction of Mr. Garrow into Parliament, and that altho' some of those whom H.R.H. formerly honoured with his countenance have not made him the most grateful return for such a distinguished honour, he may rely on my constant attachment to his person, and zeal for his service.

We all unite in the best wishes to you and Mrs. MacMahon, and believe me [etc.].

[P.S.] Tho' out of Parliament, pray continue to communicate with Lord Percy, as it is C[arlton] H[ouse] and not the Minister whose wishes I am anxious he should follow.

32 SIR VICARY GIBBS[5] *to* [COLONEL MCMAHON]

Russell Square, March 14th 1812.

ON my return from the House of Commons last night I had the honor to receive the Prince Regent's commands that I should take into my con-

1 Sir William Garrow (1760–1840). In February 1806 he succeeded William Adam as Attorney-General to the Prince of Wales. At this time he was without a seat in Parliament. He was appointed Solicitor-General in June 1812, Attorney-General May 1813, and a Baron of the Exchequer, 1817. Knighted, July 1812. See No. 36.

2 Jonathan Raine was elected for Launceston, the Duke of Northumberland's borough, on 8 May 1812.

3 This letter is missing.　　　　4 Probably Viscount Strangford. See No. 37.

5 Attorney-General since April 1807. Appointed a puisne Judge in the Court of Common Pleas, May 1812; Lord Chief Baron, 1813; Chief Justice of the Common Pleas, 1814–18. As Attorney-General he waged incessant war against the democratic press. [1751–1820.]

sideration a scandalous paragraph in the British Press[1] of yesterday. I found at the same time a reference from the Secretary of State touching a paragraph upon the same subject in the Morning Chronicle of the 9th. inst.[1] and perhaps it will be most convenient that we should report upon these together. I would not however pursue this course without knowing whether it suits His Royal Highness's pleasure, and this you can probably inform me [of] without troubling His Royal Highness again.

I am very glad that you are better and hope to hear soon of your perfect recovery.

33 Sir Vicary Gibbs *to* [Colonel McMahon]

Russell Square, March 15th 1812.

In obedience to the Prince Regent's commands, signified to me by your letter of yesterday, I have considered the paragraph to which you refer me in the British Press of the 13th. instant, and think it not only indecent and offensive to the highest degree but clearly in the eye of the Law a libel for which the author or publisher, if he were prosecuted, *ought* to be convicted.

Whether it be adviseable to make it the subject of a prosecution or not is a question of more difficulty.

After the experience which I have had of the temper of juries in trials for libel I cannot be assured, even in such a case as the present, that they would convict, for, however the generality may be disposed, one prejudiced and obstinate man may and sometimes does tire the rest into a bad verdict, and I apprehend that whatever mischief might result from leaving such a publication unnoticed would be increased beyond all calculation by an unsuccessful attempt to convict the publisher.

1 The British Museum does not possess a copy of this newspaper. The *Morning Chronicle* of 9 March contained the following paragraph, with its scarcely veiled allusion to the Tory influence of the Prince Regent's reputed mistress, the Marchioness of Hertford:

"Lyceum—On Saturday a new farce, under the title of *Turn Out*, was performed at this place.... One joke was caught at with avidity by the audience as applicable to existing circumstances, and was highly applauded. Miss Duncan, the fair favourite of a politician, says, affects to be struck with the grandeur of political projects and offers to assist the Patriot's labours [*sic*].

"Dowton—'What! a young woman turn politician?'

"Miss Duncan—'Why not? Have we not a sufficient number of old ones?'

"The audience burst into a loud peal of laughter at this poignant allusion; for though John Bull is too manly to turn the finger of scorn at a Lady for feminine foibles, yet, when a woman forgets the just decorum of her sex so far as to exert a malignant influence over the Counsels of the State, the annals of the Empire may teach her to expect sarcasm."

It is on this account only that I feel it my duty to point out the chance of failure in such a prosecution.

For myself, I have not the least objection to filing an Information, but the consequences may be of so much importance to the public that I think the measure should be well considered before it is resolved on.

34 THOMAS EDWARD WYNN BELASYSE[1] *to the* PRINCE REGENT

Lower Grosvenor Street, March 16th 1812.

WITH the highest respect I venture to lay my humble request at your Royal Highness's feet.

By the death of Lord Uxbridge[2] the Constableship of the Castle of Carnarvon is become vacant. It is an office that had long been held by different branches of my family, and was held by my late father[3] for upwards of twenty years.

I now beg leave humbly to state to your Royal Highness, that upon the question of the Regency being agitated in the House of Commons many years ago, I did strongly urge my father to vote in favor of your Royal Highness's claims. I felt grateful for the notice your Royal Highness had condescended to honor me with at that early period of my life, and I had no other way of proving my gratitude but by my father's voting as he then did. Upon his so doing, Mr. Pitt[4] immediately took from him the Constableship of the Castle of Carnarvon as well as the office of Receiver General in North Wales.[5] Lord Uxbridge was appointed to succeed my father in the Constableship, which caused my family's interest in the borough of Carnarvon, which they had long represented, to be materially injured, and my father in consequence lost his seat for that borough after having represented it for twenty five years.[6]

I most humbly entreat your Royal Highness's gracious consideration of these circumstances, and as I am now the only one of my family of an

1 He took the additional surname Belasyse when he married Charlotte, the eldest daughter and co-heir of Henry Belasyse, fifth Earl of Falconberg, who died in 1802.

2 Henry Paget, first Earl of Uxbridge (1744–1812), father of the first Marquis of Anglesey, the distinguished soldier.

3 Glynn Wynn, brother of the first Baron Newborough. (d. 1807.)

4 The Younger Pitt (1759–1806).

5 He had been given this office of Receiver General of Land Revenue in North Wales and Chester in 1781.

6 Between 1768 and 1790.

age to hold this situation, my cousins Lord Newbrough[1] & his brother[2] being both young and under my care, I do most earnestly hope that your Royal Highness will not deem me presumptuous in requesting that your Royal Highness would be graciously pleased to recommend that I should be appointed Constable of the Castle of Carnarvon.

35 VISCOUNT FORBES *to* COLONEL McMAHON

Bunny Park, March 17th 1812.

FEELING that my political opinions do not in the least degree accord with those of the Ministers, in whom His Royal Highness the Prince Regent has thought it expedient to repose his confidence, I feel it my duty to entreat, that you will, in the most submissive terms submit to His Royal Highness my wish to resign the situation in his Household, to which His Royal Highness was graciously pleased to appoint me, as it would not be consistent with the respect due to His Royal Highness, to vote in opposition to his Ministers whilst I retained a situation in his family.

I must ever retain the most warm and dutiful sense of gratitude for the distinguished honor it pleased His Royal Highness to confer on me, but I feel that under existing circumstances it is impossible for me to act otherwise than I do, without a total dereliction from all political consistency.

If this mode of communication be improper I must beg of you my dear Sir to point out to me the most respectful manner of stating my determination to His Royal Highness. You will much oblige me by giving me as early an answer as you can supposing you should consider that my resignation would come better through any other channel.

With many apologies for the liberty I take, I remain, my dear Sir [etc.].

1 Thomas John Wynn, second Baron Newborough (1802–1832).
2 Spencer Bulkeley Wynn, third Baron Newborough (1803–1888).

Maidstone, Wednesday, 18th March, 1812.

Your favour of yesterday was delivered to me in Court where I have been engaged laboriously ever since, and in half an hour I am to go into the Crown Court to try prisoners in assistance of Mr. Justice Grose.[1] Your letter requires an immediate answer and I have not a moment to write.

It was impossible for me not to feel the deepest sense of gratitude for the gracious recollection with which I have been honoured by His Royal Highness the Prince Regent upon the present as upon many former occasions, but if I may be permitted I would presume to say that at the present very advanced age of the Parliament I should, as it regards any views or objects of my own, very much prefer not to be returned upon the opportunity which now offers.[2] At the same time I beg leave to repeat, what I had before occasion to say, that if the service of His Royal Highness should be considered as in any manner to render my attendance desirable, or it shall be the pleasure of His Royal Highness to command it, I can have but one duty most implicitly and gratefully to obey.

I am sure you will have the goodness to make every allowance for the very hasty manner in which, without the power to correct, I am obliged to dispatch this. You will say everything for me which you know I feel.

37 The Duke of Northumberland *to* Colonel McMahon

Alnwick Castle, 18th March, 1812.

I am very glad to learn from your letter of the 13th. that the Regent's first Levee went off so well; and it afforded me much satisfaction to find that H.R.H. marked strongly his displeasure towards a certain noble Lord who, in addition to everything else, had the audacity to talk of publishing a conversation which passed at the Regent's private table. It is highly necessary the Regent should now be firm. He has had a fine opportunity of judging of the true caracters of different men; and of discovering the real motives of their pretended attachment to him.

His Royal Highness can now clearly discriminate those whose attachment to his Royal person was truly sincere, from those who only pretended to feel such an attachment to answer their own private purposes; who cared only for H.R.H. as much as conduced to their views of

1 Sir Nash Grose (1740–1814). Judge of the King's Bench, 1787–1813. Knighted, 1787.
2 See No. 31.

aggrandisement; and I sincerely hope he will by his conduct towards them make them sensible that they have incurred his displeasure.

I foretold you may remember, my dear Colonel, upwards of a year ago, that there woud be a violent struggle when H.R.H. assumed the reins of Government, and the event has proved, I was correct. *Firmness* and *firmness alone* will now ensure H.R.H's future tranquility and happiness. Shoud he be unfortunately persuaded to give way in the least at this present moment, they will do what they threaten, storm the Closet and, having taken the R[egent] prisoner, they will compel him to act in every particular as they please.

God grant that H.R.H. may preserve firmness enough to overset all their designs against him. The struggle will be short and when they find that H.R.H. will not yield and is not to be intimidated, they will be too happy to accept the good things of this world, upon H.R.H's own terms. It now depends entirely upon the Regent himself whether these proud, haughty and ungrateful men shall in future be his servants or his masters. I am most sincerely grieved at what I hear about Lord Moira's conduct. The Regent's partiality towards him for so many years merited a far different return. It is impossible the P.R. can ever forgive or forget it. The insult offered to the Prince and the indignity offered to the Order, in refusing the Garter, when H.R.H. was graciously pleased to signify his intention of decorating him with it, added to the ingratitude of forsaking H.R.H. at the present most critical juncture, can never be overlooked by the Regent.

At all events I hope the Regent will not permit the word *Compromise*, much less the thing itself, to enter into any arrangement or negotiation in which H.R.H. is any way concerned. It woud, in my humble opinion, be highly unbecoming the dignity of his situation.

I hope the letter I did myself the pleasure of writing to you on the 14th. pleased the Regent and was satisfactory to yourself?

I am obliged to you for what you say respecting Lord Strangford,[1] for whom you know how much I interest myself.

I trust the P[rince] R[egent] has now nearly compleated his arrangements,[2] which I can for some time merely look upon as temporary and not finally settled.

Present the offer of my most dutifull attachment to H.R.H. and be assured I ever am, with the most unfeigned regard, my dear Colonel, [etc.].

1 Percy Clinton Sydney Smythe, sixth Viscount Strangford and first Baron Penshurst (1780–1855), Envoy Extraordinary and Minister Plenipotentiary to the Portuguese Court 1808–15. The Court was resident in Brazil from 1808 to 1821.

2 The Household appointments were gazetted early in March; the political changes were not completed until April, when Sidmouth and some of his friends took office.

38 Benjamin West[1] to Major-General Turner

Newman Street, March 19th 1812.

Your letter to me by the command of His Royal Highness the Prince Regent, I had the honor to receive last night, respecting Sir Wm. Beechey[2] being permited to have the large picture of the King at a Review from Windsor, in order to repair it, and afterwards to send it to Hampton Court. On this subject I have written to Sir William, and I will see that the Regents commands are carried into effect.

With respect to the commands with which I was honored by the Prince Regent, concerning the pictures in the several Royal Palaces, and naming those pictures of the first class amongst them—I have accomplished—and will early in next week, beg of you to name a day for me to call on you for this business, as well as to mention some resolves which are now forming in the Royal Academy, to be laid before the Prince Regent, for the honour of his inspection, and if approved, to sanction, agreeable to the Laws of the Institution.

39 Viscount Forbes to Colonel McMahon

Bunny Park, March 20th 1812.

In answer to your very obliging letter which I received this morning I can only say; that in tendering my resignation to His Royal Highness I thought I did that, which was most respectful towards His Royal Highness and for this reason; that feeling I must vote in opposition it is only right that I should state my intention and so leave it to His Royal Highness to say whether under those circumstances he will allow me to remain one of his household.[3] Of course I cannot but feel highly honored in retaining so distinguished a mark of His Royal Highness's gracious favor but I can do so only with the understanding that I shall be considered as perfectly free on *every* question which will come befour the House of Commons.

I wish this to be understood and I own I cannot see how it is to be compassed unless you take an opportunity of mentioning it to His Royal Highness which you will much oblige me by doing. I have the most grateful sense of His Royal Highness's goodness to me and regret that circumstances should oblige me to appear so unworthy of it but I should be truly so, if I acted otherwise.

1 The painter, and President of the Royal Academy. [1738–1820.]
2 The painter. [1753–1839.] Knighted, 1793.　　　　　　3 See No. 35.

Alnwick Castle, 20th March 1812.

MAY I desire you to present the enclosed to the Regent. Lord Percy having informed me that he has received his summons to the House of Peers, I have thought it right to assure H:R:H: how sensibly I feel the honour he has done him.

I hope the Regent was not displeased with my letter to you on the 14th & I trust that you will be able to settle every thing with Mr. Crespigny about Mr. Garrow. Mr. Wilson wrote to me about the probability of your wanting another re-election, & I referred him to you.

Excuse my scrawl for I have only just time to save the post.

41 THE EARL OF MOIRA *to* COLONEL MCMAHON

Hockerill, March 20th 1812.

I WAS so beset with intruders & variety of business before I left town that I could not send the enclosed[1] to you: So I avail myself of my first halt to do it. You will perceive it to be the answer to my last, the tenor of which I mentioned to you. The best procedure will be for you to submit at once his difficulties to the Prince; putting the matter on it's true ground, namely his delicacy about voting against the Ministers of His Royal Highness while in the Prince's service, at the same time that his obligations to his constituents bind him to a particular line in Parliament. He, as well as myself, has the justest sense of the Prince's peculiar kindness in nominating him to be one of His Royal Highness's Aide-de-Camps: And it is that which occasions his embarrassment.

Broughton, of the Foreign Office, spoke to me as I was preparing to get into my chaise to ask if I could have any interest for his getting the Agency of New South Wales, become vacant by Chinnery's[2] flight from the Treasury. Perhaps by speaking to Arbuthnot[3] you could forward the views of Broughton, who is an excellent man & every [way] calculated for the thing. It was thro' Broughton that a secret business respecting a French spy was managed, with the privity of the Prince. The Ministers got hold of it & knocked it up.

1 Missing: presumably a letter from Viscount Forbes. See Nos. 30, 35 and 39.

2 One of the Chief Clerks in the Treasury. He absconded in March after embezzling £70,000 (it was said) over a period of years. Besides a large salary he enjoyed several lucrative Colonial Agencies, but had been living beyond his means. His dinner parties were "select" and "exquisite", but he "ill disguised, under tolerable French and Italian, and a profusion of civility, the quill behind his ear". In the summer he was reported to be living at Gottenburgh.

3 Charles Arbuthnot (1767–1850), (Parliamentary) Secretary of the Treasury, 1809–23, and the Duke of Wellington's confidential friend.

Tehran, 20th March 1812.

HAVING received your gracious commands to make your Royal Highness duly acquainted with Mirza Abdul Hassan Khan's situation at this Court, I presume to approach you with the following account.

From the favorable reports I was authorized to make of the Mirza's conduct in England,[2] but most particularly from the intimation that your Royal Highness was pleased to be interested in his welfare, His Persian Majesty has really shewn a very sincere wish to raise him to a situation of dignity and emolument at Court and about his own person. The head of the Council however, who is supposed to have occasioned the death of the late Grand Vizier (the Mirza's uncle) from hatred to the family and jealousy of the Mirza's insinuating manners, secretly opposed his elevation, although he repeatedly promised me his best support towards it. Whilst the discussions respecting the Definitive Treaty were pending I could not shew my resentment at this duplicity as the person in question was not only the Prime Minister but the principal plenipotentiary.

Since the signing of the Treaty however I have used my personal influence with the Shah, and I am happy to say, without much irritating the Premier, I have had the good fortune to fix the poor Mirza in a lucrative situation of high dignity far exceeding his most sanguine expectations.

He begs that I may lay his "humble and grateful duty and acknowledgements at your Royal Highness's feet for this great and most unexpected blessing, all the consequence of your Royal Highness's gracious commands to me, the morning we had the honor to take leave of your Royal Highness at Carlton House". Your Royal Highness will have received ere this His Persian Majesty's letter which, as it was extremely well meant, I presume to trust will not be unsatisfactory to your Royal Highness. In truth I must do him the justice to say that he never speaks of your Royal Highness but in terms of profound respect and rapturous admiration.

The Definitive Treaty which I have just concluded will be laid before your Royal Highness probably at the same time that this humble Address will be presented. If my exertions and conduct here should fortunately

---

1 Ambassador Extraordinary and Plenipotentiary in Persia, 1811–14. (1770–1844.)

2 He visited England in the capacity of Ambassador in 1810, delivering his credentials on 17 January, and presenting the Queen with three boxes of jewels, several shawls, and a carpet. A few days later he was introduced to the Prince Regent, who presented him with a clock, invented by Congreve. He left England in July, accompanied by Sir Gore Ouseley and his secretary, James Justinian Morier.

be honored by your Royal Highness's distinguishing approbation I shall indeed be the proudest and happiest of human beings.[1]

Your Royal Highness's Arab horse and some trifles, the produce of this country, will accompany the ratified Treaty to England.

I have the honor to subscribe myself with the deepest sense of respect, gratitude, devoted attachment and obedience, [etc.].

43 THE DUKE OF NORTHUMBERLAND *to* COLONEL MCMAHON

Alnwick Castle, 22nd March 1812.

I HAD the pleasure of receiving your letter of the 19th, by the post last night, and I beg you will believe me, that it ever has, & ever will afford me the greatest pleasure whenever I can do any thing that can tend to your benefit, or the accomplishment of any wish of your's. I coud have wished that on the present occasion H:R:H:'s desire, of having his Attorney General, Mr. Garrow, returned for Aldeburgh for the remainder of the Parliament, had taken place, because you know how devoted I am to H:R:H:.

Mr. Garrow however declines the offer, in his letter[2] to you, which I herewith return. The very short, and precarious time, which any body would have to sit, together with the expence of the election, & its taking a professional man out of the course of his business, will make it equally objectionable to Mr. Raine. In this case therefore I think it will be most adviseable, to give up the remainder of this Parliament, & return the seat into Mr. Crespigny's hands. Especially as the shortness of time before the day of nomination will hardly permit me to look out for a friend and be able to arrange every thing, before the day of election. Indeed I do not even know upon what terms Mr. C[respigny] would consent to make the transfer. May I therefore beg of you to be kind enough to inform Mr. C[respigny] of my intentions of releasing him for the remainder of this Parliament, & that I return this seat to him.

I am very sorry to give you all this trouble, which however is not my fault.

Knowing that your time is so much occupied, especially at your first taking possession of your two new offices, I will only detain you, to desire you will offer my duty to the P:R: & accept yourself of the com-

1 For English relations with Persia at this time, when a petty war between Persia and Russia was in progress, see Professor C. K. Webster's *Foreign Policy of Castlereagh*, I, 90.
2 No. 36.

pliments of congratulations & the good wishes of myself and family. Be so kind as to present our compliments to Mrs. MacMahon. Adieu my dear Colonel and be assured I ever am with the greatest truth [etc.].

44 VISCOUNT MELVILLE[1] *to* COLONEL MCMAHON

Park Lane, 22nd March 1812.

IF you will have the goodness to return the inclosed [missing] to me at the India Board tomorrow morning, I will direct a copy of it to be sent *officially* to Mr. Tyrwhitt,[2] with a request that he & any other gentlemen interested in the matter will appoint a time to converse with me on the subject of their application.

I suspect they are not aware how much the conquest of Java may operate to the prejudice of the tin trade from this country, however advantageous that acquisition may be in other respects. The East India Company will now have neither the power nor the commercial means of preventing this competition, if Java (as will probably be the case,) is retained under the dominion of the Crown.[3] These hints are for your own private information at present, but it will be my duty to point them out also to the Cornish gentlemen.

I am afraid that in the course of a day or two, with the Prince Regent's permission, I shall have to intrude on His Royal Highness for a short time on some Indian topics now under consideration.

45 SPENCER PERCEVAL *to the* PRINCE REGENT

Downing Street, March 23rd 1812.

MR. PERCEVAL presents his humble duty to your Royal Highness. He is just returned from the House of Commons, & proceeds immediately to acquaint your Royal Highness that he brought before the House, the

1 Robert Saunders Dundas, second Viscount Melville (1771–1851); at this time President of the Board of Control. First Lord of the Admiralty, April 1812–27, 1828–30.

2 Sir Thomas Tyrwhitt, Private Secretary to the Prince of Wales, 1796; Keeper of the Privy Seal and Private Secretary to the Prince, 1797–1804; Auditor and Secretary of the Duchy of Cornwall, 1797–1804; Deputy Warden of the Stannaries, 1804; Lord Warden of the Stannaries, 1805–12; Knighted, 8 May 1812; First Gentleman Usher Daily Waiter, June 1812 to 1832. (d. 1833.)

3 Sir Samuel Auchmuty's force conquered Java from the Dutch in August 1811, but the island was restored at the peace.

4-2

consideration of the provision to be made for their Royal Highnesses the Princesses.[1]

Mr Creevy[2] opposed the Speaker's leaving the Chair, and proposed to postpone the consideration of the question for a month—not objecting to some liberal provision being made for their R. Highnesses but thinking it necessary to have a previous enquiry into the state of the Consolidated Fund, before that additional charge was brought upon it. The House however resolved itself into the Committee, and the Vote for £9000 pr An^m for each of their R Highnesses was proposed. It was opposed on various grounds by Mr. Tierney, Mr Ponsonby,[3] Mr Bennet,[4] Mr. Whitbread, Mr Will^ms Wynn,[5] Mr. Wrottesley,[6] Mr. H. Thornton.[7] It was supported by Mr. Perceval, Mr. Freemantle,[8] and Col. Ellison.[9] The objection in general was not to the grant or its amount, but to the time. Some thought there should be a previous enquiry into the state of the Civil List, that it might be seen whether such a reform might not be effected in the Civil List, as would produce a saving equal to the amount of the grant required. Mr. Ponsonby thought the grant not too large but saw no reason for accelerating the period at which the provision should take place, conceiving that it would be right to leave it as under the former Act to take effect at the demise of the Crown. Notice was taken by some of the speakers of the situation of Her R. Highness the Princess of Wales.[10] Mr. Perceval thought it right to explain what had been done by your R. Highness in the arrangement for her debts, and the encrease of her income. Mr. Perceval was called upon particularly

1 The proposal was to increase the annuity which had been previously settled on each of the King's daughters (the Princesses Augusta Sophia, Elizabeth, Mary, and Sophia) from £6000 to £9000, exclusive of the grant of £4000 each from the Civil List.

2 The Whig politician and diarist (1768–1838).

3 Leader of the Whig Opposition in the House of Commons, 1808–17. [1755–1817.] His father was the second son of the first Earl of Bessborough.

4 Henry Grey Bennet (1777–1836), second son of the fourth Earl of Tankerville.

5 Charles Watkin Williams Wynn (1775–1850), Lord Grenville's nephew, and leader of the Grenvillite party in the House of Commons. Under Home Secretary, 1806–7. In Opposition from 1807 to 1821. President of the Board of Control, 1822–28.

6 Whig M.P. for Brackley (d. 1825). The brother of Sir John Wrottesley, first Baron Wrottesley.

7 Henry Thornton (1760–1815), the banker, friend of Wilberforce and member of the "Clapham Sect".

8 Sir William Henry Fremantle (1766–1850), a member of the Grenville party. Joint Secretary of the Treasury, 1806–7; Commissioner of the India Board, 1822–26. Knighted, 1827.

9 Richard Ellison, M.P. for Lincoln.

10 The Prince of Wales, in order to please his father, had married his cousin, Princess Caroline of Brunswick-Wolfenbüttel (1768–1821), in 1795. After the birth of their only child, Princess Charlotte, in January 1796, they separated. Caroline went to live at Blackheath and the Prince resumed his connexion with Mrs Fitzherbert, whom he had secretly married in 1785.

to say why he did not either bring forward a charge against Her R. Highness or propose an adequate provision for her. It was alleged that he must either in his character of counsel to the Princess or as Minister to your Royal Highness be enabled to state the grounds of the separation. Much more was said to the same effect. Mr. Perceval said that he did not conceive it to be his duty in any character to say anything upon a subject, which however much it might be to be [*sic*] lamented, it did not appear to him could with any propriety be discussed in that House— but that as to bringing any charge against Her Royal Highness he certainly had not any to bring forward. With respect to voting any encrease to Her R. Highness's establishment, he had received no commands for that purpose, but if he could collect that it was the sense of the House that some additional provision should be made for Her R. Highness he had no doubt he should receive authority for it. This conversation lasted for some time, but the resolution was agreed to without a division and it will be reported tomorrow. Mr. Perceval does not doubt that the Bill to carry the resolutions into effect will pass tho' probably not without some more discussion yet without any difficulty.

46 SPENCER PERCEVAL *to the* PRINCE REGENT

Downing St, March 24th 1812.

MR. PERCEVAL presents his respectful duty to your R. Highness. He acquaints your Royal Highness that Lord Jocelyn,[1] has made those arrangements which were necessary previous to his formally accepting your R. Highness's gracious offer of the situation of Comptroller of the Household, so as not to interfere with his Parliamentary situation. And Mr. Perceval is humbly to represent to your R. Highness that his Lordship waits your R. Highness's commands as to the time when he should pay his duty to your Royal Highness & receive the wand of his office.

1 Succeeded his father as third Earl of Roden in 1820. (1788–1870.) M.P. for Louth County. His appointment as Vice-Chamberlain of the Household was gazetted on 18 August.

47. THE EARL OF MOIRA *to* COLONEL MCMAHON

Holkham, March 26th 1812.

MANY thanks to you, my dear friend, for having so kindly satisfied Ld Forbes' scruples. I was in great anxiety about it. I would not on any account that a step from any one connected with me should seem to exhibit abandonment of our dear unhappy Prince.[1] God knows, sufficient vexation (without that) is coming upon him rapidly. Accept my truest congratulations for the distinction conferred on yourself.[2] It is one which you have earned so honorably that the universal assent of the public ratifies the favor & renders it a real dignity. Long may you enjoy it; with increase if it be possible of the honest estimation which you receive from your country & which you should contemplate with no ordinary satisfaction.[3]

48 VISCOUNT FORBES *to* COLONEL MCMAHON

Bunny Park, March 26th 1812.

I FEEL most grateful for His Royal Highness's gracious goodness in permitting me to remain his Aid de Camp.[4] I must ever feel it my highest distinction to serve His Royal Highness in any capacity. I congratulate you most sincerely on yʳ appointment and remain [etc.].

49 BENJAMIN WEST *to* MAJOR-GENERAL TURNER

Newman Street, March 28th 1812.

THE two papers which will accompany this letter, I take the liberty to place in your hands for the purpose of being privetly laid befor His Royal Highness the Prince Regent for his consideration. The first of them is the copy of an Address proposed to be presented to the Prince Regent: prepeared by the President and Council of the Royal Academy, and sanctioned by the General Assembly of Academicians. Which

---

1 See Nos. 30, 35 and 39.

2 McMahon's appointment as Keeper of the Privy Purse, and Private Secretary to the Prince Regent, was gazetted on 17 March.

3 In 1813, however, Peel, the Irish Secretary, said that Lord Forbes was "decidedly in opposition". (Add. MSS. 40283, fo. 129.) But he seems generally to have supported the Government.

4 See Nos. 35 and 39.

Address is now writing by Mr. Tomkins[1] on velum (as was customary to be done to those which the Academy had the honor of presenting to His Majesty) and which Mr. Tomkins will have finished in the ensueing week. In the week following—should it be the pleasure of the Prince Regent to condescend to receive the Address—His Royal Highness will be graciously pleased to signify the day in that week to be waited on: I hear beg leave humbly to remark, that when ever my predecessor, and myself had the honor of presenting an Address to His Majesty, we were only accompanied by the Secretary, and Treasurer of the Academy; but, should the Regent honour the Academicians by receiving their Address —he will be graciously pleased to signify, in what manner, it is his pleasure to be waited on, with the Address.

The second paper, is a statement of the institution of the Royal Academy, as founded, and patronised by His Majesty from the year 1768.

Your communication with His Royal Highness the Prince Regent respecting the contents in this letter, will be ever considered a favour by [etc.].

P.S. I have the gratification to state, for the information of His Royal Highness the Prince Regent—that in obedience to the commands with which I was honored, respecting the collection of the Royal pictures— that I am prepeared with the statement of them for his inspection, when ever he m[a]y be pleased to signify his pleesure to see me on the subject.

50. *Extract from the Minutes of the* SUBLIME SOCIETY OF BEEF STEAKS, *Saturday, 28 March* 1812.

RESOLVED that our illustrious brother the Prince of Wales being now Regent without restrictions and effectually Sovereign of this country, his seat in this Society is necessarily become vacant.

A motion having been made and seconded, a resolution passed accordingly that the name of the Prince Regent be continued to grace the Records of a Society of which H.R.H. has been so many years a member.[2]

1 Peltro William Tomkins (1759–1840), the engraver.
2 The Club adjoined Covent Garden Theatre. Writing on 4 March 1814 Farington the diarist remarks: "The old custom is kept up of having *Beef Steaks* only for dinner, and port wine and punch only for drink. The Dukes of Sussex, Norfolk and Argyll were there and several other Peers, and in all about 30 persons. The Club consists of 12 persons only—the remainder of the company came by invitation. Captn. Morris and others sung songs, and pipes and tobacco were allowed. Mr. Green remarked [on] the enormous quantity which the Duke of Norfolk ate, and said after dinner, according to his custom, he slept."

51 THE EARL OF MOIRA *to* COLONEL MCMAHON

Holkham, March 30th 1812.

ON looking over my papers, I have thought it but right to send to you the enclosed from Hammersley.[1] To understand the circumstance to which he alludes relative to me, you should remember the representation I made to the Prince of Hammersley's misbehaviour to me & my solicitation that H.R.H. would punish it by not appointing Hammersley his goldsmith in case of a demise.

Subsequently, believing Hammersley to have sufficiently smarted from his apprehension of that consequence, I informed him thro' his son in law, Ward, that I would petition the Prince to discharge from his mind the unfavorable impression caused by me; & this prayer I did make to the Prince. At the same time I suggested to the Prince that he might, in the event pointed at, fairly desire that Hammersley should make you & Bloomfield[2] participators to a certain degree in the very large advantages of the appointment.

Sir Rd Phillips[3] has written soliciting my interest (he has a good notion how things stand) for his printing the *Delicate Investigation* which he says is to be published according to Perceval's version.[4] Surely there cannot be any truth in such a report! God bless you.

52 WILLIAM ADAM *to* COLONEL MCMAHON

Woburn Abbey,
Tuesday March 31st 1812.

EVER since I came here I have intended to send to you these inclosures: but I have been so unremittingly engaged in business that I have not till now had leisure to explain the business. I now take time by the forelock

1 See No. 8.

2 Benjamin Bloomfield, first Baron Bloomfield (1768–1846). He had been in the Prince's household as a Gentleman Attendant since 1808. On 10 March he was appointed Chief Equerry, and in June succeeded Sir Thomas Tyrwhitt as M.P. for Plymouth. Knighted, 1815; Auditor of Duchy of Cornwall, 1816; Keeper of the Privy Purse, 1817. Peerage, 1825.

3 Sir Richard Phillips (1767–1840), the bookseller and publisher. Knighted, 1808.

4 In 1806 the Prince of Wales accused his wife of misconduct with Sir Philip Sidney and Captain Manby of the Royal Navy, and of having given birth to a child in 1802. The King appointed four members of the Grenville Ministry to examine the charges. She was acquitted of the graver charge, but the allegations of improper relations with Captain Manby, etc. could not be so easily disproved, and the King censured her for her levity and indiscretion. She was defended by Perceval, who, while the Talents Ministry was still in office, printed a pamphlet respecting her case, but before it was published, the Tories returned to power, and *The Book* was suppressed. A few copies, however, got into circulation, and it was said that the Portland Government spent £10,000 of secret service money in buying them up.

and to secure ag[ains]t interruption or farther delay I write at 7 in the morning.

You will observe that the note which incloses Lady Berkley's[1] two letters—was a Mem^m taken down by me from the Prince's statement to me—on my going through the other paper with his Royal Highness, on the 22^d.

I went on the same day to Lady B. when she stated to me that respecting Lord Fife's[2] conversation H.R.H. recollection was not accurate. That that conversation took place in 1792, immed^y on the old Countess of Berkley's[3] death & long before the present Lady Berkley's acquaintance with His Royal Highness. This seemed so marked that I should, notwithstanding the variance in the Prince's recollection, have without any farther trouble to H.R.H. allowed it to stand as in the paper.

The other fact—regarding the introduction of Lady B to H.R.H. is again so marked by H.R.H.s particular recollection that I parted from Lady B. with an understanding that I was to alter that to H.R.H's recollection, and from her long letter you will see she still agrees to that: but unfortunately she states in that letter (I have underscord it to catch your eye) that they were not at Weymouth in 1796. It would never do that the Prince sh^d state that to have happend in 1796 which from the Berkley's not having been there could not have happened in that year. It is clear that according to the Prince's recollection of one introduction, without name, and another when Lady B. was declared the Wife that there must have been two—and the circumstance of going to Hayman the Conjurer fixes it. But it must have been 1797 & not 1796. It is material to have this cleared up: And all this detail is to get you to ascertain that date in order to have Lady B's paper corrected by it. The paper may then be copied, and what I settled with her was that one copy with my attestation sh^d be deposited in the Duchy Strong Box—one given to her—and that I should read it to the Ch[ancello]r—that she seems now to wish to have suspended. I refused to deposit one with the Ch^r. So much for Lady B.

Now for another subject, to which I have turned my thoughts with all the earnestness that belongs to what is interesting to you. I observe

1 The wife of the fifth Earl of Berkeley. [d. 1844.] She was the daughter of a publican and butcher named Cole. He married her, secretly, on 30 March 1785, and publicly, on 16 May 1796. After his death, in 1810, his eldest son (b. 1786) presented a petition to the Crown for a writ of summons as Earl of Berkeley, but, the secret marriage not being proved, the House of Lords decided against his claim, and the title went to the eldest son born after the public marriage. The papers relating to the case are in the Windsor archives.

2 James Duff, second Earl of Fife (1729–1809).

3 After the death of her husband, the fourth Earl of Berkeley, in 1755, she married Lord Nugent.

that Wynn[1] has given notice of a motion for your appointment. I presume with a view to question its regularity as well as its fitness. This has led me to think a great deal about it, and when I return to my books I will confirm my cogitations by investigation. In the mean time it will not be amiss to state to you—that altho' the prerogative cannot be excercised in the appointment of new Judicial offices it can as to new Executive— of that the Sovereign is the judge—and if the salary is defrayed out of what he possesses the Commons have no controul but by Address— which the fitness of the appointment might defeat in the present instance. It is worthy of remark—that some of the great Executive officers are all comparatively of modern date—the Secritaries of State are so much so that they have no rank given to them by the Statute of Henry the Eighth regulating precedence—nor are they noticed in that Statute. In modern times the creation of Executive situ[a]tions both individual & collective have been constantly in use. The late Commission of Naval Review was of this description. These hints when pursued may be useful in the day of discussion, and I will pursue them farther, & communicate with any body that you shall suggest, whom you may think best to use them in the House of Com[s]. As to the fitness of the appointment, I had the honour to state to the Prince that the extent & nature of the Sovereign's b[usine]ss, so much encreased since the commencement of the King's reign, required a confidential person of character & station. That the arrangements must either be made by Pages, or by such a person, & there could be no question as to the unfitness of the former. As to the legality of the appointment another illustration is afforded by the very circumstance of your being out of Parl[t].[2] The Act of Queen Ann[3] which renders you incapable of sitting in Parl[t] implies that the Sovereign has the power of making new offices.

I shall be in Town on Thursday for the India Court, & see you on Friday.

1 Charles Wynn, who raised the question of McMahon's appointment as the Prince Regent's private secretary, in the House of Commons on 14 April.
2 McMahon resigned his seat before the appointment was made.
3 The Place Act of 1707.

Wob[ur]n Abbey,
Tuesday, March 31, 1812.

...MY writing this additional note has arisen from my having recd, since I closed the large packet,[1] a letter from my son Wm from Exeter, where he is upon the Circuit. I shall conclude this with copying a passage of it that you may see the natural bias of those you[n]g minds which have risen under my care. I am induced to this by having felt very poignantly the cruel report communicated of my nephew to the Prince: and I assure you it has born very much on my mind to have had it stated that any person connected with me should have been concerned in a systematic plan of libel and that upon the Prince. And altho' it was a mistake to suppose that I had a nephew of the name of Adam, yet I have a nephew residing in London of the name of Lock. And the same disposition which conveyed the story under a mistaken name might repeat it under a corrected one.

My nephew is a conveyancer most laboriously employed in his calling —and is quite incapable of what is supposed—as much as the person who wrote the following paragraph in the letter received this morning from the Western Circuit. They are intimate friends & having been educated together their minds are framed on the same modell. I can add too that I took some pains for the sake of truth to ascertain whether such a Club had an existence and I find it be [*sic*] be totally *without* foundation. It is hard upon innocent individuals to have such imputations cast upon them—and rather singular that it should be thought even by the mind that conveyed the poison that a person who lives with me as a son—(tho' only a nephew) should be supposed to participate in the malignant contrivances.

Now for the extract from William Adam's letter—"What can the Opposition mean by the line they have taken about the Princess of Wales? I can understand its being a ground for attacking Perceval for his personal shabbiness in deserting her, but to take up her cause as an injured person is too bare faced and in my opinion too blackguard to suceed with any body. It is the highth of of [*sic*] factiousness & must do them a great deal of harm: But Tierney has not the most remote idea of what belongs to a gentleman."

These are thoughts which were never meant to pass beyond my view but I cannot reesist imparting them to your friendly & confidential perusal. They are the spontaneous free communications of one of the most perfect beings that I know.

1 Correspondence relating to Lady Berkeley.

Rio de Janeiro, April 4, 1812.

I AM unwillingly obliged to trouble you once more on the subject to which my last letter referred.

I do beseech you, in the most earnest manner, to lay me at the feet of the Prince, and to submit to His Royal Highness with the assurance of my most humble and dutiful respect, that it is altogether impossible that the British interest at this Court should keep it's ground, during the state of irritation and dissatisfaction into which the Prince of Brazil is thrown, by the preference shewn to Spain in the question of the Embassy. The public service is quite at a stand; and the Prince of Brazil takes every opportunity of expressing his vexation and resentment at the slight which he avers has been put upon him. I am sure that if His Royal Highness were once made acquainted with the real state of this affair, he is too just and too considerate to suffer the feelings of his Ally to be thus hurt by a circumstance which is so easily remedied. The secret source of mortification is the fact of an Ambassador having been sent to Spain, at the very time when a similar compliment was refused to this Court, and that too, on the plea, that an Ambassador had *not* been sent to the Spanish Government.

If the difficulty consists in any personal objection which the Ministers of H.R.H. may entertain with regard to *my* being the Ambassador, I am ready, should His Royal Highness judge proper, to resign my present situation, rather than that His Royal Highness's interests at this Court should suffer, as they now, most undoubtedly do. I would submit to any sacrifice, sooner than behold the decline of the British influence at this place, after so many years employed in upholding it.

Pray forgive this long *Jérémiade* and believe me to be, ever, with the sincerest regard, [etc.].

55 THE EARL OF MOIRA *to* COLONEL MCMAHON

St. James's Palace, April 5th 1812.

THERE is a point on which you should tomorrow take the pleasure of the Prince Regent, and communicate it to me. On Wednesday next the election (made annually) of a Grand Master for the Free Masons is to come on at the Quarterly Communication. It seems inconsistent, if not indecorous, that the Sovereign of the country should be subjected to the forms of an election. It is admitting the possibility of another sentiment than one. Might it not be more consonant to the Regent's situation that he should desire to be considered as simply Patron of the Craft, and that the Duke of Sussex[1] (or any other of his brothers whom the Prince will deign to name) should be proposed as Grand Master?

Perhaps I refine too much on this head: but, as the thought came across me, I could not but conceive it right to have the matter laid before the Prince for His Royal Highness's determination.

56 The Duke of Northumberland *to* Colonel McMahon

Alnwick Castle, 10th April 1812.

It is impossible for me to say how sensibly both the Duchess & myself feel the kind & gracious expressions which the Regent has been pleased to order you to make use of, on account of the recent calamity which has befallen our family, and we return you and Mrs. MacMahon our thanks, for your condolence on the same melancholy occasion.[2]

I apprehend we may now daily expect some account of the consequences, which have attended the siege of Badajos. Let the event turn out which way it will, it will most probably be attended with consequences the most interesting, if not the most decisive, of any thing that has as yet taken place in the Peninsula. This movement of Lord Wellington's & the styles of this movement, accord more with my ideas, than any his Lordship has as yet undertaken. God grant it may be as successfull, as it deserves to be. Indeed I have reason to believe that affairs in the Peninsula wear a more favourable aspect, than they have ever done before.

I was a good deal pleased with a letter I received last night from N: America. It was written by an Englishman, who has been for many years in that country, & who I believe knows more of the real sentiments of the generality of the people than almost any other person. At least I never found him mistaken in the information which he has sometimes thought proper to send me, & as in this instance his opinion corresponds so exactly with mine, I must of course suppose him to be right. After having detailed the events which have taken place, & the real feelings of the different parties in that country, he adds "Since the report of the Secretary of the Treasury, people's minds have been a good deal

1 Augustus Frederick, Duke of Sussex (1773–1843), sixth son of George III.
2 The Duke's second daughter Julia died on 20 March at the age of twenty-seven.

changed, & the war mania seems to be wearing away—The same manly, firm, & temperate conduct continued on the part of the British Government, as of late so conspicuously & wisely manifested, must effect every favourable result they can wish for; and I feel persuaded that *forbearance*, but *not concession* on the part of the British Government, will defeat the machinations of those men, who appear so violently opposed to its influence & prosperity."[1]

I shall wait with impatience till the arrival of the post on the 12th to know what is decided on Mr. W: Wynne's Motion.[2] This new mode of attacking personally the Prince Regent on every step he takes, is not only very indecent, & insulting, but, I should suppose, cannot fail of making the breach between H:R:H:, and the two noble Lords[3] & their party too wide, ever to be closed again. Indeed the insults and ingratitude which he has met with from those, who have always basked in the sunshine of his good opinion, & favour, are more than it can be possible for H:R:H: ever to forget or forgive. He has now had a good specimen of the nature of interested attachments.

I am really quite distressed at the conversation you have had with Lord Cast[l]ereagh, about Lord Strangford. What in the name of God has he done to merit all this? I cannot possibly conjecture what it is. Either his Lordship must have been guilty of some most criminal offence, or have been most maliciously & scandalously misrepresented. I hope in God on the proper close examination of his conduct, the latter will be found to be the case. Shoud it prove so, this will not be the first instance, where I have known the ruin of a most deserving servant of the State, effected by malevolence & falsehood. I really shall be quite unhappy till I learn what this most unpardonable offence is which Lord Strangford has committed.

[P.S.] I am very glad Mr. Wettier[4] likes his cup. He has always been very kind to me, in procuring me what I wanted about my kitchen establishment, and I was happy in an opportunity of convincing him, that I am not ungratefull.

1 The United States declared war against Great Britain in June 1812, the Orders-in-Council, our insistence on searching American ships for escaped English seamen, and our destruction of American trade with France, being the chief causes.

2 See Nos. 31 and 60.

3 Grey and Grenville.

4 John Baptiste Watier. He is described in the *Court and City Register* as the Prince Regent's maître d'Hôtel, 1811–14; as Clerk-Comptroller of the Kitchen, 1815–22. Philip Watier was Assistant Confectioner, or Assistant Pastry Cook, 1813–20.

[10th April 1812.] 9 p.m.

H:R.H. having enquired at the Levee as to the truth of the Russians having entered Memel, Lord Castlereagh transmits the result of his enquiries relative to the Article in the Times on this subject.

58 JOHN WALTER[1] *to* EDWARD COOKE[2]

Printing House Square, April 9. [1812].

MR. WALTER presents his respects to Mr. Cooke, and informs him, that the statement enquired after was founded only on the authority of a private letter from Paris. Letters from the same place, and of a later date, Mr. Walter learns, have been this day received which are wholly silent on the subject; and it is therefore apprehended, as doubts were expressed in to-day's paper of the truth of the news, that it may be now held still more doubtful.

59 BENJAMIN WEST *to* MAJOR-GENERAL T. H. TURNER

Newman Street, April 13th 1812.

HAVE the goodness to make the following known, with my humble duty to His Royal Highness the Prince Regent should I not have the honour of seeing him.

First.

That I hope the Prince Regent will be graciously pleased to signify, what is his pleasure I am to report to the Council and General Assembly of the Royal Academy, on the subject of their Address to His Royal Highness, which myself, and the Keeper of the Royal Academy had the honour to present on Thursday last at the Levee.

Second.

On receiving the accompanying letter from Sir Wm Beechey—I went to the Queens Library in Green Park, and there saw the picture of His Majesty at a Review, which by the command of the Prince I had brought from Windsor. I find the picture in so ruinous a condition, that makes it

1 The second son of John Walter, founder of *The Times*. At this time he was its chief proprietor, and joint-editor with John Stoddart. [1776–1847.]
2 Edward Cooke (1755–1820), Under-Secretary for Foreign Affairs, 1812–17.

necessary to be lined before Sir William can make a restoration of it: should lining the picture be approved of by the Regent, I will order its being done.

Third.

The committee is now arranging the various works of Art, sent into the Royal Academy for exhibition—and I hold it a duty on me, for the information of His Roya[l] Highness the Prince Regent; that the arrangement will be compleated on Thursday the last day of this month, the dinner will be on Saturday the second of May—and the Exhibition will open to the public on the fourth. It would be gratifying to know, in what way it should be the Regents pleasure to honor the Exhibition this year with his presence—that the Council and myself might prepear for such an occurrence.

Your communication of the Prince Regents conclusive pleasure on the above heads, will be highly esteemed, by Sir, [etc.].

60 THE DUKE OF NORTHUMBERLAND *to* COLONEL MCMAHON

Alnwick Castle, 18th April 1812.

SENSIBLE how much your time must now be engrossed by business, I woud not trouble you with a letter just at present, coud I resist the pleasure I feel, in finding that you have overcome the opposition offered to you by your enemies, & that your appointment as Private Secretary to H:R:H: the Regent is at length confirmed to you, and acknowledged, by the House of Commons. These repeated insults offered to the R[egent] will I hope have the proper effect both on H:R:H:, and the publick. It will show him the true caracters of those, who have so long pretended an attachment to him, & have received such marked kindness, & attention from H:R:H: It will convince him, that gratitude does not form any part of their carater. It will likewise tend to convince H:R:H: of the real value of a true, & really attached friend, & servant. The publick will receive the benefit of learning from their conduct how little dependence is to be placed on such men, who would willingly sacrifice their Sovereign, their country, & every thing, to their presumptuous & mad ambition; and that their professions, & protestations of regard, attachment, & devotion, are only binding upon them, as far as suits their own private convenience. In my own opinion, much good may arise from their unmeasured violence. They have opened their true caracters so very soon to H:R:H:s that it is to be devoutly hoped every future professions will be treated with that contempt they merit, & that H:R:H: can never be deceived by them again.

I was happy to find, from your letter of the 10th, that so very little coud be charged against my friend Lord Strangford. I positively know that this accusation against him is a compleat misrepresentation. That he has most superior influence over the Regent of Portugal I know; but I know likewise, that he has made use of it, to obtain advantages for this country, which without such influence he never coud have obtained. In one instance most assuredly he has proved the falsehood of the accusation you mention; when he, by his influence, actually persuaded the P[rince] of Brazil to trust to him, an Order under his Royal Sign Manual, for the removal of an old & faithfull servant (who was also brother to his Prime Minister) from the Regency of Portugal, for having given some offence to either Ld Wellesley, or Ld Wellington if Lord Wellesley himself thought it of sufficient consequence, to make use of such an order of removal; and this Lord S— prevailed upon the Regent to do, without even the knowledge of the Prime Minister, whose violent opposition to this removal of his own brother, woud probably have been the means of preventing H:R:H: from putting his Sign Manual to any such order. This fact must of course be known to our Regent, & therefore I trust will do away any evil impression, which Lord Strangford's enemies may attempt to give H:R:H: of his Lordship's conduct, by the misrepresentation of his Lordship's proceedings. Surely a person, having such influence over the Court to which he is sent, is of inestimable value to the Court from whence he is accredited, & deserves honours & rewards instead of marks of disapprobation. Of Lord Strangford's attachment, & devotion, to the Prince Regent, personally, I am certain, as well as of his most anxious desire to do every thing to the utmost of his power, & ability, for the advantage and good of this country....

61 BENJAMIN WEST *to* MAJOR-GENERAL T. H. TURNER

Newman Street, Aprl 18th 1812.

THE commands of His Royal Highness the Prince Regent, which you honoured me with, I communicated to the Council of the Royal Academy —when it expressed the high since [*sic*] it had for the honor His Royal Highness had confered on the Institution of the Academy, by taking it under his gracious protection—and to sanction its Laws and regulations by signature.

The President and Council being deprived the honor of laying the business of the Academy before His Majesty for the last two elections, which annually appoints its President and others for conducting the concerns of the estableshment; have caused the business on the Kings part to accumulate: it will therfore be necessary for myself and the Secretary —to shorten the business for the Prince Regents signature, to be permited the honor to lay the papers before him, and explain their contents, from a summery of the whole. This part of the business, I must be permited to state, somewhat presses; as the catalogue of the works of Art for exhibition, cannot with propriety be compleated until some of the Academical elections being sanctioned by the Prince Regents signature. I have therefore humble to hope—that the Regent will signify his commands for the papers to be layed before him.

With profound respect, I have the honor to be [etc.].

Turn over [*sic*]

Sunday Aprl 19th.

THE Regent having been graciously pleased to signify his intention of honouring the Exhibition of the Royal Academy with his presence on the 2nd of May—I am anxious that so high an honor to the Arts should be met on the part of the Academy with every possible attention and profound respect. I do therefore propose, that a proper gaurd [*sic*] be at the door of the Academy to receive the Regent—as was the usage when His Majesty honoured the Exhibition with his presence: and that a Band of musick should be in the new room adjoining the great room where the dinner is—during the time of the dinner. When the dinner is over to have the vocal musick as usual.

Should the above arrangement meet the pleasure of His Royal Highness the Prince Regent—or should His Royal Highness be graciously pleased to signify any other adjustment—the Council and myself will be proud, to be honored with his commands.

Should the Regent approve of the Band of musick in the adjoining room to the dinner room—perhaps His Royal Highness the Duke of Yorks Band might be permitd to attend on such an occasion, with a proper selection of musick.

Yesterday at 5 oclock, I removed by the orders of the Earl of Yarmouth[1]—the two portraits of Rubens and Van Dyke [*sic*] from the upper Libary in the Queens Palace.

The Rubens I find in good condition; but the Van Dyke much damaged—I placed both the pictures in the care of the porter in the hall of Carlton House.

62 *Abstract of Proceedings of the* ROYAL ACADEMY *requiring the Royal Signature.* 21 *April* 1812

A REGULATION respecting the mode of admitting students into the schools of the Academy.

A Regulation respecting the times of admitting students.

Regulations respecting the institution of some new premiums for the encouragement of the students.

A Regulation respecting a new classification of the students.

A Regulation respecting the mode of filling up vacancies occurring among the Academicians.

A Resolution repealing an old law which excludes painters in water colors from becoming candidates to be admitted Associates.

A Regulation of the annual order of Lectures in the Royal Academy.

A List of the officers elected & appointed for the Year 1811.

A Resolution allowing the Secretary £150 pr Ann. in lieu of the advantages of residing in the Academy.

A Resolution to allow the Deputy Librarian a salary of £60 pr Ann.

The election of Henry Howard[2] to the office of Secretary.

The appointment of Thomas Stothard[3] to the office of Deputy Librarian.

1 Francis Charles Seymour, afterwards third Marquis of Hertford (1777–1842). At this time he was Vice-Chamberlain of the Household, and in August 1812 he was appointed Lord Warden of the Stannaries in Cornwall and Devon. His father, whom he succeeded in 1822, was now Lord Chamberlain. The Marchioness of Hertford, the Prince Regent's reputed mistress, possessed considerable personal and political influence at Carlton House, and as she and her family were strong anti-Catholics, that Manchester House influence was exercised invariably in favour of Perceval and the ultra Tories. Castlereagh's mother was Lord Hertford's sister. Napoleon thought it strange that the Prince Regent should choose as his mistress a lady who was over fifty and already a grandmother. "Il paraît que vous aimez les vieilles femmes en Angleterre." The Princess of Wales and many others thought that Lady Hertford was "a woman of intact virtue". "It is only a *liaison* of vanity on her part with my better half, but it will not last long, she is too formal for him." It lasted until 1820, when she was superseded by Lady Conyngham.
2 The painter (1769–1847).
3 The painter and book-illustrator (1755–1834).

5-2

The election of David Wilkie,[1] James Ward, Richard Westmacott[2]—Robert Smirke Junr[3] & Henry Bone[4]—Academicians.

A List of the officers elected & appointed for the year 1812.

The election of P. Reinagle[5] Academician.

A Resolution to augment the remuneration allowed to members attending the General Assemblies & Meetings of Council.

One signature will be sufficient for all the above proceedings.

The six Diplomas of the Royal Academicians elect, require to be signed separately.

63 THE DUKE OF NORTHUMBERLAND *to* COLONEL MCMAHON

Alnwick Castle, 24th April 1812.

I REALLY am shocked to perceive how certain persons are insulting the P:R:, from whom H:R:H: had reason to expect a very different treatment. As for Mr. Tierney's motive for all his rancour, I cannot conceive from whence it proceeds. I had always understood he was rather of a quiet caracter, & a great protegée, & friend of Lord Moira's. As for his idea that the Princess should be placed in the situation of a Queen, & called the Princess Regent, & receive an income as such, nothing surely can be so completely ill founded. It has already been declared that the Estates of the Kingdom may call whoever they like to the Regency, & that the P: of W: as eldest son to the King has no claim to the situation. Does therefore Mr. Tierney & his associates pretend then to assert, that if Lord Grey, or Mr. Perceval had been called to the Regency, Lady Grey, or Mrs. Perceval, were immediately to be treated as the Queen, & take upon themselves the stile & title of Princess or Lady Regent, & have a corresponding establishment settled upon them thro' the intervention of Parliament? The idea is too extravagant, & absurd, not ever to have struck those gentlemen; tho' their understandings appear to be driven from them by their disappointed ambition.

1 He was knighted in 1836. [1785–1841.]
2 The sculptor (1775–1856). Knighted, 1837.
3 Sir Robert Smirke (1781–1867), the architect who designed the British Museum and the General Post Office; the second son of Robert Smirke (1752–1845), the R.A.
4 The enamel painter (1755–1834).
5 Philip Reinagle, the animal and landscape painter (1749–1833).

Poor Brogden[1] was very miserable at being shut out on the question of Mr. Wynne's Motion,[2] & Mr. Morris[3] still more angry at the newspaper having been pleased to print his name in the list of the minority. Such kind of misrepresentations are scandalous. Capt. Bennet[4] is going to apply for the Chiltern Hundreds, & Raine[5] will come in for Launceston, so that I hope we shall be all right at last.

I was rather surprised at what you inform me of the Queen's[6] having seen some passages in some of my letters, but am very glad to find they have met with Her Majesty's approbation. They may be the means of making her better acquainted with my sentiments & caracter, having great reason to believe that I have been much misrepresented both to H:M: & the King, from the most unjustifiable, & vindictive motives. The Duchess & myself are very sensible of Her Majesty's condescension, in offering us her compliments of condolence on our late most afflicting loss.[7]

I am very happy to find you think Lord Strangford is in a way to advance in honours, & emoluments, instead of being recalled. I am convinced that he does not deserve the reflections which have been cast upon him, & I am sorry to say, that I have reason to think some of the many misrepresentations which have been made about him, has been for the purpose of covering their own conduct, & the shamefull neglect of not sending him any instructions how to act, altho' he repeatedly sollicited the Minister of his Department to do so.[8] I believe if this matter shoud be sifted to the bottom, it will be found, that not unfrequently he got neither letter, nor dispatch, for many packets, one after another, at a period when he was in the most critical, & distressing situation, in consequence of the repeated applications he received from Spanish S: America, & the appearance of great dissatisfaction, on their part, that no positive answer was given to them. But what coud he do in such a dilemma, unable to procure any instructions from home how to act?

I hope now you have got rid of all the intended attacks upon you, & that they will leave you alone to enjoy the comfortable situation

1 James Brogden, Tory M.P. for the Duke of Northumberland's borough of Launceston, and a London merchant. (? 1765–1842.)

2 See Nos. 31, 60.

3 Edward Morris, M.P. for the Cornish borough of Newport and Lord Erskine's son-in-law. (d. 1815.) The error is repeated in Hansard.

4 Richard Henry Alexander Bennet. Succeeded Earl Percy (who elected to serve for Northumberland) as M.P. for Launceston, 17 July 1807.

5 See No. 31.

6 Queen Charlotte, wife of George III (1744–1818).   7 See No. 56.

8 Wellesley had not only frequently absented himself from Cabinet meetings but had also been most negligent in answering despatches.

with which the P:R: has rewarded your meritorious attachment, & fidelity.

I must beg of you to renew the offer of my most dutifull attachment to H:R:H:, & to accept yourself of the compliments & best wishes of the Duchess, my family, & myself & to present the same for us to Mrs. Mac-Mahon. Adieu & believe me [etc.].

64 RICHARD BRINSLEY SHERIDAN[1] *to* COLONEL McMAHON

Sat Night, April 25th [1812].

THE statement made at the close of the debate[2] last night in the House of Commons, respecting the Prince's *authorised pledge* to the Irish Catholics under the Duke of Bedfords administration, *must not* remain uncontradicted or at least unexplain'd. I cannot describe the mischief it will do to his honor & character, while a statement of *the truth* can only do him honor.

I have had a long conversation with G[eorge] Ponsonby on the subject this evening, and I shall entreat a few minutes audience of his R[oyal] H[ighness] tomorrow on a subject, in my humble judgement, of such consequence to his character, which there is a manifest combination to endeavour to destroy.

I have been in unaccountably bad health & spirits for the last ten days or you should have seen me. I enclose you a letter from Adam which will shew you that waiting for my *brief* it was not my fault that I only gave a vote on the last question respecting you.[3]

1 The dramatist and Whig politician (1751–1816). At this time he was M.P. for Ilchester and one of the Prince Regent's old friends. But now that the Regent had thrown over the Whigs Sheridan was finding it difficult to reconcile his personal attachment to the Regent with the loyalty he owed to his Party. In 1811 he had countenanced a project to break up the Party—the project of a Whig Ministry from which the party leaders, Grey and Grenville, were to be excluded. Grenville disliked him as a dissolute man, and Grey was hardly civil to him—"from an honest but somewhat overcharged disdain of all trickery and artificial characters".

2 The debate on Grattan's motion on the Catholic question, which was rejected by 300 to 215. The statement was made by George Ponsonby. See No. 6.

3 Charles Wynn's motion respecting McMahon's appointment as Private Secretary to the Prince Regent. Sheridan voted with the Prince's friends against the Whigs.

April 28th 1812.

Among the other cares of Empire which assail the Prince, there are some Masonic points to which His Royal Highness's attention must be solicited.

At the last Grand Lodge it was voted that an office of Grand Organist be created & be distinguished with a blue apron. This was done in consequence of Samuel Wesley's[1] having offered to play gratuitously on the organ at all Masonic ceremonies in the hall; & the Lodge wanted to designate him as the person to fill the place. I acceded (being in the chair) to the establishment of the office: but I resisted the nomination of any individual by the Lodge, on the ground that the Grand Master alone ought to confer distinctions. Pray take the Prince's pleasure as to appointing Samuel Wesley.

The Grand Feast is on the 13th May, when the officers for the year ensuing are to be appointed by the Prince. Have the goodness to ask whom His Royal Highness will please to have declared Grand Wardens.

My absence from London will hereafter incapacitate me from fulfilling the duties of Acting Grand Master; so that I shall have to entreat His Royal Highness graciously to fix on some other person. If there would be any convenience in my being nominated anew at the Grand Feast, so as to give time till the Quarterly Communication in November for the choice of another, I would bow implicitly to the Prince's wishes.

66 Spencer Perceval *to the* Prince Regent

Downg St, 4 o'Cl. A.M.
Tuesday morng [5 May 1812].

Mr. Perceval presents his humble duty to your Royal Highness & regrets to acquaint your Royal Highness that he in vain atempted to oppose Mr. Bankes[2] Bill for the abolition of sinecures. The House divided this morning upon it.

134 for the Bill—& 123 against it.

1 The son of Charles Wesley the hymn-writer, and nephew of John Wesley. [1766–1837.]
2 Henry Bankes (1757–1834), M.P. for Corfe Castle, and an independent Tory.

Pall Mall,
Monday Morning, 5th May 1812.

(Copy.)

IN the report of the debate of last night in the H[ouse] of Commons on Mr. Bankes' Bill, it is stated in most of this morning's papers that in allusion to my appointment as Private Secretary to the P[rince] R[egent], and in mentioning my name on the occasion, you coupled the epithets of *"gamester* and *spendthrift"* so closely to it that many of my friends have read it with concern as to be seemingly intended for me. Although I readily confess, Sir, that with the consciousness of having never either gamed or being rich enough in my life to be extravagant I could not possibly take the application to myself, for those who have best known the habits of my life can fully bear me out, that I never had any transaction in the world which could give room for either imputation. I know too well, Sir, to presume the questioning of any gentleman's conduct on allowed public grounds, or even to feel sore on such, whenever respect and delicacy is shown to personal feelings, and I feel that no man can have more to acknowledge on this score than I have reason to do for those considerations which have (with this single exception), so invariably observed towards me on the several occasions wherein my name has been brought forward this session of Parliament in that House. I have no doubt, Sir, that upon calm reflection of those words, so used, you will at once perceive how they may be attended with essential prejudice to me, and that you must readily acknowledge they cannot belong to my character.

In this persuasion, Sir, I will not doubt for a moment that as a man of honor and spirit you must feel for my situation, and take such immediate steps as shall remove the injustice and misapprehensions on this subject.

68 WILLIAM HENRY LYTTELTON *to* COLONEL McMAHON

48 *Davies Street, Berkeley Square,*
May 5th 1812.

IN answer to your letter, which I have just received, I am happy to have it in my power to assure you that in the course of my speech, delivered last night in the House of Commons, I did not use the words *"gambler"*

1 William Henry Lyttelton, third Baron Lyttelton (1782–1837), Whig M.P. for Worcestershire. Succeeded to the title, 1828.

and "spendthrift", and consequently could not have applied them directly or indirectly to yourself. As I imagine that this declaration cannot fail to remove all "misconception" on the subject, and to be perfectly satisfactory to your feelings, I will only add that I have the honour to be, [etc.].

69 WILLIAM HENRY LYTTELTON *to* COLONEL MCMAHON

48 *Davies Street, Berkeley Square,*
May 5th 7 o'clock [1812].

YOU only do me justice when you suppose me anxious to contradict and correct any false statement of words used by me when such statement may prove injurious to the character of an individual. This feeling has already prompted me to write to the Editor of the Morning Chronicle, desiring him to substitute, in the last sentence of the report of my speech given in his paper of to-day, the words *Gaveston*[1] and *Spenser*[2] for "*gamester*" and "*spendthrift*".

I now subjoin for *your* satisfaction (at the bottom of this sheet), the whole of that sentence, according to my best recollection of what it was, and this you are at liberty to insert in the newspapers, or otherwise to make public in whatever way you may think fit.

[P.S.] The sentence referred to above "I had rather vote hundreds of thousands to a Nelson or a Wellington than a single farthing to a Gaveston or a Spenser."[3]

1 Piers Gaveston, Earl of Cornwall (d. 1312), Edward II's favourite.
2 Hugh le Despenser (1262–1326) and his son, of the same name, succeeded Gaveston in Edward II's favour.
3 His speech is accurately given in *Hansard*.

12th May 1812.

I CANNOT possibly begin this day without returning you thanks for your attention of sending Adolphus[1] to me last night, which I felt doubly, as I know how much your own mind must have been shocked with the horrible event[2] he had to communicate. I most anxiously wish that you may be fortunate enough to replace this loss with a person equally attached to yourself & the country. The steadiness you have shewn since you have been placed in this situation has insured you the good opinion & esteem of the country & I trust that in his successor you may be able to find combined together equal talents & integrity, as I am sure it will be your wish to do so.

It will be better I think not to fix any particular time for the next Drawing-room, but to leave it to circumstances.

I hope you have not essentially suffered from this blow & beg you will let Col. McMahon write me word how you really are.

71 *Minute of the* CABINET [*written, and communicated to the* PRINCE REGENT, *by* LORD ELDON]. 12 *o'clock, Night of the* 13th *May* 1812.

THE Chancellor, understanding himself to be authorised by the Prince Regent, to learn the sentiments of the Cabinet, whether they would consider it to be their duty, if called upon by His Royal Highness, to carry on the administration of the Government under any member of the present Cabinet whom His Royal Highness might think proper to select as the head of it, requests that the Cabinet will be pleased to express their sentiments upon this point, that he may be enabled to lay them before His Royal Highness.

In answer to this, the Cabinet expressed that they would feel it to be their duty, if called upon by the Prince Regent, to carry on the administration of the Government under any member of the present Cabinet whom his Royal Highness might think proper to select as the

1 Adolphus Frederick, Duke of Cambridge, the seventh son of George III. (1774–1850.)
2 On the 11th Perceval, the Prime Minister, was assassinated in the lobby of the House of Commons by John Bellingham. The Government, though it had been strengthened in February by the substitution of Castlereagh for Wellesley as Foreign Secretary, and in April by the accession of the Sidmouth group, was now forced to seek additional support. Lord Liverpool, who succeeded Perceval as First Lord of the Treasury, was authorised on the 17th to invite the co-operation of Canning and Wellesley, the leaders of the two Tory groups which now remained outside the Government; but they refused to form part of a Cabinet which was opposed to Catholic emancipation.

head of it. They consider it to be at the same time incumbent upon them most humbly to submit to His Royal Highness that, under all the present circumstances of the country, the result of their endeavours to carry on the Government must be very doubtful. It does not, however, appear to them to be hopeless if the Administration is known to possess the entire confidence of the Prince Regent.[1]

72 THE DUKE OF NORTHUMBERLAND *to* COLONEL McMAHON

Alnwick Castle, 15th May 1812.

SENSIBLE how much your time is engaged, I had not intended troubling you with any letter, in answer to your's of the 2d; but this terrible event which has taken place, of the assassination of Mr. Perceval, makes me very anxious to enquire after the Prince Regent, who must have been most particularly affected by this circumstance. Nothing coud possibly have happened, which woud have embarrassed H:R:H: so much.

1 The draft of this Memorandum is in *Twiss*, II, 209, but it is undated and differs in some respects from the original here printed. The opinions of individual Cabinet Ministers as to the possibility of their continuance in office, with both the Whigs and the Wellesley-Canning group in opposition, are in *Twiss*, II, 210–11. The Cabinet decided that it would have less chance of parliamentary support, if office should not previously have been offered either to the Whigs or to Wellesley and Canning. Castlereagh decided that he would not allow personal considerations to interfere with an offer to his old enemy Canning with whom he had fought a duel in 1809, and on the 15th wrote a letter of resignation to the Prince Regent, which, however, was not accepted. There is no copy at Windsor, though the Prince Regent must have seen the letter; the original is in Add. MSS. 38191, fo. 29.
"Upon a full consideration of the present state of public affairs, I deem it my duty humbly to entreat your Royal Highness's gracious permission to resign the Seals of the Foreign Department.
"Your Royal Highness will I trust do me the justice to believe that no other motive than a dutiful attachment to your Royal Highness, and solicitude for the preservation of the great interests confided to your Royal Highness's care, could dictate this request at the present moment; but it does appear to me essential that your Royal Highness in the construction of your Administration, more especially in that branch of it which concerns the House of Commons, should find yourself wholly unfettered by arrangements which originated under circumstances now altogether changed.
"The impressions under which this act of public duty is performed, as it can apply to none other of your Royal Highness's present servants, will I trust not be suffered by them for a moment to influence their line of conduct.
"I rely with humble confidence on your Royal Highness's gracious favour and indulgence for interpreting favourably the feelings I have presumed to submit; they are alone the result of a deep sense of personal gratitude to your Royal Highness, and of the ardent desire to augment your Royal Highness's means of extricating the country from its present embarrassments."
When, on the 17th, Lord Liverpool opened negotiations with Canning and Wellesley, he made it clear that Castlereagh, who was to succeed Perceval as Chancellor of the Exchequer, was to retain the "Lead" of the House of Commons.

Before this, I take it for granted, he must have decided on Mr. Perceval's successor, & the arrangements necessary to be made in consequence. It woud therefore be useless for any person to presume to give any caution, against H:R:H: submitting to deliver himself up into the hands of those, who have already treated him with such indignity, nay even insult; & who if they once get into power, will indisputabily carry into effect those threats, of making him submit to their will, & pleasure, which they have so often flung out amongst their friends, & correspondents. I most sincerely hope H:R:H; will on this critical occasion act from the dictates of his own head, and heart, without listening to the advice of those, who may perhaps be someway interested in the advice they may give, and at any rate have not H:R:H's good sense, & understanding. This, you know my dear Colonel, has ever been what I have wished H:R:H; to do; & whenever he has done so, he has fully proved the correctness of my judgement.

I am very sorry to find, by letters from my Regiment,[1] that the disturbances are become of a very serious nature. I have great reason to fear, that a number of diabolical emissaries are spread over the whole country, administering illegal oaths, & distributing the most wicked, & treasonable papers, amongst those whom they can seduce. Every preetence is made use of, such as dearness of bread, want of employment, weight of taxes, stagnation of trade, &cr &cr &cr to influence the minds of people; make them dissatisfied, & unhappy; and encourage them to mobs, & insurrection; quoting the speeches of the Opposition, to prove the truth of what they alledge, & that they can no longer entertain any hopes of redress, but by their own exertions. In short such I fear is the present state of a great part of the country, that unless the most vigorous measures are pursued without delay, & prompt punishment immediately follows the commission of these illegal acts, the most dangerous consequences are to be apprehended. I wish I may be mistaken, but I confess this is my opinion. "Principiis obsta"—is a maxim I have always thought a very wise one, on these occasions; & always carried into execution myself, wherever I have been concerned, and have always found it to answer. Too much lenity in the commencement, is cruelty in the end, and never answers the purpose. Firmness, in compelling every person to submit to the laws of a country, is the only sure means of procuring its peace, tranquillity, and happiness. But I must stop—I am perhaps interrupting you from attention to serious business to read my useless opinions. I will therefore conclude with desiring you to present my duty to H:R:H:, & to accept yourself of the compliments of myself

1 He was appointed Colonel of the Royal Regiment of Horse Guards in January 1807.

—the Duchess, & the rest of my family, & to present the same for us to Mrs. Mac-Mahon.

[P.S.] I have the pleasure to say that I now feel myself considerably better, & hope before long to get about again. I find Lord James Murray[1] has been in waiting. I hope the P:R: approves of him?

73 QUEEN CHARLOTTE *to the* PRINCE REGENT

Windsor, the 17th May 1812.

I T was my wish to write by dear little Charlotte[2] yesterday morning, but I mus[t] fairly own that my head was so full of the Old Bayly that I could do nothing untill I new the issue of the tryal.[3] Thank God that it has ended as it ought.

I only grieve that the execution could not take place immediately after the condemnation, tho it must be owned that two days for recollection & preparation for the prisoner to go out of the world is a grant worthy a christian & religious nation.

I feel extreamly hurt at the accounts from Nottingham;[4] the inhabitants there seem to be so very unfeeling that I cannot help thinking that both French principles & money encourage them, & I wish most sincerely that you could at least get Lucien[5] out of the country as I hear from every quarter, that under the appearance of great quiet, he is busily employed in the early part of the day when no body is about with many people & that he has many spyes amongst his attendants who take care to be at home by five in the morning to avoid being seen. This is perhaps what you know better than I can relate, & I hope you will pardon me for naming it, but my heart is so full that it must come out.

The best part of this letter will be to acquaint you that I have had a conversation with Charlotte for a full hour on Fryday morning to which the event of last Munday[6] was the best introduction, as also the report

1 The Duke of Northumberland's son-in-law, and the second son of the fourth Duke of Atholl. (1782–1837.) He was appointed a Lord of the Bedchamber in March 1812 and created Baron Glenlyon in 1821.

2 The Prince Regent's daughter (1796–1817).

3 Bellingham was tried at the Old Bailey on the 15th, and, though undoubtedly insane, he was hanged three days later.

4 When the news of Perceval's assassination reached Nottingham a mob collected and "manifested their savage joy by the most revolting excesses". The military had to be called out and the Riot Act read.

5 Lucien Bonaparte (1775–1840), who, after quarrelling with his brother, the Emperor, had found an asylum in a very curious captivity in England.

6 The day of Perceval's assassination.

of a Proclamation being ordered to be published on account of the anonimous letters sent to you.[1] My great wish was to impress upon her mind that she ought to look upon you as the only source of her happiness & that it was her duty to obey you in every thing, & that she ought at no time to consider herself as agrieved when you disapproved of any thing in her conduct, for that you as her father must of course not only by right but by experience know better what was for her good. That she ought to be carefull about fancying particular friendships at her time of life; nay, that in her situation she ought to be civil to every body but to shew no partiality, & that your character was greatly raised by following that course, & that I was sure that she must both see & feel that political friendship never could be depended upon, & that any of the Royal family taking a part against the Crown was lowering it most essentially. After that I spoke to her about her manner, not finding fault but pointing out the necessity of mending what appeard trifling to her, but what might be prejudicial to her in the world. And I have the pleasure to tell you that she told L[a]dy De Clifford[2] that she was much pleased with her

---

1 The anonymous letters, sent to McMahon and the Prince Regent, are as follows:

(i) To Colonel M'Mahon, Carlton House, Pall-Mall.

"Provisions cheaper—*Bread or Blood*—Tell your Master he is a *Damn'd unfeeling scoundrel*, and if he don't attend to the above, *Death* shall be his portion, and that soon, it's come to the point now, and we are determined to strike the decisive blow.

      May 12/12   Vox Populi.

(ii)   To His Royal the Prince Regent.
            With speed.   Windsor.

George, Prince of Wales. Take care of yourself for your life is in danger. You shall meet the same fate as Mr. Percival if Billenghall is *hung before this reach you*. You blackguard you shall be shot before three months is *elapsed* if Billenghall is hung you shall be shot as sure as
               I remain, an enemy of the damned Royal Family.

The Proclamation, printed in the *London Gazette* on the 19th, is as follows:

"Whereas it has been humbly represented to His Royal Highness the Prince Regent that the following anonymous threatening letters have been sent to the Right Honourable Colonel McMahon,

His Royal Highness, for the better apprehending and bringing to justice the persons concerned in writing and sending the anonymous letters above-mentioned, is hereby pleased, in the name and on the behalf of His Majesty, to promise His Majesty's most gracious pardon to any one of them (except the person who actually wrote the said letters) who shall discover his, her, or their accomplices therein, so that he, she, or they may be apprehended and convicted thereof.

                            R. Ryder.

And, as a farther encouragement, a reward of One Thousand Pounds is hereby offered to any person making such discovery as aforesaid (except as is before excepted) to be paid on the conviction of any one or more of the offenders by the Right Honourable the Lords Commissioners of His Majesty's Treasury."

2 Princess Charlotte's governess since January 1805. She died in 1828 at the age of eighty-five.

conversation & that the more she thought it over the more right she thought I was.

I think it right to inform you that I have just been below to see the dear K[in]g: he looks well in the face & certainly has gained flesh. I was there about ten minutes. He was quiet upon the whole but gave some indication of his disease.

I long to hear that you are more comfortable & wish most heartily that you may soon see an end to all your troubles which will be the best news to hear by, my dearest son, [etc.].

74 CLAUDIUS STEPHEN HUNTER[1] *to* COLONEL MCMAHON

Old Bailey,
¼ before 9 o'Clock [18 May 1812].

YOU will be pleased to hear that everything at the execution[2] has gone off perfectly quiet; the crowd was not so large as I have before witnessed. The Sheriffs & myself had much conversation with him and in the full conviction that he was instantly going into the presence of the Almighty, he declared again and again that he was unconnected with any party whatever and that he did the *deed to redress two private wrongs.*[3] Every precaution has been taken to preserve the peace as you will know but the place has been more quiet than you could suppose.[4]

The Marquis Wellesley to the Earl of Liverpool, 18 May 1812. (*Parl. Deb.* XXIII, Appendix.)

1 Lord Mayor of London, 1811–12. Created a Baronet, November 1812. (1775–1851.)
2 Bellingham had been hanged three-quarters of an hour earlier.
3 For his imaginary grievances, see the account of his trial in the *Annual Register*, 1812, Chronicle, pp. 52–6.
4 A large body of police and soldiers was on duty, and police notices were posted up everywhere, urging people to stay at home, and reminding them that when the murderers Haggerty and Holloway were executed (February 1807) thirty people were crushed to death by the crowd.

Downing Street,
2 o'clock, Monday. [18 May 1812.]

I DO not return to Carlton House as I understand that at this hour His Royal Highness is to see Lord Liverpool, but in case I should be wanted a note from you will find me at home and any orders which it contained should be obeyed immediately.

I have seen Canning who could at the first moment go no farther than to assure me that he had listened with the most dutiful respect to the suggestions which the Regent had deigned to make, and with the most anxious wish to shape his conduct in that way which would be most conducive to the interests of His Royal Highness.

I found that Canning was entertaining a most anxious hope that His Royal Highness would send for Lord Moira, considering it, as he does, of the very utmost importance that his Lordship should be secured.

Canning was further of opinion that it would be disadvantageous to the service of His Royal Highness if Lord Wellesley should not receive authority to make some specific proposal to the Opposition which might bring over to us some of the best of that body, and by connecting such persons with some of the present Ministers an Administration might immediately be formed.[1]

I ventured this morning to take the liberty of mentioning to His Royal Highness that unless Lord Wellesley should have reason to be pleased with his reception at Carlton House it might have the effect of throwing him entirely into the hands of the Opposition.

Canning had not seen Lord Wellesley since his Lordship's last visit to Carlton House.

1 Wellesley asked Liverpool on the 17th whether any members of the Opposition were to be invited to take office. Liverpool replied that he had not been authorised to make any proposal to the Whigs.

Windsor, the 21st May 1812.

THIS letter is to convey my thanks for the beautifull presents I received by the hands of the Duke of Cumberland[1] on Tuesday last. Sorry I am that I can not have any distant hope of your seing your beautifull gifts shine at dinner to morrow at Frogmore where I had hoped to have the pleasure of your company, yet I flatter myself that easier times will soon procure me that satisfaction.

With infinite concern do I see by today's papers that the correspondence as well as the conversation between L[o]rd Liverpool, Marquis of Wellesley and Mr. Canning (not Cunning) is published.[2] This is the first time I ever remember such a transaction being given out in the public prints, and I can not help reflecting with pleasure how well the dear King judged the characters of those two individuals, by proving themselves such as he always described them to me. Still I think with your firmness all will do well, and showing steadiness of principle the country will stand by you in your distress.[3] And now with my best and sincere wishes for your speedy relief I subscribe myself [etc.].

77 RICHARD BRINSLEY SHERIDAN *to the* PRINCE REGENT

Bruton St.,
Thursday Eve[nin]g, May 21, 1812.

I CANNOT but be aware that at a moment so critical as the present and while so many important public considerations must press upon your Royal Highness's time and attention, any intrusion upon either from the suggestion of private feelings, however dictated by duty and attachment, requires the gracious indulgence of your Royal Highness to pardon it.

Not to trespass a moment longer than necessary I have only frankly to say that my object in now taking the liberty of addressing you is to express my extreme concern that your Royal Highness could for a moment, if I understood McMahon right, have thought me capable of

1 Ernest Augustus, Duke of Cumberland and King of Hanover (1771–1851), fifth son of George III. Created Duke of Cumberland, 1799. Succeeded on William IV's death, in accordance with the provisions of the Salic Law, as King Ernest I of Hanover, 1837. In politics a reactionary Tory.

2 The correspondence relating to Liverpool's overture to Wellesley and Canning. See *Parl. Deb.* xxiii, Appendix.

3 The Queen and the Duke of Cumberland were believed to have exerted their influence with the Prince Regent against both the Whigs and the liberal Tories.

the vanity and silliness of being a party to the misrepresentations in the newspapers which stated me to have mix'd in the recent consultations at Carlton House. There is nothing more repugnant to my temper and nature than to be characterised as a medler of that description, and I had myself authorized the contradiction of the paragraphs alluded to before I had the honor of calling at Carlton House.

Undoubtedly duty would require of me, as of every other Privy Councellor, to submit my humble opinion at the expressed command of your Royal Highness upon any subject regarding which it might be required, and I only humbly take the freedom of adding that I can lay my hand on my heart and declare that that opinion never has in a single instance, nor ever can be if ever again required, been formed or given but upon grounds and motives proceeding from the most sincere, grateful, and ardent attachment and devotion to your true interests, honour, and happiness.

My object in presuming to have wished to see your Royal Highness on Tuesday last was, as I explained to my most esteemed friend and your Royal Highness's most faithful servant, Col[one]l McMahon, to prevent the possibility of my canvass at Stafford[1] being misrepresented as being in any way a declining on my part still to have the honour of owing my seat in Parliament to your gracious protection and partial recommendation.

To continue to be your servant with unaltered and unalterable zeal, anxiety, and affection is the hope and pride of my private wishes and ambition, but I feel confident that I can in no way be usefully so but by preserving the independence and consistency of my public course and political character, now doubly endeared to me since allowed and sanctioned by your Royal Highness's gracious approbation.

I wish to avoid giving way to gloomy thoughts respecting the possible results of the present awful crisis of unprecedented difficulty and danger, but I can from my soul aver that under any condition of calamity, public or private, I should find a degree of consolation in the very worst events in proportion as they aforded me an opportunity of proving the true sincerity with which I am and ever will be, [etc.].

1 In the Parliament of 1807–12 Sheridan sat for the nomination borough of Ilchester, but since November 1811 he had been canvassing the electors of Stafford, whose member he had been in previous Parliaments. But at the general election he was at the bottom of the poll, the figures being, 482, 347 and 255.

Present

The Lord Chancellor	Earl of Harrowby[6]
The Lord President[1]	Viscount Melville
The Lord Privy Seal[2]	Lord Mulgrave[7]
Earl of Buckinghamshire[3]	Viscount Castlereagh
Earl Bathurst[4]	Mr Secretary Ryder[8]
Earl Camden[5]	Mr Vansittart[9]
	Earl of Liverpool

Your Royal Highness's confidential servants having taken into their consideration the peculiar pressure of public affairs at the present moment, humbly recommend to your Royal Highness to adopt without delay, such measures for forming an Administration, as to your Royal Highness may seem expedient, in consequence of the Address of the House of Commons;[10] and they beg leave to assure your Royal Highness that they will in the meantime continue to carry on the business of Government in their respective Departments, if such shall be your Royal Highness's pleasure.

1 Henry Addington, first Viscount Sidmouth (1757–1844). Prime Minister, 1801–4; President of the Council, April to June 1812; Home Secretary, June 1812 to 1822.

2 John Fane, tenth Earl of Westmorland (1759–1841). Lord Privy Seal, 1807–27.

3 Robert Hobart, fourth Earl of Buckinghamshire (1760–1816). Appointed President of the Board of Control, April 1812, and also Chancellor of the Duchy of Lancaster (succeeding Perceval) in May. A member of Sidmouth's group.

4 Henry Bathurst, third Earl Bathurst (1762–1834). President of the Board of Trade, 1809–12; Secretary for War and the Colonies, June 1812 to 1827; Lord President of the Council, 1828–30.

5 John Jeffreys Pratt, second Earl Camden and first Marquis of Camden (1759–1840). Succeeded to earldom, 1794. President of the Council, 1807 to April 1812, when he readily made way for Sidmouth, at the same time agreeing to remain in the Cabinet without office until the end of the Session. He was promised a marquisate, and the honour was conferred in August. See No. 136.

6 Dudley Ryder, first Earl of Harrowby (1762–1847). At this time a Cabinet Minister without portfolio. President of the Council, June 1812 to 1827.

7 Henry Phipps, first Earl of Mulgrave (1755–1831). Master-General of the Ordnance, 1810–1818, when he voluntarily made way for the Duke of Wellington. Created Earl of Mulgrave and Viscount Normanby, September 1812. He was opposed to Catholic emancipation until the summer of 1812, when he declared that since there was no longer any probability of the King's recovery, the Catholic question ought to be finally settled. He was so anxious that Canning, Wellesley and some of the Whigs should join the Government that he offered to make way for one of them.

8 Richard Ryder (1766–1832), second son of Nathaniel Ryder, first Baron Harrowby. Home Secretary, 1809–12. Some thought him an incompetent Minister, but Perceval considered him a useful colleague. He suffered from ill-health and was never again in office

9 Nicholas Vansittart, first Baron Bexley (1766–1851). Succeeded Perceval as Chancellor of the Exchequer, May 1812. A member of Sidmouth's "connexion".

10 On the 21st Stuart Wortley's motion "That an humble Address be presented to his royal highness the Prince Regent, humbly praying that he will be pleased to take such measures as will enable him, under the present circumstances of the country, to form a strong and efficient Administration", was carried by 174 to 170. The Government thereupon

Cleveland House,
Saturday Night May 23rd [1812].

IMPRESS'D as I must be with a conviction that any intrusion upon your Royal Highness's time must at this particular moment be greatly inconvenient & unwelcomely received from so humble an individual as myself, yet I can not refrain from presuming to make known to your Royal Highness my very anxious desire to offer you my feeble services in whatever may be most consonant to your wishes.

As it is generally presumed & understood, that it is your Royal Highness's pleasure to make such a change in your confidential servants as will most probably do away those scruples which I have lately most conscientiously entertained respecting some great & important political subjects, I shall feel in such an event much pride in obeying any commands with which you may honor me, & shall be happy to exert to the fullest extent my feeble abilities in whatever your Royal Highness may think me worthy of your notice.

resigned. The Prince Regent first invited Wellesley to ascertain the views of all parties on the Catholic question and the prosecution of the Peninsular War, so that a Ministry could be planned. But Liverpool and his colleagues positively refused to serve in any Administration of which Wellesley should be a member. On the 20th the *Statement* of the reasons for his resignation of the Foreign Secretaryship in February was published in *The Times* without his knowledge and consent. Accusing not only Perceval but also the rest of his colleagues of downright incompetence, it naturally excited their indignation. *The Times* said that it had been for some time in circulation among his friends. "The principal allegations were never for a moment concealed from that person whose reputation they seem most to affect. The friends of Lord Wellesley indeed felt the necessity of being put in possession of some such statement, on the accuracy of which they could rely, in order to be enabled to rectify and refute the numerous misrepresentations and falsehoods which were circulated by the adherents of Ministers, and even, it is said, by persons in office, and intimately connected with the Government, respecting the causes of his resignation. They accordingly applied to a gentleman in his Lordship's confidence for such information as might satisfy their minds on this point, and put it in their power to contradict the false reports by which it was daily attempted to assail the character of Lord Wellesley. At the same time it appeared that an erroneous impression of the motives of Lord Wellesley's resignation had been conveyed, through some means or other, to Sir Henry Wellesley, Lord Wellington (his Lordship's brothers) and to other friends of his Lordship in the Army. Under these circumstances therefore the gentlemen above alluded to applied to Lord Wellesley himself for some notes of the causes of his resignation, from which the statement now published was prepared, and given to a few friends of Lord Wellesley's in confidence, for the purpose above mentioned. That statement was not intended for publication; at the same time there is nothing in it which is not strictly true; and above all, which was communicated to Mr. Perceval himself, by Lord Eldon, at the desire of Lord Wellesley." The Ministers were angry with him, too, for publishing his correspondence with Lord Liverpool respecting the formation of a new Government, on the 21st, whilst delaying until the following day the publication of Liverpool's explanatory letter on the Catholic question. The Ministers believed that Stuart-Wortley's motion of "no confidence" would never have been carried but for Wellesley's equivocal conduct. The Whigs, though agreeing with him on the Catholic question, made difficulties about the conduct of the war (24 May). See No. 80.

[*c.* 24 May 1812.]

LORD WELLESLEY has the honor humbly to acquaint your Royal
Highness, that in preparing to execute your Royal Highness's commands,
for submitting to your gracious consideration, the plan of an Administration properly adapted to the present crisis of affairs, he has deemed it to
be necessary in the first instance, to advert to certain practical principles,
which should, in his humble judgment, constitute the basis of the
system of measures, calculated to meet the actual exigencies of the
country.

It appeared to be desirable to reduce these leading principles within
the narrowest compass, which the situation of affairs could admit;
omitting for the present the discussion of many questions, which (however important in their nature,) may not be deemed of such instantaneous
pressure; or may not be expected to involve so much difference of
opinion.

With this view, Lord Wellesley, upon the most mature reflection,
considered, that the practical principles, upon which an Administration
might be constituted, in the present crisis, might be safely comprised in
the two following propositions.

1st That the state of the Laws affecting the Roman Catholics, and the
claims of that body of His Majesty's subjects should be taken into immediate consideration, with a view to a conciliatory adjustment of those
claims,

2dly. That the War in the Peninsula should be prosecuted on a scale
of adequate vigour.

It appeared to Lord Wellesley to be indispensably necessary, towards
the due execution of your Royal Highness's commands, to endeavour to
ascertain the views and dispositions of all parties, with regard to these
general principles, previously to submitting any names of persons to
your Royal Highness, for the purpose of filling the several offices in your
Royal Highness's service.

He therefore conceived it to be his duty to open a communication with
the principal persons of all parties, carefully confining that communication to the point of ascertaining their respective sentiments on the two
propositions stated in this paper.

In these communications, Lord Wellesley was particularly cautious to
explain, that he had received no authority from your Royal Highness to
form an Administration, nor to communicate with any particular party
or description of persons: But that your Royal Highness had been
apprised of the necessity of Lord Wellesley's holding such intercourse

with all parties as might enable him to prepare a plan for your Royal Highness's approbation.

He also explained, that in this transaction he was merely the instrument of executing your Royal Highness's commands, neither claiming nor desiring for himself any station in the Administration which it was in your Royal Highness's contemplation to form.

Under these circumstances, as Mr. Canning and he agreed in the general principles already stated, he requested Mr. Canning to communicate them to Lord Liverpool, believing that to be the channel of communication which was likely to be most agreeable to Lord Liverpool.

Mr. Canning transmitted to Lord Wellesley the annexed Minute of his conversation with Lord Liverpool[1] together with the answer from Lord Liverpool[1] and a letter from Lord Melville.[1]

From Lord Liverpool's letter, your Royal Highness will observe, that "he & his colleagues do not think it necessary to enter into any discussion of the principles stated in Mr. Canning's Minute, because they all feel bound, particularly after what has recently passed, to decline the proposal of becoming members of an Administration, to be formed by Lord Wellesley."

Lord Melville's letter is particularly submitted to your Royal Highness's notice.

Lord Wellesley made the communication stated in the paper No 4 to Lords Grey and Grenville[1] and received from them the answer[2] marked No 5.

He also received the letters[1] from Lords Lansdowne[3] & Holland marked Nos 6 & 7 expressing their concurrence in the Memorandum (No 5) received from Lords Grey and Grenville.

Lord Wellesley also communicated with Lord Moira, Lord Erskine, and Mr. Sheridan, who all expressed their concurrence in the principles already submitted to your Royal Highness; and Lord Wellesley takes the liberty of humbly recommending the letter from Lord Moira[1] (No 8) to your Royal Highness's particular notice.

The examination of these papers will afford your Royal Highness an opportunity of determining,

1st Whether the principles proposed by Lord Wellesley are such as your Royal Highness may be graciously pleased to approve as the basis of a new Administration.

1 Dated 23 May. See *Parl. Deb.* XXIII, Appendix.
2 Dated 24 May. *Ibid.*
3 Sir Henry Petty-Fitzmaurice, third Marquis of Lansdowne (1780–1863). Chancellor of the Exchequer in the "Talents" Ministry, 1806–7, and one of the leading Whigs.

2dly Whether it is your Royal Highness's pleasure that Lord Wellesley should proceed to propose for offices the names of any persons who have appeared to be disposed to concur in these principles.

3dly Whether any negotiation shall be opened with Lords Grey and Grenville for the purpose of explaining any difficulty or misapprehension which may exist respecting the management of the War in the Peninsula; and any other points of discussion which may occur.[1]

George Canning's statement to Viscount Melville, 26 May 1812. See *Parl. Deb.* XXIII, Appendix.

81 THE DUKE OF NORTHUMBERLAND *to* COLONEL MCMAHON

Alnwick Castle, 26th May 1812.

I HAVE to acknowledge the receipt of your two letters, of the 19th and 23rd, and lament sincerely the very disagreable situation, in which Mr. Stuart Wortley's[2] motion has placed His Royal Highness. It has undoubtedly only left him a choice of difficulties. I trust however H:R:H: will still preserve his firmness of mind, & not be in any way alarmed by these struggles for power, & dominion; for which you may remember I endeavoured to prepare him, in a letter to you, before H:R:H: accepted the Regency. This, depend upon it, my dear Colonel, is the very last struggle that will, or indeed can be made, on either side. Shoud H:R:H: consent to give himself up into the hands of those who have already treated him with such indignity, & insult, you know full well what in my opinion the consequences of such a step woud be; but shoud H:R:H:, altho' he has authorised Lord Wellesley to submit to him an arrangement for the formation of a new Administration, object to admitting into his service, and confidence, the heads of that party, who have in their conduct, and language, treated H:R:H: in a manner that

1 The Prince Regent gave Wellesley no immediate authority to continue negotiations, and on the 25th urged Lord Liverpool and his colleagues to reconsider their decision not to unite with Wellesley and Canning. For the Cabinet's reply, see No. 84.

2 James Archibald Stuart-Wortley-Mackenzie, first Baron Wharncliffe (1776–1845), grandson of the Earl of Bute, the Prime Minister. Peerage, 1826. His motion of 21 May was not inspired by Canning. At this time he was an independent member, and a Canningite only after 1823. He had uniformly supported the Perceval Ministry and had been opposed to Catholic emancipation (he changed his views in April 1812); and in the course of his speech on 21 May he said: "With respect to his motion, it came before them utterly destitute of any other influence than that derivable from its own merits. He had made it upon his own free motion. He had consulted with no one. Indeed, he was then actually ignorant whether his motion would be seconded or not."

no private individual woud submit to, without strongly resenting it, and declare, that till he had received an ample apology for such insults, & was fully convinced from their conduct of their contrition, he never woud admit them into his councils. If, I say, my dear Colonel, H:R:H: shoud take up this line of acting on the present occasion, I will engage for it, with all their pride, & hauteur, they will readily submit to any reasonable, and proper terms, rather than forego the whole object of their lives. To conduct the affairs of a State a person must be endowed with great political courage, & firmness. Without these necessary qualifications, they soon become mere puppets, & are played upon by every arrogant, artfull, & ambitious demagogue, who continues to make their lives miserable, by keeping them in almost continual alarm; either for the purpose of forcing himself into power, or of preserving the power he already is in possession of. I confess, as far as I am capable of judging, the Prince, in the situation in which he now finds himself, coud not have selected a more proper person than Lord Wellesley to place at the head of his affairs. Ld. W: certainly has many faults, which in a great measure disqualify him for that elevated, and arduous situation; yet when I look around me, & consider the total want of proper abilities, & caracter, as well as the disposition of those, who are likely to be his Lordship's competitors, I cannot help, with all his failings, to give him the preference. He is possessed of three qualities, which are absolutely necessary to the Prime Minister in the present times, & the present situation of the country. He has certainly great abilities, firmness, & energy, in his composition, whenever he is pleased to exert this latter; and I shoud really hope that under the controul of H:R:H:'s good understanding, & goodness of heart, his Lordship may prove an usefull Minister for the country. You must acknowledge, my dear Colonel, I am very impartial; for I have not the slightest connection, or even acquaintance with the noble Marquis, & you know besides, I have no great reason to be extremely pleased with him, for his cruel, and I believe most unjust, attack upon my friend Lord Strangford. Great care, & attention, however, I shoud suppose necessary to check him on some occasions, & prevent his bad qualities from frustrating, what otherwise his great abilities woud perform; & I trust in God our worthy R[egent] will never forget the great difference that exists, between admitting, & learning advice with patience, & being dictated to. Plans may be formed, & measures proposed, by the Minister; but the final adoption of them must absolutely depend upon the Regent. It is he who must decide upon them, & no infraction of this rule, in my humble opinion, ought ever to be permitted.

I own I shall wait with impatience, till I learn the result of Lord Wellesley's endeavours to form an Administration, & the Regent's decision on the men & measures to be employed & brought forwards. It is the most anxious moment I ever felt; as I look upon it as decisive of H:R:H:'s future comfort, or torment. I confess I look with dread at the consequence of the universal & total emancipation of the Roman Catholicks, from all those wise & necessary restraints, under which they have been placed by the good sense of our forefathers, & which their experience convinced them were necessary for security of the State, & the Constitution. Allow me likewise to say, I cannot help lamenting a little the probable consequence which will ensue to my poor friend Lord Strangford, when Ld. W[ellesley] is cloathed with full power. As he is great he shoud be mercifull. But I fear when interested views, which relate to his own family, are in the way, they supercede every thing else, & become one of the great faults, which lessen so much his caracter.

Adieu, my dear Colonel; present my duty to H:R:H: The Duchess, & my family, unite with me, in compliments & the best of wishes to you, & Mrs. Mac-Mahon.

P:S: I hope in God, altho' the P:R: has given Ld. W[ellesley] carte blanche, he does not mean to give himself up blindfold into his hands, but select his own Administration from amongst the names, which Ld. W: shall lay before him.

82 THE EARL OF MOIRA *to* COLONEL MCMAHON

Tuesday Morning. May 26th 1812.

I HAVE just had a letter from Lord Wellesley, in which he says that he has reason to think it would be pleasing to the Prince Regent if I solicited an audience from His Royal Highness. Altho' this is grounded upon what passed in the interview with which the Prince honored Ld Wellesley yesterday afternoon, it strikes me as just possible that Ld Wellesley's desire of facilitating the course of matters now in suspense may have made him give me the counsel more from his view of that expedience than from accurate observation of the Prince's wishes. Let me, therefore, refer myself to your advice. If His Royal Highness really did desire to see me, nothing on earth could be so truly gratifying to my heart (which has never swerved in a single feeling respecting him) as the being admitted to his presence. Should you think it right for me to ask the audience, let me know at what hour I ought to be at Carlton House.[1]

Viscount Melville's communication to George Canning, 27 May 1812 (*Parl. Deb.* XXIII, Appendix).

83 THE EARL OF LIVERPOOL *to the* PRINCE REGENT

Fife House,
May 27. ½ p 2 p.m. [1812].

LORD LIVERPOOL has the honour to submit to your Royal Highness a Minute of Cabinet to which your Royal Highnesses confidential servants then present have just agreed.

84 *Minute of the* CABINET. [27 *May* 1812.]

Present

The Lord Chancellor	The Viscount Melville
The Lord President	Lord Mulgrave
The Lord Privy Seal	Mr Secretary Ryder
Earl of Buckinghamshire	Mr Vansittart
Earl of Harrowby	Earl of Liverpool

Earl Camden & Viscount Castlereagh absent at their own desire.[2]

Your Royal Highnesse's confidential servants having received the communication made to them on the 25th inst by your Royal Highnesse's commands through the Lord Chancellor, the Earl of Liverpool, & Viscount Melville, have taken that communication into their most serious consideration and have most anxiously and repeatedly deliberated upon the same, and they beg leave most humbly to submit to

1 A reconciliation now took place between Moira and the Prince Regent, who had been estranged since February. "Such a scene I never heard of", wrote Creevey on the 27th. "The young monarch *cried* loud and long; in short he seems to have been very nearly in convulsions. The afflicting interview was entirely occupied with lamentations over past errors, and delight at brighter prospects for the future under the happier auspices of his old and true friend now restored." (*Creevey Papers*, p. 157.) Thomas Grenville, too, said that the Prince "hung round his neck in tears". "It was a *scène larmoyante*," wrote Lord Grenville, "but Moira says that nothing in the least distinct passed about politics or arrangements." (*Regency Memoirs*, I, 330, 332.)

2 Out of delicacy. See No. 71 n. Camden was Castlereagh's uncle.

your Royal Highness their decided conviction that no beneficial result is likely to arise to your Royal Highnesse's service from any further attempt being made on their part, under the present circumstances, to bring about an union between your Royal Highnesse's servants and Marquis Wellesley and Mr. Canning.[1]

85 VISCOUNT MELVILLE *to the* PRINCE REGENT

Park Lane, 28th May, 1812.

IN obedience to the commands which Lord Melville received from your Royal Highness to-day, to state in writing for your Royal Highness's information the reasons which induced him to entertain in common with his colleagues the opinion submitted by your confidential servants on the 27th. inst. that no beneficial result would arise from any further proposal being made to Marquis Wellesley and Mr. Canning to unite with your Royal Highness's present servants, Lord Melville humbly submits to your Royal Highness that, though individually he did not object to act with Marquis Wellesley and Mr. Canning, he was satisfied that such a union with the present servants of your Royal Highness would not have had the effect of strengthening your Government unless it could be accomplished with their general concurrence.

But when he observed that for various reasons as connected with the agitation of the Catholic question, or with Lord Castlereagh's situation in the Government, or from both those considerations, a majority of your Royal Highness's servants would probably solicit your permission to retire from the Administration if any proposal were made to Marquis Wellesley and Mr. Canning, it appeared to Lord Melville to be hopeless that any beneficial result would arise from making such proposal, and he was therefore of opinion that it ought not to be made.

1 The Prince Regent, through his private secretary, sent the following reply (dated 27 May, 10.30 p.m.) to the Cabinet Minute:

"Colonel McMahon is commanded by His Royal Highness the Prince Regent to state his commands to Lord Liverpool to attend himself and to desire the attendance of his colleagues at Carlton House tomorrow morning at twelve o'clock, as the Prince is desirous to learn from each of his servants the grounds of the opinion which they have communicated to His Royal Highness in the Minute of this day." Add. MSS. 38247, fo. 328. Liverpool's reply is in *Yonge*, I, 393, Bathurst's in *Bathurst Papers*, p. 176. The differences between the reasons of the "Protestants" and those of the "Catholics" will be noticed.

28th May, 1812.

IN obedience to the commands of your Royal Highness, Lord Mulgrave most humbly states the grounds of his concurrence in the written opinion submitted to your Royal Highness through the Earl of Liverpool.

A very great diversity of opinion being manifest amongst the confidential servants of your Royal Highness, in discussing the question of a further negotiation with the Marquis Wellesley and Mr. Canning, Lord Mulgrave became strongly persuaded that any further attempt to bring about the proposed union would not be attended with a result beneficial to your Royal Highness's service; because with such diversity of opinion, and under the various circumstances which had intervened, it did not appear that negotiation could be further pursued in a way likely to afford the prospect of establishing an Administration in any respect stronger than that which had been deemed insufficient by the Address of the House of Commons presented to your Royal Highness.

87 VISCOUNT SIDMOUTH *to the* PRINCE REGENT

White Lodge, Richmond Park,
May Ye 28th 1812.

IN obedience to your Royal Highness's commands, Lord Sidmouth humbly submits to your Royal Highness the grounds of his concurrence in the Minute of Cabinet presented yesterday to your Royal Highness by the Earl of Liverpool.

It appeared to him that the public declaration required by Marquis Wellesley and Mr. Canning, as a part of the basis of the proposed union that your Royal Highness's confidential servants would take into their consideration the Roman Catholic claims, was highly objectionable and likely to prove illusory; as, however reasonable such a demand might appear under other circumstances, he could not but understand it at present as implying much more than the terms of it may seem to import.

It must be presumed that those claims had long engaged the anxious attention of your Royal Highness's servants: it was known that they had recently been brought under the consideration of Parliament and supported to a certain extent by the persons now desirous of a public pledge that they should be considered in Cabinet: the least therefore that Lord Sidmouth conceived could be intended by such a proposal was that your Royal Highness's servants should take a new view of the question and he thought that those by whom the proposal had been made should state their own view of the subject, both with regard to concession and securities: as far indeed as it could be inferred from what had passed in the present Session Lord Sidmouth was convinced that it differed materially from the opinions which he had repeatedly expressed in Parliament and which remain unchanged: that no hope was entertained of Mr. Canning's acquiescence in an arrangement by which the chief conduct of the business of Government in the House of Commons would be placed in the hands of Lord Castlereagh and which, on grounds, with a recapitulation of which he will not presume to trouble your Royal Highness, Lord Sidmouth conceived to be due to the obligations of honor and good faith as well as to the eminent pretentions of Lord Castlereagh, and to be not less material to the strength and efficiency of your Royal Highness's Government; an object which it had been the principal motive of the proposed union to promote: that a change in this arrangement must deprive the Government of the assistance of Lord Castlereagh whose resignation had been once already tendered to your Royal Highness; and that then it must be considered how far Mr. Canning's splendid talents in debate could alone compensate for the lamented loss of Mr. Perceval and the retirement of Lord Castlereagh, who, when united, were not more than sufficient to contend with the abilities opposed to them.

That, as therefore he perceived no reasonable hope remaining of an union at once creditable and satisfactory to the parties, and advantageous to the interests of the country, Lord Sidmouth was of opinion that any further attempt to accomplish it would have no other effect than to increase irritation and to prolong and augment all the inconveniences and embarrassments to the public service which the delay in forming a Government had already occasioned.

88 THE EARL OF WESTMORLAND *to the* PRINCE REGENT

28th May, 1812.

IN obedience to your Royal Highness' commands I have to state: I was of opinion that upon your Royal Highness's reference a proposition ought to be made to Mr. Canning; that a sense of duty to the King, to your Royal Highness and to the country required us to make every effort to obtain the aid of Mr. Canning's talents in support of the Administration.

I concurred in the Minute delivered to your Royal Highness on the ground that the sentiments expressed by several members of the Cabinet in discussing the proposition for a negotiation, as well as the little disposition to facilitate overture which seemed to be manifested on the part of Mr. Canning, afforded little expectation of a beneficial result therefrom.

89 THE EARL OF BUCKINGHAMSHIRE *to the* PRINCE REGENT

Hamilton Place, May 29th, 1812.

IN obedience to your Royal Highness's commands that Lord Buckinghamshire should state the grounds upon which he had concurred in the communication made to your Royal Highness by your confidential servants on the 27th. instant,—he has the honour humbly to submit that, with the sentiments he entertains upon the subject of the laws affecting the Roman Catholics, he could not become a member of an Administration founded upon a principle of concession, unexplained as to its extent and unaccompanied by any intimation of the nature of the securities intended to be provided for the maintenance of the Protestant Establishment.

That the communications which had already taken place with Lord Wellesley and Mr. Canning had afforded no satisfaction upon these points, nor had any disposition been shewn by them to preserve to Lord Castlereagh the situation in which he stands in the Government and in the House of Commons.

Under this impression Lord Buckinghamshire has dutifully to represent to your Royal Highness that he conceived a further communication on the part of the confidential servants of your Royal Highness to Lord Wellesley and Mr. Canning would have occasioned a delay which, under present circumstances, might be highly inconvenient without, as far as Lord Buckinghamshire could judge, the prospect of a beneficial result being produced.

29 May 1812.

Your Royal Highness, having commanded me to assign my reasons for concurring in the Minute of Cabinet, I take leave to represent that I was not led to concur by the judgement which I had formed upon the principles upon which it had been proposed that an Administration should be constituted. As to the proposal that the Roman Catholic claims should be taken into consideration by Cabinet, I conceive it to be the duty of Government to consider in Cabinet the claims of any body of His Majesty's subjects, and to decide upon them bonâ fide whenever the attention of Government is called to that consideration by any member of Cabinet acting upon his sense of his public duty. It certainly has not, as yet, been ascertained to what extent the persons proposing this principle think that concession might or might not be made. I cannot presume that they, at present, think that absolute concession should be made: or that, whilst they propose that the Catholic claims should be made the subject of consideration, they are ready, with others, to avow that all the Catholic claims should be, and must be, immediately granted. Such enquiry and consideration as could be had by any persons enquiring and considering with those who should avow such to be their present decided judgment upon all the Catholic claims I do not deem to be that enquiry and consideration which is meant in the true spirit of the principle proposed. It appears to me that, under present circumstances, a refusal to concur, with the persons stating this principle, in a fair consideration, in Cabinet, of those claims,—in a fair consideration whether any and which of them may be reasonably granted, and with what securities for the Protestant interest,—cannot be justified by an apprehension that the result of it, though perhaps unsanctioned by such consideration itself, might be entire concession, or probably would be too much concession.

I do not think such apprehension as well founded as others may deem it to be: but, if I thought the apprehension better founded than I conceive it to be, I could not, on the other hand, suffer myself to overlook the fact that a refusal—under present circumstances—to concur in such a consideration of these claims in Cabinet, will almost necessarily lead to a change ensuring either immediately or speedily, the entire establishment of all the Catholic claims. If such establishment is a public evil there is little prospect of avoiding it afforded by refusing to consider the claims in Cabinet.

Enquiry and consideration carried on at present, even with those who mean to give to enquiry and consideration their just effect, may, too probably, lead to some evils—but, attending to all the circumstances

[95]

which, *at this day*, demand attention, the refusal to enquire and consider will not, I fear, avert those evils, and will, I fear, produce many other evils.

As to the war in the Peninsula, I have always thought that it should be carried on with all the means that this country, acting justly to itself, could apply to the prosecution of it, and so I have understood it to have been carried on, judging upon all the information ever brought before me as to the extent of the country's means. And when I judge of the effect of refusing—under present circumstances—the consideration of the Catholic claims, I have not lost sight of the probable consequences of such refusal, not only with regard to the Catholic question but with regard also to the great question of public policy involved in this principle, which has been stated as to the war in the Peninsula, which I cannot believe will be vigorously prosecuted if changes take place in the Administration, introducing into the Government those who have not acknowledged the policy of prosecuting it at the expense even of the means hitherto applied for that purpose.

It was not, therefore, by the nature of the sentiments which formed my own opinion upon these points that I was led to concur in the Minute, importing that we thought no further proposition made to those who had brought forward these principles, would be beneficial: and I add that, although I have strongly felt the difficulties which publications—whether authorized or not authorized—have thrown in the way of making propositions, yet I have not thought that those difficulties ought to prevent the tender of any proposition which would be useful.

I concurred, however, with my colleagues in the Minute of Cabinet because, attending to the differences of opinion which appeared to prevail among your Royal Highness's servants, I could not discover any further proposition which they were likely to agree in tendering to Lord Wellesley and Mr. Canning, and which it was also likely that those persons would accept and act upon; and because, therefore, I was unable to convince myself that the tender of any further proposition was likely to produce that general co-operation between them and your Royal Highness's servants which might be useful to your Royal Highness's service, or would, by any beneficial effects, compensate for the evils which delay in constituting the Government might occasion.

All which is most dutifully submitted to your Royal Highness's wisdom.

29 May 1812.

IN obedience to the commands of your Royal Highness to Lord Harrowby to state in writing his reasons for concurring in the Minute of Cabinet of the 27th. of this month, Lord Harrowby begs leave humbly to submit that he thought any further attempt on the part of your Royal Highness's confidential servants to obtain the accession of Lord Wellesley and Mr. Canning to the Administration perfectly hopeless, considering what had passed during and since the former attempt for that purpose; that he thought it also useless because it was evident to him from the discussions which had taken place, in obedience to the commands of your Royal Highness, amongst your confidential servants, that even the success of such an attempt (however improbable) would be attended with the loss of as much strength on the one side as might be gained on the other.

As these reasons alone would have been sufficient to induce Lord Harrowby to concur in that Minute, he humbly trusts it is unnecessary for him to trouble your Royal Highness with the statement of any other ground of opinion or feeling more peculiar to himself. He begs, however, to be permitted to add that he should have thought it his duty to allow them more or less weight in his decision according to the degree of probability that the service of your Royal Highness could be effectually promoted by the sacrifice of what appeared to him to be due to them.

92 RICHARD RYDER *to the* PRINCE REGENT

Great George Street, May 29, 1812.

IN obedience to your Royal Highness's commands that each of your Royal Highness's confidential servants should transmit to your Royal Highness in writing the reasons which induced him to concur in the Minute of Cabinet of the 27th. inst. Mr. Ryder has the honour of humbly submitting to your Royal Highness that it was evident to him from what passed in the course of the repeated deliberations which took place amongst your Royal Highness' servants, on that occasion, that no further attempt at an union with Lord Wellesley and Mr. Canning could be made at the present moment by your Royal Highness' servants collectively: and that the loss of strength which must follow from such an attempt being made in the only manner in which, under such circumstances, it could be proposed would, in his opinion, counteract and defeat every beneficial practical object that could be expected from such a measure.

Mr. Ryder does not presume to intrude upon your Royal Highness with other considerations which undoubtedly influenced his decision upon the question, because he is of opinion that, exclusive of whatever weight might justly be attached to them, the reason he has already ventured respectfully to lay before your Royal Highness was in itself conclusive.

93 NICHOLAS VANSITTART *to the* PRINCE REGENT

Great George Street, 29 May 1812.

MR. N. VANSITTART, in obedience to His Royal Highness's commands calling upon him to state the reasons which induced him to concur in the Minute submitted to His Royal Highness on the 27th. inst. by the Earl of Liverpool, begs leave humbly to submit that he has so recently had the honor to be called into His Royal Highness's confidential Councils that he has had very imperfect means of judging from any observations of his own with respect to the subjects referred to in that Minute, and has therefore been principally guided by the opinions of others of His Royal Highness's servants with whom he has usually been accustomed to agree; but that he has had sufficient opportunities of observing that such a diversity of sentiments prevailed, with respect to the extent to which the claims of His Majesty's Roman Catholic subjects could be safely admitted, as to render it, in his opinion, highly improbable that an arrangement could be formed between His Royal Highness's present servants and the Marquis Wellesley and Mr. Canning on terms which could afford a probable prospect of a stable and efficient Government.

Downing Street,
Friday [29 May 1812].

I BROUGHT with me from the Levée[1] Long[2] & Manners Sutton.[3]

They were both loud in their praises of the Prince, & said that no human being ever showed more firmness than he has done.

I do think it most cruel towards His Royal Highness that some means should not be devised to save him from the worst of the Opposition.

I see but one way of doing this, viz; the persuading Lord Wellesley to transfer with cordiality the commission to Lord Moira. Many of the best of the Prince's present servants would serve in an Administration formed by Lord Moira; but they all feel it a point of honour to act differently with regard to Lord Wellesley.

It will however be difficult to persuade Ld Wellesley to give up the commission to Lord Moira, thinking that his honour is committed not to do it. This I can tell you *confidentially* I got from Pole,[4] who feels as his brother does, & this I shd have mentioned to His R. Highness, had it been possible to have done it at the Levée.

Were it not for this circumstance an arrangement might be made, & Lord Liverpool might be brought into the Cabinet after the Catholic question had been disposed of.

I am not imagining that what I am writing can be worthy of His R. Highness's notice, but this I leave to your consideration. I had yesterday some conversation with Lord Liverpool which proved to me that he finds himself so committed upon the Catholic question as to make him feel that he had better be out of the Govt., & this it is wch has given me an idea that he might be brought in after that question has been considered.

1 The Prince Regent held a Levée at Carlton House on the 29th.
2 Charles Long, first Baron Farnborough (1761–1838). At this time Joint-Paymaster-General of the Forces and a Whip. Peerage, 1820.
3 Charles Manners-Sutton, first Viscount Canterbury (1780–1845). Judge-Advocate-General since 1809. Speaker of the House of Commons, 1817–35.
4 William Wellesley-Pole, first Baron Maryborough (1763–1845), one of Lord Wellesley's brothers. Irish Secretary 1809–12; Master of the Mint, 1814–23. Peerage, 1821. A member of his brother's political group, he declined Lord Liverpool's offer of the War Secretaryship in May 1812, and consequently remained out of office until 1814.

Downing Street,
Saturday, 6 o'clock [30 May 1812].

IT was unlucky that I called just after you went out, for I wanted to tell you that Mr. Martin[1] having given notice of a motion for Wednesday next, in case an Administration should not be formed on that day, I have sent to every part of England to get a full attendance.

I had been told that the Prince, in the event of a motion, would wish me to do so. But it is very necessary I should learn from you whether any progress has been made as I ought not to bring members up unnecessarily. Do on this account write me word what has passed today, and I am anxious to hear from you before I go out to dinner.

96 THE DUKE OF NORTHUMBERLAND *to* COLONEL McMAHON

Alnwick Castle, 30th May, 1812.

BY the post last night I had the pleasure of receiving your letter of the 27th. with its accompanying papers; and am concerned to perceive there is so much difficulty in forming such an Administration as His Royal Highness woud wish for. Lord Wellesley coud not have contrived a more certain method of preventing H.R.H. from receiving the aid and assistance of any of Lord Liverpool's friends, than by establishing the emancipation of the Catholics as the first of the two principles laid down on which the new Administration was to be formed. It was perfectly clear this was done with a view of catching the Lords Grey and Grenville with their friends; but in this it woud appear that he has been disappointed; for however anxious that Party may be in the Catholic cause it is as determined a measure with them, shoud they ever come into power, to withdraw our troops from the Peninsula and abandon the Spanish cause. Nor is this kind of system new to them, for when Buonaparte was in Poland, opposed to the armies of Russia and Prussia, with a large corps of observation from the Austrians a little in the rear of his right flank and directly cutting off his retreat to France, shoud he have been worsted and they shoud have chosen to act, the Lords G[rey] and G[renville] most positively refused to send the Allied Courts any assistance, although repeatedly pressed to do so particularly by the

---

1 Richard Martin (1754–1834), "Humanity Martin"; one of the founders of the R.S.P.C.A. The substance of his proposed motion (which was withdrawn on 2 June, Wellesley having been instructed to draw up a plan for a new Ministry) is in *Parl. Deb.* XXIII, 313.

Court of Petersburg. Had they at that time in conjunction with the Court of Stockholm landed ten thousand men from the Islands of Usedom and Wollin in the rear of the French army, Buonaparte must inevitably have been ruined. Though most earnestly pressed to do this, with a plan given them for the execution of this measure, they most positively refused all aid; and instead of it formed their absurd plan for the passage of the Dardanels and the conquest of Egypt.

I take it for granted, I am to suppose, from Lord W[ellesley] having laid down the two principles as the ground on which the new Ministry was to be formed, that he had brought the Prince Regent to consent to these measures in his first interview with H.R.H., as I can hardly bring myself to believe that his Lordship woud venture of himself to propose these or any other propositions, as sine qua non, without H.R.H's directions, particularly the first, to which the P[rince] R[egent] had formerly signified his disapprobation. Shoud this first proposition form the basis of the Administration which H.R.H. shall establish, I most sincerely hope the measure may answer H.R.H's expectations, and that the great care our ancestors have taken not to allow the Catholicks any acquisition of power (& in which I cannot but think they have acted with great wisdom), may on trial be found to have been perfectly needless. It must however be confessed that the trial is a very hazardous one, which ought not to be risked without the most serious consideration of all those consequences which may possibly attend it. I likewise most sincerely hope that those who have behaved with so much insolence and insult towards H.R.H. and whose object has been to storm the Closet and make the Regent their prisoner, may not falsely flatter themselves that they have gained their point, and by their uninterrupted violence induced H.R.H. at last to consent to this their favourite measure. Shoud they conceive this and act accordingly I fear H.R.H. will find them very troublesome and headstrong servants. God grant however this may not be the case. Surely if the P[rince] R[egent] does Lord Wellesley the honour of entrusting him with the direction of the affairs of the country, his Lordship is in duty bound to give up one of his two favourite principles if H.R.H. shoud wish him to do so. Indeed I carry my opinion much further and insist upon it that in every case and every measure it is the undoubted right and indeed duty of the Minister to propose, yet the ultimate decision on the subject does and ought to depend entirely upon the pleasure of the Sovereign, or whoever occupies his situation. Otherwise he is a mere tool and puppet in the hands of his Ministers. This, I insist upon it, is agreeable to the Constitution of the country. Whereas to allow any Minister to govern without controul is in direct contradiction to the Constitution, and highly dangerous to the State. You see, my dear Colonel, I give you my opinion with the utmost freedom. Was I not to do so I must cease writing, for I am incapable of saying what I do not think. Truth and honesty I have always thought the best policy; this path I have always pursued and I am now too old to alter. I have no interested views to gratify nor ambitious object to obtain. My sincere attachment to the Prince and the love of my country are the sole motives of my actions, and the sole causes which coud induce me, at my age and in my situation, to trouble my head with politicks.

I beg you will present my duty to H.R.H. and assure him I am perfectly sensible of, and most properly gratefull for, that partiality he is graciously pleased to show me. Accept, with Mrs. MacMahon, all our comp[limen]ts and believe me, [etc.].

97 THE EARL OF MOIRA *to* COLONEL MCMAHON

[31 May 1812.]

A SUDDEN light has struck across Ld Wellesley & me. He happened to ask me what was the particular assertion advanced by Ld Grey which the Prince deemed so offensive.[1] None suggested itself to my recollection: none occurs to Ld Wellesley's memory. Perhaps some very incorrect statement may have been made to the Prince. Would His Royal Highness deign to communicate to us the particular point that we may assure ourselves there is no error.

98 CHARLES ARBUTHNOT *to* COLONEL MCMAHON

Sunday, 6 O'clock. [? 31 May 1812.]

THE Prince had better not mention to Lord Wellesley anything about Lord Melville because His R[oyal] Highness has not yet had any communication with him, and for other reasons which I will mention to you tomorrow morning. I am quite sure of Melville, and the Prince may have him when he likes, but this ought not to be mentioned to any human being at present. Pray attend to this.[2]

1 The Prince Regent took offence at Grey's speech in the House of Lords (19 March 1812) when he implied that by keeping the Perceval Ministry in office, the Prince had broken his pledges to the Irish Catholics. Grey explained the matter in a letter to Moira (31 May), printed in *Parl. Deb.* XXIII, Appendix.

2 The Prince Regent sent for Wellesley on the night of the 31st, and next morning gave him full authority to form a Government. Wellesley was instructed to offer Melville a Cabinet post because of his great political influence in the House of Commons.

Monday, 6 o'clock. [1 June 1812.]

KNOWING yr zealous anxiety about me, I think it right to lose no time in observing to you that as the Govt. is to be formed *by* Ld. W[ellesley], my friends can have nothing to do with it,[1] & I of course shall follow the same line. I am therefore very desirous that you shd consider me as out of the question, tho' I never shall consider out of the question all that you have done & are wishing to do for me.

[P.S.] If you shd know anything this eveg, pray I beseech you write me a line, as you may easily imagine that I am now very curious.

Any time this evening I shd be glad to hear from you. At all events I shall call at ½ past 10 tomorrow. Adieu.

100 THE MARQUIS WELLESLEY *to the* PRINCE REGENT

Apsley House,
1st June 1812. ½ p 7 P.M.

LORD WELLESLEY has the honor to acquaint your Royal Highness, that he saw Lord Grey this afternoon, and communicated your Royal Highness's commands.[2]

Lord Grenville being absent from town, Lord Grey desired to defer his answer to your Royal Highness's orders untill to morrow. His Lordship however candidly stated, that the first impression on his own mind was, that the proposal, as made by Lord Wellesley, must be declined.

As Lord Wellesley expects to receive from Lords Grey & Grenville a written answer to morrow, it appears to him to be unnecessary to intrude upon your Royal Highness this night; he is however ready to attend your Royal Highness's orders at a moment's warning; he will not fail to submit the answer from Lords Grey & Grenville, as soon as he shall receive it.

1 The Prince Regent expressed a wish that some of the members of the late Cabinet would join Wellesley, and in particular mentioned Melville and Eldon, though he was disposed to recommend Sir William Grant for the Great Seal.

2 Wellesley was authorised to inform Lords Grey and Grenville that they might nominate four or five members of the Cabinet according as it should consist of twelve or thirteen, and that Canning, Erskine and Moira were to be in it. The Whigs declined office on these terms. Grey's account of this interview is in *Dropmore MSS.* x, 277, and Wellesley's Minute of the communication to Grey is in *Parl. Deb.* XXIII, Appendix.

Monday Evening, June 1st 1812.

I should think myself deficient in the respect and duty I owe to you were I to close this day without conveying to your Royal Highness in a few words my humble congratulations on the wisdom and magnanimity of the part you have taken in giving to Lord Wellesley the powers with which you have invested him this morning—At the same time I should be insincere if I attempted to dissemble the deep regret I have felt at an apparent alteration in your manner towards me—produced solely I must beleive by my expressing an opinion that a proscription of Lord Grey[1] in the formation of a new Administration would be a proceeding equally injurious to the estimation of your personal dignity and the maintenance of the public interests.

Long indulgence, Sir, on your part, in allowing me to speak the truth to you leads me not to hesetate, or consider it as presumptuous to say that you grievously wrong'd me if you supposed I ventured to press this my opinion on you from any undue partiality to the noble Lord in question or any of those with whom he is allied—I have never profess'd or affected any such motive—and with great submission I must express my surprise that your Royal Highness could for a moment have entertained this notion. My object I can with the utmost sincerity declare was founded on what I considered best *for your honor* & *your interest* and *the general good of the country.*

Junius says in a public letter of his address'd to your royal father— "Fate that made you a King forbad your having a friend".[2] I deny his proposition as a general maxim. I must feel confident that your Royal Highness possesses qualities to win and to secure to you the attachment and devotion of private friendship in spite of your being a Sovereign. At least I am entitled to make this declaration as far as relates to myself —and I do it under the assured conviction that you will never require from me any proof of that attachment and devotion inconsistent with the clear and honourable independence of mind & conduct which constitute my sole value as a public man and which have hitherto been my best recomendation to your gracious favor confidence and protection.[3]

1 Grey had never troubled to conceal his indignation at the Prince's conduct in February, and, as Lord Holland said, "his unguarded exposure of the Prince Regent's duplicity in all companies...sank deep in the Royal mind....We all incurred the guilt, if not the odium, of charging his Royal Highness with ingratitude and perfidy. We all encouraged every species of satire against him and his mistress."

2 "The fortune, which made you a King, forbade you to have a friend." (Letter xxxv.)

3 A portion of this letter is quoted in Moore's *Life of Sheridan*, inaccurately, however; and Sheridan's biographer, Sichel, erroneously states that no trace of the original remains.

Minute of a Communication made by the Marquis Wellesley to Earl Grey, 1 June 1812. (*Parl. Deb.* XXIII, Appendix.)

Earl Grey's and Lord Grenville's reply (3 June) to the Marquis Wellesley's Minute, 1 June. (*Ibid.*)

102 THE EARL OF MOIRA *to the* PRINCE REGENT

Wednesday Afternoon, June 3d 1812.
Seven o'Clock.

LORD MOIRA, with his humblest duty, informs your Royal Highness that Lord Wellesley this afternoon made in the House of Lords a statement of the unprosperous termination of the negociation.[1] It appeared to be the decided sense of the House that no details should then be laid before them; obviously, from the fear that such an exposition might prevent the renewal of treaty. Untill the effect of what has taken place in the two Houses shall be ascertained, which cannot be the case before tomorrow morning, Lord Moira most respectfully submits to your Royal Highness that all proceedings must pause.[2]

103 THE EARL OF MOIRA *to* COLONEL MCMAHON

June 4th 1812.
¼ past 11.

THE Prince's injunction shall be strictly obeyed; and indeed, all the steps which I am taking are calculated upon the decisive assumption that it is no longer of any use to look to the Opposition.

1 *Parl. Deb.* XXIII, 332.
2 Wellesley's commission to form a Government was now withdrawn, and on the 4th Moira was instructed to plan a Ministry. At the same time, believing that the negotiations between Wellesley and the Whigs had failed from a misunderstanding, Moira sent written explanations to Grey and Grenville, but they declined to pursue the subject by unauthorised negotiations. Then, in order to deprive the Whigs of their last pretext for complaint—in that no offers had been made to them—Moira on the 6th was given full power to treat with them, and, as he had expected, and as the Prince Regent had doubtless intended, they declined office, on the ground that Moira refused to acquiesce in the removal of any of the Household— in changes, that is, which had been usual when a new Government was formed. Moira considered that the removal of Lord Hertford and his son Lord Yarmouth "would have been an unnecessary humiliation of the Prince, and would have set the seal of office to accredit every ribbald tale of scandal that had been circulated in this town". The Hertfords intended to resign if the Whigs came in. See No. 117.

June 4th [1812]. 5 o'Clock.

I HAD not the good fortune to find the Chancellor at home, but I shall try to fix an interview with him.

Enclosed, you have Lord Wellesley's final decision.[1] I was with him this morning; & he was in good humor, tho' I could not gain upon him.

I have an answer from Lord Grey,[2] resting entirely upon his former objections. It is clear that they do not mean to accept any terms whatever. The only point to be determined is, whether one should take from them the last shadow of excuse which they might attempt in saying that *I* had made no overture to them; my letter being to be considered as an explanation of a matter already defunct. The expedience of this, as a ground for detaching many partisans of the Opposition, must be canvassed with Ld Melville & Canning. I shall see them immediately.

105 COLONEL MCMAHON *to the* PRINCE REGENT

Pall Mall, Thursday June 4th 1812.
½ past Nine o'ck.

I HAVE the honour to send your Royal Highness, four distinct letters, which will better serve to explain, than anything I could otherwise detail, the political operations of this day. In suggesting to Lord Moira the essential propriety, & advantage, of his *immediately* communicating with the Lord Chancellor, Y.R.Hss will find an answer in his Lordship's note to me, of this evening, bearing date "5 o'Clock", covering Lord Wellesley's final letter. Lord Wellesley had however, at their meeting in the morning, when he equally declined any component part in the new Administration, nevertheless, offered his best interposition with Mr. Canning to enter into office, but I own, I cannot with any share of confidence, subscribe to the sincerity of this profession, when I read Mr. Cannings letter of late this evening to Lord Moira, as written subsequent to his interview with Lord Wellesley, & his Lordship's proffer'd mediation being antecedent to such interview, for Canning's letter to Lord Moira, bears no evidence, of any such disposition on the part of Lord Wellesley. Erskine's letter goes certainly to establish that

1 Dated 4 June. (*Wellesley Papers*, II, 113.) Wellesley refused to take the *second* place in the projected Moira Government.
2 See *Parl. Deb.* XXIII, Appendix (4 June); and *Life and Opinions of Earl Grey*, p. 291.

Lord Moira's letter to Ld Grey of yesterday was no *renewal* of overture to the Opposition, & only a mere individual correspondence.

Mr. Ponsonby held to-day at one o'clock a numerous meeting of the Opposition, where I learn that nothing more pass'd than in reading them the correspondence between Lord Wellesley, & the Lords Grey, & Grenville, & without deciding on any specific course of proceeding. The general, & prevailing sentiment, I have understood every where to-day, is an abhorrence of the factious, & intollerant views of an obnoxious Opposition.

106 THE EARL OF MOIRA *to the* PRINCE REGENT

June 5th, 7 o'Clock.

LORD MOIRA humbly acquaints your Royal Highness that he stated in the House of Lords this afternoon your Royal Highness's having never indicated any person (except Marquis Wellesley the negociator) for the Cabinet, but that the fullest scope was given for the discussion of that point.[1] He further declared that your Royal Highness had not made any reservation of seats to be filled up according to your subsequent direction; and above all he asserted his knowledge that your Royal Highness had not only soared infinitely above personal animosities but that you had not signified an exclusion against any individual whatever.

The paper[2] of which the enclosed is a copy was carried by the Duke of Bedford to Lord Grey, who told Lord Moira in the House that an answer should be immediately sent. Lord Moira anticipates that they will decline the interview.[3] In that event, Mr. Canning & Mr. Huskisson[4] have professed their readiness to take office.

1 "With regard to the nomination of individuals it was understood to be a mere statement of a wish on the part of the illustrious personage...and it was naturally believed that the names introduced would be acceptable" to Lords Grey and Grenville.

2 Moira's letter to Grey and Grenville, 5 June. (*Parl. Deb.* XXIII, Appendix.)

3 The reply, dated 5 June, of Lords Grey and Grenville is in *Parl. Deb.* XXIII, Appendix.

4 William Huskisson (1770–1830), one of the leading members of Canning's party. Huskisson refused the Chancellorship of the Exchequer "from a firm conviction that the interests of the Government cannot be adequately maintained in the House of Commons, especially at this moment, unless this office, united to that of First Lord of the Treasury, is held by the person who leads the House". Canning, therefore, meant to be First Lord of the Treasury, Chancellor of the Exchequer, and leader of the House of Commons. Moira, he suggested, should be Home Secretary, "with the portefeuille and station of Premier", and leader of the House of Lords. Melville should be First Lord of the Admiralty, Canning's friend, Lord Granville Leveson-Gower, should be Foreign Secretary, and Wellesley-Pole Secretary for War and the Colonies. "Lord Wellesley may be prevailed upon to go to Ireland, but he will not accept any other situation, and on his acceptance will depend the

June 5th 1812. Half past Eleven P.M.

Lord Moira humbly lays before your Royal Highness the answer which he has received from Lord Grey & Lord Grenville.

With great submission he solicits your Royal Highness's observation of that part of the letter in which the disposition is expressed to receive a communication of your Royal Highness's pleasure thro' any channel whatsoever; tho' they object to unauthorised communication.

Lord Moira, that nothing may be left indistinct, most respectfully entreats your Royal Highness's permission to propose a meeting with Lords Grey & Grenville, tho' their obvious endeavours to evade a conclusive discussion leaves scarcely a hope of any efficient result from the interview.

The Earl of Moira to Earl Grey and Lord Grenville, 6 June 1812. (*Parl. Deb.* XXIII, Appendix.)

Minute of a Conversation between the Earl of Moira, and Earl Grey and Lord Grenville, 6 June 1812. (*Ibid.*)

108 The Earl of Moira *to* Colonel McMahon

June 7th 1812. 3 o'Clock.

Lord Liverpool, tho' he answers that he cannot come into office *at present* without fallaciously misconstruing the terms of our pledge for considering the Catholic question, has promised his most zealous support. He is much flattered by the way in which we addressed him.[1]

decision of Mr. W. Pole." Castlereagh should be asked to take a peerage "and to take office not immediately but before the opening of the next Session". Huskisson, and, doubtless, Canning too, thought that if these proposals, "or something not materially different", were unacceptable to Moira, there would be no chance of forming a Government. (Add. MSS. 38738, fo. 258.)

1 Liverpool and Eldon had complained that Moira and his friends "had not had the politeness to ask for the support of their Party, though they were disposed to give it handsomely without sharing in government with us". "This little point of honour" was "gratified" on the 7th. In spite of Liverpool's answer, Moira still hoped to form a Ministry representing all parties. He was supported by Canning and his friends, and hoped to persuade Wellesley to go to Ireland as Lord-Lieutenant. Of the Whigs he hoped to secure Sheridan, Erskine, the Duke of Norfolk and even Whitbread; and of the Tories, Melville, Eldon and others. But unexpected difficulties arose, and when on the 8th Moira reported progress, the Prince Regent decided to revive the old Tory Ministry under Lord Liverpool. Moira's explanation of his failure is in *Hastings MSS.*, pp. 295–7.

Downing Street,
5 o'clock. Sunday [? 7 June 1812].

You understood that Lord Melville would be most happy to obey His R[oyal] Highness's commands to accept office, and that if H.R.H. wished to see him he w[oul]d be most happy to wait upon him to state the same himself. Indeed, as I stated that I had been ordered to give the message to Lord Melville it may be desirable that His R[oyal] Highness should see him. Lord Melville will be a great accession of strength to His R.H.

If, now that our friends act with the new Government, I could be appointed Secretary to Ireland it would certainly please me, but of this and of other things I will speak to you tomorrow morning.

110 THE DUKE OF NORTHUMBERLAND *to* COLONEL MCMAHON

Alnwick Castle, 7th June 1812.

I HAVE had the pleasure of receiving your letter of the 3d, together with the very interesting papers which accompanied it. No man in the kingdom can lament more than I do the very disagreeable situation in which H:R:H: is placed by the conduct of the different parties; and perhaps it might have been as well if H:R:H: had determined at once, to keep in the late Ministers, and dissolve the Parliament. Mr. Stuart Wortley has much to answer for. He has done a mischief to this country, far beyond any thing, which any attempt of Buonaparte's coud have effected. Most truly and most sincerely do I sympathize with the Prince Regent's feelings. What must these be, if H:R:H: is driven to the necessity of taking those into his Councils, who basely, & most ungratefully deserted him, at a moment when he stood in the greatest need of them? He never can have any regard for, or confidence in persons, who have proved to him, that their attachment to H:R:H: was of the most selfish nature, and only continued, as long as it was their interest. And yet altho' they deserted him in the most brusque, & brutal manner, they are not unwilling to return, and perhaps feign the same attachment again, whenever their interest, & ambition lead them to suppose they shall be greatly benefitted by so doing. Even the two noble Lords[1] are not unwilling to accept of office, provided H:R:H: will consent to their having all the power, and submit himself to their will, and pleasure. Shoud the Prince

1 Grey and Grenville.

Regent's generosity make him consent to overlook such unpardonable ingratitude, and indignities, as he has met with from those, from whom he had an undoubted right to expect a very different return for the great partiality, with which he had honoured them, I am certain at least he can never in his heart forgive them; much less forget the treatment he has received from them. What security can H:R:H: have if such men are to become his Ministers, that they will not desert him again, whenever they think it for their advantage to do so. H:R:H: knows by experience, that no kindness, or even affection on his part, can bind them to him; and therefore I hope he will make the proper use of them, & keep them in, or turn them out, just as it suits his convenience at any time; for it is absolutely impossible that they can ever again enjoy his confidence, or good opinion. It is impossible for anybody to have shown more nobleness of mind, or more true patriotism, than the Prince Regent has done, in his attempts to form a strong, & powerfull Administration. He has even offered to sacrifice his own private feelings, to, what has been thought, the good of the publick. If he has not succeeded it has not been his fault, & the impartial, and thinking part of the Kingdom, must ever admire his conduct, & feel the obligations they owe him, upon this occasion. I beg you will present my most dutifull assurances of *continued* attachment to His Royal person, & the happiness I shall feel, if I can in any way be made usefull. Accept yourself of the compliments and best wishes of the Duchess, myself, & all my family, & offer the same for us to Mrs. Mac-Mahon. I have the pleasure to be, with the most sincere regard, [etc.].

111 GEORGE CANNING'S *Memorandum*

Carlton House, June 9, 1812.

LORD LIVERPOOL stated to Mr. Canning yesterday that he (Ld. L.) had understood from H.R.H. the Prince Regent that Lord Moira had "recommended to H.R.H. to fall back upon his old Government."

Mr. Canning had previously heard from Lord Moira, in the presence of Colonel MacMahon an account of what had passed between H.R.H. and his Lordship; in which, to the best of Mr. Canning's recollection, no mention had been made by Lord Moira of this supposed recommendation.

He therefore took the liberty of calling upon Colonel MacMahon, to inquire whether he (Col. MacMahon) had heard Lord Moira mention this recommendation: though hardly conceiving it possible that a point so important should have escaped Mr. Canning's attention.

2. It is very generally reported by the friends of the Administration that Lord Moira gave it as his opinion to the Prince Regent, that "every thing had been done that could be done to give effect to the vote of the House of Commons".

This opinion Mr. Canning does not recollect to have been stated to him in Lord Moira's report of what passed at his Lordship's audience with the Prince Regent. And he was equally anxious to learn from Col. MacMahon whether he (Col. MacMahon) had heard Lord Moira state any thing to this effect, which had either escaped Mr. Canning's attention at the time, or his recollection since.

Mr. Canning has troubled Col. MacMahon on this occasion only because having yesterday foreborne to request an audience of the P.R^t. on the avowed ground of his general concurrence in what had been stated to him by Lord Moira as the substance of his Lordship's conference with H.R.H. he felt it necessary, & due to Lord Moira as well as to himself, to endeavour to ascertain from Col. MacMahon *his* impression of what had passed in his presence: in order that if he, Mr. Canning, should have omitted to notice two points of such importance, on which he would have had the misfortune to differ from Lord Moira, (had he been aware that they were stated to him),—he might without loss of time set himself right; & might guard himself against being implicated in a supposed agreement upon those particular points, by the expression of his general concurrence.

112 THE EARL OF MOIRA *to* COLONEL MCMAHON

June 9th [1812].

You must let me have a line (secret) to say that Ld. Wellesley's concurring with me in the publication of the papers will not displease the Prince. It is not an authority he wants; but with a proper delicacy he wishes to be satisfied that the Prince would not take it amiss. The note should be addressed to me, as if in answer to a question of mine, & after having shown it to him I will destroy it.

He told me he had not been summoned for the Chapter on Friday, & he seemed uneasy at the possibility of being left out.[1]

1 Lord Moira was installed as a Knight of the Garter on the 12th.

[June 9th 1812.]

BE assured that the P[rince] has a thorough sense of the delicacy of Ld Wellesley's attentions on every occasion. His Lordship had full power to explain the late negociations in any way: So that whatever mode of communicating them to the public he may adopt in concert with you cannot be unsatisfactory to the P[rince], only you will feel that H:R:H: could not properly make himself a formal party to the publication.[1]

114 HENRY BATE DUDLEY[2] *to* COLONEL McMAHON

Coles, Tuesday [9 June 1812].

I AM in the midst of a click of the most indignant oppositionists, the Duke of Bedford, Ld Albemarle,[3] Coke,[4] Edw Coke[5] &c. They came down to dinner much depressed under an idea that Lord Moira had accepted the Premiership. My presence was evidently a political restraint to them, and I experienced a great drawback even in their agricultural friendship, and experienced a coolness from them all, evidently for my own political offences, and probably more so from those of the author of the *Lover of Opposition* being imputed to me. Though this is a sacrifice which I own hurts me, you may be assured that I did not demean myself on this occasion for want of a proper portion of pride, and equal reserve with their own, which I had the satisfaction to find they felt: for this morning they were more communicative. The Duke had letters from *Rob Adair*,[6] & Lord Albemarle from *G. Walpole*,[7] & Coke from *Tierney* detailing what passed to a certain hour last night in both

1 Wellesley's correspondence with Grey and Grenville was published in *The Times* on the 12th.

2 The journalist and clergyman (1745–1824). He had been editor of *The Morning Post* for some years, when in 1780 he founded *The Morning Herald* in the Whig interest. In 1812 the *Herald* became the Prince Regent's newspaper and Bate Dudley was given a Baronetcy.

3 William Charles Keppel, fourth Earl of Albemarle (1772–1849). The Prince Regent had recently tried to detach him from the Opposition by offering him the Mastership of the Horse, with the prospect of a Garter. (Albemarle, *Fifty Years of my Life*, I, 334.)

4 Thomas William Coke, first Earl of Leicester (1752–1842), Whig M.P. for Norfolk and one of the leading figures of the agricultural revolution. Peerage, 1837.

5 Coke's brother, M.P. for Norfolk.

6 Sir Robert Adair (1763–1855), the distinguished diplomatist and last surviving friend of Charles James Fox. At this time Whig M.P. for Camelford. K.C.B., 1809. He declined to join the Carlton House party and in March rejected the Prince Regent's offer of a Foreign Mission.

7 General George Walpole (1758–1835), second son of Horatio, second Baron Walpole. Whig M.P. for Dungarvan.

Houses: Their joy was boundless *on learning* that Lord *Moira* had *"got out of the d—d scrape as they termed it"*, for one of the *Seymours* had told Lord Albemarle just before he left London that Lord Moira had not only kissed hands, but was at that hour transacting business with the American Minister, which *that Seymour* s[ai]d he had from Lord *Robt. Seymour*,[1] but which Lord Robt denied to the Duke of Bedford having so said. They affected a triumph at Lord Liverpool's having *presumed* to become Minister, and *Coke* said (wch is the *main purport* of *this letter*)— "that now he trusted the House of Commons "w^d do their duty, and *impeach the Chancellor*: if they did not he did not care into what public contempt they fell." This sentiment was concurred in by the whole click.

They are to receive a pacquet from Tierney & others by an early coach to give the detail of his 2 nights proceedings & to regulate their stay here, or flying hence to Parliament. I trust we shall meet tomorrow in Sloane Street.

P.S. George Walpole has *written them* word that Lord Moira had *"thrown up his cards"*, a Brookes's[2] phrase: & that they cannot account for Mr. Wortley's motion[3] being postponed till Thursday.

115 THE BISHOP OF SALISBURY[4] *to* MAJOR-GENERAL TURNER

Seymour St., June 10, 1812.

LADY DE CLIFFORD has informed me that it is the pleasure of the Prince Regent that the Princess Charlotte and her establishment should be removed to Windsor.

I must therefore beg of you to take the earliest opportunity of laying my humble duty at the feet of His Royal Highness with a request that I may be honoured with His Royal Highnesses commands, without which I cannot presume to give any directions to the preceptors or masters who are under me.

It is my intention, should it meet with His Royal Highnesses approbation,—to go to Windsor on Saturday.

1 The third son of the first Marquis of Hertford who died in 1794. [1748–1831.] His eldest brother was now Lord Chamberlain of the Household.
2 The Whig Club.
3 On 11 June Stuart-Wortley's motion regretting that an efficient Administration had not yet been formed, and entreating the Prince Regent to form one that would be entitled to the support of Parliament, was rejected by 289 to 164.
4 John Fisher (1748–1825), Bishop of Salisbury since 1807. From 1780 to 1785 he was preceptor to Prince Edward, and in 1805 was appointed to superintend Princess Charlotte's education.

Alnwick Castle, 12th June 1812.

As I am convinced that your time, my dear Colonel, must now be much occupied, I merely trouble you, to acknowledge the safe receipt of your letter of the 8th, with its accompanying papers, and to say, that as the Prince Regent has named Lord Liverpool to be the First Commissioner of the Treasury, I take it for granted the return to office of the old Administration will be followed by an immediate dissolution of Parliament. This measure will of course become necessary, to prevent the eternal motions, which will otherwise be made in the House of Commons by Mr. Wortley—Mr. Tierney, & their adherents; assisted, & encouraged, by the two great Lords,[1] and their party. Shoud such a measure be intended, I shall feel myself most particularly obliged to you, if you will let me know it, as soon as you can do so consistent with the duties of your situation.

I beg you will offer my duty to H:R:H: and congratulate him, on what I look upon as a victory; which if properly followed up, with perseverence, and firmness, will relieve H:R:H: from a great deal of future embarrassment. As his insulters are desperate, they will be for a short time the more violent, but he must not mind that, & all will become right again, & they as humble, & submissive, as they are just now haughty & arrogant. Adieu. Accept the kind wishes of us all, & offer the same for us to Mrs. Mac-Mahon.

117 THE EARL OF MOIRA *to* COLONEL MCMAHON

Sunday night. June 14th 1812.

ALL argument with Sheridan (and I have used to the utmost extent of his patience whatever could be urged) has been unavailing. This much, however, I have gained; that I have made him limit definitely the substance of what he is to address to the House.[2] The amount is this. He

---

1 Grey and Grenville.

2 Sheridan had been violently attacked in the *Morning Chronicle* for his alleged treachery to the Whigs during the recent ministerial negotiations. Lord Yarmouth, the Vice-Chamberlain, had told him that most of the Household intended to resign if the Opposition came into office, but Sheridan failed to pass on the information to Grey and Grenville, and was heard prophesying at Brooks' Club that the Household would remain. His explanation, begun on the 17th, and completed two days later, failed to satisfy his party, whose confidence he now completely and irretrievably lost. The Prince Regent and Moira strove hard to prevent Sheridan from making a public explanation because they doubted his discretion, and were probably afraid that he would disclose the fact that from the first they had really intended to exclude Grey and Grenville from the Ministry, that Moira's negotiations with them were meant to fail, and that the aim was to break up the Whig party by detaching such members as Erskine, the Duke of Norfolk and Whitbread.

will assert that he never gave to the Regent any secret counsel on the subject of the negociation; and he will declare that what L[or]d Yarmouth said to him respecting the projected resignation of the Hertford family was not communicated in any manner which should make it incumbent on him (Sheridan) to impart the determination to L[or]ds Grey & Grenville directly or thro' me. If he keeps to this no harm will be done, and I think he will be precise to the point as I understand Whitbread concurs with him and is keen to vindicate his own judgement by showing how the Opposition have erred in all their constructions. Do not think I have pressed the Prince's wishes feebly. I insisted on them till Sheridan became absolutely violent. It is on Wednesday he is to make the motion which will be in itself of some nugatory nature and only framed to let in the explanation. He means previously to ask an audience of the Prince. I do not think it will be possible for His Royal Highness to gain on Sheridan's resolution, and all that can be effected, I apprehend, will be the binding him strictly to the line which I have described.

118   BENJAMIN WEST *to* MAJOR-GENERAL TURNER

Newman Street, June 15th 1812.

AGREEABLE to the annual arrangements in the Royal Academy—the Exhibition in that place will close on Saturday next (the 20th inst) for this year: I therefor request, that you will be pleased to make known this circumstanc, with my humble duty to His Royal Highness the Prince Regent—that should it be his pleasure to honour the Exhibition with his presence before the pictures are taken down, that he will be graciously pleased to signify his commands, that I may give orders for the works of Art not to be removed, untill after he has inspected them.[1]

1 The Prince Regent, accompanied by the Dukes of York and Cumberland, visited the Exhibition. "He staid full two hours", wrote Farington. "The *portraits* principally occupied his attention, and he continually referred to his catalogue for the names of the portraits. . . . A guard of soldiers had been ordered to attend, and [the] floors of the Exhibition rooms were covered with green baize. These marks of respect he appeared to be pleased with."

Bruton Street, [16 June 1812].

UNQUESTIONABLY I shall obey the Prince's commands by waiting on him tomorrow at the time he is pleased to command, but I am really so ill that I have not left my bed today but to receive L[or]d Yarmouth for an hour tonight—between whom and myself there remains not a shade of difference, and further, I do most humbly hope and implore that His Royal Highness would press no more that I should submit to the attacks so foully levelled at me and forfeit my pledge to vindicate myself. To act [thus] would render me the most disgraced and dishonoured man living and I could never show my face again. Surely surely my dear friend I may be trusted with the discretion that my devotion to the Prince will guide me thro' the whole of the *very little* I shall have to state and that I shall not utter one word that will not be in maintenance of his honor. I am aware of the points he dislikes my touching on and of my anticipating part of the Lords debate. Not one word that I shall utter can lead to any such result. Pray let me have another line. Upon my honor I can scarcely hold the pen I am scrawling with.

[P.S.] I mean a line graciously dispensing with my attendance tomorrow. N.B. Received at 10 o'clock A.M. Wednesday 17th. June. [Endorsement.]

120 LORD ELDON *to the* PRINCESS OF WALES

17th June 1812.

THE Lord Chancellor humbly begs leave to communicate to your Royal Highness the Princess of Wales that he has been commanded by the Prince Regent to inform your Royal Highness that it is his pleasure that the Princess Charlotte of Wales should at present reside at Windsor; and that the Princess Charlotte, for the purpose of waiting upon your Royal Highness at Kensington, should come from Windsor once a fortnight, the same regulation that the company should be the Royal Family only being attended to, which His Royal Highness thought it fit should be observed upon the Princess Charlotte's coming to Kensington from Warwick House. The Prince Regent has further commanded the Lord Chancellor to state that it is His Royal Highness's pleasure that the Princess Charlotte should not receive visits at Windsor, as the Princess

Charlotte is residing in a house, appropriated for the use of the Prince Regent.[1]

121   LUCIUS CONCANNON[2] *to* COLONEL MCMAHON

Palermo, 18th June 1812.

I WRITE to you every two or three years in the most liberal way possible—*you* not in any hurry to answer and *I* expecting none.

I must own however that your last letter, dated October 1806, ought to satisfy me for the remainder of my life, since it contained an assurance, "by His R.H's command that he was always my friend and would be happy to serve me upon every occasion".

I can safely assert that this sentiment has been my consolation in exile and my incentive ever since to do what could be most worthy of His R.H's approbation.

I came here from Vienna with Dispatches of importance to Lord William Bentinck,[3] and arrived in the Bay of Palermo on the 25th. of May. It was thought necessary that someone should go as quickly as possible, and for that purpose the only road was thro' Italy to Naples and try to embark there. It was a ticklish service and not without danger and therefore I volunteered it. No small labour was requisite to get a false passport signed by the French Minister at Vienna as well as by other Ministers, but it was managed and Mrs. C. and myself set off as a Danish merchant and his wife going to Smyrna.

We travelled thro' the Illyrian Provinces, Bologna, Florence and Rome to Naples and should have arrived here in 33 days if the wind had been favorable,—instead of which we were driven back three times after waiting five weeks at Naples, and at last after having experienced every storm during the months of March and April arrived at Tunis in a Neapolitan vessel unobserved and untaken by the numerous English cruisers which they told us infested these seas. At Tunis we luckily found an English gunboat who brought us to Palermo in two days.

Here another misfortune awaited us. Lord Malpas[4] and Dr. Arm-

1 From this time the Princess Charlotte's intercourse with her mother was more and more restricted, and, though in her seventeenth year, she was forced to live a life of seclusion at Windsor under the watchful eye of the Queen.

2 He was in Parliament from 1818 until his death in 1822, and joined the Whig Party.

3 Envoy Extraordinary and Minister Plenipotentiary at Palermo, 1811–14, and Commander-in-Chief of the British military forces in the Mediterranean.

4 Succeeded his father as fifth Earl and second Marquis of Cholmondeley, 1827. (1792–1870.)

strong sailed that very night (25th. May). The son of our respected
friend whom everybody loves would at any time have been a cheering
sight to us, and particularly here, as I had several things to say to him
from Vienna as well as to Armstrong who is a most excellent and worthy
fellow. They came alongside us in the moment of departure. Lord
Malpas with the greatest kindness, as soon as he heard of our coming,
had already left his lodging at our disposal, and everything it contained,
for the term which belonged to him till the end of August, and it has
been the greatest comfort and advantage to us in every possible way.

As soon as our *quarantaine* was expired I saw Lord William and have
had long conversations with him since. I brought him several strong
letters of recommendation as unluckily he was almost the only one of the
family that I did not happen to know. Lady William was an old
acquaintance. They have both been particularly kind to us and our reception here would flatter people more difficult than ourselves. To shew
you that it is not meant to treat us with coldness or formality, Lady
William called yesterday to ask us to dinner for tomorrow, and we had
a long chat. Her Ladyship had received a letter from Lord Malpas since
his departure and speaks of him with much feeling and affection.

Of London friends we found Admiral Freemantle,[1] Lambe[2] who
awakened all my sorrow for poor *Penn!*[3] Gen[era]l MacFarlane,[4]
Orby Hunter[5] and his wife, &c.

I go to Lord William when he sends for me, never otherwise. He
made me give him, in writing, all my observations upon Italy, particularly upon the present state of Naples and all I knew of Austria. The
gentleman knows how to ask questions, believe me.

He is extremely popular here, shrewd, sensible and penetrating, with
a total absence of *hauteur*, pomp or nonsense—perfectly at his ease himself, he seems not to imagine how anybody can be otherwise.

In our last interview he sucked me so dry that I came home in the
shape and likeness of a squeezed lemon—that the simile may go no
further and your poor friend not be thrown on a dunghill, I have thought

1 Vice-Admiral Sir Thomas Francis Fremantle (1765–1819). K.C.B., 1815.
2 Frederick James Lamb, third Viscount Melbourne and Baron Beauvale (1782–1853),
William Lamb's brother. In 1812 he was Secretary of Legation at Palermo, an appointment
which he probably owed to his mother's influence with Lord William Bentinck.
3 Peniston Lamb (1770–1805), William Lamb's elder brother.
4 Sir Robert Macfarlane. He served on the Staff in Sicily, as second in command under
Lord William Bentinck. He was permitted to accept the Grand Cross of the Neapolitan Order
of St Ferdinand, conferred for his services in Italy, especially at the capture of Genoa in 1814.
K.C.B., 1817. (? 1770–1843.)
5 He won distinction in the literary world by translating Byron's works into French.
He died in 1843.

of applying to *two men* for whom I certainly have a very sincere regard—Lord Cholmondeley[1] and yourself—and I shall enclose this letter open to his Lordship—I have no other excuse to offer for troubling either of you.

My request is that *one* of you—and in that case I should prefer Lord C.—or both of you, which would be still better, would have the goodness to mention, in the shortest way possible, my situation to His Royal Highness. There it is, with as much brevity and truth as I can state it.

The manner of Lord William towards me is every day more encouraging and affable. I cannot guess whether he means to offer me anything here or not. Some of my letters, particularly one from Gen[era]l Nugent, expressed a strong hint of that kind. Of *this* I am quite sure, that I cannot ask him. *That* to me is quite impossible.[2]

I received from Mr. King at Vienna for this journey £200—it has cost above five hundred. I have not mentioned this to Lord William, nor do I conceive any claim is to be made anywhere for the overplus, authorized as it might be by the extreme state of nudity of circumstance in which we arrived—added to the misfortune of having lost the best part of our baggage at Tunis in changing ships at night and in a gale of wind. Supposing it were to be said to His Royal Highness in these words—"Sir, Concannon is at Palermo. He has performed a duty (or a service if you please); being on the spot he wishes to be employed there, or in any of those seas. His views are humble, his zeal is great, and to your Royal Highness alone he would wish to owe any employment, however trivial, that you may have the goodness to recommend him to."

This is the *basis* at least of what I beg *you* my good friends to represent. I don't know that there is anything here to be given away—places may be full, and God forbid that I should wish to eat the bread of such another poor Devil as myself, but Sicily is not the only part of the world where service may be found to go hand in hand with duty and attachment!

Can it be offensive to His R.H. that I should offer these services and sollicit his protection? No. Have *I* any claim to such protection?

1 George James Cholmondeley, fourth Earl and (1815) first Marquis of Cholmondeley (1749–1827). Appointed Lord Steward of the Household, March 1812.

2 Concannon was offered nothing: he was distrusted both by Bentinck and the Government at home. Bentinck wrote to Lord Bathurst on 25 October: "Many thanks for your private letter of Sept. 4 relative to Mr Concannon. I remember him of old and all the reports about him, which very possibly are well founded. But he was trusted by all the Archduke's party at Vienna and they had great confidence in him. He remained at Vienna for three years and completely succeeded in deceiving them if he was dishonest. If he could be relied upon his information would be of the first kind, for in knowledge of the world and acuteness he excels. *I* certainly would not trust him." (*Bathurst Papers*, p. 218.)

Certainly none. Will it injure you or Lord Cholmondeley in His R. Highness's opinion if you intercede for an old friend? Oh, no. I am myself a witness to the contrary. I applied to him once, upon a similar occasion, and remember well what he did *then* for the person which even my obscure application reminded him of.

May I then be permitted to hope that neither you or Lord Cholmondeley will refuse to do as much for me?

I must wait an answer for four months in a burning climate, and with very small resources. It requires some patience but we have been in long habits of acquaintance with that accommodating virtue.

In the worst of cases we may return amongst you, but we shall never be found either discontented or ungrateful.

Adieu, My dr Colonel.—

122 THE MARCHIONESS THOMOND[1] *to the* PRINCE REGENT

G George Street, June 20 [1812].

THE kind sentiments your Royal Highness was pleased to express for my late uncle Sir Joshua Reynolds,[2] can never be effaced from my recollection, and it is with gratitude & pride, that I lay the best portrait he ever painted of himself, at your Royal Highness's feet. I could in no way so well exemplify my duty & love to him, as by doing what I know, living, would have gratify'd him most, nor can I in any way more fully evince *my* respect towards your Royal Highness.

The deep sense I have of your Royal Highness's goodness to my uncle, and your gracious condescension in accepting his portrait from my hand, will ever be a source of the most heartfelt satisfaction, since it must be accompany'd with the idea that it is his patron (and may I presume to say his friend) who thus honours his memory.

1 The second wife of the first Marquis of Thomond, who died in 1808.
2 The portrait painter (1723–1792).

St. James's Square,
Tuesday night [23 June 1812]. Half past Twelve.

LORD CASTLEREAGH has the satisfaction to acquaint your Royal Highness that the Order in Council[1] was very favorably received by the members from the manufacturing Counties, to whom it was communicated at a meeting this day. The Opposition generally expressed themselves satisfied with what had been done and declared in debate that if America hesitated to receive it as a liberal measure of conciliation they were ready to support your Royal Highness in asserting the rights of the Crown.

In the course of the evening a proposition was brought forward by Mr. Parnell[2] to pledge the House to a consideration of the question of tithes with a view to their modification in the next Session. Owing to the small attendance of the friends of Govt the proposition was only negatived by a majority of 3. The numbers were, Ayes—36, Noes—39. Mr. Parnell, Sir J[ohn] Newport,[3] Mr. Barham,[4] Knight of Kerry, Mr. Smith[5] and Mr. Tighe spoke in favour of the question. Mr. Pole and Lord Castlereagh against it.

124 THE DUKE OF NORTHUMBERLAND *to* COLONEL MCMAHON

Alnwick Castle, 26th June 1812.

I HAVE to thank you for two letters, of the 18th, and 22d. The Prince has certainly acted a very noble and generous part, in having fixed your salary as Private Secretary on his Privy Purse, instead of the Civil List,[6] and in having given up the erection of the barracks.[7] I most sincerely wish the H: of Commons may be gratefull for these concessions on the part of His Royal Highness; but I confess my experience leads me to doubt, whether such concessions are attended with any permanent ad-

1 Printed in *Parl. Deb.* XXIII, 716. It revoked the Orders in Council of 7 January 1807 and 26 April 1809, so far as American shipping was concerned, but the concession came too late to avert war with the United States.

2 Sir Henry Brooke Parnell, fourth Baronet and first Baron Congleton (1776–1842). Succeeded to baronetcy, July 1812. Peerage, 1841.

3 [1756–1843.] Whig M.P. for Waterford. Chancellor of the Irish Exchequer in the Grenville Ministry, 1806–7. Created Baronet, 1789.

4 Joseph Foster Barham, Whig M.P. for Stockbridge.

5 John Smith, Whig M.P. for Nottingham.

6 Castlereagh announced this in the House of Commons on 15 June.

7 In Marylebone. (*Parl. Deb.* XXIII, 559.)

vantage. I remember after the Peace in 1763, His Majesty gave up to the publick the enormous sum paid by France, as the difference due on the exchange of prisoners.[1] This sum woud have sufficed to have built a most magnificent palace, & made many other material improvements, without requiring the aid of one shilling from the publick. The plans were drawn; the estimates made out; but His Majesty having been assured, that the giving this large sum up to the publick, just at that time, would tend much to increase his popularity, did so. Unfortunately however it was almost immediately forgot; H:M: received neither thanks, nor the popularity promised him; and there is no doubt the people woud have been better pleased, to have seen hundreds of workmen employed in building the magnificent palace, as at first intended. This, and several other instances which I recollect (for few Sovereigns have made such concessions to the publick as his present Majesty) have convinced me that all such concessions, however inconvenient to the Sovereign, are never received by the publick with that gratitude, which ought to attend them; and indeed H:R:H: himself has felt the truth of this observation from the second motion made in the House of Commons, notwithstanding all the sacrifices he made, in order if possible to have formed such an Administration as the House seemed to point at, in their first Address.

It has been the cause of most serious grief to me that any of those, whom I have brought into Parliament, shoud have taken so improper a line upon Ld. Milton's[2] motion.[3] Indeed I did not know that Mr. Northey had done so, till I received your letter of the 22ᵈ They were certainly all three[4] apprized of my wishes, and Lord Percy's. As for Mr Raine, I woud not propose him to my friends at Launceston till Lord Percy in writing fully explained to him the part I wished my friends to take in Parliament, and till Mr Raine had in answer consented to follow that line of conduct, in every particular; and Lord Percy has now in his possession Mr. Raine's answer, & a copy of his own letter. After this what can I say in extenuation of Mr. Raine's conduct? All I can do, is to have advised Mr. Raine to call at Carlton House, and endeavour to ex-

1 Horace Walpole wrote in 1765: "We have had a sort of day in the House of Commons. The proposition for accepting the six hundred and seventy thousand pounds for the French prisoners passed easily...." (*Letters*, VI, 174, ed. Toynbee.)

2 Succeeded his father in 1833 as third Earl Fitzwilliam. (1786–1857.)

3 It was an amendment to Stuart-Wortley's motion on 11 June. It regretted that a strong and efficient Administration had not been formed, and entreated the Prince Regent at once to form a Government equal to the exigencies of the times. This amendment was rejected by 289 to 164, but *Hansard* does not give the list of the minority.

4 William Northey and Edward Morris represented the Cornish borough of Newport, and Jonathan Raine was one of the members for Launceston.

plain to you his motives for that vote, and to afford you such security, for his future good conduct, as shall satisfy H:R:H: that there will be no repetition of it in future. Indeed I have received his verbal assurance, that the vote proceeded from a mistake (which certainly was a strange one) & that in future he will be more guarded. I have likewise written a very strong letter to Mr. Morris, whose answer I have not yet received, but expect every day. To Mr. Northey I shall write immediately; for these are not times, when I will allow my friends the least latitude, of not supporting His Royal Highness, and his Government, on every occasion. I am full as angry with Mr. R—, as the Chancellor can possibly be. My utmost exertions will ever be employed in the Prince's service. He has found sufficient ingratitude in other quarters, although his magnanimity has, in one instance, so nobly forgiven, & seems to have forgot it....

125 COLONEL MCMAHON *to the* EARL OF KENMARE[1]

Pall Mall, June 26th 1812.

Copy

THE "Patriot" newspaper having published (what I have the honor to now send your Lordship a copy of) in Dublin on the 19th inst., that the Prince Regent had written to your Lordship some pledge or promise on the subject of the Catholic question, & which is certainly not within H.R.Hss's recollection, I have no doubt that your Lordship will have the goodness to state what such document may be, & of what date, or as your high & respectable name has been brought forward at the late meeting, on this occasion, that you will kindly cause this error to be set right.

126 SAMUEL PEPYS COCKERELL[2] *to* MAJOR-GENERAL TURNER

Saville Row, 8 July 1812.

HAVING already been honoured with your attention on the subject of the Marbles discovered at Egina, I hope you will permit me the liberty of this letter, and will have the goodness to mention the purport of it in

1 Valentine Browne, first Earl of Kenmare; a Catholic Peer. (1754–1812.) He died on 3 October.

2 The architect (1754–1827). He was the father of the more distinguished architect, Charles Robert Cockerell (1788–1863), who in April 1811 discovered at Ægina the remains of the temple of Jupiter Panhellenius.

such quarters as you may think useful. My object in writing it being to remove an erroneous impression which I have heard thro' different channels has been felt concerning these Marbles, namely, that absolute engagements had been made on the part of the discoverers for their disposal to this Government which they have since declined to perform.

The fact being, that the proposal which I suggested on their part for the consideration of the Government was conditional, leaving the proprietors to accept or decline it in case the Marbles should not be appropiated, before directions, which might be given here, should reach Athens; and optional on the part of Government to accept or decline them if brought here, according to their merit upon inspection.

The account of the discovery, which I had the honour to transmit to you on its receipt in July last, stated that the purchase of the Marbles had been proposed to Mr. St. Canning[1] at Constantinople for the British Government and by the German co-proprietors[2] to their Ministers, that they were valued at from six to eight thousand pounds, and that Mr. C:R: Cockerell and Mr. Foster were so desirous to secure them to this country, that they were willing to relinquish all advantage from their half share in them, rather than let them be removed to any other.

In the communications I afterwards had with the Foreign Office, it was perfectly well understood that I had no direct authority relative to their disposal: I therefore could only suggest a means of their being brought to England, and of their eventually becoming British property, provided the proprietors should accept the proposal forwarded to them from hence.

Unfortunately however the discoverers, not foreseeing the probability of any such arrangement here, and judging the collection too interesting to be seperated, being themselves of different nations, whilst they felt themselves bound by no specific engagement to dispose of their property in one way more than other, entered into a bond to each other, not to divide it: but to offer it *entire* to the different Courts and public of Europe, at public sale, on the 1st of November next, and this agreement had been accordingly made public before any intimation reached them of the measures taken here.

Under these circumstances it was impossible for Mr. C: R. Cockerell and Mr. Foster, the English proprietors, however disposed they might have felt to sacrifice their individual interests in the property, to force

1 Stratford Canning, first Viscount Stratford de Redcliffe (1786–1880) ; at this time Minister Plenipotentiary at the Porte.
2 Cockerell was accompanied to Ægina by Baron Haller von Hallerstein (architect to the King of Bavaria), Foster, the Liverpool architect, Mr Linckh of Würtemberg, and Baron Stackelberg of Esthonia, who shared the ownership of the Marbles with him.

their co-proprietors to recede from their common engagement: which was at this time become universally known in those countries, and in which were intimately concerned the Sovereign Princes at whose expence the German artists were travelling and these refusing their consent to any alteration in the plan agreed on, were with great difficulty persuaded to permit the Marbles to be conveyed to Malta, under the condition of the sale not taking place 'till the first of November next.

I hope however, being now there, they will ultimately be secured to the British nation.[1]

127 FREDERICK JOHN FALKINER[2] *to* COLONEL MCMAHON

Cheltenham, July 10th 1812.

EXCUSE me, but a part of the conversation I had with you upon the 25th of June has given me very great uneasiness. You said you had thought I had voted against His Royal Highness; that I most positively deny. You mentioned His Royal Highness did not consider me as one of his friends; I can only say I never did an act of any kind to forfeit his good opinion. In your letter to me in July 1806, when I wrote to you to apply to His Royal Highness to do me the honor to appoint me one of His Royal Highness Aid de Camps, you then stated he "was only allowed one, that His Royal Highness looked upon me as one of his steadiest friends & when he had an opportunity, my services should not be forgotten"; & in reply to my letter in April 1807 you state "His Royal Highness hoped his friends may be ready to rally round him, in whatever may concern his personal interest", & that I was ready and willing no one can deny.

I really feel quite sorry that you should have mistaken me, I am also sorry you had left Carlton House, before Ormonde & I called on you that day, as I was & am unhappy until I cleared up that point. When you mentioned Bradshaw[3] for whom I have the greatest love & regard, I do not think that the member representing for so many years the first & most independent County in Ireland ought to be classed with Honiton.

In truth it gives me pain to occupy one moment of your time, but I think it only in justice to my own feelings, knowing all my life time my sincere attachment to the Prince, & my devotedness to his service, as a

1 The Marbles were sold at Zante to the Crown Prince of Bavaria and are now at Munich.
2 M.P. for Dublin County up to 1807. Created a Baronet, November 1812. See No. 134.
3 Augustus Cavendish Bradshaw, M.P. for Honiton; appointed a Groom of the Bedchamber, August 1812. It was said that he had declined the appointment in March "because he expected better and because he cannot afford the expense of re-election".

supposition that any misrepresentation of my conduct in Parliament could have been made to His Royal Highness. I can only say that on my return to represent the County of Dublin (which nothing but accident lost me) His Royal Highness will not find a more faithful supporter.[1]

128 THE DUKE OF NORTHUMBERLAND *to* COLONEL MCMAHON

Alnwick Castle, 13th July 1812.

I HAVE to thank you for your two letters of the 1st and 8th.

I was at first much alarmed at the account I read in the papers of the King's state, as they represented it in such a manner as to induce the belief that it proceeded from a paralytic stroke. Your letter however afterwards satisfied me that it was a violent paroxysm of his disorder. A stroke of the palsy, in addition to the malady with which H: M: is afflicted, woud be terrible indeed.

However anxious I shoud have been in behalf of Mr Raine, had he conducted himself properly, yet I cannot help thinking, my dear Colonel, that he has deserved the disappointment he has met with by the very unjustifiable part he chose to take on Ld. Milton's motion. Shoud he make any more mistakes of that kind (which however he has assured me shall never happen again) he must take the Chiltern Hundreds; for I am determined His Royal Highness shall be supported by all the aid I can have the honour, & pleasure, of affording him....

P:S: I hear the Luddites are all known, & many taken—I trust they will all be executed, & a public declaration made, that nobody, who creates such disturbances in the Kingdom, must ever expect pardon. This is the only way to stop these riots.[2]

1 He was elected for Carlow borough on 24 October 1812.
2 The Luddite disturbances in the Midlands and the North in 1811 and 1812 were partly a revolt of the workers against the introduction of labour-saving machinery, but chiefly the result of low wages, poverty and unemployment.

Killarney,
Thursday July the 15th 1812.

ON my arrival here yesterday evening, I had the honor of receiving your confidential & obliging letter[1] of the 26th of last month, which from the knowledge you have of my devoted attachment, respect & gratitude I have towards His Royal Highness, the Prince Regent, you may easily conceive, has given me the greatest sorrow & uneasiness. But various delays I met with in my journey from London to this place, on the one hand & the uncertainty where to direct to me on the other, are the cause, which I much regret, of my apparent delay in answering you on a point of so much interest.

I never had the honor of receiving any *written document* from His Royal Highness relative to the Catholick question as stated, I have no doubt thro' mistake or from ill grounded reports, in the extract from a speech of Counsellor Finlay's as it was reported in the Patriot Dublin newspaper of the 19th June to have been made by that gentleman at the agregate meeting of the Catholicks of Ireland. Tho' many & great have been the marks of condescension & kindness which I have been happy enough to receive from His Royal Highness, I never had the honor of receiving from him any thing in his writing, nor could I know his hand writing, having never seen anything written by His Royal Highness. I hope Counsellor Finlay will lose no time to have the mistake he fell into rectified, as I shall & must necessarily do so myself. I have communicated with him thro' a friend of his on the subject, for I am not acquainted with him personally, but, as you may well judge, without letting him know from what quarter I had received information of a circumstance so painfull to my feelings. I did not arrive in Dublin till the 3d of July, so I did not see the speeches made at that meeting nor hear a word of my name having been introduced at it. Indeed I own to you I seldom read the speeches made at these meetings or any others except a few of those made in Parliament, nor have I for these many many years been in the habit of assisting at them no more than my son Lord Castlerosse[2] from whom I might have had the means of hearing of what was said of me.

I beg leave to add that in order to obviate any suspicion of evasion or any sort of subterfuge on my part, I stated to the person I wrote to that I could equally assure Counsellor Finlay that not only His R. Highness had never honoured me with any document or promise or pledge *in writing under his own hand,* but that I never had received any such things *in writing from any person by the commands of His Royal Highness.*

1 No. 125.   2 Afterwards second Earl of Kenmare (1788–1855).

Permit me to request of you to take the earliest & most favorable opportunity of presenting to His Royal Highness the homage of my most sincere & devoted & respectfull attachment & gratitude. There is nothing I would not forfeit rather than His Royal Highness's good opinion of me which I should have merited, could I have been capable of such an act of impropriety & indiscretion as the one attributed to me by disclosing a correspondence on matters of so delicate a nature, had it so happened that I ever had been honoured with such a distinguished mark of his confidence on such weighty & important State concerns. How could any one think me entitled in any shape to such a thing? that is what I wonder at most. I request my best respects to Mrs. McMahon & have the honour to remain my dear Colonel, [etc.].

130 THE EARL OF MOIRA *to* COLONEL MCMAHON

Donington, July 20th 1812.

...After balancing a little, I thought it right to send yesterday to the Prince a letter I had received from Bishop Warburton.[1] The delusion of thinking the Irish Catholics inactive or in good temper may be fatal. Warburton has stumbled on something which alarms him: Yet I am sure it is nothing beyond what I have long known. Indeed, no private information ought to have been requisite for the fixing ones opinion on that subject. The invariable operations of the human mind made it sure that when the Catholic body once attained the point of methodizing the management of its' numerical force, no middle policy was left. We must win them, or make up our minds to Bonaparte's having them.

131 THE EARL OF MOIRA *to* COLONEL MCMAHON

Donington, July 21st 1812.

MY conscience chides me because (if I mistake not) I omitted saying something to you about Ld Wellesley before I came out of town. He had not then leagued himself with the Opposition. I urged him strongly to avoid connection with them; & I believe the advice made impression. My counsel was that in the event of the Prince's desiring him to form an Administration, he should not think of sending to them at all: and I told

1 Dr Charles Warburton (? 1755–1826), Bishop of Limerick, 1806–20.

him that I had striven, I believed efficaciously, to make some of the other
Party withdraw the objection they had made to treating with him. Sense
of their own interest will lead them to affect being satisfied with the explanations which he made in the House. You see I look forward to a
possibility of a change of Ministry.[1] The state of the country, tranquil but
deeply dissatisfied, will force that measure; and when the necessity comes
it will be very sudden. I am cutting down all establishments here with
an unsparing hand, & fashioning rigidly the plan of my future life. It
promises me more gratification than I have experienced in active scenes;
so that the preparations for it are not as uncomfortable as you might
think.[2]

132 WILLIAM HOLMES[3] *to* [*unknown correspondent*]

10 *Grafton St*,
Wednesday Morning [22 July 1812].

I LOST not a moment in communicating to Mr Canning (thro Mr.
Huskisson) the plan as suggested yesterday.

Mr. Canning will at $\frac{1}{2}$ past eleven this day solicit thro Colonel
McMahon an audience of the Regent, for the purpose of communicating
what has passed between Lord Liverpool & himself since he was last at
Calrton [*sic*] House, & at the same time to express his regret that all
hopes of any arrangement are now at an end.[4]

Should His Royal Highness condescend to propose to Mr. Canning to
enter into his service, upon Lord Castlreaghs making a distinct dis-
claimer of any superiority over Mr. Canning either in the House of
Commons or Govmnt, & taking only that lead & managemᵗ of the House
which usually belongs to the situation of Chancellor of the Exchequer
when not joined with the premiership, the withdrawing of motions &c

1 See No. 136.
2 He was nearly bankrupt at this time. In his early years, it is said, he lent large sums of
money to the Prince of Wales which were never repaid. Lord Carlisle declared in February
that Moira had decided to go abroad, "urged by his circumstances and the abominable
treatment of the P[rince]". His friend Thomas Moore said in June that the only thing that
could save his reputation as a statesman was "what I suppose he reckons upon, the present
Ministry giving up the Catholic question, in which case he will, of course, go to Ireland"
[as Lord-Lieutenant].
3 The well-known "Billy" Holmes, the Tory Whip (d. 1851).
4 The negotiations for the entry of Canning into the Cabinet broke down on 27 July,
on the question whether Castlereagh was to retain the "lead" in the House of Commons. As
in May, Castlereagh was willing to let Canning have the Foreign Secretaryship. Canning's
blunder kept him out of office until 1816.

&c to be subject of mutual consultation, Mr. Canning will respectfully request to be allowed to consult his friends on the proposition & in the event of their acceding to it, he understands that he will receive his Royal kind wishes for the success of this arrangem[e]nt.[1]

I hope you will not deem it intrusive in me to candidly state to you my opinion that unless some arrangement is entered into before the House is up, it will be very difficult to prevail on Mr. Canning or his friends, to listen to any terms next Session, the consequence of which will be, the dissolution of the present Govermnt. In this opinion I can venture to positively state that the best friends of the present Ministers agree with me.

I shall wait on you at eleven o'clock & remain [etc.].

1 The Prince Regent's views are given in Sir C. Stewart's important Memorandum of his conversation with the Prince Regent respecting the conflicting claims of his brother Castlereagh and Canning. It is undated, but was probably written on 12 June. The Prince Regent said that Castlereagh "by his manly and honourable conduct had not only gained his complete confidence and high opinion but his affectionate regard and love. That H.R.H. felt there could be no competition between him and Mr. Canning. He avowed in his judgment the solid and useful abilities of the one added to his mild and gentlemanlike manner had an irresistible influence with H.R.H. far superior to anything he ever felt or could ever feel for the other. But it was impossible to deny that Mr. Canning's great powers of debate, especially of retort, were of that nature as linked with a number of the House of Commons and had such a commanding hold of theirj udgments as to make his accession to the present Government a point of nearly vital importance.... That Lord Castlereagh should consider in the part he might now have to act that the salvation of his Prince, of his country, of the existence of the Monarchy itself depended upon the noble and generous conduct that he might pursue. That it never should be forgotten that no man had been called on to make or had made such sacrifices as himself. That in the instance of his dearest and most valued friend Lord Moira who had treated H.R.H. (worked on as he was by the faction of which he was a victim) *infamously*. But that nevertheless when it was suggested for the sake of the country, that he should be called into his presence again, he did not hesitate, but offered him his hand and banished from that moment all feelings of the past. That in Castlereagh's transactions with Mr. Canning everything was most favourable, most triumphant to the former, the public opinion, the satisfaction he manfully demanded, the magnanimous spirit that guided him in the whole transaction. H.R.H. believed there was but one opinion in the country as to this business and in proportion as Lord Castlereagh stood elevated so ought he to be the first to show conciliation and generosity. H.R.H. said he was certain the House of Commons so strongly felt Mr. Canning's powers that they would have him sooner or later and it was in vain to resist it. It must be either his accession or the Government being again thrown at the mercy of the Opposition.... Lord Castlereagh was to consider what Lord Castlereagh would do if placed as the Prince, seeing what was so evident to all. Would he shut his eyes and not endeavour to accomplish that understanding which was alone wanting to make the Government solid in all its parts.... If Lord Castlereagh could place his honour in his hands, H.R.H. would guard it as his own, and he could not for his life and soul conceive what had passed between the two individuals which the weighty, enormous and difficult crisis of the country ought not to soften down and bury in oblivion....

"H.R.H. however was not explicit on any mode in which he saw that the difficult points of bringing Lord Castlereagh and Mr. Canning together in the House of Commons could be obviated without the one yielding to the other.... H.R.H. finished his conversation by declaring he was satisfied that every real friend of Castlereagh's, Yarmouth, Hertford and Camden, if he considered the question deeply would advise him to take the generous part he might now do to save the State, and not to stickle at little objects which were nothing when arrayed against the magnitude of difficulties that surrounded us." (Londonderry MSS.)

Carlton House, Thursday July 23d 1812.

Copy

THE Prince Regent being still prevented by the continuation of the complaint in his hand and fingers from writing, without considerable pain and difficulty, has commanded Col. McMahon to have the honor to acknowledge the receipt of Lady De Clifford's letter of yesterday, and for which His Royal Highness returns many thanks: and to state that the Prince consents to Princess Charlotte's visiting the Princess of Wales tomorrow at *Kensington,* according to Her Royal Highness's desire, notwithstanding it had been previously conditioned that such visits were only to be made once in a fortnight; nor does His Royal Highness wish to precisely adhere to the *once* a fortnight, whenever it may be desired weekly provided that it shall not either be injurious to Princess Charlotte's health, or break in upon the occupations incident to the education, that Her Royal Highness may proceed to *Kensington;* but as the repetition of such visits shall be granted, so it is presumed the Princess of Wales cannot require to see the Princess Charlotte in future at Windsor, where Lady De Clifford is requested to have the goodness to refuse such interviews, if applied for. That the Prince from the good opinion he has always entertain'd of Lady De Clifford, and the great regard he has always borne her Ladyship, relies confidently on her strict attention to those instructions. That His Royal Highness highly approves of Lady De Clifford's letter of yesterday, more especially, as the want of such precaution, on a recent occasion, had led to very unpleasant consequences.

134 FREDERICK JOHN FALKINER *to* COLONEL McMAHON

Cheltenham, July 24th 1812.

I HAVE this day received a letter from the Duke of Richmond[1] saying he had sent my name to Lord Sidmouth to have me created a Baronett as this mark of favor will be of great use to me in my County.[2] I will be much obliged if you will have the kindness to present my duty to His Royal Highn[ess] the Prince Regent & to hope that his Grace's recommendation will be honoured by his sanction. I am just going to Scotland & if

1 Charles Lennox, fourth Duke of Richmond and Lennox (1764–1819). Lord Lieutenant of Ireland, 1807–13; Governor-General of British North America, 1818–19.
2 See No. 127.

you will have the kindness to direct to me at Sir Ch:ˢ Ross,[1] Balnagour Castle, Ross Shire, N.B.

I hope in the most perfect confidence you will tell Ormonde the name of the person I mentioned in my last letter.

135 LADY DE CLIFFORD *to the* PRINCE REGENT

Windsor Lower Lodge,
Saturday July 25, 2 O'clock.

YOUR Royal Highness having so graciously received my former letter, makes me venture to trouble you again, as I am anxious to tell your Royal Highness, that when we went to Kensington yesterday, I mentioned to the Princess of Wales, what you had said about her coming to Windsor. She answered, that if your Royal Highness permitted Princess Charlotte to come to her once a week, she would not think of going to Windsor, & that she had told Lord Liverpool so, when he waited on her with your Royal Highness's message, which she said she made Col St Leger[2] write down in Lord Liverpools presence, & which she showed to Ld Liverpool, who said it was correct. I beged to have a coppy of it which I enclose to your Royal Highness as I received it. Thinking that it was possible, that Lord Liverpool did not write down what had passed at the meeting, & that your Royal Highness might like to see it. If I have done wrong, I hope you will have the goodness to tell me, as believe me no one is more [etc.].

136 THE EARL OF MOIRA *to* COLONEL MCMAHON

Donington, August 18th 1812.

BROUGHTON has written earnestly to ask whether I think there is any chance of getting young Dilke into a clerkship of a public office. You may remember my mentioning the lad to you. He is 17 years of age, & of very promising turn. My answer has been that I really have no channel thro' which it can at present be effected, & that I believed you had as little opening. In truth I know that nothing can be more ungracious

---

1 Sir Charles Ross, of Balnagowan, sixth Baronet (d. 1814).
2 Vice-Chamberlain of the Princess of Wales' Household.

than these Ministers. The victory in Spain[1] will not strengthen them, any more than it will alleviate the distresses of the English manufacturers. It will add great weight to Ld Wellesley; & that will be all in a scale opposed to their interests. I have peculiar grounds for thinking that the P[rince] begins to be seriously sensible of their inadequacy & to ponder on the natural consequences of the disesteem in which they are held. They have just now led him to do a thing which has an inconvenient effect. A Marquisate bestowed on Ld Camden, who could have no possible pretension to the distinction[2] (unless the having produced a rebellion in Ireland be a service to the State)[3] will lower any reward conferred on Ld Wellington;[4] & indeed, without that contrast, must make every body stare.

By the end of the week I will dispatch another basket of venison to you. We do not leave this till Tuesday the 25th.

Offer my best compliments to Mrs. McMahon, & believe me [etc.].

137 THE EARL OF LIVERPOOL *to the* PRINCE REGENT

London, Augst 20, 1812.

LORD LIVERPOOL presents his humble duty to your Royal Highness, and having communicated with your Royal Highnesses confidential servants, upon the subject of the provision which it would be proper to connect with the honours recently confer'd upon Marquis Wellington, in consequence of his great and meritorious services, they are all of opinion that it would be more adviseable to propose to Parliament to vote a sum of money, than to make any addition to the annuity already granted: and they are further of opinion, that under all the circumstances, and adverting to the state of Lord Wellington's private fortune,[5] and the expences to which for publick purposes he has been necessarily exposed, that sum may not improperly be fixed at one hundred thousand pounds.

Lord Liverpool humbly requests therefore if this opinion should meet with your Royal Highnesses gracious approbation, that you would be pleased to authorise Lord Liverpool to inform Lord Wellington, that it was your Royal Highnesses intention to give directions to your confidential servants to propose to Parliament upon its next meeting, to grant a provision to the extent above stated.[6]

1 The Battle of Salamanca, 22 July.   2 See No. 78 n.
3 His policy as Lord-Lieutenant contributed to the outbreak of the Irish Rebellion of 1798.
4 Wellington was promoted to a Marquisate on 18 August.
5 "I know that at this time he is rather poor", said Liverpool. "An income of nine or ten thousand is after all a poor support for a marquess."
6 See *Parl. Deb.* XXIV, 179, 201 (4 and 7 December 1812).

Whitehall, August y⁰ 21st 1812.

Lord Sidmouth has the honor of acquainting your Royal Highness, that, in obedience to your Royal Highness's commands, a prayer has been prepared by His Grace The Archbishop of Canterbury[1] of thanksgiving for the successes of the Allied Army in the Peninsula of Spain, and Portugal in the present campaign, and particularly for the late victory near Salamanca, which prayer will be forthwith read in the churches, and chapels of England, and Ireland; but that with a view to a similar proceeding in Scotland, an Order by your Royal Highness in Council is deem'd to be indispensably necessary. It is therefore Lord Sidmouth's duty humbly to request the commands of your Royal Highness, for causing a Council to be summon'd for that purpose.

139 The Earl of Moira *to* Colonel McMahon

Donington, August 27th 1812.

A circumstance has occurred, not worth explaining to the Prince directly, which I wish you to understand accurately in case it should hereafter be touched upon. The Princess of Wales sent to Mrs. Rawdon[2] & my niece,[3] desiring that they would pass a couple of days at Blackheath with her. Nothing could be more unexpected, & nothing could be more inconvenient as they were on the point of going out of town. They applied to my sister to know if they could with propriety excuse themselves. She said that the invitation was to be construed a command; that they were to know nothing of the Princess but her rank; & that they ought to go. I think that a swelled face or a nervous headache might have been called up on the occasion: but perhaps female opinion is the best on the subject. What I want you to be enabled to assert is, that the honor was never courted by them; because it might give the Prince some jealousy. The Princess had but the slightest knowledge of them: And it is possible that some indistinct notion of giving the Prince a fidget by the appearance of an oblique attention to me may have caused her to take the step.

You see that the advancement of Lord Camden has had all the effect I apprehended of making Ld Wellington's deserts seem not sufficiently

1 Dr Charles Manners-Sutton (1755–1828), Archbishop of Canterbury, 1805–28.
2 Moira's sister-in-law.
3 Her only daughter, who married Lord George William Russell in 1817.

acknowledged by the Marquisate.[1] When I reflect how the application of all my earlier life was devoted to the study of my profession as a science; when I may to you without vanity say that I have experienced in myself the power of readily employing in an hour of difficulty the principles so acquired; & when I feel that my attachment to the Prince has barred the field of fame against me, I cannot at times repress a sigh.

140 The Earl of Moira *to* Colonel McMahon

Donington, August 31st 1812.

You say, my dear friend, that you wish I were safely moored in Dublin Castle.[2] It would some time ago have been an appointment advantageous for myself as well as for others. I think I could have done essential good in Ireland to the people & still more to the Prince. What is to be done in that country must be effected by the influence of opinion; for, in truth, what is wanted is the establishing a different tone from the higher ranks towards the lower classes. While my popularity was fresh, I could have compassed that object; and, I know, I could have settled the tythes, a much more important point towards the tranquillity of the country than the removal of Catholic disqualifications. The merit of this attention to the real comfort of the population of that country would have referred itself to the Prince, & he would have had the notoriety of that country's attachment to weigh upon the calculations of the discontented here. There would, besides, have been much in point of appearance not unworthy of consideration in that arrangement. All that, however, is gone bye.

Tho' I have never said it to the Prince, I have not concealed from you that there never has been, even since the incalculable service which I rendered to them, the least semblance of disposition in the present Ministers to show me any degree of courtesy. Estranged of course from them & having sacrificed for the Prince all political intercourse with the other Party, I have nothing to do with public life. There is a sort of vanity which makes it painful to proclaim the necessity of striking sail. That dose of physic might have been avoided had I been sent to Ireland; an arrangement which could have taken place (supposing the Prince to have wished it) had that decision been made on Ld Wellesley's motion[3] to which you must ultimately & very speedily come.

1 See No. 136.   2 As Lord-Lieutenant.
3 Wellesley's motion on the Catholic question (1 July 1812) was rejected by 126 to 125.

After that division, I saw the part which befitted me. I have finished the gulp. I have declared here my inability to maintain longer my past stile of living or to reside at this place. I have told every one that I have been seeking a retreat where I can live on a narrow income: And I have cut off every establishment at Donington as a mansion which I am no more to inhabit. Lady Loudoun has a generous pride in this which makes it quite easy. I, therefore, dismiss wholly any view of public situation; and I have been delayed here only till we shall decide between a small place in Essex & another in Monmouthshire, as we must before we move from this determine to which our furniture &c is to be sent. Accommodate your mind to this. It is not what you wished: but for myself it is the best.

141 THE DUKE OF NORTHUMBERLAND *to* COLONEL MCMAHON

Alnwick Castle, 4th Septr. 1812.

I FEEL much obliged to you, for your letter of the 28th of last month, and partake most sincerely with you of the joy, which the victory near Salamancy [*sic*], for this I allow to be a victory. I am sorry to find so many of my friends amongst the list of killed, and wounded. I find that half the Royal Regt. of Horse Guards are under orders to join the Marquis.[1] Two squadrons are too small a body to send of so distinguished a corps. If the Prince Regent woud restore to us (& heavy cavalry are wanted) the two squad^{ns} of which H:R:H: knows we have been cheated, we coud spare at least 4 squadrons to be sent extremely well. The Regt. was so popular at Warrington that, I understand, we coud have raised & compleated there two squadrons in a fortnight, and no augmentation of troops can be so cheap to Government, as our recruits cost nothing, for we give no bounty money, nor receive any allowance, like the other Regts. in the Service.

I lament much to receive so bad an account of Lord Moira's affairs. I always feared it woud come to this. I confess I think he is quite wrong, not to take your advice. The situation of Governor General in India, is the only one, in which he can hope to clear himself from his present embarrassements. Ireland woud be his certain destruction.[2] It is however to be hoped, that the regard the Prince Regent has for Lord Moira will prevent H:R:H: from ever consenting to an appointment which woud be his Lordship's certain ruin.

1 Wellington.
2 The Duke of Richmond, however, was able to save money whilst Lord-Lieutenant. (*Bathurst Papers*, p. 183.)

I am very happy to find you receive so much benefit from Cheltenham waters.

It is very easy to conceive that the duties of your office as Private Secretary to His Royal Highness must be very severe, and enough, as you justly observe, to wear out both the body and mind. You must however recollect not only that it gives you free access to the Prince at all times, & that it may be looked upon as nearly a permanent situation, whereas the office of one of the Paymasters General to the Forces, is a very precarious one, & infallibly the possessor of it changed, on every change of Administration. You woud therefore probably hold it only for a very short period, and if you once lost it, very possibly you might not easily obtain it again. Besides, entre nous, when the Prince had lost the habit of seeing you constantly there woud be great danger of your successor taking your place in H:R:H: affections. These are matters well worthy of your serious consideration, before you decide upon the step to which you allude.

As nothing has yet been done with respect to Lord Strangford I much fear his enemies have, by their insinuations, & false statements prevailed against my friend. If this is the case, I own I am much grieved, & disappointed, because I know for certain his Lordship is not culpable. What is a poor Foreign Minister to do, if he can get neither directions how to act, nor answers to his dispatches? I know Ld. Strangford is a very meritorous Foreign Minister, & has done more for this country, by the weight he has obtained with the Prince Regent of Brazil, than any other Minister, since the time of the late Lord Tyrawley.[1]

The Duchess, my family, and myself unite compliments to you, & Mrs. Mac-Mahon, to whom we all beg leave to offer our comp.ts of condolence, on the loss of her mother. Adieu, my dear Colonel, & believe me [etc.].

142 COLONEL MCMAHON *to the* PRINCE REGENT

Carlton House,
Septr 12th 1812. 3 o'Clock P.M.

I HAVE been with Arbuthnot in a rage at the diabolical Morning Chronicle of this day, & I am proceeding in quest of Dudley[1] &c.ª for

1 James O'Hara, second Baron Tyrawley (1690–1773). Ambassador in Portugal, 1728–41 and 1752–56.
2 The editor of *The Morning Herald*, the Carlton House newspaper. See No. 114.

something *must* & *shall* be done er'e night, to silence this miscreant, & to counteract him on Monday. I have reason to think Ld. Byron[1] employ's himself in this way, & from his having given a seat in his box at the Cheltenham Theatre on the evening before I left it, to Mrs. Mary Anne Clarke,[2] it is not improbable he may make her an auxilliary. I shall however, Sir, lose no time in trying everything that can possibly be done.[3]

1 The poet (1788–1824).

2 The Duke of York's discarded mistress (1776–1852), who tried to ruin him in 1809 by accusing him, as Commander-in-Chief of the Army, of selling commissions.

3 *The Morning Chronicle* of the 12th contained a long Article entitled *The New Epic*, in which the Prince Regent and his reputed mistress, Lady Hertford, were held up to ridicule. "The New Epic" was written by "Rosa Matilda".

"We resume our observations upon this wonderful poem. Venus, the next in order and the most splendid of all the planets, finds an appropriate representative in a venerable lady—all astronomers know that this planet's appearance is of a yellowish white, and that she is most admired in her evening declination, when hastening after the setting sun, from whom in reality she borrows her brilliancy. Rosa Matilda, who seems to be at least as good an astronomer as she is a poet, tells us that the memorable transit of Venus over the Sun's disk in 1761 (when a pretty Quakeress * was said to be enamoured of a youthful modest swain) was nothing compared with the transit of 1811–12.... We remember in April 1795 every one was delighted with the sight of Venus in conjunction; but shortly after, the Sun was observed to recede more and more from her every day, and to become, as it were, *apparently* retrograde— since when that planet seems in opposition, and has lost much of her brilliancy, though she still emits a mild melancholy lustre—consequently, we presume, there could have been no transit; the poet however is positive, and contends that at two o'clock p.m. every day, for several stated months, through a glass well stained, Venus might be seen from the Royal Observatory, reposing on the right limb of the Sun's disk...."

"[Rosa Matilda] thus opens the flood gates of her indignation upon the unfortunate Whigs.

> "Rail on, ye ragged raggamuffins, rail!
> Ye dirty lees of Whitbread's dirtier ale;
> No language can be hyperbolical
> To sketch a set so diabolical,
> Thieves, cut-throats, robbers, rascals, all the crew!
> And wh——s they *would be*, were they women too.

"Here, in the high fermentation of her wrath, sex itself is forgotten, and Lords Grey and Grenville are suddenly metamorphosed into a pair of flaunting cyprians.... She then turns to the P[rince] R[egent], to whom she again abuses them...

> "They're like the mud you tread beneath your feet,
> Your pretty, pretty feet, so dainty small and sweet;
> But thou art like a nosegay in full blow,
> Culled for the village holiday—*all shew*!
> Made of lillies, hyacinths and roses,
> All sorts and kinds of Covent-garden posies."

Nothing, apparently, was done to "counteract this miscreant" in the columns of *The Morning Herald*.

* Hannah Lightfoot.

Government House, Cape Town,
September 12th 1812.

I WISH I could express all my feelings in this letter. I have seen in a paper the gracious recollection of His Royal Highness, and I may say I am in possession of all I wish, in being his immediate servant. I have always declared, though my situation is among the first in Royal disposal, it is but a secondary object in comparison with the happiness I should feel, in performing whatever duty His Royal Highness may be pleased to command. I have no view but the sole gratification to prove myself a zealous devoted adherent—such has been the cherished idea from those early moments of life, which His Royal Highness is pleased to remember, and may the remainder testify that the recollection has not been misplaced.

I cannot quit this station without special leave. May I employ you "to have sent out to me" such a conditional permission as will enable me to place the Government in the hands of the Lieutenant Governor, till the future disposal may be decided. Or, if in any shape, *I* or my appointment can be made useful, or turned to account, do with me as my gracious royal master pleases.

Our intelligence, or letters reach no further than the 3d May, but rumours circulate through the meeting of ships at sea, that Mr. Percival has been assassinated, and that the animosity of parties is carried to the utmost extent. Such things make me the more anxious to be at home and share in whatever may be the case. A ship the General Wellesley, that ought to have come here direct, and which I believe, has all our letters, is gone to Rio Janeiro, so we are left in painful anxiety.

In all this ignorance I can only recur to the subject of most interest in my mind, to take the most favorable moment to place me and my devoted sentiments at the feet of the Prince of Wales.

To you, my dear friend, I can never adequately say how obliged and grateful I am for uninterrupted kindness.

Accept my most sincere and affectionate regards.

1. General Sir John Francis Caradoc, Lord Howden (1762–1839), who exchanged the name Cradock for Caradoc in 1820. He was Governor of the Cape from 1811 to 1814. Peerage, 1819.

Fife House, Sept. 15, 1812.

LORD LIVERPOOL presents his humble duty to your Royal Highness, and having had the honour of calling at Carlton House this morning, Col. Macmahon deliver'd to him your Royal Highnesses message, respecting the *confidential letters*.[1]

Lord Liverpool is apprehensive that considerable inconvenience may arise from the delay of sending these letters till Friday next. The event to which they refer, is so generally believed to be likely to take place, that the greatest activity prevails on the part of the opponents of your Royal Highnesses Government, whilst the friends relying upon the usual confidential and early communication, are in most quarters taking no steps whatever. Lord Liverpool fears likewise that the delay will have the effect of offending the Duke of Rutland,[2] Lord Lonsdale[3] & many others, who naturally expect such a mark of confidence on the part of Government, and may in some cases suffer seriously from the want of it.

Lord Liverpool has in obedience to your Royal Highnesses commands defer'd sending the letters, which it was his intention to request your Royal Highnesses permission to send by the post of to-day, but unless some very important consideration should influence your Royal Highness's mind, he humbly solicits your leave to be allowed to write confidentially to such of the friends of Government tomorrow, to whom an early communication of the intended purpose may be most material.

145 THE DUKE OF NORTHUMBERLAND *to* COLONEL MCMAHON

Alnwick Castle, 15th Septr. 1812.

MANY thanks for your letter of the 11th, & the information it contains.

It has been very much my wish, whenever a dissolution took place, to procure some situation in the Administration for my friend Mr. Brogden.[4] His superior knowledge in all matters relating to trade woud be very usefull to the publick, & H:R:H: woud be certain of having, in him, a

1 Letters informing the Government's influential supporters that Parliament was about to be dissolved.
2 John Henry Manners, fifth Duke of Rutland (1778–1857).
3 William Lowther, first Earl of Lonsdale (1757–1844).
4 He was appointed a Junior Lord of the Treasury on 3 October, but held that office only until December 1813. He was afterwards for many years Chairman of Ways and Means in the House of Commons, and represented Launceston until the Reform Bill.

person most zealously attached to his wishes on every occasion. As I wish for no employment myself, I trust I shall not be deemed very unreasonable, in having at least one friend provided for. If H:R:H: is inclined to gratify me in this very earnest wish, I will beg of you to send for my friend Brogden, & arrange it between him, & Ministers. I am convinced he will be very reasonable on the occasion.

I have just received a letter from Lord Strangford, in which he says, things have taken a very pleasing turn for him since the appointment of Lord Castlereagh to office. His Lordship, he says, is really a man of business. He not only gives him employment, but does him the honour of answering his Dispatches & appears to be so kind, as to read them, & attend to them. It is truly a pleasure, Lord Strangford observes, to transact business, with such a Secretary of State, & he will engage for it more will be done in six months with Lord Castlereagh, than in two years with his predecessor. He now receives proper directions, & knows how to act without those apprehensions to which the unconquerable silence of his Lordship's predecessor continually subjected him.

I hope affairs now look well both in the Peninsula, & in the North. I woud not however trust Bernadotte[1] too much. Timeo Danaos et dona ferentes. Adieu. Present my most humble duty to the Regent, & accept for yourself & Mrs. MacMahon the comp^ts of the Duchess, my family, & myself.

146 PETER STUART[2] *to* COLONEL McMAHON

85 Hatton Garden, Tuesday Sept 15, 1812.

INDULGE me in the liberty of assuring you, that, as soon as you read the pamphlet[3] in vindication of the Prince Regent's Government, you'll immediately be induced to recommend a compliance with my request; and that, from particular circumstances, which are altogether uninteresting to you, the receipt of the *one-half* of the sum at this time (previously to the period formerly mentioned) would be more service-

1 One of Napoleon's Marshals, he was elected heir to the throne of Sweden in 1811. The old King's health began to fail, and Bernadotte became the real ruler. He refused to co-operate with Napoleon in the invasion of Russia; on 17 July 1812 Russia and Sweden signed a Peace Treaty with Great Britain at Örebrö, and in 1813 Bernadotte joined the Allies against his former master. He succeeded Charles XIII as King of Sweden and Norway in 1818. (1764–1844.)

2 The brother of Daniel Stuart (1766–1846), the journalist. They jointly owned *The Morning Post* between 1795 and 1803. Peter Stuart started a Tory paper, *The Oracle*, before 1788, and the Tory evening paper, *The Star*, in 1788.

3 See No. 200.

able than five times that sum at the end of October. But earnestly intreating you to make liberal allowances for this intrusion on your more precious time, and as earnestly intreating you to favour me with your friendly answer on the receipt of this, I remain, [etc.].

147 THOMAS CHOLMONDELEY[1] *to the* PRINCE REGENT

Vale-Royal, September 17th 1812.

AGITATED by the fear of offending and incurring a displeasure which I could not support, yet encouraged by recollecting the repeated marks of gracious condescension and goodness with which, however unworthy, I have been honored by your Royal-Highness; I venture to approach as a petitioner, humbly laying myself at your Royal Highness's feet & entreating pardon for my presumption. I am grieved to state that the representation of the County of Chester, which I have so long had the honor of enjoying,[2] will inevitably be disturbed at the next general election; and tho' I have received such strong assurances of support as scarcely to admit a doubt of my success, yet the expence of a contest in a large and populous County is so tremendous, that victory in my case would be almost ruin.[3] Thus unhappily circumstanced I venture Sir, though with the greatest timidity, to entreat your Royal Highness's gracious protection by conferring on me the honor of a seat in the Upper House of Parliament. And however great this request, yet I trust that it will not meet the disapprobation of your Royal Highness's Ministers when they recollect my steady attachment to them and their principles, without an instance of change, during the last seventeen years.

To mention any pretensions of mine to this distinguished honor from family and long Parliamentary service, or to enumerate the many instances where it has been obtained in cases similar to my own, would be presuming too much, and trespassing too far, on your Royal Highness's valuable time. But if with condescending goodness your Royal Highness will so far honor an humble individual as to take into consideration a request on which his future welfare wholly depends, it shall be his constant endeavour by the most unbounded gratitude and deepest attachment to testify the feelings of a warm and faithful heart entirely devoted to your Royal Highness's service. With the most profound duty and respect I am [etc.].

1 (1767–1855.) He was raised to the peerage as Baron Delamere in 1821.
2 Since 1796.
3 Davies Davenport and Wilbraham Egerton were returned for the County on 20 October.

Westminster, Septem.^r 17, 1812.

ABOUT the beginning of the present Reign, in a celebrated trial for a libel against Government, it was observed, by a very eminent Judge, "That the British Constitution could never be beat down by paper-shot". If that great Judge had lived till the present day, his Lordship would probably have thought differently; for no reflecting man can *now* fail to be of opinion, that, for several years past, the great majority of news-papers, and other periodical publications, circulated throughout this country, have had a direct and immediate tendency to set His Majesty's subjects at war with their rulers, and to sap the foundations of our whole political establishment. *Some* of these publications content themselves with attacking the characters of those statesmen and senators whose principles they affect to disapprove; others proceed to the length of throwing dirt upon *all* publick men without distinction; while *not a few* have been daring enough to revile their *Sovereign himself*, and to pay compliments to our enemies, at the expence of our *own Liege-King*.

Such, unhappily, is but too just a character of all the news-papers which are said, in common language, to be friendly to *Opposition*. They tell us, with unblushing effrontery, that they proceed upon "true Whig-principles". What meaning they affix to this antiquated term, it is of little consequence to enquire. The doctrines which they are, daily and hourly, disseminating, make it but too plain, that they have departed very far indeed from those principles, by which the most zealous patriots were actuated at the glorious Revolution in 1688. Were any one, even the most popular, supporter of Whiggism, of *that* day, to rise now from the dead, and to peruse a single page of those inflammatory writings by which the publick is every day insulted, he would be penetrated with as much horror, as would the highest-flying Tory that ever existed. It is almost unnecessary to observe, that the British Government has, for more than a century, been, and could only be, a Whig-Government; and that the present Administration is, as every Administration in this country must necessarily be, a Whig-Administration: For a Whig-Government, means now, as it has all along meant, nothing else than a Government established by Laws equally binding upon the King and the subject.

While the newspapers thus described have been spreading their dangerous doctrines far and wide, they have met with but little resistance from any quarter. Certainly with none, of material consequence, from those papers which are commonly called *Ministerial.* Men are not quite agreed in opinion, with regard to what a Ministerial paper, in this country, is. *Some* people think it enough to constitute a Ministerial news-paper, that it uniformly takes part with the Administration of the day; and, according to this definition, we have plenty of ministerial papers, such as they are. *Others*, with a little more malignity, tell us, without much hesitation, that such and such a news-paper is in the pay of the Treasury. If such persons really mean what they say, on this subject, it is greatly to be feared, that there is no such thing as a Ministerial paper in Great Britain; because it has never yet been proved, to the conviction of any sensible man, that Government are in the habit of bestowing a single fraction of publick money for the support of any news paper whatever, or of giving them any kind of encouragement, except perhaps by ordering a few copies for the use of the publick offices; a species of encouragement so trifling, as would never create a political bias in the mind of any editor, who is in tolerable credit.

These remarks are intended to apply chiefly to the *daily* newspapers, to the multiplication of which, beyond all possible bounds, there is just one barrier, namely, the considerable *expence* which their readers must incur, before partaking of the poison which they contain. A London daily paper cannot be bought in town at less than £8. 10. –, *per annum*; nor in the country at less than £9. 4. –; an expence very unsuitable to the pockets of those who are most likely to be misled by false doctrines. But what shall be said of the *weekly* papers, which can be read for one sixth part of the expence? What shall be said of the *Sunday's* papers? It is a fact, not very generally known, that in the morning of every Lord's day, there are published, in London, no less than eighteen different news-papers, under the following names:—

1. Monitor and Recorder[1]	10. Phoenix
2. Englishman	11. National Register
3. Observer	12. Independent Whig
4. Sunday Advertiser	13. Bell's Dispatch
5. Review	14. Antigallican
6. British Neptune	15. Tribunal
7. Bell's Messenger	16. Rifleman
8. The News	17. Beacon
9. Examiner	18. Constitution.

There can be no harm certainly in publishing a news-paper on Sunday; on the contrary, it affords a fair and proper relaxation to those who are immersed in business throughout the week; and, were the pages of such

1 Some of these newspapers are not noticed in *The Times Handlist of Newspapers.*

papers filled with matter fit for the eye of a loyal subject, or of a good christian, they would deserve every sort of encouragement. But, when it is found, upon experience, that, *with very few exceptions*, these Sunday's papers abound in nothing but the most libellous and scandalous matter; (setting at nought every establishment, civil or religious, in the country, and not seldom throwing defiance in the teeth of Mr. Attorney General) no one who wishes well to his country can mark the progress of this growing evil, without the strongest feelings of apprehension and alarm.

Those who have reflected deeply upon the passing events of the last twelve months, must have come to this conclusion, that the *licentiousness of the Press* has arrived at its utmost height; and that it has, at last, become an *evil*, which *nothing* but the *Press itself* can cure. In former times, even sensible men were accustomed to boast of the *liberty* of the Press, as a priviledge enjoyed by Englishmen beyond all other nations; and, after all the clamour that has recently been heard, it is a privilege enjoyed, at this moment, in its utmost possible extent. It is, however, a privilege which never meant more, and which never can, or ought to, mean more, than "the right, competent to every man, of printing and publishing what he pleases; *with a fair responsibility to the law of the land*". Such was the result of the maxims established by our forefathers: *but* they *also* knew, that, if a man published *slander* against his neighbour; if a man published *treason* against his Sovereign; or if a man published blasphemy against his God, he was just as much amenable to the laws of his country, as he who robbed his fellow-subject on the highway.

While such is, and has been the law for a long period of time, the liberty of the Press has not only not been diminished, but has been greatly inlarged, in the course of the present most auspicious reign, which has added more to the *liberty of the subject*, than has been added in all other reigns which have occurred since the Revolution.

In the year 1792, an Act (introduced into Parliament by a very popular member, *Mr. Fox*) was passed into a law, by which it was declared, that, in all subsequent trials for libel against Government, the jury should be entitled (contrary to the former law) to decide upon the *whole merits* of the trial; whether arising from the *character* of the publication, or from the *simple fact* of publishing. One should have conceived, that this was going the utmost possible length, which, in reason, could be desired. But still some men are not satisfied. Mr. Fox is *quite* forgotten; and the calumniators of the *present* day care just as little for his memory as they care for that of Oliver Cromwell, or of any other person who ever acquired the silly appellation "Man of the People". Nay, a still farther step has, of late, been taken; because it is most evident, that the effort *now* is, not to maintain the liberty of the Press (every one knows what *that* is) but to put an end to *all* responsibility whatever, for *criminal publications*. If a man is sentenced to imprisonment for such delinquency, a subscription is immediately opened for his relief, and motion after motion made in the House of Commons for his enlargement. If he happens to be acquitted, instantly we have *publick dinners* in honour of the *independent jury* who acquitted him, and not seldom proposals for having the head of Mr. Attorney General placed on a lamp post!

These are awful things, which could only gain credit by being universally known to be *true*.

The moment seems, therefore, to have arrived, when *something effectual* MUST be done; and nothing appears so *very* efficacious, as the remedy that has been already hinted at, namely, that the *poison* of the Press should be counteracted by the *antidote* of the Press.

It is a curious circumstance, that, after the British Empire has suffered so deeply from the wickedness of periodical publications, it is the only country in Europe which does *not* possess an *official Government newspaper*. By this expression, it is by no means intended to convey the idea of a *controversial Ministerial newspaper*. That idea is absurd, and has always been so; because, no one who does not *absolutely* adhere to the Administration of the day, *out and out*, will *ever look* at a paper, which, in the vulgar and daily acceptation of the word, may be called "Ministerial". The important object would be, to have a daily publication issued out to the country, and understood as containing a *fair* and *impartial* picture of publick measures, and of publick events; a publication to which should be immediately communicated every circumstance, occurring with reference to national affairs, whether from the publick offices, or from other authentic indubitable sources of intelligence.

It is most piteous and most woeful to see how these things are garbled at present; and they are garbled, only because no one official person seems to take the least charge of them. It is said to be a sort of perquisite at the Post-Office, by which some obscure persons there shall make so much a-week for giving out news, in any manner which their utter incompetence may dictate; and the consequence is, that, in no two news-papers, is the same story told in the same words.

It appears, therefore, high time, that *Government* should take this most important business into *their own hands*. It should be recollected (and that speedily) that we are now engaged in a war of a *very unusual* description, and that the enemy must be fought by his own weapons. The French, for the last twenty years, have been endeavouring to get the better of us at every point. They made their first effort upon the ocean; and *there* we have *extinguished* them. They made an attempt at *accelerating* the *conveyance* of *troops*, which we have more than equalled by our own *waggon-train*, and other establishments for similar purposes. They have tried to surpass us in the department of the *Ordnance*, and in the service of *Light Artillery*; while it is well known, that, so long ago as the year 1799 our own Horse-Brigades (with the effectual co-operation of Sir Sidney Smith[1]) conquered the "Invincibles", even with that their own boasted engine of warfare, in the plains of Damascus.

It may be said, that, in all these particulars, Great Britain has *followed* the example of France. So she has; but she has followed France *effectually*; just as the great Wellington is *following* the French troops at this moment. But there are two modes of warfare in which Great Britain has taken the lead, and in which, down to this hour, the British Service has had no competitor. The important inventions of Colonel Congreve's[2] rockets, and of Colonel Shrapnell's[3] spherical case-shot, are entirely unknown in France; and every naval officer can testify the efficacy of the one; while the whole British Artillery will subscribe to the universal destruction inflicted by the other. It is, indeed, scarcely possible to read any one dispatch from the *great Wellington*, without being quite convinced, that, unless Colonel Shrapnell's wonderful invention had been acted upon, even *that* illustrious officer could not have peppered the enemy to half the amount that he has done. Perhaps, at this moment, the *whole Peninsula* might have been lost.

There is just one circumstance in which the little Corsican usurper has got the start of us; and we have not yet met him on *that* ground. It is a mortifying truth, that, ever since he seized the Government of France, he has, upon the Continent of Europe, done more mischief, and more for the furtherance of his own crooked purposes, by means of the *Moniteur of Paris*, than he has ever, during his whole life, effected by the united efforts of the cannon and the sword. His plan has, indeed, been uniformly that of circulating *lies*; of suppressing truth, when it happened to be unpleasant; and of embellishing any thing that might be accidentally favourable. But, (laying aside the meanness and wickedness of his attempts to impose, on a nation very willing, and even most anxious, to resume its allegiance to a legitimate Sovereign) it cannot be denied,

1 The Admiral, who successfully defended Acre against Napoleon. [1764–1840.]

2 Sir William Congreve (1772–1828), the inventor of the Congreve rocket. In March 1812 he was appointed one of the Prince Regent's Equerries, and succeeded as second Baronet in 1814. See No. 151.

3 Henry Shrapnel (1761–1842), afterwards Major-General. His invention was adopted by the War Office in 1803.

that the present ruler of France has, so far, made out his point, as to render the *Moniteur* the *exclusive* vehicle of *Government intelligence*, and to hold out every article as of doubtful authority, or of no authority, unless it has been sanctioned by *previous* insertion in the *official* pages of the *Moniteur*.

But, if the authority of Government can give so much currency to *falsehoods*, how much *more* must such authority give currency to plain and unvarnished *truth*! The fair object in *Great Britain*, is, *not to deceive* the people, but to prevent the *possibility* of their *being deceived*. The Government is so free, the Press is so free, and the debates in Parliament are so open and accessible, that, even were it possible to suppose our rulers desirous (as they certainly are not) to impose on the publick by disguising their measures, they *have not the power*. That is *not* the danger; but there is *another*. The danger *is*, that almost every measure of the State is misconstrued, and leads to a discussion as useless as it [is] pernicious to the country. Every news-paper maintains what it supposes to be the sentiments of its patron. Right or wrong, this is the ground uniformly taken, and taken without disguise. To seize on a very familiar example: Marquis Wellington has, in the course of this Summer, done things which are *only* NOT *miraculous*. *Some* of the publications say (very fairly) *not merely* that *he* has done every thing within human power, *but* that those *Ministers* who sent him out, judged well. *Others* say, the Peninsula has been almost betrayed; because a *greater* force was not sent thither many months ago. In writing such nonsense, this class of writers attempt to pay court to a noble Marquis,[1] who is said to have retired from office, because he could not prevail on his colleagues in the Cabinet to send over to the Peninsula a larger force than happened to exist in Great Britain. A *third* description of editors abuse the whole proceedings in Spain and Portugal; because, forsooth, *their* patrons had long ago *predicted* (in the very words of Bonaparte) that the English would very speedily be driven *into the sea*!

These are the unfortunate results of throwing Government intelligence open to every adventurer: And perhaps there is not one object of deeper importance to the State, than that the matter should forthwith be taken into the most serious consideration of those who are entitled to watch over the national security, and the national character. The portentous aspect of the times in which we live, does not dictate *much* discretion or much choice, with reference to the course most fit to be pursued. It is of little consequence to the country, or to the cause of Europe, that our warriors by sea and by land have put down our most implacable enemies,

1 Wellesley.

and are just as ready to put down all others; if there are so many *canker-worms* preying on our vitals, as are every day to be found in the shape of disaffected news-papers.

The humble individual, who, with the most dutiful respect, submits these loyal sentiments to his Sovereign, is most anxious to have it distinctly understood, that he has thus expressed himself, from a perfect consciousness, that he is discharging the first duty of a good subject. He has not the vanity to suppose, that he has now put forward a single idea that can properly be called *new*. He feels, that his conscience is very nearly discharged of its responsibility, when he has impressed the subject, as strongly as he could, on the minds of all whom it may concern. The ground which he has now ventured to chalk out, has hitherto been untrodden; but it is truly British ground; and it is ground pointed out alike by the wishes of our friends, and by the example of our enemies.

Surely one must be blind and stupid indeed, not to see, and to feel, the interesting situation of this mighty Empire at the present moment. Engaged in a complicated warfare, we have a young Sovereign just seated on the throne; a Sovereign who has made every sacrifice of feeling and of private comfort for the good of his country; who entertains warmly at his heart those principles of sacred honour towards foreign States by which his Royal father has been actuated throughout his whole Reign; and, who, amidst difficulties the most trying, amidst calumnies the most treasonable, and with an amiable and worthy Minister assassinated almost by his side, has, with unexampled firmness, shown to an admiring nation, his unalterable determination to bestow his Royal confidence upon no man who has not, by well-proved conduct, manifested himself as the real friend of the King and Constitution.

Under such circumstances, it is not *quite* so easy to be silent. Every true British subject should rally round his Prince, and contribute to the great national cause such services as may be within his competence. The warrior should fight, the Minister should advise, the senator should legislate, and the poet should sing. Be it the province of others, in a humbler sphere, to render *their* tribute also. If *they* shall be so fortunate as to stem the torrent of defamation, to explain to their countrymen (and the British character, *when left to itself*, is loyal without measure) the pure and unspotted conduct of their Sovereign Prince; the labours of such persons, although less conspicuous and less tremendous than those of a Wellington or a Nelson, may not perhaps prove less useful to the vital interests of the country. They, at least, will not, or should not, be less the dictate of ultimate attachment and devotion to the high and illustrious personage who now sways the scepter over the first Kingdom in the world, and presides over the most beautiful and perfect Constitution of Government, that was ever contrived for the aggrandizement and happiness of human nature.

149 CHARLES FOX CRESPIGNY *to* COLONEL MCMAHON

Aldbro', Saxmundham, 20 Sept 1812.

HAVING heard of your return to town I lose no time in writing to you as I promised on the subject on which you spoke to my brother at Cheltenham. To you who are acquainted with the proofs which I have given of it I need not make any protestation of the very sincere wish I feel to have it in my power to support the Prince Regents Ministry—a disposition which I would have great additional pleasure in indulging on account of its allowing me at the same time to meet any wish of yours. But, my dear Sir, the fact is that every application which I have had occasion to make to Ministers (& I have made several thro' Mr. Arbuthnot) has been treated with such a marked unwillingness to oblige me in any instance, that I consider it a paramount duty to myself no longer to intrude myself among their adherents.

I accordingly feel myself under the necessity of forming a connexion with the Duke of Devonshire[1] or the Marquis of Lansdown both of whom I have reason to know are desirous of having the disposal of my influence at the next general election on any terms I choose to fix. I will however defer making any conclusive engagement with either of them until I hear from you, if it will be convenient to you to favor me with a line by return of post.[2]

150 AUGUSTUS CAVENDISH BRADSHAW *to* COLONEL MCMAHON

High Elms, Watford, Sepr 20, 1812.

ROUMOURS have reached me within these few last days that our excellent friend Lord Moira has been persuaded to accept the Government of India! I hope & trust it is true as I am sure every sincere & real well wisher to him is most anxious to see him in some great situation & I shd think none could be so advantageous to himself & the country as that to

1 William George Spencer Cavendish, sixth Duke of Devonshire (1790–1858).
2 Crespigny returned two Tories for Aldborough on 13 October: Lord Dufferin and Andrew Strahan. See No. 153.

India. It would be a new era to India; a new splendour to the whole thing, particularly if Lady Loudon accompanied him. I declare, poor as I am, I would not go to the eastern hemisphere with any other nobleman in England, but if Lord Moira went I should be proud & delighted to attend him. I shd of course go alone as Mrs Bradshaw wd remain at home with her only son.

I have received always the most marked & kind attention from Ld M. for which I owe & feel eternal obligation. I wd write to him myself if I was sure there was any truth in the reports. If there is do pray take an early opportunity of stating to him my anxiety to belong to his suit.

Independent of myself I declare I shd feel happy to hear he had accepted, for he is too honorable & good a man to have any connection at home with the present political statesmen. I shd also think the appointment wd be highly gratifying to the Regent. I hope to God it is true.

I shall not see you for some time as I have no thoughts of going to London before Christmas & hope you will soon get to Margate or some other quiet place.

151 COLONEL CONGREVE *to* COLONEL MCMAHON

Liverpool, 20th Sept. 1812.

THERE is I am sorry to say no good to be done by my remaining at this place—the *party* to whom I have been sent down—are not only *pledged* to Mr. Canning, but have actually *subscribed* their *monies*.[1]

Had I been here three days earlier or had any notification either of my coming been sent down—or of that of any other Ministerial candidate, the probability is that Government wd have had two members returned for this place—and now from this splitting of the Church & State Party, which has taken place by their inviting Canning in despair of getting any person to oppose the progress of the *down right* democrats— it seems not improbable that they may not have *one*—Helas!

Under these circumstances having no ground under my feet I shall hasten back to London without delay—as it wd tend neither to *usefulness* nor *dignity*—and also that I may not be quite cut out in the general scramble. I have left a very active & intelligent friend here to make the most of any circumstance that may turn up for the Government cause but I am quite sure I have no business to *appear* here—at least to *continue* to

1 "Congreve, the rocket-man, stands on the Prince's interest", wrote Brougham on the 29th. "I suppose the Prince is anxious to make him entirely his own", Grey replied. (Brougham's *Memoirs*, II, 57, 59.)

appear here—as things have turned out. Mr. Bolton[1] has already, & indeed before I arrived, here apprised Lord Lowther[2] of the changes that had taken place.

I hope the measure I have decided on will be approved of and remain [etc.].

P.S. For God sake, my dear friend, aid me in some other arrangement—for if I am now to be left out after all these hopes & fears & fags—and after the various tantalising expectations which I have had—it will be hard indeed—nay it will be disgracing me in the eyes of the world—who—will not rightly comprehend this last operation.[3]

152 LEWIS GOLDSMITH[4] *to the* DUKE OF CUMBERLAND

76 *Charlotte Street, Fitzroy Square*, 21 Sept. 1812.

THE very gracious reception I always experienced from your Royal Highness has induced me again to become importunate.

In a former interview I already had the honor to inform your Royal Highness that the Treasury assisted me to establish the Antigallican & I have continued to receive pecuniary aid, but it is always so uncertain that I really am at a loss to know if the Treasury mean to continue their aid or not; and it is for this reason that I humbly request your Royal Highness to ascertain from Lord Liverpool or Mr. Arbuthnot whether they mean to give me some kind of permanent support or not, it is fit that I should know it & not be left as I often am in the most embarrassed situation.

I can assure your Royal Highness that Bonaparte as well as his dupes on the Continent not only wish the Antigallican to be suppressed but myself exterminated, this wish is not confined to persons on the Continent it is equally the ardent desire of persons in this country.

1 Colonel John Bolton, a well-known Liverpool merchant and a friend of the Lowthers and of Canning. Brougham called him "the purse" of the Canning party. (*Memoirs*, II, 106.)

2 William Lowther, second Earl of Lonsdale (1787–1872). Succeeded his father, 1844.

3 He was returned for Gatton on 5 October by the influence of Sir Mark Wood. See No. 164.

4 The political writer and journalist (1763?–1846); conducted *The Anti-Gallican*, afterwards *The British Monitor*, an anti-French weekly paper started in January 1811. In announcing it to the public, Goldsmith said that he had been "urged by the most distinguished political characters in the country, of different parties and connexions, to establish a political periodical paper". "It professes itself of no party, yet will ever be ready to assist those who are leagued in determined opposition against the cruelties and aggressions exercised by the present tyrant of the Continent." Goldsmith had already, in 1810, published a highly scandalous "Secret History of the Cabinet of Bonaparte, including his private life, character", etc.

If your Royal Highness wishes to be informed what sensations my writings make on the Continent principally at Vienna & at St. Petersburg I can appeal to a Count de *Bruges*, who is recently arrived from those places. He is well known to Lord Castlereagh.

I humbly request to call your Royal Highnesses attention to a proposal which I have made to Ministers since my return to this country, viz to Mr. Percival, Mr. Arbuthnot & to Lord Castlereagh.

No man so well as myself knows the effects which certain publications have on the mind of Bonaparte, & which he very recently evinced by his angry replys to General Barclay de Tolly's[1] Address to the Germans. I therefore proposed to establish a kind of office distinct & separate from any of the Government offices, the object of which should be for the persons employed in that establishment to write pamphlets, to reply to articles written in the disaffected prints, but principally to write pamphlets in all languages to be distributed on the Continent. Persons in office are too much occupy'd in the daily routine to pay any attention to those objects, but which every person who knows any thing at all about Bonaparte is convinced that it will be of the greatest utility. In a conversation I had a short time since with Lord Yarmouth, his Lordship told me that he perfectly agreed with me in what I have just stated, & even said that he thought it would be of great use to have the Antigallican published in French as well as in English.

The establishment which I propose should be under the direction of the Foreign Office, and the Treasury.

I also informed your Royal Highness that I have ready for the Press a very important work which I intend calling the *Secret History of Bonaparte's Diplomacy*; detached pieces I have already given in several numbers of the Antigallican, but situated as I am I feel very much discouraged to continue my exertions. I have no fortune, no friends, & am, by telling so many truths constantly encreasing the number of my enemies, could I however but have the *verbal assurance only* of your Royal Highness or of the Prince Regent that I shall not be persecuted or deserted whoever may be the Ministers of this country, I will have no objection to do every thing in my power to serve my Sovereign and my country, and I cannot help remarking that I am either worth *something* or *nothing*.

Relying on a continuation of that gracious kindness which I ever experienced from your Royal Highness, I humbly beg leave to subscribe myself with gratitude & profound respect, [etc.].

1 A Russian General of Scottish ancestry, who distinguished himself against Napoleon. (1761–1818.)

153 [Charles Arbuthnot] *to* [Colonel McMahon]

[Sept. 21, 1812.]

I don't see what I can write more to the purpose than the inclosed,[1] wch you may send to Crespigny if you think it will do any good. Only beg him to return the letter to you. I trust you will be able to bring him to reason.[2] I am afraid I shall be too late for the post.

154 Brigadier-General George Porter[3] *to* Colonel McMahon

Govt. House, Gosport, Sept. 22, 1812.

I am induced to trouble you from the conviction I have, of the certainty of a dissolution of Parliament, speedily taking place, and feeling my position a little unpleasant. In the event of this taking place, any situation that I may afterwards be honored with from the condescencion and kindness of His Royal Highness the Prince Regent, will occasion a re-election, and altho' of course I should chearfully do this, yet if I could avoid the expence, it would suit my circumstances much better. I may perhaps appear to be most troublesome and encroaching, but emboldened by the gracious and gratifying promise of His R.H. communicated by you, would it be too much, if I was to express my hopes, that I might be gazzetted to some appointment previous to a new election for which of course I should receive *no salary*, untill an actual and effective vacancy should take place. As the situations in the Houshold are not I apprehend limited, I should concieve this might take place without incorrectness, and it would save me some hundred pounds. If I ask any thing unreasonable, pray do not attribute it to any other cause but the natural anxiety I feel to be placed in some way which would be most gratifying to me.

I go to Stockbridge on Saturday and stay till Tuesday; will you have the goodness to direct to me there, during that time—before and after to Gosport. I sincerely hope you are quite recovered and that Cheltenham has quite set you up.

1 Missing.   2 See No. 149.
3 M.P. for Stockbridge until 1820.

Downing Street, 23rd Sept. [1812].

I HAVE been so overwhelmed that I have never had one single moment to run up to Carlton House.

I now want you to do a very great favour.

If the Regent will make a point with Lord Chichester[1] to order Brooks, Francomb, Gorringe & Chambers to vote for Mr. John Pelly Atkins,[2] & for Dr. Sherrard Beaumont Burnaby they will be sure of their elections, & we shall keep out Leach[3] & Ellis.[4] But I ought to tell you that Ld Chichester is shy of interfering, & that if he does not *order* these men (who rent land of him) how to vote, they will vote for our enemies. Pray get His Royal Highness to authorise yr writing to Ld Chichester, it is of the utmost consequence.

Thanks for sending Crespigny.[5] It will do with him.

156 THE EARL OF MOIRA *to* COLONEL McMAHON

Sept. 26th [1812].

Return Sutton's Note.

I ENCLOSE to you a confidential note, which is worth your perusal for the inference it furnishes. When Sir Thomas Sutton[6] first meditated to stand for the County of Surrey, he spoke to me on the subject; & I saw he was beating about the bush how to connect himself with Government yet not to seem deserting me. I made all easy, as is my way in such cases, by advising that he should address himself to Mr. Perceval, tho' I had no intercourse with the latter but on the contrary was in professed opposition to him: Sir Thomas did so; explained his political principles; & was assured of Mr. Perceval's support. Lest this should not be distinctly known to Ld Liverpool, Sir Thomas asked me for an introduction to Arbuthnot. I gave him a note, which stated the ground Sir Thomas stood upon with Perceval. With this preliminary explanation, you will

1 Thomas Pelham, second Earl of Chichester (1756–1826). Joint Postmaster-General, 1807–23, and Postmaster-General, 1823–26. A Sussex landowner, he had some electoral influence in the borough of Seaford.
2 An Alderman of the City of London.
3 Sir John Leach (1760–1834). He was soon to be the Prince Regent's confidential legal adviser, and in 1818 was appointed Vice-Chancellor of England, and knighted.
4 Charles Rose Ellis, first Baron Seaford, and Canning's closest friend. (1771–1845.) He and Leach were elected for Seaford on 5 October. He was raised to the peerage in 1826.
5 See Nos. 149, 153.
6 Elected M.P. for Surrey, 12 October 1812; died, November 1813.

see in the conference a distinct exhibition of the sentiments of Arbuthnot & Ld Liverpool towards me. This, coupled with what I know of the objects of another person in the negociations with Canning & Ld Wellesley, informs me what ground I stand on.

157 WILLIAM JOSEPH DENISON[1] *to* COLONEL MCMAHON

Denbies, 27 Septr. 1812.

OUR friend Taylor[2] has this morning written to me, with the offer of a seat, through the kindness & condescension of His Royal Highness, the Prince Regent.

Pray have the goodness to lay my most humble duty at the feet of His Royal Highness, with my most gratefull thanks for this as well as for every other mark of kindness he has uniformly condescended to shew me; but at present I have no intention of coming into publick life.

With my best wishes for the health, happiness & prosperity of His Royal Highness, as well as your own; believe me [etc.].

158 THOMAS BEST *to* [COLONEL MCMAHON]

Belvidere House, Borough Road, 30th Septr. 1812.

FROM your natural disposition to kindness and good nature; I am induced to sollicit your friendship & interference on the present occasion, and the dissolution of Parliament affords an opportunity at once of your most essentially serving & obliging me by a seat, & I hope you are convinced that in any situation in life I should allways consider myself highly honored by the very obliging favor of your condescension in directing me by your advice & opinion, & particularly in this & believe me Dear Sir[3] [etc.].

1 The senior partner of Denison, Heywood & Kennard, the Lombard Street bankers. Whig M.P., 1796–1802, 1806–7, 1818–49. Lady Conyngham was his sister. He left a fortune of over two millions. (1770–1849.)

2 Michael Angelo Taylor (1757–1834), Whig M.P. for Ilchester and a member of the Carlton House party.

3 His hopes of a seat were not realised. See No. 169.

Leatherhead,
Thursday [*c.* end of September 1812].

I HAVE received this morning a letter from Burgess[1] repeating a conversation you have had with him. I say little now because it will bring me to town tomorrow. With the utmost frankness I am compell'd to declare that it has not been in my power to make any effort with respect to a seat, & that after our last conversation I should have thought it disrespectful to our Royal master's declared intention if I had busied myself on the subject had I even had I had [*sic*] an opportunity. The very place however which Burgess mentions to me has been voluntarily offered to [me] & I requested it might be kept open which has been promised me. Apart from personal motives I confess I am on *political* grounds anxious to be in Parliament an[d] to take a line which I think the P.R. will not disapprove of. No more now, I shall see you tomorrow.

160 RICHARD BRINSLEY SHERIDAN *to* [COLONEL McMAHON]

Saville Row,
Wed. Night [*c.* end of September or early October 1812].

I WILL call on you tomorrow—and, our gracious master willing, I shall be glad to be honor'd with an audience of ten minutes. I grieve to observe the existing mismanagement of his honor & character. At five in the evening I set off with Attersol[2] for Wotton-Bassett—most relunctantly [*sic*] incurring the expence,[3] but with a hope that my presence in the House may afford an opportunity of being useful to the Prince.

1 Henry Burgess, a solicitor, of Curzon Street, Mayfair, and Sheridan's friend.
2 John Attersoll, then patron of the borough of Wootton Bassett (Wiltshire).
3 £4000, a sum which Sheridan proposed to borrow from the Prince Regent. James Kibblewhite and Attersoll himself were returned for Wootton Bassett on 7 October, and the House of Commons saw Sheridan no more. Wellington wrote in July 1816: "I believe there is no doubt that upon several *important* occasions Sheridan took a line in Parliament different from that of his party, and rendered essential service to Government. If this conduct was not the principal cause of his being out of Parliament in the latter years of his life, it had at least tended to separate him from the party and was in some degree the reason of his being abandoned by some of his old friends belonging to it, and probably the cause of the poverty and distress in which he has left his family." (*Bathurst Papers,* p. 421.)

161 SIR ROBERT BARCLAY[1] *to* COLONEL MCMAHON

Rock Office, 1st Octo[r] 1812.

THE inclosed is from the House of Messrs. Barclays Tritton & Co., bankers in Lombard St. If the seat of Westbury is wanted you have of course (with this House) a safe channel of communication thro' me.

Messrs. Barclays & Co's influence at Yarmouth must be also great appertaining as they do to the Norfolk banks, with whom they are closely connected.

If you wanted my services in this, a line will reach me at the Rock Office tomorrow between the hours of 12—till 2.

Wilson I know is in want of a seat for Mr. Vernon of Orwell Park but I shall not write to him until Monday.[2]

162 [Enclosed] J. H. T[RITTON] *to* SIR ROBERT BARCLAY

Thursday [1 October 1812].

THAT to which I alluded was Westbury. There is also an opening at Yarmouth. I will attend to your letter.

163 JOHN NASH[3] *to* COLONEL MCMAHON

East Cowes Castle, Isle Wight, Oct. 2, 1812.

WILL you have the goodness to make known to H.R.H. that Holmes[4] (to my very great astonishment) has embraced the Marquiss Wellesleys politics & returns two of his friends for Yarmout[h][5] and himself & brother[6] for Newport. As I have no object in Parliament but the Prince I of course am out of the question in this arrangement. If H.R.H. considers that I can be useful I do not mind an expence not exceeding 3000 £ & if any such arrangement can take place I will come up immediately.

1 [1755–1839.] In 1813, he was appointed collector of the internal revenues at Mauritius.
2 Benjamin Hall and Benjamin Shaw were elected for Westbury on 10 October, and Edmund Knowles Lacon and Lieutenant-General William Loftus for Yarmouth on the 7th.
3 The architect, who laid out Regent's Park, planned Regent Street, and enlarged Buckingham House. (1752–1835.)
4 Sir Leonard Thomas Worsley Holmes (1787–1825).
5 Richard Wellesley and Sir Henry Conyngham Montgomery were returned for Yarmouth (Isle of Wight) on 7 October.
6 Richard Fleming Worsley Holmes (d. 1814); elected for Newport (Isle of Wight) on 6 October.

Lord Wellesleys son[1] is a great crony of Holmes and will I suppose be one of the Yarmouth members—but knowing Holmes as well as I do the whole is unintelligible to me. Will you favor me with an answer and believe me to be [etc.].

164 SIR MARK WOOD[2] *to* COLONEL MCMAHON

[Octr 2. 1812.]

See me for *one minute.*

I SCARCELY think it worth while to trouble H.R.H. again.

My own mind is made up—to go out of town—and to leave at Sidmouths the accompg letter—provided you perfectly approve.

You are wellcome to take a copy of it—and show it to a certain personage. Wm. Congreve Esqe and Sir Mark Wood Bt. will fill both Gatton seats—provided the P[rince]'s offer to Ld E.[llenborou]gh[3] is declined, but I only hold my situation for the P. and I think H.R.H. will not have a more strenuous supporter.

It shall however be vacated the instant it is thought right.[4]

165 SIR MARK WOOD *to* VISCOUNT SIDMOUTH

Gatton Park, October 2nd 1812.

AFTER the most mature consideration of the subject of our conversation yesterday evening I feel that it will be totally impossible for me to withdraw from Parliament, to make room for any other person excepting for Mr Law[5]—and as in consequence of your previous arrangements, he was the sole object of your solicitude, I the more regret, that there should be any change upon the present occasion, altho I readily enter into all the feelings of Mr Laws friends that his political *debut* should be as free and

1 Richard Wellesley, one of Lord Wellesley's illegitimate children by the woman whom he afterwards married as his first wife.

2 M.P. for Gatton since 1802 and patron of the borough. Created a Baronet, 1808. [1747–1829.]

3 Edward Law, first Baron Ellenborough (1750–1818). Lord Chief Justice of England, 1802–18. See No. 165.

4 Lieutenant-Colonel Congreve and Sir Mark Wood were elected for Gatton on 5 October.

5 Edward Law, first Earl of Ellenborough (1790–1871), afterwards Governor-General of India. Eldest son of the first Baron Ellenborough, the Lord Chief Justice (1750–1818). He was elected for St Michael on 13 February 1813, and generally, though not invariably, supported the Government.

as unfettered as possible; but as Mr Law will in the situation which has been so graciously offerd be as free as air—and under no other restraint than that which must actuate every honorable and independant mind, no longer to accept of an obligation than he felt himself perfectly easy under it.

Whenever therefore Mr Law feels himself in that situation, not to be able to give his free and unbiassed support to His R.H.s Government— of which yourself and your highly respected friend[1] form so esential a part—he will be perfectly at liberty to retire, without having incurred one penny of expence. I therefore trust and hope that upon further consideration all difficulties will be removed and that I shall have the satisfaction of returning Mr Law—for Gatton.

It is true that in the event of my placing Mr Law in Gatton I have received the most unquestionable assurances, at a very early period of another seat for myself upon equally liberal and gratuitous terms, but to make any exchange or to place any other person there must totally change the state of the case, and I could neither expect nor ask to return to Parliament myself. Exclusive of this important consideration after the enormous sacrifices which I have made during these last 18 years[2] (without ever having received the smallest acknowledgement whatsoever) in support of Government, no Minister could with any conscience ask me so to degrade myself as to retire from Parliament to make room for any man, excepting upon such an unforeseen and unexpected emergency such as that in which Mr. Law has been placed by unavoidable events.

It must not be forgotten that even had I not been unexpectedly called upon for the fullfillment of a voluntary offer which I made two months ago—to an illustrious personage—(the circumstances of which so far as relates to Aldborough, you are not unacquainted with) and even had every thing remained in the exact state in which it was at the time I made you a voluntary offer, yet you could not have been so unjust as to have expected that I would have accepted of any recommendation—but a person—whom I could be certain of his better supporting my own political friends, or of withdrawing upon being fully indemnified all expences. It is true that in the case of Mr. Law I should most probably have dispensed with such a promise or pledge, as I should just as soon have suspected yourself, as I would Mr Law, of any intention to desert

1 Lord Ellenborough was a member of the Sidmouth "connexion".
2 He claimed to have returned twenty members in the Tory interest between 1794 and 1812: Milborne Port, one (1794); Newark-on-Trent, one (1796); Gatton, four (1802 and two by-elections in 1803 and 1805); Shaftesbury, two (1802); Gatton and Shaftesbury, two each, 1806, 1807 and 1812. (Add. MSS. 38368, fo. 206.)

the Prince's Government, but after the conduct of Mr. Greenough[1] last Session, recommended to me, particularly by the Duke of Portland,[2] it evinces the expediency upon all matters of business, of having a clear and explicit understanding.

Scarcely any private gentleman in England has made those liberal and gratuitous sacrifices for the support of Government which I have done during these last 18 years, and I have the satisfaction of feeling that altho I have conferd many obligations I have never received any favor or service from any Minister or any man within the King's dominions nor have ever provided for a single friend. Had Mr. Percival lived I had from him every assurance of providing for every friend in the most hand-some and most liberal manner—which Lord Liverpool as well as other Cabinet Ministers—are well acquainted with, but his premature death has disappointed the expectations not meerely of individuals, but of the country. Should Mr. Law accept of the very gracious offer which has been made to him of coming in for Gatton, I will in course return[3] till such time as another similar situation can be found; and as the whole of this arrangement is upon the most liberal and gratuitous footing as well in regard to Mr Law as to myself, this I trust after Mr Curwen's[4] Bill cannot fail to have to every thinking and reflecting mind its proper weight and value.

I shall expect a line from you by this night's post—meerely to say whether or not the offer now made be declined or accepted. If accepted, it will not be necessary for Mr. Law to attend unless it be in every respect convenient and agreeable to himself. He shall not incur a single farthing of expence. I am My dear Lord [etc.].

166 THE EARL OF MOIRA *to* COLONEL MCMAHON

Cheltenham, Octr 2d, 1812.

LET me trespass on you so far as to beg that you will send the enclosed to my house, with a direction that it is to be immediately forwarded into the City.

1 George Bellas Greenough (1778–1855), M.P. for Gatton, 1807–12, and a member of Canning's Party. This accounts for Sir Mark Wood's dissatisfaction. Canning tried, but failed, to get Greenough a seat at the General Election.
2 William Henry Cavendish Bentinck, third Duke of Portland (1738–1809). Prime Minister, 1807–9.
3 Probably *retire* in the original.
4 John Christian Curwen (1756–1828), Whig M.P. for Carlisle. His Bill to prevent the purchasing of seats in the House of Commons was passed in 1809.

The Duke of Norfolk called upon me & said "He was endeavoring to make himself as strong as possible & wished to be regarded as an humble adherent of the Prince's if His Royal Highness would let him."[1] Colhoun's money is ready if an opening be found for him.

167 VISCOUNT MELBOURNE *to* COLONEL MCMAHON

Brocket Hall, Octr. 4th 1812.

THE bustle of the moment, and the animosities created at this particular period, affects every one more or less, and from the unfortunate differences in political opinions between me and my dearest connections,[2] I have been represented as no well wisher to His Majesties present Government.

And that no such impression may be made on His Royal Highness the Prince Regents mind, I will be much obliged to you to take an opportunity of informing His Royal Highness with my humble duty, that to all the various applications I have had for my interest and support in the several places wherein I have property, that I have uniformly engaged myself in favour of Government candidates, as conceiving such conduct the most servisable to His Royal Highness the Prince Regent. I am no politician, and of little weight or consequence any where, but I glory in having been devoted in attachment to His Royal Highness the Prince Regent, invariably for now full thirty years and it will ever be my greatest pride & comfort that in the course of so long a time I have been constantly honoured by His Royal Highness attention, kindness, friendship, and protection, and I trust I shall never forfeit these distinguished honours, during the remainder of an already advanced life.

Your kindness to me, Sir, on many occasions, has incouraged me to trouble you with this letter. I hope you received all the benefit you could wish from your stay at Cheltenham, and I have the honour to remain, [etc.].

1 Two months later Romilly said that since the beginning of the Regency the Prince had "slighted and shunned the Duke". All the Duke's members in the Parliament of 1812–18 belonged to the Opposition.
2 See No. 16.

Gatton Park,
Sunday Evg [4 Oct 1812].

I RECEIVED the inclosed yesterday afternoon from Lord Sid[mou]th—, which speaks for itself. I am gratified to learn from you, that my letter to Lord S.[1] was approved of. Not only yourself but an illustrious person will see from the state of the business, the absolute necessity of acting with the greatest caution and circumspection, to prevent the construction which both S[idmouth] and E[llenborough] will otherwise to a certainty put upon it, of a previous arrangement. This becomes fully more necessary for the honor of a certain personage than even for mine; and after this shall have been fully called to the attention of an illustrious person, my duty is only to obey. The return for Gatton will be Sir Mark Wood Bt. and Wm. Congreve Esq. The earlier I am placed elsewhere the better for us all, so that honor be safe.

I hope you prevailed upon a certain personage to read my letter to S. Lord S. answer you can return when we meet in town. The election is tomorrow.

Whoever is *through you* recommended to succeed me, *depend upon it*, shall be seated without one farthing of expence. I shall have the pleasure of seeing you in the course of a day or two.

169 THOMAS BEST *to* COLONEL MCMAHON

Belvidere House, Borough Road,
Monday 5th Octr 1812.

THE candor with which you have acted towards me, is the most indubitable proof (if any had been necessary) of your sincerity; and the explicit manner which you have been at the pains of informing me on the subject, is at once evincing of your wish and intention if possible to serve me, but alas! I can not serve myself, and I think it the least that is due to your kindness & friendship, to state without any mental reserve whatever, what my whole and sole object was, merely that I might have succeeded in obtaining a situation without putting the Prince to any further trouble, by voting and making myself usefull to Ministers, and thereby obtaining what my necessities required, and I now have only to impress on your mind that I feel your conduct, MOST *gratefully*; and believe me My dear Sir with sincere regard and esteem[2] [etc.].

1 No. 165. 2 See No. 158.

Foreign Office, 5th October 1812.

Dispatches have been received from Mr. Baker[1] dated Washington the 24th of August.

The result of his conferences with Mr. Monroe[2] are—

1st—that the official notification of the repeal of the Orders in Council had produced no effect upon the Government.

2d—that the Government of the United States would take no measure to terminate or suspend hostilities, till they heard the result of the negociation given in charge to Mr. Russell[3]—but they hoped the result of that negociation would be favorable for peace.

3d—that they had given orders to General Dearborn not to continue the suspension of hostilities agreed to by him with Sir George Prevost.[4]

4th—that with regard to the vessels & cargoes which sailed for America after the repeal of the Orders in Council, they would be seized by the collectors at the different ports, that they would be restored to the consignees on their giving bonds to the amount; the payment of which would possibly not be required, as on the meeting of Congress some legislative measures would be recommended for the purpose of affording relief in these cases. On Mr. Bakers asking, if goods loaded on account of British merchants would be included in the arrangements Mr. Madison[5] said, there was no disposition in the Government to separate the case of the British goods, and in the event of a friendly intercourse, an arrangement would be made respecting the bonds, provided Congress did not make provision generally to include them with the others.

Mr. Gallatin[6] was to issue a circular, ordering the collector to restore the goods seized under the Non Importation Act on bonds being given for the amount.

5th An exchange of prisoners agreed to.

Mr. Baker thinks the measures taken by England will have such an effect as to prevent the Government being able to continue the War.

The House of Representatives had agreed to a resolution for taking possession of East Florida, but it was rejected by the Senate.

1 Anthony St John Baker. Secretary of Legation at Washington, 1811–16, and Chargé d'Affaires there, 1815–16.

2 James Monroe (1758–1831), the American Secretary of State, 1811–17, and President of the United States, 1817–25.

3 The American Chargé d'Affaires in London.

4 Governor of Lower Canada and Governor-General of British North America. He was in charge of the military operations during the war of 1812–14. [1767–1816.]

5 President of the United States, 1809–17. [1751–1836.]

6 The American Secretary of the Treasury. [1761–1849.]

Cholmondeley Castle, Oct. 5th 1812.

I MUST beg you will have the goodness to assure the Prince Regent from me that if I had not been detained here upon very *particular business*, I should have been anxious in person, at the first moment of the dissolution, to have taken His Royal Highness' pleasure in person, for my guidance, with the small Parliamentary interest I now possess.

Lord Yarmouth slept here on Saturday night, in his way to Ireland, when I was much vexed to hear from him that Government when he left London was not sure of Lord Clintons[1] boroughs. I lost no time in sending to beg Lord Charles Bentinck[2] would go down to Ashburton from me.

I did not wish to disturb the boroughs, when Mr. Long I understood was in treaty for them. It is well know[n] I otherwise was anxious to have tried the three seats at my own expence.

I am authorised to say I was pretty sure of Ashburton by a letter from my lawyer dated Exeter Oct. 1st saying there would have been very little doubt of my success if I had sent Lord C— Bentinck down in time.[3]

With respect to Callington I can only say neither trouble or expence should have been spared by me to have effected so desirable an object for His Royal Highness in case of Lord C[linton's] hostility.[4]

Will you have the goodness to let me find on my arrival in London a line from you. I hope to be there very late on Wednesday or early on Thursday. Believe me [etc.].

1 Robert Cotton St John Trefusis, eighteenth Baron Clinton (1787–1832). Canning's friends had some hopes of getting Lord Clinton's boroughs. Clinton was said to be in opposition in 1818 (see No. 749), but his brother Charles certainly voted with the Government in the Parliament of 1812–18.

2 Lord William Charles Augustus Cavendish Bentinck (1780–1826), third son of the third Duke of Portland (1738–1809). Appointed Treasurer of the Household, August 1812. M.P. for Ashburton, 1807–12. See No. 173.

3 John Sullivan, a member of the India Board, and Richard Preston, who voted with the Opposition, were returned for Ashburton on 8 October.

4 Two ministerialists were elected for Callington on 9 October: William Stephen Poyntz (Lord Clinton's father-in-law) and Sir John Leman Rogers, whose place was taken on 4 March 1813 by Charles Rodolph Trefusis, who succeeded his brother as nineteenth Baron Clinton in 1832.

Cawdor Castle, Nairnshire, N.B.
7th Oct 1812.

Yours of the 1st inst which reached me this morning requires an immediate answer & claims my warmest acknowledgements for the nature of its contents.

From the urgency of the occasion I presume that a discussion of them might be even now too late.

But I may mention that I am at present engaged in election arrangements respecting this County with considerable prospect of ultimate if not of immediate success & that whatever conduct I may feel myself bound to adopt in public life it is impossible that I should ever experience any abatement of that attachment of which you much gratify me by adverting to some of the early proofs.

Accept my dear Sir of my grateful thanks for your communication & permit me to assure you that I have the honour to be [etc.].

173 Lord William Charles Augustus Cavendish Bentinck *to* Colonel McMahon

24 *Grosvenor Place*, October 7th 1812.

It is impossible for me to express the distress I am in at finding that Lord Cholmondeley's borough of Castle Rising is to be given to Mr. Cavendish Bradshaw.[2] I have had many difficulties to struggle through for some years but now from the Prince Regents goodness to me I hoped to go on a little better, & eager to retain my place went to a considerable expence to be re-elected for Ashburton. Lord Cholmondeley had talked of contesting that place for the Parliament but having altered his entention I lost my seat there but was made quite comfortable from receiving a letter from him offering to bring me in for Castle Rising.

My brother[3] does not take any part in politicks & will not bring any body in. On an income of eighteen hundred a year it is impossible I can either buy a borough or contest an election. I must therefore lose my

1 The Whig philosopher and politician (1765–1832). On 8 May 1812, a few days after his return to England from Bombay, he was offered a seat in Parliament by his old friend Perceval, but he replied on the 11th, the day of Perceval's assassination, that he could not accept a seat at the hands of an anti-Catholic Prime Minister. Lord Cawdor offered to return him for Nairnshire on the understanding that he remained a Whig, and he was elected in June 1813. See Nos. 211 and 212.

2 See Nos. 127, 150.   3 The fourth Duke of Portland (1768–1854).

place unless His Royal Highness will be graciously pleased to allow me to come in for Castle Rising.

The expence of my last election which was upwards of six hundred pounds has so involved me that added to other expences I have incurred counting on my salary I must be ABSOLUTELY RUINED if I lose my situation in His Royal Highnesse's family.

I understand from Arbuthnot that I am supposed to have made a promise of bringing myself into parliament; this never was the case— and had this promise been proposed to me as the alternative I must have given up all hope of the place from the first, knowing I could have no chance of keeping such a promise. For God sake lose no time in laying my case before His Royal Highness & forgive the trouble I am giving you but I really am so extremely distressed I hardly know what I am writing.

174 CHARLES ARBUTHNOT *to* COLONEL MCMAHON

Downing Street, Thursday, [8 October 1812].

LORD CHOLMONDELEY seems by his letter to me to be highly displeased at my not preventing the Prince from substituting Cav: Bradshaw.[1]

You know that this in no way depended on me, but make him feel that the Prince was resolved. You will see Ld. Choly to-day.

Pray let me know whether I can have the box on Saturday.

175 AUGUSTUS CAVENDISH BRADSHAW *to* COLONEL MCMAHON

High Elms, Octr 10, 1812.

YOUR official communication that I am returned for the borough of Castle Rising I have just received. Of course I was surprised & highly gratified at the event. I have only now my good friend to request you will express to His R.H. the Prince Regent how grateful I feel for this additional mark of H.R.H. gracious kindness to me. I hope I need not say this last gracious condescention was not wanting to make the first object of my life in whatever situation I am placed devoted in every way to forward the prosperity & happiness of my Royal master. I wish I could better express to you one half of what I now feel but must trust to you to make my humble devotion at the feet of His Royal Highness the Prince Regent.

1 See Nos. 127, 150, 173.

Prince Royal's Camp, Borders of Georgia,
October 13th 1812.

I PRESUME to approach your Royal Highness at the request of H.R.H. Abbas Mirza, Prince Royal of Persia, to inform you that he has given me a few articles of presents, which however unworthy he prays your Royal Highness's acceptance of.

I have in consequence taken the liberty of forwarding to your Royal Highness's feet the following articles by my Assistant Secretary the Honble Robert Gordon,[1] and have humbly to beg that your Royal Highness would order some of your servants to honor me with an acknowledgement of the receipt of the same, that I may have it in my power to render the Prince Royal's heart glad, by knowing that you have graciously condescended to accept these marks of his unfeigned attachment and veneration.

1 long shawl, sky blue, with fine ends.
1   do   do scarlet,   do   & border.
1 piece of white flowered shawl.
1 striped   do   do   handkerchief   do
4 shawls
A persian ink stand painted by a man of great celebrity about 180 years ago.
A Persian helmet.
A   do   sword with gold clasp.
A coat of chain armour.
A suit of (Char aineh) body armour
I have the honor to remain with the highest respect and most dutiful attachment, [etc.].

177 *Memorandum* [*by* CHARLES ARBUTHNOT, *October* 1812].

THE numbers to-day make no alteration.

The contests bear a favourable look; & it is believed that Gascoyne[2] will succeed.

In answer to former applications for seats, & particularly for Evelyn,[3] I am informed by Peel[4] that he has no seat to give me.

1 The distinguished diplomatist and brother of the fourth Earl of Aberdeen. [1791–1847.] Afterwards Minister at Vienna and Constantinople.

2 Isaac Gascoyne, Tory M.P. for Liverpool, 1802–30. [1770–1841.] See No. 178.

3 Lyndon Evelyn. Returned at a bye-election for Dundalk on 2 January 1813, by Lord Roden, the patron of the borough.

4 Sir Robert Peel, second Baronet (1788–1850). Afterwards Prime Minister. Irish Secretary, 1812–18.

Liverpool, Saturday, 17 Octr 1812.

THE friendly interest which you are kind enough to take in what concerns me, must be my apology (as it is my inducement) for troubling you, among the first of my friends, with the intelligence of my success at this place.

It has been complete, and flattering beyond my most sanguine expectations.

I hesitated (as perhaps you know) to accept the invitation which was sent to me, first on account of the expence—which I dared not encounter, and secondly, because I felt it almost ridiculous to suffer myself to be proposed to a town in which I had not a single personal acquaintance.

The first of these objections was presently removed.[1] The second was overcome by the assurances which I received from the leading persons of Liverpool—and I must say that these assurances have been realised to a degree that even now I can hardly *believe*, much less account for.

After a contest of 8 days I was placed yesterday by a majority of 500 above my antagonist Mr. Brougham[2]—& by about 100 above my colleague General Gascoyne. And scarcely any support has been tendered to me without being accompanied with an intimation that I may rely upon it, as long as I choose to represent Liverpool. The numbers at the final close of the poll were

Can.	1631
Gasc.	1532
Brough.	1131
Creev[ey]	1068

Tarleton[3] declined early & had but 10 or 11 votes.

My friends are in general safe in their returns to Parliament. Three only have failed—Dent,[4] Lord Binning[5] and Taylor.[6] But *I* am returned or to be *returned* for *two* places besides Liverpool[7]—so that I shall be

1 On 3 October Canning said that his Liverpool friends had subscribed over £6000 to meet the cost of the election, and on the 17th declared that it had not cost him a farthing.

2 Henry Peter Brougham, Baron Brougham and Vaux (1778–1868). Lord Chancellor in the Reform Ministry, 1830–34.

3 General Sir Banastre Tarleton (1754–1833). Fought under Clinton and Cornwallis in the American War. Whig M.P. for Liverpool, 1790–1806 and 1807–12. Created Baronet, 1815.

4 John Dent, M.P. for Lancaster, 1790–1812; without a seat, 1812–18; M.P. for Poole, 1818–26. (d. 1826.)

5 Thomas Hamilton, ninth Earl of Haddington (1780–1858). M.P. for Callington, 1807–12, and for other boroughs, 1814–27. Succeeded his father, 1828.

6 William Taylor, M.P. for Barnstaple, 1806–12.

7 Canning was returned for Petersfield, a borough belonging to his friend Hylton Joliffe, on 9 October, and for Sligo borough on 5 November.

able *nearly* to replace my old number;[1] and I have had the satisfaction of being assured of support in new quarters where I had no title to expect it.[2]

If therefore the Government intended the dissolution (as I hear they do not scruple to avow they did) against *me*, they are as great bunglers in their miserable home politicks—as they have shewn themselves abroad in their *vigorous* war-measures against America (for instance) and their wise, well-timed but most circumspect and deliberate Swedish expedition.[3]

But though I have not suffered by their good intentions you may believe I do not the less *gratefully* acknowledge them.

P.S. I do not frank to you, because I hope you are returned to Parliament—though I have seen your return contradicted.[4]

If you are kind enough to acknowledge the receipt of this, your letter will find me here for the next ten days: as I am obliged to wait for a publick dinner which they propose giving to me.

179 THE EARL OF YARMOUTH *to* COLONEL MCMAHON

Saturd^y 17. [October 1812.]

PRAY forward the enclosed.

I shall be quite quietly returned for this County [i.e. Antrim] but the Dowager of Downshire[5] has raised a flame in Down—a ball under cover of a christening afforded her an opportunity of commencing an extensive canvass which she has since enlarged—she subscribes 2000 & if Lord D[ownshire][6] permits her to lead his freeholders she will perhaps beat Castlereagh & at any rate cause much bloodshed & disturbance as the threshers are numerous in Down & have already burst into Downpatrick

1 Canning had a following of fifteen in the House of Commons on the eve of the Dissolution, and of twelve in the new Parliament. Joshua Spencer, who was never a member of Canning's party, was elected in his stead, for Sligo, on 5 April 1813. Canning's cousin, Colonel George Canning, took his place at Petersfield, on 24 December.

2 This probably refers to Sir Leonard Thomas Worsley Holmes' offer of his boroughs to Canning and Lord Wellesley.

3 Referring to Castlereagh's negotiation with Sweden, which issued in the Treaty of Örebrö (17 July 1812). Thornton was sent to Sweden in a warship.

4 McMahon was not in Parliament after 1812.

5 The Marchioness of Downshire (d. 1836), wife of the second Marquis (1753–1801).

6 The third Marquis of Downshire (1788–1845). The Downshires had defeated Castlereagh at a bye-election in July 1805, but he recovered the seat in 1812 (21 October), the two rival interests sharing the representation of the County.

& killed two people—the Dragoons are gone there from hence. Lord D. has promised not to interfere but if he suffers mama to dictate to his tenants it will only be keeping the word of promise to the ear & Cast. will have to parade his on Putny Commn.

I think Croker[1] will be at least hard run in Downpatrick.

God bless you, my dear Mc. I am now going to canvass in the County of Down.

180 EARL BATHURST *to the* PRINCE REGENT

Brighton, Octr. 18th, 1812.

LORD BATHURST most humbly submits to your Royal Highness the copy of a letter Lord Bathurst has received from Prince William of Orange,[2] in answer to one which Lord Bathurst thought it his duty to address to His Serene Highness, announcing to him your Royal Highness having been pleased to appoint him an Aid de Camp to your Royal Highness.

Lord Bathurst at the same time communicated to His Serene Highness your Royal Highness's considerate kindness towards him, in selecting that military reward, which would not deprive His Serene Highness of the advantage to be derived by his situation with Lord Wellington, in which it must be both his wish and interest at present to remain.

181 EARL CONYNGHAM[3] *to* COLONEL MCMAHON

Dublin, Octr 20th 1812.

MY submission to the Prince Regents will must ever be my duty—the marks of his goodness will ever be remembered with gratitude by me. On my arrival in Dublin I waited on the Lord Lieutenant, and I feel

1 John Wilson Croker, the Tory politician and contributor to the *Quarterly Review*. Secretary to the Admiralty, 1809–30. M.P. for Downpatrick, 1807–12. In 1812 he lost his seat, but Lord Castlemaine brought him in for Athlone. [1780–1857.]

2 William, Hereditary Prince of Orange (1792–1849), afterwards William II, King of the Netherlands, the son of William VI, Prince of Orange, under whom Holland and the Austrian Netherlands (Belgium) were united in 1814. Prince William became engaged to the Princess Charlotte in 1814, but the engagement was quickly broken off. (*Vide* 1814 Letters.) He was now serving on Wellington's Staff in the Peninsula.

3 Henry Conyngham, first Marquis Conyngham (1766–1832). Lord Steward of the Household, 1821–30. By 1820 his wife had supplanted Lady Hertford as the King's mistress.

happy to inform you, I have returned S.ʳ James Stewart[1] & Genl. Hart[2] for the County of Donegall, two members you may depend upon. I have started Col.ˡ FitzGerald[3] for Clare.

The very kind interest you took when last I had the pleasure of seeing you in London with regard to my wishes, & your most kind promise of laying those wishes before His Royal Highness—will I hope plead my apology for informing you that the Duke of Richmond[4] has recommended me in the event of a promotion—to a Marquisate—or an English peerage —but every thing depends on the Prince—his orders will be obey'd. May I therefore again entreat of you to lay my name before him—for the Marquisate or English peerage—whenever His Royal Highness may think fit.

I almost flatter myself with your pardon for this bore—and in return I beg leave to inclose a most curious epistle from an old friend of ours— a man most useful in this country. Pray keep the letter till we meet as I purpose going to England next week.

182 The Duke of Northumberland *to* Colonel McMahon

Alnwick Castle, 20th October 1812.

...I have indeed had a lucky escape at Aldeburgh, I find however there was a kind of opposition at New Romsey, & a petition to Parliament against the return is threatened; but I fancy it will come to nothing....[5]

183 Charles Arbuthnot *to* Colonel McMahon

Downing Street, 23rd Octr 1812.

ALTHO' I believe that the less said the better, I think you will agree with me that the letters wch you saw this morning justified me sufficiently in

1 Sir James Stewart, of Fort Stewart, Co. Donegal. Succeeded his father as seventh Baronet, 1801. (d. 1827.)

2 Lieutenant-General George Vaughan Hart (1752–1832). Served in America and India. Peel, the Irish Secretary, said that Hart was returned "on Lord Abercorn's interest, who has a larger property in the County than Lord Conyngham".

3 Lieutenant-General Sir Augustine Fitzgerald (d. 1834). He was returned on 3 November. Created a Baronet, 1821.

4 The Lord-Lieutenant.

5 See No. 240.

assuring His Royal Highness that I had full reason for considering Mr. Johnstone[1] & Mr Holmes[2] as friendly to Government. I am thoroughly convinced that the loss of men like them will never materially injure any Government; & tho' we shall have the *Middle Party*[3] sounding their numbers loudly, yet we may rest assured that with regard to the *national feeling* the triumph of Government has beyond all example been complete. Long came to town this morning, & he is every day feeling this more strongly. This also is told me from every quarter; & I am convinced that the sentiment is very general.

I was very much amused with hearing that Mr. Holmes was my first cousin. A relation of his married a relation of mine in Ireland; but till I got acquainted with him in the House of Commons I did not know of his existence, & having always thought him a very vulgar low sort of man, it has been my unvarying endeavour to stand aloof from him.

I think you will be of opinion that were his letters to me to be published, they wd not much raise him in the world's estimation, for you have seen the manner in which he represented himself as a friend of Government.

184 WILLIAM MCMAHON[4] *to* COLONEL MCMAHON

Merrion Street, 24 Oct. 1812.

I LAST night was favored with your letter of the 19th inst. With respect to Lord Manners[5] I consider your conversation with him of much value because it pledges him not to oppose, but still the serious desideratum remains in the structure of our Government. For the main point will be to put me in nomination, & this is the business of only three people the

1 Two Johnstones were elected in 1812 who had been in the 1807–12 Parliament: George Johnstone, for Heydon; and Andrew Cochrane Johnstone, for Grampound.

2 Rather curiously, this must be William Holmes, the Tory Whip, for the other Mr Holmes elected in 1812 (Richard Fleming Worsley Holmes, for Newport, Isle of Wight) was a new member, belonging to the Wellesley party. "Billy" Holmes' letter to Lord Liverpool (No. 132) suggests that he was acting with Canning in 1812, but he was never referred to by Canning and his friends as a member of their group, nor did the Treasury Whips label him a Canningite either before or after the dissolution. He was returned for Grampound in 1808 and for Tregony in 1812. He never voted against the Government after 1812 (so far as appears from the division lists in *Hansard*), and he was appointed Treasurer of the Ordnance in June 1818. His father was a wealthy brewer, with a large estate in Sligo County, and was High Sheriff of the County in 1810. Arbuthnot's family was settled in County Mayo, and his mother was the daughter of John Stone, a London banker, and the niece of Dr Stone, Archbishop of Armagh.

3 The Canning-Wellesley group.

4 [1776–1837.] Colonel McMahon's brother. Created a Baronet, 1814. Appointed Master of the Rolls in Ireland, 1814. See Nos. 323, 324.

5 Thomas Manners-Sutton, first Baron Manners (1756–1842). Lord Chancellor of Ireland, 1807–27.

Lord Lieuten^t,[1] his Secretary,[2] or the Chancellor; because if the recommendation be forwarded to the Secretary for the Home Department[3] at your side with the authority of the Lord Lieuten^t in the ordinary form it presents an herculean difficulty to overset that & substitute another in lieu of it. This I therefour confide to your anticipation.

As to Mrs. O'Halloran I reluctantly discuss her character particularly when it is impossible she may be served. My first decided dislike to her arose from her trip to annoy you in London & nothing has occurred to even mollify my disapproval of her measures. I confess I regard her as formidable from her infatuation in letter writing & her general disposition & after a series of persecution I have recently set her at defiance.

As to the office which is the basis of her letter I have no doubt whenever I have the happiness of talking with you for a few minutes I shall convince you of these two propositions; first that I was despoiled of the office by a very origin^l & oppressive proceeding by Government compared with other cases, & next that I yielded at the peculiar juncture to what I consider rank injustice from considerations of expediency as to you & myself which a prudent view of the question must ever sanction. However to come to the point; I went yesterday to the Castle & the result of my exertions there has been, that I was assured Mrs. O'H:'s son should be put on the Excise list—this enters him a supernum^y guager [*sic*] & upon the present Excise system is the initiation of office. Friends & exertions may afterwards put him in a valuable office. I acquainted Mrs. O'H: with this; but she doubts much about it's acceptance & I can do no more.

As to any arrangement for her; I am quite ready to do any thing you say I ought, & I quite agree you are not called upon to join, & therefore I can propose no plan on the subject but in deciding I must beg leave to apprize you of *these facts*—*My family Civil List* consists of a small income I give my mother in addition to her own limited estate—the provision of another sister's female child who has always acted quite to my satisfaction & Mrs. O'Halloran's son—these three persons with some slices for debts which I have paid for Mrs. O'H: form a serious charge upon a fund which is nothing but the precarious professional income which I earn & my sentiment has been ever this—I regret that my aid is so limited but I consider it my first duty to acquire such an independence as will place me above want for myself or my children if my health fails— if fortune favors me that my health is steady a promotion awaits my exertions without affecting philosophy I shall always be willing liberally to share any superfluous wealth with my kindred & connections.

1 The Duke of Richmond.　　2 Peel.　　3 Sidmouth.

Windsor, October 24, 1812.

Copy

I DID not fail, in compliance with your wishes to acquaint Her Majesty with your intention of taking the earliest opportunity of speaking to her upon the subject of Charlotte, and shewing her at the same time the enclosed paper, which I herewith return, from Lord Liverpool.

Her Majesty at first listened with much complacency, and seemed to view in a right light the necessity of her enjoying more liberty and passing a part of her time in London, but there was a very visible alteration in her manner when I stated to her the wish that our sisters should occasionally accompany her. She said however but little, the only remark she made was that the late Princess of Wales's[1] daughters[2] had gone into public, without their mother, to which I answered that the cases were by no means similar; that the Princess of Wales's daughters were under the protection of their mother, and therefore it depended upon her in what manner she chose them to appear in public, but that Charlotte was to all intents & purposes without a mother, or if possible, in a worse situation, and therefore she required the support & protection of the female part of her family, and that our sisters were now of an age to do that. To this she merely said that she had not adverted to this circumstance & dropped the subject.

It is now perfectly open to you to speak to her & I have no doubt that, if you do it with gentleness & firmness, and can make her sensible of our sister's situation, she will be easily got the better of.

All our sisters desire their love and thanks for what you are doing for them. They are determined to be stout, and trust that you will support them.

I have told them of course not to begin the subject with the Queen, but should she speak to them upon it, not to deny that I had mentioned it to them.

The Queen seems anxious to see you & I hope that you will be able to come tomorrow.

1 Princess Augusta of Saxe-Gotha, the wife of Frederick Lewis, Prince of Wales (1707–1751); the parents of George III. (d. 1772.)
2 The Princesses Augusta (1737–1813); Elizabeth (1741–1759); Louisa Anne (1749–1768), and Caroline Matilda (1751–1775).

Pall Mall, Novr. 8th 1812.

NOTWITHSTANDING I have not hitherto been able to arrange that an immediate publicity might be given to a certain important subject[2] for the reasons I explain'd to you yesterday, & that it cannot but actually appear that no strong measure has yet been taken by the adverse party to warrant such an anticipation of it at the present moment after so many years of forbearance still, the proposed channel of communicating it, is so truly respectable, & desireable, that I am satisfied the period cannot be very far distant when such a step will be gladly adopted, & the sug- gestion (as it has been) most thankfully remember'd. At this time how- ever to have anything said upon it might be liable to a prejudice which I am sure, after your so recent & confidential a perusal of the case (as a transaction merely between ourselves, altho' in point of substance, pretty well known to you before) you would be very far from wishing to arouse. I am therefore induced from those considerations to hope that you will have the goodness to abstain from any part of it's discussion just now, & to await a little it's further progress. Be assured I feel most sensibly your past kindness, & cannot conceal from you how truly, & greatly, I should hold myself personally obliged & endebted to you for a con- tinuation of such kindness in future, on those peculiar points which I have already described to you, for being sincerely anxious for the possession of your friendship, I would gladly owe you an obligation that should un- feignedly cement us thro' our lives, & without any possible imputation on either the consistency or the value of our respective characters, for believe me that at all events, I am & ever shall be, with the most sincere regard & esteem, [etc.].

187 JAMES PERRY *to* COLONEL MCMAHON

Tavistock House, 9 Nov[r] 1812.

ON my return home last night, I was favoured with your obliging letter. I trust you will believe that it never entered into my mind to make use of the knowledge I possess in regard to the Delicate Investigation (coming to me as it did confidentially) without your express permission. Indeed I feel myself committed against all mention of what I knew pre-

1 Editor and proprietor of *The Morning Chronicle*, the leading Whig newspaper. (1756-1821.)
2 The charges against the Princess of Wales.

viously, unless the discussion should be taken up by others; in which case I am sure you would relieve me from all difficulty on the subject. The accurate perusal of the whole case serves to confirm me in the opinion I had formed from early knowledge of the particulars, that His Royal Highness has it at all times in his power to vindicate his own proceedings, and to settle the public judgement forever on the point of the Princess' conduct. It rests of course with him to decide on the proper time to make the case known, and until that time shall arrive, you may depend on my silence.[1]

In respect of other matters you are well aware of my long and ardent wishes for His Royal Highness' popularity; but you must be sensible that I cannot wholly abstain from animadversion on such matters as I think calculated to affect the country; but it is only where his measures or partialities are connected with the public interests of the realm that I have anything to do; And I should feel the most sensible gratification in having to hail his return to the sentiments that made me devoted to his service, with the most disinterrested feeling, for thirty years of my life.

Permit me to express to you the grateful sense which I have of your confidence, and my conviction of the integrity with which in your faithful attachment to His Royal Highness, you have constantly exerted yourself to promote his true honour and secure his happiness.

I have the honour to be [etc.].

188 GEORGE CANNING *to* COLONEL MCMAHON

Hinckley, Novr. 11, 1812.

You must not suppose from my long delay in thanking you for your letter of the 19th that I was insensible to the kindness which dictated it, & to the warmth with which you entered into my success at Liverpool.[2] I was detained at that place for ten days after my election by feastings— & had afterwards to make a circuit by Manchester for a similar purpose, before I could get quietly home—which I did not do till the end of last week.

I stay here till the end of this week—& by the end of *next* week I mean to be established at Gloucester Lodge.[3] Should you have any occasion to

1 The depositions taken against the Princess of Wales in 1806 were published in *The Morning Herald*, the Carlton House newspaper, on 13 March 1813. See No. 195.
2 See No. 178.   3 His house in London.

write to me, a line directed *there* would be duly forwarded to me on my journey. I should be very glad if you could tell me that it is true, as I have heard, that poor Sheridan is to find a refuge at Gatton. He lost Stafford, I hear, by his own (or his agent's) mismanagement.[1]

P.S. I hope you received the Liverpool papers with which I took the liberty of troubling you from time to time.

189 ROBERT THORNTON[2] *to* [COLONEL MCMAHON]

India House,
late Wedn[y] Eveng 11 Novr 1812.

LORD BUCKINGHAMSHIRE[3] has made no communication to the Chairman in contradiction to the arrangement before settled with his Lordship that Lord Moira was to be proposed to succeed Lord Minto[4] as Governor General, & likewise to be appointed Commander in Chief, but *without* a salary for the latter appointment.

Thus the Chairman on giving notice to the Court that he should take their sense by ballot next Wednesday had no power to do any thing, but lay before them these propositions exactly as stipulated with Lord Buckinghamshire. Finding this to be the case, & that we, the Chairs, could only proceed in the course predetermined, I persuaded Sir T. Metcalfe[5] to state in his place to the Court, what was a fact, viz[t] that he heard out of doors that Lord Moira was expecting the salary of both appointments, & that *we* had probably some misconception on the subject. The Chairman was obliged to say, he hoped not, but that it would be cleared up by the next Wednesday.

I own it will be very hard & difficult, tho' perhaps *not impossible*, to get the Court to vote the two salaries. It can only be done by the *strongest* interference of Government thro' the regular channel, Ld Buckinghamshire, & we must be forced to state it as their requisition, not as our own opinion or we certainly should be foiled. If I were to take

1 See Nos. 159, 160.
2 M.P. for Colchester; a Director (and in 1812 Deputy Chairman) of the East India Company.
3 President of the Board of Control.
4 Sir Gilbert Elliot, first Earl of Minto (1751–1814). Governor-General of Bengal, 1807–13. Barony, 1798; earldom, 1813.
5 Sir Thomas Theophilus Metcalfe (d. November 1813). A Director of the East India Company, and father of Lord Metcalfe, the Indian administrator and Governor-General of Canada.

the liberty of advising it would be that Sir Hugh Inglis[1] should *only* be addressed about this thro' Lord Buckinghamshire, or Lord Liverpool. Sir Hugh may make some objections, but I think he might be brought to put his shoulder to the proposition, & then it would be carried.

He is to wait upon Lord Buckinghamshire tomorrow morning at ten o'clock to report what passed in the Court, & he will not forget to communicate Sir T. Metcalfe's remark. Sir Hugh said to me, "I am very glad that Metcalfe made it, & that will take the load from us".

Lord Buckinghamshire would be very jealous, if he knew how far I *interested* myself in this matter, but gratitude, & a feeling that high & most respectable characters deserve a liberal reward for very important services, must plead my excuse. I *know you* will keep all this secret, & as every thing passed in a *secret* Court, tho' hereafter it may be known, I rely that you will not allude to my having prompted Sir T. Metcalfe to remark as he did.

I am going out of town this night to a public meeting at my borough where I am a steward but shall return on Sunday. Sir Hugh Inglis leaves town on Friday evening & will return Tuesday evening.[2]

On Wednesday next we shall both be likely to see Lord Buckinghamshire about ten o'clock before we proceed to the Court to settle the Governments of Bengal & Madras. With sincere regards I am ever [etc.].

190 COLONEL MCMAHON *to the* PRINCE REGENT

Carlton House, Novr. 12th, 1812.

THE enclosed *very confidential letter*[3] from Mr. Thornton, I think it right to lose no time in transmitting for your Royal Highness's particular & immediate information, as besides the secrecy enjoined for the reasons it assigns, I have held it absolutely necessary to preserve it with the same secrecy from the knowledge of Lord Moira, lest from the view he might take of the Commr. in Chief's salary being withheld by the parsimonious

1 A Director, and in 1812 Chairman, of the East India Company; father of Sir Robert Inglis, the Tory politician. (d. 1820.)

2 Moira owed his appointment as Governor-General of Bengal to the influence of the Prince Regent, not at all to that of the Government. He went to India to escape from his financial and political bankruptcy. Had the Liverpool Ministry given up the Catholic question he would have gone to Ireland as Lord-Lieutenant. "The Catholic claims," he wrote on 12 November, "if they cannot be overborne, are to be baffled. I can take no part in such a system: and it is desirable to be out of the way when the unavoidable consequences of such policy shall break forth. I could not support the Prince against my principles and my feelings; it would be the extreme of distress to me to go into ranks hostile to him, and I could not hope that I should be suffered to remain in any retreat."

3 No. 189.

arrangement of Lord Buckinghamshire, together, with the not thoroughly digested feelings of Lady L[oudoun] on the entire subject, so desirable a measure, looking to so many beneficial consequences from it, should after all Y.R.Hss's labours in bringing it so near to maturity, & accomplishment, be in a moment dash'd down, & frustrated, & which I fear might be the case if those proceedings were to come to their knowledge. The whole difficulty seems to arise from a desire on the part of Lord Buckinghamshire to protect the personal interest of Sir Geo: Nugent[1] (who was A.D.C. to the Marquis of Buckingham,[2] when his Lordship was Chief Secretary to him at the same time in Ireland)[3] for as it is not denied that Lord Moira is to have both the name, & powers of Commr. in Chief, a Lieutenant General, commanding the Army under him, would at once do away every objection on the score of pecuniary expenditure to the Company, supposing the Company to refuse making up the inconsiderable difference between such a Staff situation & Sir G. Nugent's present pay. I apprehend, Sir, it will be very material that before next Wednesday, Lord Buckinghamshire should be apprized by Y.R.Hss thro' Lord Liverpool, & by whatever mode you shall think proper, (such as your commands to me, in a line *ostensible* for Lord Liverpool, should it be your pleasure; at the same time returning me Thornton's letter for my guidance) that Y.R.Hss expects the Government, & Board of Controul, will give all their weight to this question at the India House on that day, for at present I understand the Control has a positive ascendancy, if chosen to be exerted, of 16 out of the 24 India Directors. Lord M[oira] and Lady L[oudoun], knowing nothing of all this, continue in high spirits, & pursuing their preparations for India. He wrote fully yesterday to the D[uke] of N[orfolk], & *thinks well of it*. I have seen Sheridan this evening, & was sorry to find that his boasted security appears to have turn'd out as I fear'd very visionary, for he last night got notice that two of his creditors had disclaim'd any further forbearance while he remain'd out of Parliament, & he sets off to'night for Hampshire. There is nothing stirring worth observation, & everything continues right & comfortable. I shall see Lowton[4] again tomorrow, & intended

---

1 Commander-in-Chief in India, 1812–13. Pursuant to a Resolution of the Court of Directors, 18 November 1812, Sir George Nugent, upon the arrival of Lord Moira in October 1813, assumed the appointment of Commander-in-Chief in Bengal and held it until December 1814, when this separate provincial appointment merged into the general appointment of Commander-in-Chief in India.

2 George Nugent-Temple-Grenville, first Marquis of Buckingham (1753–1813). Lord-Lieutenant of Ireland, 1782–3, and 1787–9.

3 Lord Buckinghamshire was Chief Secretary to the Lord-Lieutenant, 1789–93.

4 A solicitor whom Lord Thurlow had recommended to the Prince of Wales in 1805 as a person to be employed to collect evidence respecting the conduct of the Princess Caroline.

also to put myself in the way of Ly D[ouglas] but understanding that Sir J. D[ouglas][1] had written to Y.R.Hss, I thought it might be better to pause until I heard further.

191 COLONEL MCMAHON *to the* PRINCE REGENT

Carlton House, Novr. 16th 1812.

DOBLE with the box containing the various papers bearing your Royal Highness's signature arrived safely, & in good time this morning. In obedience to the most kind, & gracious letter which I had the honor & happiness to receive from Y.R.Hss, I have waited upon, and seen both Lords Liverpool, & Buckinghamshire, & have distinctly explain'd to each, the precise conditions on which the Governor Generalship, & Commander in Chief of India, had been proffer'd to Lord Moira, & that it was a *sine qua non* expectation in Y.R.Hss's mind, that those conditions should be strictly fulfill'd; by their jointly obtaining the consent, & ratification of the Court of Directors on the question to this effect, standing for Wednesday next. They both pleaded that in their respective interviews with Lord Moira, he had only ask'd to have the same appointment, & powers, which Lord Cornwallis[2] possess'd there, & that Lord Cornwallis had left the military salary with General Lake,[3] & that whether Sir G. Nugent should be recall'd or not, or to remain in a lesser gradation of command under Lord Moira, the salary, & allowances of Lord Moira would thereby in no shape alter, & that Lord Moira had not ever convers'd with either of them on the subject of salary, & only on the powers which were to belong to him, & in those they were perfectly agreed. I merely observ'd that the act of Lord Cornwallis in generously giving up the salary of Commr. in Chief to Lord Lake, they must please to recollect, was an act of his own free will, & might have personal motives for it's grace & favour, whereas it would now become a stipulated condition, strip'd of any such incentive. Lords Liverpool, &

1 Sir John Douglas and his wife had alleged that the Princess of Wales was delivered of a child in 1802. This was the main charge which was the subject of the "Delicate Investigation" in 1806. After his revival of the charge in 1813 he was suspended from employment in the Duke of Sussex's Household, and expelled from a masonic lodge. He died in 1814. His wife was enjoying a pension of £200 a year in 1823. In 1813 Princess Caroline received the following anonymous communication: "Does Her Royal Highness the Princess of Wales know that L—y D—g—s has lately been caught in a crim. con. affair with a M—e officer of Woolwich. The servant who discovered them has been put into solitary confinement."

2 Charles Cornwallis, first Marquis and second Earl Cornwallis (1738–1805). Governor-General of Bengal, 1786–93, and 1805.

3 Commander-in-Chief in India, July 1801 to July 1805.

Buckinghamshire were however to consult over the matter again this evening. I have since seen R. Thornton, & have agreed with him (to prevent the appearance of any failure in the appointment in the eye of the public) *not* to postpone the ballot on Wednesday next, with a view to this adjustment, but to carry at once the appointment of Lord Moira to be Governor General & Commr. in Chief, & to let the salary of the latter be fought after Y.R.Hss's return to town, when, as Thornton rightly observes, they will move you, Sir, to elevate Lord Minto to an Earldom, & then it will be entirely in your pleasure in the granting the one, to command the other point, should you think proper, & I have deem'd it adviseable to say *nothing* to Lord M[oira] until his appointment is irrevocably concluded.

This has been a day of such violent & incessant rain, & I have been so occupied in the above transaction that I have not been able to see Lowton since his interview with Sir J[ohn] D[ouglas], nor has he written to me this evening as I expected. Neither have I seen Ld M. but tomorrow I will write more fully, & in the mean while leave nothing unattended to, & at present *all*, thank God, is quite right.

192 COLONEL MCMAHON *to the* PRINCE REGENT

Carlton House,
Novr. 18th 1812, Six o'Clock P.M.

EXCEPTING, that your Royal Highness should know why such a deficiency in all points of information has happen'd to'night, I would not have presumed to trouble you with so uninteresting a letter; but Lowton who had promised I should punctually receive by half past 5 a detail of his proceedings, has made me no communication whatever, & the excessive storm & rain of the day, has not allow'd me a moment to seek him. Lord Moira having again received no answer from the D of Norfolk, imagines he defers a reply until he returns to town, which will not be before next Monday.

The ballot at the India House was not expected to take place sooner than seven or eight o'clock this evening, but there is no apprehension of any failure in the appointment. As all other things continue right, I console myself for this dearth of news, in the hope that Y.R.Hss will excuse it, by thinking on this occasion, that "no news is good news".

Carlton House, Novr. 19th 1812.

THE election yesterday at the India House was very successfully managed (thro' the exertions of Sir Hugh Inglis & Mr. R. Thornton & especially the latter) & Lord Moira appointed Govr General, & Commr in Chief of India. The appointments were put separately. On the first division for Govr General there were 17 to 6, & on the second for Commr. in Chief 14 to 7, there having been but 23 Directors present (Grant[1] not attending) & two not choosing (from personal motives towards Sir Geo: Nugent) to vote on the latter question. The Court did not break up till 10 o'clock, & no resolution has taken place on the subject of the Commr. in Chief's salary, although much observation attended it. Lord Moira from waiting on the Chairs, the Board of Control &c.ʳ I have not been able to see today, but I am to be with him early tomorrow in order to prepare him on several points which Thornton has instructed me to explain to him. Lowton's occupations in attending for those two days past on Lord Ellenborough's sittings has prevented his pursuing Edward's business in the way I could have wish'd & expected, but I enclose your Royal Highness his note of this evening, by which he promises somewhat for to'morrow. I likewise enclose a note from Lord Liverpool of this morning respecting Y.R.Hss going to Parliament on Monday the 30th. The news from the North[2] goes in an accompanying box from Lord Castlereagh. Everything else right & pleasant.

194 THE EARL OF LIVERPOOL *to* COLONEL MCMAHON

Fife House, 19th Novr. 1812.

LORD LIVERPOOL presents his compliments to Colonel MacMahon & understands, upon a reference to precedents, that there does not appear the smallest ground for the difficulties stated by Sir Isaac Heard,[3] and that there can be no objection to the Prince Regent opening the Parliament in the House of Lords from the Chair of State or Throne.

1 Charles Grant (1746–1823), a Director of the East India Company, and father of Lord Glenelg.
2 News from Russia. Napoleon began his retreat from Moscow on 18 October.
3 [1730–1822.] Garter King-of-arms.

195 James Perry *to* [Colonel McMahon]

Strand, 20 Novr. 1812.

I DID myself the honour to call at your door this morning to thank you for your most obliging note of yesterday; and at the same time to ask you whether I ought to permit the insinuation of The Herald[1] to pass unnoticed respecting the Princess of Wales *political* advisers. It was my intention to have said a few words to justify my friends against the scandal; but I should be glad to know your sentiments on the subject.

196 Peter Stuart *to* Colonel McMahon[2]

85 *Hatton Garden*, Sunday Nov. 22/12.

As one gentleman to another, I am ashamed to say, that I have now written to you twice or thrice without the smallest notice on your part. Let me know, my dear Sir, how to please, or in what I have offended, and *two months* shall not elapse in vain after your promise of a satisfactory interview on the subject.

Had I written for the sake of popularity, I need not appeal to your own good sense, that, with the knowledge, powers, and DOCUMENTS, which I possess, I could have much easier produced a pamphlet of fifty times the public attraction; but I am a child of attachment and affection, and wish to shew my duty and attentions to a Prince whose patriotism and discernment will I hope always be proverbial, and from whom I had been uniformly taught to believe I might, whenever in his most gracious power, expect every gratification of protection and patronage. You perfectly know what I mean; and as many transactions of a delicate nature have passed between us, allow me to hope that I shall hear from you for an interview in the course of a day or two.

The pamphlet, pardon the presumption, presents a double claim—that from the Prince Regent, and that from his Ministers. His Royal Highness has therefore only to issue or hint his commands or wishes, when there must be an immediate concurrence of sentiment—provided my worthy friend, Colonel McMahon whose partiality I have constantly experienced, recommends it.

Inclosed are two papers,[3] whose public authorities in my favour are

1 *The Morning Herald.* Its proprietor was Henry Bate Dudley, whom the Prince now created a Baronet. (See No. 114.) The British Museum does not possess a copy of its files.
2 He had addressed his earlier letter (No. 146) "Dear Colonel". No. 200 is addressed "Sir"; No. 202, "My dear Sir".
3 Missing.

highly respectable. Several other publications have also made similar declarations; so that I cannot help thinking that I have in this instance alone been of considerable service both to the Prince Regent and to his Government.

197 QUEEN CHARLOTTE *to the* PRINCE REGENT

Windsor, the 22d/Novbr 1812.

YOU will receive through the hands of the Earl of Liverpool, copies of another letter from the Princess of Wales, which she desired might be communicated to you, & with it also my answer to her which only touches upon those subjects which relate to myself alone. I do hope that it will be found very mild & moderate & therefore meet with approbation.

I shall not allow myself to make any further remark upon the contents of the Princesses letter leaving that to yr own judgement, but I can not possibly pass over in silence the very *indiscreet manner* which is the most delicate expression I can make use of, in which she reproaches me for having acquiesced in yr wishes to have Charlotte established at Windsor, accusing me of being the cause that her education is not properly followed up, which I can explain in no other way than that she means, that my love for you & affection for the child upon this occasion is a matter of imprudence.

There is one satisfaction I feel at this moment, that you have quite the right on your side, & that pursuing the same course you have hitherto done all just people will approve of it.

I have now no more to add than that I am [etc.].

198 COLONEL MCMAHON *to the* PRINCE REGENT

Carlton House, Novr. 25th 1812.

YOUR Royal Highness's approbation to the choice of Mr. Abbot[1] as Speaker to the House of Commons, was pronounc'd at 12 o'clock today by the Lord Chancellor,[2] & being then form'd into a House has continued

---

1 Charles Abbot, first Baron Colchester (1757–1829), Speaker of the House of Commons, 1802–17.
2 Eldon.

ever since till 4 o'clock in swearing in members at the table. Notwithstanding the many rumours to the contrary, I have *good* authority for believing that neither Lord Wellesley, or Canning, have the most distant intention of joining the Opposition. Lord Temple,[1] I understand has been trying to intrigue for those few days past with the former, but to no effect; & there certainly has been something, in the air of coquetting, between Lords W[ellesley] and Holland.

If anything should come forward in Parliament respecting the P[rince]ss of W[ales] I am inform'd that Lord Essex[2] is to give H.R.Hss the amiable mantle in the H. of Lords. I have nothing material now to communicate, & I hope Y.R.Hss shall find everything quiet & right on your arrival tomorrow.

199 SAMUEL WHITBREAD *to* COLONEL McMAHON

Dover Street, Nov. 26, 1812.

BY the alteration effected in the Pit of Drury Lane Theatre for the protection of the Prince Regent's box I have every reason to believe, from observation, that the object is attained: and that His Royal Highness cannot now be annoyed by the intrusion which was so offensive to His Royal Highness when he honoured the Theatre with his presence. Should anything further prove necessary, it will be done.

I shall shortly have it in my power to lay before you an account of the extra expences incurred by the alteration, and additional furniture necessary to render his present box commodious and fit for the reception of His Royal Highness; and I have reason to hope the charges will not be deemed in any way extravagant.[3]

The Prince Regent to Queen Charlotte, 2 December 1812. (*Taylor Papers*, p. 78, but there dated Tuesday night, December 1, 1812.)
Queen Charlotte to the Prince Regent, 2 December 1812. (*Ibid.* p. 74.)
The Prince Regent to Queen Charlotte, 3 December 1812. (*Ibid.* p. 81.)
Queen Charlotte to the Prince Regent, 4 December 1812. (*Ibid.* p. 82.)

1 Richard Temple Nugent Brydges Chandos Grenville, first Duke of Buckingham and Chandos (1776–1839), son of the first Marquis of Buckingham (1753–1813). Created Duke, 1822. At this time, M.P. for Buckinghamshire.
2 George Capel, fifth Earl of Essex (1757–1839). A Whig Peer.
3 Drury Lane Theatre, destroyed by fire on 24 February 1809, was re-built in 1811–12 and re-opened in October 1812, largely by Whitbread's efforts.

85, *Hatton Gardens*,
Monday, Dec. 7/[18]12.

A SERIOUS illness, from which I am now almost recovered, has prevented me from seeing you sooner.

Excuse me for saying, that although I have often reflected on your advice with every degree of esteem, yet I have never been able to collect confidence equal to the irksome task of addressing such an august personage as His Royal Highness the Prince Regent.

Permit me therefore to assure you, that I must beg leave to commit my case to the management of a much abler and a far more persuasive advocate. Past experience teaches me, that I may repose with the greatest hope on your friendship; and I must intreat you to use your influence at this time in my favour with His Royal Highness the Prince Regent, whose affable deportment, liberal sentiments, and patriotic conduct, have justly endeared him to a nation whom he was happily destined to govern.

Allow me, Sir, to request, that after offering my most humble duties to His Royal Highness the Prince Regent, you would represent, that four months ago I had the satisfaction of being the author of a pamphlet intituled [*sic*] "*Thoughts on the State of the Country*", &c &c that this pamphlet has had the singular good fortune of being the *first* and *only one* in vindication of the PRINCE REGENT and HIS GOVERNMENT; that its author, like most authors, is at this time far from being rich; that he is still considerably more than two hundred pounds *minus* by paper, print, &c &c; that some other embarrassments, not indeed to a great amount, may also be superadded; that His Royal Highness's most gracious notice of the author might serve to stimulate some abler writer in so just a cause; and that as literary men have often been rewarded by *permanent* situations under Government, a hint to that effect from the Prince Regent, in favour of the present writer, would by the Minister—whose cause is also warmly supported—be construed into a Royal command.

You can, Sir, fully testify, that on many occasions I have availed myself of opportunities to prove my duty and attachment to His Royal Highness; and as often as it may be within my power, I shall zealously embrace the same line of conduct.

Earnestly soliciting you, Sir, to submit these facts to the Prince Regent, by most humbly requesting on my part, that he would condescend to hear the contents of this letter, recommended to His Royal Highness's consideration by your better judgment and discretion, I have the honour of being, [etc.].

Windsor, the 11th Decbr 1812.

IT is a pleasure to take up the pen when it is to convey congratulations upon a succession of such glorious news as you have of late communicated to me in so kind a manner. The surrender of General Augereau[1] with a corps of 2000 men to the Russians is the strongest proof of discontent in the enemy's army, & tho necessity may have induced the General to such a step, I can not think it would have been executed if Napoleons downfall was not foreseen by his own friends if one may call them by that name who are forced to serve under him: and you have my sincerest prayers & wishes that this may be followed up with an account of the tyrants personal fall as soon as possible.

I am very sorry to learn that the gout still continues upon you, & hope that during this very severe weather you will take care not to expose yourself too soon into the cold air. I shall with great pleasure come to town on Tuesday next, when I hope to find you better & to assure you by word of mouth how sincerely I am [etc.].

202 PETER STUART *to* COLONEL MCMAHON

85 *Hatton Garden*, Dec. 16, 1812.

WHEN I last saw you, I thought you seemed displeased that I had applied to any other person. Permit me to say, that it was very natural I should present a copy of the pamphlet to a noble personage whose family was particularly noticed in it; but I assure you, upon my honour, that *I never made the smallest mention of your name, or the most distant allusion to it, or to that of any other individual connected with the Prince Regent.*

I cannot charge my memory with any thing but the kindest and most cordial friendship on your part towards me. I recollect it with great satisfaction and pleasure; am one of the very last men in the world to forget favours; and should be exceedingly sorry, indeed, that you entertained any improper impressions of an interference which was very handsomely meant to serve me, without in the most remote degree offending you, or any other gentleman whatever.

The noble personage, indeed, has no idea, even at this very moment, that I have the smallest knowledge of you, or ever saw you. I am particularly cautious in making use of distinguished names as those with

---

1 Pierre François Charles Augereau, Duke of Castiglione, Marshal of France (1757–1816).

whom I am acquainted; and, had you not noticed the noble Lord's recommendation, his name would have never even been hinted at by me.

Now allow me, my dear Sir, to avail myself of this opportunity of requesting that you would make an effort to introduce some amendment to to [*sic*] the last act of Royal condescension, otherwise I shall not be enabled to pursue my plan of a weekly paper in support of the Prince Regent. It is truly hard, that the vindicator of the Prince Regent and his Government—and the very first writer who has attempted the task—and now considerably minus—should not receive a compensation equal to the one-half of what was given for the suppression of a book advancing vile and calumnious insinuations against a Royal Duke.

I cannot fail of receiving, with the most grateful respect, whatever His Royal Highness is pleased to bestow; but let me hope, that, even on the score of old services—which you know were numerous and confidential—that some amendment be recommended. I was always some years ago given to understand that the *modicum* advanced would be doubled or tripled as a *permanency*, whenever His Royal Highness by the accession of power, was enabled to do so. These suggestions are submitted with every degree of sensibility and most dutiful attachment to His Royal Highness the Prince Regent.

Begging three or four lines from you, and that our friendship for each other may not cease, I am, Dear Sir, [etc.].

203 JAMES PERRY *to* COLONEL MCMAHON

Strand, 16 Decr. 1812.

I DID myself the honour to call at your door, but was not so fortunate as to find you at home. I have since fortunately seen Mr. Adam to whom I communicated the fact that I have this day received an advertisement of which I inclose you the copy. It carreis [*sic*] on its face the evidence of its origin by the promise of *fac similes*. I understand that it is a garbled narrative with observations—I submit to you whether it will not be adviseable to be before hand, that the whole truth without a remark may be laid before the public at once.

[*Enclosure*]

(*Copy*)

Illustrious Personages

In the press and speedily will be published in

one Volume 8°.

AN authentic narrative of facts with correspondence and *fac similes* to prove the authenticity of the letters to such as may be acquainted with the handwriting of the parties. Among the parties to this correspondence are the heads of the Royal Family and it relates solely to matters in which that Family and these Kingdoms have an equal interest.[1]

204 JAMES PERRY *to* COLONEL MCMAHON

Pall Mall, 17 Decr. 1812.

I AM sorry that I missed seeing you when you did me the honour to call. I write this at your own table; for I am most anxious to learn your determination on the notice which appears in the papers of this day.

I suspect the volume will be published on Saturday—and all the journals in the Kingdom will teem with extracts. If you agree with me in the prudence of giving the first impression, my notice must be written this evening; in which I should say that to prevent misrepresentation I would lay the whole before the public without a comment. Let me hear from you; I shall be in the Strand.

1 This advertisement was in *The Morning Chronicle* on the 17th (for *personages* read *personage*). Lady Charlotte Campbell wrote, on 2 December: "I have only observed the advertisement (of the letters the Princess of Wales wished to have published) once inserted in the *Morning Chronicle*, and it is not, I find, yet generally understood, as being a genuine document. I am in hopes that some compromise may be offered from the other side; and the less that is said about it, therefore, I think, the better. I dread the publication of these epistles, as, however great it may make her wrongs appear...yet it will give colour to a charge of breach of trust in making letters public that were never written to meet the public eye." (*Diary*, I, 164 [1838 ed.]) "Mr. Conant, the police magistrate," she wrote on 20 December, "went to Messrs Longman and Rees, and asked what they meant by the paragraph they had put in the newspapers, concerning a publication of letters....Mr. Conant threatened them with the law and foretold their ruin, and the Lord knows what—but Messrs Longman and Rees replied, they should take care not to publish anything actionable." (I, 199.)

Southill, Decbr. 20, 1812.

I HOPE this will be the last time of my giving you any trouble on the subject of Drury Lane Theatre, but I am now enabled to state a sum which I hope will be thought moderate, & which I think the Committee may fairly be content to receive for the alterations & addition of furniture &c, consequent upon the exchange of boxes between His Royal Highness the Prince Regent & Lord Holland: & I have taken the liberty to address you now, because I am very desirous of closing every account before the new year begins.

You have seen what has been done, & His Royal Highness has been graciously pleased to express his approbation of it. I will not state items but if the sum of £600 should not be thought too much, I will undertake to say the Committee will be satisfied with it.

The whole is paid but it will form a refund.

In this is not included, nor is it at all intended to include any charge for the alteration in the Pit for the protection of His Royal Highness's box.

I feel that I have occupied so much of your time I will say no more.

206 PRINCESS MARY[1] *to the* PRINCE REGENT

Decr the 28, [1812].

I MUST begin this letter with stating in consequence of the Queen having shown me a letter she wrote to you to-day that I never named Miss Scott[2] with an idea of *presumeing to recomend her* or any body else to be placed about your daughter.[3] The real fact is that upon the Queen saying she was of opinion that should the Dss of Leeds accept the situation offered *she* never could undertake it without an assistant & that Charlotte was much too old to have an other Sub Governess therefore according to her ideas it ought to be some young woman who *she could admit* into her society & dine with us &c &c., not understanding the sort of person & rank the Queen wished, I certainly did say "Do you mean

1 Fourth daughter of George III (1776–1857). In 1816 she married her cousin, William Frederick, second Duke of Gloucester (1776–1834).

2 Lord Eldon's daughter.

3 At the end of 1812 Lady de Clifford resigned her post of Governess to Princess Charlotte. It is generally stated that she resigned on account of ill health, but the real reasons are given in Nos. 216, 217, 508 and 509. The Dowager Duchess of Leeds, the second wife of the fifth Duke of Leeds (1751–99), was then put in charge of Princess Charlotte's education.

a young woman of Miss Scott's time of life & her rank"—not with the smallest idea it should be repeated out of the room or *represented* that I named her in preference to any body, for though I have heard all that is most amiable & good of the Chancellor's daughter, and find her most *agreable* in *society* & believe her to be a very *sensible* woman & well informed, yet I really don't pretend to *know her* beyond what I have seen of her in our assembly room, therefore *never could have* recomend[ed] a *person* I am so little acquainted with (if such a thought *had entered my head*) as to do so *ill judged* & so *important* a thing as to presume to recomend any body—as I feel fully sensible I am perfectly unfit to judge who is *proper* or fit to undertake so very arduous a *situation*. I only pray God whoever is with your daughter may do her duty HONESTLY by *you* as *well* AS HER and do you both *justice* in your diferent *situations*.

The King has passed a quiet day, he has been shaved & it went off well. Dundas attempted to make himself known to the K. but no conversation took place, as the King was fully occupied with his own ideas.

207 QUEEN CHARLOTTE *to the* PRINCE REGENT

Windsor, 28th Decbr. 1812.

SINCE I had the pleasure of seeing you my thoughts have been chiefly occupied with our conversation, & after our breakfast yesterday morning myself & the sisterhood had above an hours consultation upon the subject, & as you wished that we should fairly state our oppinion I am encouraged to relate what passed in the female Council.

By some things that Lady De Clifford dropt to some of your sisters it is evident that *she herself* was the *cause* of Charlotte's *dislike to Windsor* by *representing the manner* in which it was *done* as *being kidnapped* there, and very offensive to the childs feeling. Therefore would it not be better when you have settled with the Dutchess of Leeds to let Lady De Clifford mention the step she has taken of asking her dismission to the child that it may not come upon her like *a coup de foudre* & she have it in her power to complain of not having been fairly dealt with, besides that it may lead her to complain of it *at a place where she will be listened to*. Moreover I am sure that the old lady tho very desirous that we should not nam[e] her interviews with you, that she has informed your daughter *of it*, but how *far* she has put her into the *secret I do not know*.

If the Ds of L. can be persuaded to come to your assistance it is of the utmost consequence that with her almost every individual servant should be changed, & those which are to succeed them, chosen by her, my reason for this is that Charlotte has an eye to a German servant, nursery maid to the Duke of Brunswicks[1] children now in Germany which is the reason that she always made her sick servant better for fear of having one taken which was not her own choice & this Lady De Clifford *knows.*—Mrs. Gagerine's[2] daughter as well as those of Lion [? Lyon] have been *too much her companions,* a society which must be broke at *once,* for you know very well "que telle société devient pernic[ie]use par la vile flatterie dont elle est d'ordinaire accompagnée".

I most sincerely wish that the D. of Leeds may be persuaded to come into your proposal, but I fear her health will not permit her to undertake such a charge without some assistance. By this I do not mean another Lady of the Bed Chamber nor a Sub-Governess but a person as a Companion the Dutchess could put trust & confidence in when she is necessitated to absent herself & to which you may at any time when Charlotte gets an establishment make her a Bed Chamber woman or leave her as a Companion. Your sister Mary has named one which I think would be a trouvaille in Miss Scott the Chancellor's daughter. She is sensible, chearfull & a very agreable woman in society, universally beloved & well spoken of, & I am sure known by the Dutchess, & I can not help thinking that when the proposal is made to the Dutchess such an indulgence being held out to her would make her undertake the charge with less difficulty, & this the more you consider it the more you will find assistance necessary.

I have now opened my mind with that of [the] sisterhood most sincerely, & beg it may remain amongst us alone excepting to Lord Chichester & beg you will not give any directions to Ldy De Clifford untill you have seen Lrd Chichester & untill you have seen me again as perhaps by that time I may be informed of more things necessary for you to know, & when you shall think it fit for me to come up to London I shall be ready even to stay a day or two that it may be settled but pray see Lord Chichester first to whom alone this may be shewn but to nobody else.[3]

1 Frederick William, Duke of Brunswick (1771–1815), the Princess of Wales' brother. He fought in the Peninsular War and was killed at Quatre Bras.
2 Princess Charlotte's dresser. She died on 1 July 1813.
3 Lady Chichester was the daughter of the fifth Duke of Leeds by his first wife.

Downing Street,
Thursday Morning [? December 1812 or early in 1813].

AFTER leaving Carlton House I sought Street,[1] but could not find him—I wrote to desire that he would call upon me either in Downing St., or at the House of Commons. Hearing nothing of him, I went from the House between 8 & 9 to the Adelphi where he lives, & as he was not at home I sat down & wrote the heads of such an article as I wished to appear in to-day's Courier; & I left word that he should be with me very early this morning—According to my desire, he came to me a little while ago, & I had much conversation with him upon the several subjects respecting which the Regent did me the honour to speak to me.

In a few words I will give you an idea of what passed between us.

I first discussed with him the possibility of *buying over The News.*[2] He deprecated the idea of making the attempt, observing to me that such a Sunday paper would not be useful if bought, & that any attempt now made by us would inevitably produce *against us* the same kind of disclosure as was now, in the case of Lady Perceval,[3] so injurious to the Princess.—Here I interrupted him by saying that I had understood that the idea of purchasing the *News* had originated with himself, & that he had mentioned it to Yarmouth—No, replied he, it never entered into my thoughts that it w'd be useful or practicable to purchase *The News*, but in the course of conversation I merely remarked that if in the present instance *that paper* c'd be induced to make public all that he knew, our cause would gain greatly. I then asked him whether he could be instrumental in making the attempt to obtain such publicity, & this he has promised to do.

If we succeed, I shall rejoice; If we fail, I shall not be surprised; but at all events I do venture to persuade myself that both for his own sake &

1 Peter Street, to whom Daniel Stuart had transferred the management of his newspaper, *The Courier*, in 1811.

2 See No. 148. The Princess of Wales declared at the end of November that this paper had been bought by Carlton House, and that the editor was intending to publish "a correspondence, which he declares to have passed between the Princess herself, and Lady Anne Hamilton, and Lord Perceval, which Correspondence her Royal Highness says is a forgery". (Lady Charlotte Campbell's *Diary*, I, 161.) This correspondence was published in *The News* on 4 April 1813 and was copied by *The Courier* on the 5th.

3 Bridget, Viscountess Perceval (d. 1826), the wife of John, Viscount Perceval, who succeeded his father as fourth Earl of Egmont in 1822. For her connexion with *The News* and the Princess of Wales, see the pamphlet, "The Important Trial of John Mitford, on the prosecution of Lady Viscountess Perceval, for perjury at Guildhall on Thursday, 24 February 1814, before Lord Ellenborough, forming a clue to the discussions which took place relative to the affairs of H.R.H. the Princess of Wales, in the beginning of the year 1813. By the Editor of *The News*. London, 1814." The editor and proprietor of *The News* was Thomas Adderley Phipps.

for his Government's sake the Regent will approve of my not being ostensible in this business. I do not wish to make professions; but I think I may say that when I can really be of use I shall not be found backward in the Regent's cause, & that if I wish to unite discretion with zeal it is from a conviction that one false step might be most injurious to His Royal Highness.—It was sometimes thought during the general election that I might have done more—Has not the Parliament proved a good one, & has it not been incalculably advantageous even to the Regent himself that my name has never once been called in question?

After having finished what we had to say respecting *The News*, I asked Street as oftentimes I have asked him before whether he could put me in the way of getting a good *morning* paper. His answer was, Why mine is a London as well as a country paper; & by attempting to have *two avowedly Party papers* you would destroy the efficiency of each. I then said to him, I am quite sure, Street, that when you were half drunk at Lord Yarmouth's you held different language; & I am equally convinced that were I to set up a new morning paper, you would be the first to cry it down & to be jealous of it. He laughed & owned that it might be so, & that no Party ever had or ever could have more than one organ:— That this was the case with the Opposition in respect to the Morning Chronicle, & that such always had been & ever must be the case with all Parties.

He left me with an assurance that he would have the article in this day's Courier, & that he would do all in his power to prevail upon the editor of *The News* to make a general disclosure.

For brevity sake I have given you but the outline of what passed.

My task is no easy one I assure you. I did not like to trouble the Regent yesterday with long explanations; but in truth I believe that I might make it clear as noonday that had the whole discussion in the Courier been from the first left to Street & me, the result sh^d have been far different. The Regent very much mistakes me, & I w^d fain add very little knows me if he thinks that I would be lukewarm where he is concerned. It would be strange indeed if I were not bound to him by ever the warmest feeling of gratitude & attachment; but I scruple not to say that on his account & on his account solely I did disapprove of the line which was pursuing.

I did not attempt to silence Street; but I told him that clamour and declamation would be idly kicking against the pricks, & that we should be fighting with the air until we had new facts to go upon—I swear that weeks & weeks ago I foretold to Street all that has happened. I sh'd rejoice to be confronted with him; & I know that he would now declare that I was right. It was by the violence (not resting upon new facts) of some of the articles in the Courier that we turned the public against us; & it was this which from the very beginning I had so greatly dreaded. I always said to Street, let us be quiet—Our appearing so will set the others off the guard, & the instant that they have committed an imprudence we will strike the blow—I was not listened to; & as I could do no good I withdrew. At length the imprudence was committed. Lady Perceval was notoriously the agent of the Princess. It would not have answered our end to have done other than attack the agent; but seeing that the moment had arrived when I might attempt to do good, I went to Street & urged him to insert an article—The one which he did insert was tamer than what I should have advised, but he was afraid of risking the popularity of his paper.

I have written a much longer letter than I had intended. I will only add that my heart and soul will be at work when I see the means of doing good; & that if I have been thought lukewarm or supine I have been misjudged. I saw that the work was in other hands, & I had neither the means nor hope of doing good.

209 Augustus Cavendish Bradshaw *to* Colonel McMahon

Friday Even. [? 1812].

I RECEIVED the enclosed[1] & as I understand from the servant by the usual Treasury messenger. If so I imagine they do not wish to remove me & want my support. Anxious as I may be, (in the unpleasant situation in which I stand as to vacating &c &c) to retain my office I should be equally as well satisfied to loose it & vote against them shd that be the sentiment of *the Prince* & indeed shd his Royal Highness remain neutral I will take no part without his consent & approbation.[2]

210 The Prince Regent *to the* Duke of Northumberland

Copy. *Carlton House*, 4th Jany. 1813.

IT is with the most heartfelt concern that I have received officially through my brother[3] by your Grace's particular desire, your request to retire from the Service, as well as from the command of the Regiment of Royal Horse Guards.

1 Presumably a "Treasury Note". 2 Bradshaw resigned his seat early in 1817.
3 The Duke of York, the Commander-in-Chief of the Army.

I had flattered myself, my dear Duke, that the steadiness of my friendship *personally* to you for so many years, and the uniformity of my sentiments and conduct during that long series down to the present moment, might have secured me, (at least in your Grace's opinion) against even the suspicion of any want of attention, still more of neglect towards you in the most distant degree. Relying, my dear friend, upon your giving me full credit for those feelings, and for such conduct towards you, I wrote you about three weeks since, a letter, which I had hoped would have proved highly satisfactory to you in its explanation as it was entirely dictated by those sentiments. However it is with the deepest regret that I now find I have failed in the object I had so much at heart. Still I cannot help cherishing the flattering hope, that all this misunderstanding may, and has arisen from some unfortunate misapprehension, or from some inconceiveable misrepresentation; I therefore have desired and directed my brother to be silent upon the subject, and to suspend all steps in consequence of it, until I have the pleasure of hearing from you again, when I cannot but hope, that upon a reconsideration of the whole of the case, you will bring yourself to view it under different colors, assuring you at the same time, my dear Duke, that whatever your decision may ultimately be, I shall never cease to entertain through life for you the same sentiments of affection, regard, & esteem, that I ever have done, and with which I remain, [etc.].

211 COLONEL MCMAHON *to the* PRINCE REGENT

Bath, January 8th 1813.

IT was my intention to have written your Royal Highness by Wednesday's post the result of my interview with Sir Jas. Mackintosh, but the enclosed note will explain the reason why he defer'd seeing me till yesterday, when it became too late to communicate the particulars of our conversation; but by this delay I have derived the further advantage of receiving this morning the letter (which I likewise enclose) that will still better detail to Y.R.Hss his general disposition with the circumstances attending his immediate situation.

I am quite sure that he is eager to manifest a personal devotion to Y.R.Hss, & that nothing will ever induce him to depart from the respect which belongs to that feeling, but he is unluckily I perceive already too deeply engaged with Ld. Cawdor[1] to come in for the County of Nairn,

1 John Campbell, first Baron Cawdor (d. 1821). Raised to the peerage, 1796.

to shake off at this time a connexion which he does not appear to be over firmly wedded to, & which a little attention and address in the progress of the Session may entirely wean him from.

212 SIR JAMES MACKINTOSH *to* COLONEL MCMAHON

Bath, 8th Jany 1813.

IN consequence of what passed yesterday I take the liberty of requesting that you will lay my humble duty before His Royal Highness & assure him of the gratitude which I feel for the high honour which he does me by his gracious remembrance of my efforts in his service.[1] It is still farther enhanced by your intimation that His Royal Highness would be disposed to shew that remembrance whenever any change of circumstances should allow.

Dispositions so gracious & condescending cannot fail to embitter my regret at the painful & unexpected necessity under which I feel myself of declining for the present any public station connected with the political Administration of Great Britain.

The trifling services which His Royal Highness is pleased to recollect must have derived their whole value from the sincerity of that dutiful & respectful attachment towards him which they manifested & which has actuated me throughout my whole life. No part which I may take either in or out of Parliament in discussing the measures of any Administration can affect the steadiness of that attachment. It may I trust rather afford me opportunities of proving its constancy, & the consistency of such sentiments with the independent discharge of political duty.

I took the liberty of mentioning to you that I was engaged in the composition of a History of Great Britain from the Revolution & you seemed to think that there would be no impropriety in humbly soliciting His Royal Highness's orders for copies of such papers or extracts of papers from public offices as might be material to my work & might on due consideration not seem unfit to be communicated.[2]

If you should continue to be of that opinion I should consider your mentioning it to His Royal Highness as an additional proof of the kindness which I have always experienced in our personal intercourse.

1 Mackintosh had been Recorder of Bombay from 1804 to 1811.
2 His *History of the Revolution in England in 1688* was published in 1834, two years after his death.

The repositories particularly meant are the Paper Office[1] & His Majesty's Library.[2] It is the History of the establishment of His Royal Highness's family in this Kingdom & if my talents were equal to the purity of my intentions & to the magnitude of the work it might be thought on national grounds to deserve the assistance which I now very humbly solicit.

213 THE REV. JAMES STANIER CLARKE[3] *to the* PRINCE REGENT

Library. [1813.]

I s it your pleasure, Sir, to allow me the audience of a few minutes this morning; that I may receive your Royal Highness's further instructions respecting Sir James Mackintosh's access to the very valuable Stuart Papers.[4] I should not, Sir, discharge my duty, as the faithful and devoted servant of your Royal Highness, if I did not feel very nervous, & watchful, over every thing in the Department you have been pleased to place me, which in the most remote degree may affect your Royal Highness's kind & liberal courtesy to every one.

At the beginning of the French Revolution Sir James Mackintosh printed his celebrated pamphlet styled Vindiciæ Gallicæ in answer to Mr. Burke, and this work, Sir, was so tainted & poisoned with the venom of democracy that I cannot sleep until I am well assured of the present principles of Sir James in his intended History.

It is for your great & superior mind, Sir, to decide respecting this.

214 THE DUKE OF NORTHUMBERLAND *to* COLONEL MCMAHON

Alnwick Castle, 8th Janry 1813.

I MUST trouble you to deliver the accompanying letter to H:R:H:. I confess it is a bitter pill to be made to swallow, after 53 years services; but after finding every attempt to recover that indulgence, for the Regt, which it cannot be denied it has enjoyed for 78 years, wholly ineffectual, and that the past services of an old General, now fourth on the list,

1 Now the Public Record Office.
2 Now the King's Library, in the British Museum.
3 The Prince's domestic chaplain since 1799, and Librarian, at Carlton House (1765?–1834).
4 Then preserved at Carlton House; now at Windsor. "I go to the Library at Carlton House four hours of three days in the week to make extracts from them", wrote Mackintosh on 3 April 1813. See No. 249.

entitle him to no weight in military affairs, when compared to the future expected services of an half pay Captain of Light Dragoons, it is high time for those, qui ont blanchis sous l'harnois, to retire, before they are quite flung up into the garret as useless lumber.

You are a witness, my dear Colonel, of the zeal, and devotion with which I have on all occasions exerted myself for H:R:H:, as well as of the steady and immoveable attachment I showed towards H:R:H; when many of those, to whom he had been most kind and attentive, (nay even Lord Moira himself) shamefully abandoned him.[1] In so doing I was not actuated by any interested motives whatsoever. It was a most sincere affection (if I may be allowed to make use of so familiar a term) that united me to his interests. That same attachment will still continue, on my part, let H:R:H: decide in this business as he may think proper. I cannot help however thinking that some misrepresentation has taken place on the subject and we all know, my dear Colonel, misrepresentations can do a great deal of mischief. Nay, even H:R:H: himself has formerly felt the truth of this remark, otherwise I cannot bring myself to think, that for the mere putting an officer into the Blues, H:R:H: woud have deviated from what had been usual for the last 78 years, & have stopped the promotion of the Officers, in a Regt long distinguished for its bravery, & good discipline, just at the moment a considerable part was ordered upon foreign service. Nay, I am even vain enough to think, that your wishes woud otherwise have possibly had some weight with H:R:H:. But as I before said, let H:R:H: decide whichever way he may, in this business, my attachment to him will remain unchanged. Whether Captain Murray, or the Regiment and myself as their present Colonel, may carry the day, I may in the first case, feel sore & hurt and withdraw from the service, but I will still, as an independent, tho' private individual, make use of my influence, and property, to render H:R:H: every service in my power towards the support of his Government. May the Almighty God ever shower down blessings on his head, & may his government of the country be ever attended with glory and happiness.

Adieu my dear Colonel. We all unite in the offer of our regards to you and Mrs. Mac-Mahon. Clouds will sometimes pass between us & the sun, but I hope some favorable breeze will soon disperse them.

I cannot conclude without repeating to you, that I am most thoroughly convinced that you have done every thing that the most sincere friendship coud dictate, to avert this unpleasant denouement.

1 See No. 37.

Alnwick Castle, 8th January 1813.

I HAD the honour of receiving your Royal Highness's letter on Wednesday night, but as the post does not leave this place upon a Thursday, it was not in my power, to have the honour of sending your Royal Highness an answer sooner.

Nothing, be assured, Sir, can flatter me so much, as there is nothing I value so highly, as the continuance of your Royal Highness's good opinion, and esteem; and there are few things in this world, to which I woud not rather submit, than endanger the loss of them.

But I must intreat your Royal Highness to consider there does not appear to be any instance of an Officer being appointed from either the half pay, or from another Regiment to any vacant commission, in the Royal Regiment of Horse Guards, of a rank superior to that of a Cornet, during the whole time the Duke of Argyle [1]—the Duke of Somerset [2]—the Duke of Richmond [3] (grandfather to the present Duke)—Lord Ligonier [4]—Lord Granby [5]—Field Marshal Conway [6]—and the late Duke of Richmond, [7] were Colonels of the Regiment. For the instance of Major Johnston, which has been quoted, took place between the death of the Duke of Richmond, and the appointment of Lord Ligonier; and Captain Dashwood was not appointed to the Regiment upon any vacancy, but came into it by an exchange with Captain Asheton; which tho' extremely unusual, took place, in consequence of the recommendation of the Colonel of the Regiment.

The appointment of the Honourable Captain Murray therefore, Sir, was such a marked deviation from the usual mode of appointment to the vacancies in the Royal Regiment of Horse Guards, which had continued for the space of 78 years, during the time the above mentioned Officers were the Colonels of the Regiment, as coud not fail appearing to the Army, and the publick in general, a strong proof of your Royal Highness's displeasure towards either the Regiment, or their Colonel. This, Sir, has naturally made a very deep impression in the minds of the Officers of the Corps, and has compelled me to be desirous of resigning my

1 John Campbell, second Duke of Argyll (1678–1743).

2 Algernon Seymour, seventh Duke of Somerset (1684–1750). Appointed Colonel of the Blues in 1740.

3 Charles Lennox, second Duke of Richmond (1701–1750). He held this command for a few months before his death.

4 John Ligonier, first Earl Ligonier (1680–1770). Appointed Colonel of the Blues in 1753.

5 Appointed Colonel of the Blues in 1758.

6 Henry Seymour Conway, Sir Robert Walpole's nephew (1721–1795). Appointed Colonel in 1774.

7 Charles Lennox, third Duke of Richmond (1735–1806).

commission as Colonel, and of quitting the Army. Especially after finding that all my efforts, and representations, upon the occasion, have proved wholly ineffectual. As the cause therefore still exists, which originally induced me, Sir, to form this resolution, your Royal Highness cannot be surprised at my renewing my request, that you will be graciously pleased, in consequence of these circumstances, to permit me to retire from the command of the Royal Regiment of Horse Guards, and from the service.

To whatever final decision your Royal Highness may please to come, upon this subject, permit me, Sir, to assure you, that as my attachment to your Royal Highness originally proceeded from the most pure, honourable, and disinterested motives, it will ever continue the same; and that I have the honour to be, with the most profound respect [etc.].

216 PRINCESS MARY *to the* PRINCE REGENT

Janry the 10 [1813].

I AM commanded by the Queen to inform you that last night at Frogmore Charlotte[1] took me on one side & told me that Lady de Clifford had seen you Friday before she left town & that in consequence of Lady de Clifford informing you *she had told* Charlotte of her resignation with *your* leave she had acquainted her of the Dss of Leeds's appointment.[2] Charlotte expressed great *sorrow* and regret at the Dss of Leeds being put about her as *Governess* & gave me to *understand* that she was ready to receive any body you appointed as Lady of the Bed Chamber but never would *submit to obey any body* in the capacity of Governess. She desired me to state these her feelings to the Queen as she did not wish to conceal them. In short this morning I acquainted the Queen of all that passed between us on the subject and the Queen determined to have a conversation with Charlotte before Lady de Clifford & the Bishop of Salisbury as well as myself & fairly represented the *situation* YOU was placed in as her father as well as her *duty* towards you as a daughter & pointed out strongly the necessity of her submiting to whatever proposal you thought proper & that whether it be Governess or Lady of the Bed Chamber the *same authority* must be *given* as *she was too* young to be her own *mistress* and that as a FATHER she had no right to expect you would *consult her* & untill all was *arranged you could not speak to her.*

The Queen lamented very much Lady de Clifford feeling herself under the necessity of acquainting Charlotte of her *resignation,* as the *Prince*

1 Princess Charlotte.　　　　　2 See No. 206.

certainly never intended she should have heard it but *from himself,* but she was greatly mistaken if she thought any father *was bound* to tell a child of what he might think *proper* to do *by her* as *he* must know best *what was most best* for her good. In the situation of the Royal family any change can not be made immediately as it requires great care & judgement to find proper people & the Queen strongly said nothing but aff[ectio]n for the *Prince* & the family could induce any body to accept so *responsable* a *situation.* The Queen said the Prince had accepted Lady de Clifford's resignation with great regret, but upon Lady de Clifford stating she felt she had lossed Charlotte's CONFIDENCE it was impossible to ask Lady de Clifford *to stay* & she was hurt to find Charlotte *appear* to *feel* her going *so little* considering Lady de Clifford had been 9 years with her & given up so much of her time to her. Charlotte said she should have liked Lady de Clifford as a lady. The Queen ran over Charlotte's manners in general as not what would please in the long run in the world and her want of civility some days to people and over civility at other times.

The Queen in short said every thing she could to make her *sensable* of *her duty* towards *you* & of the consequence that might arise if she did not submit to the commands of a father. I think the Q. did it with great dignity, any way it was not by way of finding *fault* but from the aff[ectio]n she had for your child. Lady de Clifford was violently affected. The Queen hopes that as she has compleately paved the way for *you,* YOU will loose no time in haveing a conversation with Charlotte, but I think it right to state the Queen has got a very bad cold & is quite unequal to comeing up to town & coughs a great deal. Therefore if you *will* speak to Charlotte you must come down to Windsor. Charlotte has shown me a copy of a letter you must have received by this time from her, *which* will be *proof enough how determined she is.* The Q. has not seen the letter or did she name *it to her* but I told Charlotte I had acquainted the Q *with it.* In consequence the Q. hopes instead of deterring you from speaking *to her* it will *hasten your so doing.* Lady de Clifford did not know of the letter till it was gone.

The Queen begs for Godsake the Dss of Leeds may not hear of this.

[P.S.] I find Charlotte has sent a copy of her letter to you to Lord Liverpool[1] & the Q. hopes you will be *very very firm.*[2]

1 It is sometimes wrongly said that she wrote a letter to Lord Liverpool.
2 "The Prince was violently angry when he heard of the letter", wrote Miss Knight, "and took Lord Eldon (the Chancellor) down with him to Windsor, where, in the Queen's room, before her Majesty, Princess Mary, and Lady de Clifford, in a very rough manner the learned Lord explained the law of England as not allowing her Royal Highness what she demanded, and on the Prince's asking what he would have done as a father, he is said to have answered, 'If she had been my daughter, I would have locked her up'. Princess Charlotte

Sunday Mg. [10 Jan. 1813].

I THROW myself on your indulgence most respectfully to assure you, that I am most ready & willing on all occasions to meet your will, wishes & pleasure. That in humbly representing my feelings to you, I most sincerely hope I shall not be taxed with the name of disobedient, or disrespectful. Allow me then to say that I felt very much hurt at never having been informed of the resignation of Ly de Clifford & consequent alteration. That I was the last to know of it & not till every one talked of it & it reached my ears by hearsay, & more particularly as the once kind & grateful promise you gave me of there never being a third person between us gave me hopes. Through Lady de Clifford I know of her resignation as a Governess, & sincerely regret it as she is a true & sturdy friend, but had she remained I could never have looked upon her as such. The coldness that has latterly arisen between us has arisen from that & from the hope I entertained of having a Companion in a Lady made me more easily agree to our separation.

I trust my dear father will pardon the freedom & candor with wh I have addressed him upon so interesting a subject to me. I feel the difference of my age. I cannot help judging from the view of other young people of my own age who cease to have Governesses at 17. I think it my duty also to state, before any final arrangements are made with the Duchess of Leeds that I have no *personal objection* to her, none therefore to her being appointed as *my* Lady, but that under the name of Governesses as such, either her or any one else I never can & never will accept or submit to, or look upon in such a light. As a person recommended & approved of *by you* I shall be happy to receive her or anyone else from *your hands* as a Companion & Lady, you will never I trust have cause or her either to complain or disapprove of my conduct towards her.

I earnestly hope you will take this, as well as my request into consideration & not look upon my fixed determination either as disaffection or obstinacy towards you. Grieved I should be indeed, as I wish you to believe me ever, [etc.].

heard all this with great dignity and answered not a word; but she afterwards went into the room of one of her aunts, burst into tears, and exclaimed, 'What would the King say if he could know that his grand-daughter had been compared to the grand-daughter of a collier?'" Cp. Lady Charlotte Bury's *Diary* (I, 193 [1838]).

Harley Str. [12 January 1813].

May I beg the favor of you to take a favorable opportunity to present my most humble duty to the Regent, and assure His Royal Highness that nothing but an ardent desire to do something worthy his approbation has prevented me from executing the commission which His Royal Highness was graciously pleased to honour me with. I have nearly compleated four portraits of Mr. Percival, all different views of his face; and when they are compleated I will do myself the honor of sending them to Carleton House for His Royal Highness's inspection, that he may choose *that* which he shall consider the best.

219 Princess Mary *to the* Prince Regent

Windsor, January 13th 1813.

My mother has so heavy a cold that she has commanded me to write to you for her, for she has very wisely determined to stay in bed the best part of the morning.

She first desires me to say that she will do every thing that lays in her power concerning Lady De Clifford, she would most willingly offer her an apartment at Frogmore, but she fears that she might take it ill. Therefore she will take her into the Castle for that night, for she would not for worlds put it into Lady De Cliffords power to say that she had not been treated like a gentlewoman & that she had been turned out of the house at a minute's warning, for she must pack up her things which must take some little time.

The next thing is, my mother entreats you to be very careful how you word your letter to Lady De Clifford. She wishes you (for your own sake) to express how sorry you are for the *reason she gave you* for her resignation; thank her for the time she had given up, in consideration of which you would leave her the 1200 a year, & nothing more should be added, as if you approve of her conduct it might do a great deal of harm.

About Mrs. Gaggrin, Sir Henry Halford[1] will see her to-morrow. She is at present so ill that it is impossible that she should be moved, but as soon as that can take place you may depend it shall be done. But every thing that is done must be done with that degree of prudence to prevent mischief. In short, I am commanded by the Queen to assure you she, as

1 [1766–1844.] Physician to George III, George IV, William IV and Queen Victoria. Created a Baronet, 1809.

well as all those belonging to you, are anxious to meet your wishes in every thing for Charlotte's good & sincerely do we pray that your present anxiety & trouble may be crowned with success.

My mother sent for me when I had got thus far in my letter to tell me she had received one from the Dss of Leeds, saying that in a few days she hoped to be here. The Queen upon mature consideration wishes me to ask you if you do not think that it would be better to drop this to Lady De Clifford? that she may not say you had taken her by surprize, & she thinks it is more for your dignity not to appear to have any mystery, as it might imply your being apprehensive of some misconduct on her part, for if she has a mind to do mischief there has been time enough already for the purpose.

You will answer this by any one you think proper *this evening* as my mother will not open her lips till she hears from you.

220 THE PRINCE REGENT *to* LADY DE CLIFFORD

[*c.* 13 January 1813.]

I LAMENT very much the necessity under which you have placed me of accepting your resignation, in consequence of what you have stated to me to have passed between my daughter and you. It remains therefore only for me to thank you for the good intentions and affection, which you have manifested towards her during the many years she has been in your care.

As a proof of my regard I desire you will retain the same allowance, which you have hitherto received, & I remain, Dear Madam, [etc.].

221 PRINCESS MARY *to the* PRINCE REGENT

Jany the 14th [1813].

I HAVE had a long conversation with Sir Henry[1] & I am *delighted* to hear all he tells me. Some, I think much, will depend of *quiet* upon Miss Knight[2] being about Charlotte (though I said the other day she would be of more use not ATTACHED to her) but I find from our friend Sir Henry,

1 Sir Henry Halford.
2 Ellis Cornelia Knight (1757–1837). Lady Companion to Queen Charlotte, 1806–13; Lady Companion to Princess Charlotte, 1813–14. She was the daughter of Admiral Sir Joseph Knight, who died in 1775.

Miss Knight WOULD LIKE TO ASSIST THE Dss of Leeds from *real* affn for Charlotte & as Charlotte has such an opinion of Miss Knight & Miss Knight so *well* acquainted with *our House*, Charlotte will *receive* her with open arms & GRATITUDE.

Of course we must not tell the Queen Miss Knight *would* like a situation about Charlotte in *preference* to REMAINING *about* the Queen, that would never do, but as Sir Henry in his conversation with the Q. has brought her to promise not to object should you propose such an arrangement, for God sake do when you come down to-morrow & before you *introduce* the Dss, urge it to the Queen with all your powers of *persuasion* as the greatest FAVOUR SHE can possibly DO YOU (when SELF is in question we know by experience it is *difficult* to GAIN HER). She will make ten thousand objections as to *rank, health*, &c &c but you may contrive to arrange the first by tacking Honble, to her name & Sir Henry will UNDERTAKE THE REST. In short I am in very good heart to-day from Charlotte's *manner* yesterday & from all Sir Henry tells me about her to-day.

This is quite for YOURSELF ALONE & I have only to say God bless you.

222 SIR HENRY HALFORD *to the* PRINCE REGENT

[? 14 January 1813.]

MY interview with the Queen last night was perfectly satisfactory, as I found Her Majesty full of approbation of your Royal Highness's letter to Lady de Clifford, and entirely disposed to concur with you in whatever else your R.HIs had thought it right to say, and to do in the conduct of this most interesting affair. But my conversation with Her Majesty this morning, at her bed side, (for she has a heavy cold) has been still more comfortable.

Her Majesty was pleas'd to desire me to give her her lesson, by which I was enabled to explain your Royal Highness's further wishes and views respecting Miss Knight, and other parts of the Pss Charlotte's arrangements—and when I left her chamber, the Queen gave orders instantly for a message to be sent to Lady De Clifford, to bring her to the Castle, in order to a final termination of her Ladyship's charge.

Her Majesty intended to say exactly what your R.H: conceived the Queen would say to Lady De C:, and gave good reasons for not intending to separate the Pss Charlotte from Lady De C. this day, but having it in view to hint delicately to Lady De C. that she might go tomorrow morning, and intending to desire the Pss Charlotte to come to the Castle, and to detain H:R:H: here after the ride.

On the subject of Miss Knight, the Queen did more than hesitate at first, but Her Majesty permitted me at length to prevail upon her not to make any objections to her assisting the Dss of Leeds, and being attach'd officially to Her Grace, and I flatter myself your Royal Highness will find the Queen tomorrow disposed to yield to your request, or, shall I say? to your incomparable powers of persuasion when you come to talk to her.[1]

I am the more earnest about Miss Knight, because I have had a conversation with the Pss Charlotte this morning, and infer from it, that this arrangement would do much to all[a]y that feeling of irritation which has discover'd itself so strongly within these few days. The Princess understands *perfectly* that I never can or will have a secret from your Royal Highness—that I do and will tell your R:Hs every thing. Yet compatibly with this Her R:Hss is disposed I think to give me her good opinion and something of her confidence. In my conversation, therefore, I had no difficulty in offering Her R:Hs my humble opinion upon the propriety of her continuing still under a GOVERNESS, by stating particularly that the custom of this Kingdom which had now acquired almost the force of the law of the land, had held the future Sovereign under Governors until 18 years of age, and that I supposed the Constitution thought it necessary perhaps to the condition of reigning hereafter, that the presumptive heir to the Throne had submitted to be governed for 18 years. I say H:R:Highness heard this with complacency—asked if Princesses were under the same necessities as Princes, and then remarked that she did not want exceptions to be made in her favor. She inquired who was to assist the Dss of Leeds, I said your Royal Highness wish'd Miss K. and I believe intended to ask the Queen to spare her. She expressed great satisfaction, said she had a high opinion of Miss Knight, and believed that Miss K: thought well of her, the Pss.

I said what I knew to be just of the Dss of Leeds, as to her gentleness, and the generosity of her nature. Her remark was, that she believed she had not much sense, and would therefore be mild and managed *by the Castle.* I answered that the Dss would shew only half the sense for which I gave her credit, if she did not make the Princess's happiness and fame the exclusive object of her attention. Yes, she replied, but the Dss may be more disposed to consult the tempers of the *ruling powers*, than of

1 The Queen wished Miss Knight to remain with her, and never forgave her for entering the service of Princess Charlotte in accordance with the wishes of the Prince Regent and of the Princess herself.

those who are *to rule*. It terminated by my assuring Her R.H. that as I had no authority from your R.H. to say any thing of yourself, the Pss must receive it as my most disinterested opinion that every word I had heard your R.H: utter on this subject convinced me that you had but one object in view—her happiness, and that as she would certainly find her father on all occasions her best friend, she might and ought to look up to your R.H: for every indulgence compatible with her present and future happiness. I left the Pss quite in comfort, I assure your R:H:, and have the best hope that this matter will terminate quietly after all, and entirely to your R:H:s satisfaction.

Miss Knight to the Duchess of Leeds, 15 January 1813 (Miss Knight's *Autobiography*, I, 239, where the letter is dated the 16th).

223 THE DUCHESS OF LEEDS *to the* PRINCE REGENT

Lower Lodge, Windsor,
Saturday night. [16 January 1813.]

I TAKE liberty to forward to your Royal Highness a copy of the proposal I made to Miss Knight this morng: & regret the result of her consideration upon the business.

I am, I own, sincerely disappointed of the sanguine hopes I had entertained of having so very desirable an assistant being granted & really am much distressed about it.

I shewed Her Majesty the copy of my letter to Miss Knight, but thought it better to withhold her answer, & will be most obliged to your Royal Highness to put it in the fire if you think proper.

Miss Knight told me that from her high sense of gratitude towards Her Majesty she felt she could not quit her service unless the Queen commanded it, & she is most afflicted at the contrary feelings that harrass her mind. Her Majesty seems still to think she has not made any decision, so I humbly hope your Royal Highness will order Miss Knight to attend you at Carlton House & hear what she may further think on this very important point.

It is impossible for me to see any other person at present, & I think the Queen may alter her sentiments. I will exert myself as long as I can without help, & I am encouraged so to do, by Princess Charlotte's most amiable & gratifying kindness, which has been really beyond description. Her conduct does honor to both Her Royal Highness's head & heart & proves her duty & affection for your Royal Highness.

I had the honor of dining tête a tête with Princess Charlotte to-day, & her conversation was quite delightful.

With every sentiment of respect & gratitude, I have the honor to be, [etc.].

[P.S.] May I beg your Royal Highness to return me the copy of my letter to Miss Knight.

224 THE EARL OF MOIRA *to the* PRINCE REGENT

Jany. 18th 1813.

IN obedience to the commands of your Royal Highness, I lost no time in waiting upon Miss Knight. I luckily found her at home, and I stated to her in the strongest terms all that your Royal Highness had directed me to urge. I represented the infinite importance involved in Princess Charlotte's having about her a person for whom Her Royal Highness had testified a flattering prepossession; a consideration which made me of opinion that Miss Knight should feel herself bound by duty to the Royal Family & to the country to declare her acquiescence without further hesitation. Miss Knight pleaded her apprehension that her submission to your Royal Highness's orders might be misconstrued into a relinquishment of the Queen, to whom she was devoted by every tie of attachment & gratitude. I assured her it was impossible that the procedure could be so erroneously viewed by any one: but that, above all others, the Queen would be the person who must the most surely comprehend & acknowledge the service rendered to Her Majesty as well as to the rest of the Royal Family. I told Miss Knight that if the opinion of her departed friend Lady Ailesbury[1] could weigh with her, I could distinctly assert the solicitude expressed more than once by my sister, that Miss Knight should be placed in the family of Princess Charlotte: and if vigilant anxiety for the happiness & dignity of the Queen could influence the question those sentiments would not be believed to have existed any where more actively than in the breast of my poor sister. So far was she from imagining that such an appointment could appear a dereliction of the Queen, she was certain the public would regard it as a proof of Her Majesty's earnest forecast for the general good when she deprived herself of so faithful an attendant in favor of the young Princess.

1 Lord Moira's eldest sister. She died on 8 January 1813 at the age of 60. "Lady Aylesbury", said Miss Knight, "had been to me more than a sister, and her death was a heavy blow to me."

In fine, Sir, I have the satisfaction of reporting to your Royal Highness that I have overborne Miss Knight's doubts, & that she has authorised me to express her submission to your commands.

With every sentiment of affectionate & respectful duty, I remain, Sir, [etc.].

225 THE EARL OF MOIRA *to the* PRINCE REGENT

Jany. 20th 1813.

THE necessity of laying before your Royal Highness the letter[1] which I have the honor to enclose gives me great concern. I am perfectly aware that the generosity of your Royal Highness would not allow Miss Knight to become a sufferer in consequence of her disposition to obey your commands; therefore my regret only points at the obstacle your Royal Highness's views experience. It is almost superfluous to add that I am ready to make any further representations to Miss Knight that may be consonant to your Royal Highness's wishes. Perhaps, in order to satisfy Miss Knight's honorable delicacy, it may be well first to take some step for reconciling to the Queen Miss Knight's acceptance of the station proposed for her.

There will be some satisfaction to your Royal Highness in the information that Mr. Whitbread has no notion of bringing forward any discussion respecting the Princess.[2] He accepts with every acknowledgement the permission offered for his perusing at Carlton House, on his return to town, the documents relating to the subject.

226 MISS KNIGHT *to* [*the* EARL OF MOIRA]

Tuesday ev^g, [19th January 1813].

I HAVE had the severe mortification to find by a letter which I have this evening received from Her Majesty, that I have much offended her, and that she thinks me very ungrateful. However miserable in having occasioned so much trouble to His Royal Highness the Prince Regent, and, in having disappointed for the second time the wishes he condescended to form for my entering his service, my only comfort must now be to withdraw myself entirely, and neither appear ungrateful to

1 No. 226.   2 The Princess of Wales.

Her Majesty nor to His Royal Highness by accepting the honourable situation now offered me; or retaining that in which the goodness of Her Majesty had placed me. This is the only step now left me to take with honour, and I hope, my dear Lord, you will say all I am incapable of saying in the present agitated state of my mind to the Prince Regent.

227 THE QUEEN *to the* PRINCE REGENT

Windsor, the 20th Jany, 1813.

YOU can not be more surprized at the contents of Miss Knight's letter than I am myself, having understood by the letter you sent yesterday, as also by the one she wrote to me, that *she had accepted* through Lord Moira your proposal upon *which I gave her by a letter in answer a full dismission for ever*, but not in the manner she required it by giving my full approbation to the step she had taken. This it was out of my power to do as the two letters written on Saturday & Munday the one refusing & the latter accepting the offer are so contracdictory that unless she took me for an idiot I could not pass it over in silence & stated in my answer that I was always desirous to act consistently. She could not suspect me of retracting on the Tuesday the words I made use of on Fryday to yourself & the Dutchess of Leeds & on the Saturday to herself, viz. *that I would not biass her either way to accept or to refuse but that I would abide by her decision.*

This I have done by saying that from this moment she & I parted for ever & that I would only add my sincere wishes that she might be far far more happy in her new situation than she could have been in my family. I made use of no other words I do assure you & you may be sure that I can not nor should have stood in your way at any time, the proof of which I have given you by declining speaking to her myself as I feared that by my great partiality for her, I might make use of some expressions which might lead her to think I wished her to decline, & I even went so far as to refuse seing her on Sunday when she called at the Castle.

Miss Knight is at this time as much her own mistress as you are your own master. Dismissed my service since yesterday, I do certainly not mean to offer her to come back again to me, & therefore I can not possibly understand why she should feel any reluctance to oblige you.

I answered this as quick as I could & am sorry that you should so continually meet with unexpected difficulties. Ld Moira's eloquence has great power over her, therefore you have much to hope from his assiduity & that he may succeed is the sincerest wish of My dearest Son, [etc.].

[P.S.] If you think this letter can prove of use to you I have no objection to Miss Knight's seing it.

228 SIR HENRY HALFORD *to the* PRINCE REGENT

[*c.* 21 January 1813.]

YOUR ROYAL HIGHNESS will have been convinced by the style of Her Majesty's answer to your letter of yesterday, that the Queen has not yet abated any thing material of her anger against Miss Knight. From the best observations, however, which I can make on all I have seen and heard here, I cannot hesitate to express a hope that your Royal Highness will immediately confirm Miss Knight's appointment, or rather refuse to accept her resignation of it, leaving it to her friends to reconcile her to undertake the duties of it as soon as possible, without regarding any coldness which it may please Her Majesty to shew her when she presents herself. I must confess that I think the resentment goes deep, and will not be eradicated in any length of time, but Miss Knight cannot want zeal to serve your Royal Highness after the extreme condescension and kindness which you have shewn her. I am going to write to Miss Knight a letter of comfort and encouragement as far as I can give it her, and have only to intreat your Royal Highness not to allow this subject at least to aggravate the ten thousand cares which must press upon you at this moment any further.

I have seen the Duchess,[1] and have thought it best not to give the slightest hint of there having been any new impediment in the way of Her Grace's receiving Miss Knight's assistance, and she expects to be join'd by her at Warwick House on Saturday or Sunday, which will be the best way of Miss Knight's commencing her office.

1 The Duchess of Leeds.

[? 21st January 1813.]

THE KING has passed a perfect quiet composed day & every appearance of irritation is over for *this moment*.

I am grieved to the heart you have had so much anxiety and worry on the subject of Miss Knight, but I hope & trust (notwithstanding the Queen's most unaccountable *selfish* behavour) we may still see Miss Knight in the situation of all others every *well wisher* of YOURS *ought* to pray *she* may be *in*. I was sure by what the Queen told me, she had *wrote* a very *unkind letter* to Miss Knight & after having promised you & the Dss of Leeds over & over again she would not *bias her* it is the more *wonderful* the Q has *exposed herself* so in all this *business* and really will *hear no reason*.

Her rage is so great at Miss Knight having refused at *first* & accepted *after*. When your letter came this evening (which by the by she never showed me) she let me read Miss Knight's letter to Lord Moira & her own answer to your letter, and of course I said all I could to try & convince her of Miss Knight's attachment to her & that by accepting the situation about your daughter was the strongest proof she could give of *love* & *duty* & that when she consider'd the dreadful situation you was placed in & all *your* DIFICULTIES it was *hard* to put any in the way of his placing so proper a person about Charlotte as Miss Knight.

I said it was *your* duty to try to get proper people for your daughter & Lord Moira as your friend equally justified to leave no argument *untried* to assist *you*, & the moment Miss Knight found *if she did not come forwards & accept* the Queen would be blamed in the world as they would say SHE WOULD NOT GIVE HER UP. I felt certain that idea at once decided her to take it & therefore the Queen was her FIRST OBJECT. Instant after lunch backwards & forwards she allowed Eliza[1] to soften some expressions in her letter to you, for though it is wrote out of temper I assure you it is very much less violent than she first intended & she is so far come round as to feel ALARMED FOR FEAR SHE SHOULD NOT ACCEPT.

Therefore I trust Lord Moira may *persuade her*. I think her letter to Lord Moira does her the greatest possible *honour* for she never could return to the Queen after *such a letter* & such a *conduct*, but as the Q says she *hopes* Lord Moira may *talk her over* Miss Knight had better *take it*, and if she could make up her mind to cold nods and looks for a little time I should hope (if you with your usual kindness support Miss Knight) it may all *blow over*.

1 Elizabeth, Princess Mary's sister (1770–1840). Married, 1818, Frederick Joseph Louis, Hereditary Prince of Hesse-Homburg (d. 1829).

I had a comfortable conversation with the Dss of Leeds this morning who appears very well satisfied with Charlotte & was then in high spirits at the thoughts of Miss Knight having accepted & had told Charlotte of it who was all joy. I most sincerely hope the Dss & Charlotte may never hear of all that has passed since, as it does not make the Q appear amiable.

230 A. MACKENZIE *to* COLONEL MCMAHON

Bath, 27th Jany 1813.

I AVAIL'D myself of an early opportunity to communicate your wishes on the subject of our last conversation, and I am now enabled to say, that all is arranged in that quarter *exactly* as you wish.

Since we parted, I find, by report, that the Princess Charlotte of Wales is likely to have an establishment. You are so well acquainted with the nature and extent of my attachment to the Prince, and know how ardently I desire to serve in *any* shape near His Royal Highness's person, that I need not say, how *infinitely* I should value and prefer an appointment that would enable me to do so, to *any* other that the utmost range of ambition could offer. In belonging to Her Royal Highness's establishment, I should feel that I might be enabled to serve, and to have occasional opportunities of seeing the Prince, to whom I am so much devoted, and I trust I should not be an unworthy appendage to the young Princess's Court. These considerations induce me anxiously to desire to belong to it; and I therefore entreat of you my good friend to convey, in whatever manner you may judge best, these my most ardent wishes to the Prince. I commit to your friendship for me, the most cherished object of my ambition, and I feel that it cannot be in better hands. I need not add that pecuniary emolument is *totally out* of my consideration.

I get strength and health daily. The baths have lately been of much use to my complaint. Adieu, [etc.].

231 THE MARQUIS OF WELLINGTON *to the* PRINCE REGENT

Fre[s]neda, January 27th 1813.

WHEN I was lately at Lisbon Mr. Aston delivered me the letter which your Royal Highness had been pleased to address to me; and I had the pleasure of seeing him more than once while I was there.

I hope that your Royal Highness will permit me to avail myself of the opportunity of acknowledging the receipt of your commands regarding Mr. Aston to return your Royal Highness my warmest thanks, for the numerous favours which your Royal Highness has conferred upon me. Not only have all the means which the resources at the disposal of your Royal Highness could command, been given to support the efforts making in this country with my directions, but I have been encouraged in every manner to act with confidence in the support of your Royal High-ness; and I have been favoured & rewarded to a degree not only far beyond my deserts, but far beyond what any subject has yet been by his Sovereign.

I can evince my gratitude for such favours only by devoting myself to serve, and to forward the views of your Royal Highness, with the same zeal which first attracted your notice.

I have the honor to be Sir with the utmost gratitude & respect your Royal Highness' most obliged & most faithful humble servant.

232 FRANCES, COUNTESS OF JERSEY[1] *to* COLONEL MCMAHON

Jany. 27th [1813].

I HAVE received your letter of yesterday, & in justice to myself, I must remind you of your calling upon me on the 12th of August 1811, & asking me "why I would not have a pension"? I answered I cannot *ask* for one. You then said that the Prince felt hurt that I was in an uncomfortable situation & that the moment the restrictions were taken off it would be the first thing he should do, to grant me one & we entered as much further into the subject as to agree that such a thing could be done without its being made public. All that passed in this conversation, as well as your answer to a letter which I wrote to you upon the subject (in which you told me I must address myself to the Prince & *ask* for a pension) I understood to be indirect messages from him, nothing but what I looked upon as an absolute promise from him would have induced me to do so. I thought my letter to him a mere matter of form & now I find that I have put myself in the disgraceful shape of a beggar! I do entreat that you will relate these facts to him in order that if I have been

1 Frances, daughter of the Rev. Philip Twysden, and wife of George Bussy Villiers, fourth Earl of Jersey, who died in 1805. He had been Master of the Horse in the Prince's Household, and she was the Prince's mistress at the time of his marriage. They finally parted in 1798. [1753–1821.]

mistaken, if I have misunderstood his intentions & your assurances, that I may no longer feel in the humiliating state in which I must remain while my way of thinking upon the subject remains unexplained. Many of my friends have at different times advised me to apply for a pension, have urged that as the widow of a faithful servant of His R.H. left without a sufficient income to support my rank, I might hope that I had some claim to one but I felt that it was quite impossible to *ask*, and no power, but a command from him could have forced me to take a step so repugnant to my feelings of respect to His R.H. or of delicacy to myself. Should you dislike to show this letter to the Prince, or to state to him all that has passed, I have no objection to writing to him when I shall *most fully* explain that no blame can attach to the part you have acted, that all the distress which I now endure is owing to my having miscomprehended you when I saw you here.

Pray let me have an immediate answer to this letter, I shall be wretched till all *is* explained.

233 LIEUTENANT-GENERAL WILLIAM KEPPEL[1] *to* COLONEL MCMAHON

Park Place, Jany 28th [1813].

THE kind act of friendship which you communicated to me yesterday, deserved a warmer return than my disappointed feelings permitted me to offer you at the moment, but I trust you know me, and judged me as I am. But how be otherwise than surprised and disappointed, when having been thought worthy to fill the situation of His *Majesty's representative* for seven years (a situation I trust I did not dishonour) I am to-day judged unworthy to to [*sic*] possess that which every brother Officer may hope to obtain, and how not be hurt in the extreme, to see that that which is the birth right (generally speaking) of every British subject, (to look with merit to reach it, to every honour in the State) should be by accident of birth, and an old Act not suited to the present day, withheld from him perhaps who may have the good fortune most eminently to serve his country, and shut out from that which the meanest member of the community, may not dispare to reach. That I should have

1 Sir William Keppel (d. 1834), who was gazetted G.C.B. on 1 February 1813, was apparently an illegitimate son. The sixth Earl of Albemarle described him as his father's first cousin. (*Fifty Years of My Life*, I, 238.) He served in North America and the West Indies, became a Lieutenant-General in 1803, Colonel of the fourth Battalion of the 60th Regiment in 1806, and a General in June 1813. He was appointed a Groom of the Bedchamber in March 1812, and Governor of Guernsey in November 1827.

been judged not deserving of what I ambitioned, might have been the case, but that an excellent and amiable master should have thought the reasons offered to him sufficiently weighty to stop his hand, and follow his inclination (for so I wish to flatter myself it was) and towards one of his family, for many reasons, hurts me to a degree. From Ministers I had no expectations, or did I wish to take the place of any body, but I did I confess, hope that I might have been included in the list. How humiliating to think that the lowest individual, a highwayman, or a pick pocket may pretend to that to which I am forbid to hope.

But I am afraid there is an indisposition, where I ought to have received a better return.

234 CHARLES ARBUTHNOT *to* COLONEL MCMAHON

Downing Street,
Friday [Jany 29, 1813].

I FOUND it impossible to call upon you after I had seen Ld L[iverpool]. I will call tomorrow mg, & indeed we shall meet at dinner.

Ld L: said that the including our friend in the present batch was impossible; & he certainly feels much the objection of birth; & he thinks that the deviation in favour of some marked brilliant service ought not to form a precedent. He allows Keppel's general merit, but he does not think that good conduct in the W. Indies is such brilliant service as wd authorise a deviation.

I will explain more fully when we meet. He would be glad to be kind to Keppel having a very good opinion of him, & perhaps between us something satisfactory might be done on a future occasion.

Till we meet, aff. yrs.

235 THOMAS SHERIDAN[1] *to the* EARL OF MOIRA

Rossie Priory, Feb. 1st [18]13.

YOUR letter has very sensibly afflicted me. I am utterly at a loss to conjecture, by what calumny it has been attempted to injure me with His

1 [1775–1817.] The only son of Richard Brinsley Sheridan by his first wife, Elizabeth Linley. He died at the Cape whilst holding the office of Colonial Treasurer to the Governor, and left his family in a "dreadful situation". The Duke of York asked Lord Bathurst, the Secretary of State for War and the Colonies, "to give every assistance in your power towards obtaining them some assistance and provision from Government". (*Bathurst Papers*, pp. 443–4.) See Nos. 292 and 377.

Royal Highness, but assuredly no man on earth ought with greater justice to be reproached with the deepest ingratitude, were it true that I had ever been found wanting in attachment to His Royal Highness. That I did think & continue to think the principles of Mr. Percevals Administration alike injurious to the people & hazardous to the Sovereign, I do not deny, & certainly I have never sought to conceal that opinion, but of His Royal Highness I ever did, & ever must, speak but one language. From my childhood to the present hour, spight of very many omissions on my part, His Royal Highness has been to me an *unalterd, beneficent* and *steady* friend. I know not the favor he ever refused me, or the obligation he hesitated to confer; no Party or politics can ever interfere with that respect, affection & gratitude, I so justly owe him. This *I* have said *always,* & *every where.* Good God! who was I to conciliate, with whom was I to obtain credit by a contrary conduct? The favor & protection afforded me, by His Royal Highness, is matter of notoriety. What possible motive can be conceivd, for my thus wantonly branding myself with the crime of ingratitude, & lowering myself in the estimation of every one whose good opinion is worth possessing! Unfortunately my Lord, in a case like the present, I can call no evidence, I can make no appeal—were it permitted, that appeal should be to His Royal Highness himself. I would intreat him to say, whether in the many happy hours he has allowd me to pass in his society, he ever noticd in me a disposition to calumniate those who were absent, or whether on the contrary I have not always evincd an inclination to defend them, tho persons perhaps, perfectly indifferent to me. Most happy should I be to leave the decision with His Royal Highness, & allowing me to assume that it would be favorable, can it be thought, that His Royal Highness is to prove the exception, & that towards *him alone* I am to be treacherous & malignant. Something of this my Lord I intreat you to say for me. When you shall have left this country, I know of no other mediator who will interest himself in my behalf, & all I ask is to be restored to that place in the good opinion of His Royal Highness, with which he has hitherto honord me, and which I feel fully conscious, I have done nothing intentionally to forfeit.

150 *Bond St.*, Febry 7th 1813.

I wou'd this day be the most miserable being were it not my faith so strong in your Royal consideration benevolence and kindness to my self. I alude to the publication in the news papers of the narative that accompanied my memorial[2] to your Royal Highness—how it was obtained by them I cannot discover and all the consolation I have for the shock it has given is my conviction that your generous mind wou'd not easily believe me capable of giving any sanction or colour to a proceeding so absurd. I shou'd never think of intruding those observations on your Royal Highness but that I am told I gave it to the paper. Whatever be my most sanguine hopes of remuneration or however sharp my necessities they stand in no compition [*sic*] with me to that of being sensible that your Royal Highness will not believe I cou'd do so and that too when my memorial was most graciously taken into your consideration. May God bless you Sir with health & happiness and preserve you from any thing like the affliction I have expearanced [*sic*] & I beg your Royal Highness to believe me [etc.].

237 JOHN LANDSEER[3] *to* MAJOR-GENERAL TURNER

Foley Street, 9 Feby 1813.

As it is very probable that the Prince Regent will commune with you upon the subject, before he returns an answer to our petition, I send herewith a small pamphlet which contains a record of all that has passed upon the subject: and as H.R.H. formerly desired you to learn what were Mr. West's sentiments respecting our claims, I have the honour to enclose a note lately receiv'd from that gentleman, which clearly shews that he is *with us*.

I left you a proof yesterday of a view which I have lately engraved of the Alhambra. It falls far short of its fame—at least externally—but

1 [? 1761–1815.] The wife of Sir William Hamilton, the diplomatist (1730–1803); and Nelson's mistress. Her extravagant manner of living involved her in debt, and she died in poverty and obscurity at Calais.

2 She claimed, *inter alia*, to have procured and sent to the British Government a copy of the King of Spain's letter to his brother the King of Naples in 1796, expressing his intention to declare war against England. Her claims were not altogether imaginary but her memorials for a pension were ignored. See No. 244.

3 [1769–1852.] The painter and engraver; father of Sir Edwin Henry Landseer (1802–73).

knowing you were curious in architectural matters, I thought you might like to possess it.

Mr. West's note, & the pamphlet, I should be glad to have returned. The former I shall have to read to the petitioners when they meet, & should wish to keep as a record: the latter is perhaps written too hastily & too warmly for me to wish it to be seen except by those immediately concern'd.

238 THE EARL OF MOIRA *to the* PRINCE REGENT

Feby 9th 1813.

THE persuasion that what I have to communicate will be pleasing to your Royal Highness induces me to take the liberty of this intrusion. I went this day to the Duke of Sussex, on pretence of Masonic arrangements; & I soon led the conversation to the rumored discussion of the Princess's case in Parliament.[1] He reprobated the measure of bringing it forward; saying that they who could advise it were as little friends to the Princess as to the rest of the Royal Family, for it must be ruinous for her. On that, I expressed my happiness at hearing him hold that language, as I had feared his having been drawn into consultation. He declared, & repeated it with strong asseverations, that he had not had any communication with the Princess for some months: that, the last time he was summoned by her he had answered "It was his duty to wait "upon her if she commanded it but he should be happy if she would dis-"pense with his attendance:" and that he should consider any private negociation with her a personal offense towards your Royal Highness of which nothing on earth should make him guilty. This was said with such distinctness & earnestness as to leave no doubt whatever on my mind.

1 On 14 January the Princess of Wales wrote a letter to the Regent complaining that additional restrictions had been lately imposed upon her intercourse with Princess Charlotte. The letter was returned unopened, and after it had been published in *The Morning Chronicle* on 10 February, the Prince Regent decided to submit the matter to his Ministers and other members of the Privy Council for his own justification. Having examined the evidence on which the 1806 charges were based, they reported on the 27th that the intercourse between Caroline and her daughter should continue to be subject to restraint.

Castle Windsor, the 12th Febry 1813.

M Y first occupation this morning must be that of returning you thanks for your attention of ordering Lord Liverpool to inform me of your visit to your daughter. Ever since that imprudent letter appeared in public print I felt convinced that it could not be passed over with silence & I admire the mildness in which you informed Charlotte of this distressing affair.[1] Many difficulties I fear must still arise upon this subject but I feel confident that by uniform unimpassioned conduct on your side which is so happily the line you have taken that I doubt not it will defeat the intentions of your adversary. I wish you would take an opportunity of telling Charlotte that you informed me of the purport of your conversation with her, & that tho' I felt very much for her distress I thought it more delicate not to write to her upon the subject.

I hope you will not suffer essentialy from all this vexation & take care of yourself by which you will greatly oblige, [etc.].

240 THE DUKE OF NORTHUMBERLAND *to* COLONEL MCMAHON

Alnwick Castle, 16th Febry 1813.

I HAVE to thank you for your kind letter of the 11th. Conscious that my conduct, and correspondence, on a late occasion, was highly respectfull I must confess I was not a little surprised, to find an attack was commenced against me, by a paper, said to be patronized at Carlton House. The contents of your last letter has therefore afforded me some satisfaction.

Of your friendship, my dear Colonel, I can never doubt; of your sincere attachment I have received too many proofs, not to be thoroughly convinced that I may depend upon it, on all occasions. Such friendship, as yours, that is always steady, & is not laid aside, & forgot, for some present momentary object, is not only desireable, but invaluable, and as such, do I regard, and esteem it.

Indeed, my dear Colonel, I know so well the value of a true and disinterested friend, that not the most artfull, or insinuating persuasions, and arguments of any insidious, and interested adviser, will ever have

---

1 The Prince Regent told his daughter "that an investigation was being made with respect to the conduct of her mother, on the result of which depended her ever being allowed to visit her again, and that in the meanwhile her usual visits must be suspended...". "Princess Charlotte was dreadfully overcome", adds Miss Knight.

influence enough with me, to risk ever the loss of such a treasure, by any act of mine.

The Duchess, and all the rest of my family, desire I will offer their compliments and best wishes to you, and Mrs. Mac-Mahon. To these, I hope you, & Mrs. Mahon, will allow me to add my own.

I have just received an account of my friend Sir J: Duckworth's[1] re-election for New Romsey, so that I shall now commence the political campaign, with *eight* firmly attached votes in the House of Commons. I hope therefore those whom it most concerns will remember the following verses of the poet.

> "Attentions, by attention gain,
> And merit cares, by care
> Thus, my firm friendship you'll obtain,
> Such friendship, is but rare."

Adieu My dear Colonel, and be assured I ever am with the utmost truth, [etc.].

241 VISCOUNT CASTLEREAGH *to the* PRINCE REGENT

St. James's Square,
Tuesday 11 P.M. [23 February 1813].

LORD CASTLEREAGH has the honor to acquaint your Royal Highness that Sir F. Burdet's motion for a Regency Bill has been negatived by a majority of 166—the numbers were for the leave to introduce the Bill 73—against it 238.[2]

The debate was strictly confined to the question, and perfectly temperate on both sides. There was not only no allusion to the Princess of Wales, but an obvious tone against the introduction of that topick into the debate. Sir F. Burdet took pains to profess respect for your Royal Highness, and disinclination to advert to any subject that could give

1 Sir John Thomas Duckworth, first Baronet (1748–1817), the Admiral. Elected for New Romney on 8 October 1812, he was re-elected on 12 February 1813 after he had resigned his seat for some obscure reason by taking the office of Steward of the Chiltern Hundreds. (House of Commons' *Journals*, LXVIII, 113 [3 February 1813].) See No. 182.

2 Sir Francis Burdett (1770–1844), the Radical member for Westminster, held the Whig view of 1788 that, in the event of the death or incapacity of the Sovereign the exercise of the Sovereign's functions devolved, as a matter of right, upon the heir apparent. Had Burdett's Bill passed, Princess Charlotte, whose legal and political advisers and friends were Whigs, would have become Regent automatically in case of the death or disability of her father.

pain. Mr. C. Johnstone[1] was present but shewed no inclination to say a word.

Lord Wellesleys and Mr. Cannings friends divided with the majority. *Sir G. Webster*[2] with the minority.

The list of speakers is submitted.

242 COLONEL JAMES WILLOUGHBY GORDON[3] *to* COLONEL McMAHON

H[orse] G[uar]ds, Feb. 25, 1813.

I AM very sensible of your kindness in mentioning to me the Prince's observation upon the subject of the newspaper, and I have no difficulty whatever in explaining fully to you everything I know relative to it.

When the Duke of York was so abominably abused in 1809 by *all* the old papers without exception, & particularly by those in the interest of Government, I endeavoured but without success to stop the abuse, and I remonstrated with the Government who I thought rather winked at it than otherwise: in this difficulty I took up a very obscure paper called The Pilot,[4] which at that time was hardly known, and what with my assistance and that of my friends, we soon brought it into notice, and it became a very powerful advocate & support of the Duke in his greatest extremity.

When the Duke's business was over, the paper became established, & I dropped all assistance or acquaintance with it, and since that period I have had no more to say to The Pilot than to Mr. Cobbett,[5] or any other writer: except that I have endeavoured more than once to stop the current of abuse which I saw levelled against Carleton House. I however soon found, to my surprize, that the paper was quite above any control of mine, and was written to sell, & not to instruct. The editor expresses himself grateful to me, but that gratitude does not extend

1 Andrew James Cochrane-Johnstone (1767–1834), Lord Cochrane's uncle. On his first marriage he assumed the additional surname of Johnstone. They were both found guilty of a stock-exchange fraud in 1814 and were expelled the House of Commons. At this time Cochrane-Johnstone was persistently ventilating in Parliament the Princess of Wales's grievances against her husband.

2 Sir Godfrey Vassal Webster, fifth Baronet (1789–1836), M.P. for Sussex. He usually supported the Government. His divorced mother married Lord Holland in 1797.

3 Quartermaster-General of the Forces. Created a Baronet, 1818. (1773–1851.) In 1809 when the Duke of York was involved in the unpleasant Mary Anne Clarke scandals, Gordon was his military secretary.

4 A short-lived evening paper, started in 1807.

5 William Cobbett, the Radical journalist (1763–1835).

beyond a personal feeling, and I doubt much whether I could induce him to alter one sentence of writing.

In short, I am well convinced that the less we have to do with them the better.

As to the discussion upon the Princess,[1] perhaps you will recollect that I have for some years prohibited Mrs. G[ordon] from visiting in that quarter, & of all men I should not be suspected of being an advocate there.

I wish you would have the goodness to do me justice with H.R.H. who certainly should never feel one painful moment, if it was in my power to prevent it.

243   THE DUKE OF NORTHUMBERLAND *to* COLONEL MCMAHON

Alnwick Castle, 28th February 1813.

I HAVE lived too long in the world not to know, that a true and attached friend is the greatest blessing, of which a man can be possessed; and I am much mistaken, if a certain person will not e'er long be fully convinced of the truth of this assertion, and have cause to know, by fatal experience, the difference in value between a sincere, honest, & disinterested friend, & one whose attachment only proceeds from false and selfish motives.

I lament most sincerely that this business of the Princess's is brought forward; because I know it is a subject which particularly agitates the Prince. However little my feelings have been considered on a late occasion, I can assure you any thing whatever which can affect H:R:H:'s feelings, will ever give me the greatest pain. With regard to Ministers, nothing on earth coud embarrass them so much, & probably the knowledge of this is the very cause why it is brought on at present. A very deep laid plan is formed for removing them from the Regent's Counsel, privately & I must say insidiously countenanced & encouraged by a person who, unfortunately for the Prince and the country, possesses too much of H:R:H:'s confidence & high opinion at the present moment. This last is, of course, entre nous, my dear Colonel; but the affection I ever shall feel for the Prince makes me miserable to perceive the scheme that is laid, for delivering him blindfold into the hands of those, who I know are his inveterate enemies. You may remember, my dear Colonel,

1 The Princess of Wales.

formerly my predictions usually were fullfilled. Woud to God my present one may prove erroneous.

All here unite in compliments, & the very best wishes to you, and Mrs. Mac-Mahon, & be assured I ever am, [etc.].

244 LADY HAMILTON *to* VISCOUNT SIDMOUTH

Copy

150 *Bond St.*, 28 Feby 1813.

THE necessity that urges me to address your Lordship again upon my affairs is not more galling to me than the fear of being thought intrusive. My claims having now lain so long brings my situation to that point, *as* to leave me no other means of appeasing creditors than by shewing them my hopes of payment from Government to enable my satisfying them.

Your Lordship need not be told of the beseting importunities of tradesmen upon every expectant of fortune; or that an unprotected unsuspicious widow not tinctured with parsimony shou'd get entangled in their snares. This my Lord cou'd not have been my case were this expectancy never cherish'd, and so generally sanction'd by authorities of the highest consideration, *nor is that all*, for it was in the undisturb'd conviction of these claims being satisfied, "that my husband felt authoris'd to curtail my jointure £500 a year: and the like cause and feeling influenced the Duke of Queensbury[1] to recind £500 p an and £1000 of what he at one time actually bequeathed to me. But for those unfortunate claims and pretensions thought so irresistable by all my friends, Lord Nelson's provision for me wou'd have been of a different nature to that which by some management or contingencies has proved totally unproductive to me. It is easy then to see how much better wou'd be now my situation had not myself and friends been flatter'd by those pretensions and how much yet more so, *had* I hoarded what I expended, and rescued (as I might) what I cheerfully sacrificed for the publick benefit: or even had I not perform'd any services to the State that cou'd give me a colour of title to remuneration but even here my Lord the sum of my wayward grievance and hard fate does not end. The ardency with which I patronized and urged on to glory the hero of

1 The fourth Duke (1724–1810), with whom she had been on terms of friendly intimacy. He was notorious for his profligacy. His will became the subject of litigation and she derived no benefit from it. Nelson left her an annuity of £500, £2000 in cash, and an estate valued at over £12,000.

the Nile ended in the loss of my friends invaluable life; its true a gratefull country bestow'd upon him both living and dead those rewards he so richly merited: but then behold my Lord how I have fared for my zeal in promoting his and my country's glory.

The most false and infamous aspersion as well upon his honor as mine has been promulgated no doubt to bar my meed of praise and considera-tion. And I now feel it high time to speak and to give the lye eternal to the black infamy cast upon us.

Lord Nelson was not more brave than he was honorable and noble minded: wou'd it be either to have a criminal intercourse with the adored wife of his best his bosom friend.[1] Sir William Hamilton was not only the best of husbands to me; but also the father, friend, and monitor, to him I owed every thing, he was the kind benefactor and protector of my virtuous widow'd mother[2] who from the day of our marriage lived with us untill Sr William's death,[3] and afterwards with me untill her own: he was not only the gentleman & scholar—but also a man of the highest spirit and most tenacious both of national and private honor: to the hour of death he and Lord Nelson loved one another like brothers and there was no knowing either without feelings of the highest veneration and esteem, they seem'd to have but one heart they certainly had but one purse. In vindications of this nature I feel my Lord as innocence and honor ever must, *a horror* the grossness that necessarily attends the proof.

Then my Lord it was impossible that in Italy such a connexion cou'd exist. I was never seperate from the side of my mother or husband, and save in the hours of rest with him was always surrounded by company and domesticks. Alike was our situation in our nearly shipwreck'd pas-sage to Palermo with all the Royal Family Court and train. In our travels home I was never apart from my husband my mother or Miss Knight, the present Lady Attendant to Her Royal Highness the Princess Charlotte of Wales, who travel'd with us, whom immediately on her mother's death[4] I took under my roof, and who lived with me three years. On our arival in London Lord Nelson and Sir William took different lodgings, his Lordship was immediately after employed upon the coast and seldom came to town; upon his last visit Sir William *died in his arms* with a satisfaction not alloy'd, my Lord, by any base suspicion of his faithfull wife and bosom friend; nor had he room to harbour such. Immediately after Sir William's death Lord Nelson left the house and

1 There is no doubt that Lady Hamilton's child Horatia (b. January 1801) was Nelson's daughter: he acknowledged the child as his.

2 Mrs Lyon.   3 6 April 1803.   4 In 1799.

soon after the country upon his professional duty. When on his return after *about three years* absence, he found me living at Merton with the present Earl[1] and Countess Nelson his sisters and their grown up children, he remain'd with us but 25 days when he finally departed to go off Cadiz in that short time he was so immers'd in publick and private business as to afford his family and myself very little of his society. Now I appeal to all of the said family by whom he was during that time surrounded if such a connexion was possible. And I appeal to Admiral Sir Thomas Hardy,[2] to Miss Knight[3] and to every one that witness'd our manner of life, habits and intercourse in Italy if such a connexion there was not equally impossible. Yet my Lord that it is the force of this unfounded aspersion that makes Ministers fearfull of bringing forward the consideration of my memorial.

Then my Lord I pray you to believe that it wou'd afford me more pride and pleasure than any remuneration, that cou'd be offerd, to have this base aspersion thoroughly canvass'd, as I wou'd then be enabled to develope facts that wou'd undeceive those who are ignorant, and to confound the malignant: above all to rescue the memory of my beloved husband and my brave lamented friend from the odium thus cast upon their fame and honor as well as upon my Lord.

245 PRINCESS CHARLOTTE *to the* PRINCE REGENT

[March 1813.][4]

I AM this moment returned from my drive in the Park, & do not delay an instant informing you that I met the Princess,[5] who stopped her carriage & spoke to me for five minutes as she came to town to see the Duchess of Brunswick.[6] I trust this circumstance will not happen again, but as it was entirely unexpected by me I wished to give you the earliest inteligence, as I make it a point *never* to have *any concealments* from *you*.

I hope you will come soon to me,[7] which will give much pleasure to My dearest Father, [etc.].

1 William Nelson, second Viscount and first Earl Nelson (1757–1835). The Admiral's brother. He married Sarah, daughter of the Rev. Henry Yonge.

2 Sir Thomas Masterman Hardy, first Baronet (1769–1839), Nelson's flag-captain in the *Victory*. Created a Baronet, 1806.

3 See her *Autobiography* for her life in Naples and her intercourse with the Hamiltons.

4 From a paragraph in *The Times*, 10 March 1813, it would appear that this incident occurred on the 8th.

5 Charlotte was not allowed to see her mother without her father's permission.

6 Princess Caroline's mother, who died on 23 March 1813, at her lodgings in Hanover Square.

7 Her father neglected her, and, says Miss Knight, scarcely saw her once in two months.

Newman Street, March 1st 1813.

THE ingenius artist Mr. Heaphy[1] will have the honour to present you this letter—he has requested it of me, as having been informed that you were the proper person for him to see respecting the rooms in Pall Mall —formerly the Royal Academy.

Your permiting Mr. H. to see you on this business will greatly oblige him, as well as Dear Sir, [etc.].

247 VISCOUNT CASTLEREAGH *to the* PRINCE REGENT

St. James's Square,
Tuesday Morning, 2 A.M. [2nd March 1813].

LORD CASTLEREAGH has the honor to acquaint your Royal Highness, that the debate on Mr. Grattan's[2] motion has been further adjourn'd, the Speaker being unwel—there is every reason to hope that it will be terminated *tomorrow* or rather *this* night.[3]

Lord C. takes leave to apprize your Royal Highness that Mr. Speaker this evening received a letter from the Princess of Wales, but without any date, or signature.[4] The purport of the letter is, to complain of being judg'd without being heard, and wishing only for acquittal or condemnation & further desires that the letter may be read to the House of Commons, of course with a view to Thursday's debate. Lord C. will pay his duty to your Royal Highness tomorrow on this subject.

The names of the speakers in tonight's debate are submitted—those who vote for the Committee are mark'd with an F.—those against with an A.

1 Thomas Heaphy, the elder (1775 1835), the water-colour painter.
2 Henry Grattan (1746–1820).
3 Grattan's motion for a Committee on the Roman Catholic claims, brought forward on 25 February, was carried, after a debate lasting four days, on 3 March by 264 to 224.
4 See Colchester's *Diary*, II, 429, where the letter is dated 1 March 1813.

1 *Alpha Cottages, Marylebone Park,*
March 4th 1813.

HAVING done myself the honor of calling at Carlton House several times with Mr. West's letter of introduction but understanding that you were not likely to be in town at a time that I could see you, I take the liberty of writing to explain the business that induc'd me to call.

Through the pressure of the times my works have the last two years totally ceas'd selling, which oblidges me to form an Exhibition of as many of my works as I can get together as Mr. Wilkie did last year.[1] But a difficulty occurs through not getting a room in a good situation. I have applied to Mr. Christy for those rooms that he holds of the Prince Regent nearby adjoining Carlton House, but he gives them up on Lady Day next through their being so out of repair. The large room and small private room would be every thing that I could wish, its situation being so good. What ever repair they may want for the term of three months (from Lady Day to Midsummer Day) I could do. Mr. Wyatts[2] model of a theatre is in one of the rooms but as there is a smaller room and nobody at present goes to see it I presume that it would be no inconvenience to Mr. W.

Should you be able to accomplish my wish it would be doing me a most essential service.

I feel much hesitation at troubling you with the above request but I hope you will accept of my apology having been inform'd that the only channel to obtain it is through you.

249 SIR JAMES MACKINTOSH *to* COLONEL MCMAHON

15 *Great George St.*, 6th March [1813].

LORD MOIRA informed me yesterday that His Royal Highness had been pleased to grant me "the fullest access" to the invaluable collection of papers formerly belonging to the Stuart family which he has just received, & his Lordship added that he thought I might immediately apply to you to ascertain the mode in which I might avail myself of this most gracious permission. I am very anxious to do it as soon as possible as some of them must relate to the commencement of my History.

1 See Cunningham's *Life of Wilkie*, I, 341–54.
2 Benjamin Dean Wyatt (1775–1850?), the architect, who designed Drury Lane Theatre in 1811.

If you would have the goodness to ascertain the times & places which are thought proper for my examination I should esteem myself particularly obliged to you.

Your good nature & kindness induce me in confidence to observe to you that the examination of these voluminous papers would be conducted with far greater ease, quiet & advantage of every sort at this house than any where else if it were thought fit to entrust them to my care for a short time. My health does not yet allow me always to go out—but I could always carry on the inspection of the papers at home. The matter might be accomplished in half the time & the accommodation to me in making extracts &c would be very great. They might in that case be delivered to me by the catalogue which would be a sufficient security. In this way Lord Hardwick[1] & some other Noblemen have had the goodness to allow me the full use of their papers.

If you think this suggestion fit to be mentioned to His Royal Highness it would be the greatest favour to me to do so.

The very great obligation conferred by him would doubtless be enhanced in the heghest [*sic*] degree & his most gracious intention of granting me the fullest access would be completely carried into effect.

But this I entirely leave to your judgement. I shall take my chance of finding you at home between one & two but you should be gone abroad I beg the favour of an answer as soon as you can.

250 BENJAMIN WEST *to* MAJOR-GENERAL TURNER

Newman Street, March 16th, 1813.

I EMBRACE the first moment to write you this letter for the information of His Royal Highness the Regent—that I have made the last inspection of Mr. Wil[kie's] picture he has the honour of painting for the Regent by his commands, which I had the gratification to convay to Mr. Wil[kie]. The picture will be ready to present to the Regent by the 25th inst. His commands on what day and hour he may signify for seeing the picture—and by whom present, will be obayed.[2]

1 Philip Yorke, third Earl of Hardwicke (1757–1834).
2 See No. 256.

St. James's Square,
Wednesday [17 March 1813].

Lord Castlereagh has the honour to acquaint your Royal Highness that Mr. Whitbread abandoned his intention of moving to prosecute Lady Douglas,[1] concluding his speech with a motion to proceed against the editors of the Morning Post and Morning Herald for publishing the depositions.[2] This proposition was withdrawn in favour of a motion of Mr. Tierney's to bring the editors to the Bar for the purpose of ascertaining from whom these documents were received. The latter motion was negatived without a division.

Mr. Cartwright[3] and Mr. Lascelles[4] made useful speeches and the sentiments of several of the Country Gentlemen were rendered favourable by a previous meeting this forenoon at the Foreign Office.

Lord Castlereagh submits to your Royal Highness the list of speakers.

252 Queen Charlotte *to the* Prince Regent

Windsor, the 18th March 1813.

I cannot be silent to day my dearest son for I feel anxious to congratulate you upon the good turn things have taken last night in the House & also thank you for yr amiability in acquainting us with it so early. Indeed yesterday was a heavy day full of anxiety, but now as the Co[u]ntry Gentlemen begin to represent yr present conduct in this affair as forced upon you by yr adversary[5] I live in hopes that all will turn out to yrs & our satisfaction. This is the fervent prayer of yr affectionate mother.

1 On 17 March Whitbread presented to the House of Commons a petition from Sir John and Lady Douglas stating that they understood their original depositions were taken under such circumstances as might prevent any prosecution for perjury, but reasserting the truth of their charges against the Princess of Wales and desiring to re-swear the same facts in such a way as might remove all obstacles to a prosecution for perjury. Whitbread was advised that there were technical difficulties in the way. See No. 190.

2 On 13 March.

3 William Ralph Cartwright, M.P. for Northamptonshire; an independent country gentleman. (1771–1847.)

4 Henry Lascelles, second Earl of Harewood (1767–1841), another independent member. Styled Viscount Lascelles after the death of his elder brother in 1814; succeeded his father, 1820.

5 Cartwright, for example, said that no good could result from parliamentary interference. "He lamented the nature of these publications, but blamed those whose first publication of the Princess's letter [see No. 238] had naturally led to them, as the source of all the mischief that might ensue. That letter contained paragraphs calculated strongly to excite public

March 19th [1813].

I am the last man to give you trouble unnecessarily, well knowing from tryed & experienced friendship you wd not let an opportunity pass of serving me, but a circumstance has come to my knowledge which I will state to you with my wishes on the subject & leave it to your judgment & friendship as to making any stir in it.

I understand since the failure of Mr. Chinery of the Treasury[1] it is the intention of Government to remove to the Treasury Mr. Fruin[2] the Chairman of the Board of Customs, which will leave a vacancy at that Board.

I must confess a situation of that kind wd be a provission for me for life, though attended with considerable labor, for I am much afraid, my good friend, that any place I might get in which I was obliged to *pay for a seat in Parliament* would leave me little or nothing to live upon & you know from the *circumstances of my life* I am obliged to live entirely at home at my own expense & consequently am very poor, taking into consideration the sums of money I have expended in Parliamentary persuits. I hope you will excuse this letter. Upon this occasion as upon all others I will be guided by your better judgment, urged as I know it is by true and disinterested friendship. You must not trouble yourself by answering this.

254 The Duke of Northumberland *to* Colonel McMahon

Alnwick Castle, 19th March 1813.

Let me assure you, once for all, my dear Colonel, that the sense I feel of all your acts of kindness, and friendship, must make every letter from you acceptable whenever you have time and inclination to write to me. If it conveys to me only an account that you & Mrs. MacMahon are enjoying good health, it cannot fail to be interesting to me, because that will be intelligence which I shall rejoice to receive. Sincerity & gratitude are certainly plants which do not flourish much in a Court; but my educa-

opinion in a certain direction, and he could easily enter into the feelings of persons who deemed it right that there should be no partial statements of this important business, but that, if any part came forth, then that all should appear before the country." Lascelles, too, said that the publication of the depositions against the Princess of Wales was in some degree to be attributed to the provocative publication of her letter of 14 January to the Prince Regent.

1 See No. 41.

2 Richard Frewin (1742–1822) was appointed a Commissioner of Customs in 1786, became Chairman of the Board in 1810, and retired in May 1813. Henry Richmond was appointed to the vacant Commissionership, and Bradshaw's hopes were never realised.

tion & habits of life, were formed in a camp, & not in a palace, and altho' I have been compelled to quit the profession, I never will quit the manly and open caracter of a soldier. I lament much, altho' I am by no means surprised at the account you give me in your letter. It was so easy to foresee what has now happened, that at the very commencement of this ill advised business I predicted to my friend Mr. Brogden that it woud be attended by consequences of a much more serious nature than I imagined were generally apprehended. All this might easily have been avoided thro' the advice of sincere, honourable and wise friends, on either part. On Her Royal Highness's part nothing coud be expected from such confidential friends, as are said to be consulted by her.[1] Who His Royal Highness's confidential friends now are, I know not; probably the same to whom H:R:H: has given his confidence, and to whose advice he has thought proper to adapt his measures, since the begining of October last. How far their advice has been in general wise, or has tended to increase H:R:H:'s private happiness, or publick dignity & popularity, it woud very ill become me to be a judge. Most devoutly do I wish they may be able to bring H:R:H: thro' this business, with honour, credit & dignity. Ministers are most sincerely to be pitied; who are obliged to bear quietly & almost tacitly, the whole attack of the Princess's Party, as well as the odium & unpopularity which the violence of Party has contrived to attach to the business, without daring to clear their own caracters from the appearance of duplicity; one of the meanest vices of a truly low and dishonourable mind. I feel myself most truly happy, that the difference between their Royal Highnesses, was a subject on which, as you well know, my dear Colonel, I never woud enter, and which I ever avoided to have any concern in, always foreseeing that it woud some day or other come to a most serious crisis; & that I coud not approve entirely of the conduct on either part.

Most sincerely do I feel for the state of irritation which I am convinced this business will occasion to the Regent, & for the fatal consequences which may arise from it to the State. Tho' my own feelings were very little considered on a late occasion, yet I interest myself most zealously for whatever affects those of H:R:H:, and most devoutly do I hope H:R:H: will call for, & attend to wise, cool & well experienced counsel on this business, before he finally decides on the measures he will pursue. I confess the crisis is very critical & delicate; which might in my opinion have been easily avoided. I write the more freely to you, my dear Colonel, for as I have lost H:R:H:'s favour & confidence, my opinion and advice will not be required, nor indeed can they be expected.

1 Whitbread and Brougham were the Princess of Wales's principal advisers.

We all unite in compliments & the best wishes to you & Mrs. Mac-Mahon. H:R:H:'s present confidential friends have brought an old house about your ears; may you all get clear of it before it falls & crushes you. Adieu; & believe me, [etc.].

255 SIR JOHN LEICESTER[1] *to* SIR THOMAS TYRWHITT

Hill Street, March 19, 1813.

I TRUST you will excuse the liberty I take in troubling you with a few lines.

No one knows better than you, the sacrifices I have made in three Parliaments or the circumstances attendant upon the last, with the view solely of lending every feeble assistance in my power to the Prince Regent; or my anxious wishes for everything that concerns His Royal Highness welfare.

Since we have had any conversation upon this subject I have the additional motive of an infant son to inter[e]st any mark of His Royal Highness favor.

I am sure you will believe it is the furthest possible from my wishes to be intrusive, and that I am well aware what claims & expectations must press on all sides. But having heard from my friends that a creation of Peers is intended soon to take place, and urged by them, I leave it entirely to your goodness to recal me to His Royal Highness recollection, should he be pleasd graciously to bestow the honor of an Irish Baron. Anxious only to bear any mark of His Royal Highness' patronage, believe me [etc.].

256 BENJAMIN WEST *to* MAJOR-GENERAL TURNER

Newman Street, March 24th 1813.

THE picture which the Prince Regent honoured me with his commands to commission Mr. Wilkie to paint for him; with that princely liberality —by saying—"let Wilkie make choice of the subject—take his time in painting it—and fix his own price": is at No 29 Phillimore Place, Kensington, Mr. Wilkie's residence.

1 Sir John Fleming Leicester, first Baron de Tabley (1762–1827). M.P. for Yarmouth, Isle of Wight, 1791; Heytesbury, 1796; and Stockbridge, 1807. He was one of the Prince Regent's earliest friends, and a great patron of English painters, and was raised to the peerage in 1826.

I have frequently seen the picture in its progress to its finish; its subject is a youthful company playing at Blindmans Buff: you will find the subject is supported with that perspecuity every where appropriate to its character—life with mirth and good temper is seen in every group and in every figure—it places the painter in this class of Art prieminent to the Flemish Schools in mantal capasity, and is not inferior to them in deleniation—it does honour to Mr. Wilkie and the country.

257   QUEEN CHARLOTTE *to the* PRINCE REGENT

Windsor, the 28th March 1813.

I TAKE the earliest oportunity of returning you thanks for the communication you sent me of Windsor being the place fixed upon for the poor Dutchess of Brunswick's interment.[1] I hope not to appear too medling if I suggest that as the whole is under the Lrd Chamberlains direction either Lrd Harford[2] or Lrd Jocelin should attend the procession, & also if possible Count Münster[3] as the family Minister. All those that belong to the Establishment here will be at the Church door to receive the body as a respect due to the King & attention which, could he know it, he would be highly pleased with.

I am glad to hear that the meeting at Black Heath is gone off so well, as also to learn that this act of yours has given universal satisfaction in the world.[4] I hope this will stop all further proceedings tho I will own I always live in terror of something new, but provided if what ever may arise does but come unprovoked I feel courageous that all will go well.

Sophia[5] is better to day which gives me great comfort to inform you of, the day is so fine that we are all going out & I hope you may enjoy the fresh air in yr pritty garden which will contribute to yr health in which none can be more interested than [etc.].

1 See No. 245.

2 Francis (Ingram) Seymour, second Marquis of Hertford (1743–1822). Lord Chamberlain of the Household, 1812–21.

3 Count Münster had been one of the Hanoverian Ministers of State since 1805. In 1806, when Prussian troops occupied the Electorate, he retired to England. In March 1812 he was appointed one of three commissioners for the protection and management of the King's private property. (1766–1839.)

4 On the 25th the Prince Regent gave his daughter permission to visit her mother. She went the following day, accompanied by the Duchess of Leeds and Miss Knight, who reported that they passed "a very quiet and comfortable day".

5 The fifth daughter of George III and Queen Charlotte (1777–1848).

March 31st 1813.

THE gracious interest which your Royal Highness has testified on the occasion of this strange attack upon me from Mr. Whitbread far overpays any dis-satisfaction which so unworthy a procedure has excited. Indeed, the measure of that dis-satisfaction is so trifling that I have no merit to assert for letting it be outweighed by your generous feelings on the subject. I know not well wherefore, but I cannot find in my heart to be aggrieved by this occurence. Perhaps the reason is, that the conduct befits the porter-brewer, & that I am conscious I ought not to be angry with what is only the nature of the animal.[1]

With the truest devotion I remain, Sir, [etc.].

259 LORD ELDON *to the* PRINCE REGENT

Bedford Square, March 31, [1813].

THE LORD CHANCELLOR, offering his most humble duty to your Royal Highness the Prince Regent, takes leave, (after apologising, on account of the extreme pressure of business, for presuming to make this communication in this form, instead of personally waiting upon your Royal Highness) to mention that it was his intention to have postponed humbly taking your Royal Highness's pleasure upon the nomination of a Vice Chancellor till Easter: but the unexampled weight of business, which must be earlier disposed of, has obliged him to allow that purpose.

He thinks it right to state that he had entertained a wish that he might be permitted to mention the name of Lord Redesdale,[2] who had been Chancellor of Ireland upon this occasion, but his Lordship declines giving that permission. The Chancellor therefore begs leave humbly to recommend to your Royal Highness the name of Mr Atty General[3] whose anxiety to have this situation, as it is represented to the Lord Chancellor, he thinks himself bound to attend to, considering the claims incident to his present situation.

The Chancellor takes leave to mention that the Cabinet have not yet formed their report upon the papers lately transmitted to the Chan[r]— but probably will do so on this day.

1 On 27 March the newspapers published a private letter written by Lord Moira which Whitbread considered as reflecting upon the Princess of Wales. Four days later he raised the matter in Parliament. (*Parl. Deb.* xxv, 460.)

2 John Freeman-Mitford, first Baron Redesdale (1748–1830). Lord Chancellor of Ireland, 1802–6.

3 Sir Thomas Plumer (1753–1824), Attorney-General since June 1812; created first Vice-Chancellor of England, under the provisions of 53 George III, cap. 24. See *Twiss*, II, 238–43.

London, 3 April 1813.

RECEIVED of H.R.H. the Prince of Wales (by payment of the Rt. Hon. John McMahon) four hundred and sixty seven pounds which has been owing to me since the years 1796 and 1797 for the subscription of two boxes at the Opera House and some masquerade tickets.

W. TAYLOR.

261 THE EARL OF MOIRA *to* COLONEL MCMAHON

Saturday Night, April 3d [1813].

THORNTON has been with me, to detail a little artifice which is practising against his election to the Chair.[1] It is an attack upon him & Sir Hugh Inglis for having gratified me *solely* with five cadetships which is attempted to be construed as a bribe to me, to make me promote the friends of Sir Hugh & Thornton in India. They thence wish you to copy the enclosed & address it to Sir Hugh Inglis; *to be confidentially shown to only one person.* It must be on gilt paper, & sealed with red wax, to correspond with the date. Thornton will call upon you at *eleven* tomorrow, to explain this more fully.

262 THE DUKE OF NORTHUMBERLAND *to* COLONEL MCMAHON

Alnwick Castle, 4th April 1813.

I HAD the pleasure of receiving your letter by the post last night, and as I am just on the eve of my departure from hence for the South, I have taken up my pen to answer it directly, lest the hurry of business just before my leaving this place shoud prevent me, if I delayed it.

I much fear the letter written by H:R:H: the Princess Charlotte, and the visit to Black Heath,[2] will not induce those who are evil minded to put an end to those very mischievous discussions which have lately irritated the publick mind, unless this intercourse between the Princess of Wales and her daughter is to continue perfectly free and uninterrupted in future. Then, of course they must be silent, at least for a time, as Her

1 Robert Thornton was elected Chairman of the Court of Directors of the East India Company in 1813.
2 See No. 257. "Charlotte" is obviously a slip for "Caroline".

Royal Highness will have carried her point, & gained the victory. How Mr. Whitbread coud make such a speech, as the last I saw in the papers, I am at a loss to conceive, as I had always heard him spoken of as a sensible man. His conduct however throughout this unfortunate business certainly does not tend to confirm this report.[1]

I am much concerned on Lord Moira's account, for the very unpleasant situation in which he is placed, by this ever to be lamented discussion. It has done more mischief in lowering the caracters of all the parties concerned in the estimation of the respectable country gentlemen, & the middle class of inhabitants of this country, than is easy to conceive; and so far has answered the purpose of the instigators of the measure.

I coud say much on military matters, did I not recollect that my military experience & services are not of the least consideration, nor fit to be put in comparison with those of an half pay Captain of Light Dragoons.[2] I shall therefore conclude with offering you the compliments of the Duchess, my family, & myself, & desiring you to present the same for us to Mrs. Mac-Mahon.

Adieu My dear Colonel, & be assured I ever am, [etc.].

263 FRANCES, COUNTESS OF JERSEY *to the* PRINCE REGENT

April 6th 1813.

AT the risk of your displeasure of your thinking me presuming, I must entreat that your Royal Highness will read this letter. I have been three weeks in Staffordshire, at my return I hear from various quarters, it has been asserted that I have been in Her Royal Highness the Princess of Wales's confidence, & one of her *advisers* in the late transaction; that I was in the habit of meeting her at Lady Oxfords[3] & that I went out of town at the moment I did in order not to appear to be one of her counsellors. I entreat that your Royal Highness will believe that I do not intend by this letter to force myself into your Royal Highness's presence any longer than while I justify myself—but Sir I have long smarted under the effects of the malice of my enemies without knowing of what I have been accused, and now that I am possessed of a specific charge

---

1 See No. 258.   2 See Nos. 214, 215.

3 Jane Elizabeth, daughter of the Rev. James Scott, and wife of Edward Harley, fifth Earl of Oxford. Sir Francis Burdett, Lord Archibald Hamilton, and Byron, were the most notable of her lovers. From the doubtful paternity of her four children, they came to be known as the "Harleian Miscellany". She was born in 1772 and died in November 1824; her husband died in 1848.

against myself, I will not end my life under so vile an aspersion. Permit me then to assure you by every thing most sacred, that I have never directly or indirectly had any communication with the Princess since I sent to her my letter of resignation, & that I have never been in Lady Oxfords house since last Summer when I was there at a Ball. If your Royal Highness recollects my character, you will remember that to *advise* was never my taste, & if *truth* respecting me has reached your Royal Highnesses ears you will know that I have ever expressed myself with that dutyful respect, & attachment to your Royal Highnesses interests which I ought to feel. If your Royal Highness could imagine what I have suffered from this accusation you would pardon my venturing to enter into an explanation.

Should you be graciously pleased to make it known to me, that you are not offended at the liberty I have taken and that you believe what I have asserted you will relieve me from great unhappiness.

264 ROBERT FULKE GREVILLE[1] *to* COLONEL MCMAHON

The Rangers Lodge, Richmond Park,
April 6th 1813.

MR. SMITH[2] of St. George's Row, who probably you know as an artist of very superior abilities in water colour drawing, has intimated to me, from himself & brother artists (whose works in oil and water colours are to be exhibited at the ensueing Exhibition at Spring Gardens, the latter end of this month) their wishes & humble hopes that His Royal Highness the Prince Regent would in his gracious goodness give patronage to their Exhibition by honoring it with his inspection, *previous* to its being opened to the public.

Should His Royal Highness be pleased to honour them with so flattering a mark of his condescension, would you have the goodness to mention to His Royal Highness, that the *23d & 24* of this month APRIL, are the ONLY TWO DAYS when all the pictures *could* be ready, & *prepared*, for such particular distinction, & that *the Exhibition* of *the painters in oil* & *in water colours* in their room in Spring Gardens, opens on the Monday following, viz. on April 26th.

1 The third son of the eighth Baron Brooke. He was the diarist's second cousin once removed, and one of George III's Equerries from 1781 to 1797. [1751–1824.]

2 John Smith (1749–1831), for some years Secretary and President of the Watercolour Society.

Mr. Smith is the principal manager this year. If there is no impropriety in the request, I shall be most thankful to you if you will have the goodness to mention the wishes of these artists (& which have been communicated to me by Mr. Smith) to His Royal Highness the Prince Regent, & if His Royal Highness should be pleased to signify his pleasure to you, may I hope to receive any communication which you may be permitted to make, & which I would carefully report to Mr. Smith, for his own, & for the information of his brother artists.

266 THE MARQUIS OF STAFFORD[1] *to* MAJOR-GENERAL TURNER

Cleveland House, April 10, 1813.

I HAVE desired Mr. Gillam, the Secretary of the British Institution, to wait upon you, in order to receive from you His Royal Highness the Prince Regent's orders respecting the pictures which His Royal Highness has been so gracious as to allow to be sent to the approaching Exhibition of the works of Sir Josuah Reynolds.

266 THE EARL OF MOIRA *to the* PRINCE REGENT

Portsmouth, April 10th 1813.

IT is impossible for me to be on the eve of such long separation from you & not to express once more my ardent prayers for every blessing to your Royal Highness. That anxiety for your welfare will not cease but with my existence.

I leave you, Sir, in a state of affairs more likely to become seriously embarrassing than I think is calculated by those around you. Were I asked in what manner the impending troubles are to be surmounted, I would say "The Prince has only to recur to the generosity & magnanimity of his own nature in order to rise above all political difficulties. A cold & creeping system suits so little with the scale of these incidents which the present unexampled crisis must daily offer, that a Sovereign pursuing it would unavoidably be regarded by his people as unequal to what the times demanded. The Prince should soar & dazzle the public eye,

---

1 George Granville Leveson-Gower, first Duke of Sutherland (1758–1833). Succeeded his father as second Marquis in 1803; created Duke of Sutherland, 1833.

& be admired". Pardon me, Sir, if there be any presumption in this suggestion to the dignity of your spirit. It can have no reference to myself. My interests are put into a line in which their relation must be remote indeed from ought that passes here. Nothing personal can be contemplated by the liberty I take: and if it require excuse, that excuse will be found for it by your goodness, in the habit of that earnest solicitude for your fame & happiness which your Royal Highness has for so many years condescendingly allowed me to indulge.

With unalterable perseverance in that disposition, I remain Sir, [etc.].

267 THE EARL OF MOIRA *to* COLONEL MCMAHON

Portsmouth, April 11th 1813.

HAVING to write to Ld Melville by an express, I cannot refrain from troubling you with a line. We are now ordered to convoy the India men round the Cape of Good Hope.[1] Ld Melville asked me whether I should object to convoying them as far as Madeira. I answered that I should not, because it could not make a difference of above three or four days. This addition may be three or four weeks augmentation to the length of our voyage; as we are to be tied to the pace of any bad sailer or any crippled ship in the squadron. I feel this for Lady Loudoun;[2] I feel it more for the Prince. It was the profession of His Royal Highness that I should go out in that dignified stile which should rebut the popular imputation that he was only studying to get rid of me, & which should testify that he still condescended to feel an interest for me. Every single advantage held forth has failed me. The having a line of battle ship[3] cannot be considered a distinction. I ask whether after the fate of the Java any Ministers would on public grounds have allowed me to go out in a frigate?[4] As it is, I can only be regarded as being permitted to take my passage (paying cursedly for it too) in a ship that is to convoy the trade. Indeed, indeed, this is not decorous. I speak not as to myself but as to the testimony which the Prince wished to give of his earnestness to make this mission creditable to me. Lucrative it cannot be after the annulment of advantages proposed, but honorable it might have been

1 Warships convoyed fleets of merchant vessels during the Napoleonic War.

2 She and her three eldest children accompanied Moira to India.

3 *The Stirling Castle,* commanded by Admiral Sir Home Riggs Popham (1762–1820).

4 The *Java* frigate, whilst on its way to the East Indies, was destroyed off the Brazilian coast on 29 December 1812 by the more powerful American frigate *Constitution.*

made; & it is a pity to have the grace of the measure frittered away thro' these intrigues of the Board which baffle the kind dispositions of Lord Melville.

[P.S.] We go aboard tomorrow, & shall sail I imagine on Tuesday morning.

Miss Knight to the Prince Regent, 13 April 1813. (Miss Knight's *Autobiography*, I, 228, where the date of the letter is not given.)

268 THE EARL OF MOIRA *to* COLONEL MCMAHON

Stirling Castle, Spithead,
April 14th 1813.

To the representation which I made of the heavy delay ensured to our voyage (as we have two notoriously execrable sailers in our convoy) Ld Melville has pleaded that he should be unjustifiable did he not give the India ships & storeships the benefit of our protection. When a man in office has a mind to be ungracious there can be no difficulty in finding an excuse of public service for being so. Do not say any thing further on the subject. I am silent: but I shall not forget all that I have experienced. The wind is unfavorable or we should have put to sea today. We are in hopes it may veer so as to enable us to sail early tomorrow. I shall have to put a packet to Adam[1] under cover to you, to be dispatched by to-morrow's post, so you will hear the last of us, in an English port at least.

269 THE EARL OF MOIRA *to* COLONEL MCMAHON

Spithead, April 15th 1813.

THE wind is adverse; & we were forced to annul a signal which we made at day-break for our convoy to weigh anchor. Luckily the breeze is so weak as not to be likely to last. We shall wait patiently aboard to take advantage of the earliest change. The foul wind, however, may last long enough for me to have your answer. Therefore let me ask you if there is any truth in a report which Sir Home Popham has this day mentioned to me, that the Directors had a Secret Court in which it was proposed to

1 William Adam. See No. 18.

annul my appointment. I cannot imagine that such a circumstance occurred; because one cannot comprehend what ground could be advanced for so extravagant a procedure. Pray forward the packet to Adam; as likewise that for Ld Erskine. The former by a safe hand.

God bless you, My dear friend.

[P.S.] There is one J: Johnson, whose letter I enclose. Your saying a good word for him (as the phrase goes in Ireland) may be useful. I will beg you to do it if occasion serves, as it is only for advancement in his line.

270 PETER STUART *to* COLONEL MCMAHON

85 Hatton Garden, April 15/13.

PARDON me for stating, that if you could prevail upon the Prince Regent to allow me, through your medium, the loan of £150 *at this time*, it would save me and mine from *much serious consequences*, and be the means of re-animating in His Royal Highness's service a man who has been uniformily zealous for the interest of the Prince and his friends. The acknowledgment shall be given to you for its repayment in the course of a twelve month; and I would pledge myself thus to close all pecuniary concerns whatever for efforts of attachment which I have always found warmly commended.

A long series of illness, and other causes which can be mentioned when I have the pleasure of seeing you, induce me reluctantly to impose this kind task *for once* upon your friendship; and with your permission, I'll wait upon you between ten and eleven o'ck next Monday.

271 SIR WILLIAM MANNERS[1] *to* COLONEL MCMAHON

Oxford Street, West end,
April 16 [1813].

ALLOW me to ask you two questions. Since I last had the honor of writing to you, a great change in politics has taken place.

Parties being nothing to me, my Parliamentary interest will always

1 The son of John Manners, of The Grange, Grantham (a natural son of Lord William Manners, M.P. for Leicestershire), and of Louisa, Countess of Dysart (1745–1840). He was M.P. for Ilchester, 1806–7, and was created a Baronet in 1793. [1766–1833.] He married Catherine Rebecca (d. 1852), daughter of Francis Grey.

[SIR WILLIAM MANNERS *to* COL. MCMAHON, 16 APRIL 1813, *cont.*]

follow the politics of Carlton House. Have you any friends of the same sentiments desirous of securing seats for the next Parliament without trouble, opposition, or even attendance. If you have, & will refer them to me, or name them, I will enter into arrangements with them to their satisfaction, either for Ilchester, where I have reduced the votes to fifty two, all of whom are tenants at will, or for Grantham, where I own by inheritance & purchase the chief part of the parish, & have the Duke of Rutland at my command. Therefore any opposition there is now out of the question.

My second question is, whether you can form an idea at what time the promise of the peerage will be realised to me.[1]

[P.S.] I will return your letter, if you desire it.

272 PETER STUART *to* COLONEL MCMAHON

85 *Hatton Garden*, April 18,/13.

I FEEL myself exceedingly obliged by your very friendly letter of this day.

I acknowledge it both inadvertent and indecorous to have submitted any proposition for a loan—even through your kind medium—to such a very high character as the P.R.; but, at the moment, it occurred as the most delicate way of urging a temporary relief, fully persuaded that I ought to offer you the return of it at the time mentioned, even should its appropriation be ordered for a charitable purpose.

Pardon me for mentioning a fact which can be proved by respectable witnesses, and which, although *I do not attempt to state as a claim*, has, by a species of over-zeal, been the origin of my present difficulties. For

1 See No. 597. In March he had written to Perceval on the subject, and Perceval had replied on the 18th, saying that the Prince Regent had been advised to refrain from creating any new Peers of the United Kingdom. "It has been therefore and still is out of my power to tell you at what time you may expect it. As this is the case it is unnecessary that I should at present trouble you with any inquiries into the particulars of this written promise, which at least is so far out of the ordinary course of matters of this description as to put me under the necessity of making such inquiries before I can satisfy myself that it is consistent with my duty to advise H.R.H. to grant this peerage, for you must be aware that, by the Constitution of the country, H.R.H. cannot, either as Regent or King, exercise any of the prerogatives of the Crown but under the advice of some responsible Minister and consequently that such Minister has a duty which requires him to know the circumstances which are connected with any promise which he may be desirous to carry into execution." Perceval sent a further elaborate reply on the 28th. (Add. MS. 38191, fos. 220, 232.) Liverpool declared on 10 October 1812 that he could have had three seats from Sir W. Manners. (Add. MS. 40181, fo. 15.)

several years I knew of an important series of *"the Book"*,[1] and some months ago gave securities for the purchase, in order, as has always been my endeavour, to SUPPRESS every thing of the kind whose publicity could be supposed to have the smallest tendency to wound the feelings of the P.R. or any of his illustrious family. And when I thought I was about to obtain the well-earned approbation of my conduct, out came suddenly and unexpectedly the contents of Pandora's box, and all my efforts of suppression were dissipated in idle dreams. For this exertion of loyalty I have already sustained, as could be easily proved, a greater loss than the sum stated. But although I most solemnly aver, that I now communicate the *real truth*, I beg it to be clearly understood, that the relief now solicited, may not be considered as on that account, but for past services, and in A VERY SERIOUS EXTREMITY OF DANGER.

Have the goodness to put it on any footing which your better judgment may direct; and be assured that although my humble efforts can never cease in support of the P.R., yet that it is the *very last time* which any application from me of a *pecuniary* nature shall ever be made for any services which I may have rendered. Barring this obstacle, my prospects are immediately flattering, being about to be connected with a publication by which I will be enabled to serve myself and friends. Nothing but the *most serious extremity*, which I have for the two last months combated in vain, could have induced me to apply wth most dutiful respects and most humble devotion to the P.R. Excuse me for earnestly requesting a favourable answer on the receipt of this, which I hope in God may be before Wednesday next; and I beg and pray that you will *for this once* save from a dreadful abyss, [etc.].

273 PETER STUART *to* COLONEL MCMAHON

85 *Hatton Garden,*
Wedy Morning (Ap. 21) [1813].

PARDON me for thus obtruding myself again upon you so soon after my last letter; but the time is so rapidly approaching, that I tremble for the issue, if not prevented by your kind interference.

In my humble and dutiful representation to His Royal Highness the Prince Regent, please put the affair in the most favourable point of view which your friendship can suggest, and which His Royal Highness, in the plenitude of his goodness, will condescend to admit. Such an effort

1 Perceval's defence of the Princess of Wales.

at this time will impose upon me the most grateful and permanent recollection.

In the hope and belief that my request—submitted only at *the utmost
extremity of danger*—will be complied with, I pledge myself *never* again
to make any application of a *pecuniary* nature for any services, and to
cancel at once any reference whatever to the annuity which was several
years regularly paid. But your better judgment and discretion may perhaps think it improper at this time to glance at such an act; and therefore
I leave my case to the benevolent construction of His Royal Highness as
viewed through your friendly medium.

I am glad to find that you are returned to town; and very impatiently
hope that you'll allow me to call upon you this day, or early to-morrow,
to save me and mine at this time from the most dreadful consequences.

274 THE EARL OF MOIRA *to* COLONEL McMAHON

April 22d 1813, 10 A.M.
10 Leagues S.W. of the Lizard.

A SHIP, apparently homeward bound, seems inclined to speak to us:
So I get this ready to apprize you that we have cleared the Channel. The
wind is as fair as it can blow, & strong. Thanks to the convoy attached
to us, we can avail ourselves but insufficiently of it. With double reefed
topsails we go too fast for some of the ships which have put out every rag
of canvas they can carry.

[P.S.] Pray send this key to the person who has charge of my house.[1]
The convoy will make the difference of six weeks in our voyage.

May 1st, Lat 36.35, Long 12.

The ship did not come to us: but we have this day stopped a Spaniard
bound to Cadiz; & I risk this by him. We have had a formidable gale;
quite a hurricane. Most of our convoy have lost masts. The Indefatigable frigate has lost two. We came off with having every sail
shivered to pieces. We are however all well. Adieu.

1 His London house, in St James's Place, was sold by auction in May for 14,200 guineas,
presumably for the benefit of his creditors.

85 Hatton Garden,
Mondy morng April 26, 1813.

YOU may well remember, that on a former occasion when I was indebted to your friendly efforts, I declined every reference to any other person than yourself in matters respecting His Royal Highness the Prince Regent.

Suffer me therefore, at this extreme crisis, to draw upon you, at any date or dates you please, for one hundred pounds; and thus to close at once all pecuniary affairs. I promise faithfully to return it to you in the course of nine or twelve months; and it will at this time render me uncommon service. I hope you'll consider my past exertions in favour of the Pr. Regt. and yourself in some degree entitled to the indulgence of such a loan.

Allow me to wait upon you tomorrow morning for this purpose; and thus oblige Sir, [etc.].

276 THE REV. SIR ROBERT PEAT *to* COLONEL MCMAHON

Parsonage House, New Brentford,
12 May 1813.

SIR ROBERT PEAT presents his respectful compliments to Colonel McMahon; requests to have the honor of a few minutes conversation with him respecting an intended publication which has come to Sir Robert's notice relating to the Princess of Wales, which in his opinion may produce much irritation on the public mind.

Altho' Sir Robert never had the honor of being presented to His Royal Highness the Prince Regent, yet from having been so many years upon his list of Chaplains, added to other circumstances, he cannot help feeling much interested in any thing that concerns the Prince.

Sir Robert trusts this feeling will apologise (if an apology be necessary) for interfering in a subject, which concerns him, no further, than in shewing his desire to seize every, even the most trifling, occasion, of proving his attachment to the Prince—and the obligation he is under, for the polite manner, in which Colonel McMahon received him at Carlton House.

Sir Robert will wait on Colonel McMahon tomorrow at 11 o'clock, and take the chance of finding him disengaged.

16 May 1813.

I CANNOT express to you how much delighted I am with yr most kind & affectionate letter. I shall not object to your visiting your mother upon the occasion of her birthday, but I confide so much in your own discretion, sense of propriety, & what you must feel is the delicacy of both our situations at the present moment, that you will see how desireable it is to make this merely a morning visit, & not to extend it to that hour of the day when you might be subjected to society, of the nature of which I cannot be apprized, which I might not approve of and which consequently I have every reason to rest satisfied that you would not wish to meet.[1]

I cannot conclude, my dearest child, without once more expressing to you the extreme gratification your very affectionate & delightfull note has given me, and how truly & affec^tly I remain, [etc.].

P.S. I was in the very midst of dinner when I receiv'd your note & therefore could not answer it till my company broke up.

278 The Duke of Cumberland[2] *to the* Prince Regent

Stralsund, May 20th 1813.

AFTER a most tiresome and disagreeable passage of 36 hours I landed here at 4 o'clock yesterday morning, not having been in bed since the night previous to my landing at Gottenburg last Friday morning. I had most fully intended to have started from hence the moment my carriages were landed, and that I could obtain horses, which is *not* to be done like in dear England where I can send to Martin etc. for 4 horses, but *here* before a stranger leaves a place there are soldiers, noncommission'd officers, officers etc for two or three hours long to enquire who you are and the questions of the Lord knows how long. Well we all thought the Prince Royal[3] was still at Carlscrona, when lo and behold in my little pied à terre at the captain of the packet boats when I was waiting for my carriage and horses came a general officer habillé et brodé with his yellow

1 Miss Knight, Princess Charlotte's Lady Companion, wrote: "On the 17th of May we had visited the Princess of Wales on her birthday, but were not allowed to dine there."
2 On 2 May the Duke left England for the Continent in the hope of getting a military command in the Allied Army, and also the Governorship of Hanover, to which, however, his brother, the Duke of Cambridge, was appointed in the autumn, after the French had been expelled. Before leaving London the Duke disposed of his wine cellar and his stud of 16 horses.
3 Bernadotte.

ribband on his coat (which by the by *all* the general officers wear *eternally* here) an Aide Camp and an officier d'Ordonnance of the Pr[ince] R[oyal] who desired to see me. The General told me he had received orders from the Pr.R., who had heard of my having arrived at Gottenburg, to meet me wherever I was and beg me to come to his headquarters. I said that I was merely a passenger and meant to proceed to Strelitz as soon as I could get my horses. He then said that he really thought that I ought to wait as the account of the safety of the roads was not yet known. I then thought within myself that the wisest thing I could do would be to make a merit of the necessity of staying....He then told me that there was a house prepared for me, and that he recommended me to go there directly. I went there in one of the P.R. carriages & found guard of honour, of a Captain, colours, and 100 men of the Grenadiers of the Queen. In about a quarter of an hour the P.R. came in person attended by *all* the General Officers, officers of State to the number I suppose of 200. Nothing could be more polite really than he is, and much less of the Frenchman than anyone could suppose. He said, "Qu'il le regardait comme un des plus beaux jours de sa vie de voir un Pr. Anglais chez lui, que c'était la première nation de l'univers, et qu'il n'oubliait jamais tout ce qu'il devrait au Pr. Regent d'Angleterre. To which I replied that the very last words the Prince Regent had said to me, on leaving him that day 3 weeks was that "He desired me should I meet with the Pr. Royal of Sweden to express to him in his person how much he was satisfied with him and that he put his whole confidence in him for the defence & recovery of his German dominions, that there was not one of the House of Brunswick who did not feel grateful to him for his conduct to the country of Hannover when in command there....He then took me by the hand and pressing it said "V[otre] A[ltesse] R[oyale] peut dire au Pr. Regent qu'il me comble de bontés et qu'il trouvera en moi un homme franc et toujours digne de sa confiance."

He then wanted to speak to me respecting the conduct he had met with from Russia. I stopped him & said, "Mon Prince, je ne suis que soldat, et ce n'est que dans ce caractère que je me présente ici, voulant servir dans la bonne cause, quant aux politiques je n'ai pas le désir de m'en mêler, n'y étant pas chargé du Pr. Regent mon frère, & en même temps je suis assez franc pour déclarer à V.A. que je ne m'y entends pas. I hope *this* answer will satisfy you. To which he replied, Prince, permettez moi de vous répondre deux mots, quand au premier je suis sur que vous agissez franchement en me disant que le P. ne vous a pas chargé de commissions, mais quand au dernier vous m'excuserez quand j'observe que vous êtes connu d'être très lié avec le Pr. Regent votre frère & que nous savons qu'il vous aime. To which I replied that I did not deny I had the satisfaction of living a great deal with you but that really my living so much with you was from attachment reciprocal to each other, but that as to *affairs* je ne m'en mêlais pas.[1] So far I hope I have acted as you could wish. Well, in about a quarter of an hour after, he went away. I went and returned his visit, when I found the whole garrison. He immediately came up to me and taking me by the hand took me to his closet (alias) his bedroom, when he said that since he had seen me he had received a courier from Mr. Alopeus[2] who had written him a most extraordinary letter which he begged to communicate to me. I then again repeated what I had said before, namely that "I was no politician but merely a soldier, to which he said, "ainsi soit il alors comme soldat. Je vous prie de lire cette lettre & ma réponse que je vous donne à garder. I thought *refusing this* would be absurd, and I took it and *confidentially* I give it you, but trusting to your honour *not* to commit me with Castlereagh, for I suppose M[ajor] Gen[era]l Hope[3] who arrived *here* last night and had an interview with the P.R., will have learnt all this and will of course communicate it to him, but perhaps by my sending it to you, you will get it a *few* hours sooner and will shew it to Munster. That I applaud his answer most fully I do, and at the same time talking of Hamburg I could not help telling him of the necessity of saving it if possible, for the effect of its being taken would be bad chez nous, first on acct. of the communication with England then being cut off, & 2ndly that our merchants would feel severe losses.[4] In short he seemed to feel this and ordered in my presence the different battalions to march forward this morning, & *all* the cavalry he has as yet on this side of the water, which only consists of Myran's Hussars, 3 squadrons about 600 men; the other transports are expected & I suppose by Hope's being arrived they are also; when all his forces are arrived they will consist as he told me of 36,000 infantry & 4000 cavalry. What I have seen of the infantry they

1 This is not a very candid statement. The Duke of Cumberland was a strong Tory politician, closely connected politically with Lord Eldon, and he had been instrumental in keeping the Tories in office in the spring of 1812. Referring to the 1812 negotiations, he wrote in 1827: "I was happy enough after six weeks hard labour to place the late Administration in their seats." (*Bathurst*, p. 635.) Cp. *Romilly*, III, 42: "Lord Eldon has been every day closeted with the Duke of Cumberland.... We have even had the Duke of Cumberland coming down to Westminster Hall, and sending for the Chancellor out of court."

2 Prussian Ambassador to several Courts (d. 1821).

3 Sir Alexander Hope (1769–1837). He had just been sent on a confidential military mission to Sweden, and, with Edward Thornton, the British envoy to Sweden, he now went to Kiel to negotiate a peace between Great Britain and Denmark, which had been in alliance with France since 1807. The Treaty was not signed until 14 January 1814.

4 In March the French had evacuated Hamburg but they reoccupied it on 30 May, the Russian General Wallmoden being inadequately supported, and threatened by a Danish as well as a French army. Bernadotte besieged and captured the city in December.

are really *fine* men young and active. I have only seen detachments of the Hussars which appear to me a very pretty Regt.—nice little horses about 14 h[ands] to 14 h[ands]. 2.

Having now related to you all the material I will now just add a few lines regarding less interesting points. The P.R. is a man about 49, as tall as I am, very thin, black complexion, dress very much recherché. He wears a plain blue coat, one row of buttons buttoned up to the top with a blue and gold sash and a small order round his neck with a red ribband which I am told is a Freemason's order instituted or rather revived by the present King.[1] The oddest thing is his wearing the blue ribband over his right shoulder to which is suspended a small sword like the one you have of the Pr[ince] of Peace.[2] He wears white pantaloons, *high* Hussar boots and gold spurs, a black hat with a black feather round it and the yellow cockade. I dined with him; there was over 70 people there. I saw Potzo di Borgo[3] who had been sent here from the Emperor,[4] and General de Suchtelen, the Russian Ambassador, who appears a most agreeable man. His son is also here, and Chief of the Staff attached to Walmoden.[5] Lt. Colonel Cooke[6] is also here. Mr. Thornton is not yet arrived, at least *not* to my knowledge....

Now God bless you. Excuse the length of this letter, but I hope it may amuse you a few minutes, and do let me have *a line* from you to say you are satisfied with what I have done. I set off for Strelitz this day,[7] but must travel all night to get there. I had not been in bed from last Friday till last night and I got up at 5 this morning to write this to you. God bless you and do not forget [etc.].

1 Charles XIII (d. 1818).

2 Manuel de Godoy, Duke of Alcudia (1767–1851), the Spanish statesman and favourite of Charles IV. In 1795 he received the title of the Prince of the Peace, for having negotiated at Basle a Treaty of Peace between France and Spain. The sword, and a belt, were given by Napoleon to Godoy, together with the Grand Order of the Eagle, instituted by the Emperor himself, and afterwards named the Legion of Honour. The sword and belt were sold by the Supreme Junta at Seville, with the personal belongings of the Prince of Peace, in 1809, and purchased by Lord Wellesley, who in 1811 presented it to the Royal Collection. The sword was made at Versailles.

3 Count Pozzo di Borgo (1764–1842), the Corsican, an inveterate enemy of Napoleon. Since 1803 he had been in the service of the Tsar, who sent him on many diplomatic missions.

4 Alexander I (1777–1825).

5 Count von Wallmoden-Gimborn, the Russian General, who was opposing Marshal Davout on the Lower Elbe.

6 See his letters dated 21 and 22 May 1813, in *Castlereagh Corresp.* IX, 18–21. He reports that the Duke has "done good by his manners and conduct towards the Prince Royal, who appears highly satisfied with him".

7 He left on the 21st. "He says that he will await the arrival of the Emperor's instructions at Strelitz", reports Lieutenant-Colonel Cooke, "but I rather suspect that he will go on to Berlin, as I know two of his *aides-de-camp* are already gone."

Strelitz, May 26 [1813].

HAVING just an opportunity of writing you a *few* lines I do it in great haste. I received yesterday a copy of a letter from Cathcart[1] to Castlereagh which I do *not* like and therefore without pretending to know a word of the matter have written straight to their two Majesties[2] asking permission to join their army. If they refuse I shall then join the Pr. Royal of Sweden who believe me is sincerely the friend of the good cause & there I will serve, which being nearer *our* country will be much more preferable to me.

I hope this will meet your approbation for I do not like to remain here a burthen on my uncle[3] who is all kindness to me. I cannot sufficiently express my gratitude. The two uncles are grown very old. Ernest is ailing but still when roused his spirits return. The misery they have suffered surpasses all belief. My cousin the Her[editary] Prince[4] is very gentlemanlike charming young man, very well inform'd and perfectly loyal in his opinions, hating Bonaparte as we do. La cousine Solms[5] is charming but also very sickly, and like her sister[6] most determin'd in her antipathy to everything French. The Duke has raised a Hussar Regt. which I am to inspect for him this day & as soon as they receive their arms, which I hope they will use, they will be ready to march. He has parted with 2 thirds of his plate to equip and mount them. The country is really most beautiful, the finest woods possible, & interspersed with very fine pieces of water.

I have the satisfaction of telling you that *here* they are all for *you* and not one single supporter of the Pss.[7] On the contrary elle est mieux connue ici que chez vous. A curious thing I found out she was upon the point of being married to the son of the Dowager Landgravin of Hesse

1 Sir William Schaw Cathcart, first Viscount and Earl Cathcart (1755–1843). Ambassador and Military Commissioner with the Russian Army, 1813–14.

2 Alexander I and Frederick William III.

3 Charles Louis Frederick, Duke of Mecklenburg-Strelitz; Grand Duke, 1815. (1741–1816.) His brother, Prince Ernest, died in 1814.

4 Prince George, who succeeded his father as Grand Duke of Mecklenburg-Strelitz in 1816. (1779–1860.)

5 Frederica Louisa Caroline Sophia Alexandrina (1778–1841), daughter of Charles Louis Frederick, Duke of Mecklenburg-Strelitz, Queen Charlotte's brother. She married, first, Prince Frederick Louis Charles (d. 1796), the brother of Frederick William III of Prussia, by whom she had two children (Frederick William Louis, b. 1794; Frederica Wilhelmina Louisa Amelia, b. 1796); having been divorced, she married Prince Frederick William of Solms-Braunfels, who died on 13 April 1814, leaving three sons and a daughter. Finally, on 29 May 1815 she married at Strelitz her cousin the Duke of Cumberland; the marriage was solemnised according to the rites of the Church of England on 29 August 1815 at Carlton House.

6 Theresa, Princess of Tour and Taxis.

7 The Princess of Wales.

Darmstadt, Pr. George[1] (who is here) when *your* proposals stopped it. This fact I never heard before. Now God in Heaven bless you & think now & then of [etc.].

[P.S.] Do remember me to ALL my *friends*.

280 SIR WILLIAM MANNERS *to* COLONEL McMAHON

Oxford Street, May[2] [June] 4 [1813].

I UNDERSTAND from the best authority, that a creation of English Peers is immediately to take place. Indeed the appointment of Lord Whitworth,[3] announced in this day's papers, to be Lord Lt of Ireland, is a convincing proof of that fact. I cannot for a moment doubt, but that a certain Royal written promise in my possession will be now performed.[4] I could wish to know therefore whether I ought not to write to Lord Liverpool on the subject, to whom perhaps His Royal Highness the Regent has communicated the matter.

281 COLONEL McMAHON *to* SIR WILLIAM MANNERS

Copy.

Pall Mall, June 5th 1813.

I WAS honor'd with your favor of yesterday's date, and I can venture to assure you, from the best authority, that you have been misinform'd as to there being any immediate intention of creating English Peers, & that the recent elevation in rank of Lord Whitworth is by no means to be consider'd as a creation, or affording precedent for others, but arising entirely from the unavoidable necessity of enabling his Lordship to fill a great & important station in the service of Government, such as might occur in the appointment of a Secretary of State, or of a Lord Chancellor.

1 The Princess of Wales is reported to have said of him, "He turned all de women's heads except mine. I like him very much, but he was very perfide to me—a false perfidious friend. It was he who was the lover of the late Queen of France, and he was the real father of the last Dauphin." (Lady Charlotte Campbell's *Diary*, I, 32.)

2 Obviously a slip.

3 Charles Whitworth, Earl Whitworth (1752–1825). Lord-Lieutenant of Ireland, 1813–17. Barony, 1800; viscounty, 1813; earldom, 1815.

4 See No. 597.

Strelitz, June 7th 1813.

I HAVE been so much knocked down by a piece of news I received in my last letters from London that I have hardly been able to collect my thoughts except upon that subject, for believe me I never have had such a friend or ever again shall meet with one so highly honourable and dis-interested, having never had any object in view but my honour and character; as the blow was unexpected, so much the deeper is the wound inflicted by it. Excuse my having mentioned thus much to you, but as you are the only brother with whom I have been in the habits of talking freely what concerns myself I have not been able to conceal my feelings from you. To describe all the misery I have felt and with a lacerated heart to appear quiet and undisturbed has been no great soother. However man must act like a man, and I must exert myself especially at a moment when it appears to me that things are in a very ticklish state; that there have been very great and shameful blunders committed on all sides there is no denying, that *our* interests are *not* sufficiently taken care of is too manifest for me to dwell upon, but still something may be done, and if the report is founded which was received here yesterday that Austria has joined the Coalition, Europe may be saved.[1]

On the other hand Hamburgh and Lubeck are lost for the present and even it is reported that the Danish troops formed the advanced guard upon the last occasion. Nothing can equal the good feelings of this part of Germany, every man is ready to turn out, *all* that is wanting is money and arms, offers I have had without end of joining me in any undertaking for the rescue of Hannover, but from what I can learn unless there is some ostensible presence of the family nothing will be done there.

I have had a message from a Colonel Lutzen who has a legion of 3000 men that he wishes to put himself under my orders, and his proposals as far as I have learnt are perfectly fair and honourable for us. He said his corps are to act in the first instance and *all* those who join on entering the country are to be raised *not* for him but for US Hannoverians. This I merely mention *now* to you as a *private* information, for till I receive it officially and see it in black and white I will not enter into any com-munication with him. The melancholy state we are in is that as our only communication with England must go by Gottenburg so much time is required for an answer that the opportunity perhaps may slip through our fingers.

1 The report was premature. Austria did not declare war on France until August.

I have therefore sent to Minister Bremer[1] to talk to him on the subject, and then shall know more of the matter.

The King of Prussia has written me a very kind answer to my letter and says "he shall be very happy to see me at his Headquarters whenever I choose". From the Emperor I have received NO answer though I know he has written as Ld. Cathcart informs me His Im. Majesty has written, but *where* that letter is it is *not* for me to *pretend* to know; therefore I shall [go to] his Hd.Qrs. as soon as I get tidings of the arrival of my horses. Your commission respecting the sashes has been obeyed and I hope upon my arrival at Berlin to find them ready and I shall forward them by the first courier that goes. Pumpernickel I shall send with this letter. I cannot describe to you how I long to get into activity and if by my feeble means I can in any way succeed in recovering Hannover for you it will be the proudest day of my life, and believe me my zeal and endeavours shall be most active. Pray let me have a line from you, I entreat you. I hear the D. of Brunswick in driving over the country, passed through here and never came near me. Best love to all *my friends* both male and FEMALE, the latter I hope to see after the end of the campaign. Uncle Ernest is laid up with the gout again, since two days most dreadfully so. Mr. Douglas Kinnaird[2] called *here* yesterday upon me in his way to Berlin.

God bless you and do not forget [etc.].

283 THE EARL OF MOIRA *to* COLONEL McMAHON

June 10th 1813.
Lat. 6 North, Long. 20.

A SHIP bound for Liverpool has just met us & gives me the opportunity of telling you that we are all well. Our convoy delays us so distressingly that I foresee we shall be forced to give up the plan of stopping at Rio Janeiro. Were these the regular India ships one should feel happy to sacrifice convenience for their security: but we have none but extra ships, of no value, & such bad sailers that the Directors would not suffer their fleets to be encumbered by them. By such a conveyance I can say nothing more. Offer my humblest duty to the Prince, & believe me, [etc.].

1 The Hanoverian Minister of State.
2 Douglas James William Kinnaird (1788–1830), younger brother of the eighth Baron Kinnaird. Byron's friend.

16 *Clarges Street*, 14th June 1813.

THE Session being now pretty near a close, and no question expected in which the personal interests of the Prince Regent are concerned, I propose returning next week to the duties of my Diocese, where, I trust, my presence will be much more useful in opposing & checking the mischievous spirit of prejudice & clamour which some angry & disappointed politicians are now endeavouring to spread against the wise, firm, & constitutional conduct of our illustrious & beloved Regent.

This clamour however, and this prejudice will soon be got the better of by time & a little wise management in the government of Ireland. I have not the honor of knowing our newly appointed Viceroy,[1] but I am happy to understand his character is firm & conciliatory. From a feeling of duty, as well as anxiety for the wellfare of our Prince Regent's Government I shoud experience much satisfaction in affording any useful information or assistance to His R. Highness's Viceroy—and to you I can say in confidence my dear Sir, that the management of the Church department is that in which a Lord Lt. (especially a stranger) is most likely to fail—unless assisted by the confidential opinions of some person whose professional experience & station enable him to point out the errors into which any man (unacquainted with clerical arrangements) is subject to fall.

The want of attention to this point (tho' quite unintentionally in the D. of Richmond) has occasioned serious inconvenience, which would be too tedious to explain at present, but which was felt by the head of the Church & other Bishops.

The patronage of the Church in Ireland is vastly extensive, and tho' in general, it must be applied to the support of the Government by the Lord Lt., yet, in the higher orders of it, I wou'd most conscientiously wish the occasional interference of the Prince himself in favor of some worthy individuals—such interference (now & then) wou'd have the happy effect of upholding the dignity of the Irish Church and attaching it's members to the person & Government of His Royal Highness.

I propose seting off on Monday next the 21st for Limerick, but shall previously have the honor of paying my duty of leave at Carlton House —and with truest feelings of gratitude & attachment to our Royal master, believe me, [etc.].

1 Lord Whitworth.

35 Brooke St., Holborn,
17 June 1813.

IF there be anything that I abhor beyond all others it is the yielding to the pressing demands of necessity & asking for assistance. The poorest of all His Majesty's subjects, I was ill prepared to sustain a loss of £50 last autumn in an election pamphlet written if not by the command, with the approbation of the Premier, who when the service was performed refused even the expences I had been at. Had he not been the Minister of H.R.Hss the P.R. I should not have silently sate down with it.

You know the pamphlet I lately wrote & thinking it would serve the cause of justice I have at a very great expence gained the necessary information for providing in any way that may be deemed expedient & for this purpose I have sent to Lord Sidmouth to request an interview in order to communicate what I have learnt; feeling with you that it would be very improper for you to interfere in it.

Well, for the pamphlet & before I have received 1/- from the book-sellers my printer poor fellow presses me for the money. I know his necessities & my own inability. I do not ask for any remuneration for time, labour or expences—when my services are completed they will be duly appreciated but in the mean time I am at the lowest ebb of distress.

I suffer many privations & contentedly living in hope but until I get my money from the booksellers I am in great distress to pay my printer. I have exhausted every means & I am truly pained to say that on you, on whom I have no claim but the very reverse, I can only rely. To say I will repay it in a month or six weeks cannot have weight having forfeited the character of punctuality. I will therefore only say—you know my exertions, you know my intelligence & you know the prospect of repayment by me & I must leave it entirely to your own generous heart to decide. I may add that I am sanguine enough to hope that my exertions will afford me the means of clearing off old scores.

I shall receive the produce of the pamphlet in about two months & I think I had better send you my draft at that date which if paid into your bankers shall be duly honored.

I shall send at eleven tomorrow for your answer which if favorable

1 Possibly J. Scott Byerley, who published an edition of Machiavelli's *Prince* in 1810, "to which is prefixed an Introduction, showing the close analogy between the principles of Machiavelli and the actions of Bonaparte". "I do not hope", he wrote, "that the heir-apparent will display all the virtues of his sire, but I can venture to predict that *England's ruin* will be *more remote* on his accession to the throne." His "superior talents, to prove their superior transcendancy, only demand a field for action".

will relieve me from a heavy load & shall be most gratefully paid & acknowledged in every way.

P.S. I pledge you my honor most solemnly & wish to stake your friendship on it that this shall not be like the last.

286 J. BYERLEY *to* COLONEL MCMAHON

35 Brooke St., Holborn,
18 June 1813.

IF you knew the pressing urgency of my affairs at this moment you would I am sure pardon my importunity. I have the pleasure of inclosing you a draft for £50 as security & it is not improbable that I may be able in a fortnight not only to pay this but the former as I am in treaty for the sale of my M.S. If you do not feel it right from the former disappointment what you please in part of it will be gratefully considered.

The truth is my time & little resources have been expended in *the good cause* but *le bon tem[p]s viendra* & if I can only rub on for a little time all will be right.

I conjure you my dear Sir leave a line [for] me in the morning for tomorrow is of the utmost importance to me.

287 THE DUKE OF CUMBERLAND *to the* PRINCE REGENT

Strelitz, June 18th [1813].

I AM still here, but having at length yesterday received the account of my horses and baggage being arrived at Stralsund I shall *now* upon their arrival here immediately set out for Reichenbach the Headquarters of the K. of Prussia where I shall hear what H. M. says. If I can get service there, bien, if not return, and with your permission then serve under the Pr. Royal of Sweden who I look upon as the truest friend to England. *This* would suit me best as it is the nearest our own country, but I do entreat you to give me a letter to the Pr. in order that I may be employed in some way. If it suited the views you have I could without difficulty raise a corps of 10,000 men in six weeks as there are plenty of men, and no difficulty of getting horses; arms and ammunition are the first to be promised. Upon my arrival here there was a report I was to raise men, and my doors were crowded with peasants who wanted to enlist, so you see the spirit is very good. I am sorry to say the Germans hate the Russians and the manner they are treated here by this Commission under Stein[1] & Alopeus is not calculated to mend matters, for the style of his letters to the Princes here is really rude and more the language of conquerors than friends. The Pr. Royal is equally disgusted with their proceedings. There is at this moment no less than 40,000 men quartered in the Dutchy of Mecklenburg Schwerin, among which are the new levies from Hannover.

Walmoden is quartered at Hagenow but I have not seen him, nor does he seem to wish to see me, the cause I know not exactly, though I suspect it. Nothing can exceed the civility and kindness with which the Pr.Roy of Sweden has treated me, and I am certain we should agree perfectly. I suppose you will have read the proclamation the K. of Pr. issued on the signing of this infernal Armistice[2] to his country. It does him honour, and every exertion is making to increase the Army. The Duke here is doing everything in his power and had he but the means he would produce a battalion of 1000 to 1200 men very soon if required.

Minister Bremer came here Sunday and passed three days here. He is now gone to Doberan a seabathing place in Schwerinsche where he [is] remaining till the war begins again.

Our cousin the D. of Brunswick has given general disgust here in Germany. I understand he did not manage his affairs well at the Head Qrs. of Prussia, and did so much worse at Stralsund that the P. Royal would not speak to him at last, in consequence of which he has sold all his horses and is returned to England. Now if it comes to the worst and if through *your* recommendation I cannot somehow be employed *here* as I might hope, rather than show myself in England without having served, I will join some new corps as a *volunteer* and at least prove myself worthy of being a descendant of the Gwelfs, for to return without seeing a shot fired I should consider an eternal disgrace.[3]

Let me entreat you, dearest brother, to give me a letter to the K. of P. or P.Roy of Sweden that I may be employed, for as to situation I care *not* what it is, all I want is to have an opportunity of shewing the world I am not living upon the fat of the earth without doing something for it.

1 Heinrich Friedrich Karl, Baron von Stein (1757–1831), the Prussian Minister; at this time the Tsar's unofficial adviser.

2 The seven weeks' truce of Pläswitz (4 June) between Napoleon and the Allies. Both sides were temporarily exhausted, and needed time to prepare for a final effort to end the war.

3 It was the Cabinet that refused him a command. Castlereagh wrote on 14 July to his brother Sir Charles Stewart: "You must try to reconcile the Sovereigns at headquarters to let him witness as a volunteer what is going on. He cannot have a command, and, to guard against jealousy, it is better he should not be with the Prince Royal." (*Cast. Corr.* IX, 33.)

Perhaps when the levies in Hannover are formed you will then allow me
to resume my situation as senior Lt. General of Cavalry which patent
I still possess signed by H. M. 1796 and which I never resigned, and which
he desired me *not* to do. There is a free corps of 3000 Infy. & 750 Cavalry
of the Prussians which have offered themselves *to me*, but untill I see how
things turn out I have declined giving any answer.

Your sashes I hope to send by the first messenger and I shall send *you*
a *hat* and feather from Berlin. God bless you.

288 JOHN BAYFORD *to* COLONEL MCMAHON

Doctors Commons, 19 June 1813.

I HAVE recd the commands of His Royal Highness the Duke of Sussex
to enquire of you relative to the Address & Petition, by him lately presented to His Royal Highness the Prince Regent, from the Society of
Freemasons, praying His Royal Highness to be graciously pleased to
allow himself to be designated, Patron & Protector of the Craft. A meeting of the Grand Lodge is fixed for Wednesday next, when it will be
necessary for the Duke of Sussex to make some communication on the
subject of the Address: and he has therefore directed me to write to you
to express his hope, that he may by that time be empowered to signify
to the Fraternity His Royal Highness the Prince Regents gracious
pleasure thereon; humbly trusting that the Prince Regent will be pleased
to notice the humble Address & Petition of the brethren by acceding to
their dutiful and loyal wishes.

289 COLONEL MCMAHON *to* JOHN BAYFORD

Copy.   *Carlton House*, June 19, 1813.

I HAD the honor to lay your letter of this morning before the Prince
Regent who commands me to request you will have the goodness to
acquaint His Royal Highness the Grand Master, that the Prince Regent
has the highest pleasure and satisfaction, in accepting the wishes of the
Honorable Society of Freemasons, & becoming the Patron of that laudable & distinguished Institution, together with His Royal Highness's
best thanks, for the obliging & handsome manner in which that wish has
been expressed.

George St, June 19th 1813.

MR. COPLEY presents his compliments to Col. McMahon, [and] will be greatly obliged if he will have the goodness to obtain for Mr. Copley, the commands of His Royal Highness the Prince Regent, relative to the destination of the picture, which Mr. Copley has had the honour to paint of His Royal Highness, attended by the late Lord Heathfield,[2] Genl. Turner, Col. Bloomfield, Baron Eben,[3] Col. Quinton[4] &c:

Mr. Copley is most anxious that it should be placed in a situation suitable to such a work, and which he humbly presumes to flatter himself would be of importance to his name and reputation as an artist.

[P.S.] Mr. Copley takes the liberty of adding that the picture is 1500 Gs.[5]

291 VISCOUNT MELBOURNE *to the* PRINCE REGENT

Whitehall, June 20th 1813.

IT is with the greatest reluctance, that I venture to trouble your Royal Highness on a subject, upon which I have so often been honoured with such gracious assurances from you. But your Royal Highness will I hope forgive my present anxiety, under the peculiar circumstances of Lord Whitworth's advancement to an English Peerage.[6] After your Royal Highness' repeated promises for a period of nearly thirty years, in addition to a letter you wrote to Lady Melbourne in October 1806 from Rufford, stating that you had written to London to insist that if any Peers were then made, I should be included in the number.

1 The portrait-painter, and father of Lord Lyndhurst, the Lord Chancellor. (1737–1815.)
2 Francis Augustus Eliott, second Baron Heathfield (1749–1813), a Lord of the Bedchamber, 1812–13.
3 Equerry to the Prince of Wales, 1807–13.
4 Colonel George Quentin, of the 10th, or Prince of Wales' Own Royal Regiment of Light Dragoons.
5 This picture was exhibited at the Royal Academy in 1810. Amongst the Prince Regent's accounts there is an unsigned Memorandum (? by Robert Gray) dated 26 September 1814: "Mr. Copley—a large painting of the Prince, with Lord Heathfield, General Turner, Colonel Bloomfield and Baron Eben, with Colonel Quintin in the background—finished about two years. Price 1500 Gns. The account has been sent to Colonel McMahon long since, and the picture still remains at Mr. Copley's." "20 October: Saw Colonel McMahon and informed Mr. Copley that His Royal Highness never intended to purchase the picture, having sat merely at the request of the artist, and understanding it to be a public work, like the Death of Lord Chatham."
6 See Nos. 280, 281.

It is the pride of my life to know the eagerness and ardent zeal your Royal Highness has shewn in the repeated applications you have made, & altho' they have been unsuccessfull, the recollection of your unbounded kindness on those, and many other occasions can never be forgotten by me. I could interpret this condescending goodness of your Royal Highness's in no other sense than that you were determined to take the earliest opportunity of distinguishing my long and faithfull attachment to your Royal Highness's person, by that mark of your regard.

Feeling as I do Sir the strongest sentiments of respect and devotion towards your Royal Highness I should have thought it my duty to remain silent and wait your Royal Highness's pleasure had it not been for the conversations you honoured me with in February 1811 and also in February last. In the first your Royal Highness said that if any new Peers were made that I should be one of them, unless it were for any great military or naval victorys, but that any advance from one rank to a higher one in the Peerage was not to be considered as a new creation, on that point your Royal Highness condescended to be particularly explicit. In the last conversation I learned from your Royal Highness at Carlton House, that before Mr. Percival's death, you had settled with him that I should be the first in any addition made to the Peerage, and that Mr. Percival mark'd it down as your Royal Highness's own promise, that your Royal Highness had also spoken to Lord Liverpool to the same effect. And that you would speak to him again, then it might become proper for me to wait upon his Lordship as the Minister through whom the recommendation would officially be laid before your Royal Highness.

It has been lately strongly reported that it was recommended to your Royal Highness to advance some gentlemen to the English Peerage, but I could not for a moment allow myself to think, (nor do I now) that your Royal Highness would have consented to my name being omitted. For under the sanction of all the assurances I had received and with the deepest sense of gratitude towards your Royal Highness I have waited untill the moment in which I learn from the Gazette Lord Whitworth's advancement to the rank of an English Viscount.

I most humbly submit to your Royal Highness that there appear to be various opinions conserning Lord Whitworth's advancement, some persons thinking it to be a new creation, and an addition to the English Peerage, and this with all duty and respect to your Royal Highness, is the way in which I consider it. Other persons say it is only an advancement in the Peerage; he being already a Peer of the United Kingdoms. If it be considered as a new creation I suffer great mortification at not being thought of by your Royal Highness at this time; if considered as an advancement, your Royal Highness has reserved to yourself that power, and conceiving that I am in the same situation as Lord Whitworth in the Peerage, I should have been highly honoured and gratified, had your Royal Highness been graciously pleased to confer so distinguished a mark of your Royal Highness's favour upon me.

I am very sensible that I am taking a great liberty in presuming to lay this representation most humbly at your Royal Highness's feet, and you will I trust, pardon me, and with your accustomed condescention, make some allowance for the additional mortification which this circumstance must naturally create in me. And that your Royal Highness will be assured that in the request I now humbly make to you to be admitted to the honor of the English Peerage, I have no other feeling, than that which rendered this distinction valuable from the first, that of owing to your Royal Highness, so flattering a testimony of your sense of that sincere and devoted attachment which I have ever borne to your Royal person.[1]

292 THOMAS SHERIDAN *to* COLONEL MCMAHON

(?) *Garton Maynooth*, June 20th 1813.

You have not to learn that I am out of favor with the Prince, for Moira told me how friendly an interest you had taken upon the occasion. I will first thank you for that, & I do assure you that these evidences of un-chilled regard, wh: I thank Heaven I experience from all quarters, more than repay me for all my poverty & privations, & I sometimes doubt if I could have experienced the same *share* of happiness, had my circumstances rendered it unnecessary to call them forth. Secondly I request your advice as to how I should best proceed. The inclos'd will save me a world of explanation—it shows that I have made up my mind to ask a favor—the reason why and what I conceive the properest mode—but I will state further *to you* why I consider myself in some degree entitled to H.R.H.'s consideration, tho' I see no means of suggesting it to him. You may perhaps remember an offer made me by the Duke of York *to take me into his family giving me a regular commission—a Lieut. Col[onel]cy in the then Army of Reserve with the pay & promotion in the Line, as rapidly as propriety wd. admit of, towards rendering that rank permanent*; a finer opening for a young man it was impossible to imagine. His R.H. & the

1 See No. 16.

Duke were unfortunately at that time on bad terms and after due consultation with Mrs. Fitzherbert[1] and all the circle about the Prince it was decided that I ought to refuse as the acceptance wd. look like an abandonment of my avow'd patron. It is on this circumstance I found any claim I may have on His R.H. I ask no great favor, I seek employment and I will not affect the false modesty of saying anything needlessly humble of myself; I think myself qualified to fill any situation such as I now aim at, without discredit, and I will add stoutly that the Prince wd. not do an unpopular act by serving me. I have already stir[re]d this among some of my friends but I wd rather be obliged to the Prince than anyone, nor will I believe his good will towards me is to be destroyd by some damnd lie wh my whole life & conversation is a contradiction to (for tho I cannot ascertain *what* it is, I have said, it is something *in abuse of him personally*, it seems) there being no occasion when he has been *individually* attacked and no subject in wh he is *personally* interested that I have not done my best towards his support. If you deem it wise to submit the inclosure to his inspection I am sure you will be glad of the opportunity of serving me—if not, give me y[ou]r advice how I ought to proceed and believe me [etc.].

293 SIR PHILIP FRANCIS[2] *to* COLONEL MCMAHON

29 June 1813.

I REQUEST you will be so good as to make my excuse, in proper form, and with all due acknowledgements, to His Royal Highness for not availing myself of the honour done me by his invitation to the Fête tomorrow night. The truth is that, between age and infirmity, I am quite unequal to it. All which I must leave to you to represent for me in your own terms.

1 Maria Anne Fitzherbert, the Catholic lady whom the Prince of Wales secretly married in December 1785. Her first and second husbands died in 1775 and 1781. [1756–1837.]
2 The reputed author of the *Letters of Junius*, and a member of the Governor-General's Council at Calcutta, 1774–80. [1740–1818.]

Tuesday night, 29 June 1813.

M Y dear McMahon, for now I shall never give you any other title, since that alone expresses the true affection I have ever felt for you. Please God, you shall not have that thorn in your pillow to night, of thinking that I ever could doubt of your sincerity to me, and of your hearty zeal for me on all occasions, great or small. I am also as sure, as I am that I exist, that you would have had a real pleasure in obliging Catharin[1] about little Mary.

As to *my* not going to the Fête, I once more assure you that I told you the true reason, and that I had no other. If I had meant any thing else, I should have conveyed it by a more direct course, and not on any account have given you a painful commission. I am sorry now that I used that *chilling name*; which I would not have done, if I had not thought it possible that you might be obliged to shew my letter. On the whole however I do not regret having written that letter, because it has drawn from you an answer which could not have come from any but an honest and generous heart.

I have now but little value for any thing else in this life; and, even if this feeling were not so strong in me as it is, I have had too much and too long an experience of this world not to know that, in prudence merely, old friends and tried friends are not to be lightly parted with, because it is very difficult if not impossible to replace them. So I wish you a good night & also to Mrs. M[cMaho]n who I see is fretting like gummed velvet.

[P.S.] I called on Bloomfield; & would have favoured him with my commission, if I could have found him.

The Prince Regent to the Marquis of Wellington, 3 July 1813. (*Wellington Desp.* x, 532; Miss Knight's *Autobiography*, I, 244.)

295 THOMAS HARRIS[2] *to* COLONEL McMAHON

Cov[en]t Gard[e]n Theatre,
Wednesday, July 14th [1813].

A s we close our Theatre tomorrow night I take the liberty of sending our Treasurer for the remaining half of the Prince Regent's subscription[3]

1 Probably Francis' daughter (b. 1772), who married George James Cholmondeley.
2 Manager of Covent Garden Theatre.
3 £262 10s. for the half year. [Endorsement.]

for his private box, which would be of some assistance towards our new and splendid decorations. I am happy to say that by throwing back the Pillaster on the stage we shall be able to render the view from the box *more* compleat and I trust that the *outward* embellishment will be found to be more consonant with the interior.[1]

With many apologies for this intrusion on your valuable time.

296 ROBERT GILLAM *to* MAJOR-GENERAL TURNER

British Gallery, Pall Mall,
14 July 1813.

I AM commanded by the Directors of the British Institution, to inform you that the Exhibition of Sir Joshua Reynolds's pictures at this Gallery, will be closed on Saturday the 14th of August; and to beg that you will have the goodness to lay before His Royal Highness the Prince Regent, the request of the Directors, that he would be graciously pleased to permit them to retain His Royal Highness's picture of the Duke of Orleans,[2] until the end of November next, for the study of the artists attending the British School.

The Marquis of Wellington to the Prince Regent, 16 July 1813. (*Wellington Desp.* x, 532.)

297 THE BISHOP OF LIMERICK [DR WARBURTON] *to* COLONEL MCMAHON

Dublin, 20th July 1813.

I HAVE made a delay here of a week, for the purpose of talking with our heads of the Law, upon the subject of the late violent & indecent proceedings of these R. Catholic meetings, and their abominable personal abuse of our illustrious & belov'd Prince.

I had an idea that some public step shou'd be taken against those vile libelers, but after discussing the subject with the Chancellor,[3] the Chief

1 There is a description of the new Covent Garden Theatre in *The Gentleman's Magazine*, September 1809, p. 880. In December 1809 it was decided to reduce the number of private boxes from 32 to 10, and in 1810 the number was further reduced to six. The yearly rental of each was £400.

2 The famous Égalité. Louis Philippe Joseph, Duke of Orleans (1747–1793). The picture was exhibited at the Royal Academy in 1786.

3 Thomas Manners-Sutton, first Baron Manners (1756–1842).

Justice,[1] the Chief Baron,[2] and Mr. Sergeant McMahon, I am inclined
to think with them, that any notice taken of it (on the side of the Prince)
wou'd be a triumph to those blackguards, who are looking for such an
event to encrease their consequence with the mob.

The object of O'Connell[3] & his associates, is revolution. The Crown is
the chief object of their vulgar & abusive attack; and I have no doubt
their treasonable conduct will very soon call for the interference of the
Attorney General. Indeed I am of opinion that forbearance has been
carried too far, and it is seriously to be lamented, that measures have not
yet been taken to prevent these unconstitutional & dangerous meetings,
where not only the powers of a Parliament are exercised, but the very
forms of it are assum'd by it's members.

A departing Viceroy naturally declines the adoption of any new
measure, but his successor will find it absolutely necessary; and with an
Attorney General (such as Lord Clare[4] was) these treasonable meetings
wou'd (and ought to be) very soon annihilated.

O'Connell is now about going our Munster Circuit, and in the provincial papers he has already issued his proclamation for holding his
little mischievous parliaments at the assizes towns of Limerick, Tralee,
&c, &c.

All this may appear of little consequence to people at a distance, or
unacquainted with the real state of things in this country, but to any
thinking man, who resides in this country, and watches the progress of
things, it must be evident that those meetings, if permitted to continue,
will very soon produce events of the most serious & alarming nature.

At a fete given by the Duke of Leinster[5] a few days ago, I met a
number of R. Catholic gentlemen, (amongst them, Dr. Troy,[6] the R.C.
Archbishop of Dublin)—in our walk thro' the grounds the conversation
turn'd upon the fate of the C[atholic] question in Parliament; in which
they complain'd of the Prince's non-performance of his pledges to them
&c, &c. Fortunately, I had in my pocket the two letters, which H.R.Hss
honor'd me with. I beg'd to assure them that the public mind had been
totally misled upon that point, and that I held in my hand the disavowal
of the noble person whom they had just mentioned—(Lord Kenmare).[7]

1 John Toler, Baron Norbury (1745–1831), Chief Justice of the Common Pleas, in Ireland,
1800–27. Earl of Norbury, 1827.

2 Standish O'Grady, first Viscount Guillamore (1766–1840). Lord Chief Baron of the
Irish Exchequer, 1805–31.

3 Daniel O'Connell, the Irish agitator (1775–1847).

4 John Fitzgibbon, Earl of Clare (1749–1802). Irish Attorney General, 1783; Lord
Chancellor of Ireland, 1789–1802.

5 Augustus Frederick Fitzgerald, third Duke of Leinster (1791–1874).

6 John Thomas Troy, Archbishop since 1784. (1739–1823.)   7 See No. 129.

I then read to them your letter,[1] and Lord Kenmare's answer. They express'd much surprize, but acknowledged that the thing had been differently understood before.

I ventured to assure them also, that the Prince never did or cou'd be understood to make any pledge or promise further than an expression of his wish to remove restrictions, as far as the principles of our Protestant Constitution wou'd permit—that there cou'd be no doubt the same benevolent disposition still existed in his Royal mind; but they themselves must know, that the British Constitution is founded upon Protestant principles, which the Regent, nor the King can ever violate.

My friend Dr. Troy did not quite assent to the full extent of my argument, tho' he cou'd not deny the obligation imposed upon the Monarch, or reigning Prince by his oath of office.

We at length sat down to our repast in very tolerable good humor, and they all join'd me in drinking the Prince Regent's health.

I am just now seting out upon a tour of visitation through my diocese, where I shall feel it my duty to use every means of counteracting Mr. O'Connell's mischievous impressions, and with truest feelings of affectionate devotion to our Royal master, believe me, [etc.].

298 QUEEN CHARLOTTE *to the* PRINCE REGENT

Windsor, the 22d July 1813.

THIS morning I was agreably surprised by a pacquet of letters from Germany. The Duke of Cumberland writes chearfully & happy but in his usual stile damns the Armistice[2] and expects some further difficulties in his journey to the different Royal personages. He means to go to, fully determined however not to follow the Emperor to Prague nor the King of Prussia to the baths in Silesia, & he ends with assuring me that he will come back to England without a wife.

I have also received a letter from my brother the Duke[3] part of which I send you a copy, as his own words must express his wishes as well as his wants & that of the country much better than I can do. I take it for granted that the Duke of Cumberland will according to his promise have represented to you the true situation of my brother, for being an ocular witness he can speak more to the purpose than I can, & I am fully persuaded that as far as lays in yr power to alleviate my brother's distresses

1 No. 125.   2 See No. 287.
3 The Duke of Mecklenburg-Strelitz.

you will be inclined to favour his requests. As his sister & a German born I need not say how truely I feel interested in what concerns my family & my country, nor do I pretend to make upon this occasion a complimentary excuse for troubling you with this statement, as a want of feeling for my relations & country which I still love dearly must of course lower me much in yr eyes.

I saw S[i]r H[enry] H[alford] this morning & am sorry to hear that he left you so uncomfortable upon a certain object. I hope that after so many storms double the number of sun shining days will follow which is the wish of [etc.].

298A THE DUKE OF CUMBERLAND *to the* PRINCE REGENT

Berlin, July 22ᵈ, [1813].

HEARING that the King[1] was arrived at Charlottenburg, I directly posted off for this place where I arrived last Saturday & saw H.M. but I had no private conversation with him till *this* day, though I have seen him once at table & once at a Review, but unfortunately the anniversary of the death of the Queen[2] was on Monday on which day he shuts himself up and never sees a soul; nothing in the world could be more kind & civil than he was he talked of England, of the satisfaction he derived from *all* the kindness he had received from *you*, I told him that my object was to serve and not be an idle spectator of what was going on, that in case the war went on, which I trusted in God it would do, I hoped he could allow me to join his Army; this he acceded to & said that at present *he* himself was only a *visitor* at the Russian Head Quarters but that he should take care to mention my wishes to the Emperor. Now though it is not my business to say so, still it appears very odd that *he* should acknowledge himself as a *vassal* to Russia which faith this does. My real hope & wish is to be employed, and I think I might be of some use to the cause could I be employ'd with that part of the Army which is to be employed at the coupures, the greatest part of which is to be composed of the Hanoverian levies & German Russian Legion now in British pay. I therefore beg to submit to you could *I* not be employ'd there, as far as zeal & activity can go you may depend upon my using every every exertion in my power do, dearest brother, reflect upon this & answer my request. The spirit here

1 Frederick William III.
2 Louisa, daughter of Charles Louis Frederick, Grand Duke of Mecklenburg-Strelitz. She died, deeply lamented by the Prussian people, in 1810.

is perfect in every way, & I trust & hope that the great news from the Peninsula will be a stimulus to the potentates not to bow down to that monster, who will try any thing he can to ruin what has been done. I have seen yesterday about 11,000 Prussians arriv'd here of the Land Wehr or Militia which are capital uncommon fine men, there was 10 battalions of Infantry, & 9 Squadrons of Cavalry also Landwehr, very useful men & really better mounted than I expected. The Black Hussars I also saw now the Life Hussars renown'd for their bravery & courage, but certainly never was I more disappointed than at their manœuvre, I assure you our Brigade beats them out & out.

I am in hopes your sashes will now be finished in a few days, the truth is they have so much to do, they hardly can get any thing finished; the appearance of the troops in my humble opinion has lost prodigiously especially the Cavalry. They have *all* got shoulder straps as broad as my hand resembling the old French contre epaulettes. The King has procured a complete set of *each* heavy & light Cavalry as well as Infantry which I shall send over to you. Dearest brother, do pray let me hear soon from you, & grant my request,

Tell Tom[1] that his nephew Sir Tyr. *Johns* is *here.*

299   SIR WILLIAM BEECHEY *to* COLONEL MCMAHON

Harley Str. in bed,
July 24th 1813.

MAY I beg the favour of you to present the sketch, sent herewith, to the Regent for His Royal Highness's approbation or rather his opinion of it, the likeness is not to be considered of course, nor the air of the person, only the general idea, and arrangement of the subject in regard to its composition & colour &c. I have also sent *not a copy*, but the original picture which His Royal Highness was graciously pleased to approve of Mr. Percival, and which has never been copied. I have to entreat His Royal Highness will pardon me for not sending it sooner, but I was under a promise to Lady Arden[1] to let Mrs. Percival have her choice of all the pictures I have attempted of Mr. Percival but who has lately declined seeing any of them. A most melancholly accident which has confined me five weeks and will I understand confine me three months

1 Sir Thomas Tyrwhitt.
2 Margaret Elizabeth, wife of Charles George Perceval, first Baron Arden (1756–1840), the Prime Minister's elder brother. She died in 1851 at the age of eighty-two.

longer prevents my having the honor and happiness of accompanying my works, and receiving His Royal Highness's commands in person.

Confiding in your usual goodness to pardon the trouble I give you on this occasion, I beg leave to subscribe myself, with most sincere esteem & respect, [etc.].

300 BENJAMIN WEST *to* MAJOR-GENERAL TURNER

Newman Street, July 27th 1813.

MR. WILKIE waited on me yesterday to say that the picture he had the honor to paint for His Royal Highness the Prince Regent had been sent to Carlton House when it was taken from the last Exhibition at the Royal Academy—and as I had favoured him with the Regents commands for painting that picture, he requested me to inform him, to whom he was to apply for payment.

My not knowing any one so proper at Carlton House as yourself, for me to gain him that information—I do it with a full assurance, as knowing your politness to me in all intercour[se] respecting the Fine Arts and your friendship for them—to make this communication solely to gain Mr. Wilkie the information he has requested.

301 SIR GEORGE DALLAS[1] *to* COLONEL MCMAHON

Henrietta Street, Cavendish Square,
Thursday July 1813.

A FRIEND in need, is a friend indeed.

I am, at this moment, placed in a situation of singular anxiety—three years of hopes and labour at issue, suddenly!

You are no stranger to my well founded expectation of succeeding to Sir George Barlow.[2] My pretensions you know. My claims I will be bold to say challenge competition—essential public services rendered to

1 [1758–1833.] He had been in the service of the East India Company as a Revenue Collector in the time of Warren Hastings, but he was not allowed to succeed Sir George Barlow as Governor of Madras. Lieutenant-General [Sir] John Abercromby was temporary Governor from May 1813 to September 1814, when the Right Hon. Hugh Elliot took his place, the appointment being made on 3 December 1813.

2 Sir George Hilaro Barlow (1762–1846), Governor-General of Bengal, 1805–7; Governor of Madras, 1807–13.

His Majesty's Government—the voice of the Proprietary—the pledged support of the leading Directors, and late Chairs—three Governors General of British India addressing the President of the Board of Control in my favor—and super-added to these, a speech in support of Administration at the late General Court, where I was invited by the Directors and Government to take the lead, and which led to an *unanimous* acceptance of the Charter, to which, by both parties, the greatest importance was attached. They who heard it, but know its effect—and the value of such a service, at *such a moment*, to Govt, when the Regent's speech was to give such just importance to the advantages likely to be secured for the public by the terms of the new Charter.[1]

What can beat down this? A man of straw! *Mr. Wallace!*[2] Is this just? Is it a fair return to me, under the confidential memorandum I enclose for your perusal?

My friends therefore raize me to exertion, and secretly urge me to endeavour to ward off such an act of injustice. The Chairman, Mr. R. Thornton was with me by nine o'clock this morning and I enclose you, under his hand, for your *most secret perusal*, a voucher I received yesterday, of what are the sentiments of the Court of Directors, of which the Prince Regent cannot yet be aware. The Deputy Mr. Elphinstone[3] has also expressed to me the same opinion.

Lord Wellesley is out of the Cabinet, who headed them all, and destined for me this situation had he remained in it, as far as his influence, and personal request of it for me could go. Under these circumstances, unless His Royal Highness the Prince Regent will condescend to espouse my pretensions by recommending me to Lord Liverpool as a subject honored with his countenance, I must succomb.

His R.H: knows that the Carnatic is the key of our Indian Empire; and he well knows, at this feverish crisis there, the importance of placing at the head of the Government there a person adequately qualified, in all respects.[4] My friends will never receive Mr. Wallace without a battle—he may be forced upon the Court—and they must perhaps submit: but is it fair, with so many great authorities in my favor, to crush that voice

1 In 1813 Parliament passed an Act renewing for a further period of twenty years the East India Company's Charter. The Company was deprived of its monopoly of the trade with India, but retained its monopoly of the China trade until 1833.

2 Thomas Wallace, Baron Wallace (1768–1844), at this time a Commissioner of the Board of Control. Peerage, 1828.

3 William Fullerton Elphinstone, third son of the tenth Baron Elphinstone, and Mountstuart Elphinstone's uncle. Deputy Chairman of the Court of Directors, 1813; Chairman, 1814.

4 Sir George Barlow's period of office was marked by an alarming mutiny in the Madras army and great discontent in the civil service—the outcome of his policy of retrenchment.

which has so recently been raised in support of the Prince Regent's Government?

P.S. I shall thank you to return to me the enclosure with expedition that I may lay it before my brother.[1] It is only to satisfy your mind completely of the strong ground on which I stand, & for yr eye only.

302 JOHN INGLIS[2] *to* COLONEL MCMAHON

Mark Lane, 31st July 1813.

I AM desired by the Committee appointed to manage the subscription now raising for the releif of His Majesty's North American subjects[3] to beg, that you will be pleased to lay before His Royal Highness the Prince Regent, their humble acknowledgements for the generosity, and liberality, with which His Royal Highness has been pleased to manifest his gracious countenance and approbation of this undertaking.[4]

303 THE DUKE OF CUMBERLAND *to the* PRINCE REGENT

Strelitz, Aug.t 6th 1813.

I HAVE received within these two days no less than three letters purporting to contain messages from you, from Castlereagh, Münster & Thornton.[5] As I am fond of direct and open communication I propose answering all three letters not individually to them but to you yourself: I am convinced you know me well enough to be assured that the object of all my letters to you has been to state to you fairly and honestly all that strikes me upon the Continent, feeling that in so doing I am cherishing the wellfare of a brother for whom I feel the most sincere & affectionate attachment which neither time, nor absence will ever diminish, & I trust that nothing will ever occur to make you change in your kind

1 Sir Robert Dallas (1756–1824), Solicitor-General since May.

2 Of the house of Inglis, Ellice & Co. A Director of the East India Company and of the East India Docks; Deputy Chairman of the East India Company in 1814, and Chairman of the London Docks. (1748–1822.)

3 Who suffered from the American invasion, in the spring of 1813. York, now Toronto, was captured in April, and the Parliament House was burnt.

4 The amount was £500.

5 Not the British envoy to Sweden, but Colonel Charles Wade Thornton, the Duke's Equerry, who was in England.

affection to me; as there is no [one] who values your friendship more than I do. What I mentioned to you some time ago with respect to the possibility of raising troops in this part of Germany I did from the best motives, being convinced that the means there pursued were not sufficiently pursued to accomplish the object, I am still of the same opinion & am the more strengthen'd in it from conversations I have had with persons fully acquainted with every thing that has been done and if I am *not* very much mistaken the report of Sir C. Stewart[1] who has since inspected the levies will in a great measure confirm what I have said. You must recollect I speak to you the language of a private individual who is a spectator, & who not being in any official situation hears many things which others either do *not* hear, or do *not* communicate for fear of offending. The Hanoverian levies have not advanced with that success it was reasonable to hope for, & indeed I believe I may say they have in part failed; but certain it is that those actually raised are not in so forward a state as they ought to be by this time; they feel dissatisfied at seeing so few of their countrymen employed, and finding themselves under the command of a Russian General, which alone can account for the tardyness with which they have come forward, as the spirit of this part of the country surpasses every thing of the kind hitherto known.

The Russian German Legion[2] amounting to about 8000 men, part of which I have seen, three Battalions which passed through here and are uncommon fine, are most anxious to be turned over to the British Force, as they feel that being in the Russian service they are not considered on a par with the Russian troops and therefore it is a great pity that when the connection was made they were not raised to be taken into our service, as such a force in addition to the 15,000 to which I understand our levies are to be extended, would give your Government an influencing voice here, which the P. Royal of Sweden possesses by having an Army of 30,000 men to back all he proposes. With respect to my proceeding to the Head Quarters at Reichenbach, I must observe that I have regulated my movements according to the events which have taken place on the Continent; the Emperor in his answer to my letter of the 26th of May asking leave to pay him a visit there, replied "He could not then receive me, but that he would let me know when he could". The

1 Castlereagh's half-brother; at this time Minister to Prussia. See No. 287 n.
2 By the terms of the Treaty of Peterswalde (24 July 1813) between Great Britain and Russia the British Government agreed to take into British pay a corps of Germans raised in Russia. Subsequently the British Government made an agreement with Count Münster on the part of the Government of Hanover, to arm, equip, and pay a corps of Hanoverian troops amounting to 15,000 men at an estimated expense of £600,000 a year; and the Russian German Legion, to the extent of 6000 men, was to form part of this force.

Armistice immediately ensued, & their Majesties quitted Head Quarters, & even had they remain'd there, I should have felt an awkwardness in proceeding there, not knowing what might have been the feeling of my own Government with respect to the Armistice. However with respect to the Emperor, I have since learnt from a *person* of *distinction* that H.M. answer was *not his own act and deed*, but was I am sorry to say at the suggestion of ONE I should have least expected it from; & in a conversation I had with one of the Foreign Ministers who accompanied the Pr. Royal of Sweden here, he observed upon my not having as yet seen the Emperor, "Monseigneur, croyez moi, nous Russes sommes tous indignés, je connais le dessous des cartes. I told him as far as I was individually concerned I did not regard it much as the King of Prussia's answer had been so civil; but that as the brother of the Pr. Reg[en]t of England who had done so much for Russia, I had a right to be treated as he treated the P.R. of Sweden, for that as to birth the Emperor & myself were upon a par. He said I can tell you the Emperor feels he has acted wrong & will repair what he has done. You will think I hope that I have acted right in saying what I did, as I find it is necessary to make these Russians feel that we Englishmen do not feel ourselves inferior to them in any respect. The King of Prussia on the contrary has behaved to me with the greatest possible kindness and civility, and having said he hoped to see me very soon at his Head Quarters I propose setting off on the 10th; my visit will be to him, & when there shall write to the Emperor to ask his leave to visit him. Ch⁵ Stewart will accompany me, who is what he ever has been a thorough Englishman, feeling for the honour of his Prince & country & not toadying Foreign Powers at the expense of what he owes his master.

The Pr. Royal of Sweden came here on the 1st insᵗ to review Major General Tchernicheffs corps of Cavalry which he inspected the morning of the 2ᵈ. The corps consisted of one Hussar Regᵗ. two Dragoon Regᵗˢ. & five Cossackes. The Hussars was [name indecipherable]¹ Regᵗ about 800 strong remarkably well mounted and very fine body of men, looked upon as one of their best Regᵗˢ of Hussars. The front rank is armed with piques as the Russian Light Cavalry are, they are cloathed in scarlet, the officers cloathing very like the English General of Hussars. The two Dragoon Regt. were Riga & Finland Regts both equally well mounted, about 600 each they are cloathed in green, the former with red cuffs & collars, the latter white, the former the best of the two. They wear helmets which make them look very well & according to my opinion are preferable to those worn by the British Cavalry as they have no horse

1 The Duke's handwriting is sometimes unreadable.

hair to them. These three Regts manoeuvred very correctly indeed & are very rapid in their movements. As to the Cossacks any thing more contrary to our idea of tactique I never saw, they have no one signal or word of command, but are continually hallooing & galloping about like a pack of fox hounds. It certainly is very interesting and amusing to see them manoeuvre for once, as they skirmish as if they were in actual battle knocking each other off their horses, & to make it still more natural on the 2^d inst they fired ball cartridges up in the air, so much so that the balls hissed over our heads, & the Pr. Royal found it necessary to stop it. There was also two pieces of flying Artillery which appeared to be very rapid in their motions.

General Moreau[1] is arrived at Stralsund and the Pr. R. has sent an A.D. Camp to invite him to join him. The P.R. proceeded that same evening to Gartow to inspect the Hanoverian levies and means to be the 10th either at Oranienburg or Potsdam where his H. Quarters are to be fixed for the present. He will have a corps of 80,000 effective men which he can collect at any time in 36 hours. Munster says my absence affords my enemies an opportunity of abusing me, & that you advise my return, to which I can only reply, no individual living is more happy to obey your wishes than myself, but knowing as well as I do your high sense of honour, and regard for character, I am convinced that you would not wish me to return home at a moment when there is an appearance of hostilities recommencing,[2] I should in such a case indeed expect to be abused by every one, for you have no idea how the D of Brunswick is abused & despised by all ranks for his strange conduct in going away as he did.[3] Upon my soul I had much rather that the first canon ball should destroy me than quit the Continent *now* at this moment. As for enemies everybody has some, mine at any rate cannot injure me here, & you knew when in England I did not care for them. Mens conscia recti carries one through many difficulties. If by my return to England I could feel conscious of being of any material service to you, I would lay down my life to prove my affection but you are now safe thank God, the more you are known, the more you must be adored, & your name goes here further than any Princes. Was I to consult my own pleasure only on this occasion I should not have quitted my own comforts in England and the happiness of your society and all my other friends there for the fatigue, *expense* & inconvenience of such a tour as this, but feeling as I do our evident desire

1 Jean Victor Moreau, the French General whom Napoleon banished in 1804 for his alleged participation in Cadoudal's plot. He was killed at the Battle of Dresden, fighting on the side of the Allies. (1761–1813.)

2 Austria joined the Allies on 11 August and hostilities began again on the 17th.

3 See No. 287.

to uphold our family name, to secure our national interests, & to aid by every effort in my power your dignity and the support of your Government, I feel I have availed myself of an opportunity that seemed to be presented to one of the House of Brunswick to manifest his zeal for the great cause of Europe; I certainly should have preferred to have seen service with a British Army, but being alas convinced that there did not exist a chance of my being so employed there remained for me no alternative but that of repairing to this great field of military operations or of giving up all idea of ever seeing service again. I long to hear the first canon shot, and every one in this part of Germany burns with the same desire, I expect every thing from the spirit of enthusiasm which pervades this part of the Empire. The van guard of the Swedish Army consisting of 4000 men pass through here this day on their road to Berlin, commanded by Major General Baron Schultzheim. I understand the 2^d Reg^t of Foot Guard forms a part. Now God bless you & believe me wherever I am that I ever shall be Dearest brother [etc.].

P.S. To confirm what I have said above respecting the *advantage* our Gov^t would have in having an *actual* force even of 23,000 men, do you think that in that case the Pr. R[oyal] would have let Hamburgh been taken, and certainly England must deplore the loss of that place.

304 THE EARL OF CARHAMPTON[1] *to the* EARL OF LIVERPOOL

Paines Hill, August the 6, 1813.

ON the 19 of June last I had the honor to enclose to your Lordship a statement of my claims for a seat in Parliament, accompanied with a letter addressed to your Lordship requesting that after you should have perused it, you would do me the favour to lay it before His Royal Highness the Prince Regent, that the claim so made would be acknowledged and that I should procure the fulfillment of His Majesty's gracious promise to me. I feel at no time the smallest doubt; nor do I now feel the least uneasiness; but to this claim I subjoined the suggestion of substituting one thing for another & am sensible how far the favour I solicited is superior to the thing claim'd. I am also aware that of my pretending to be honour'd with such a mark of His Royal Highnesses indulgence I must not be

1 Henry Lawes Luttrell, second Earl of Carhampton (1743–1821). The opponent of John Wilkes at the famous Middlesex election, 1769; M.P., 1768–84, 1790–94, 1817–21. Succeeded his father in the (Irish) peerage, 1787. Master General of the Ordnance (Ireland), 1797–1800.

allowed to judge, at the same time I feel it incumbent on me to acquaint your Lordship that so far as the favour asked is separate and distinct from the claim made, it is the first I have ever in the course of a long life solicited from the throne.

That there has been no notification made to me on this subject has I confess given me some uneasiness; tho at the same time there may be reasons which prevented your Lordship from acknowledging the receipt of my letter, and untill I am acquainted with them the very great respect I have for your Lordship will not permit me to believe that they would be dispenced with.

305 THE EARL OF LIVERPOOL *to the* EARL OF CARHAMPTON

Fife House, August 6th 1813.

I HAVE this moment received your Lordship's letter of the 5th of August, referring to a communication which you made to me on the 19th inst.

I should certainly not have omitted immediately returning an answer to your former letter if you had not desired that I should lay it, together with the papers inclosed, before His Royal Highness the Prince Regent. As the pressure of Parliamentary business at the close of the Session is very considerable—as that period was at a short distance, and as the delay could have no material effect upon the question itself, I thought it would answer every purpose if I placed your letters together with others of importance, to be laid before His Royal Highness for his consideration, during the recess of Parliament.

I am not yet enabled to return your Lordship any answer in His Royal Highness's name, or by his command to your communication. But I should mislead your Lordship if I did not apprize you that I have reason to know that the Prince Regent is so circumstanced with regard to the creation of Peers of the United Kingdom, that I do not think there is any probability of his being able to comply with your Lordships wishes in that respect.

Louisbourg, August 10th 1813.

AFTER my long silence you will be surprised to see my handwriting, however I trust that it will not be unpleasant to you to hear from one that is sincerely attached to you, and who troubles you so seldom with a line from the fear of appearing indiscreet; even now I should not have ventured to break in on your precious time if the King had not desired me to present his compliments to you dear brother, and beg of you to do me the favour to grant Count de Gallatin leave to go over to England. This gentleman who is one of the King of Wurttemberg's Privy Counsellors and Chamberlains, has been named by him to settle the business regarding that part of the late Dutchess of Brunswick's[2] fortune, which was settled on her daughter, the late Princess of Wurttemberg[3] by her marriage settlements and which of course belongs to her children. The Princes's of Wurttemberg having applied to their father to send a gentleman to England to transact this business with the Duke of Brunswick, the King made choice of Count de Gallatin and has obtained a French passport to allow him to go over to Great Britain: but fearing that the Count might be exposed to many unpleasant difficulties on the English coast unless he has also an English passport, wishes that you would have the goodness dearest brother to send me by return of the post by the same banker which will have the honour to present this letter to you, a permit or licence signed which gives Count de Gallatin leave to land in England and to go to London, or wherever it may be necessary for him to meet the Duke of Brunswick's trustees to settle this business.

It gives me great pleasure to think that I shall have it in my power to write openly to my family and to receive a true account of the health of my beloved relations. Pray dearest brother do have the kindness in your answer to let me know whether my mother's health has suffered from the fright she met with last May;[4] and whether the King continues in the same unhappy state which has made us all so wretched of late years.

1 Charlotte Augusta Matilda, George III's eldest daughter (1766–1828). In 1797 she married Frederick William Charles, Prince of Wurtemberg, to whom Napoleon gave the title of King in 1806. She had no children. For her own account of the troubles which his fidelity to Napoleon brought upon the country, see No. 364.

2 See Nos. 245, 257.

3 Augusta, daughter of Charles William Ferdinand, Duke of Brunswick (d. 1806), and sister of the Princess of Wales. She was the King of Wurtemberg's first wife, and died in 1788.

4 At five o'clock in the morning of the 2nd May a Miss Davenport, assistant mistress of the wardrobe, and daughter of the housekeeper at the Lower Lodge, Windsor, tried to force her way into the Queen's bedroom, "with the most distressing shrieks and screams imaginable". Mrs Beckendorf, the Queen's dresser, managed to summon assistance; the unfortunate woman, who had shown symptoms of insanity in childhood, was put into a strait-waistcoat and sent to a lunatic asylum.

I beg that you will be so good as to present my duty to the Queen and my affectionate love to all the dear family. I cannot be quite silent on the approach of the 12th. Pray accept of my best congratulations and be convinced of the sincere wishes I form that you may see many many happy returns of that day and that every new year may bring with it some fresh blessing.

I must now take my leave and remain with the sincerest affection [etc.].

307 FRANCES, COUNTESS OF JERSEY *to* COLONEL MCMAHON

August 12, 1813.

I HAVE written, since you think I am not forbidden, & am sure it is most respectful to do so. I send my letter to you for I think it better not to let my ser[van]t go to C.H. am not I right? Now my good friend I must thank you for all the trouble which you have taken. I hope Cheltenham will strengthen & prolong a life so valuable as yours is to the best of masters & I am sure you join with me in heartfelt rejoicing on this day[1] & prayers that the glory & happiness of his reign may not be interrupted by the malice of his enemies. Pray tell me when you have received this & believed most sincerely your friend.

I did not venture to say, what I will in confidence to you, how *much* I am distressed that what you sent came from a very different fund than I intended. Do you understand me?

308 SIR GEORGE DALLAS *to* COLONEL MCMAHON

Henrietta Street, Cavendish Square,
Tuesday night, Augst 1813.

IT is impossible I can adequately express my sense of your kindness.

I wrote to you that I considered, after (or rather *before*) the *service I had rendered*, the faith of Government pledged to me.[2] I enclosed to you the narrative of the Secretary of the Board of Control,[3] Mr. Meheux[4] waiting on me (they being in the secret of my views) *to solicit this service from me*. I did not transmit to you Sir J. Macpherson's[5] attestation to the fact, who they employed first to wait on me. I now lay it before you. He is ready to come forward, and, viva voce, to confirm it. Since then,

1 The Prince Regent's birthday.   2 See No. 301.
3 Thomas Peregrine Courtenay (1782–1841).
4 Assistant Secretary to the Board of Control.
5 Sir John Macpherson, first Baronet (1745–1821), Governor-General of Bengal, 1785–86.

I have laid them before Lord Buckinghamshire[1] and Mr. Meheux admitting the facts, the difference, if any, is between them. In the teeth of this I had no sooner rendered the service than Lord B. who is under great obligations to myself, sends a quiet Treasury mandate to the Directors to nominate that worthy but really incompetent man Mr. Wallace. I assured him he could not propose *"a more obnoxious measure to the Court"*—he would not believe me—sends for Thornton—persists in the measure and forces on a Court this day, from whence I had secret communication that they would not adopt him—and what has been the consequence? This moment I have a secret dispatch from a principal Director to say, in the following words—"We are this instant come to an almost *unanimous* resolution not to swallow the DOSE, and to communicate this civilly to the Board of Control". I give you my honor this is an accurate statement.

I have another letter this evening from a most leading Director, Mr. Twining,[2] wishing me to come forward. Under these circumstances I intend to address Lord Castlereagh tomorrow, and since all that is eminent in that Court would like to have me there, as I have reason to know Lord Moira also would, with whom I could so harmoniously cooperate, I ought not to give way when such powerful friends and claims support me, even though Lord B: adopts Wallace. My hope is, that Castlereagh will properly represent the case to Lord Liverpool. I have abstained from delicacy from making my brother a party to this pursuit, not to commit him in any degree, or chill his ardour in the Ministerial cause. If I can, under the rejection of Wallace, get Government to adopt me, (who have been so long on the ground with such claims) my friends will do the rest. There are two or three Opposition Directors for Tierney, who has talents, but no *temper* for the situation.

His R.H. the Duke of Cumberland has long been made acquainted with my views. I have no authority to use his name, but think, if he were on the spot, he would go to the Prince and lay my wishes at his feet. You know the Duke's hand, and will recognize the fragment I enclose. I was also the author of the little scrap I enclose from the Morning Post, just on his recovery,[3] as you will see from our friend Col[onel] Thornton's letter which accompanies it. Whatever may be the result of this business, *my voice is the Prince's,* and it shall never be found, with angry feelings, to mix with the polluted stream of faction.

1 President of the Board of Control.
2 Richard Twining (1749–1824), a tea-merchant, and Director of the East India Company.
3 Presumably from the injuries he received on the night of 31 May 1810 when, it was alleged, he was murderously attacked in his apartments in St James's Palace by his valet, Sellis, who was shortly afterwards found dead in his bed with his throat cut.

Bruton Street, 15 August 1813.

WHETHER the papers you have done me the honor to lay before His Royal Highness the Prince Regent shall be read or by an accident overlook'd I cannot tell. There certainly may be papers of more importance or at least in the opinion of Ministers more important to be read than mine, yet I am not without hope if they shall meet the eye of His Royal Highness they will interest his attention. But be that as it may, my Lord, if your Lordship had found time to cast *your* eye over them you must have perceived that without meaning the smallest disrespect to your Lordship it was decorous and proper that my claim, the reliance I had on the promise of our most gracious Sovereign and my reasonable expectations of the fulfillment thereof should in the first instance be made known by myself to His Royal Highness relying as I do on his known perspicuity to see that although it is a case out of the common routine of business it is precisely for that reason he will have the goodness to bestow upon it the consideration I presume to say it deserves.

That it is of such a nature as to interfere with Ministerial arrangements (though I confess I cannot see how) may be more or less possible—the novelty and unexpected appearance of it I know will not recommend it to any Minister, but these real or supposed impediments I should hope will be easily got over: It is not made on the usual ground of vote interest or exertion in support of Ministerial influence, it bottoms upon a broader base and rests upon a foundation which I should hope no Minister would like to shake—the sacred word of the King—it requires neither artifice or intrigue to support it nor will any such means be resorted to.

That any difficulty will be thrown in my way from the incapacity of His Majesty to make good his p[r]omise to me I will not readily believe. I send your Lordship the original letter of Lord North[1] to me as it gives me an opportunity of recapitulating without the appearance of egotism some of my services at that day. From the cowardice of the Cabinet and the irresolute and vacilating conduct of the Parliament all the springs of the Executive Government were relax'd and lost their elasticity: the mob were uppermost; disorder and confusion triumphd. I put myself at the head of my own Party; I beat the mob and cleard a passage for His Majesty to his palace where otherwise his safe return was more than doubtful, and by so doing I became the most unpopular man in England. But when I saw myself abandoned by that Cabinet and that Parliament I had it in my power to become perhaps the most popular man in England

---

1 Frederick North, Lord North (1732–1792), Prime Minister, 1770–82. Succeeded his father as second Earl of Guilford in 1790.

by abandoning them in my turn and refusing to sit for Middlesex, which from every principle, from every feeling I had as a gentleman and a man of honor I was prompted to do; and certainly would have done though Lord North advised His Majesty not to grant me the Chiltern Hundreds.[1] All my friends and my family importuned me to it; and nothing but His Majesty's interference and request could have prevented me from so doing. He was sensible not only of the injury I should sustain but of the services I had performd and such My Lord is the origin of the promise of which I now claim the performance.

Many of my friends know I have that promise, all of them know my services and the hard conflicts I have had with insurrections and rebellion in Ireland[2] and I feel it incumbent on me to shew them and the world that not for any obloqy that can attach to me am I apparently prescribed [*sic*] from both Houses of Parliament.

I have not ask'd for an hereditary Peerage, the Crown could not bestow it upon me, I have no family to inherit it. I only ask to be placed where (if I had not turnd my back upon and absented myself from a scene of vice and profligacy that in my mind injured and disgraced His Majesty's Government)[3] I should have been placed twelve years ago. My services have been long and I might venture to say arduous. The claim I make or the favour I ask is short and transitory. But if I shall be put into a seat in the House of Commons where only I can claim it; instead of the House of Lords where I have presumed to ask it; my knowledge of the Peerage of both countries will prevent me from feeling that the latter is refused to me on the score of its being beyond my pretentions to aspire to.

I am the last male branch of the Luttrells of Somersetshire. My family have possess'd large property both in England and Ireland, descending from father to son for more than six hundred years. These things I do not value much, but it is galling to have seen some persons whom I remember scarce gentlemen and of otherwise strange description and equivocal loyalty preferred to me and so thrust out that plain men have conceived Government must have some good though secret reason for treating me as it has done.

I beg your Lordship will excuse this letter unintentionally made so long and that you will communicate to me the alternative I am to expect

---

1 See *George III Correspondence* (ed. Fortescue), II, 308 (2 January 1772).

2 He was Commander-in-Chief of the Army in Ireland from 1796 to December 1797, at a time when the United Irishmen were making preparations for rebellion.

3 In 1800 he resigned the office of Master General of the Ordnance (Ireland) to which he had been appointed in August 1797.

from the decision of His Royal Highness in this business, so soon as it shall be in your Lordship's power so to do.

310 SIR HENRY HALFORD *to the* PRINCE REGENT

Windsor Castle, August 21, 1813.

I AM not without a hope, on good grounds, that matters go on here in a less unsatisfactory manner than they did. The Princess Charlotte seems more thoughtful and mild in her manner than she was—and Her Royal Highness express'd to me the day before yesterday a grateful sense of Her Majesty's attention and kindness to her.

But the Princess is really not well. She looks ill—and has complain'd for some time past, but more lately of a pain in her left side. This is not accompanied, however, with cough. Nor has the Princess any difficulty in lying down on either side—nor is the skin hot, tho' Her Royal Highness pulse is quick. I am inclined to think it muscular only—but it has seem'd prudent to apply a blister, and Her Royal Highness assented readily to this last night. For the rest, I am not sorry that Her Royal Highness's complaint gave me a good opportunity of speaking in very decided and forcible terms on the necessity of a regimen—and the Princess has determin'd to give up wine altogether at present.

I felt sure that it would be highly interesting to your Royal Highness to receive this account—and I thought it my duty to send it.

The Ladies[1] seem to have recover'd somewhat from the impression which your Royal Highness's most temperate but most forcible remonstrance occasion'd, and they are both pretty well.[2]

I hope your [Royal Highness] feels every possible comfort and advantage to your own health from the air of the sea, and from a short retreat from your great cares. Pray, Sir, continue to make me happy by your good opinion, and to believe me most faithfully attached to your Royal Highness, and always your Royal Highness's most humble, and grateful servant.

1 The Duchess of Leeds and Miss Knight.
2 The Prince Regent had recently complained of their having allowed Princess Charlotte to drive along the Chiswick road one day when the Duke of Devonshire, who was displaying too much interest in her, was giving a breakfast party at his Chiswick house. They were also censured for taking her to the studio of Sanders, the portrait painter, the Prince insisting that she should sit for her portrait at her own residence, Warwick House.

Prague, Augt. 23 [1813].

I ARRIVED *here* last night having travelled night & day from Langestatt the moment I received my passports. I have been detained here this day on account of buying carriage horses to convey my carriages to the Army. I hope to join the Army in two days when we expect a battle. I saw the Grand Dutchesses[1] today & you may tell William that my taste was not at all struck with their beauty though I think them very amiable, the widow is vastly pleasant & I prefer her to the Pss. of Weimar. I met Paul Esterhazy[2] here who married our cousin the daughter of Pss. Turntaxis[3] [*sic*] who is a charming little woman, & also have seen Hardenberg[4] from Vienna, his brother & Ompteda,[5] also Reden all of whom I was most happy to see. I trust to be able to leave *this* in the course of tomorrow & shall write to you from the Army. Stewart[6] has left this, this eveng. It does one's heart good to hear with what respect every one talks of YOU, and I feel proud at thinking that *you* dearest brother are looked upon as the main spring of all that is going on *here*. With the assistance of Providence I hope to be able to give you favourable accounts of *all* going on. Do not forget me but think now & then of one who loves you dearly. I suppose you are *now* setting off for Ragley. Pray remember me kindly to the dear landlord and landlady[7] & say my thoughts are often THERE. Pray do this for me in your best manner, & please God to spare me my health & life, we shall meet there again. God bless you & prosper you is the sincerest wish of [etc.].

1 Julia Henrietta Ulrica, daughter of Francis, Duke of Saxe-Coburg-Saalfeld, and Prince Leopold's sister. She married the Tsar Alexander I's brother, the Grand Duke Constantine. The Grand Duchess Catherine (1788–1819), the Tsar's sister, married, in 1809, Prince George of Oldenburg (1784–1812), and, second, in 1816, the Prince Royal of Wurtemberg, who succeeded his father as King later in the year.

2 Prince Paul Anthony Esterhazy (1786–1866), appointed Austrian Ambassador in London in 1815. In June 1812 he married Maria Theresa, daughter of the Prince and Princess of Tour and Taxis, and granddaughter of Charles Louis Frederick, Grand Duke of Mecklenburg-Strelitz.

3 The Princess Tour and Taxis, and Louisa, wife of Frederick William III of Prussia, were the daughters of Queen Charlotte's brother, the Duke of Mecklenburg-Strelitz, by his first wife. Sir Thomas Lawrence, who saw the former at Aix-la-Chapelle in 1818, said she had "a very fine figure and manner". (Williams, *Life of Sir Thomas Lawrence*, II, 117.)

4 Count Hardenberg, Hanoverian Minister at Vienna. Prince Hardenberg (1750–1822), the Prussian Chancellor of State, was his cousin.

5 The Hanoverian Minister at Berlin.

6 Sir Charles Stewart.

7 The Marquis and Marchioness of Hertford.

Aug. 27th 1813.

I t is satisfactory to me to be able to assure your Royal Highness that the Princess Charlotte is better than she was last week—tho' Her Royal Highness has suffer'd severely from her blister. In Her Royal Highness's present circumstances there is more lowness and nervousness, the effect of her disease and her remedies, than disease itself, and I believe it will not be prudent to enjoin too rigid a regimen.

Her Royal Highness has been extremely tractable, and has permitted with great good sense and good humour all that was necessary for her recovery.

For the rest, I may venture to assure your Royal Highness that matters go on pretty well on the whole. To speak with that honesty which your Royal Highness always approves, there appears to me much more want of common sense and a knowledge of the world in the *Governesses*[1] than of tractability in the Princess—and the consequence of this is, that some difficulty or other occurs perpetually to disturb the Lodge, and to create an anxiety in the Castle, which might be prevented by the exercise of a very little firmness and discretion in the first instance.

In short there is too ready a compliance with the hasty, quick desires of the Pss without considering any *consequences*. When these appear at length in their full light, and it is necessary to retrace their steps, disappointment and ill-humour follows—and the place of residence, or the tempers of others are found fault with, when the whole mischief has really been created by themselves. I could illustrate this by an instance or two in which they have called upon me to interpose—but I would not have your Royal Highness's peace disturbed by these small vexations. The Queen is all good sense and kindness—and I have only to lament that Her Majesty's continued dislike to Miss Knight prevents that access on the Chevalier's part which would be essentially useful to the Princess Charlotte, by promoting her attachment to the Royal family, and facilitating her governance.

When I have the honor of waiting upon your Royal Highness, I will take courage to speak still more fully, and to explain all that I have observed.

Pray, Sir, continue to me your Royal Highness's usual consideration and goodness, and believe me ever with most cordial respect and attachment, [etc.].

1 The Duchess of Leeds and Miss Knight.

9, Blackheath Hill, 6th Sept. 1813.

Be assured that nothing could induce me to trespass on the sacred retirement of a watering place, but the urgency of a case which compels me to depart, though very reluctantly from common forms.

I have been thoroughly sensible that during my present undertaking it would be highly impolitic for there to appear any correspondence between us. Therefore I have refrained from even sending once to trouble you for a frank, & at the festival I forebore to pay my personal respects to you on the same grounds, & I trust my conduct herein met with your approbation. The ticket you so kindly honored Mrs. Byerley with, compelling me to stay late on her account, I caught a violent cold being previously very unwell, & I have never been an hundred yards from home excepting on the day the bill was due, which you so obligingly gave me cash for, in order to attend to its being regularly paid, for those matters I never trust to any one lest by accident the confidence placed in me should appear to be abused. And I have the pleasure of inclosing you the draft to shew you it was so done.

My continued ill health together with that of Mrs. B. who has been ill these 5 mos & is now only just convalescent enough to go to Brighton in the hope of a complete recovery; with the contingent expences of doctors, physicians & nurses have terribly shaken my little finances, for while at increased expenses I was unable to meet them by any exertions of my own. I did hope that no casualty would have compelled me again to ask your generous & friendly aid of a temporary loan but beaten down as I am by affliction I trust I may be pardoned in once more asking it. Had I been in health I should not have needed it but all I have been able to do has been to prepare my M.S. more carefully for the Press & I declare to you most solemnly that the *loan* of £50 at present wo'd be equal to the present of £500 at another time. I need not say I shall feel grateful for your assistance on this trying occasion, but I will say that if you can conveniently oblige me you may rely on its being punctually paid according to the tenor of the inclosed.

I have several little matters & disclosures of perhaps some moment to communicate on a certain subject, but as I have studiously avoided any mention of your name in the course of the work perhaps you would not even wish that these anecdotes should be communicated to you. One relates to one of the Royal Dukes & throws a strong light on his subsequent conduct.

On these matters however you must decide & my pleasure will be obedience. The gent^n on whom I have drawn living at Hammersmith I

[288]

thought it better he should draw upon me & I make it payable at my bankers where I keep my cash (when I have any,) having drawn out of their hands within the last two mos £150. Waiting your answer with much anxiety, [etc.].

314 THE PRINCE REGENT *to the* QUEEN

> *Ragley*, Tues.ᵞ night,
> Sept.ʳ 7th 1813.

WHAT a kind, Oh! what a kind kind, very kind dear letter I have been favour'd with from you; never no never never, can I find words sufficiently strong or powerful, to express to you the full tide of all my gratitude, for your affection, kindness, goodness, & attention to me & to my wishes. But since I feel myself wholly unequal to the task, I will not presume to trespass upon your precious time, with weak & fruitless attempts at such expressions, as can only be *really* felt by the heart, & do not admit of being traced by the pen, therefore I must & I do throw myself upon your indulgence, to fancy to yourself to interpret to yourself, & to say to yourself for me, *all* that heart can feel, or that pen can trace.

As to the subject itself which gave rise to this most amiable & delightful of letters, I acknowledge candidly to you, that treated & managed as it has been by you, (& as indeed you always do every thing with your very superior understanding, judgment & taste) it does not in itself & as taken in the abstract, occasion me any uneasiness only this, that alas! one can not help seeing, & that one can not disguise from oneself, in whichever way one turns it & views it but that it arises from a sort of natural & intuitive spirit of restlessness & premeditated systematick kind of dissatisfaction that let one do what one will to please & to endeavour to please, one can never, & never is to succeed; & this, from my own cool deliberate & constant observation, I am quite sure, I am quite convinced is the real & positive truth, that it is a constitutional evil, a constitutional perversity in temper & nature, which I fear nothing now can correct or eradicate, (though it might have been & ought to have been so in earlier days:) The only possible chance that there may be, (at least according to my calculation, & which I am sorry to say, that I set but very, very, very, little reliance or dependance upon) of any amelioration or improvement in this respect, is, that by degrees, & perhaps in time there may be some appeal, or rather some interior monitor that will make an appeal to the heart; but there again, there must be a heart to be able [to] appeal to, & how alas! can we flatter ourselves with any such ameliatory hope either from what we have seen or observ'd as yet, but more especially if we reflect & recollect, *that part* of the stock from whence this has sprouted fourth, & drawn its origin & source.[1]

These however are only *private* & certainly not pleasant reflexions for ourselves, but which in the complete abandonement de mon coeur, & the unbounded confidence I place in you my ever dearest mother, I can not, & could not help adverting to.

With respect to the intimacy itself (it really is such complete stuff & nonsense) for I can not give it, nor allow it to be favour'd with a worthier denomination, as that would truly be stamping too great a ridicule upon worthier feelings, to call it by any other appellation; never till now did I know that it existed, as I have been kept in total ignorance that that particular person (who I believe to be perfectly harmless by the bye in themselves) had ever had an opportunity of conversing with the other young person (& much less had I any idea, that they had been in the habits of visiting; a circumstance which you well know, not in an in[di]vidual & solitary instance perhaps such as the present but as in a general point of view & as a general principle I have always so much & so uniformly disapprov'd of, & have so constantly wish'd to prevent on account of the bad consequences which are certain & sure to arise out of such habits. But all this is to be ascrib'd to the infamous treatment I have experienced from those in whom I had so sadly misplac'd my confidence, & whose whole, sole & only object & principle has been & was as I am now convinc'd from the very first to the last to deceive me systematically, & by the most cautious & artful means possible to keep me entirely ignorant & in the dark upon every thing that was going on & forwards & I am afraid that a day will hardly pass now, without some little something or other arising or shewing itself, to convince us more & more of the truth of what I have just been stating; & really therefore those that are at present about her, should rouse & call forth a little good sense & resolution, to check this spirit wherever & whenever they discover it, & should check instantly though with mildness yet with firmness instead of constantly & perpetually as they appear to me to do giving way to it, & encouraging it. I have now said so much to you my beloved mother upon this unpleasant topic which you have managed in so very masterly a manner that I really am quite asham'd of myself, & therefore I will not bore you much longer certainly not upon this &

1 At this time the Prince Regent was trying to persuade his daughter to marry the young Prince of Orange, and refused to allow her to marry her cousin the Duke of Gloucester; and he suspected that she was too much attached to the Duke of Devonshire.

hardly upon any other, for I perceive that my scrawl is already of a most unwarrantable length.

We leave this most beautiful place on Saturday; our party has been a most delightful one, & we have passed our time very gaily & happily. Poor dear William[1] has been in the very highest force, & enjoy'd himself beyond all conception, & his looks & his health & his spirits so improv'd (which I am sure that you will be pleas'd to hear) that I think you will hardly know him again when you next see him. Münster arriv'd here yesterday as upright as a pole, not at all in a crokeing humour but seeming to view the general state of things upon the Continent more en couleur de rose, than I almost ever knew him, but I candidly acknowledge to you, that I am both most impatient an[d] anxious for dispatches from the Continent for some decisive blow must have been struck by this time, & God grant that it may be a propitious & a successful one for us & all our Allies.

You surely must long ere now be tired to death with the sight of my horrid scrawl, indeed I am quite ashamed of it myself, there are so many erasures, blots & interpolations in it; the only excuse I have to offer for this, is, that I have not only been scribbling in great haste, & therefore had no time to recopy what I had written, but I let my pen trace every thought as it occurr'd in its own mishapen & crude state, prefering writing to you in this natural & easy way, to any studied language which must savour of mere ceremony & form. Now then adieu my dearest & most beloved mother, remember me with all possible love to the dear sisterhood, & believe me, whilst I have life, Your ever & most affectionate & dutiful son.

P.S. I perceive that I have another apology to make you, now, as upon going to fold up my scrawl, I find that I have begun it upon a sheet of paper, much smaller than the rest, but it happens to be a single one, & I had no more of the same sort, & I thought I knew you, & your usual indulgence too well, not to hope, & to trust that the circumstance of my writing in such haste, accompanied by the assurances of my sincere regrets at having been guilty of such an inadvertance, might & would ensure me your kind & gracious forgiveness.

1 His brother.

Headquarters. Teplitz. 7th Sept. 1813.

HERE we are still and since last Wednesday we have had nothing but reviews, the Russian troops are certainly beautiful, the Cavalry Regt. Cuirassiers really the finest sight I ever saw. We saw 76 squadrons together, namely 12 Cuirassier Regt. Russian, the Pr[ussian] Horse Guards equally fine and completely resembling the R[ussian] except having no cuirasses, the R. are cuirassed both behind and before; the Household Cavalry consist of two Regt. of Cuirassiers, Les Chevaliers Gardes, and Garde à Cheval, a Dragoon Regt., a Hussar Regt. & a Hulan [sic] Regt. The Hussars are dressed in scarlet and gold & Hulans in dark blue with crimson kapkas, the whole division of Guards both cavalry, infantry & artillery are under the orders of Constantine[1] who is also *Inspector* of *all* the Russian Cavalry, Supt. Adjt General to his brother the Emperor & colonel of the Gardes à Cheval, & Hulans of the Guard. The Russian Foot Guards are magnificent and have the finest military bands you ever heard, the Pr. Foot Guards are in the same manner brigaded with them as the Horse Guards and Light Cavalry Guards are with the Russian Horse Guards. The Hussars of the Russians I do not like at all. I think they are the least good of their cavalry, their artillery is magnificent & I really think it would be very well worth while for an English Artillery officer to come & see them, for it is a thing not to be described, it is peculiar to themselves. The Austrian army I saw also; I do not think it is so fine as it was 20 years ago. The Regts. are not half so strong as they were but expect daily to be recruited. Their Hussars are still very good. I have seen both Schwarzenburg[2] and Merveldt;[3] the latter is just appointed to a corps. I was present last Sunday at a small skirmish & mean tomorrow to return to the outposts which are commanded by Major Genl Zeithen[4] [sic] of the Prussians. I propose in a few days to go & see Blucher's army if there is nothing going on here, who has distinguished himself very much indeed. Esterhazy desires particularly to be laid at your feet. No news as yet of the Dwarf.[5] I suppose he is afraid of advancing. God bless you.

1 The Grand Duke Constantine (1779–1831). He renounced his claim to the succession in 1822, consequently Alexander I was succeeded three years later by his youngest brother, Nicholas I.

2 Karl Philipp, Prince von Schwarzenberg, who commanded the Austrian armies. (1771–1820.)

3 General Merveldt. In 1814 he became Austrian Minister in London. (d. 1815.)

4 General Count von Ziethen. He commanded a corps in the Waterloo campaign.

5 Sir Thomas Tyrwhitt. See No. 393. At the end of July the Prince Regent held a Chapter of the Most Noble Order of the Garter at Carlton House to elect the Tsar a member of the Order. Sir Thomas Tyrwhitt was a member of the deputation which left London on 8 August to confer this honour. He took with him a new travelling carriage "to encounter the bad roads of Germany".

Head Quarters, Teplitz, 13th 7^{ber} 1813.

W E are still *here* though there have been all this week marches & counter marches the advance Guard under Witgenstein[1] has been duly engaged there was a pretty smart affair at Perna last Wed^y I just arriv'd there in time to see it the attack begun early in the morning & we carried everything as I understand, at 2 o'clock I got there it being some thirty miles from *here* I arrived in time for a precious good dinner at Perna [Pirna] which had been prepar'd for Bonaparte who was to have his H. Quarters there that night, while we were at dinner reports came in that the enemy was advancing with force, Witgenstein gave orders for other Divisions to advance & we sat on quietly till then; when he thought it prudent to order the horses we mounted and rode out of the town which is very pretty, on the high road to Dresden about two miles we saw plainly the attack was having every success, and both General Ziethen of the P[russians] and Pahlen of the Russians declared they could not keep their position. Witgenstein immediately ordered the Division of Grenadiers of the Russians to advance and support them, but they being 3 English miles in the rear came up rather late however after obstinately fighting we kept Perna that evening, but were obliged to retire that *night* to Gottlieb [? Gottleuba] the two following days they made attacks again and our outposts were forced to give way as far as Colm [Kulm] about 10 Eng miles from hence; it must appear surprising to you all that we *here* with such a prodigious force do nothing by God it drives one wild but the *fact* is *that* the antipathy among *our* troops to each other destroys every thing and I pity Schwarzenberg from the bottom of my soul, for he cannot do anything, as I have but *this moment heard* of a messenger's setting off for England I can only write you a few hurried lines but will write you a long letter soon. I was going to say that the Russian Emperor is *not* what I expected, and I see plainly *here* at his Head Quarters there is nothing to be done or learnt, I shall now visit the P of Sweden where I have always received *civility* and shall be nearer *our* own possessions. The K. of P. is *all* I can wish and so is the Emperor of Germany, but there are too many cooks in *all* business here. Ch^s Stewart is already gone to Prague & from thence as soon as he can move he goes to Bernadottes Army.[2] I shall then have my equipage & hope to see a great

1 Wittgenstein, the Prussian General, was Commander-in-Chief of the Allied Army after Kutusoff's death in April.

2 Sir Charles Stewart wrote to his brother Castlereagh on 21 October from Leipzig: "The Duke of C[umberland] is going immediately to Walmoden to enter Hanover with him. I fear there will be a breeze there, but I shall go to Walmoden the very first inactive moment." (Londonderry MSS.)

deal. The last victory of Bernadottes, the news of which arrived here yesterday has given universal satisfaction & a feu de joie was fired last night. I wish this might act as a spur to them *here*, but I am sorry to say there is no unanimity *here* whatever and it must end in each Power collecting its own forces together & then it may do. However coute que coute *I will stay it out*, at least if there is no other activity I see a great deal & learn a great deal.

I like the Continent and though I have been put to very great difficulties still I prefer this life, Do not forget me but think now & then on your [etc.].

The Dwarf[1] I believe is lost no one has heard of him.

317 CHARLES WESLEY[2] *to* COLONEL MCMAHON

No 4. *Buckingham Street, Fitzroy Square,*
Sep. 14th 1813.

I TAKE the liberty of addressing you on being directed so to do by Mr. Robert Gray,[3] Somerset House.

I have had the honour to attend by command of His Royal Highness the Prince Regent, his organ at the Pavilion, Brighton, during the residence of His R.H. at that place.

When the Prince most graciously appointed me Organ Performer to His Royal Highness, I was order'd to apply to the Duchy of Cornwall and Lancaster Office for my professional remuneration, which I allways received from Mr. Rt. Gray, till on this last application he inform'd me that he had now, nothing to do with things of this kind, and that it belonged to your department, which I trust Sir, will excuse this trouble, and therefore have the honor to enclose the account for the allowance which His Royal Highness graciously assigned me.

1 Sir Thomas Tyrwhitt.

2 1757–1834. The eldest son of John Wesley's brother Charles, the hymn writer (1707–1788).

3 Of the Duchy of Cornwall Office. At this time he was also Steward to Princess Charlotte. He had formerly been Deputy Commissioner of Accounts to the Prince of Wales. See No. 534.

[*Enclosed*]

Journey to and from Brighton, and attendance on His Royal Highness The Prince Regent from the 18th to the 26th of August.

Fifty Pounds.
Charles Wesley,
Organ Performer in Ordinary
To His Royal Highness.

50 £.

Sept. 14. 1813.
Buckingham Street,
No. 4, Fitzroy Square.

318 THE DUKE OF CUMBERLAND *to the* PRINCE REGENT

20th 7ber [1813].

UNDERSTANDING Cathcart means to send off a messenger for England this evening or tomorrow morning early, I take up my pen, dearest brother, to add to my letter, since writing which I have had the satisfaction of assisting at two affairs of the advanced Guard; the first was Friday last when I luckily happened to be upon the identical spot when the attack began, which was at the abatti[s] that we had made at the entrance of a wood upon the road leading up to the mountains called Nöllendorf. Here the French showed their rascality. The evening before, our advanced posts had been strongly attacked & repulsed down the hill, the identical hill that had on Tuesday last cost us near 800 men to take, in one of the charges made by the Prussian cavalry. Young Lt. Colonel Blucher who commands the Pr. Boris Hussars (formerly Wolfraden) was wounded in four different places & taken. As is the custom a trumpeter was sent in early Friday morng with a letter to enquire after him, it was delivered & an answer was promised to be sent. I just arrived at this moment & a report was brought to Major Hildesheim who commanded that post, that the answer was ready to be delivered. He ordered an officer & a drummer to advance & receive it, when the officer perceived a French officer of cavalry at the other side of the abatti with a section of infty & no trumpeter. He beat, & receiving no answer halloed to the Frenchman to halt, upon which this rascal ordered his men to fire. Thus began the affair. After two hours fighting like lions the Pr. having twice expended their ammunition, were forced to retire and in the course of three quarters of an hour they debouched with 6 pieces of cannon, with which they regaled us nobly. All this time their infantry being engaged with ours, we had tried all in our power to prevent their advancing with our canon, and for two hours there was a fire of the Devil himself, shot, shell and grenades wizzing among us. I saw one poor fellow knocked down & a groom with a led horse had his arm shot off by the same ball. The moment that spectacle began, every one of the Cossacks who attended Witgenstein, near 200, took to their heels & the devil a one did I see again until we got to Culm, about a German mile in the rear, when we took a position which was protected by two battalions, one on the right of the road with 24 pieces, 12 pounders, & the left by an equal number. Luckily for us the fog was prodigious & it rained torrents, which induced General Ziethen who commands the advanced guard of Kleist's army to propose attacking the enemy with the bayonet, and this was followed by the other battalions when we drove them back to the abatti. Further we could not go on account of night coming on. Colloredo, who commands a corps of 20,000 Austrians, at this time fell upon their left flank, and a most dreadful carnage took place of which we saw the effects the next morng, as the roads and fields were covered with dead bodies. I am sorry to say, but tis as true as the Gospel, that *all* this might have been prevented had three Russian battalions who were the support of the outposts, advanced when ordered so to do, but the antipathy between Prussians and Russians is so great that they won't support each other, and I heard Zeithen then cry out, "By God this won't do, we must be separated, the Prussians do not trust the Russians & vice versa", but mind this is for yourself as I make it a rule to tell you the plain honest truth and you ought to know the fact. I have now been five weeks at these headquarters & no man has endured more than I have, and to *you alone* I acknowledge I am so disgusted with the conduct of the Emperor of Russia that I am determined to leave it and shall visit Blücher and the Crown Prince of Sweden's and *our own corps.* Quit the Continent I shall not, for I still think much may be done; but believe me it must be done in a very different way. I beg, dearest brother, you will not commit me nor show this letter to the *big Wigs* as I call them, the only one you may is to *Bags,*[1] but as to all the rest I have shaken hands with them for ever.[2] I speak to you openly as a brother & not as Regent. Depend upon it the temporizing system that now is going on is our ruin. Schwarzenberg who is a very old friend of mine and who speaks de coeur

1 Lord Eldon.
2 Probably because they were opposed to his having a military command.

ouvert is perfectly of the same opinion, the armies must be united and each fight for themselves. I mean the Russians alone, the Pr[ussians] d[itt]o though they and the Austrians agree fully. Let me ask you how is it possible for Schwarzenberg to do any good if every order he issues is to be explained, debated upon, and very often even disobeyed by Barclay de Tolli who is completely supported by the Emperor his master. This has been the case no less than three times these last three weeks. Schwarzenberg told me no later than last night, ma foi je suis à plaindre. Vous connaissez ma position, d'honneur je quitterais [the mounting here makes three words illegible] si je ne savais pas que l'Empereur mon maitre serait peutêtre trahi car l'on me nommerait un successeur qui n'aurait pas les nerfs de combattre avec la partie Russe et tout irait au diable. Can you ever conceive anything more horrible. I have had many conversations with the K. of Pr. who is by God the best of them, most faithfully attached to England and the good cause, and has proved himself so by his endeavours, but he is as if he was subjugated and resigned to his fate, not acting like a Sovereign but like the vassal of the autocrat. It grieves me to say this for I am convinced he has *talents* to command, and in the affair of Friday last I was by his side in the eveng when he came out and he instantly in the coolest manner made dispositions and placed himself the Prussian batteries when the balls were falling pretty thick round him. His fault is he has no confidence in himself, and why he should not I cannot conceive, as he has more sense in his little finger than the Russian[1] has in his whole frame. This is language I only hold to you, for alas all one can do now is to palliate and soften down things, not to encrease feuds. On the other hand I am sorry to say that C[athcart] is all Russian and will not see things as he ought to do, and this is very strongly felt by *all*, not only by every Englishman but by Austrians and Prussians. The overbearing manner of the Russians is dreadful, and all I can say is that if H. I[mperial] M[ajesty] offered to make me Field Marshall of his armies and give me the command, the Devil a bit would I accept. The fact is *he* wants to command the armies of the Allies himself. In this he was foiled by the Emperor of Austria, and how could he think of such a thing, for to command such a body of troops, God knows is no sinecure, every hour, yes every minute day and night are occupied and I heard him tell the Emperor of Austria that for the common routine of business he was occupied *ten* hours a day. On Saturday Merveldt with his corps d'armée made an attack on the left wing of the enemy, which I suppose induced them to retire, for last night we were enabled to resume our former posts, we made about 400

1 The Tsar.

prisoners who were litterally starved to death, so much so that they laid on the ground expiring with fatigue and hunger. We experience, God knows, the same. I have hardly been able to get anything myself to eat, and the poor soldiers who are constantly laying out a bivouac in the wet have had nothing but bread this whole week. I am afraid we shall lose a great number of men by the dysentry. What do you think, Witgenstein has lost in killed and wounded since the 8th when we had the affair at Pirna no less than 10,000 men, so this must prove to you we have had fighting enough, but in spite of that we are still *all* in the same position, and every day longer we stay here, every day our difficulties must increase. Our horses have no hay or oats, so exhausted is the whole country, and the troop horses look like dog horses. Excuse this long letter but I thought you would like the *real* & *true* state of things as they strike me, and those who are fair & candid. I must say the Austrians are exerting all their efforts but they are deficient in many things, they are in want of cavalry for from their false economy introduced by Metternich[1] & Wallis[2] their Regts are now but 800 instead of 1200 men, they expect a reinforcement of 10 Hussar Regiments that are now raising in Hungary, which are all volunteers commanded by *ten* Hussar general officers, but they cannot possibly arrive for 3 months, & 62 battallions of infantry; in short every exertion that human power can exert they are doing at present. In this moment I have had a visit from Prince Hesse Hombourg,[3] General of the cavalry in the Austrian service & Colonel of a Hussar Regt., green pelices & dollman red pantaloons, who tells me he has received orders that *all* the Hussar Regts are to be increased to 13 squadrons, consequently they will have 26 Rittmeisters, 105 Lieutenants, and each squadron is to be 130 mounted, which will make each Regiment 1690 men besides sergeants and corporals and trumpeters, but this will take time to accomplish and a pity it is that this was not thought of five months ago. No news whatever of the Dwarf.[4] I suppose either the prostate gland stops him or he is sunk into some bog in Poland.

Best love to *all*. Remember me kindly to the worthy host and hostess of Ragley[5] where I perceive you went the 30th. and suppose you are still there. My thoughts have transported me often there, and I longed for a few quiet days there. God knows when we may meet, but wherever

1 Prince Metternich, the Austrian Foreign Minister and Chancellor (1773–1859).
2 Who had reorganised the Austrian finances.
3 Frederick Joseph, Hereditary Prince of Hesse-Homburg (1769–1829). In 1818 he married Princess Elizabeth, the daughter of George III, and succeeded his father as Landgrave in January 1820.
4 Sir Thomas Tyrwhitt.   5 The Marquis and Marchioness of Hertford.

I am and whatever may happen to me you may depend upon the faithful and everlasting attachment, dearest brother [etc.].

[P.S.] I am sorry to see by the newspapers that you sprained your leg again. However by perceiving you went your tour I trust it was of no consequence. Vyse[1] left me last week for England to join his cara sposa who has produced him a second son. Remember me to Yarmouth and *campus florius*.[2]

319 THE PRINCE REGENT *to* QUEEN CHARLOTTE

C[arlton] H[ouse], Wedy Evg, ½ pt 8.
Septr 22d 1813.

Great Events, Great Events, Great Events.

I AM delighted at having it in my power to be once again able (under the blessing of a divine Providence) to be the channel of communicating to you the most satisfactory & important intelligence. In primis Mecklenbourg is entirely free'd from the French; & Swedish bulltins have been this instant receiv'd to the 8th & 9th inst stating the the [*sic*] Prince Royal of Sweden had, after a long & well contested action taken 18000 prisoners & 60 peices of cannon from the French who were commanded by Marshal Oudinot.[3] I am too much elated at this moment to be able to make any comment, but my first impulse was & is, before I can allow myself to collect my ideas, to communicate to you best & dearest of mothers these most joyful tidings. After once more endeavouring to express my boundless gratitude to Almighty Providence, for these its immesurable blessings, & mercies, so incalculably & bounteously shower'd upon us of late, I subscribe myself in the greatest haste, my ever dearest mother, [etc.].

P.S. Since writing the above, one of the printed bulltins has been sent by Lord Castlereagh which I inclose. How fortunate also that the good news should have reach'd us on this day. I shall fly & embrace you the first moment I am able. If you receive this as I hope you will whilst you are at supper, pray drink a bumper all round, men, women, & children,

1 Richard William Howard-Vyse (1784–1853), the son of General Richard Vyse, Comptroller of the Duke of Cumberland's Household.
2 Sir Benjamin (then Colonel) Bloomfield.
3 Charles Nicolas Oudinot, Duke of Reggio (1767–1847). He was defeated at Gross-Beeren, near Berlin, at the end of August: a battle which saved the Prussian capital.

to the health of the Prince Royal of Sweden, & do not quite forget poor me, who have I think, some little merit at having been the first to set them all at work. Pray do not hurry yourself to answer this. My servant has orders to stay all night & wait your orders in the morning.

320 DAVID WILKIE *to* COLONEL MCMAHON

24 *Phillimore Place, Kensington,*
Septbr 27th 1813.

HAVING thro' the medium of Mr. West, President of the Royal Academy, been honored with the command of His Royal Highness the Prince Regent to paint a picture for his collection, the subject of which together with the time of painting it, & the price of the picture, His Royal Highness was graciously pleased to leave to me, I did in obedience to His Royal Highness paint a picture, the subject *Blindman's Buff*, which I completed in April last & delivered at Carlton House & in an interview, which I had the honor to have with His Royal Highness, he was pleased to express his approbation of the picture.

Considering the business, as a private concern with His Royal Highness, I take the liberty Sir, to address you on the subject, & beg leave to state that the price is five hundred guineas, & that I shall feel myself greatly obliged to you, if you will do me the favor to acquaint me with His Royal Highness's pleasure.

321 THE EARL OF LIVERPOOL *to the* EARL OF CARHAMPTON

Copy.

Fife House, 29 Septr 1813.

THE PRINCE REGENT having read over the papers wch I laid before His R.H. at your Lp's desire has commanded me to acquaint you that he very much regrets that it is not in his power, under all the circumstances, to comply with your wishes respecting a Peerage of the United Kingdom.[1]

With regard to a seat in the House of Commons, the particulars detailed in your Lordship's statement were never before known either to His Royal Highness or to his Government, & they were therefore entirely unacquainted with them at the time when it might have been

1 See Nos. 304, 309.

practicable for them to have assisted your views if they had understood that they had been directed to this object.

In the present state of things I can say no more than that adverting to the nature of the transaction to which you refer, to the period at which it occurred, & to the fact that for more than 15 years your Lordship had chosen to forego the advantage in question in consequence of your preferring to hold an office[1] not tenable with Parliament, for wch a compensation has been since granted, they cannot consider your Lordship as, under all the circumstances, having a claim upon them for a seat in the House of Commons, even if they had the means of ensuring it to you, which at the present moment do not exist.

322 Peter Stuart *to* Colonel McMahon

85 *Hatton Garden*,
(Morning), Wedy Sept 29/13.

A s another testimony of loyal attachment and humble duty to His Royal Highness the Prince Regent, permit me to communicate to you the inclosed for your better judgment and superior consideration. If you think it worthy of your notice, I'll wait upon you any time to-day or tomorrow you please, to mention particulars.

The publication will extend to about 12 sheets, or about 200 pages— the MS. is completely prepared—and intended for immediate publicity, or at the meeting of Parliament. It was offered to me in the way of business; and I did not suffer a single moment to elapse before I thought it incumbent upon me to give you the information. But whatever be your determination, I fully expect that I shall not in this instance be transferred with my secret to any other gentleman; and relying implicitly upon that honour which I have so often with the greatest pleasure witnessed, I am, [etc.].

1 The office of Patent Customer at Bristol.

Treas[ury] Chambers, 2nd Octr 1813.

UPON looking over my papers I found the letter wch I showed you from Ld Manners.[1] It is so satisfactory for yr present purpose that I again put it into yr hands, advising you at the same time to write to Ld Manners yourself with a view to recal to his recollections *his own idea* respecting the expediency of yr brother being the Master of the Rolls whenever there was a vacancy.[2]

Direct to Ld Manners, the Duke of Rutland's, Cheveley Park, Newmarket.

I *have already* written to Ld Manners, but it will not be amiss for you to let him know that *thro' yr agency* the present Master of the Rolls[3] might be induced to resign.

Pray tell Mrs. McMahon with my very best regards that I have had Mr. Macnamara with me, & that I have paid him all the attention wch she can desire.

I have not seen the R[egent] Ld Lowther dines with him every day. He & Croker are going to Ld Yarmouth in Suffolk. This is a sort of mess wch is not very reputable, & I don't at all fancy Mr. Brown's notion that *I* give news.

P.S. The *R.* is now sending for Harrison[4] to Carlton House.

Harrison is a very good man, but I cannot think it for the Prince's interest to be taking up every new person.

Drayton, 5th Octr. 1813.

I BELIEVE I may truly say that I never had greater pleasure in sending any letter than I have in sending the inclosed; & I am sure that I shd be a brute if I had not joy in promoting yr wishes.

I shall call yr brother *my* Master of the Rolls, & so I beg you will tell him.

You have surely now nothing to do but to write instantaneously to Ld Manners, & to tell him that I have communicated to you his letter. I shd trust that the final settlement of this business cannot now be de-

1 The Lord Chancellor of Ireland.   2 See No. 184.
3 John Philpot Curran (1750–1817), Master of the Rolls, in Ireland, since 1806.
4 Sir George Harrison, Assistant Secretary to the Treasury since August 1805. Knighted, 1831. (d. 1841.)

layed; & if I can be of further use, tell me so, & you will not find me inactive.

Upon the strength of Lord Manner's letter you will of course communicate with Curran; & altho' I am not positively sure of Ld Manner's present direction, I would write to him at the D. of Rutland's, Cheveley Park, putting on the outside that the letter shd be forwarded in case his Lordship shd have gone away. Not a soul knows of our negotiation, & no one therefore can intrigue against you. I shall of course write to thank Ld Manners for his letter, & shall treat the affair as being as good as finished under his auspices. At all events you *must* write to thank him.

Don't fancy I am so mean minded as to be *jealous*; but it did seem odd that Harrison shd have been sent for the other day to meet Nash, & that there shd have been a very great deal said to him about Wharton[1] & not one single word of me. But however this is quite between ourselves.

[P.S.] I am on my way into Lincolnshire, but direct to me in Downing St.

325 LORD MANNERS *to* CHARLES ARBUTHNOT

Cheveley Park, Octr 3d 1813.

I LOSE no time in answering yr letter, and assuring you of my zealous co-operation (so far as I ought to appear in it) to carry into effect the plan suggested by you, and I apprehend the necessary steps to be taken, in order to attain this object, will be, for the Master of the Rolls upon the score of ill health to apply for leave to resign his office, and to have the retiring pension; and upon that being done you must obtain from the Prince Regent a strong recommendation of Sergt McMahon as the successor. The first step will be popular throughout Ireland; and when it is known that the circumstance of Sergt McMahon being the intended successor, was an inducement to Mr. Curran to resign, I think there will be little or no complaint by the profession of any part of the transaction.

I am anxious not to appear very conspicuously in the matter, as I fear there are some at the Bar who consider themselves better intitled, and will be disappointed at the preference, but I hope to reconcile them to it —and I do not doubt of satisfying the Lord Lieut. that the commands of the Regent ought not to be opposed.

I shall be particularly gratified by the success of this measure on account of our friend Col. McMahon, to whom I beg of you to give my best regards.

1 Richard Wharton, Joint Secretary of the Treasury, 1809–14.

4 Buckingham Street, Fitzroy Square,
Oct. 7th 1813.

NOT having been favour'd with an answer since I had the pleasure of addressing you, I take the liberty of enquiring whether a letter came to your hands, in which I enclos'd the little account of my journey to Brighton when I had the honour of obeying the command of His Royal Highness the Prince Regent, and which Mr. Robert Gray of Somerset House was accustomed to settle on my return to town, who directed my application to you.[1]

327 THE DUKE OF CUMBERLAND *to the* PRINCE REGENT

Strelitz, Oct. 10th 1813.

I ARRIVED here about a week ago having left the H.Q. still at Teplitz, and as I mentioned in my letter there I proposed visiting Walmoden's corps which is now at Ratzeburg or [illegible]. I feel myself much more comfortable at being nearer my own countrymen than where I was before, for certainly the life and situation of a volunteer at H.Q.s is of all others the most vile, and I can assure you that nothing but feeling my *departure* at this crisis from the Continent, after what I have read in public print of *being ill-used*, might strengthen that report, makes me stay [in] the neighbourhood. However I think the time fast approaching that I can hail you with the good news of the recovery of your dominions upon the Continent which to *me* I acknowledge will be the happiest of my life, and when that day is arrived then I shall forget *all* the unhappy & uncomfortable time I have passed since I have left home. But *all this* I mention merely to yourself as I know that *this* will be nuts to MANY in England and alas when I come to consider that some of those persons who will feel *rejoiced at this* are nearly connected with myself, I cannot help saying that this among many other reasons has made me resolve upon not returning home for some time; as I know that *I* am not *popular* among those, for God knows many things have within these last five months come to my knowledge which have given me more pain than I can find words to express, believe me, dearest brother, you have no man whether brother or friend more affectionately or more sincerely attached to you than I am. I believe you knew me *too well* to think me capable of expressing to you any other opinion but what flows from the

1 See No. 317.

sincerest feeling of attachment to you. My object is to remain at Hannover & as Adolphus has declared to you he will not serve any more in a military capacity, and will not reside abroad, I am most ready to do so, & if you will entrust me with any command there, you may depend upon my exerting every nerve for your service. When I say this I do it *merely* for yourself, for if you have any other person in view for that command, then do not let me stand in their way, for in that case I shall reside either at Berlin or Vienna as I may like but at the same time I must say from having lived so many years in Hannover I think I might be of use, & you must be aware that in the actual situation of things *one of your own family* ought to be there. Do pray read this letter with attention and do communicate to me your answer if not in your own hand writing at least through some confidential person, for from the reason already mentioned I wish *not* this to be *public* that I have made an offer you have not accepted. I am fully persuaded of your good wishes and friendship and therefore I trust you will receive this letter as it is meant by me. I have still the rank of *Senior General Officer* in the Hannoverian service; as all my seniors are *dead*, therefore I am not demanding anything that is unjust. I propose going to Walmoden in a day or two when you shall hear from me again. Tyrwhitt arrived here the day before yesterday. He is remarkably well and has written to you upon the subject of his staying still upon the Continent, which I think you will approve of. God bless you and let me hear from you soon.

328 THE EARL OF CARHAMPTON *to the* EARL OF LIVERPOOL

Paines Hill, 14 of Octr 1813.

THE PRINCE REGENT, assisted with your Lordship's advice I presume, does not think proper to place me in that situation in the House of Lords, of which the Irish Ministers, at the time of the Union, deprived me, as a punishment for not supporting that measure. The scenes which I witnessed & the means that were then resorted to, made me disdain to have any part in it, and in my own justification, I have collected facts, which will I trust, satisfy my friends at least, that I did not, by withholding my support, forfeit the character of uniformity of conduct & disinterestedness, which in a very long life I have endeavour'd to preserve. To the Prince Regent's decision on that point, I most submissively bow down. What I humbly claim as matter of right, stands upon a very different foundation. Your Lordship rests the refusal of a seat in the House of Commons, on the grounds that neither His Royal Highness nor his Government had hitherto been made acquainted with the particulars detailed in my statement; to my having for so long a period as 15 years chosen to forego the advantage in question; & that a compensation had since been granted, as it should seem (if your Lordship's argument has any connection with the facts of the case) for that forbearance. I trust that the facts do not warrant any one of the conclusions which yr Lordship has drawn from them, & still less, any conclusion militating against the truth or justice of my claim.

Ministers have certainly not been made acquainted with the particulars to wch my statement relates, (tho I cannot conceive how that should in any respect weaken their force) nor should they now, if the Legislature had not removed the incapacity under wch I labored, of demanding that situation wch I look to, & which has been guaranteed to me, by the express word of my Sovereign.

Secrecy, while it could be preserved, without injury to my honor, it was incumbent upon me to preserve; but it cannot be expected, that I should submit to an implied slur upon my character, by witholding my claim, whenever the world sees that there is no longer any legal bar to my sitting in either House of Parliament.

If it be observed, as yr Lordship seems to hint, that I might at any time during 15 years have rendered myself eligible, I admit the fact, but by no means allow the conclusion that my not having done so, should operate as an obstacle to my getting a seat in the House of Commons, now that I am by operation of law, again rendered capable of sitting there.

For a considerable period I was employed in my military capacity, in highly confidential situations in Ireland (for my conduct in which I received the repeated thanks of that Government) & while on that account, necessarily residing there, a seat in the English House of Commons was of less value to me, the more so, as I then had a seat in the House of Lords of that Kingdom. It is however the first instance I believe, & I trust it will be the last, where the delicacy or forbearance of the claimant should be urged as a reason on the part of Government for not noticing or recompensing his acknowledged services, performed as mine were in its immediate support, as well as in that of the peace, honor, nay safety of my Sovereign, & of his family.

I have concealed my claim out of respect to His Majesty. If yr Lordship is of opinion that the motive was a weak or mistaken one, it is at all times in my power to remove at least this objection to it, by showing that no personal consideration has sufficient weight to keep me longer

silent with reference to the period which has elapsed, since the transaction took place. It may be vexatious enough that I should be alive 43
years after the event (a circumstance which few of the witnesses of the
Middlesex election in the year 1769 could have ventured to predict)
but if I should chance to live 40 years more, I shall not while I exist relinquish my pursuit, nor be made to believe by any authority, short of
his own, that the Prince Regent will see his Royal father's express
promise violated.

His Royal Highness tho' very young, was yet old enough to have
participated in that safety, which, at the hazard of my own life &
character, I insured to his father & himself, & he will not I trust leave me
to be the only man in England, who cannot be a candidate for any
borough upon equal terms with another, in consequence of the part which
I took upon that occation.

If your Lordship supposes, that the office which I held in the Customs,
was given to me as a recompence for the surrender of my claim to a seat
in the House of Commons, I beg to assure you, that you are altogether
mistaken. My brother having thro' the interest of my father, obtained
the patent of Customer of Bristol, was desirous from the embarrassed
state of his circumstances, of alienating it to me, for a valuable consideration. To this Lord North acceded, almost as a matter of course. I held
the office for several years by a trustee; sat & voted in Parliament, as
Mr. Fane my brother's predecessor had done, & I should probably have
continued to do so at this instant, if an Act had not passed, which by the
death of the trustee, rendered it equally dangerous (as I have had the
honor of detailing more at length, in the statement transmitted to your
Lordship) for the Minister & myself if I had continued to sit & vote in
the House. Antecedent to that Act Mr. Pitt did not urge it as an objection, wch perhaps he might have done, that I held the office in question
but when my trustee died & that my being the possesor must have
directly appeared or the office have been abolished. He then said that
I must resign my seat or surrender the office as his connivance would
then have been obvious to every man in or out of Parliament. For the
reasons already assigned, I decided as I did, but without abandoning my
right to a seat whenever my own choice or other circumstance should
render it not unsafe, or myself eligable. In another view, I think that it
rather fortified my existing claim, than weakened it, for assuredly as
long as on any account, or for any reason whether of a public or private
nature, I remained out of Parliament & did not exact the performance
of the promise made to me, so long did I benefit that & all other succeeding Administrations (yr Lordship not eccepted) by leaving my seat

20-2

to be filled at their disposal, & by a friend of their own. That my silence has grown out of the nature of the case, & not from any doubt of the validity of the claim, appears clear from what occurred in Mr. Pitt's Administration, many years after the events had happened, on wch His Majesty's promise to me was founded. Mr. Pitt then as little acquainted with the transaction & his Royal master's share in it, as yr Lordship now is, having as I know in the first instance satisfied himself directly from the King, did not deny my right, allowing that the claim was from its nature irresistable.

If it be a maxim of law that Nullum tempus occurrit regi, I hope that a feeling of a similar nature will prevent an implied statute of limitations from being pleaded on the part of His Majesty, to a debt of gratitude, even to the meanest of his subjects.

I trust that I have now shewn yr Lordship that the place which I held was not a recompence for my being out of Parliament, but an office purchased for valuable consideration, & consequently that neither this, nor the other objections stated to my claim do in fact apply. Out of respect to your Lordship & in justice to myself, it is incumbent upon me to remove those objections which (the value of your time not admitting of much consideration of the documents submitted by me to you) you have on perhaps a cursory view of my case, urged against me, & to express a hope, that you will upon reconsideration not think them sufficient in honor or conscience to defeat my claim. Should I however be disapointed in this expectation, as I then mean to solicit an opportunity of appealing to the Prince Regent in person, it will be but fair, that if you found the advice which you may give, that the covenant with me shall be broken through, upon the reasons which yr Lordship has stated to me, you will make His Royal Highness acquainted with this, my reply to them.

329 *A Statement of Facts on which* LORD CARHAMPTON *claims a Seat in Parliament from* HIS ROYAL HIGHNESS THE PRINCE REGENT

IN the Administration of the Duke of Grafton[1] and in consequence of a vote of the House of Commons expelling and incapacitating Mr. Wilkes to sit,[2] I voluntarily vacated my seat and successfully opposed him in the election for Middlesex.[3]

1 Augustus Henry Fitzroy, third Duke of Grafton (1735–1811), Prime Minister, 1768–70.
2 17 February 1769.
3 Luttrell was defeated by 1143 votes to 296, but two days later the House of Commons resolved that he had been duly elected.

When Lord North became Minister I was present at the timid de-liberation of the Cabinet, and when I saw it was resolved to give way and to rescind the vote against Mr. Wilkes I wrote a letter to Lord North (a copy of which I have the honor to enclose markd No. 1.) and I received from him in his own hand writing the answer mark'd No 2 now in my possession a copy of which is also annexd to this statement.

Having gone down to the House to exculpate myself, Mr. Robison[1] the Secretary to the Treasury informd me that Lord North wishd to see me before I took any further steps, which produced the letter from me to his Lordship markd No 3.

In the conference I had with him the following day had I been in-fluenced by any other motive than a just sense of the injury I was about to sustain, and an anxious desire to justify my my [*sic*] conduct as well to the House as to the public at large, had ambition or emolument been my object no difficulties opposed me in the gratification of either; but I neither askd nor would accept anything but what I had a right to demand, what it had never been customary to refuse, and what could only place me on a level with every other man in Parliament.

This request Lord North advised the King not to grant, but His Majesty well knowing the zeal and disinterestedness with which I engaged in this contest, and finding that I would not come to any com-promise with his Minister without the sanction of His Majesty in future; desired Lord North to tell me that he guaranteed me a seat in Parliament during my life hoping I would not agitate this subject any farther. Whether my acceptance of this accommodation was was [*sic*] right or wrong it is now too late to decide, but from it originated all the disputes that existed between me and my family and that lasted for so many years.

My brother Mr. Temple Luttrell was Customer of the Port of Bristol which office was obtained for him by his father and by an arrangement between us was made over by him to me; but I being in Parliament it was held in trust for me which had been the practice of former occupants sitting in Parliament, and I continued to sit and was returnd by Lord North during his Administration.

When Mr. Pitt became Minister he dissolved the Parliament and I found myself left out in the next. I remonstrated with him on this breach of faith, quoted the sanction of His Majesty and was at length put in nomination for Bossiny; but that borough refused (as was signified to me) to return me alledging they would return any other man in

1 John Robinson (1727–1802), the Tory politician and party organiser. Secretary of the Treasury, 1770–82.

England but Colonel Luttrell. I replied to this subterfuge as I ought and was returnd for Plympton.[1]

An Act of Parliament having pass'd while I sat for this borough by which certain offices were to cease after the death of the then possessors:

Amongst these offices that which I held was included; and Mr. Whitby my nominee dying shortly after; Mr. Pitt stated to me the consequences as well to himself as to me if I continued to sit holding such an office which could not then be concealed; and I being on the staff of Ireland[2] and in that situation confidentially employed in quieting the disturbances which then prevailed there, and being involved in law suits with my family originating from political disagreements I preferred taking the Chiltern Hundreds[3] and keeping my office to remaining in Parliament and losing it, it being clearly understood that when I should be again eligible my right should revert. By an Act lately pass'd that right now reverts; I just now cease to be a Custom House officer, and I trust my claim to a seat will appear to His Royal Highness indisputable.

I was left out of the Representative Peers at the Union, for what reason must be explaind by those who thought proper to pass me by on that occasion.

Disgusted at the scene that was passing before me; and seeing the country likely to become Catholic I took no part in that measure.

Of my services I am not in the habit of speaking at any length; I had borne the brunt of insurrections and rebellion in Ireland till my life which was constantly in danger was perhaps less saved by the conviction and execution of some of those who conspired against it, than by a total neglect of its preservation for I never skulkd from the active performance of my duty at any time. Indignant at such treatment were my services out of the question the circumstance of my family possessing property in In [*sic*] Ireland descending from father to son for six hundred years might have entitled me to more consideration; I felt the injury like a man not used to bear one; I resented it by the only means in my power I sold everything I had in Ireland and quitted a country where the conduct of a corrupt and cowardly Government exposed my life to assassination, wounded my feelings, robbed me of the weight and influence I had in it, and where I found it was no longer safe or honorable for me to reside.

It may be observed that I am at a time of life when it is unwise for me to enter into these pursuits or to urge those claims: this would be a just

1 19 June 1790.
2 As Lieutenant-General of the Ordnance.
3 William Manning was elected for Plympton in his stead on 14 February 1794.

observation if there was any period of a man's life when he ought to be indifferent to injuries that strongly affect him in every point of view; that must attach to his memory when he is no longer able to be the guardian of his own reputation; and when he has neither sense to feel, energy to resist, or spirit to defend himself against them. I am not exactly arrived at that period and though my life is probably scarce worth five years purchase; I sincerely feel that I have been so long excluded from both Houses of Parliament, and I seize the first opportunity in my power to convince the world that not for anything discreditable to myself have I been so excluded. In this feeling I trust His Royal Highness will participate, and instead of the seat which I have a right to claim; if His Royal Highness shall graciously please to place me in the situation in the House of Peers, where I had every right to expect I should have been placed so many years ago for my life (and an English Peerage can do no more) I should be proud to owe that obligation to His Royal Highness.

[*Enclosures*]

H. L. LUTTRELL *to* LORD NORTH, 28 *May* 1772. No. 1

In consequence of what has passed in the House I am decided to take the step I informed your Lordship and General Conway I was determined on doing.

Consistently with my principles and with what I have declared both in public and private I cannot hold the seat for Middlesex which now ought to be filled by Mr. Wilkes.

I ask the Chiltern Hundreds which His Majesty will I trust not refuse me, as he is well acquainted with the disinterestedness of my conduct, with how much personal hazard I voluntarily and highmindedly undertook the task of stemming the popular fury audaciously aimed even at His Majesty and tending to render the Parliament contemptible.

LORD NORTH *to* H. L. LUTTRELL. *Downing Street,* 29 *May,* 1772. No. 2

I obeyed your commands in laying your request before the King, accompanying it with the advice which I told you when I had the honour of seeing you in Downing Street I should think it my duty to give to

His Majesty, and I am in consequence authorised to inform you that you cannot at present have the Stewardship of the Chiltern Hundreds.

If the office for which you solicit were likely to produce any advantage to yourself or your friends I should have been very desirous of contributing to the success of your application, but as it would be unpardonable in me to promote by any act of mine a new election for Middlesex, you will not be surprised that I offered my advice to the King not to grant your request in the present instance.

H. L. LUTTRELL *to* LORD NORTH [n.d.]. No. 3

I shall have the honour of waiting on your Lordship tomorrow, Mr. Robinson having communicated to me your wish that I should do so.

Mr. Robinson having however thought proper, sitting near me in the House to endeavour to feret out of me in conversation something of my intention with respect to the matter in question; I was obliged to change my seat, telling him I was apprehensive many in the House seeing us apparently in close conversation together, might think that I was under the guidance of your Lordship as Minister, which certainly not being the case I would not suffer him to exhibit an appearance of.

330 SIR MARK WOOD *to* COLONEL MCMAHON

Gatton Park, October 18th 1813.

IF you can without much trouble or inconveniency, discover, through what channel of information the young man whom you mentioned to me, (I think of the name of Greaves) heard that I had it in contemplation to dispose of Gatton, I will be much obliged to you—as I wish to trace to its source the channel of so confounded and malicious a report. You will farther oblige me, should you ever accidentally hear any such report—to give it the most decided contradiction, and to add—that you learnt from me, that I had put it out of my own power ever to part with Gatton—that estate being strictly entailed upon my son—& failing of him my daughter.

I think it not improbable, but that the rumour may have arrisen from a late transaction betwixt Sir John Nicholl[1] and myself—which about six weeks ago was settled by the intervention of the Speaker.

1 [1759–1838.] M.P., 1802–32; Dean of the Arches and Judge of the Prerogative Court of Canterbury, 1809–34.

About 12 years ago I purchased from the Crown the whole of the late Paul Bonfields[1] [*sic*] interest in the burrough of Shaftesbury, which lost me upwards of 75 thousand pounds, but having had a great deal of trouble in the management of this property—and Gatton being sufficient to gratify every political view, about five years ago I enterd into an agreement with Sir John Nicholl, and (Sir John's nephew) Mr. Robert Peter Dyneley, to sell them the same estate for 50 thousand pounds.

Some months after Sir John repented of his bargain and applied to me to let him off—his nephew at the same time assuring me on the part of Sir John, that it would make no difference in point either of payment of money, nor security, and altho I had lived long enough in the world, to have known a great deal better, yet I was fool enough to let him off—tore the contract and accepted of a new one, with the name of Sir John's nephew alone.

I put the nephew in possession of my estate, but year after year went on and no money was fourthcoming; even the common interest remained unpaid.

To my applications to Sir John he turned a deaf ear, and finding by fair means impossible to compel him to behave like a man of honor; I at last threatened to publish the who[le] of the transaction and correspondence and to distribute them amongst the members of both Houses of Parliament. This brought matters to a crisis—Through Sir William Scott,[2] the Speaker accepted of the reference and very *judiciously* and *lawyer like* gave it against me, but at the same time recommended to Sir John Nichol to advance 10 thousand pounds—which Sir John offerd to do, but which I have declined accepting of.

If therefore you should ever by chance hear this business mentioned you have my authority—and I intreat of you as my friend—to give my statement of it.

The burrough of Shaftesbury I now consider as *close* and *certain* a burrough as any in England. At least three fourths of the property belongs to Mr. Robert Dyneley, and exclusive of the burrough interest will pay a man at least 4 pr c. for his money. I was consulted in the nomination of Wetherell[3] and Kerrison[4] and of course highly approved of them

---

1 Paul Benfield, who amassed a fortune of over half a million in India, and subsequently, it is said, returned nine members to Parliament. (d. 1810.)

2 Lord Eldon's brother, and Judge of the Admiralty Court, 1798–1828. Created Baron Stowell, 1821. (1745–1836.)

3 Sir Charles Wetherell (1770–1846), afterwards Attorney-General. Knighted, 1824. Elected M.P. for Shaftesbury, February 1813.

4 Edward Kerrison, the other member for Shaftesbury.

from their political principles—and untill my money be paid, I think it is but fair that I should have a vote in the business.

It would however be much more desirable to me to have my money. Robert Dyneley told me a few days ago that he was treating with a party for the sale and that the price was 55 thousand pounds. I know not who the party is, nor whether friend or foe but I think if young Greaves's father can command the property he says, the sooner he applies to Mr. John Dyneley (brother to Robert Dyneley) of Grays Inn, the better, as I should be extremely sorry that the philistines should get hold of Shaftesbury.

Exclusive of Mr. Greaves, should you hear of any of our friends, who may be desirous of purchasing a property of this sort, I will be much obliged by your mentioning it.

I will give them a line to Mr. Dyneley. I beg of you to excuse this trouble and to believe me with great regard, [etc.].

331 THE EARL OF MOIRA *to the* PRINCE REGENT

Calcutta, Octr. 19th 1813.[1]

IT is impossible for me to let the Stirling Castle go home without repeating to your Royal Highness the humble tribute of my unalterable & most affectionate devotion. Distance or time cannot make any change in a sentiment so long interwoven with my existence. On the contrary, I am disposed to think that whensoever my recollection turns to your Royal Highness (& indeed the recurrence is not unfrequent) it rests with more grateful contemplation on your kindness than when the sense excited by the daily opportunities of intercourse was confused by the whirl of the busy circle around you. I dare to believe that I, too, shall gain by the reflection of your Royal Highness upon me when so far removed.

As yet my view of all here must be very imperfect. The scene is vast & the occupation incessant. Never before, I am persuaded, was dominion conducted with such silent regularity as is the case with regard to the territories of the Company. All is quiet & well within them. On their borders the spirit is not so placid. Breaches, not formidable but likely to be very troublesome, have been postponed by management till the palliatives will serve no longer: and our task, whatsoever may be it's extent, will be necessarily the heavier from the preparation to which protracted discussions have excited our adversaries.

Be the future what it may, it will ever find me Sir, [etc.].

1 Moira arrived at Madras on 11 September, sailed again on the 18th and reached Calcutta on 4 October.

Calcutta, Octr. 20th 1813.

MY writing to you by this ship (the Radnor) is more to excuse my sending under your cover a heap of letters for other people than really to address yourself. Pray frank such of the packets as are to be dispatched by post.

I wrote to you at large by the Stirling Castle. In the mean time (lest this ship should arrive before her) I may tell you that all is going on well. There was a possibility of some hitch. Ld Minto, excellent in his intentions & most amiable in personal character, had let down Government so sadly that it was questionable whether folks here might not have become so wedded to the levelling system as to hang back against the effort to re-establish the decorations of authority. Luckily, the public feeling took the right turn; & the communication of our intention to observe an etiquette somewhat analogous to that of Dublin Castle was cordially hailed by all classes.

I am satisfied that the sentiment arose from their conviction of the mischiefs obviously creeping forward from the other line. In business, my colleagues manifest the most satisfactory desire to support me zealously. The Secretaries are men of sound & ready talent; so that one perceives judicious discrimination as well as habitual facility in their mode of laying subjects before one. Altogether, I find great ground for confidence: The affairs to be managed are immense. Still, with method so well established & with such able functionaries to aid one, I see that due periods of relaxation may from time to time be secured after I shall have cleared away some of that accumulation which comes upon me now as if it were an arrear in all the branches.

I have given to a Lt. McCawdlish of the Stirling Castle a letter for the Prince; enclosed to you, that you may lay it before His Royal Highness. To a younger Lieutenant (Martin) I shall give a letter soliciting your good offices. The officers of a ship employed on such a mission look with a sort of claim to the Governor General to forward their promotion. Sir H. Popham begged me to solicit it for the eldest Lieutenant. I answered that altho' I saw every reason to believe that gentleman to be a very good officer, I had tact enough to discover much difference between his demeanor towards us & that of other officers. In short that altho' he could not but be civil to us it was always in a way that implied "I must behave with due politeness but you are a damned troublesome set": Therefore, altho he was a Campbell, I should decline interesting myself for him.[1] Sir Home represented that it would stigmatize the man

1 Moira was Earl of Loudoun and Baron Campbell in the Scottish peerage.

for ever if I passed him over. At last, I agreed that I would recommend Lt. Campbell formally & as a matter of course to the First Lord of the Admiralty;[1] but that I would not back the application with any private interest. Let the recommendation of Campbell take it's fair chance; but I shall be particularly glad if the promotion can be obtained for the other two, giving McCawdlish the preference.

There is not in this country an Arabian horse fit to send to the Prince. I must write to the Resident at Bussorah to get a proper one for me.

Sir G. Nugent stays.[2] The civilities which I have shown to him have produced that resolution. It was not for my private interest to make remaining here appear eligible to him; but it was right, so I am satisfied with having done it.

We are all well. The heat has been unusually great for the last fortnight; but the sultry season is this day breaking up with a tempest of wind & rain.

Offer my truest & most affectionate duty to the Prince; & believe me, [etc.].

Kindest regards to Mrs. McMahon.

333 THE BISHOP OF LIMERICK [DR WARBURTON] *to* COLONEL MCMAHON

See House, Limerick,
21st Octr. 1813.

MY young friend & neighbour Lord Clare,[3] has been requested by Lord Whitworth to *move the Address*. He hesitated a little, and was kind enough to ask my advice.

Finding his hesitation arose from an unwillingness to *pledge* himself, *so early*, to any Ministry, I advised his accepting the invitation upon the fair ground of "approving the measures of the Prince Regent's Government". He has consented, and sets out for London immediately.

Without a particle of the fiery enterprizing genius of his father, Lord Clare is a young man of much promise—a good scholar, mild & conciliating in manner, with an excellent understanding; extremely popular in his County, and will certainly make a respectable nobleman.

1 Lord Melville.   2 See Nos., 190, 191, 193.
3 John Fitzgibbon, second Earl of Clare (1793–1864). Succeeded his father in 1802. The Earl of Digby moved, and Lord Clare seconded, the Address at the opening of the Session (4 November 1813).

Feeling gratefully alive to every circumstance, touching the person or Government of our Royal master, I take the liberty of troubling you with this little private communication; and with most cordial congratulations upon those great events which enable the Regent to meet Parliament, under circumstances the most glorious to the nation, & most honorable to H: Royal Highness's Government, I have [etc.].

334 JOHN NASH *to* COLONEL MCMAHON

Cranbourne Lodge, 24 Octr 1813.

HIS R.H. THE PRINCE REGENT commanded me to request of you to signify to Lord Liverpool H.R.H. wish that the road & plantations in Windsor Park as shewn by the annexed plan should be immediately carried into effect. I saw Mr. Harrison on the subject who suggested that the regular mode on this and all such occasions is to address the Prince Regent's pleasure to Lord Liverpool individually who will thereupon cause the necessary Minute to be made by the Board of Treasury.

I apprehend something like the enclosed letter clad in your better terms and accompanied with the enclosed plan will produce the authority wanted.

I have only to add that the season for planting will not admit of delay.

335 THE QUEEN OF WURTEMBERG *to the* PRINCE REGENT

Stutgard, October 28th 1813.

HAD I only consulted my own inclinations I should yesterday have indulged myself in conversing with you, but knowing how much your time is taken up by serious business I denied myself that pleasure and commissioned Charlotte to express to you in my name every thing that is kind and affectionate. However the King thinks that it will give you pleasure to be acquainted with the various changes which have taken place last week in our political horizon and has kept back the messenger that I may give you an account of them. I am not very fond of entering into political discussions which little suit the pen of a woman, but encouraged by the desire of doing something agreeable to you, I hasten to comply with my husband's advice.

I need not dear brother give you an account of the unexpected turn which affairs have taken in Germany nor of the great advantages gained by the Allied Armies, which your Ministers will have certainly acquainted you with. The Wurttemberg troops which made part of the French Army suffered dreadfully in most of these battles and behaved with a steady courage that did them honour in the eyes of friends and foes. Such was the state of things when the King heard that an Army of Austrians was forming near the frontiers of his Kingdom, without his being informed of their destination and about eight days ago these reports were followed by a message from the Emperor of Austria, to engage the King to enter into the new Coalition, or in case of his refusal to threaten his dominions would in a few days be exposed to be treated as the country of an enemy. Seventy thousand men commanded by General Wreden[1] [*sic*] were at that moment within two days march of Stutgard. This of course required some deliberation, one cannot change sides without taking time to decide on a step of such importance and particularly when the situation of the Kingdom of Wurttemberg is known; Stutgard being within three days march of Strasbourg is exposed to fall into the hands of the French every time they cross the Rhine, and many days or rather weeks must elapse before Austria could send a sufficient body of men to free the country from the dangers it would be exposed to. These reasons must ever have great weight, but present necessity makes the King give up all other considerations and he has not only yielded to the Emperor of Austrias demands and sent part of his troops to join General Wreden's Army but has also sent Count Zeppelin[2] to conclude a Treaty with the Emperors of Austria and Russia. I hope that this Treaty will be very advantageous for Württemberg as the dominions of none of the other Sovereigns are so much exposed to the first inroads of the French. This I hope dear brother will be the first step towards renewing a friendly correspondence between the Courts of London and Stutgard which none will rejoice in more sincerely than myself who am much attached to my family and have felt sadly vexed at being so long deprived of all direct accounts of those so justly dear to me. I will now take my leave and only add the King's best compliments to you and beg you to be convinced of the sincere affection with which I remain, Dear brother, [etc.].

1 General Wrede commanded the combined Austrian and Bavarian army operating in South Germany.
2 The Wurtemberg Minister for Foreign Affairs.

Camp near Maraghah, October 31st 1813.

AT the same time that this humble address will be presented to your Royal Highness you will be informed by your Ministers that I have had the good fortune to conclude a Treaty of Peace between the Russians and Persians, the attainment of which had baffled the attempts of both parties for the last ten years.[1]

Although the affairs relating to Persia (unfortunately for me) create little interest in England, yet the reverse being the case in Russia I have already received the most grateful acknowledgements from General De Rtistchew [Rtischev], Governor General of Russia and the line of Caucasus, and having learned from Mr. Campbell, the gentleman whom I had sent to Teflis as acting assistant Secretary, that the Emperor of Russia would probably solicit your Royal Highness to recompence me for what he is pleased to term "this most important service" which I have rendered him, I feel that it would be derogatory to the duty I owe your Royal Highness as well as undeserving the uniform gracious favor and protection with which you have honored me, were I to allow your Royal Highness to be surprized by the application without your first learning from myself the degree of participation I had in it.

The fact is, that when my unceasing exertions had encouraged General De Rtistchew to give some hopes to the Emperor that a Peace might be concluded through my mediation he repeatedly (I suppose by command of his Sovereign) requested me through Mr. Campbell to name the honors, distinctions or recompense most agreeable to myself, that he might write to the Emperor to have them granted. I at first declined everything, declaring that I considered it a happy discharge of my duty to use every exertion in the cause of your Royal Highness's most honored Ally; but at length when pressed on the subject I suggested as delicately as I could that the dearest ambition of my heart would be best gratified were His Imperial Majesty to write to your Royal Highness in my favor.

General De Rtistchew has now given me to understand, through Mr. Campbell, that such a letter will be written and a recompense solicited perhaps more suited to the Emperor's idea of my services and to the elevated situation I fill as your Royal Highness's representative than to my own personal deserts. I should therefore consider it in a measure treasonable to the feelings of your Royal Highness's generous heart, and to my own devoted attachment, were I not to apprize you of what has passed, although it is possible still that General De Rtistchew reckons upon more than the Emperor may comply with.

1 See No. 176.

Let the result be what it may, your Royal Highness's continued favor and protection allow me to hope you will not be displeased to find (should such application take place) that the conduct of your faithful and dutifully attached servant has obtained such a recommendation to your Royal Highness's approbation.

I beg leave to apprize your Royal Highness that I have not as yet been honored with your commands respecting the curiosities and productions of Persia.

337 THEODORE EDWARD HOOK[1] *to* [COLONEL MCMAHON]

Bruton Street, Monday [? 1813].

I AM truly sorry to be under the necessity of troubling you again on my account & can only trust as I have done before to your kindness to excuse me.

By letters from the Mauritius we find that the situation of "Collector of Registration Fees" for my holding which my Lord Bathurst in his letter to you on the subject gave his sanction conditionally—has been given to our friend Mr. Power, which through the mistake of the person who told me I did not understand and therefore applied for a wrong *nomination*. It is the *"Deputy Secretary to the Government"* that Govr Farquhar[2] has *left vacant* and if your kindness would induce you to make the application for *that* to Lord Bathurst my views will again be as good as before, otherwise my situation will be a very inferior one.

Lord Bathurst said that he should have no objection to ratifying any appointment the Governor might assign to me—it is no great assumption to say that he (the Governor) would wish me to have the best appointment which *could* be allowed me though from motives of delicacy he has left the *"Deputy Secretaryship to the Government"* unfilled.

It may be of some use to observe that out of the very few appointments he has originated one of Assistant Paymaster to which he proposed Mr. Lautour[3] (Mr. Farquhar's brother's) name will not be accepted by that

1 [1788–1841.] The novelist and wit. In October 1813 he was appointed to the offices of Accountant-General and Treasurer of the Mauritius. For the Prince Regent's personal interest in him, see *Bathurst Papers*, 190–1, 205.

2 Sir Robert Townsend Farquhar (1776–1830), Governor and Commander-in-Chief of Mauritius, 1812–23. His father, Sir Walter Farquhar (1738–1819) was the Prince Regent's physician.

3 Sir Robert Farquhar married one of the daughters of Joseph Francis Louis de Lautour, of Madras.

gentleman who has now gone into the Guards and declines going to the Mauritius, so that in point of fact ther[e] would be *no addition* to the number of names the Governor may have transmitted.

I remain with many apologies for the intrusion, [etc.].

338 THEODORE EDWARD HOOK *to* COLONEL MCMAHON

8 *Bruton Street*, Sunday [October 1813].

IT is with an unfeigned feeling of gratitude I have to announce to you that Lord Bathurst has been pleased to appoint me Treasurer and Accomptant General of the Island of Mauritius.

Permit me dear Sir to make my warmest acknowledgements for the many kindnesses I have received at your hand, they will remain for ever impressed upon my mind and cannot fail to incite future conduct in the confidential situation in which I am now placed, which may prove that I am not unworthy the favor & protection which has been so generously and graciously afforded me.

Should there be any pacquet which you might wish to have conveyed to Mauritius I shall be proud to be the bearer of it, if sent to Bruton Street before Thursday on which day I leave London finally.

339 MISS MARGARET MERCER ELPHINSTONE[1] *to* CAPTAIN CHARLES HESSE[2]

Copy.

Plymouth Dock, October [1813].

I HAVE for some time had reason to expect the arrival of a packet from you, under cover to Lord Keith, in consequence of a letter that was addressed to you from London in the month of August last. I am now de-

1 [1788–1867.] The only child of George Keith Elphinstone, Admiral Viscount Keith (1746–1823) by his first wife. She was the close friend and confidante of Princess Charlotte. In 1817 she married the Comte de Flahault, Napoleon's Aide-de-Camp, and afterwards French Ambassador in London.

2 Captain Hesse, a dashing young officer of the 18th Hussars, was the reputed son of the Duke of York by a German lady of rank. He served with Wellington's army in the Peninsula, and was wounded at Waterloo. His parentage naturally brought him into contact with Princess Charlotte, who fell in love with him when she was about sixteen. She wrote him some rather indiscreet letters, and, whilst he was in Spain, she sent him presents, which she experienced much difficulty in getting him to return. For some time after August 1814, whilst the Princess of Wales was living on the continent, he was in her Household, and her enemies alleged that she too had a fancy for him. He returned to England with her in 1820. In later years he had a *liaison* with the Queen of Naples, and this becoming too notorious, he was expelled from

sired to inform you, that the disappointment has been severely felt in a quarter, where any inattention or disrespect ought not to have taken place, and I am also commanded to require an immediate compliance with the directions contained in the letter, alluded to, as a further delay must inevitably produce the unpleasant consequence of a full and explicit disclosure of every thing that has passed.

I am also anxious to know if a parcel reached you safely that was given in charge to Capt. Vernon of the Challenger Brig, who sailed from hence about the end of August.

The answer to this letter, if sent to Sir George Collier[1] at Passages, will be forwarded by him to my father [etc.].

340 THE PRINCE REGENT *to* QUEEN CHARLOTTE

Carlton House,
Wed? Ev? ½ pt 6. Novr. 3d, 1813.

Now that I have recover'd a little the use, both of my senses & of my poor hand, after the first effects of the glorious intelligence[2] which I was so fortunate as to be able to forward to you this morning, will you in the first place pardon me for troubling you with a few lines so soon again, & in the next place will you (but entirely entre nous) indulge me (perhaps) in a little peice of superstition, which is, in accepting of the accompanying trifle on *this day*,[3] putting it in your pocket & taking a pinch of snuff out of it, before you retire to rest, as it bears upon it the effigies of *one* who I hope you will *now* think is *no disgrace to you*, to his family, or to his country, & who as far as his mite could go, has contributed *that*, *to his utmost* in aid of & towards the accomplishment of all the great & splendid events & success, with which it has pleased divine Providence, to bless & to crown our joint, combined & allied exertions & arms. I hope you will not be offended with me for this further little intrusion & that you will forgive the great liberty I am taking with you, which

the city under an escort of gendarmes. He was engaged in several affairs of honour, and was ultimately killed in Paris in a duel by Count Leon, a natural son of the Emperor Napoleon.

For further letters dealing with Princess Charlotte's letters and presents, see Nos. 370, 387, 395, 396, 418, 434–6 and 547 A. For the Princess of Wales's attempt to corrupt her daughter, see Nos. 508, 509 and 547 A; also No. 876 n. For his rank in the Army see Charles Dalton, *The Waterloo Roll Call* (London, 1890).

1 Commodore Sir George Ralph Collier, the son of Vice-Admiral Sir George Collier (1738–95). His ships were co-operating off the Spanish coast with Wellington's army.

2 Of Napoleon's overthrow at the Battle of Leipsic (16–18 October).

3 Princess Sophia's birthday.

believe me is neither dictated by vanity or self presumption, but purely by that never ceasing affection & veneration, with which I remain, my ever dearest mother, [etc.].

P.S. No further particulars or details have as yet reach'd us.
P.S. Pray pardon my griffonage as well as blotting & mistakes as I write in great haste.

341 QUEEN CHARLOTTE *to the* PRINCE REGENT

Windsor, the 4th Novbr 1813.

M Y first occupation must be this morning to convey you my thanks for the beautifull present I received last night, it is in every sense so exquisitely elegant that which most to admire, the taste or the workmanship is very difficult for me to decide, but I do not feel the same distress to express how sensibly I am of the kind & affectionnate letter which accompanied this dear gift & trust that I never shall forfeit but always deserve such a blessing.

The news of yesterday are indeed of a nature so great as to give us hopes that the wretched state of the Continent must now draw near to an end of their misery, & I am convinced that the steadiness of this Government has greatly contributed to the decided part our Allies have at last taken to oppose the tyrannical oppression of the upstart Corsican self made Emperor who I trust will still fall into our hands & will be made sensible that human power can not outdo the will of the Almighty.

Indeed we may be proud that the unshaken steadiness of this country during twenty years when it stood nearly alone has at last been the cause of opening the eyes of the world & that it should have fallen to your share to add to the example & to see our wishes so blest makes me not less proud to sign myself [etc.].

[P.S.] The sun shines, may every blessing attend you.

Hannover, Novr. 9th, 1813.

You would have been apprized by the letter I addressed to you on the 2nd. inst. from Domitz of the intention I had formed (after mature deliberation with your old Ministers Decken and Bremer and Lt. General Walmoden on understanding from the Prince Royal of Sweden that he was to be the 4th. at Cassel with his Army), to avail ourselves of so eligible an opportunity of proceeding to Hannover without loss of time and reinstating the old Govt, there being actually at that moment no Govt. in the country. In acting in conformity with that idea I could be governed by no other motives than those which were connected with the wellfare of the State, the interest of your Government, and a desire as a member of the House of Brunswick to shew an attachment to the country not less ardent than that distinguished loyalty which it has so long manifested to our family.

Previous to stepping into my carriage, the horses already to it, my baggage forward and the Ministers already gone, who had announced two days before my intention of being the 4th. at Hannover I received a Dispatch from Sir C. Stewart dissuasive of the measure, which at *that* time I did not concieve to be official but which I found upon his arrival here yesterday he designed as such. I am frank and honest enough to acknowledge to you that *even* had I *then* known it to be official I should have felt myself bound to proceed as *my personal honor and character were committed*, and had I not so proceeded the publick expectation wd have been exceedingly disappointed; and knowing as well as I do *your high sense of honor and spirit* I feel confident that could you have been situated as I was, the only member of the family then on the Continent and on the very confines of Hannover, you would have acted as I have done. Thus far did I think myself bound to act, namely in assisting to replace your Ministers, & further I give you my honor neither directly or indirectly have I meddled nor will I interfere unless in any way authorized by you. Upon the arrival of the Pr. R. of Sweden here the 6th. I rode out to meet him and complimented him as the restorer of the country and I have the satisfaction to add that he addressed me in the following words. "Mon Prince vous avez fait votre devoir en venant ici, et si j'eusse été en votre place j'en aurais fait autant, car l'honneur le demandait de vous". Thus I am authorized to conceive that my *presence* cannot *in any way militate* against the arrangements of the P. of S. My continuance here cannot in the least operate against Adolphus' return to Hannover should *that* be *your* wish and he be so disposed; on the contrary no man will be more happy to see him here and embrace him *more cordially* than I shall, and

I am confident that you cannot employ any brother more faithfully attached to you than he has ever been. I shall write to him by this same messenger to explain myself to him and to tell him that although at this moment I am residing in his house he must consider me as only preparing it for his reception, and that the moment I shall hear of his coming I shall immediately look about to procure myself one either by purchase or hire as I can manage.

I have the highest gratification in assuring you that the most enthusiastic feeling of satisfaction has been universally expressed upon the re-establishment of your Government; and for my own part attached as I have ever been to this country I feel tenfold more so from all I have witnessed since my arrival here.

I hope and trust that my proceedings, dictated as they have been by the purest motives, will meet with your approbation, and I do not say too much when I assure you that they have been replete with good effect here, and the warmth of my attachment to you will ever actuate my best energies for the wellfare of your Government.

I send you by this messenger a Hannoverian sword knot which I am proud in being the *first* to offer you. I also send you the pattern of the sash which you directed me to get made after the pattern of the Prussian one. There was no time to get *one* completed but *this* is a sample of the web. When finished it will cost but 25 dollars or 5 £ English, that is to say to go twice round the body with crépines. Those for the General Officers should have bouillons to them and they will cost 5 dollars more which will make a General Officer's sash cost about 6 louis.

Let me know by return of post if this sample meets your approbation. It is exactly as the Prussians wear them in black and silver, and the Russians in black orange and silver. I should think Lieven[1] could show you his. Once more let me congratulate you dearest brother on your having recovered your hereditary dominions and believe me ever, [etc.].

343 THE EARL OF MOIRA *to* COLONEL McMAHON

Calcutta, Novr. 14th 1813.

YOUR brother is arrived & at all events should have been kept here. Our knowledge, however, of the brevet leaves me no merit in such an arrangement. It is true, we have no notification of it from the Horse Guards, nor even a Gazette on which I could act. We only see it, in a

1 Count Lieven, the Russian Ambassador in London (1774–1839).

newspaper or two, as extracted from the Gazette & therefore out of doubt. Herewith I transmit a letter for the Prince. It was written near a month ago: being, however, only expressive of sentiments which never can alter, the date does not signify. There is not in all this country a single horse that I could bear to have enter his stable as from me. I have sent to Bussorah to try for something of the right description. The only thing worth sending was a small provision of coffee, which Sir H. Popham will deliver to you for His Royal Highness. As it was a present from the Shereef of Mecca to a great Arab merchant here, it has the fairest chance possible of being superior in quality; and I obtained it under the assurance of it's being such as is not to be bought in any common course.

We are all well. The cool season has set in, & the weather is really pleasant. One cannot stand the sun in the middle of the day: But the air is bracingly fresh from four till seven in the morning; our time for riding. The evening also, & the night, may also be reckoned approaching to cold.

Expenses here are heavier than what you imagined. We shall manage tolerably, but we shall not make a purse. All descriptions use their best efforts to make the situation agreeable to us, & show high satisfaction at Government's being put on a proper footing. Believe me (but this is quite between ourselves) it was full time that a little dignity should be given to it. Some of the persons in the highest Public Departments have explained to me the mischiefs they felt & the still greater evils they had feared from the manner in which it was let down. The peculiarly amiable character of Ld Minto softened the censure which would otherwise have attended it; and even with that sense of his private merit it was with difficulty that an Address to him was carried thro'; principally I may say by means of my declarations in his favor.

I have soothed Sir G. Nugent, & have done every thing for his protegés, & he stays. This of course is not advantageous for me in a pecuniary forecast; but it was right for me to do. There is a Mr. Lethbridge, a Cornish man, who was Sir Home's secretary in the Stirling Castle. He is a very clever, accomplished, well behaved young man; of excellent moral character & good connections. If you can be serviceable to him thro' Tyrwhitt or Tucker,[1] pray be so for my sake. We all liked him exceedingly; & had I not been already over-loaded I should have kept him here; if he would have sent for his wife. Satchwell cannot be transferred to the Civil Service, & thence begs me to take him off the list of cadets (as he dislikes the military line) & plant him in Java. I am

---

1 Benjamin Tucker, Surveyor-General of the Duchy of Cornwall.

endeavoring to learn what line will be advantageous for him there, & I shall dispatch him. I wrote to you, from some place on our passage, about looking eventually to the Government of Madeira for Ld Granard.[1] He would suit perfectly for that station; & the Prince, I know, would like to do something in return for his long attachment & sacrifices.

God bless you. I write hastily; being surprised by an unexpected call for my letter.

344 THE DUKE OF CUMBERLAND *to the* PRINCE REGENT

Hannover, Nov[r] 15th 1813.

As there is a messenger now going over to England I seize with eagerness this opportunity of writing you a few lines to tell you that the Prince R of Sweden leaves *this* tomorrow as he says for Minden & Bremen and what his ulterior objects I know not.

Everything is going on *quietly* here, but as I told you in my last I should do nothing unless authorized by you I make no enquiries but ready to act if called upon; you must excuse my saying that in my humble opinion *no time should be lost* and that whatever military force you choose to have ought without loss of time to be formed, first not to let the spirit that now is so ripe for every thing be damped and 2[dly] because depend upon it our adversary will move Heaven & earth to renew his Army, but alas *here* is nobody to arrange the military part, therefore if Adolphus is to come the sooner he comes the better, as the person who is to superintend *this* ought to be here.

I am convinced the idea of a Landwehr here is premature and the example of Austria and Prussia will not do here, for *there* they have so many old soldiers & plenty of men who have borne arms, that is not the case here, therefore in my opinion first of [all] an *Army* a regular Army should be formed, and that once formed then have as many Landwehr battalions as you chose. This is the time for the organization of an Army and I am confident if the *will* is *there* the means must be found. Hannover must become respectable by its own forces & ought to have a standing Army from 25, to 30,000 men, and then add to that as much Landwehr as you choose. This country is very populous and therefore there are plenty of men, you may have the *best country* and believe me if *the will* is there the means must be found, but if the old narrow minded slow system is to be

1 George Forbes, sixth Earl of Granard (1760–1837), the father of Viscount Forbes, for whom see Nos. 30, 35, 39, 47–8.

followed you won't have an Army these six years. Excuse my saying this but I think 'tis my duty to say to you what strikes me. 4000 stand of arms & cloathing for 2000 men I understand Stewart (?) has promised to send for tomorrow from Stralsund and then I hope to see something in the shape of a military force and by the time this force is got together *your* further orders may arrive. Gracious God when one sees what other countries have done, which are hardly so big as provinces *here*, what ought not this country to do, ay & it will do for it is devoted to you. Mecklenburg Strelitz has raised a Hussar Reg^t 750 strong & 100 in the depot making in all 850 men this my uncle[1] has *lent* to the King of Prussia for *he* pays them and fills the vacancies which is a heavy weight upon him the formation of the Reg^t cost him 123,000 dollars, & he has parted with his jewels, plate & the greatest part of his stables to pay it, therefore it was I was so anxious that England had taken it into its subsidies [*sic*] that this good man might not be ruined entirely for the good cause and if in any shape you could manage this with Castlereagh & Bathurst it would [be] a very *great thing* done, & being so very nearly related to us, I think they would do it.

Your proclamation which has been so long expected arrived *here* this morning & I understand the Ministers mean to publish it in a couple of days. God grant dearest brother that you will put your plan into execution and come *here* next Summer when I shall have the happiness of embracing you again & I hope then you will have a good Army, if proper steps are taken you ought to have it. By God the English Govt must assist *you here* for one or two years & then we shall do very well. Hanover suffer'd for England. Pray let me know if the *sash* meets your approbation & then I will instantly order *you* one and in 3 weeks you shall have it pray also give your directions for the Govm^t officers uniforms, & I hope at least if *not to be employed* at least you will give me the rank of General of Cavalry, for at present *here* I am but Lt. General of Cavalry made so in *1798*. In case Dolly[2] comes may I take possession of the house that was the *Prefecture* and arranged very handsomely for him I have not seen it as yet as Field Marshall v Stedingk of the Swedes is quarter'd there. If you think I can in any way be of service here, you have but to let me know, & I shall act according to your orders, at least I may be of some service as to the formation of your troops; but for Gods sake be not deceived by those who recommend the Landwehr system, it will not answer. I have been present at several conversations with Walmoden who perfectly agrees with me in this opinion. Only conceive

1 Charles Louis Frederick, Duke of Mecklenburg-Strelitz.
2 The Duke of Cambridge.

that beautiful Riding House is now full of horses: I believe there are near 6 to 700 Swedish Hussars horses in it. All that must be got into order as soon as possible in order that by next Spring your horses may be placed there, & it will demand a great deal of purification. I have seen old Leuthe: il est le meme & I could not help recollecting his conversation with you about the poor dear King's present. I leave this open as I am expecting the P. Royal of Sweden who told me this morn^g when I called upon him that he should come & speak to me, therefore I leave this letter still open.

After 2 hours conversation till a late hour with the P.R. he desired me to tell you that he meant to proceed and retake *Hamburgh* which he thought a most desirable thing for all Europe & especially for *England* that his [? desire] was to act in every way (?) as England could wish it, that his politics were Englands, and that after taking Hamburg he should await further orders & then perhaps proceed to Holland and Belgium. He does not approve of the plan sent from France first & he means to send you *his* opinions, I own I am of his opinion that it is a most dangerous thing the passing the Rhine & our not having one single fortress as yet on ours, Magdeburg, Stettin, Austrian Torgau, Dresden, Konigstein all in the enemy's hands, nothing I believe but God Almighty has brought us out of the scrape & I trust He will not forsake us. The Pr is very earnest about the levy of your troops & is completely of opinion that you must have a regular Army first. His plan is to have first that force raised & then proceed to the Landwehr. Henry can describe to you our conversation in as few words as I could manage it, believe me ever [etc.].

345 MISS MARY SEYMOUR[1] *to the* PRINCE REGENT

November the 24th 1813.

MY dearest Prinny,

FOR as you kindly commanded me always to call you so, I hope I am not wanting in respect in continuing to do so; you will I hope, receive my most grateful thanks for the very kind and affectionate letter, which you

1 [1798–1848.] The Prince Regent's daughter by Lady Horatia Seymour, the wife of Lord Hugh Seymour, Lord Hertford's brother. Lady Horatia died in July 1801 and her husband two months later. In his will he appointed his brother, Lord Henry Seymour, and his wife's brother, Lord Euston, as his executors and guardians of his children. Lady Horatia's friend, Mrs Fitzherbert, had taken charge of Mary during her mother's last illness, and wished to adopt her. The executors, ignorant of the child's parentage, would not consent to such an arrangement, and Mrs Fitzherbert, with the Prince's approval, appealed to the Court of Chancery, which, in 1805, decided against her claims. Her counsel, Erskine and Romilly, advised her to appeal to the House of Lords. The matter was settled on 14 June 1806. Lord

were so good as to write. It gave me additional pleasure, as it is some time since I have had the happiness of receiving a letter written by yourself. I must likewise thank you, for the truly handsome, and magnificent ornament which accompanied it; it is very beautiful, and I shall have great pleasure in wearing it, as being your gift.[1]

I have not yet rode, but intend doing so in a few days; the horses are very well, and Adonis is as great a favorite, as formerly. I ride dear little Sancho occasionally, but have almost outgrown the little fellow.

346 THE PRINCE REGENT *to* QUEEN CHARLOTTE

C[arlton] H[ouse],
Wed[y]. night, Novr. 24th 1813.

IT has pleas'd the Almighty to bless our arms again & with another most signal victory under that undaunted Commander Field Marshal Lord Wellington, the accounts of which I receiv'd at too late an hour this evening, to think of disturbing you with the joyful tidings until tomorrow morning.[2] Lord Worcester[3] brought the Dispatches, & the narrative is very short. Soult[4] had been forming for himself a strong intrench'd position or camp for at least the last two months; our glorious Commander thought it right to attack it, & to storm it, which was no sooner determin'd upon than executed, & the moment our gallant fellows shew'd themselves before their redouts & intrenchments, the French abandon'd them, & fled from all quarters, leaving in the action & pursuit above two thousand kill'd, at least as many prisoners, with fifty eight pieces of ordinance [*sic*]; & with a very very very insignificant loss on our side, & not an Officer either kill'd or wounded; such were Lord Worcester's words. I can not, (though quite worn out with the joy of the business of this thrice happy day,) think of going to my rest till I have had the happiness of imparting with my own hand to you, these additional

Hertford himself agreed to undertake the guardianship of his niece, on the express understanding that he should be unfettered in its exercise. He at once asked Mrs Fitzherbert to deputise for him, and his relatives had to accept the situation. It was this *cause célèbre* which brought the Prince into close relations with Lady Hertford, and which, consequently, ended his connexion with Mrs Fitzherbert. See Wilkins, *Mrs Fitzherbert and George IV*.

1 The 23rd was her birthday.

2 On 10 November Wellington broke the French lines on the lower Nivelle. His dispatch to Bathurst was printed in a London Gazette Extraordinary on the 25th.

3 Henry Somerset, Marquis of Worcester, who succeeded his father as seventh Duke of Beaufort in 1835. (1792–1853.)

4 Marshal Soult (1769–1851) commanded the French armies in the Peninsula.

glad tidings. I shall only add a milion of thanks to you for your most kind of letters, & implore of you to assemble the Band of musick some how or other in the course of tomorrow, & for *good luck's sake*, at least to make them play *Landes Vater*. And now God bless you a million & a million of times, prays [etc.].

P.S. I receive the Russian Orders tomorrow.[1]

347 COLONEL McMAHON *to* VISCOUNT WHITWORTH

Carlton House, Novr. the 24th 1813.

I AM commanded by the Prince Regent to acquaint you of the anxious inclination which His Royal Highness has long possess'd to serve and distinguish the present Bishop of Limerick, and how desirous he is to earnestly recommend him to your Lordship's notice & favor.

As the rank & income of the See of Limerick, as the Prince believes, stands high on the Bench of Bishops in Ireland, His Royal Highness would in the event of any future arrangements in the Prelacy, be extremely wishful to recommend the Bishop of Limerick to your kindness for either a removal to the Diocese of Clogher, or a promotion to the Archbishoprick of Tuam, both of those Sees being preferable more from their retirement and patronage, than from any disparity in point of their value, as Limerick is nearly as good as either. But as the translation to the one, or the other, are objects towards the comfort and happiness of Dr. Warburton, His Royal Highness cannot resist this personal application to you in his behalf.

348 QUEEN CHARLOTTE *to the* PRINCE REGENT

Windsor, the 25th Novbr 1813.

THO almost drunk with joy, there is sense enough left to return you thanks for your kind letter[2] as also for the great news which it conveyed. The hand of Providence has been particularly manifested towards us of late

---

1 At the beginning of December the Prince Regent gave "a most splendid dinner to the gentlemen of the deputation sent by the Emperor of Russia to convey the orders of Russian knighthood to his Royal Highness". It consisted of three courses, "served up with the most sumptuous magnificence".

2 No. 346.

& I am confident that by your pursuing that steady & upright conduct which always has been the character of this nation & to which I feel proud you do belong, the Almighty will support & bless our arms. Accept then my dearest son my most sincere congratulation upon this new obtained victory by Lrd Wellington over Soult & my sincerest wishes, that not only all the French, but all your interior ennemies may equally be put down.

[P.S.] In my hurry of last night I forgot to return you thanks for the account you gave of my brother.[1] I hope to see him in the Spring; at least I will not give up all hopes.

I shall most certainly have the Band & make them play Landes Vater & most heartily join in their chorus.

349 THE DUKE OF CUMBERLAND *to the* PRINCE REGENT

Hannover, Novr. 26th 1813.

I TRUST and hope that ere this you will have received my several letters explanatory of everything that has passed here on the reformation or restoration of your old Government, which thank God was re-established by a Proclamation signed by your *own* servants, and not by the Prince Royal of Sweden, a circumstance which I had very much at heart, and I feel a very great satisfaction in having assisted in accomplishing so desirable an object, as it appears that this circumstance has given the greatest pleasure to all *your* subjects throughout your dominions and has been adverted to in the different Addresses.[2]

According to my former assurance that I would not interfere in *any one* point unless called upon and authorized by you I have strictly adhered, therefore I hope you will excuse me if, as a *quiet* but vigilant spectator, I deliver to you my opinions freely, as you know by experience they are honestly meant and have no other object in view than the well-

1 Prince Ernest of Mecklenburg.
2 Bernadotte's entry into Hanover, following the expulsion of the French, was preceded by the issuing of a Proclamation on 4 November by Decken and Bremer, "Privy Counsellors of the King of Great Britain, appointed to the Electoral Ministry of Brunswick-Lunebourg". "We have not hesitated," they said, "in the name of the lawful Sovereign, to resume the government of the electoral dominions." "A son of our highly revered monarch, his Royal Highness the Duke of Cumberland, who, ever since his earlier residence among the Hanoverians, has conceived the most lively attachment to them [the Hanoverian people], is himself on the spot, and has most generously resolved actively to contribute towards effecting the welfare of the ancient inheritance of his illustrious ancestors."

fare and honour of your realms: thank God we have been now for some years in habits of such pure friendship that I trust absence will not make any difference in your kind and brotherly attachment to me, as you may firmly rely that you never had a brother who has more at heart your happiness than myself. Let me entreat you for God's sake if possible to come here next Summer yourself if it be but for *one* month, and the country will derive the greatest benefit from the presence of its Sovereign, a blessing it has not enjoyed for more than fifty years. Much may be done in the mean time, and if I might presume to offer an opinion, the first object here should be the formation of your Army for the defence and safety of the country. The population of this territory with the addition of Hildesheim amounts to eleven hundred thousand inhabitants, and actually you might have a standing Army of 25 to 30,000 men, and that being once formed, the Landwehr might be also enrolled to the number of 30 to 35,000 men, not however till the Regular Army shall have become organized; for this country cannot be compared with Austria and Prussia when their Armies have been always so extensive that most of their peasants have served, and when therefore very little is necessary to form a Landwehr. Here that is not the case, for the Army, little as it was, having been totally disbanded, it will require time to form one. And I hope now that greater attention and respect will be shewn to the military than was formerly paid here, as from change of times and circumstances a much greater force must eventually be kept up, which I have the satisfaction to tell you the country at large feels the necessity for. Both the Pr. Royal of S. and Lt. General Walmoden agree with me on the necessity of a Regular Army being formed senior to the Landwehrs, and I was present at Dömitz when the latter declared his sentiments most positively and freely to the Ministers who were much more inclined for a Landwehr than any other sort of force. It was on account of this that I pressed you, if Adolphus was to come, to send him over directly as there is litterally *no* military character to take upon himself the formation of such an Army which no other person but a General Officer authorized by you can do, and at present all arrangements are in the hands of civilians who know nothing of the matter. In speaking upon this I speak not only for the sake of Hannover but also with respect to England, for conceive what a card it is for that country, Hannover being again restored to its lawful Sovereign, by being able at any great emergency to have the benefit of being able to subsidize thirty or forty thousand men without any difficulty. Therefore I maintain that your Ministers there ought to assist you on the present occasion with the necessary means of defraying such expences which, though they may be obtained here, yet cannot be without severe sacrifices, and I am happy to say that such is the attachment of the subjects to their Sovereign that there is no sacrifice they are not ready to make at *this* time for the defence of the country. It is therefore that I am so anxious to know what your wishes are upon this subject. From all we can learn, and the Pr. R. of S. who has the very best information of all that is going on in France, we have reason to believe that by the month of April France will produce again an Army of 400,000 men, therefore it behoves all the Sovereigns in Germany to exert every nerve to encrease their Armies. If Lt. General Leiningen can be spared from England his presence would be of the greatest possible service here for the formation of your cavalry, as litterally the few remaining cavalry officers here are completely superannuated, and from the anxiety of the young peasants to enter the cavalry service I am sure much progress in that arm might be made in a short time. Here I must relate to you a very interesting anecdote. A corporal of the old Garde du Corps arrived here two days [ago] bringing with him 4 horses belonging to himself and offering them and his services for the cavalry, he having sold his farm, hearing that the land was again restored to its old Sovereign.

Artillery there is none of any description, nor even the means of providing any as they have destroyed everything in the foundry, and it will be necessary to send persons from here to Woolwich to learn the art which was first introduced here from thence during the time of Desaguliers.[1] I can scarcely describe to you the state of the dear old Palace; it is so ruined that it will be impossible to do anything with it. I went over the whole of it and it drew tears from my eyes to behold such a wretched appearance of a place where I had passed so many happy days. Everything destroyed and now nothing but a barrack which even is arranged in the very worst manner, and can only hold 1200 men, but if it had been properly arranged it might have contained from three to four thousand. Thank God Herrenhausen is in perfect order and the gardens also, so that you can lodge there perfectly well if you come here next Summer. The Riding House here which had been converted to a stable is now being restored to its former use, and I hope in the course of a week to be able to ride in it again. As to the destruction of the Palace it was sheer mischief, and Monsieur Simon, one of the Ministers of Jerome Bonaparte[2] said to Mr. de Bar who repeated it to me on seeing the Palace in its present horrible state "Que cet acte ne prouvait que sa méchanceté, et qu'il était méchant comme un petit singe".

1 Thomas Desaguliers (? 1725–80). Colonel-Commandant of the Royal Artillery, 1762. He invented a method of firing small shot from mortars and an instrument for verifying the bores of cannon.

2 His brother, the Emperor, made him King of Westphalia in 1807. (1784–1860.)

I had here last Tuesday a deputation from the country of Hildesheim consisting of 32 persons composed of the clergy, nobility, citizens and peasants. They presented me with an Address desiring me to lay them at your feet and assuring you that it was the happiest day of their lives their being incorporated to Hannover. I invited them all to dinner when your health was drunk with enthusiasm. Some of them staid till half past 12 at night and I thought I never should get the house clear of them.

God bless you and believe me ever, [etc.].

350 DAVID WILKIE *to* COLONEL MCMAHON

24 *Lower Phillimore Place, Kensington,*
29th Novbr 1813.

IN a letter[1] I had the honor of addressing you on the 27th Septm. I took the liberty of mentioning the price of a picture I had the honor of painting by command of his Royal Highness the Prince Regent, which had been delivered some time at Carlton House.

I hope Sir you will not consider me obtrusive in again calling your attention to the subject by requesting your care of the enclosed bill of the amount, which if you will be kind enough to put in the way of being taken into early consideration you will greatly oblige, Sir, [etc.].

[*Enclosed*]

24 *Phillimore Place, Kensington, London,*
2nd April 1813.

HIS ROYAL HIGHNESS THE PRINCE REGENT *to* DAVID WILKIE

For a picture—the subject "Blindmans-Buff" painted by command of His Royal Highness, & delivered at Carlton House this day—500 Guineas. } £525

1 No. 320.

Phenix Park, 3 Decr. 1813.

I HAVE to acknowledge the favor of your letter[1] of the 24th ulto respecting the Bishop of Limerick.

I hope I shall have no difficulty in convincing His Royal Highness the Prince Regent of the gratification I must feel in acquitting myself of that part of my duty which enjoins obedience to his wishes.

There is at this moment no vacancy on the Ecclesiastical Bench, or indeed any immediate prospect of any. Whenever either of those preferments mention'd in your letter shall become vacant, I shall submit such considerations as may be call'd for, bearing always in my mind the interest which His Royal Highness is pleas'd to take in the promotion of the Bishop of Limerick.

352 THE EARL OF MOIRA *to* COLONEL McMAHON

Calcutta, Decr. 6th, 1813.

No Gazette or official account of the brevet has yet reached us: so, tho' we know it to have taken place, your brother is still walking about as a gentleman at large. I hope the Duke of York has not been unmindful of my solicitation that Sir W: Keir[2] should be put upon this Staff as a Major General.

I believe I have got a horse for the Prince. Sir Evan Nepean[3] wrote to say that the Resident at Bussorah had secured for him two uncommonly fine Arabian horses; and he offered, as he supposed I might be distressed for a charger on my first arrival, to let me have one of them. I answered that if either of them were *really* of the high quality represented, & of sufficient strength for the Prince, I should feel under the greatest obligation for his letting me purchase it; and that I would in that case beg him to forward the horse to England from Bombay direct, to avoid the dangers of the voyage hither generally as long as half the time required to reach Europe. I am in this at the mercy of Nepean's judgement in horseflesh, as I cannot exercise my own: but I am forced to abide by that chance, or to incur delays which might extend to great length. Pray make this understood for me.

1 No. 347.
2 Sir William Keir Grant (previously Keir). Adjutant-General to His Majesty's forces in India since 1806. (1772–1852.)
3 Governor of Bombay, 1812–19. (1751–1822.)

I think that in a former letter I mentioned my having put Healey & Bower into Regiments of the Line. Satchwell, a very promising lad, does not like the military. There is no transferring him into the Company's Civil Service, I therefore send him to Amboyna (part of the Java Establishment) to be put into an advantageous course in that quarter. I dispatch him under the care of a person just indebted to me for an appointment, & who has then undertaken with great zeal the furtherance of Satchwell's interests. The father may rest satisfied that the young man shall be advanced as opportunity allows.

We are all well. The weather is now cool; at least till between eight & nine in the morning. One sleeps with a blanket over one but still with the under sheet spread on a cane mat & with the window open. Mosquitoes are our only discomfort at present.

Ld Minto embarks in the course of the week.[1] I believe him to be unfeignedly sensible to the attentions I have paid him. Many of those about him have been childishly petulant in endeavouring to excite dissatisfaction at the tone which we assumed; because they feared that the contrast of our show would make the narrowness of the late Government appear still more discreditable than it had done before. They have had no success & there is a general applause of our having put the Government on a dignified footing. In fact the hugger-mugger stile which had been adopted gave such disgust as overbalanced all the amiableness of Ld Minto's private character: and those testimonies of approbation with which he departs would not have been carried thro' had I not exerted every influence to suppress an opposition publicly declared to them. He would be much vexed did he know the procedure to which I have adverted. My allusion does not include Capt. George Elliot of the Navy, who is a fine young man.

I am bringing forward Vaughan (Sir H. Halford's[2] brother) but it must be done gradually. He behaved with such personal impropriety to Ld Minto as to have since lain under an absolute interdict. On my mentioning my intention to give him an appointment, my colleagues strongly represented that the intemperance of his disposition made him unfit for a judicial situation, which is his line, & the most advantageous. I do believe that his temper is rather unmanageable, but I think, also, that from taking part in Ld Minto's resentment the members of Government have exaggerated the objection. I shall explain in frank confidence to Vaughan the necessity I am under of appearing to make a trial of him by

1 He died soon after his arrival in England (June 1814). It was said that he made "an amazing fortune".
2 Sir Henry had changed his name on inheriting property.

placing him as only an Acting Judge in the first instance.[1] The notion of being under a special inspection will do him no harm.

In a former letter[2] I suggested to you the placing Ld Granard as Governor of Madeira when, as is certain to be the case, that Island shall be finally ceded to us.[3] He would do perfectly well there, as nothing is required but to be civil & hospitable, & not to offend the prejudices of the Catholics; points quite accordant to his habits. With regard to all the military duties, no man would do them better. The Prince would undoubtedly wish to mark a recollection of the sacrifices made by Ld Granard, when he commanded material Parliamentary interest, thro' adherence to His Royal Highness.

I have had the opportunity of distinguishing & benefiting Ld Liverpool's friends here in a manner that must claim his attention to mine at home. Mr. Ricketts[4] (one of the Secretaries to Government) whom I have made my Principal Secretary in consequence of Colonel Worsley being obliged from illness to decline undertaking the situation, is a very clever & a very pleasant man.

There is a Mr. Lethbridge, a Cornish man, who was Secretary to Sir H. Popham in the Stirling Castle. We all liked him exceedingly. He is a well-informed, polite, & gentlemanly person. I told him I would mention him to you, in order that you might recommend him to Mr. Tucker if he had any objects in Cornwall or Devonshire. Adieu.

353 THE EARL OF MOIRA *to the* PRINCE REGENT

Calcutta, Decr. 6th 1813.

CHANCE threw in my way an article which I thought might be interesting to your Royal Highness; and I have had the good fortune to secure it. A place in the Armory at Carlton House may be not unworthily bestowed upon it, therefore I have requested Capt. Elliot (of the Hussar) to take charge of the package for your Royal Highness. It is a box containing specimens of all the kinds of arrows made use of from the earliest time in Hindostan or any of the neighboring countries. Some are of the sort used in war; others have crescent heads, & are intended to be shot

---

1 He became the Judge at Shahabad.   2 No. 343.

3 When in 1807 the French overran Portugal, Madeira was taken under the protection of Great Britain, with an understanding that it was to be restored to the House of Braganza when Portugal was recovered.

4 Charles Ricketts, Secretary of the Public Department of the Government of Bengal.

at the necks of ostriches or other large birds. On the whole, the assemblage appeared to me very curious, not only as exhibiting the variety of inventions in that way but as displaying also the admirable quality of the steel made in the Upper Provinces of this region.

Let me thence trust that your Royal Highness will excuse the liberty I take in sending them. Should they be intrinsically undeserving of your notice, your Royal Highness may perhaps still deign to receive them with satisfaction if you construe their transmission as evincing that my mind eagerly catches at any trifling expedient by which it can prove that it rests continually impressed with the sense it ought to retain of your kindness.

At my age, & with all the contingencies attached to distance & to climate, the probability should be calculated against my ever seeing your Royal Highness again: therefore I wish, while I can still express it, to testify in every manner within my humble power that grateful devotion with which I shall be to the last moment of life, Your Royal Highness's [etc.].

354 THE DUKE OF CAMBRIDGE *to the* PRINCE REGENT

Sheerness, Dec. 6, 1813.

I CAN not let the post go out without writing you one line to thank you over and over again for all your kindness to me, and to assure you that it ever shall be the study of my life to render myself worthy of it. Your horses brought us remarkably well to Dartford and I hope they will not be the worse for the journey. Having broken one of the springs of the carriage at Rochester we were detained about half an hour when we got a most excellent breakfast and arrived here a little before three. William,[1] who has been all kindness and attention to me, is in high force. He lodges at Sir Thos Williams,[2] and I am to have a bed at the Commissioner's. Tomorrow at ten o clock I am to go on board, and I hope to get under weigh by one or two o clock.[3] Munster was very unwell indeed this morning, but the journey has certainly done him good, and I trust that a few days quiet on board of ship will make him the recover [*sic*] the fatigues of the last fortnight which have nearly knocked him up. I take the liberty of sending you the enclosed and now my dearest brother God Almighty bless you and believe me, [etc.].

1 The Duke of Clarence.
2 Admiral Sir Thomas Williams (? 1762–1841).
3 He was on his way to Hanover, to assume the Governorship.

Southill, Dec. 8, 1813.

IN the absence of the Duke of Bedford, I am directed, as chairman of the committee meetings of "The Institution for promoting the British system, for the education of the labouring and manufacturing classes of the community of every religious persuasion" to request that you will have the goodness humbly to submit to His Royal Highness the Prince Regent, the anxious wish, and sanguine hope entertained by the numerous friends of that system, that His Royal Highness will be graciously pleased to take the great interests which it involves under His Royal Highness's special protection.

It is well known, and gratefully remembered, that His Royal Highness has been a warm, powerful and munificent friend to the system of education which is now submitted to the favour of His Royal Highness, under its new designation.[1]

It's progress has been great, and the benefits conferred by its operation upon the ignorant and unenlightened of the lower classes of the community very extensive: but by the arrangements which have lately been adopted, there is every prospect of their becoming universal, provided the Institution meets with protection, from the exalted quarter wherein it is now with all humility sought.

The errors of Joseph Lancaster have been many, and it is with deep regret we are bound to acknowledge, that to those errors are attributable any partial failures of the effects which had been anticipated from the great efforts made to promulgate his invention; and to render it practically available to mankind, under the gracious and benignant patronage of His Majesty.[2]

But those errors are happily passed: and Joseph Lancaster having accepted a situation adapted to his talents and power of practical usefulness, wherein he may render the most important services to the cause, their recurrence is happily prevented.[3]

I take the liberty of sending the inclosed papers, which will thoroughly explain the footing upon which the Institution at present stands: and I trust that the foundation upon which it is placed is so firm, as that if His Royal Highness the Prince Regent shall be graciously pleased to

1 The *Royal Lancasterian Society*, founded by the Quaker philanthropist, Joseph Lancaster (1778–1838), to teach poor children reading, writing and arithmetic, changed its name in 1813 to that of the *British and Foreign School Society*.

2 George III, Queen Charlotte and the Princesses had subscribed to the Society's funds since 1805.

3 Lancaster's extravagance had reduced him to bankruptcy and the Society's trustees deposed him from the chief management of its concerns.

comply with the request thus humbly submitted to him, and to become its patron and protector, it's benefits will be rapidly diffused over every part of the extensive Empire of His Majesty, and at no remote period through out the world.[1]

356 THE DUKE OF CUMBERLAND *to the* PRINCE REGENT

Hanover, Decr. 9th 1813.

WORDS cannot express the satisfaction and at the same time the surprize I felt at 12 o'clock this day when the door opened and friend Bloomfield came in. I was completely struck dumb. Your kindness of heart and your delicacy in sending HIM to me to announce the appointment of Adolphus[2] I feel to the bottom of my soul, and perfectly calms all the disappointment that must necessarily arise to an ambitious mind as mine at being super-ceded; excuse the word for I feel I ought not to use it, but I cannot disguise to you my feelings.

I certainly understood he never meant to take any military line again and therefore had flattered myself *I* might be thought of, but I am fully aware you could not do otherwise and therefore am satisfied. Your kindness is the more marked in sending me Bloomfield first, as he is your particular friend, and 2ndly, as he must be a loss to you. It is a proof you felt for ME, and to a mind borne down with grief & misery as mine has been for these last 6 months it feels your kindness doublefold.

That you have approved of *all* I have done is REWARD *enough* for me and is a proof that your friendship for me is unaltered, and it is your love and friendship alone I look to. Promise me only to preserve me them and I shall be satisfied. Your *private* wishes communicated to me by Bloomfield shall be obeyed and I shall leave this in a few days go and pay a visit to Walmoden's corps and then between Strelitz and Berlin shall pass my Winter. My being appointed a Field Marshall is a high honour but one I have alas no right to look up to but as a mark of your favour;[3] but trust & hope that it may not be a bann to my services on some occasion or other; and should the case be that Adolphus does NOT like staying, then think of me. For many reasons I prefer living on the Continent and therefore shall look out peu à peu to establish myself somewhere, and whenever I return to England I hope my mind may be more at ease than

1 See No. 373.
2 As Governor of the Electorate of Hanover.
3 The honour was also conferred upon the Duke of Cambridge (gazetted, 27 November).

it is now. You know I have met since we met last with a disaster, which has left a sore which time alone can cure and to return would only rip it up again.[1]

Permit me to write as often as I can and you shall know all I hear and do, but for God's sake let my letters be sacred to yr self. Many thanks for your kind and generous present. Your commissions shall all be faithfully executed. At *last* shoes & sashes &c. shall be [sent] forthwith. I propose sending you a Circassian mare, a most *beautiful creature*. Blom[2] sees her tomorrow. Excuse my hurry but I am grown very nervous from much anxiety of mind. God Almighty bless you and believe me most sincerely and truly, [etc.].

[P.S.] Remember me kindly to my worthy friends in M[anchester] Sq[uare].[3]

357 COLONEL BLOOMFIELD *to the* PRINCE REGENT

Hanover, December 9th 1813.

AT one o'clock this day I reached here & was driven to the Duke of Cumberlands where I was received by His Royal Highness with the *utmost kindness*. His anxious enquiries for your Royal Highness naturally occupied the first moments, when I did not fail to convey the expression of your undiminish'd love & affection & finding His Royal Highness's feelings awakend to the utmost I thought the moment favorable to enter upon the subject of my mission, & have the happiness to assure your Royal Highness that the communication was receiv'd with fresh expressions of attachment 'though accompanied with a burst of tears & evident distress & mortification—His Royal Highness however did not hesitate a moment in coming to the decision of removing himself. I trust the measure has been as little harassing as under all circumstances, it cou'd have been. I dwelt very much upon the extreme delicacy of your Royal Highness in sending me over in order that His Royal Highness might not be expos'd to the unpleasant situation of remaining here while a younger brother was placed in supreme authority; a delicacy & attention of which

1 This does not refer to the raking up of the Sellis scandal by Henry White, of the *Independent Whig*, who, on 24 May, was sentenced to fifteen months' imprisonment and fined £200 for libelling the Duke. An unpublished letter to Lord Eldon, 1 October 1813, throws a little light on the text. "...Things have occurred since my departure from England which make me not at all anxious to return, for I should feel much misery on my return, which alas neither time nor circumstances can ever repair. Excuse these few melancholy words; you have a tender heart I know to feel the loss [of] a most valued friend..." (Eldon MSS.).

2 Bloomfield.   3 The Hertfords.

the Duke was most sensible & concluded by ordering me to assure your Royal Highness that he felt the present moment, under all your kindness, as mark'd strongly with a continuance of your love to [*sic*] towards him: I feel it particularly fortunate that a messenger shou'd arrive here, on his way to England & enable me, with so little delay, to report these few particulars. Trusting that with however little ability I may have been fortunate enough to have accomplish'd your Royal Highness's wishes, that at least as little pain has been inflicted, as the disappointment admitted: shou'd my humble & faithful endeavours meet your Royal Highness's approbation; my happiness is complete—I shou'd have stated that I was most distinct in the expression of your Royal Highness's approval of the Duke's zeal & *intention*. With the utmost veneration [etc.].

[P.S.] I saw forty very fine lads (sharpshooters) marching off, at the moment of my arrival, for Walmoden's corps, they were completely equipped—the English name, through any village, is held up to the highest admiration, as is the French to execration—The misery I have witness'd is indiscribable one voice pervades the land in which I heartily join "God bless your Royal Highness".

358 THE BISHOP OF LIMERICK [DR WARBURTON] *to* COLONEL MCMAHON

British Hotel, 10th Decr. [1813].

I HAD yesterday a long conference with the Primate of Ireland,[1] upon the Church affairs of Ireland, principally the Catholic question, to which His Grace is averse, unless sufficient guards can be devised for the Protestant Establishment, and in this I perfectly agree with him.

I fancy the Primate will attend the Levee on Monday, and I feel that it may be of use for the Prince to know it.

His Grace is a high, proud, independent man, but with honorable principles & excellent understanding. He is a constant resident in his See of Armagh, which he has much improved, and by his attention & example, the Established Church in Ireland has been highly benefited & greatly extended. Within the last seven years the number of churches has been doubled, and the resident clergy in the same proportion. Of this improvement, you will form some idea when I tell you that I have built thirty new churches since my appointment to the See of Limerick.

1 The Hon. William Stuart, fifth son of John Stuart, third Earl of Bute. Archbishop of Armagh, 1800–22. [1755–1822.] He accidentally poisoned himself with a draught of embrocation, taken instead of Sir Henry Halford's medicine.

All these little circumstances may be useful for the P. Regent to be in possession of before he sees the Primate, as I know His Grace will be highly flatter'd by the Royal notice of them—and indeed it is essential to the personal fame, as well as the public interests of our beloved Prince, that His R. Highness shou'd not only be perfectly acquainted with the affairs of the Irish Church, but that every member of it (especially the heads) shou'd be impressd with that idea.

The Duke of Richmond, without intention, but merely not understanding the thing, gave some offence to the Primate upon his becoming our Viceroy—in consequence, His Grace has never gone to the Castle, which has certainly been attended with some public inconvenience.

These few confidential hints I take the liberty of communicating to you my dear Sir, from a sense of duty, gratitude, & attachment to the person of our beloved Prince, as well as from an honest desire to promote the glory of H. R. Highness's reign by sending forth an early impression (through the heads of the Church) of his Royal favor & protection to the Established Church in that part of the Empire.

I will not offer any apology to you my dear Sir, for troubling you with these little communications, because I feel they may be useful and that you will ascribe them to the true motive.

359 FRANCES, COUNTESS OF JERSEY *to the* PRINCE REGENT

December the 12th [1813.]

IT is with the greatest reluctance that I again obtrude myself upon your Royal Highness but my situation is such that I am in a manner compelled to do so. I have only 700. per an^{m} which considering my former situation will scarcely afford me the necessaries of life. May I not hope, that as a Peeress, and the widow of a faithful servant who had the honour of holding a high situation in your Royal Highnesses family, I may have some claim upon the Royal bounty for a pension. I will not presume to enter into details which would lengthen this letter, but I am convinced that upon reading it, your Royal Highness will feel that I have suffered much before I could bring myself to write it.[1]

1 See Nos. 232, 263, 307.

Hanover, Decr. 12th 1813.

You must have perceived from the hurried manner in which my last letter[1] to you was written that my mind was little capable of adequately expressing how forcibly I felt your delicacy in the manner of making a communication to me, which must naturally have affected me much, therefore previous to my leaving this place (which I shall do in 48 hours) I shall beg your permission to enter into the whole of this business, premising that I am fully convinced from all that has passed between Bloomfield & myself that *you* felt *most forcibly* the *unpleasant task* you had to perform & that nothing but necessity compelled you to it, as your heart is too kind willingly to hurt the feelings of any man, still less those of a brother to whom you have always shewn such *particular* kindness & who received an assurance from you through Bloomfield "that your affection and friendship were as strong as ever and that they would never change".

You must recollect that one morning being with you at Carlton House the D. of Cambridge came in & after a little time you begged of me to with-draw into another room, as you wished to speak to him alone. In the course of a quarter of an hour you called me in again & after the D. of C. retired you told me you had persuaded him to consent to return to Hanover when the country should be open for him, but that he had made two declarations, vizt. that he would not take any MILITARY command, & that if he did come he would not be pledged to remain. This same conversation you repeated to me on the day that I took my leave of you and you likewise then directed me (on the morn[g] of my departure) when I should enter the Hanoverian territory to put on the Hanvorun [*sic*] sword, knot and sash, being still a Lt. General of Cavalry in the Han[overian] Service.

Ever since I landed at Stralsund (the 19th May) my constant object has been to seize the first favourable opportunity that might present itself to promote your interests in *this country*, & I had ever in view in coming over to the Continent a desire to prove to *this country* and to Germany in general that the Brunswick family was not *callous* to the sufferings of their countrymen, & that as one of its members, I wished to have a share in the great cause which was to decide the restoration or the annihilation of all the German interests. Since my arrival on the Continent I have communicated to you upon all occasions every thing which struck me that I thought might be for your advantage to know, & I have constantly

1 No. 356.

receiv'd messages from you through Thornton[1] expressive of your approbation of all that I have done.

No man can conceive the *unpleasant* & *distressing* situation I was placed in during the eight weeks that I passed at the Russian Head Quarters, *part* of *which* you know, but I have detailed the whole to Bloomfield, who will repeat it to you, as its too prolix for a letter. I bore it as long as I could for it would have been derogatory to your dignity to have submitted to it longer, however it operated this good effect, that it induced me to quit that Army & join Walmoden's corps by which means I was so locally placed as to be enabled by my personal presence to re-establish your Government without the interference of a *Frenchman*, (pardon me the expression but *that Bernadotte is and ever will be*). I certainly do take some credit to myself for my prompt decision on that occasion, for I have since seen the proclamation which *was* to have been published by the P.R. of Sweden had we not forestalled him by our publishing the one dated the 4th Nov.ʳ *sanction'd* by me, but SIGNED by your *two* Ministers.[2] You will excuse my *using* the word *sanction* but from the circumstance of my being on the frontiers of the country & *no orders* having been received from you, & being in the right line of the inheritance to the Electorate I was the *only person* they could look to at the moment; but I hope you will do me the justice to acknowledge that I acted with delicacy for I think I had the *right* as a Prince of the family to have signed that publication, but I preferred its being done by your own two Ministers.

I certainly came into the country at a moment of hasard to myself there being within the Electorate only 400 men, the P[rince] R[oyal] being with his Army at Cassel, & Walmoden at Dömitz which is the other side of the Elb[e] watching d'Avoust.[3] The French having a garrison at Prussian Mudice (?) 4000 men only seven German miles from hence, General St. Cyr being at Nimburg 5 German miles from here with 500 cavalry, Stade, Harburg & Mettenburg (?) being still in the hands of the enemy; after all this I certainly had flattered myself that from such extraordinary & unforeseen events having taken place that your decision would have been otherwise; and I am convinced that all this must upon reflection, & did strike your mind, & that you must have had very cogent reasons to have induced you to allow an elder brother who had been for 8 months active in your service to be superceded by his younger brother who has been living quietly at home & particularly as it is well known his disinclination to come here.

1 Colonel Thornton, the Duke's Equerry.
2 See No. 349.
3 After the retreat from Moscow Marshal Davout became Governor-General of the Hanse towns. (1770–1823.)

You will excuse my having dwellt so long upon this, but I think it fair to you, and to myself to disburthen my heart to you upon a subject which must be so galling to a mind actuated by enthusiasm as mine was, and feeling myself at this moment so popular with all ranks. But it is for the last time I shall ever open to you my lips upon this business, and here I beg to assure you that I feel most grateful for the manner in which you have communicated to me with so much delicacy and feeling so unwell-come a piece of intelligence, & for having assured me through Bloom-field (whose *kindness* I shall never forget to the last hours of my life) "that neither your friendship nor affection had ceased, or would cease during life", on my part I most solemnly assure you that nothing shall ever change my affection for you, & all I NOW BEG & ENTREAT of you is that should any opportunity offer for me to *establish myself* that I may depend on your *friendship* and *kindness*.

Now having disburthened my heart completely to you, I beg to assure you that with respect to the D. of Cambridge I shall ever feel he has been thoroughly brotherly, honourable & kind to me, and shall never say one word on the subject to him; on the contrary if upon any occasion he should ask any question respecting things here, he may depend on my giving him a fair & honest opinion & assisting him in every way in my power. Now adieu to this unpleasant subject for ever more.

In the caracter of a man who has been on the spot & its neighbourhood for upwards of two months I shall beg leave to state conscientiously my opinion upon the state of the Electorate having had constant & various conversations with men of the best information & soundest judgement respecting the whole country, & which I can *now* do with more ease, as it cannot be supposed that I speak for myself: in my humble opinion what led in a great measure to the loss of this country was the system formerly pursued here, & if now pursued would be still more erroneous, as the times & circumstances demand strong and decided measures, & unless vigorous energy is exerted and other measures are adopted *all* your endeavours will be of no avail, it was that *system of Departments* that ruined everything, & this country may be made one of the strongest, if a new line is pursued. I think it but fair to the D. of Cambridge to say this to you before he undertakes his task which I think will be an arduous one, especialy if the old system is to be pursued.

To render this country firm & solid it must become a military country, as all Germany is so, and unless he that is to command your Armies here is at the *head* of the *whole Government*, & thereby responsible to you for all that is done, I fear that all his endeavours will be of little or no avail, for as the old system existed all the plans & alterations proposed by the

Fieldmarshall except the *intense discipline of the troops* was obliged to be referred to the Chancery of War, of which he was not a member, and subject to the controul of that office, which however could not guarantee any measure that entailed expence without the concurrence of the Chamber of Finance, & the altercating correspondence that usually took place between these offices produced delays which occasioned serious impediments in the military arrangements & operations.

I have already stated to you my opinions in general respecting the formation of your Army, the only thing I have to say now is that I conceive the regular Army should be the first object here which ought to consist of from 25 to 30,000 men, and additionally a Landwehr of 35 to 40,000 which in time of war would double your existing force, & in peace would be of little expence, as it would only assemble in Spring for exercise, it might be said therefore that the Army would comprise 60 to 70,000 men of which I think 8,000 cavalry should always be kept up, as that species of force cannot be formed with the same facility as infantry.

Secondly it strikes me & I am happy to hear that the opinion has struck others & is acting upon now the system of taxation is to be assimilated throughout the whole Electorate which till now was not the case [*sic*].

Thirdly with respect to the State; that instead of there being four different Colleges in the Electorate & consequently four deliberative bodies, that one State General should be formed to deliberate for the whole & to which each College might send one or more members as may be determin'd upon, which would curtail & expedite business very materially.

I trust dearest brother you will excuse this long letter but as it is the last upon publick business that I shall have to trouble you with, I hope you will consider it as the fair & honest opinion of a man whose sole object has been the consideration of the wellfare of this country & the maintenance of it for you and our family, recollecting that this soil is that from which we sprung & therefore must be dear to us all.

361 QUEEN CHARLOTTE OF WURTEMBERG *to the* PRINCE
REGENT

Stutgard, December 13th 1813.

MOST difficult shall I find it to describe to you how deeply I feel your very uncommon kindness in having wished Sr Thomas Tyrwhitt to come here and give me an account of yourself and all my beloved family: words can never express the sentiments of gratitude and love I feel for you

dearest brother: one must have been nine years cut off from all confidential correspondence with the best and dearest of relations, to be able
to form an idea of my happiness at being enabled to converse with a
gentleman who has been so many years attached to you and who is so
thoroughly acquainted with the interior of Windsor. It has been a most
melancholy comfort for me to talk over the dreadful situation of my beloved father; my heart bleeds to think of all he has undergone, and I
shudder to hear that we dare entertain no hopes of any alteration for the
better. Your angelic conduct towards him my dearest brother, to my
mother, and sisters is a theme Sr Thomas kindly loves to dwell on, as he
sees how much it sooths my mind to be acquainted with every circumstance of your dutiful behaviour to our parents; and your affectionate
kindness to my sisters, whose situation would have been melancholy and
unpleasant had your good heart not induced you to step forth and have
such handsome establishments settled on them. My affection for my dear
sisters has frequently cost me tears, as I looked forwards with anxiety to
the very uncomfortable state they would have been reduced to, unless
they had met with so kind and considerate a brother who has now given
them an honourable and proper existance. Pray dearest brother accept
of my warm thanks on this subject and be convinced I feel with gratitude
every thing you have done for my sisters. Your kindness also to our poor
Amelia[1] is engraven on my heart. I admire Sr Thomas's patience in
answering the numberless questions I ask him in a breath concerning the
whole family. I rejoice dearest brother that you are in good health and
trust you will many many years enjoy every earthly blessing; which you
certainly deserve as you are always thinking of making others happy.
Sr Thomas has promised me to renew to you by word of mouth the
assurances of my love and gratitude for your kindness in wishing to see
me in England, but at the same time must mention my health not being
good, a violent cough being very troublesome for near a month; and
above all the unfortunate situation of Württemberg which does not
allow me to think it right to quit my husband at a moment in which he
requires the presence of a sincere friend who he is convinced shares in his
distresses, and not only feels for the many troubles he has to fight with,
but perhaps from being your sister may be of essential use to him and
his dominions—I hope that you are convinced dear brother this is a
sacrifice I bear to my duty and that I look forwards with impatience to
better times in which I may be allowed without impropriety to pay you
a visit in England, see my mother and sisters, and if it pleases the
Almighty still to spare my poor father that I may once again have the

1 Youngest child of George III. (1783–1810.)

painful blessing of seeing him: This would be a great comfort and I shall always look forwards to it with anxiety and hope.

I hope my dearest brother that you are too thoroughly convinced of my attachment to doubt the joy I felt at your being again in possession of your Hanoverian dominions. Pray dearest brother accept of my warmest congratulations on a subject that is so very interesting to the whole family. I only regret that our poor father cannot partake of this happiness. Much do I wish that the Hanoverian Ministers would have had the prudence to wait with their arrestations till they had received your orders, being convinced that your good heart would induce you as the Hanoverians in general are sincerely attached to our family to pass a spunge over the conduct of the few who have been mislead and not allow people to be arrested and have their old estates sequestered because they were obliged to accept of places at the King of Westphalia's[1] Court, most of the Hanoverians refused to serve another master, but others were threatned with imprisonment or the loss of their fortunes if none would attend at Court and I believe fear at last induced the few that went to Cassel to accept of places. I think it my duty to mention this and should humbly suppose that those who have been placed at the Westphalian Court, would be sufficiently punished where they have failed in being forbid the Hanoverian Court, till by their behaviour they deserve their pardon.

My dearest brother it is with great pleasure that I have read your speech.[2] The spirit of moderation that reigns in it notwithstanding the success of the Allies delights me, and wish you may soon have it in your power to contract a peace on a solid basis not only for the good of the world and our own in particular but that I fear from the various interests and dispositions of the Allies that they will in the end quarel between themselves and should they hereafter meet with any check will as usual abandon England and conclude separate peaces which would end in the total over throw of all Europe. Being personally acquainted with Emperor Napoleon I think it a duty to say that he has ever spoken of you dear brother in handsome terms and at different times expressed a wish to see the two countries at peace.

I hope my dearest brother that you will do me the favour to accept of two china flower pots of my painting and gilding and of a ring which I am assured is an Italian gem. It's being St George and the Dragon makes me

1 Jerome Bonaparte.
2 At the opening of Parliament on 4 November. In the course of his speech he said: "No disposition to require from France sacrifices of any description inconsistent with her honour or just pretensions as a nation, will ever be on my part, or on that of His Majesty's Allies, an obstacle to peace."

hope that it will please you and sometimes recall me to your thoughts.
—The King begs me to present his compliments to you and I remain
with the sincerest regard and affection [etc.].

362 THE QUEEN OF WURTEMBERG *to the* PRINCE REGENT

Stutgard, December 13th 1813.

AFTER the many proofs I have received of your constant affection for
me and particularly the great kindness you have shewn me in sending
Sr Thomas Tyrwhitt to see me, encourages me to open my heart to you
and lay before you the unpleasant situation I am in as to my pecuniary
concerns. A house I had bought with the furniture etc. and the new setting my jewels in addition to my usual expences had brought me into
difficulties, but according to a plan I made some years ago and adhered to
as far as circumstances have allowed me, the greatest part of my debts
would have been paid by this time, had not the war made me lose above
five thousand pounds on my pension and of course involved me deeper
than I know how to extricate myself unless you, dear brother, with your
usual kindness will come to my assistance. I have given Sr Thomas a note
as to the part regarding my pension flattering myself you will allow him
to settle that with the First Lord of the Treasury. But as I am convinced
you would wish to know that I enjoy a proper income to keep up my rank
I hope you will have the goodness during three years to send me two
thousand pounds a year which will quite clear me and enable me to live
in a manner suitable to my situation in life.

Nothing but your goodness to us all could have given me sufficient
courage to enter on this unpleasant subject and I trust in your affection
to forgive me should you find my demand reasonable. Adieu my dearest
brother and believe [etc.].

363 THE QUEEN OF WURTEMBERG'S *Memorandum*

Stuttgard. [13] December 1813.

AFTER a lapse of so many years, during which the course of events on
the Continent has unhappily deprived the Queen of Wurtemberg of all
direct communication with the Royal Family of England, Her Majesty
avails herself of Sir Thomas Tyrwhitt's presence at Stuttgard to charge

him with a representation to her most dear brother His Royal Highness the Prince Regent; the subject of which, Her Majesty is fully persuaded, requires only to be mentioned to His Royal Highness to secure his immediate attention and consideration.

At the period of Her Majesty's marriage the annual payment of five thousand pounds sterling was guaranteed to her during her life, but although such payment has been regularly made in England, for the use of Her Majesty, yet it is well known that, during the suspension of all commercial intercourse between Great Britain and Germany, the rate of exchange has been such that, in the annual receipt of this sum, Her Majesty has, since the year 1805 (with the exception of the two following years when the course of exchange was at par) suffered a diminution of her allowance in the ratio of more than one-fifth; amounting, in the whole, to the sum of £5,771. 9. 8 sterling, as will appear by the statement annexed.

From the manifold proofs of warm affection and regard which His Royal Highness has so often evinced towards the Queen, Her Majesty has every reason to confide in his kindness upon this occasion; and Her Majesty therefore trusts that His Royal Highness will be pleased to give such directions as may be necessary, not only to indemnify Her Majesty for the great loss which she has already sustained, but also that, in future, the intentions of the original settlement may be effectuated by her receiving in full this allowance, the diminution of which cannot but have sensibly affected Her Majesty's domestic arrangements.

Statement of the annual loss of Her Majesty the Queen of Wurtemberg, arising from the state of the course of exchange, from time to time, when Her Majesty has drawn on England for the yearly sum of four thousand pounds sterling, part of the sum of five thousand pounds sterling, the payment of which was guaranteed to Her Majesty on her marriage.[1]

1805 Course of exchange	$10\frac{1}{2}$ Fl.	2,000 Florins	£190.	9.	$6\frac{1}{4}$
1808	$9\frac{1}{2}$	6,000	631.	11.	$6\frac{3}{4}$
1809	$9\frac{1}{2}$	6,000	631.	11.	$6\frac{3}{4}$
1810	$8\frac{1}{2}$	10,000	1176.	9.	$4\frac{3}{4}$
1811	$8\frac{1}{4}$	11,000	1333.	6.	8
1812	$8\frac{1}{2}$	10,000	1176.	9.	$4\frac{3}{4}$
1813	$9\frac{1}{2}$	6,000	631.	11.	$6\frac{3}{4}$
			£5771.	9.	8

1 A copy, signed by the Queen.

Stutgard, December 13th 1813.

EVER since I left England I have met with such a singular series of events that I wish you to be acquainted with them, and therefore entreat you to read this note with attention. At my arrival at Stutgard June 24th 1797 the country was overrun by Austrian troops which continued to be quartered in the Dutchy till May 1800. During their residence in Württemberg they cost the country fifty six millions of florins which the Court of Vienna engaged to pay, but notwithstanding the length of years that has elapsed since, there appears little intention to fulfil this promise.

In the spring of 1799 the French entered the Dutchy and in the space of two months found means to cost Wurttemberg seventeen millions of florins. After the breaking up of the Congress of Rastadt in 1799 a fresh war threatened Germany, into which the King, then Duke, entered. His troops joined the Austrian army and in April 1800 were taken into British pay. The troops had marched but a few days, when the French, crossing the Rhine, entered Württemberg and drew so near Louisbourg that the Duke thought it prudent to retire to Weittingen (?) with his family, but could not remain there above a month as the enemy continued advancing. This forced him to take shelter in the King of Prussia's dominions at Erhingen (?), where a melancholy year was spent. The situation of the Dutchy of Württemberg was very wretched, at that time being totally in the hands of the French who extorted heavy contributions, of which the Sovereign was obliged to pay the moiety. However the Peace of Vienna in 1801 gave us hopes of returning home, but it was not till May that the French evacuated the country. The Congress which about this time assembled at Ratisbonne sat near two years, at the end of which was published the famous Reces de l'Empire which secularised most of the Ecclesiastical States and authorised the Duke of Wurttemberg, the Landgraff of Hess,[1] and the Margraff of Baden,[2] to take the title of Electors; which took place April 27th 1803; and they received additions to their dominions. Things remained in this state till in 1805 Emperor Napoleon crossed the Rhine and directed the march of his army through the Electorate of Württemberg. The Elector who had for months warned the Austrian Court that unless it sent him a sufficient army to join his troops and defend his dominions against the inroads of the French, he should be obliged to yield to superior force, could not contend with an army of one hundred thousand men, particularly as

1 William, Landgrave and Elector of Hesse-Cassel (1743–1821).
2 Charles Frederick of Baden-Baden; Grand Duke. 1806. (d. 1811.)

Marshal Ney[1] directed his march against Louisbourg and Stutgard, both open towns. In this situation the Elector was obliged to contract an Alliance with the Emperor of the French, who came to Louisbourg before the treaty was signed; and I must do him the justice to say, behaved not only very politely but personally to me with great attention. By this treaty the Württemberg troops were obliged to join the French army; & after the Peace of Presbourg which took place at the end of the year, the Electors of Bavaria[2] and of Württemberg took the titles of Kings and a variety of other changes took place in Germany. Though some dominions were given to these Sovereigns in addition to their old ones, the expences continued encreasing, as hardly a year passes over without a new war breaking out. And even after the Peace of Tilsit which in 1807 ended the war with Russia and Prussia, the Sovereigns saw themselves involved in heavy difficulties from the enormous expences they were drawn into, to keep up too large a military force in proportion to their revenues. Before this country could a little recover its losses a fresh war broke [out] between Austria and France in 1809, which was terminated by the Peace of Presbourg.[3] This peace being soon followed by the marriage of the Emperor of Austria's daughter[4] to Emperor Napoleon, one might reasonably have expected that quiet would reign some years on the Continent; but alas, our hopes were deceived and in less than two years a war broke out between Russia & France in 1811 and the Wurttemberg troops again called into the field. The disasters which finished the Russian campaign cost the King the greatest part of his troops; and those he was required to fit out afresh at an immense expence, have mostly shared the same fate.

After the great success of the Allies at the end of October 1812, a very peremptory message was sent to the King of Württemberg by General Wreden [*sic*] to insist that in forty eight hours he should either join the coalised Powers, or that the whole Austrian army would march to Stutgard seize on all the King's dominions and treating them as a conquered country; begin by naming an Administration who should govern them in the name of the Allied Sovereigns. You will dear brother easily imagine the effect this message had on us; as though it was to be expected that the King would be desired to join the coalition, the violent manner in which it was done was offensive. The Emperor of Austria was himself displeased when he heard how General Wreden had behaved

1 Michel Ney, Marshal of France (1769–1815). After submitting to Louis XVIII in 1814 he went over to Napoleon's side during the Hundred Days, and was shot in December.
2 Maximilian Joseph, Elector of Bavaria, 1799; King, 1805. (1756–1825.)
3 A slip for Schönbrunn.
4 The Archduchess Marie-Louise (1791–1847), daughter of Francis I.

towards the King. These preliminary steps having taken place the King sent Count de Zeppelin, his Minister for Foreign Affairs, to treat with the Imperial Courts; he returned in a few days with a treaty which dire necessity could alone oblige the King to accept of, the se[c]ret articles of which are so dangerous that they threaten the political existance of this country. This my dearest brother obliges me to have recourse to your well known affection and to entreat that you will not abandon us in this moment of danger but protect us and by ordering your Embassadors [*sic*] at the Imperial Courts to watch over our interests you will certainly stem the mischief which I have reason to fear is ultimately intended to fall on us. By the public treaty the Emperor of Austria acknowledges the King's sovereignty over all his Dominions and guarantees them in their whole extent. But by the secret articles (of which I have obtained a copy from the King that you may yourself be able to judge of the bad intentions of the Court of Vienna towards Wurttemberg) they destroy in a word all our hopes by giving another turn to their deceitful promises. I suspect these articles are much owing to the Houses of Bavaria, and Baden, who hope through the favour of Russia to agrandize themselves at our cost. Both these Sovereigns being brothers in law to the Emperor of Russia. Count Metternich has also a great dislike to the King, because he was obliged by the Emperor of the French in 1809 to sequester his estates and Count Stadions,[1] and though the King returned them to him at the peace and assisted him to pay his debts, the Count seizes on every opportunity to do him mischief. After you have read thus far you will, dear brother, see how important it is for us that this note should for ever remain a secret between us. I have entered on all these subjects with S[r] Thomas Tyrwhitt who will be able to give you more particulars. My wish is dearest brother that out of affection for me you would support my husband and order Lord Aberdeen[2] and Lord Cathcart not only never to consent to any diminution of the King's dominions but to insist on their remaining in the whole of their extent without the least exchange, and secondly that in whatever proportion the Allies intend increasing Bavaria and Baden, you will, dear brother, have the goodness to insist that Württemberg shall receive the same addition of territory.[3] Unless the King's dominions are sufficiently increased to enable him to keep a standing army of twenty five or thirty thousand men he will always be exposed to the first inroads of the French without being sufficiently

1 Count von Stadion, the Austrian Minister.
2 George Hamilton-Gordon, fourth Earl of Aberdeen (1784–1860), afterwards Prime Minister. At this time, Ambassador Extraordinary at Vienna.
3 See No. 365.

strong to defend his country till the Austrians have time to arrive, and must therefore yield to the first fifty thousand men. If on the contrary he was more powerful, Wurttemberg would serve as a tête de pont and delay sufficiently the French till the Austrians had assembled their forces. After having read these particulars, dear brother, you will easily imagine that the finances of this country are in a deplorable state, which makes me very unhappy as I do not see how the King will be able to keep up public credit unless he receives some assistance. Every day he receives fresh demands from the Allies. One moment they expect him to form magazines while the country is already eat up by the troops that are already quartered all over it. At another they insist on his forming besides the corps of troops that marches next week, a second body of ten thousand men. You have it in your power, my dearest brother, to lay us under the greatest obligations and to save the country from total ruin, if you would have the goodness to grant the King a subsidy which would enable him to fulfil with honour the engagements this country has entered into with the Allies. At the same time I should feel very happy to have contributed towards the easing my husband's mind and to owe my comfort to you—What does great mischief to the Allies is the behaviour of the Austrian troops in their friends dominions, it is impossible to be more violent in the country of an enemy. On the contrary the Russians under the command of Count Wittgenstein have kept up good discipline. I hope that this tedious note will obtain your indulgence dear brother as by this means you will be best able to judge of our situation. My trust in the many proofs I have received of your affection for me encourages me to lay our distresses before you. It is with the sincerest affection that I remain [etc.].

365 THE QUEEN OF WURTEMBERG *to* SIR THOMAS TYRWHITT[1]

[December 1813.]

LA REINE DE WÜRTTEMBERG est chargée par le Roi son époux de dire au Chevalier Tyrwhitt qu'il met toute sa confiance dans les bons offices du Prince Regent, se flattant qu'autant par égard pour les liens de parantée qui l'unit au Prince, que par égard pour sa position geographique, le Prince ne verra pas avec indifference que les voisins cherchent d'écraser le Royaume de Württemberg, qui poura toujours servir

1 The spelling of this and subsequent letters written in French has been occasionally modified to make the letters more easily readable.

soit de frontière ou de tête de Pont pour arrêter les premières attaques des Francais quand ils chercheront à passer le Rhin. Tandis que le Grand Duche de Bade n'étant qu'une lisière ne peut jamais offrire les mêmes ressources. Il est bien à désirer que le Prince Regent veuille bien prendre le Württemberg sous la protection et empêcher d'un autre coté qu'on ne sacrifie ses interêts à ceux de la Bavière qui fait sonner bien haut les services qu'elle a rendu aux Allies tandis que même leur troupes ne sont jamais complètes. Le Roi de Württemberg souhaite que le Prince Regent insiste qu'on conserve l'integrité de ses états et ne consense à auqun troque et surtout désire à la paix de garder Ulm, par ce que cette ville lui assure les frontières naturelles du Danube et de l'Iller. Il est aussi à souhaiter que le Prince Regent à la paix veuille bien veiller aux interêts de son beau frère et exiger qu'il recerve les mêmes agrandissements que la Bavière et Bade.[1]

366 THE QUEEN OF WURTEMBERG *to* SIR THOMAS TYRWHITT

Stutgard, December 14th 1813.

I CANNOT let you leave this place without returning you thanks for the polite attentions you shewed me during your stay here, and beg that you will renew to the Prince Regent, the Queen and my sisters the assurances of my affectionate attachment for them all.

I enclose the paper we talked of last night, and that you will give the Prince at a proper moment, and hope that he will read it with attention and see in it my desire to see him and his daughter happy.

I have wrote a long letter to Mr. Price and now thinking it indiscreet to take up more of your time, am with great regard, Sir, [etc.].

[P.S.] I hope that you will have a pleasant journey and arrive safely in England.

1 Queen Charlotte's appeals to her brother and the British Government were all ignored. Lord Aberdeen reported to Castlereagh a few days later that the King of Wurtemberg, who had recently joined the Allies, was intriguing with their enemies. He "has written to Bonaparte to say that the alliance has been forced on him, and that he looks forward to the time when he may be able to assist him with effect...the cause of this conduct is to be found in his hatred of Bavaria. He can never forgive Austria for granting more favourable terms to the King of Bavaria than to himself. He even made a show of not ratifying the Treaty, which his Minister, Count Zeppelin, had concluded....The King is abhorred in the country, and I should not be the least surprised if measures were taken to place the government of the State, at least for the present, in other hands." (*Cast. Corr.* IX, 110.)

[Undated: enclosed in her letter to Sir Thomas Tyrwhitt
14 December 1813].

THOSE who are sincerely attached to the Prince Regent wish him to
weigh very seriously the subject before he fixes on a husband for
Princess Charlotte, as the character and disposition of that Prince is of
high importance not only to the happiness of the Princess but to the
Prince Regent and to the whole Royal Family. Should the Prince
Regent choose a Prince who has already connections in England it is to
be feared he may be drawn to try to make himself a party, and instead of
acknowledging that he owes everything to the Prince of Wales, seek to
stand on his own legs. Therefore I should humbly presume that the best
choice the Regent could make would be a Prince of an old House but who
had very little of his own and would therefore remain dependant on him.
Nothing I dread so much as a Prince in imitation of King William 3d
(who is now cried up in every newspaper as the only example a King
ought to follow) seeking to set himself at the head of opposition and by
degrees looking forwards to set the future Queen aside and reign alone.
I should not have taken the liberty to give my sentiments on this subject did
not the House of Orange speak openly of a marriage being already agreed
on between Princess Charlotte and the Hereditary Prince of Orange.
The character he has obtained in Spain and his having been educated in
England will of course give him a Party and make him more dangerous
than a total foreigner. The Hereditary Prince of Oldenbourg[1] would
serve to unite England in closer bonds of friendship with Russia, or the
King of Prussia's nephew Prince Frederick[2] or the King of Wurtem-
burg's nephew Prince Adam, or the Prince Charles of Mecklenbourg
Strelitz would all in my opinion suit the situation better and be less
dangerous to the present Royal Family.

368 QUEEN CHARLOTTE *to the* PRINCE REGENT

Windsor, the 14th Decbr 1813.

YOUR kindness of charging the Duke of York with the commission of
acquainting me with the intended alliance between your daughter & the
Hereditary Prince of Orange calls for my most gratefull acknowledge-

1 Paul Frederick Augustus, who succeeded his father as Grand Duke of Oldenburg in
1829. He died in 1853.
2 Probably Frederick William Louis (b. 1794), son of Frederick William III's brother,
Prince Frederick Louis Charles, and Frederica, afterwards Duchess of Cumberland. In 1817
this young Prince married Wilhelmina Louisa of Anhalt-Bernberg.

ment. My congratulations upon this event you will not doubt to be sincere when I say: *may this union prove to be as happy as your own hath been fatal. C'est tout dire en peut de mots.*

I will not deny that the sudden conclusion of so serious an event did surprise me a little, but when I recollect that the proposal does arise from the same quarter from which you received a very different one before, I believe by coming into this you have prevented much distress to yourself, & however it may turn out in the end you can have nothing to reproach yourself with.[1]

I will now not detain you any longer as you must be very busy & only add how sincerely I am, [etc.].

369 THE DUKE OF CAMBRIDGE *to the* PRINCE REGENT

Cuxhaven, Wednesday, Decr. 15th 1813.

THOUGH Munster writes to you by the same opportunity, I cannot resist the pleasure of sending you one line to inform you of our safe arrival here at three o'clock this afternoon. We have certainly had a very fortunate passage, having been only three days and a half from the river. Nothing can have been more gratifying than my reception here, and everybody seems delighted at my arrival and I was assured that in the Hanoverian dominions there is an universal wish for my return. This I do not say from any foolish vanity of my own, which I flatter myself, my dearest brother, you think me incapable of, but to prove to you that the arrangements you have made are those which will give most satisfaction to the country.

I am sorry to say that I have seen here an officer of the new levies who left Hanover by order of the Hanoverian Ministry last week to fetch five thousand stand of arms for the militia, with which he arrived this morning from Heligoland. I understood he saw Ernest[2] the day of his departure who was then in treaty for a house at Hanover. I trust though that Bloomfield will have by this time arrived and that he will have persuaded Ernest to leave Hanover before I get there, which cannot be till next Sunday. The roads are so bad and the days so short that we shall not be able to get a horse thirty miles a day, and tomorrow I doubt that

1 Princess Charlotte had recently refused to marry the young Prince of Orange and had told Sir Henry Halford that she preferred her middle-aged cousin, the Duke of Gloucester. On 12 December, however, at a dinner party at Carlton House, she accepted Prince William, and the marriage was to take place in the spring.
2 The Duke of Cumberland.

we shall have our carriages ready to start before twelve o'clock, and therefore we shall only get to Bederkesa the first stage on the road to Hanover.

As Munster will inform you of all the news we have heard I will not trouble you with repeating it. Poor Munster is, I am sorry to say, suffering a good deal this evening with a rheumatic pain in his leg, and I have just left him in bed complaining that he is in more pain since his arrival here. His eyes are quite well again. I hope that a good night's rest, of which he had little or none on board of ship, may do him good, and that he may be able tomorrow to set out with me.

I will now not detain you any longer than to assure you, my dearest brother, that you will ever find me [etc.].

370 MISS MERCER ELPHINSTONE *to* CAPTAIN HESSE

Copy.

Plymouth Dock, Decr. 15th 1813.

I AM again under the necessity of addressing you, and expressing the surprise and displeasure, that is felt at your having so long delayed replying to my letter.[1] A note has since been received from you, but I am desired to say, that it does not alter the plan of conduct already firmly determined on, and that it is required that steps should be taken immediately, to forward the compliance to the commands contained in former letters as much as possible, all of which are expected to be strictly attended to [etc.].

371 WILLIAM HOLMES *to the* PRINCE REGENT

December 18th 1813.

THE kindness which your Royal Highness has condescended to shew me, together with the conviction I entertain of your gracious intentions to serve me, had led me to hope, that in the changes which Mr. Whartons retiring from the Treasury were likely to produce, Lord Liverpool would have been prevailed upon to have included my name, but the arrangements which were yesterday announced in the House of Commons[2] have extinguished every hope I had allowed myself to indulge in, & will I fear

1 See No. 339.
2 Stephen Rumbold Lushington (1776–1868) succeeded Richard Wharton as Joint Secretary of the Treasury, his appointment dating from 5 January 1814.

compel [me] to retire from a situation, where it is my pride & ambition to be enabled to remain, & give daily proofs of my devoted attachment to your Royal Highness person & Government, but being *now* left no other hope of meeting the consuming & allmost ruinous expense which my election, pitition & contest with such an opponent as my Lord Darlington have necessarily involved me in, except what I can save from my income, I feel that I ought no longer to continue a contest which can now be only maintained by depriving my family of those comforts which they hitherto allways enjoyed.[1]

Thus circumstanced I do with all humility implore your Royal Highness to pardon the liberty I take in expressing a hope, that your being acquainted with my present situation would encrease that interest which you have been graciously pleased so often to express you entertain for one who can with the greatest truth & sincerity subscribe himself [etc.].

372 THE ARCHBISHOP OF CANTERBURY (DR MANNERS-SUTTON) *to the* PRINCE REGENT

Addington, Dec: ye 18th 1813.

IN obedience to your Royal Highness's commands, I have carefully read & considered ye rules & regulations relating to y^e "British system for ye education of ye labouring, & manufacturing classes of ye community, of every religious persuasion.[2]

Nothing can be more reasonable than that they who differ from ye establishment, should be at liberty to educate their children according to their own religious opinions; always presuming, that such opinions are consistent with Christianity, & with good morals, & good order. This I apprehend, is ye view which ye Established Church of this country, not claiming to be infallible, takes of ye subject.

But surely Sir, there is a broad distinction between individual, & national education.

The Constitution in Church, & State, will be best upheld by a wise, prudent, & large religious toleration: but it would be unreasonable in ye highest degree to expect, that ye Church of ye United Kingdom, or any

1 At the general election, October 1812, Lord Darlington's two candidates for Tregony, Colonel O'Callagan and Mr Thornhill, were defeated by Holmes and Alexander Cray Grant, who were supported by the Treasury and Carlton House. The defeated candidates petitioned against the return, but the House of Commons Committee declared the sitting members duly elected.

2 See No. 355.

other Church under Heaven, should long maintain its footing among a people educated with indifference to its doctrines, & by necessary consequence, with hostility to its establishment.

I would further humbly submit to your Royal Highness's consideration, that this scheme for educating ye people, has a tendency, certainly not in ye opinions of those who framed it, but in my judgment, a strong tendency to introduce national infidelity.

The fourth rule, ye only rule in which ye subject matter of instruction is mentioned sets forth, that ye children shall be taught "reading, writing, & arithmetic; ye lessons for reading, shall consist of extracts from ye Holy Scriptures; no catechisms or peculiar tenets shall be taught in ye school, but every child shall be enjoined to attend regularly, ye place of worship to which his parents belong.

Doubtless a very excellent code of morals may be extracted from ye Holy Scriptures: but if this code be not made to rest upon ye sanctions, & peculiar doctrines of Christianity, whatever be ye excellence of ye structure, ye foundations of it will lie no deeper than those which belong to ye morality of ye heathen.

The latter part of ye fourth rule may perhaps be intended to meet this objection. "Ye children shall be enjoined to attend regularly, ye places of worship to which their parents belong." If however, nothing more be meant by this expression, than that ye children when dismissed from ye school, shall be directed to attend such places of worship, ye direction for many reasons, will fail of general acquiescence.

But after all Sir, may I presume to ask, is it safe for ye State? is it dealing fairly with ye parents of ye children? is it dealing honestly with ye children themselves? to require that they should be sent to their respective places of worship, by those who are intrusted with ye *whole* of their education, ignorant of ye doctrines, & creeds, & evidences of ye religion to which they nominally belong. These questions apply with equal force to ye Dissenter, & to him who is of the Established Church.

On ye whole Sir, if this scheme of education prevail, & become in fact, that which it proposes to be ye British system for educating ye labouring, & manufacturing classes of ye community, it is ye conviction of my mind, that ye ecclesiastical establishment of ye country will be placed in ye greatest possible danger, & that Christianity itself, under any form of worship, will hardly be safe among us.

I have plainly, & conscientiously stated to your Royal Highness, my understanding of this grave, & important subject; & I pray your Royal Highness to pardon any error I may have committed in form, or substance.

Sunday [19th Dec. 1813].

I HAVE this instant been informed that Mr. Grant cannot legally retain the situation of Commissioner for the Affairs of the Carnatic & the one he was gazetted to last night.[1] If this be the case might I take the liberty of requesting you to mention it to His Royal Highness the Prince Regent & be assured my dear Col. M'Mahon that nothing short of embarrassed circumstances, would compel me to be so troublesome to you, but believe me to be [etc.].

374   CHARLES WESLEY *to* COLONEL MCMAHON

Buckingham Street, No. 4, *Fitzroy Square*,
Dec. 21st 1813.

MR. WESLEY hath the honor to acquaint Col. MacMahon that His Royal Highness the Prince Regent hath graciously commanded that Mr. Ch. Wesley shall be paid the sum of £50. pound for his attendance at Brighton, during the time he had the honor of performing on the organ, the remuneration which His R.H. hath allway granted.[2]

375   COLONEL MCMAHON *to* SAMUEL WHITBREAD

Copy.

Carlton House, Decr. 22d 1813.

I HAVE the honor to acknowledge the receipt of your letter of the 8th instant,[3] together with the enclosed copy of Rules & Regulations of the Institution styling itself, The British System of Education. I have laid the same before His Royal Highness the Prince Regent, and he has commanded me to inform you that, although His Royal Highness is most anxious for the education of the labouring & manufacturing classes of the community, he is under the necessity of declining the proposal which has been made to him, to take this Institution under His Royal Highness's special protection. At the same time, it is not His Royal Highness's intention to withdraw the subscription which he has hitherto given to the Institution.

1 Charles Grant (1778–1866), the son of the East India Director, and afterwards Lord Glenelg, had been in Parliament since 1811. He now succeeded James Brogden as a Lord of the Treasury.
2 See Nos. 317, 326.   3 No. 355.

Hanover, Decr. 22nd 1813.

IT is with the greatest pleasure that I take up my pen to inform you of my safe arrival at Hanover on Sunday the 19th. inst. and to assure you that the joy expressed by all classes of subjects of the Electorate at my arrival clearly proves that their affections to you and the family has not decreased notwithstanding the very severe trials they have undergone these last ten years. The reception I have met with ever since I reached the Electorate which begins about six miles from Cuxhaven is beyond what I can express, and the manner in which I entered the town of Hanover exceeds everything I could expect. The loyalty shewn by all ranks and their continued cheers of God save the King and the family were gratifying to my feelings beyond measure, and I only wish that that happy day may come when we may have the comfort of seeing you here. To Bloomfield I leave the details of what has passed, which I am sure he will give you fully. I found him here to my great joy and I am happy to hear that he succeeded in his commission without being obliged to make use of the paper you gave him. I hope in a week or ten days' time to be able to give you some report of what has been done here relative to the plan for the arming of the country, and with your approbation I mean to send Bloomfield with it. In the meantime, as he very naturally is anxious to see one of the armies, he will accompany Charles Stewart who is going tomorrow to the Crown Prince's army which is in Holshtein where he can arrive in three days, so that he can be back in a week or ten days at latest. By this means I trust he will be in England time enough to attend you on your tour to Belvoir or at least to be with you before your return to town. According to my calculation he will be most probably in England within six weeks, which is the time you thought he would be absent. I must further add that it is my wish that he should stay till then, which will ennable me to write to you more fully on the state of things here. Since my arrival I have hardly even come to myself and I therefore trust to your goodness my dearest brother to excuse this hurryed letter.

Munster I am happy to say is quite well again and as he as well as Pr. Charles,[1] who sends a messenger with this, have written upon the state of the general affairs of Germany, I shall not of course trouble you with them. I have not as yet been able to write to my uncles,[2] but I hope to do so in the course of tomorrow when I shall mention your kind message to

1 Of Mecklenburg-Strelitz.
2 Charles, Grand Duke of Mecklenburg-Strelitz, and Prince Ernest of Mecklenburg-Strelitz.

Prince Ernest. He is I am sorry to say in a very weak state, and his nerves I am told, are so shook that he can hardly do anything, not even read and write, so that at present it is impossible for him to think of making a journey to England. I will now not detain you any longer, my dearest brother, than to assure you that my greatest wish is to fulfill my duty here well, and to prove to you my sincerest attachment, with which I ever shall remain, [etc.].

377 THOMAS SHERIDAN *to* COLONEL MCMAHON

Wednesday [1813].

I AM anxious to have an opportunity of taking leave of His Royal Highness before I leave England and at the same time my health renders it advisable that I should remain as little in London as possible. May I beg for your advice upon this subject, and what is the proper mode to obtain an audience on such an occasion.[1]

P.S. I come to town tomorrow and shall be at my father's house No. 14 Saville Row.[2]

378 RICHARD BRINSLEY SHERIDAN *to* COLONEL MCMAHON

Cook's Hotel, Sunday E[vening] [? 1813].

THO' since I last had the honor of paying my duty to the Prince Regent I have been often in town I have purposely abstain'd from attending at Carlton House. The anxiety express'd by His Royal Highness that I should avoid all possible risk of personal insult on the score of debt, made, I need not say, a most grateful impression on my mind, but when His Royal Highness proceeded to offer me an appartment in his own Palace with the same benevolent view to my protection I can only say that *gratitude* is too weak a word to express the feelings which that offer has indelibly planted in my mind.

And now my dear friend I come to the real purpose of this short letter. The very graciousness of the Prince's conduct towards me was the spur

1 See Nos. 235, 292. He was about to set out for the Cape to assume the office of Colonial Treasurer.
2 The house which Lord Wellesley had lent him.

that made me apply myself to a strict examination of my own circumstances and I am confident that you will hear with pleasure, & with pleasure communicate the fact to our Royal master that I am free from every personal difficulty, or embarrassment of debt—except the debt of gratitude I owe to him which it will be the object of my life honourably & faithfully to discharge.[1]

379 COLONEL CONGREVE's *statement respecting the Rocket Service, from its commencement in* 1805 *to* 1813

Copy. [? 1813]

IN 1805—I first had the honor to propose to Mr. Pitt, the construction of fire rockets for the annoyance of the enemy's coast, having by a series of experiments at my own cost, previously ascertained the powers of which this weapon was capable. Mr. Pitt with other Ministers of that day, were in consequence pleased to attend in person an experiment at Woolwich and from their own conviction of the efficiency of the weapon, ordered an establishment to be immediately formed, and in the autumn of that year granted me an allowance of one hundred pounds p month, during the continuance of the service—which was at that time paid at the Secretary of States office for the War Department.

In 1806—at the change of Administration which happened in consequence of the death of Mr. Pitt, Lord Howick, then First Lord of the Admiralty, and Lord Moira, Master General of the Ordnance, having also personally attended an experiment, determined that the service should continue and it was arranged, that the payment of my allowance should be transferred from the Secretary of States office to the Navy office; the application of this new weapon having commenced in naval operations for the annoyance of the enemy's coasts. It was accordingly paid to me at that office expressly "as preparing stores for the annoyance of the enemy"—and it is here only necessary briefly to state, that these preparations and the receipt of this allowance, have proceeded ever since according to this establishment, that during this period a great variety of rocket equipments have been sent to all parts of the world; in five of which I have myself personally attended, and that in the *present* year, the average has been greater than in any other preceeding year; not less than four equipments, on a great scale, having been formed, and the people instructed under my direction for foreign service—namely—One of 3000

1 In August 1813 Sheridan was arrested for a debt of £600, but was bailed out by Whitbread.

rockets to Sir J. B. Warren[1] on the American Station, by *Admiralty order*, with a detachment of Marine Artillery—another of the same force with a similar detachment to Dantzig—another of 4000 rockets now serving with the army of the Crown Prince, and a fourth, which sailed *last week* of 3000 rockets, equipped either for naval or land service to Passages[2]—besides which I have now orders for 11,000 rockets to be immediately prepared and am now proceeding to make rockets the actual weights and explosive powers of which will equal those of the 10 and 13 inch shell.

Under these circumstances it seems fair to presume, not only that the confidence of the Government in this weapon is increasing, but that, if my *services* in the preparation of these equipments *were deemed* at their *commencement* worthy of the salary I have hitherto received, they are *at least* equally so, at the *present moment*. Of course the extension which I have made latterly, of the uses of this weapon to the land service can not be considered as lessening my claim for its application as a naval imple- ment of warfare; nor render me less competent to receive my allowance from the Navy Board where it has hitherto been paid; even had any specific remuneration been made me for this extension to military pur- poses. No such remuneration has however taken place, and here I must beg particularly to state, that being neither in the Army or Navy I have no other emolument whatever for my services than that above men- tioned; that for this therefore I have not only produced a new and powerful arm; but have devoted myself entirely to the public service with a zeal, that has several years induced disbursements far exceeding my allowance. That by constant and unremitting attention I have succeeded in bringing this weapon to great perfection, not only as an auxiliary in naval, but in military operations and that in the actual application of it to both of these purposes, I can affirm that the destruction of enemy's property occaisioned by it has already very far indeed exceeded the whole expense incurred in the service, independent of the general effect which it is known throughout Europe to have produced in the different expeditions in which it has been employed.

I feel a confidence therefore that the foregoing statements must prove, that not only have I merited the allowance which the Government were pleased to grant me, but that the value of the services, for which that allowance was *expressly* granted, has in fact, hitherto at all events, con- tinued to increase.

1 Admiral Sir John Borlase Warren (1753–1822); served in the American and French Wars.
2 Near the Franco-Spanish frontier, on the Atlantic coast.

Belvoir, Jany 4th 1814.

I SHOULD not have thought of troubling you with one of my scrawls but, as I have just learnt from my brother Frederick that you had some thoughts of coming to London this week upon some business, it is merely, in the first place, to entreat of you, if you should do so, upon no account what-soever to think of returning to Windsor again the same day at this very very very severe and inclement season of the year, & to implore of you to make what use you please of my house (although I am unfortunately out of town, & not able personally to attend you, & to wait upon you) in short just as you are used to do when I am present. I have already written to McMahon & all the orders are given to Wettier & to the rest of the servants to hold themselves & all the apartments in readiness for your reception on any day, any hour, or any moment you may please to signify your commands, for dinners, suppers, evening parties, & in a word for all & every thing that may suit your convenience & pleasure. I only hope that all will go right, & to your satisfaction & I shall be most anxious to know that it has done so, & that you hardly missed me. One line from Eliza to my little McMahon, just to apprize him, when you are coming & he will be too proud & happy constantly to wait upon her, & to receive what orders she may be pleased to give him, respecting dinners, sup-plies, appartments, parties, etc etc etc, but which perhaps she will be so kind as to put down in writing on a little scrap of paper, as he is, poor dear little soul, so very nervous, that I am only afraid his memory might be a little treacherous, & if he was unfortunately to forget anything, to make any mistake, or that anything was wanting, I know him so well that he would be quite wretched, & the most miserable being on earth. With many apologies for this long scrawl, & in great haste not to lose the post I subscribe myself [etc.].

381 QUEEN CHARLOTTE *to the* PRINCE REGENT

Windsor, the 8th Janry 1814.

I WANT words to express my gratitude for the very kind & affectionate care you intended to take of me in your absence in case I should have gone to town. The weather is so cold & the snow so deep that I have given up all idea of venturing out of doors for fear of a second attack of the influenza which has left an everlasting remembrance behind it since last year. I have let your little nervous friend[1] know that I did not at this season think it proper to leave home, which I hope will make his mind easy.

I have been made very happy by a letter from the Duke of Cambridge. He is too modest to name the manner of his reception at Hannover, but I have received the account of it, which I read with the most heartfelt joy. He was himself so overcome with it, that he could hardly speak when he was to answer the Magistrate at the entrance of the town. I have also received a long letter from Würtenberg,[2] full of all the acquaintances she has made with the Imperial Family of Russia of which she prefers the widow of the Prince of Holstein[3] who she says is one of the most amiable creatures possible, not handsome but very pritty & pleasing in her manner, quite English & very desirous to cultivate English acquaintance. She has nothing but English servants about her little boy & begd it as a favour that they might be allowed to see your sister which was granted & produced a very crying meeting.

She expects also a visit from the Duke of Cumberland which it appears she would willingly decline on account of his dislike to the Emperor of Russia, of whom he allows himself to speak in a very disrespectfull manner wherever he goes; & she dreads therefore the consequences of the meeting between her brother & the Duke[4] who is uncle to the E[mperor] & you know easily offended. She also mentions that people in general think the D. of C[umberland] quarrelsome & dissatifyed, which would keep her in constant fear & would not give such enjoyment as a visit of a brother should produce. Her idea is that you might perhaps prevent his going to Stutgardt but I am not inclined to think so. With his disposition he would be more eager to go as he would suspect something wrong, & on the other hand I am very clear that should he be imprudent enough to let out his anger, they may stop it by telling him that such liberties can not be allowed in their house. I am clear he will leave them quick enough for he hates to be found fault with. However I leave this to your judgement & shall not say a word in my letter to her that you know it.

That the Allies have passed the Rhine is a subject upon which I congratulate you most sincerely; it gives new hopes of affairs going on swimingly & diminishes my idea of peace. Napoleon seems by his own speech & those of his Ministers to be sufficiently humbled as to acknow-

---

1 Colonel McMahon.
2 From her daughter, Queen Charlotte of Wurtemberg.
3 The Tsar's sister Catherine.
4 Peter I, Duke of Oldenburg (Grand Duke, 1823; d. 1829), the Grand Duchess Catherine's father-in-law.

ledge himself to be in a very critical situation, therefore a little more perseverance & alertness will probably bring his downfall to an end.

I understand that letters from Lrd Wellingtons Army report that there is a great party in France for the Bourbons but a still greater against Boney & that it is supposed their declaration will depend upon the further success of the Allies, for which I pray most sincerely, tho I fear it can not be obtained without great loss of blood & many lives. The latter opens the door of many promotions, if amongst those you could think of Felton Harvey if possible for your Aid de Camp it would make his mother very happy. The young man bears a good character as an officer has been in every campaign both in Portugal & Spain & has lost his arm in the service. His merits as an officer I only have by hear say & yet I think Lrd W[ellington] has frequently named him as being very active in the service. As a son & friend I know him to be all one could wish.

Our dear Sophia has had a *very good night*, the first since her illness, & the physicians assure me that she goes on much better. The King thank God is quiet & calm but feels the cold very much. His sleep is from five to six hours & he retains his appetite which I am glad of as I own I dreaded this cold season.

I hope you will return to us without any accident & rejoice that the overturn at the setting out upon the journey did not injure you.[1] That we may soon have a chearfull meeting is the sincere wish of [etc.].

382 VISCOUNT CASTLEREAGH *to the* PRINCE REGENT

The Hague, January 8th 1814.

IN obedience to your Royal Highness's orders I lost no time, upon my arrival at The Hague, in soliciting a private audience of the Prince of Orange,[2] for the purpose of executing your Royal Highness's commands on the subject of the intended alliance between the illustrious family of Brunswick and the House of Orange.

I found the Prince of Orange had already expressed through his Ambassador in London[3] his grateful sense of the overture with respect to the succession, which your Royal Highness directed me to make

1 On 27 December the Prince Regent set out on a journey to Hatfield and Belvoir Castle, but a dense fog compelled him to return, and about a mile from Tottenham Court Road an outrider was thrown off into a ditch. The Prince again set off at noon next day, and returned to Carlton House on 11 January.
2 The father of the young Prince of Orange who was betrothed to Princess Charlotte.
3 Henry Fagel.

through that channel, previous to my departure. The Prince desired I might assure your Royal Highness, that he received this suggestion as a fresh proof of liberality and kindness towards himself and his family—that your Royal Highness had, in this proposition, evinced so much consideration towards the feelings and national sentiments of his people, that he was persuaded so distinguished a mark of forbearance and delicacy on the part of your Royal Highness could not fail, if possible, to bind the Dutch nation more closely for ever to Great Britain.

With respect to the explanations on this most interesting subject, which I have been charged to make on the part of your Royal Highness, to the Allied Sovereigns assembled at Head Quarters, His Royal Highness gave me full authority on his part to assure their Majesties, that every thing which had been proposed by your Royal Highness had met with his warmest concurrence.

His Royal Highness felt the importance, that a frank but confidential communication on this subject should precede at Head Quarters, any discussion of the general interests, and that, with this precaution, the more publick and formal avowal of the intended marriage might be advantageously delayed, till the period when the arrangement might be prepared in it's details for the consideration of Parliament.

I avail myself of this occasion of humbly submitting to your Royal Highness, that I propose, whilst on the Continent, with your Royal Highness's approbation, to address whatever I may have *officially* to lay before your Royal Highness, to one of His Majesty's Principal Secretaries of State.[1] That I shall, for the better execution of the service with which I am entrusted, endeavour to restrict my personal correspondence as much as possible, leaving to the respective Ministers, as heretofore, to report, for your Royal Highness's information, events in progress; and that I propose, as Lord Liverpool has charged himself with the superintendence of the Department of Foreign Affairs during my absence, to address to his Lordship such confidential observations as may appear to me necessary for the information of your Royal Highness and your confidential servants.

---

1 A few days earlier the Cabinet had sent the Foreign Secretary to the Allied Headquarters to cement the Alliance against Napoleon and to discuss peace terms. The Cabinet's detailed instructions, dated 26 December 1813, are in Professor C. K. Webster's *British Diplomacy, 1813–1815*, pp. 123–8. "He is to endeavour to establish a clear and definite understanding with the Allies, not only on all matters of common interest but upon such points as are likely to be discussed with the enemy, so that the several Allied Powers may in their negotiations with France, and in perfect concert, and together, maintain one common interest."

24-2

Stutgard, January 9th 1814.

HAVING just heard from Adolphus that Princess Charlotte has been confirmed I should fear to appear wanting in affection to you did I not express the sincere wishes I form that this ceremony may have made a deep impression on her mind, and that the serious reflexions she will have made in preparing herself for her confirmation may through life induce her to act constantly in a manner that may please you and contribute to your joint happiness![1]

I do not intend to take up your time by a long letter but cannot deny myself the pleasure of wishing you joy of the success's the British Army has met with in Spain and of the unexpected restoration of the Prince of Orange.[2] The last year having finished so well I hope that this will happily terminate all your great plans and that before its end you will, dear brother, be enabled to give Europe a glorious & lasting peace.

Nothing has given me more pleasure of late than hearing that you had appointed dear Adolphus Governor of Hanover. He was ever adored in the Electorate and I am sure will do everything in his power to restore order and quiet in that poor country which has suffered much of late years.

The King desires me to present his affectionate compliments and I remain [etc.].

384 THE QUEEN OF WURTEMBERG *to* SIR THOMAS TYRWHITT

Stutgard, January 10th 1814.

HAVING heard from Adolphus that business has prevented your returning to England as soon as you had intended, I take the liberty to trouble you with the enclosed letters for my family, and return you many thanks for the newspapers which I have received down to the 20th. ultimate. They are very interesting and it is quite incomprehensible if I am to credit what they say about Ernest, that he can write me word that the Prince Regent approves of his conduct at Hanover. Should you, Sir, not return to London as soon as I should wish, pray be so good as to

1 Princess Charlotte was confirmed on 24 December 1813, the ceremony being performed in the private chapel at Windsor by the Archbishop of Canterbury, assisted by the Archbishop of York, the Bishop of Salisbury, and the Dean of Windsor.

2 In November 1813 the French evacuated Holland; the Dutch patriot, van Hogendorp, formed a Provisional Government, recalled the Prince of Orange, who was in England, and offered him the Sovereignty of Holland.

write to the Prince and beg of him to make Ernest delay his journey here till things are quiet. By a letter Princess Paul[1] gave me yesterday he acquaints me with his intention of spending the winter on the Continent and that he means to come to Stutgard. You will easily imagine how this plan distresses me who expect a second visit from the Great Duke Constantine[2] as also from the Great Duchess Catherine,[3] who I believe will settle herself in one of the King's Palaces till she can with safety think of going to Oldenbourg. Ernest having quarrelled with the Emperor of Russia and since that with the Prince Royal of Sweden, would keep me in hot water by his imprudent conversation, as he allows himself to say everything that comes into his head against these Sovereigns. Besides which his dirty tricks and his freedom of speech have gone on increasing since his journey to Hanover.

I must also trouble you, Sir, with a few lines concerning the private business you were so obliging as to undertake to settle for me, and beg you will consider whether as the Christmas quarter is due on February 14th. it would not be possible to send it by the same opportunity as the three which are already due. When you converse with Mr. Price[4] on this subject I should wish Sir that you would see if he has not sufficient money in hand to be able to send me an additional couple of thousand pounds as I have not bought anything in England for above six years and stand much in need of every assistance to get out of my difficulties. The encreasing wants of all ranks here make the people grow very troublesome in their demands of late; they are very anxious to be paid and the more so as they know that I am ever ready to satisfy their demands when I have money. However I cannot blame them, as the taxes, particularly the income tax falls heavy on everybody. My particular reason for wishing to have a large sum at once is that as you were so obliging to promise to send the money in ducats or louis d'or, I should by that means be able to satisfy many poor trades people, and think that some money coming into circulation will do something towards keeping up the spirits of the people who suffer much from the natural consequences of the war. I will now take up no more of your time and remain [etc.].

1 Catherine Charlotte (b. 1787), daughter of Frederick, Duke of Saxe-Altenburg, and wife of Prince Paul, the younger son of Frederick I, King of Wurtemberg, by his first wife, Augusta of Brunswick.
2 The Grand Duke Constantine of Russia, the Tsar's brother. See No. 315.
3 The Tsar's sister.
4 William Price, Secretary and Comptroller of the Prince Regent's Household.

Stutgard, January 11th, 1814.

AFTER having conversed with you on the cruel situation this country is reduced to by the war, I think it right to continue to give you an idea of the various additional sacrifices it has been obliged to make since your departure, that you may have it in your power to lay before the Regent the extent of our distresses.

You will recollect, Sir, that when you were at Stutgard I entered into many particulars concerning the poverty Wurttemberg was reduced to from the constant wars it has of late years been concerned in, and the troubles we had met with since the beginning of this new contest which encrease daily. Not only the expence of the marches and quarters of the Allied Armies has been enormous, but it has been much encreased by the Austrian cavalry being quartered for several weeks in the King's dominions. In addition to these heavy expences after the King had fulfilled all the clauses of the fallacious treaty which he contracted with Austria, the joint Cabinets have insisted on his doubling his contingent before the end of this month; therefore instead of twelve thousand men which are the number stipulated by the treaty there is now to be four and twenty thousand men under arms at the Allied Army: and what adds to the injustice of these enormous demands is that no indemnification is offered for these dreadful expences. The King is not only to continue raising battallions for the defense of his own dominions, but also to form a Landsturm which is to be compleated in a short time.

You will easily judge by this slight sketch to what a state of poverty and distress we must be reduced to unless my brother out of affection for me comes forwards and saves this country by granting the King subsidies, which is the only means to prevent the ruin which threatens this country. I enclose the printed order for forming the Landsturm that you may shew it to the Prince Regent.

I hope you will, Sir, forgive all the trouble I give you, but our situation is such that I have no dependance on any assistance but what I may flatter myself to obtain from my brother's kindness.

I now take my leave and remain with great regard Sir, your friend.[1]

1 This letter was probably written from her husband's dictation.

Stutgard, January 11th 1814.

I AM quite afraid you will be tired of my numerous letters but I cannot avoid returning you thanks for your note of December 18th which a son of Mr. Spencer Stanhopes has just delivered into my hands. Happy should I feel if I could flatter myself that Colonel Bloomfield had succeeded in his negociation, but I fear from the letter Princess Paul brought me from Ernest there is little hope that the Duke of Cumberland will return as he ought to England. The divorce of the Princess Solms[1] is much talked of and makes me very uneasy, as I dread that Ernest will forget what he owes to the Prince Regent and will obstinately persist in a marriage which must be a source of pain to the whole family. I hope that you will soon be able to quit the Continent and that you will find the Prince Regent and the rest of the family in good health.

I am glad to hear that Princess Charlotte has been confirmed and hope that the serious reflextions [*sic*] she will have made on that occasion will through life be of use to her, and make her feel doubly what she owes to her father.

387 CAPTAIN HESSE *to* MISS MARGARET MERCER ELPHIN-STONE

Hasparren, France, Jany. 12th 1814.

[*Copy.*]

I HAVE this moment had the honor of receiving a letter from you dated Decr 15th.[2] Though you mention in this letter having written to me several times before, I give you my word I never received any letter but *this* one, wh I am answering now. I must confess I am exceedingly sorry any person could ever imagine that had I received any letters, I could ever omit the common civility of acknowledging the receipt of such letters. The only cause I can fancy, for not receiving the letters you allude to, is that you may have trusted them to private conveyances, instead of sending them by *the post* which is invariably the safest and best method of forwarding letters.

The last time I ever received were dated August 10th, which I received and answered on the 10th of Octr. Since this I have never received any letters wh mentioned the subject you speak of.

The greater part of the articles demanded from me, I left in England. They are in a small trunk, containing also papers, of value to me only:

1 See No. 279. 2 No. 370.

this trunk I left in charge of a TRUE *friend of mine*, with the particular request that "should he hear of my death, to send this trunk *unopened* to the bottom of the Thames". I can rely upon the execution of his promise. Those articles I have WITH me, should they be FORCED from me, how could I find any opportunity of sending them in a safe manner to England, considering the situation I am placed in? Should I be killed, they shall be sent to *you*, without being seen by any person, before they get into *your* possession. Pray do represent this.

388 THE DUKE OF CAMBRIDGE *to the* PRINCE REGENT

Hanover, Jany 14th 1814.

HAVING written to you a long letter by Bloomfield I shall only trouble you with a few lines to say that this morning I have received the account that the hostilities between the Danes & the Crown Prince's army have ceased. It was generally believed that the King of Denmark[1] had agreed to the surrender of Norway, for which Sweden was to pay two millions of dollars, to give up Swedish Pomerania, and the Island of Guadaloupe.[2] I can not vouch for the authenticity of this account, but I only give it you as I received it. Should this prove to be true, I flatter myself that a great part of the Crown Prince's army will cross the Rhine. This will be a great blessing for this country is nearly exhausted by the requisitions for his army.

Munster is I am sorry to say still far from well. He however talks of leaving this in a few days. Indeed his presence at the Headquarters of the Great Army is of the utmost consequence, and I trust he will be able to make the journey. I heard yesterday from Ernest. He is still at Strelitz and mentions his intention of going to Berlin, and perhaps from thence to Stuttgard.

From hence I have nothing new to say. The transports with the horses are arrived and disembarked at Cuxhaven. They were to begin their march today & will [be] here I suppose, about the 18th or 19th inst. One of the black horses, an old horse of twenty four years, died on board the ship.

I will now not detain you one moment longer than to assure you that I ever shall remain [etc.].

1 Frederick VI (1768–1839).

2 The Treaty was signed at Kiel on 14 January. The King of Sweden as King of Norway undertook to make himself responsible for part of the debt of the Danish Monarchy, but there was no mention of the sum of two million dollars. Guadaloupe had been ceded to Sweden by the Anglo-Swedish Treaty of alliance of March 1813, but Sweden was persuaded to restore it to France in 1814.

Windsor, the 17th Janry 1814.

I SEND the inclosed letter for the Dutchess of Würtemberg which you will be kind enough to have directed. I have obeyed your commands and said all I could think of to persuade her comming over to England, but I have not named the little Baronet,[1] which offer will come better from yourself. And pardon me when I advise you when you write, not to say that she is invited alone, but say that you fear at the present moment the Duke[2] can not be spared at home, that little word will I am sure make all proposals and invitation be accepted kindly, tho perhaps not successfully.

The sun shines so bright that I hope there is a prospect of milder weather for your journey tomorrow.

I have so little to say that my discretion will not permit to say a word more than to subscribe myself [etc.].

390 THE PRINCE REGENT *to the* QUEEN OF WURTEMBERG

[After 17 January 1814.]

AFTER a long and painful confinement, which has scarcely left me strength to hold my pen, I am sure, my dear sister, you will not expect from me a letter of any length, tho' at the same time after so many years of interrupted correspondence, I am determined you shall see my handwriting.[3]

I have attentively read every communication you have been kind enough to make me since S[r] T[homas] T[yrwhitt] quitted Stuttgard, & would reply to them all in detail, was I not convinced that the best mode of attaining many of their objects, is your prensence [*sic*] amongst us.

And here allow me to assure you, most happy should I be, was it possible you could be accompanied by *His Majesty, the King*, your *husband*, but I am too well aware of the imperious circumstances which render his quitting his capital at this moment quite impossible.

Many of the topics upon which you treat are delicate, and you are acquainted too well with our mode of proceeding here, not to know, as it would be unconstitutional, that I could write myself upon them—but as this country is the centre of all communications from every quarter,

1 Sir Thomas Tyrwhitt, who was sent to Stuttgart to escort the Queen of Wurtemberg to England.
2 The King of Wurtemberg: a Napoleonic title which Queen Charlotte would not recognise.
3 The Prince Regent fell seriously ill after his return from Belvoir Castle on 11 January.

the Prussian Ambassador and the whole Corps Diplomatique on the spot, you will easily perceive that I can, with you here, enter upon all points and freely discuss them, which could not be the case where the King's interests and your own, left only to the care of a Minister at such a distance as he would be from you, however zealous for your interests he may be.

I am persuaded the King will see this in the light it is my anxious wish he should, and of my cordial wish to render you any assistance in my power.

Sir Thomas did not exceed the fact in the statement he gave you of the situation of our dear father. I regret most sincerely now to add that his disorder still continues the same, tho' I thank God he is free from bodily suffering, and appears to be quite happy in himself.

I beg my best compliments to the King and desire to be kindly remembered to him—and am—[etc.].

P.S. I have felt no small uneasiness on the score of your health and which adds to my anxiety to see you & I cannot close my letter without acquainting you that my daughter Princess Charlotte will shortly, with the universal approbation of all here, as well as unanimous approval of my Allies, be married to the Hereditary Prince of Orange, and surely I need not express to you how much I wish that your presence should add to the joy of our whole family upon so memorable an occasion.

391 THE QUEEN OF WURTEMBERG *to* SIR THOMAS TYRWHITT

Stutgard, January 18th 1814.

I RETURN you many thanks for the obliging manner in which you have through Madame de Gonomar(?) acquainted me with the Duke of Cumberland's intended visit. By a letter Ernest entrusted to Princess Paul who he now speaks of in raptures, he mentions his being to spend [*sic*] the whole winter on the Continent, and before his return to Windsor intending to call at Stutgard. I delayed answering him as I was too unwell to write only complimentary letters, and since those I troubled you with, have been quite confined to my bed with a soar throat and feverish cold. Today is the first time I have been allowed to sit up for a few hours and those I shall employ malgré the physical people[1] in writing.

1 I.e. her physicians.

I enclose a copy of my letter to Ernest which I beg that you will have the goodness as to shew to the Prince Regent, that he may know how I have acted and that it may not be in Ernest's power to do mischief. Tomorrow I shall write to my mother and also send her a copy. I have of late mentioned to her several times Ernest's conduct on the Continent. Princess Paul gives frightful accounts of him. He has allowed himself to be sadly familiar with her. His marriage with Princess Solms seems a thing settled between them whenever her divorce takes place. I have however avoided in every letter in which I have spoken about Ernest to mention having heard any part of his strange behaviour from you [*sic*], as, though I think it a duty to warn my mother, it would be a sad breach of confidence to expose private conversation.

Hearing that Lord Castlereagh is expected at Headquarters I have wrote a long letter to the Prince Regent to beg him to take the King of Württemberg under his protection and mentioned the pain it gave me to hear that a Minister had been appointed for Munich before a Treaty was concluded with my husband. As I am sure that you will hear of this letter I think it right to remind you that the King had hardly signed his Treaty with Austria that he was eager to have the diplomatical inter-course reestablished between the Courts of St. James's and Stutgard and frequently ordered the Count de Zeppelin to address himself to the Earl of Aberdeen who it was said was to receive full powers to treat with all those Sovereigns who had changed their political system; but nearly three months being elapsed and these powers not being arrived I have taken the liberty to advise the King to order Count de Zeppelin to write to Viscount Castlereagh and express his Sovereign's desire to conclude a Treaty with Great Britain. This was done some weeks ago but fearing that this letter might not have reached the Secretary of State a copy has been sent to him at Headquarters, and I have wrote to Lord Cathcart and begged of him to speak to Lord Castlereagh in my name that the King may obtain a speedy answer. If you are not, Sir, to return soon to London, pray send the Prince Regent my letter concerning the state of this country and Count Mandelslohe's[1] note. Every moment is im-portant at this crisis. I wish it could have passed through your hands but I hope a few lines from you will be of great use to us.

After all the trouble I have already given you, Sir, I ought to be ashamed to add to it but being convinced that you find pleasure in obliging me I must beg that you will as soon as possible by express write me word what sort of a man a Chevalier de Horn Baronet au ser-vice de sa Majesté Britannique is. He came here a day or two before you

1 The Wurtemberg Minister for Foreign Affairs.

left Stutgard, is an acquaintance of Madame de Leuthes who knew him many years ago at Ratisbonne where he was a sort of British agent, and concealed by his present wife a Mademoiselle de Gumpenberg during the time the English were obliged to leave the Continent. Some pretend he was formerly a Catholic priest. I do not know what he was but his conduct here is very singular and makes me quite uneasy. Had he not given himself out as being employed by the British Ministry I should charitably suspect him to be *un espion qualifié*. He has sent three or four express's to Lord Aberdeen without receiving an answer, pretends that he expects every day a messenger from Headquarters who is to return to London by Stutgard. This never takes place, but last night while I was ill in bed he sent to ask for letters which he would forwards by an Austrian courier to Headquarters. You will easily believe I avoided having any obligations to this unknown gentleman. You are acquainted, Sir, with the anxiety of all our dispositions and will easily imagine how we are worked [*sic*] as this man's being here in absence of an English Minister. Sometimes I cannot help fearing that justice is not done to our steady good intentions and that God knows for what purpose we are suspected and watched. This would be doubly unjust as nobody was ever so conscientious in keeping their engagements as the King. Should the Ministry think it necessary in the south of Germany to have a sort of a gentleman spy I should think either Carlsruhe or Manheim a properer place than the residence of the Princess Royal of England.[1]

We have this morning by a Russian messenger heard that the Prince Royal[2] at the head of the King's troops has beat a corps of French under General Mills and taken several prisoners. The Prince lead [*sic*] on the cavalry himself. You cannot think how happy this news has made the King. I have had a very pretty letter from Charlotte[3] and a locket with a beautiful eye and a fine noze, which has given me much pleasure. I will now take up no more of your time and remain [etc.].

1 Horn (Horne, according to Lord Aberdeen) was an agent employed by the British Government in obtaining information. Aberdeen wrote to Castlereagh, 19 December 1813: "...I desired him to fix his residence at Ratisbon, Augsburg, or Nuremberg, as I understood that his connexions were in Bavaria, and that, if anywhere, he had the means of being useful there. But it appears the Bavarian Government are as determined not to have him as the Austrian, and he has been directed to quit the country. He is now at Stuttgard. The fact is, that he was formerly a *monk* in Bavaria, so that it cannot be supposed he will be well viewed in a Catholic country, after he has turned Protestant, married, and, as they say, adopted very *philosophical* notions on these subjects. If they determine not to receive him, it is certainly a point which I shall not feel it in the least incumbent on me to press. In this case, rather than send the man home, I shall send him into Saxony, where there is no Government to object, and where there is a good deal doing which I should be glad to know." (*Cast. Corr.* IX, 106–7.)

2 The King of Wurtemberg's son, by his first wife, Augusta of Brunswick. He succeeded to the throne as William I upon his father's death in 1816. (1781–1864.)

3 The Prince Regent's daughter.

Stutgard, January 18th 1814.

[*Copy, in the Queen's handwriting.*]

HAVING been indisposed and obliged to keep my bed since I received your letter through Princess Paul, I could not answer it sooner as this is the first day I have been allowed to sit up for a few hours. I am obliged to you, dear Ernest, for your intended visit, but must for the present beg of you as a great favour to postpone it, till I write to invite you to come to Stutgard. There are many reasons which make me very anxious that you should defer our interview till quietter times. You would, dear brother, certainly be very much tired at Stutgard, the King's time of life and my bad health inducing us to lead a very quiet life which would little suit you and which is naturally duller this year as the King's two sons, Prince Royal and Prince Paul, are both absent. Pray be convinced, dear Ernest, that at some future period I shall be very happy to see you, but must now take my leave as I am still weak and remain with sincere regard & affection [etc.].

393 THE PRINCE REGENT *to* QUEEN CHARLOTTE

Carlton House, Jany 22d 1814.

ALTHOUGH I can have but very little to say that is either new or likely to interest you just now, & so soon after you have seen Bloomfield, who must have given you an account of all that has passed within his knowledge in that part of the Continent to which his journey was limmited, I can not resist taking up my pen now that I am able to do so, to thank you for your most kind letter, as well as for your most affectionate enquiries after my health, which is now thank God much improved. I have had a very disagreable & painful sore throat, that is now gone, & all that remains is still a pretty considerable degree of cold attended with some slight symptoms of lowness but which I hope to be able to shake off soon, indeed within a very few days. With regard to the visit to Studtgard which you seem to deprecate, as you say that it is much apprehended there, I can say but little as I have but little information upon that head, & I do most cordially agree with you in both hoping & wishing for manyfold reasons, such as you have assigned yourself, as well as for others, that it may not, & that it will not take place; & I have some reasons (which I will mention to you presently) for leading me to think that if the idea does exist, it is only in embryo & more as a matter of talk than of real intention, & *certainly not of desire* on his part, & that therefore in all probability it will, like all these sort of things of this nature, drop entirely to the ground, & if not revived, intermeddled, or interfered with by other persons who may chance at some unlucky moment or other to come across him, & to discuss & talk over the project with him; but then I cannot be answerable for the effects of this, nor for the strangeness nor the love of controversy one but too often meets with & witnesses in this world, in the different natures & dispositions of different men & different persons & indeed I may almost say of mankind in general. Now for my reasons. In the first place, in the very last letter which I received from him only a day or two ago he merely hints at such an intention & says "That *should* he think of making a visit at Studtgard, it would at the very earliest, only take place in the Spring". In a private letter also of the same date, to Thornton,[1] he mentions, also & merely vaguely, the same idea & nearly in the same words as he did to me; but to which he afterwards added, somewhat much stronger as testifying his extreme dislike to the thoughts of going there at all (& therefore it does seem as if the idea had suggested itself to him, merely as a matter of propriety, decency, & almost of absolute necessity, to put it in execution some time or other, & unavoidable in itself, from feeling himself on the Continent & therefore that it might be considered as an unnatural, at any rate a flagrant mark of inattention, negligence & want of interest & attention towards a sister who he had not seen, nor had any communication with, for such a number of years. He also adds in his letter to Thornton that before he takes any determination with respect to this visit, he must first wait to see the little Zemrwelgr (?), who had promised to come & see him either at Hannover or at Strelitz according to which of these places he should happen to be then momentarily residing, on his return from Studtgard, & that he must also previously know whether the Duke had as yet been recognized & acknowledged by us, as King of Wirtemberg, for if he had not, it would render his project of a journey there next to impossible, as it would be then under such circumstances & so replete with every kind of embarras & difficulty, that it would be infinitely better not to attempt it. I have now, my dearest mother, told you all I know upon this head, & my conclusion therefore is that we have not as yet received the positive confirmation & declaration from our Allies, that it is to say [*sic*] our present Allied Sovereigns that they have *actually* (though they may have virtually) agreed to the Duke of Wirtemberg's assuming the Christian name of King, & as in all probability it must & will be some time even yet before we can or shall receive

1 The Duke's Equerry.

this, formally & authentically, either from these different Courts, or even through Studtgard itself. Ernest will not think himself at liberty, according to this mode of reasoning & shaping of this business, as he has stated it, to put this project of a visit into execution, & will be too happy to have this or of any other excuse, to set it wholly aside, especially as we are well assured from all he has said & written upon the subject, he has no very lively wish or desire to put it in force.

Now with your leave I must advert to another topic, which is respecting a very kind letter which I received last night, & written by your command, from Eliza, touching the Princess Ulrica of Mecklenburg,[1] & which shall be instantly be put in effect, upon receiving your further commands; but which as the matter stands just now, I am afraid it would be attended with some difficulty, as to how to introduce in the Court Gazette, in a proper shape; for I cannot find that we have as yet in any of our offices receiv'd any formal notification of the event. But if you *have*, & that you will allow of its being thus introduc'd, "that Her Majesty having receiv'd the notification of the melancholy event of the death of her near relative the Pss Ulrica", proceeding on so & so, according to the usual terms & language in which these sort of events are notified by authority in the Court Gazette, previous to announcing a Court Mourning, it can & shall be announced without delay in the very first Gazette, and which I can have thus announced after having receiv'd your further directions; but I did not chuse to stir in it, nor to give any orders respecting, until I had stated this fact to you, & until I had receiv'd your final pleasure upon it.

You can not conceive how mortally I do hate this weather & how I shall rejoice when a thorough & confirmed change takes place, as I am all impatience to have the happiness of seeing you again, & as I live in the hopes that you may then be tempted to make the old metropolis a visit, at least for a few days, & take possession of this house, than whom, I do assure you, there is no one that can or that does look forward to that moment, with so much heartfelt pleasure & delight, as its possessor. Before I quite conclude (although you must long before this be quite tired to death of the sight of my most unwarrantable long & stupid griffonage) I can not resist, as I think it may make you & the dear sisterhood perhaps laugh for a moment (and you know, my dearest mother, that a laugh is not a matter to be dispised, especially at this season of the year, as it generally makes one shakes one's sides somewhat, & a little, & contributes in no small degree to make one warm, & is therefore

1 Princess Ulrica of Mecklenburg-Schwerin (1723–1814), the aunt of Frederick Francis I, Duke of Mecklenburg-Schwerin.

not an unwholesome sort of exercise, for it also contributes to excite & to promote a quicker circulation of the blood through the whole habit & system, a most excellent thing when or if one is a little benumb'd & torpid, & which is often the case in this excessive cold & severe weather) & I shall be the more pleas'd & flatter'd if it should prove to have this effect upon you all, because it is a little scrap of a bon mot of my own, & I take great credit to myself for my ingenuity in thinking of it & finding it out, & the only scruple I have in telling it you is the apprehension that it may blesser the very delicate feelings of my dear Eliza, as it is respecting a very great & first favourite & correspondent of hers.

Well now for it. It is a pun & a new nickname I have given our little dwarf.[1] I call him the TWENTY THIRD [*sic*] OF JUNE, & I now leave you to guess why? Pray do guess first, & do not let the impatience of your curiosity tempt you to turn over this page till you have first guessed all round a little.

This then is the explanation. What is the twenty third of June

Answer

The shortest night.

And sure there never yet was so short so diminutive a dwarf of a Knight, as this said little red dwarf of ours, & doubly now red also from the additional ribbon which now decorates the little person of his Kleine Excellence, by which name he has been received, recogniz'd, address'd, treated and travell'd through all the Courts of Germany. And I am so full of this idea and it has so completely seized hold of me respecting him, that I do assure you that I was very nearly tempted to get Sr. Everard Home[2] to go and borrow for me, out of Hunter's[3] Museum or repository, one of the large glass jars, of which there are hundreds there, containing one of the little embryos (ou peutêtre ce que l'on peut appeller aussi *fausse couche* sans se tromper beaucoup de nom) in order to tie a little bit of blue string round the neck of it, and then a little bit of red ribbon over its shoulder, and then to have sent it, as a cadeau to you to have ornamented the mantle peice o. the chimney of your sitting room, as the most exact and perfect resemblance and pourtraiture of our *little hero*, and far more I am sure, a thousand times over and over again,

---

1 Sir Thomas Tyrwhitt.

2 Sir Everard Home (1756–1832), the surgeon, and first President of the Royal College of Surgeons.

3 John Hunter (1728–1793), the surgeon and anatomist. His large museum was built in 1784–5, and his collections were bought by the nation and acquired by the College of Surgeons. His brother William (1718–1783) was Queen Charlotte's Physician Extraordinary (1764).

than any picture or painting that ever can, or that ever will be made or taken of him.

Now then adieu, my ever dearest mother, and forgive with your usual indulgence and kindness this momentary bit of farrago and nonsense, which, I am also asham'd to acknowledge, even whilst scribbling, has a visible effect upon the nervous system of my frame, which I cannot restrain. If it should fortunately have the same effect upon yours my end and purpose is answered and I shall be most happy.

P.S. No news whatever from the Continent either yesterday or today.

394 QUEEN CHARLOTTE *to the* PRINCE REGENT

Windsor, the 24th Janry 1814.

I MUST begin by thanking you for allowing Col. Bloomfield to come to Windsor. He was indeed an agreable visitor to all of us, & I rejoiced to hear him say that the Duke of Cumberland had behaved so reasonably and treated him with civility. Whether the Duke's visit to Wurtemberg will or will not be made, is by what you say very uncertain, still do I remain of the same oppinion that nothing should be named to him upon the subject, for a dislike already taken would be strengthened by it and the ceremonial manner of living at that Court will I am sure frighten him from going, and if there, hurry his departure. It is always in their power to stop his abuse of the E[mperor] of Russia by civily telling him that in their house they cannot allow such language, and I hope he has too much good breeding as to attempt offending in such a manner.

I am quite ashamed of the Duke of Mecklenbourg Schwerin's[1] inattention of not notifying to you the death of his aunt, & I would not wish by any means that you should act against the rule of putting on mourning without the proper notification. I think you will laugh when I tell you that my letter was written without a direction, & that it was quite by chance Mr. Hamilton[2] in the Foreign Office did find out who it was for. But my cousin was always very odd & was famous for acting contrary to what everybody else used to do.

I have received a letter from the Duke of Cumberland dated Strelitz.

1 Frederick Francis I, Duke (Grand Duke, 1815) of Mecklenburg-Schwerin (d. 1837). The Strelitz branch was the junior branch of the family.

2 William Richard Hamilton, Permanent Under-Secretary of State for Foreign Affairs, 1809–20; Minister at Naples, 1822–25. (1777–1859.)

I am sorry to say that he gives a very indifferent account of my brother Ernest who he says not only continues ill but is extreamly altered in looks since he left him, & very weak. I still hope that the Spring may hasten his recovery, tho' I will not deny that I fear the frequent returns of the gout in the stomach & head leave not much hope that he will gain strength sufficient to come over to England.

Your pun upon the little Zwerg we took some time to guess, but alas none could find it out, which I verily believe is owing to the cold, as really we can hardly keep ourselves warm, & Eliza bids me say *"that as you call the dwarf alias Sr T. Tyrwhytt the 21st [sic] of June if you dub him St. Thomas you will make him the shortest day.*[1] I do not think that he would be pleased with the liberty we take with his name if he could know it. I fear his Excellence will be afraid of travelling in this severe weather considering how sensible he is of having every comfort about him, which aboard he will not find. I am under great apprehensions that all his grandeur will be shriveld to nothing when he arrives & that he will become quite a mummy.

Mary received a letter from the Duke of Clarence this morning. He is in high spirits, delighted with his reception in Holland & anxious to join Sir T[homas] G[raham][2] & finishes with saying that his return is quite uncertain.

I hope to receive by Sr H[enry] H[alford] a good account of you. I regret much that the weather will not allow our meeting, but indeed it is both prudent & necessary to be carefull this severe season & of course you will be kind enough to follow this prescription of mine & not venture out to[o] soon.

I can add with truth that dear Augusta[3] is better & that Sophia has had two good nights, which is a happy circumstance, & God knows a blessing which seldom falls to her share. Below stairs everything goes on quietly. The Kg. feels the cold very much,[4] but he keeps very well & no further irritability is perceptible at present.

I fear that tho' my letter is long it is not entertaining & therefore the sooner it is finished the better. I will only add how sincerely I am jusqu'à la mort [etc.].

1 21 December is St Thomas's Day, but the shortest day is the 22nd.
2 General Sir Thomas Graham, Baron Lynedoch (1748–1843). He commanded the British force which, on 8 March, made an unsuccessful attempt to storm the fortress of Bergen-op-Zoom. Peerage, 1814.
3 Princess Augusta Sophia (1768–1840), the Prince Regent's sister.
4 It was one of the coldest Januaries on record, and the Thames was frozen over.

Carlton House, Jany 25th 1814.

I CAN not resist just scribbling one short line to offer you my most grateful thanks for the very kind & at the same time most beautiful mark of your kind remembrance & recollection, & I also send this express by one of my servants who, inclosed with it, will lay at your [feet] the accounts of the glorious & fortunate intelligence which has just reached us,[1] & for which as well as many other similar great events, within the course of the last twelvemonth, we have to offer up our unbounded thanks & praises to an all-bounteous Providence. I will not trespass upon you further at this moment than to assure you of the never ceasing devotion & attachment of, my dearest mother [etc.].

P.S. Pray do not trouble yourself to answer this, & therefore I have told my servant not to wait, as there was no answer required.

395 MISS MARGARET MERCER ELPHINSTONE *to* PRINCESS CHARLOTTE

Plymouth Dock, Janry 28th [1814].

I HAVE just received the enclosed letter[2] from Spain, wh I confess is by no means satisfactory to me, as he does not seem at all disposed to comply with the request which was repeated in my last letter, even if he had not received my former one. Fortunately I kept a copy of the first letter, which I shall certainly send for his perusal, and also add a few lines, urging the necessity of his attending strictly to the wishes your R.H. had expressed thro' me. The paragraph in which he says he has never received any letters which mentioned the subject, since Y.R.H's of the 10th of August seems to me very singular, as certainly I understood from Yr.R.H. that the Princess[3] had written to him, and received answers from him relating to it, within a few weeks. As to the nonsense of the trunk being thrown into the Thames, it by no means pleases me, as it is very uncertain, whether or not the contents might be destroyed, or into what hands they might fall. With regard to *those papers of value to him alone*, I should wish it to be explained whether he alludes to letters of your Royal Highness or if they are all already destroyed. I shd think it must be of them he speaks, for of course, papers on business, or of consequence to his family, he would never wish to have thus destroyed. As to

1 A London Gazette Extraordinary, of the 25th, announced that a peace treaty had been concluded at Kiel between Great Britain and Denmark.

2 No. 387.   3 The Princess of Wales.

the other things, I am sure there is a greater chance of their being conveyed to me safely, *before his death than after it*, which opinion I shall endeavour to *insinuate as delicately* to him as possible, as I think under your present circumstances it is more necessary than ever to be absolute about having every thing returned immediately, and I must confess this shuffling letter does not make me more lenient, with respect to his conduct, throughout the whole affair. At all events, if he cannot allow this trunk to be opened at present, we may at least exact a promise of him to return the letters the moment he comes home, or that they shd be delivered to my father, or ordered to be destroyed before him, in case of his death.

If your Royal Highness likes it, or that you think it will have greater weight, I can make my father write to him, and represent the danger and folly of his conduct. We have found Sir George Collier's letter to my father acknowledging having received my first epistle wh was enclosed to him, and wh he says *he immediately forwarded by a safe conveyance to the Army.* [The rest is missing.]

396 MISS MARGARET MERCER ELPHINSTONE *to* CAPTAIN HESSE

[*Copy*, No. 3.] *Plymouth Dock*, Feby 4th 1814.

I HAVE just received your letter, dated the 12th of Jany and it is with great regret I learn that mine written in Octr should not have reached you. My father sent it to Passages with his official dispatches, and Sir G. Collier assured him, that it had been immediately forwarded by a safe conveyance to the Army. However, I now have the honor of enclosing a copy of it, for your perusal, and I trust you will no longer delay complying with the request, which has been already but too often expressed, and return without loss of time, all the letters or presents you may now have with you.

If the parcel is sent to Admiral Penrose[1] at Passages, directed to Lord Keith, Govt. House, Plymouth Dock, there cannot be a doubt of its safety. Should it be *quite impossible* for you to allow the trunk to be opened during your absence, I am desired to say that a promise of their being restored the moment you return to this country will be accepted, but it is also expected, that in case of any accident, a written order may be given for their being immediately delivered into Lord Keith's hands, as the mode you propose of their being destroyed, is by no means

1 Vice-Admiral Sir Charles Vinicombe Penrose (1759–1830), who commanded the ships off the French and Spanish coasts, co-operating with the British army in the Peninsula.

satisfactory. I must also beg that you will answer upon your word and honor, whether any of the letters that passed before you left England are in existence, or if they were burnt, according to the agreement that was made, when the correspondance commenced. From myself, I cannot forbear adding a few words, to entreat that you will no longer trifle with feelings which ought to be both respected and admired, by any unnecessary delay in your compliance with my request, that you will consider the youth and inexperience of the person alluded to, at the time she entered into this unfortunate correspondence, and the anxiety she has since suffered from apprehension of its being known. To her, such a discovery would signify little, were all the circumstances of the case fully investigated, but to others, the consequences might be most unpleasant, and this idea, I assure you, dwells deeply upon her mind, as well as the certain ruin it would be to your views of advancement in your profession.

At the same time, neither of these considerations (tho' she feels them both most sensibly) will prevent her from informing her father of the whole transaction, should this letter not have the desired effect of inducing you to give up every trace that now remains in your possession of what has passed.

397 THE DUKE OF CAMBRIDGE *to the* PRINCE REGENT

Hanover, Feby 4th. 1814.

I CANNOT let the messenger set off without writing you a few lines to request you will have the goodness to take care of the enclosed. The death of poor uncle Ernest[1] will I am sure affect you, and I regret the unpleasant task you will have to break it to the Queen. The Duke and Ernest[2] assure me that he died perfectly easy, which is at least a great comfort.

From the accounts I had received from Strelitz ever since I have been at Hanover I did not expect to hear so soon of his death, though I doubted of his recovery, and I therefore was much struck at the arrival of the messenger.

The Prince Royal of Sweden is here and remains I believe till Sunday, the day after tomorrow. He is remarkably well bred and pleasing in his manners and our different interviews have gone off very well. On Sunday I mean to send a servant to England when I shall write more at length. The messenger is anxious to get off....

1 Prince Ernest of Mecklenburg-Strelitz.
2 The Duke of Mecklenburg-Strelitz and his nephew the Duke of Cumberland.

Stutgard, February 6th, 1814.

I BEG that you will accept of my warmest congratulations on the glorious victory of Brienne,[1] which the Allied Armies have gained over Emperor Napoleon, and of which the King has just received the account by a messenger. The French have lost seventy five peices of canon and the Emperor has retreated with the remains of his Army towards Troyes.

I do not doubt, dear brother, that Lord Cathcart will have given you all the particulars of this wonderful event, but I think it a duty to impart what I know on the subject, and to express to you the joy I feel at seeing your enterprizes crowned with success, and I have a double cause for satisfaction and gratitude to Providence as my son the Prince Royal has again distinguished himself, first by a skirmish in a wood, and secondly by taking a difficult post which he attacked at the head of the Württemberg troops. The Emperor of Russia gave him the St. George's Order of the 1st Class on the field of battle. Our troops have taken seven peices of canon which I am very proud of.

I will now my dear brother only add the King's compliments and beg of you to be convinced of the sincere affection with which I remain, [etc.].

399 The Duke of Cambridge *to the* Prince Regent

Hanover, Feby 8th 1814.

AFTER having written to you an official letter to inform you of what has been done in our military arrangements since last month, I take up my pen to write you a few lines to assure you that we really are getting on here, and that I do begin to hope I am of some use. I really feel much more comfortable, and provided I hear that you are satisfied with what has been done, I shall be happy.

In my last I mentioned having had a visit from the Crown Prince of Sweden. I am sure you would be delighted with his manners and gratified by his conversation. He has a wonderful memory and speaks remarkably well. The last morning I saw him he talked about Monsieur's[2] arrival on the Continent and said that he was decidedly for the Bourbons, though he did not dare say so to the Swedes, and, provided that a limited monarchy was established in France, he should be glad to see them again

1 On 1 February.
2 Louis XVIII's brother, afterwards Charles X (1757–1836).

on the throne. That Austria would be against this arrangement, but that he did not doubt that Russia and Sweden would side with England. This is the conversation which passed, and I have thought it my duty to inform you of it. I can not see into his heart and therefore do not answer that he feels what he said but his manner was compleatly that of a man convinced of the truth of what he is saying. He spoke very highly of you, my dearest brother, & has expressed himself flattered at the reception he has met with at Hanover. We certainly parted very good friends and he was pleased at my offering that Mr. de Hammerstein should accompany him, whom he praised very much. It is absolutely necessary that somebody should be attached to the Head Quarters of the Prince Royal to give us information of what is going on, and Hammerstein has hitherto made such very sensible reports ever since he has been there that I have insisted on his remaining, & the Prince Royal has taken it as a compliment.

I seize this opportunity of recommending most strongly to you, my dearest brother, General Decken,[1] who really has worked beyond what I had a right to expect ever since he has been here, & it is to his indefatigable exertions that we have got things into some order. I venture to propose to you his having the local rank & appointments of British Lieutenant General. Charles Steward[2] [*sic*] has got it and Decken is a much older Major General. I must add that he is not aware of my having made this application; but I do assure you he deserves it.

Wallmoden is in much better spirits. He is to follow the Prince Royal in a fortnight with the Russian German Legion, and as soon as he gets to the Rhine the Mecklenberg troops are to be added to his command. I hope in a short time after that to be able to send two Brigades of Hanoverians under Legon & I trust the Landwehr will be sufficiently exercised to relieve them. Wallmoden has given [me] the enclosed, which I forward with this letter, as it is *private*. He is delighted with the honour you have given him. The others all went off on Monday for Francfortt, & I have written to Blucher & Gneisenau[3] to send for them from thence. Your three stable servants set off today with my jager strauss who will deliver this.

I enclose the last bulletin of Bennigsen[4] which I have just received.

Before I conclude I must beg you to send me a Houssard sabre which

1 The Hanoverian Minister.
2 Sir Charles Stewart. He was a soldier before his brother gave him the appointment of Ambassador to Prussia. Entering the Army in 1794 he rose to the rank of Major-General in 1810.
3 Blücher's Chief of Staff in the Waterloo campaign. (1760–1831.)
4 The Russian General.

everybody wears on the Continent, and your taste is so good that I am sure it will be perfect and pray add a belt to it.

I am very glad to hear that Bloomfield is arrived and I hope you have got all the things which he was to take for you. Tommy[1] will by this time I hope be in England. If he is pray remember me to His Excellency.

Now my dearest brother God bless you and believe me [etc.].

400 THE HEREDITARY PRINCE OF ORANGE *to the* PRINCE REGENT

The Hague, February 9th, 1814.

HAVING to-day received the intelligence of Blucher's last victory over Bonaparte himself near Brienne, which is said to have been a most complete and decisive one in which 60 pieces of cannon have been taken, I hasten to wish your Royal Highness joy with so important an event, which seems to have been the last struggle this once so powerfull man has been able to make, and which we will hope may soon be follow'd by a general and durable peace so necessary to all countries and all nations, and for which I in particular wish for, since thereby the happy moment at which I shall be allow'd to call your Royal Highness father should become less distant.

I here take the liberty to enclose a letter to Princess Charlotte, beging your Royal Highness to be assured of the sentiments of sincere respect and attachment with which I have the honor to remain, [etc.].

401 SIR ROBERT BARCLAY[2] *to* COLONEL MCMAHON

Mauritius, 12th Feby 1814.

ALL your unabated kindness, friendship and favour to your unfortunate friend had *nearly* been lost *for ever*. After a very tedious, but *favorable* voyage to these colonies I was, (from ignorance & incapacity of the Captain of the Roxsburgh Castle) WRECKED on the coast of this Island in the night of the 30th of last month.

Fortunately & miraculously we have saved our lives. Not a soul perished, owing to the vigilance of the fishing boats, & the kind, benevolent humanity and exertion of our excellent Governor,[3] and also of my

---

1 Sir Thomas Tyrwhitt.   2 See No. 161.
3 Sir Robert Townsend Farquhar.

relation, the Commander in Chief of H.M. troops in this colony, Sir Alexander Campbell.

I enter into no particulars; we are safe, thanks to Divine Providence. My daughter (who is yet in bed at Lady Campbell's) behaved like a heroine at the fatal moment. My beloved wife will explain to Mrs. McMahon all the particulars of this dreadful catastrophe. I will not affect you now or at any time by the relation of it: I will endeavour to forget every circumstance attending this sad affliction; my health & spirits require I should do so for the sake of my unhappy wife & children, alas! I have left behind. We had but just time to save ourselves from our beds when the ship struck on the *coral* banks. Judge of my distress: I have lost nearly the *whole* of my valuable effects, in fact all the comforts that I had (*with great economy & expence scraped* together in London. If I know the heart & kindness of our worthy Governor (from what I have already experienced from him,) he is doing all in his power by his dispatches *this day* to Engd. to request the favor of Lord Bathurst to afford me some relief by way of *immediate* remuneration for my very heavy loss.

I have myself written to Mr. Goulbourne [1] the Under-Secty of State to lay my deplorable case before Lord Bathurst. His Lordship was even disposed at the moment of my departure from Engd to listen to my last application to him, & that was, to allow me an additional salary of £500 pr an for house rent &c. I stand in need greatly of this, from the pre-posterous high price of rents & every article of subsistence in these colonies; but this, I leave to the breast of Lord Bathurst to admit or refuse. My *present* application is the most pressing, I know, & have the long experience of your heart & kindness, & that you will through the benevolent recommendation of my illustrious patron H:R:H: the Prince Regent do all in your power to forward my *own* & *Governor Farquhar's* application now made to Ld Bathurst, viz. if his Lordship would kindly admit that my *salary* & per *centage* of my office to commence from *the day* of my appointment in England, in lieu from the day of my arrival here, it will nearly cover the expence of my heavy loss.

I have the satisfaction to inform you that my publick situation here is the most responsible & the most laborious of any in the colony, but I have entered into it with spirit, to fulfil the intentions of Lord Bathurst which his Lordship has been pleased to express in his dispatches to our excel-lent Governor, of my capacity & abilities to perform my important duties. They shall not be disappointed; nor above all, (if I have life &

1 Henry Goulburn (1784–1856). Under-Secretary for War and the Colonies, 1812–21; afterwards Chancellor of the Exchequer and Home Secretary.

health,) I will not discredit the illustrious patronage that I have so generously & graciously received from H:R:Hs; and sure I am, that I will endeavour to merit the distinguished friendship you have always so warmly & so *effectively* shewn to; [etc.].

P.S. My warmest regards & affection attend your amiable lady. Her commission in favor of Lt. Col. Leiseck will be attended to, if *I have any power on this Island.*

402 THE QUEEN OF WURTEMBERG *to* SIR THOMAS TYRWHITT

Stutgard, February 15th. 1814.

AFTER the polite interest you were so obliging as to shew touching everything that regards me, it appears to me but right to mention to you that the King, as soon as he had read Lord Castlereagh's handsome answer to Count de Zeppelin's letter, began to look out for a proper person to be named Minister to the Court of St. James's, and having been so good as to converse with me on the subject, I mentioned that it was your opinion that the most agreeable choice for the Prince Regent would be a military man; this induced the King to name General Count de Beroldingen, whom I once spoke of to you. He is one of the King's Aide de Camps Generaux and son to the Württemberg Minister at Vienna. I hope this gentleman will visit the Prince, as he has seen a great deal of service, lived much in the world, having been both at Paris and Vienna, and will be able if at any time it amuses my brother to give him some accounts of the late campaigns. I recommend him to you, Sr Thomas, and shall be much obliged to you for any attentions you can shew him.

Count Beroldingen will be in England about the end of March; and I suppose that soon after his arrival the Prince Regent will think of sending a Minister here. I therefore beg, Sir Thomas, you will be so obliging as to recollect everything that I said to you on this subject; and how important it would be for me to have this choice fall on a sensible quiet man, particularly as the King will allow me to invite sometimes the English Minister to spend an hour in my closet of an afternoon. Knowing my brother's great affection for me I am sure that he will not be displeased at your entering into these particulars, and that he will think of a suitable gentleman for this place; and not allow of any persons being named here who might again occasion me as much vexation & distress as Mr. Spencer Smith.[1] I hope, Sir Thomas, you will forgive my giving

1 Envoy Extraordinary to Wurtemberg, February to April 1804.

you so much trouble, but I know too well how sincerely you wish to have a good understanding kept up between every branch of the Royal family, not to be convinced that you will do everything in your power to have this settled to my satisfaction.

Pray do not forget to send me your direction and believe me [etc.].

403 THE DUKE OF CUMBERLAND *to the* PRINCE REGENT

Strelitz, Feby 17th 1814.

THOUGH I have litterally nothing worth writing about still I cannot let another post day pass without recalling myself to your recollection, for though idle, though unacquainted with what is going on in the great world I cannot but feel most anxious about all that regards you. The last victory of the Allies under Blucher at Brienne I hope will give Boney his coup de grâce and that by this time the Army may have arrived at Paris. I own my joy is great that *Blucher* was *the man*, for I wish *our* nation to feel *all* the Prussians have done this campaign, their exertions have kept pace with their gallantry, and a man must again feel himself proud to be an officer in that service, when I reflect upon all that country has done, when I consider how dreadfully low it was this time last year, & now for the things they have done & are doing, it vexes me to hear the nonsense talked by others, of the impossibility of finding *the means*. Gracious God, what means had Prussia in the first onset? a ruined country, the enemy masters of the greater part, their Army such as it was almost annihilated, & yet in less than six months they brought into the field a corps of 247,000 men. If the *will* is but there, the *means* will soon be found, and this I felt so strongly sometime back, and I took the liberty of offering these sentiments most publickly. I hope to God you will see the King,[1] the more you see of him, the more you will like him, he is not at first so prévenant as Alexander, but depend upon it on the nearer acquaintance with him you will prefer him. I do trust in God I shall have the happiness of seeing you dearest brother this summer here on the Continent, a master's eye is at all times necessary, but certainly the eye of such a one as yours is, must be, beneficial and if I *dare offer* an opinion, which I do from the *bottom* of my *soul*, it is *not* to name any new Minister till you yourself have been at Hanover to see & judge if the person recommended to you is worthy of that high confidential situation. *Excuse* my

1 Frederick William III.

saying this, but amor patriae leads me to do it; and little things that have come to my ears induce me to be so *bold* to *say this*.

I meant to have left this as last Monday and had given directions for a house to be taken for me at Berlin, but my uncle[1] has pressed me to stay till the birthdays of the Princesses are over which will be in the course of next month & then I shall start for Berlin, when I shall be most happy to execute any commissions for you either in the chabraque way or uniforms.

I understand from Thornton[2] that Ben Bloomfield is arrived, he will amuse you with his acct of all he has seen, & I should think that his honour will not be amiss for the good cheer of Woiteir[3] & Benoit's[4] hot jellies most capital in this cold weather. God bless you and think sometimes of [etc.].

[P.S.] Pray make Bloomfield *write* and let me know if *all* I have sent has reached you.

404 THE DUKE OF CAMBRIDGE *to the* PRINCE REGENT

Hanover, Feby 23d 1814.

HAVING been informed yesterday by a letter from Munster of the plans the Prussian Cabinet has of increasing its territory at the expense of the Electorate by asking for the Duchy of Lauemburg [*sic*] and some part of the principality of Göttingen, I have thought it my duty to send the enclosed Memoir to Munster which I have desired him to give Lord Castlereagh.

The Duchy of Lauenburg has shown so much patriotism & attachment to its lawful Sovereign at the time the Russians and Prussians advanced last year to the Elbe, & they have always been so loyal a people that I am confident for that reason alone you, my dearest brother, would not give your consent to give up that Province. Besides I know your wish to act as the King would have done, and I am certain he never would have been persuaded to any such concession. These considerations would make me feel perfectly easy on the subject, but as England has also a great interest in the preservation of Hamburgh, which would suffer very much from the neighbourhood of Prussia, as was the case with Dantzic, I thought it right to draw Lord Castlereagh's attention to this point and to the general politics of Prussia with respect to Germany. I of course have

---

1 The Duke of Mecklenburg-Strelitz.   2 The Duke's equerry.
3 Watier. See No. 380.   4 The Prince Regent's *pâtissier*.

consulted with the Hanoverian Ministers who are fully of my opinion, and have approved of the Memoir which I have forwarded by a messenger to Munster and which I trust you will also approve of.

Our military arrangements are going on as well as it is in our power; several batallions of militia will assemble for exercise on the 1st of next month, but the frost prevents the clothing arriving from England and till then it is impossible for them to be fit for active service.

I am going tomorrow to Bremen to see the Russian German Legion & the jagers which are on their march for the Rhine.

General Bennigsen on the 17th inst. drove the French from the Island of Wilhelmsburg and destroyed the communication with Harburg. General Tolstoy with his Division occupied it and I trust that the bridge wich has been made on the Hamburgh side may by this time be destroyed. General Bennigsen was prevented doing this on the 17th from want of combustibles. I doubt though that the Russians will be able to keep it if the French should attack them in force.

I dare not now detain you any longer than to assure you, my dearest brother, that I shall ever remain [etc.].

405 THE EARL OF MOIRA *to* COLONEL MCMAHON

Calcutta, Feby. 26th 1814.

WE have seen in the English papers a curious statement of Lady Popham's[1] (for it is assuredly her's) respecting the entertainment of my party aboard the Stirling Castle. To color the enormity of the demand for our passage, it is represented that we were ten in the cabin mess & eight at another table. The numbers are accurate: but the eight were so far from being included in the charge of £6000 that their messing was paid either by me or by themselves to the officers with whom they lived. For our my [*sic*] servants I was obliged to lay in stores separately, nothing but ship provisions being allowed to them by Sir Home.

I am vexed that any thing should ever have been said on the subject. I am not surprised at it, however, as I well know whence the attack on him came. He took care to irritate deeply the Consul & the Captain of a Sloop of War in which the Consul was to sail for England just after our departure: And I was told at Madeira of a cutting sarcasm uttered to Sir Home by that Captain in public company on the very topic of his behaviour to our servants. The slightest shade of dis-satisfaction was never

1 The wife of Rear-Admiral Sir Home Riggs Popham.

testified by Ly Loudoun or any of us. In truth, the coloring which he gave to very indifferent provision for us made it only laughable. We employed a college cook who was going to seek his fortunes in India. Now, beyond roasting & boiling a college cook has less chance of skill than any of his profession: but for the honor of the table we were always to have three or four made dishes, & they were ordinarily most comical. Common prize wines were given us for hermitage, claret, &c; and, that it might be said champagne was used at the table, towards the close of our voyage some of the saddest frothing stuff that ever came from Cooper's Gardens was produced. Just three times on the passage did he give us a bottle of old Madeira, an injudicious liberality, as it served for a standard by which we might rate our every-day wine. Of this, it is now necessary I should put you in possession. The desire of wounding him may occasion others (as he is unfortunate about exciting people to lash at him) to use us [as] the means of wreaking their ill-will; and her ladyship would not mind being poetic in her defence. The insufficiency of the provision was regarded by us all with sincere indulgence as arising from the pecuniary difficulties under which we knew him to labor; & the ostentation which accompanied it never gave rise to any thing but a good-humored smile.

His character is so freakish & his temper so little under command, that there were two or three occasions on which it was necessary to bring him quietly to recollection. This, however, was done steadily & without any thing like altercation. When he had once acknowledged himself in the wrong all remembrance of the circumstance was banished from our minds. We made it a point to show him every civility here, & made him take up his quarters in the Government House instead of occupying apartments in the house appropriated to naval officers. His expenses for us aboard could on no calculation have amounted to £2000. When wine & water was drank in our cabins, it was from a stock which I purchased for the purpose, on seeing the tone of things, at Madeira, & kept in our own locker. This is for yourself alone, & is only confided to you as a precaution against misrepresentation. I should grieve to have Sir Home placed in an unfavorable light, because, with all those injudicious tricks by which he has entailed a host of enemies on himself, there is essential good in him. He has great professional skill, much readiness of resource, & indefatigable activity in working on any subject which attracts his fancy. Material advantage may be drawn from the observations he has treasured up wherever he has been & from his suggestions on most points of service.

Sir G. Nugent has told several of his friends that he will go home in November next. The Directors cannot possibly think of sending out any other Commander of the Forces, who cannot but clash in many points with the Commr in Chief. A Lieut. General, with a dormant commission for the contingency of my death, is the only rational arrangement. In the meantime, there will be a seat in Council to be filled in the room of Sir George. Every interest should be made by Adam & his friends to secure it for John Adam,[1] Secretary in the Political Department. He is an uncommonly able & judicious man; tho' in truth he has two competitors, Dowdeswell & Ricketts, of high rate of talent as well as of excellent character. Adam is peculiarly modest & unassuming. With all my wishes for him, should I be forced to nominate provisionally, I must of necessity advance Dowdeswell to the Council; for he is the Chief Secretary, & his ability would not allow *me* to pass him over. The Directors, not being on the spot, have no such shackle on their selection; and it is understood that it must be an affair of interest with them. An overland dispatch (well worth the while) would bring to me their decision in due time.

We all continue well. The heat has come upon us again, & is more considerable than is usual so early in the year. Poor Sir W: Keir, buoyed up with the hope of remaining here on the staff is in deep mortification at his disappointment; & I am no less so. The expense of the passage home would be very heavy on him. He waits a little for chances.

406 THE QUEEN OF WURTEMBERG *to* SIR THOMAS TYRWHITT

Stutgard, February 28th 1814.

I FLATTER myself that by this time you are safely arrived in England and recovered all the fatigues of your journey, which I trust was the case before you went to Windsor, knowing that the Queen and my sisters intend to question you very closely concerning Stutgard and its inhabitants. God grant that you may have found my dear brother and the whole family in good health.

I had not intended troubling you with a letter till Count de Beroldingen's departure, but the imprudent behaviour of le Chevalier Horn[2] obliges me to have recourse to you, Sir Thomas, and beg you will speak to the Prince on this very unpleasant subject. I hope you have received my letter of 18th ultimate in which I mentioned the arrival of this gentleman at Stuttgard, his boasting of his influence with the British Ministry

1 (1779–1825.) Son of William Adam, the Prince Regent's friend and legal adviser. Acting Governor-General of Bengal in 1823, between the departure of Lord Hastings and the arrival of Lord Amherst.

2 See No. 391.

and the strange manner in which, after pretending he expected several English messengers from Headquarters, he sent his letters by an Austrian officer. All this united to his sending frequent expresses to Lord Aberdeen and Castlereagh gave me much uneasiness; but now he has taken a house out of the town of Stutgard and boasts of a promise to be named Minister either here or at Ratisbonne; however he appears to think himself certain of remaining here, as after having spent above two months at the inn, he has hired an expensive house and garden. His being a sort of spy, and having been a Catholick if not a priest would make him very unpleasant to me, particularly as he has been wanting in respect to the King, never having sought to be presented since he is here and in addition to all this Mr. George Rose,[1] I know, has a bad opinion of him, saying he is an intriguing man who has sought to be employed but that he is a spy to both parties, and that the Ministry have avoided having any connection with him, while on the other hand Sr Horn has shewn some persons Lord Castlereagh's signature, and boasts of being in the secrets of the Cabinet.

You know too well, Sir Thomas, how much I have suffered from Mr. Smith's imprudent conduct not to wish me to be spared this fresh trial.[2] Pray speak to my brother and explain to him how much my happiness would be undermined by such a man being allowed to appear here.

This afternoon I shall write you a longer letter by express and therefore will only add that I am [etc.].

407 THE QUEEN OF WURTEMBERG *to* SIR THOMAS TYRWHITT

Stutgard, March 1st 1814.

I FEAR that you will think me very indiscreet to trouble you so often with letters, but at this moment such a variety of subjects give me cause for uneasiness that I trust to your known politeness and therefore have recourse to you, who I hope are above three weeks safely arrived in England and have been able to answer the ten thousand questions which I am sure my beloved relations will have put to you concerning Stutgard and its inhabitants. I trust that you found the Prince and the whole family in good health; poor Sophia I understand is recovering of a billious fever which is a sad complaint for any body that is naturally so weak as my sister; But though very anxious about Sophia I am doubly

1 Sir George Henry Rose (1771–1855). Envoy Extraordinary and Minister Plenipotentiary to Bavaria, 1814–15.
2 See No. 402.

so about the Queen who I fear will have been sadly affected by the melancholy news of the death of her brother Prince Ernest of Mecklenbourg. You formed, Sir, a very just judgement of his situation which however did not confine him long to his house and it was only the last three days he kept his bed. He did not to the last give up the hopes of going to England, flattering himself in April or May to be strong enough to undertake the journey. This will add to the Queen's sorrow as she looked on his arrival at Windsor as quite certain. At my mother's time of life every thing is to be feared. I am sure that the dear Prince will have shewn her great duty and affection in breaking this news to her. I understand that Ernest[1] more attentive than usual sent a messenger to the Prince to acquaint him with this event. Ernest has answered me a very kind letter and does not, thank God, appear to be either astonished or displeased at what I wrote. Prince Solms has consented to be divorced from his Princess, and it is said that the King of Prussia intends to have this divorce take place in his Kingdom, as the Duke of Mecklenbourg does not wish his Church to proclaim it. The children are all to remain with their mother. In less than three weeks you will see the Great Dutchess Catherine in England; she is a charming woman and am sure will be liked by all. But pray desire the whole family to pay her a little court: she is a great favourite of her brother the Emperor of Russia and has great weight with him. At Vienna the Emperess[2] received her at the door of her bedchamber and lead her into her private apartment where they remained sometime before she went into the drawingroom where the ladies or rather the Court was assembled. I mention these trifles which are of more consequence than one thinks of in England. Pray entreat the Prince to do every thing he can to make her like England as I am sure she wishes us all well and has great influence[3]—After having spoken on all these subjects which are more or less interesting I must enter on one which causes me much uneasiness—I mean le Chevalier Horn who I mentioned to you in my letter of 18 January. He continues at Stutgard, has left the inn he has resided in since the 8th or 9th of December and hired a house which you will remember just out of the town with a pretty garden, and boasts that he is to be appointed Minister to our Court.[4] God forbid that such a very unfortunate choice should be made. He is certainly a very intriguing man, always sending expresses to Head Quarters, though it does not appear that he ever receives

1 The Duke of Cumberland.   2 Maria Louisa.

3 Castlereagh had already, on 30 January, written to the Prince Regent, informing him that the Tsar and his sister, the Grand Duchess Catherine, were desirous of visiting England. (*Cast. Corr.* IX, 210.)

4 I.e. by the British Government. See Nos. 391, 406.

answers.—I have already mentioned his history to you but least you should have lost the letter will mention it anew. Some say that he was a priest or a monk, all that he was formerly a Catholick but whether of Scotch or Irish extraction nobody can tell; during the unhappy times of Smith[1] and Drake[2] he was one of those who acted a part. Was sought for by the French as a spy while he was concealed in a convent at Ratisbonne where he spent near eighteen months afterwards he was hid in the same town by an old Mademoiselle de Gumpenberg he has since married. All this would be very indifferent to me who never interfere in what does not regard me, had he not given himself a very suspicious appearance here. By sending express's to Head Quarters and sending cards without asking to be presented on which he takes the title of Le Chevalier Horn sur service de sa Majesté Britanique. Had he at least had the good sense to address himself to one of the King of Württemberg's Ministers, and had mentioned his being an Englishman who had orders to stay at Stutgard for to forwards the correspondence with the Army, he would have been known and treated with the attention due to an English agent, but instead of this easy line of conduct he goes almost every day to the Accademie, one of the buildings which belong to the King, for to see Madame de Leuthe; and refused to attend to those who have told him that he placed himself in a strange light by not being introduced at Court while he was constantly so near the Palace. One moment he boasts of his influence in England, giving all to understand that he is a man of great consequence and as if he had the Treasury at his disposal, allowing himself to say, I know every body complains in Württemberg of the expence of the war, but that is the Queen's fault; why does not she say one word and then England will send money, as we only wish to grant supplies to all who apply for subsidies to carry on the war. At other times he says the Ministry have sent him here that he may inform them how far the toleration of the various Christian religions are allowed in Württemberg and by what Laws the Church is governed—By this strange conduct and his boasting of his influence in the British Cabinet he has found means to draw on himself the attention of every body. However the King, out of affection for me, as this Sr Horn says he is an Englishman, took no notice of all his imprudences, till he begun saying that he had the promise of being named Minister either at Ratisbonne or Stutgard. This was followed by his taking a house and assuring he should very soon be presented as English Minister. Besides which though he did not read the

1 See Nos. 402, 406.
2 Francis Drake, Envoy Extraordinary at Munich, 1800–2; Minister Plenipotentiary at Munich, 1802–4.

contents of a letter, he shewed Lord Castlereagh's signature. On this I begged the King to order his Minister at Munich to apply to Mr Rose to know what confidence ought to be placed in Sir Horn's words. He let us know that he was an intriguing man who was known to be a spy to both parties and that the Ministers avoided having any connection with him. This being the case, as I wish always to avoid every thing which can give the smallest cause of uneasiness I wrote to my brother and begged of him not to allow this gentleman to be accredited here and have also acquainted Lord Castlereagh with the very equivocal character he bears, in these parts of the world.—I suspect he was concerned in the famous story I told you, Sir Thomas, of 1807.—He pretends to be well known to the King, to have been frequently admitted in private in his library and to have talked confidentially with him, as also to have been consulted about scarce books. He speaks of the kind manner in which all the Princes behave towards him and is in constant correspondence with the Duke of Brunswick.[1]

I who am most sincerely attached to my country cannot tell you how I am grieved at the mistaken idea which the Government have of late years adopted in England, and which is so contrary to the open honest character of Englishmen. I mean the number of secret agents that are employed; they are much dearer than a common spy and really only serve to diminish the influence Great Britain would otherwise have on the Continent, as they awaken suspicions and alarm the smaller Sovereigns who dread being drawn into a dangerous scrape. Forgive my speaking so openly, Sir Thomas, but it is a duty for every Englishman or woman to say the truth on a subject which has already done Great Britain so much mischief; these secret agents seek to distinguish themselves, and form one plan more absurd than the other; which foreigners not considering them as intriguing members of society suppose to be owing to the orders they have received from Government and of course dread the having any connection with people who seem always to have some secret views. Within three months, three of these agents have drawn upon themselves the attention of different Governments, and been obliged to leave the towns they resided in. A Mr. Wills in Switzerland, a physician and other soi dissant gentleman at Vienna. It is even

1 Castlereagh wrote to Horn on 6 February: "As, in the present state of the Continent, the Prince Regent is enabled to re-establish a regular diplomatic intercourse with the different States, I am to acquaint you that his Royal Highness has no further occasion for the services of persons not regularly accredited. I cannot, however, make this communication to you without adding the expression of my entire satisfaction with the zeal and activity which you have uniformly displayed in the discharge of the several duties which have been entrusted to you." (*Cast. Corr.* IX, 243.)

rumoured there has been something of the same kind at Petersbourg.—
What makes me the most unhappy is that when I seek to avoid all connection with these adventurers they are so good as to amuse themselves
by seeking to render my attachment to my family and country doubtful,
which is as you well know, Sir Thomas, a very wicked calumny. But
when they cannot draw one into their schemes they seek to revenge themselves and destroy the reputation of those who resist their wiles.

2ᵈ Having yesterday too violent a headach to finish my letter I intended this morning to conclude it and was just taking up my pen, when
I received two letters from England which Count de Zeppelin sent me,
at the same [time] acquainting me that they had been directed to le
Chevalier de Horn. This gentleman I understand received yesterday
evening an express from Ratisbonne sent by Mr. David Horn and
directed au Chevalier de Horn Chargé d'Affaires de sa Majesté Britanique.
You will easily imagine how this distresses me. The King on being
apprized of this sent for Count de Taube, the Minister who has the
direction of the Police, and ordered him to have Sⁱʳ Horn's passport
examined it is signed by Sir Charles Steward [*sic*] and in it he is called
an Agent Diplomatique de sa Majesté Britanique en Allemagne. As he
has never sought to make himself known under that title here, the King
has desired Count Taube to ask him to whom he is accredited. You will
Sir Thomas easily believe this wears me to death pray assist me in getting rid of this odious business and join with me to beg the Prince to
name a proper reasonable Minister. You cannot think how this Sʳ Horn
by his imprudent conversation has tormented me ever since he has been
here, and I am sure my brother is too good not to be angry at my being
plagued for nothing. If they want a gentleman spy in the South of
Germany, which is however quite contrary to my opinion, do engage the
Ministers to send him some where else: it is really improper a man of so
equivocal a character should reside at Stutgard and is the source of much
uneasiness to all parties.—I have so indifferent an opinion of him that
should he unfortunately be accredited here before I receive an answer
from my brother, that I shall beg the King to delay receiving him till we
have letters from England—He is too violent for it to be safe, if peace is
once made, for him to be at Stutgard, as by his imprudent conversation
he would get me into fifty scrapes and I could not bear to see England
represented by an ex monk.—I am afraid you will be tired to death of
this volume but I have too much at heart the good understanding of those
that are dearest to me on earth not to do every thing in my power to
contribute to it. I must now take my leave and remain, with great
regard, Sir Thomas, [etc.].

Calcutta, March 6th 1814.

THE long, very long, expected ship from England brought us little satisfactory insight into our situation. That a Charter would be passed we well knew, & could nearly anticipate the terms. Therefore the simply apprizing that the Company had a new lease was nothing. All the collateral points which should have attended that information, & which were really interesting, have been overlooked.

There was not any letter from you. Most probably you waited for another opportunity, but it is right that I should mention it, lest you may have written; in which case you ought to learn that the letter has not come to hand.

The Prince having deigned to refute to a friend of mine a report that he had spoken unkindly of me, His R. Highness might possibly expect that the rumor would reach me; so that it is much better to speak to [*sic*] the matter frankly. In the first place, no degree of circumstantiality would make me credit such a tale. Secondly, could I have believed that the Prince ever did use such language respecting me, it would not have made the slightest impression on my mind. He has been in the hands of men to whom any curb of probity is a thing unknown. Tho' I have never had any hostility towards them, they never can forgive my perfect knowledge of their characters. And, too sagacious to adduce against me any broader charge which they were aware the Prince would combat, it is natural enough for them with light and dexterous insinuations to attempt indisposing him towards me in those easy moments when they had not to fear his scrutinizing their hints. If under such a transient influence the Prince had said any thing inconsistent with his former goodness, it would have altered nothing in my sentiments. It was said in olden time "I appeal from Philip drunk to Philip sober". I should have said, "I appeal from my Prince misled to my Prince himself again": and I should have had the most tranquil confidence in the result of his reflection. But, I repeat, I do not believe one word of the story.

Dr. Coghlan has written to me in agonies lest he should be thought to have claimed a recommendation from me with you without its' having had existence. Now, my dear friend, most assuredly I did mention him to you; because I remember at the same time to have told you in secret how keenly he had been fighting the Prince's battle with the Masons.

There is a Mr. F. C. Smith whom you marked on the Prince's list as one for whom H.R.H. was really interested. I have promoted him to put him into the fairest course of advantage here. I fear, however, he will not justify the being pushed forward. He is ill educated, & ignorant of the world in a strange degree.

I think I told you that I had sent Satchwell to Amboyna, to be advanced there, as I had no means of transferring him into the Civil line here.[1] He is a very good & well behaved lad; so that I am confident of his enabling me to do well for him. Aberdeen's nephew shall be benefited as soon as ever his standing will allow it. He has now all that he can, according to regulation, possess.

Adieu, my dear friend, give my best remembrance to Mrs. McMahon & believe me [etc.].

[P.S.] Pray think of what I said about Madeira for Ld Granard.[1]

409 THE DUKE OF CAMBRIDGE *to the* PRINCE REGENT

Hanover, March 8th 1814.

I WAS very sorry to hear by a letter I received from Best of the 22d of last month that you have had a fit of the gout, but I trust that by this time you are quite recovered and that your general health will be benefited by it. Since my last I have very little new to communicate from hence. Several of the batallions are assembled for exercise and between this and the 20th the greater part of the Militia will be out. Unfortunately the weather continues still very severe and the clothing & stores are not yet arrived so that at present the men make a sad appearance, but I hope before the end of the month that I may be able to make you a favourable report on the subject.

The enclosed was given me yesterday by Wallmoden just as he was setting out for the Rhine to join the Russian German Legion and the Mecklenburg troops which he is to command. It is not my business to give any opinion on the subject of his request, but I must do him the justice to say that he has certainly sacrificed himself for the good cause, and that the statement of his private affairs is perfectly correct. His father left his property in so confused a state that after a great deal of trouble to bring the affair into order, General Wallmoden & I fear all his brothers and sisters will have little or nothing to live upon after the debts are paid.

The Russian German Legion which I saw at Bremen the week before last is a very fine corps, both as to men and horses. The Artillery is

1 See Nos. 343, 352.

particularly fine and in excellent order. The clothing of the whole corps is in a dreadful state and it is a great pity that it did not remain in the country till the men were compleatly refitted.

I hope in a short time to be able to send you the whole state of the army and I regret that you will have to sign a considerable number of commissions. I would with pleasure have done this for you, but I believe it is contrary to the custom; and therefore I dare not propose it.

I will now not detain you any longer than to add the assurance of my ever remaining [etc.].

410 THE EARL OF YARMOUTH *to the* PRINCE REGENT

Saturday eve[g], March 12th 1814.

IMMEDIATELY on quitting your Royal Highnesses presence I saw Drummond the banker my Major, shewed him the letter, & had it sent to the printer of the corps by the Quarter M.S—thinking expedition in such circumstances necessary I lost no time, & right or wrong, it is done. I have however no doubt that some libeller will get prosecuted by me & possibly I may be obliged to make an affidavit also, when, where, & on what subjects I saw Baron de B.; if so obliged, I can swear with a perfect safe conscience in addition (if it would please anybody) that on the 21st I was out of town & neither by myself or power of Attorney bought or sold any stock & that I had not either real or fictitious omnium or stock either in my hands up or down, or indirectly by any other person for me.[1]

There cannot be a doubt of Berengers being the man, he has fled the kingdom.[2]

Croker I perceive thinks I ought to say something—*I* think I ought not till Parliament or a Court of Justice takes cognizance of the matter. At any rate I shall do nothing for two or three days & I hope on reconsideration your Royal Highness will think that my doctrine of taking the

1 On 21 February London was wildly agitated by a rumour that Napoleon had been killed and that the Allies were about to enter Paris. On the Stock Exchange, omnium, which opened at 27½, rose rapidly to 33, but when the rumour was discredited, the stock reacted sharply to 28½. Vast sums of money changed hands and it was alleged that Lord Cochrane and his uncle, Andrew Cochrane Johnstone, were parties to this conspiracy for raising the Funds, and largely profited therefrom. They, Charles de Berenger, and five others, were tried on 8 June in the Court of King's Bench, found guilty, and sentenced to various terms of imprisonment.

2 He was captured at Leith, and the banknotes in his possession were traced to Lord Cochrane and his uncle.

bull by the horns as far as my official military connections with B. de B. permitted was fit & proper.[1]

I do not say that this instance of your Royal Highness's kindness & condescension has either encreased my attachment or my humble affection because they had already reached the utmost.

411 THE DUKE OF CUMBERLAND *to the* PRINCE REGENT

Strelitz, March 12th 1814.

I AM very sorry to learn by letters I have received this day from Thornton that you have been laid up with the gout, but I hope long ere this you are de novo upon your legs, and for God's sake take care of yourself for you are of too great a consequence to neglect yourself. You are and have been the main spring that has set every proper feeling afloat here on the Continent, & to you *solely* and alone is owing all we have seen of late. Your letter in 1811 to the Emperor of Russia brought him first to his senses, & his acting enabled the K. of Prussia to shew himself, which one must do him the justice to say he has done to the utmost of his powers. God grant we may ultimately succeed and not allow ourselves to be intimidated by the late check our troops met with into a hurried peace, for depend upon it *no* peace will ever be a permanent one as long as Bonaparte reigns in France.[2] That man cannot live in peace, and will by his infernal machinations cause a fresh war to break out the moment he has recovered his strength. It is not for me to give you information as you must *now* have it from the best channel, Castlereagh & Co being collected together at Head Quarters, but from letters I have seen, however unpleasant a check always is, still every thing has been repaired, & I believe it was owing to too great a hurry and an unjust contempt of the forces of the enemy; these were the two causes of the disaster that took place.

However reinforcements are daily marching to the great Army & I hope if the Allies will be but *true* to one another every thing will succeed.

---

1 At the trial Lord Yarmouth deposed to Berenger's having been adjutant of a corps of sharp-shooters, and declared that in his opinion one of the incriminating letters alleged to have been written by De Berenger was not in his handwriting.

2 The Allies suffered several reverses in February, near the Marne and the Seine. Napoleon severely handled a Russian division at Champ-Aubert on the 10th, and part of the Prussian army under General D'Yorck two days later. On the 14th Blucher himself was defeated and forced to retreat to Châlons-sur-Marne, and the Austrians were driven back across the Seine after the 17th.

I see by the Cassel papers that the 2d column of Hesseners 9,000 strong left Cassel the 2*d*. Our old friend the Elector has certainly done wonders and all this shews what *can* be done *si on le veut*, for his country was in as wretched a state as his neighbors and yet he has already completed 18,000 men which are actually marched to the French territories, & he is busily employed in forming a fresh corps.

Permit me now dearest brother to thank you for the communication made to me through Thornton[1] of Charlotte's marriage with the Hereditary Pr. of Orange. As I take it for granted *this* is your wish, that she may be perfectly happy I also most sincerely wish, and believe from all I have [heard] of the young Prince that he is very pleasing; thank God this is settled for I own to you when I left England & from all I knew I was very much afraid she would prefer the *Cheese*[2] to the *Orange*. I have at length succeeded in getting a house at Berlin, and I have hired the Dutchess of Courlands[3] under the Linden which I am to take possession of the 25th. I am told it is very comfortable, and being under the Linden must be very pleasant. When there perhaps I may be able to execute commissions for you either in prints, maps, uniforms, house furniture or anything else you may want. I will do my best on that occasion as well as on all others wishing by every means to prove to you my attachment and regard, only communicate to me your commands upon these subjects by Campus florius,[4] for otherwise I fear I have no chance of hearing from him, though he promised faithfully to write to me the moment he had seen you. I am excessively happy to hear that Colonel Amshehl (?) has been appointed Colonel to the 3d Hussars, for he is a most capital officer. I own I feel very uneasy at the accounts of poor Sophy; this constant slow fever that has confined her now upwards of 4 months to her room, added to her weak state of health, makes me fear there is little hopes of her recovery, poor thing. I am positive that that constant scene of Windsor has done all the mischief, & that the only chance for her is if possible the removing her from thence & trying thus to change the scene. Now God bless you dearest brother, that my next letters may bring me the satisfactory account of the entire recovery of your health is the sincerest wish of [etc.].

1 The Duke's Equerry, who was in England.
2 I.e. the Duke of Gloucester.
3 Anne Charlotte Dorothy (d. 1821), wife of the Duke of Courland (d. 1800). Their eldest daughter was the Duchess de Sagan.
4 Colonel Bloomfield.

Stutgard, March 15th, 1814.

I AM sorry to be so often obliged to have recourse to you but your obliging politeness encourages me to hope you will forgive this trouble. I hardly know whether I ought to laugh or cry at my present commission, but to say the truth it frets me as it gives much uneasiness here because I cannot make others understand the customs of our country, as they attach more consequence to a paragraph in the news papers than it is worth. However extraordinary this appears to an Englishman it is perfectly to be excused, as, four or five days before this article appeared on the Francfort Journal, Lord Castlereagh in a conversation with Count de Wintzingerode[1] not only mentioned this paragraph which he had read in the Times, but asked an explanation of the whole, and particularly of that part concerning Lady Castlereagh.[2] When I was informed of this conversation I laughed at such nonsense and wondered that an Englishman should attach any importance to what is printed in the newspapers. —This was mentioned to me on Wednesday and Saturday evening the Francfort Journal reached Stutgard with this foolish article which was thought so important that the censor sent it sealed up and I believe that orders have been given to have a paragraph inserted in the same Francfort paper to contradict it. Pray, Sir, be so obliging as to take the same method and have an article inserted in the Times saying that every body was astonished at a report which had appeared in the Times of 22^d February, which is without foundation concerning the Queen of Wurttemberg's quitting her husband to return and settle in England.—It is very cruel when one has so many serious causes for anxiety to be constantly tormented by trifles—You would laugh, Sir, could you know the number of persons who came here on Sunday to enquire into the truth of this

---

1 The Russian General.
2 Emily [1772–1829], daughter of the second Earl of Buckinghamshire, who died in 1793. *The Times* of 19 February 1814 contained the following Article:
"The Queen of Wurtemberg. [From an Evening Paper]
"It has been stated as a mere article of Court news that Sir Thomas Tyrwhitt, after an interview with the Prince Regent and the Earl of Liverpool, waited on the Queen at Windsor on Wednesday last, with a commission with which he was entrusted by her Royal daughter the Queen of Wurtemberg. Sir Thomas certainly did wait upon Her Majesty, and we are enabled to state that the commission with which he was entrusted was of no common nature. It was to communicate to the Queen the arrangements which had been finally made, with the consent of the Court of Wurtemberg *for the departure of the late Princess Royal of England from that country*, and her future residence in her native land.
"The cause of the unexpected return of Her Royal Highness to this country, we shall not mention, except to state that Her Royal Highness's conduct has been in every instance perfectly irreproachable.
"Lady Castlereagh is said to be gone, or going, to Wurtemberg to accompany Her Royal Highness to this country."

report. I am certainly flattered by the interest so many people have shewn me though vexed at the cause.

At last le Chevalier Horn[1] has left Stutgard after having been politely desired to leave this place by the Minister who is at the head of the police. He made many difficulties, wrote a note in a very high style, threatning that the Prince Regent would resent this behaviour. He has told so many different stories that nobody can come to the truth except of his former history which I mentioned in my last—The Austrians say he was a spy at Vienna known under the name of Frederick Stambach an Augustine friar. They speak of this to all who mention Horn—Le Chevalier said at first that he had been several years employed in the Secretary of States office, and given as a sort of secretary to Sir Charles Steward,[2] who had intended taking him to Head Quarters, but Lord Aberdeen advised against his being allowed to accompany Sir Charles as he found le Chevalier was very obnoxious to Prince Metternich— Then that Lord Castlereagh had sent him word that the Regent till the peace intended having no diplomatic agents on the Continent, and when he found that on his having said this, that he was advised to leave Stutgard, he changed his story and pretends to be attached to the Embacy [*sic*] at Vienna. However he grew calmer on being informed that Mr Rose[3] and others said he was known to be a spy to both parties— I am glad to find that his assertions as to his intimacy with most of my brothers is false, therefore trust the rest has as little foundation.

I am grieved to hear that the Prince Regent has been ill. God grant his indisposition may not be of any consequence. I always tremble when I find that he has been obliged to have recourse to bleeding, as formerly he suffered much from being bled too often—I fear that you will have found poor Sophia sadly altered; I understand she continues growing weaker which makes me dread a decline.

William's returning to England is a great disappointment to me he had promised me a visit which I looked forwards to with great pleasure —Though Ernest talks of going to Berlin I understand he is still at Strelitz. The separation I find has taken place between Princess Solms and her late husband. The newspapers amuse themselves as much on that subject as on my account. I wish that they found something else to occupy them besides the Royal family. Every body plagues me to death about Princess Charlotte and accuses me of being close because I will not speak of things that I am ignorant of. I enclose the copy of the paragraph out of the Journal de Francfort and will now take my leave as I believe you will be very glad to be released from this scrawl and remain [etc.].

1 See Nos. 391, 406, 407.   2 Sir Charles Stewart, British Minister to Prussia.
3 British Minister at Munich.

Windsor, the 19th March 1814.

THE news from the Continent of yesterday fill my heart with more joy than my pen is able to express.[1] I beg you to accept my congratulation upon this happy event and also my thanks for ordering S[i]r H[enry] H[alford] to inform me of it. The next good news I should wish to receive would be that of *no peace.* Let us go to Paris and force Napoleon to surrender himself, or let England be the means of restoring the poor Bourbons upon the throne and then I think this Island will be immortal.

I wish most sincerely that you may not suffer from all the fatigues you are to go thro this day.[2] I hope Sr H. H. will be able to give me a good account of you this evening. I am just going down to the King & therefore can only add how sincreely I am [etc.].

414 THE DUKE OF CUMBERLAND *to the* PRINCE REGENT

Strelitz, March 21, 1814.

AT length Morand arrived here last night and brought me the most VALUABLE present I ever received in my life namely the beautiful box with your picture which is uncommonly like, and I hardly can find words sufficiently strong to express to you my thanks; but believe me what I *cannot express* as strongly as I *could wish,* I FEEL the DEEPER engraved in my *heart,* for I defy any one to be *more faithfully* attached to another than *I am* to YOU; all I lament is that *circumstances* have not given me an opportunity of proving to you here upon the Continent all the zeal that I feel for your service. However nil desperandum, the time may still come when such an opportunity may offer itself & you may then depend upon my exerting every nerve for you. It grieves me to the soul to hear you are still confined with the gout, but I hope & trust that as my last letters say you are so much better, that by this time at least you are able to move in your room, and that with a little care you will soon recover entirely, remember *you* are of the utmost consequence not only to *England* but to all *Europe in general,* and that you may long live to enjoy the high situation you now hold is my sincerest and most ardent prayer.

1 The news of Blucher's victories.

2 The Prince Regent held a Court at Carlton House. This was followed by a meeting of the Privy Council; subsequently the "Great Cabinet" (see No. 648) heard the report of the Recorder of London concerning the convicts lying under sentence of death in Newgate. All these were reprieved.

Thank God the good news we received early yesterday morning from the Head Quarters of the Allied Army has given us fresh spirits and God grant this may act as a spur to the crowned heads & prevent them making any peace with Bonaparte, for any peace which is made *recognising him* as *the Head* of the *French Government* must be for us English *disgraceful*, and would be of no long duration, therefore having the game in our own hands *now* God grant we may not throw it away. The account we had here of there having been in [*sic*] idea of signing an Armistice made my blood run cold, but it seems Providence has *here* favoured us again by preventing the Commissioners from agreeing on the lines of demarcation, from the last accounts I must suppose that Schwarzenberg is now actually in Paris. The K. of Prussia was not in the affair of the 9th[1] as I read a letter of his dated Chaumont that very day. He seems to be from all I can learn perfectly STEADY and very much against making peace with Bonaparte. There are every week fresh reinforcements marching from Berlin to join the Great Army.

Permit me to return you my *personal* thanks for having allowed that Regt. of Hussars now at Hannover to bear my name. I certainly was put into a very awkward state, for it was under my personal influence I may say they were raised, and I have every reason to maintain, had circumstances permitted my staying there a little longer, they would have been completed long ere this, for 2 squadrons were nearly completely [*sic*] & I had from outward and distant parts of the Electorate offers of 300 and more volunteers. Bloomfield saw a detachment and they met with his approbation. I received yesterday a letter from the Military Governor at Hannover announcing me *your consent*. I take it for granted the uniform you are painted in is the new Field Marshalls coat, and it certainly must be very handsome. I understand there is one sent out for me, but is still frozen up at Heligoeland. Do let me know if Tom Tyrwhitt procured you when at Berlin the drawings of the Prussian Army as they are now cloathed; if not tell Bloomfield to write me word & I will procure them for you, as well as any thing else that either Vienna or Berlin can afford. I assure you that en corps, the new Prussian uniforms look very well, and now that the K. of Pr. has again introduced the gold & silver lacing to the Hussars they look very well, but when they wore the worsted here, they looked horribly. I have been amusing myself in reading the new regulations for that Army which are lent me by my cousin, for they are not published in general. They seem to me to be very good though certainly there are points on which I differ very much in opinion, & cannot conceive they will answer. If by any means I can

1 When Blucher defeated Napoleon near Laon.

procure them I will, & perhaps some day or other may have an opportunity of talking over them with you. I understand Owen[1] has finished my picture for my friend Bags,[2] if you think it like, and will permit me to offer you a copy, only tell Thornton to call upon him and order it. I shall feel happy to think that *now* and then as you pass by it, you will cast a friendly look at it. I ought to apologize for writing you so long a letter, knowing you to be unwell, but really when I take up my pen I hardly know when to cease, & I always feel as if I had more to say. However now God bless you, protect you, & restore you completely to health is the sincerest wish of [etc.].

415 LORD WALPOLE[3] *to* VISCOUNT CASTLEREAGH

St. Petersburgh, March 23, 1814.

I HAVE heard from many people here that H.R.H. the Princess Charlotte of Wales has conceived a friendship for Made de Tatischeff, wife of the Minister from this country to Spain: as a proof of the high regard entertained for her by the Princess, she has transmitted to Made Narischkin (la belle) several of the notes received by her, expressive of disappointment &c that her cold shd prevent Her R.H. from seeing her &c. Tho' in themselves of no consequence, they are sent to shew Made T's importance, but produce a bad effect here, & tend to lower the Princess in the eyes of the world. If you could contrive to stop this correspondence (tho' most likely the friendship has already finished) it wd not be amiss.

I have long known, & was formerly pretty well acquainted with the lady in question, just after her divorce from her first husband, when she was a most beautiful creature, but of a loose turn; she is of a low extraction in Poland, cannot speak any language tolerably, without talent of any kind, & of a reputation whh. has for many years ceased to be equivocal.[4]

1 William Owen (1769–1825), the portrait painter.   2 Lord Eldon.

3 Horatio, Lord Walpole, afterwards third Earl of Orford (1783–1858). Secretary of Embassy, 1812–15, and Minister Plenipotentiary *ad. int.* at Petersburg, 1813–15.

4 Liverpool suspected the Tatischeffs of intriguing against the Orange match. He wrote to Castlereagh on 30 April: "There have arisen most unpleasant difficulties respecting the marriage of Princess Charlotte with the Prince of Orange. I have no doubt they have originated in a political intrigue, and they have been so far attended with success, that she has been induced to insist upon conditions being inserted in the contract of marriage of which she never thought until recently, and which (to the extent to which she is desirous of pushing them) can not be admitted. We have the strongest reason to believe that the Tatischeffs are engaged in this intrigue, and the object is to break off the marriage with the Prince of Orange and to form a connection between the Princess and one of the Grand Dukes of Russia." The Prince Regent therefore asked Castlereagh to prevent the Russian Grand Dukes from coming over to England at that moment. (C. K. Webster's *Castlereagh*, I, 541.) He said she was "a woman of slight character" and was very angry with his daughter for having made her acquaintance. (*Miss Knight*, I, 288.)

His Majesty's Ship Jason,
Late at night. March 23d 1814.

I was really in hopes of not having been under the necessity of writing again and indeed of having shaken you by the hand before this; but since the arrival of the Grand Dutchess at the Hague I have observed her anxiety to arrive in England and her irritation at not finding the ship or vessel ready to carry her over; to detail all the particulars would be useless, but various causes have combined, which I will relate when I see you. I had been in hopes when I left the Hague she was more pacified: on my arrival here I *first* saw the Admiralty orders relative to her and myself: most strangely worded indeed about the Grand Dutchess: putting before the eye of an elegant and ignorant female a cutter in preference to a frigate: but the offer of a frigate I could not, either as an Admiral in the King's service or as the brother of the Prince Regent, knowing my brother's sentiments towards the Emperor of Russia, permit the Grand Dutchess (who I know was irritated) and the favourite sister of the Emperor to be deceived about the cutter: the Chearful cutter *cannot* carry the Grand Dutchess, her son and her suite of *thirty seven* persons with *three* or four carriages. I thought last Saturday I had prevailed on her to embark with me in the Jason, more particularly as the Chearful cutter was not then in this part, being only *this* evening come in with Tyrwhitt: but the Grand Dutchess again grew uneasy and talked of want of official information and of this cutter. I have had since that two more communications with her and have been most unfortunately unsuccessful, being still more impressed with the *impossibility* and *impropriety* of the cutter carrying over the Grand Dutchess and having with Captain King's exertions properly fitted the Jason for Her Imperial Highness, I have made a *third* offer, the success of which I have not yet had time to learn.

I write this therefore to account for my absence, as the packet sails early tomorrow and I may not have her answer in time. I am sure I am quite right in what I have done and rejoice to find from Tyrwhitt the Queen of Wirtemberg recommends every attention and respect being paid this lady. I shall of course wait the arrival of the cutter and the Grand Dutchess will then come here, after having seen the Jason and Chearful I shall implore her to take the Jason, and I will attend her in the Chearful. I have requested Admiral Young[1] to represent as the King's Commander-in Chief to the Grand Dutchess the *utter impossibility* of her proceeding to England in the cutter and recommending the

1 Sir William Young (1751–1821). G.C.B., 1815.

Jason. I hope yet to see this elegant and fascinating lady landed on our shore in a manner suitable to the sister of the Emperor Alexander and agreeable I am confident to the wishes of the Prince Regent who so justly values the Emperor. You cannot conceive how much I feel for the honour of our country in not insulting a lady of her rank who is desirous of visiting the Prince Regent for whom she so justly has such an esteem and respect. George the First sent an Admiral and a whole British Fleet to fetch Peter the Great, her ancestor, and *now* a *cutter* is sent for the Grand Dutchess. At all events I have done my duty and should be most liable to censure if I had acted otherwise, knowing so well the generous and gallant sentiments of the Prince Regent.

I still hope to have the satisfaction of landing Her Imperial Highness in England to the credit of our island and trust this will be the last letter I shall have occasion to write before we meet. Adieu and ever believe me, [etc.].

417 The Duke of Clarence *to* Colonel McMahon

His Majesty's ship Jason,
March 26th 1814. Late at night.

I WRITE in a very different temper from what I took up my pen last time. I was then very much hurt at the *unintentional* but *real* insult offered to the Grand Dutchess and equally concerned to see her irritation and dissatisfaction. I have however smoothed all difficulties & with the very great exertions of Captain King I have arranged the accommodations on board the Jason as well as our means and a Dutch dockyard could provide, and the attendants of the Grand Dutchess appear to be satisfied. All her baggage and carriages are on board and she comes herself tomorrow at ten. I hope if the wind is fair she will arrive in England on Monday; she is anxious to land as near London as possible and I shall therefore run the Jason up to Gravesend if the wind is fair. She arrived this afternoon in high health and spirits at three o'clock and has quite forgot her ill humour and dissatisfaction. I returned on board to dinner and was most agreeably surprized shortly after to have a visit from Tyrwhitt who returned from Admiral Young with letters to me giving me full powers to do what I please and putting the Chearfull cutter at my most *positive* command. I shall therefore tomorrow embark the Imperial Catherine on board the Jason and unless Her Imperial Highness particularly requests me I shall leave Major Steiger to interpret on board the Jason and attend her on board the Chearful cutter.

Thank God this disagreeable affair is over. After all the marked attention I have received from all the Allies and the civil message I had from the Emperor Alexander I could not permit his favourite sister to be conveyed in an improper manner to England, more particularly being myself in the navy.[1]

I hope not many hours after you receive this to be able to shake you by the hand, in the meantime adieu and ever believe me [etc.].

418 CAPTAIN HESSE *to* VISCOUNT KEITH

Near Toulouse, April 1st 1814.

[*Copy.*]

A SHORT time ago I received a letter from your Lordship, & should have answered it before this, had I been stationary but for one day, but our Regt. has been moving about in so many different directions that I could not find sufficient time to send you the parcel I intend sending. Even now, it is only because Marshall Beresford[2] told me that he would send this letter off that I take the liberty of sending you these few lines merely to tell you, that the parcel shall be sent next week *for certain* according to your Ldship's own directions. I shall then also take the liberty of speaking more fully to your Ldship on the subject in question.

419 THE QUEEN OF WURTEMBERG *to the* PRINCE REGENT

Stutgard, April 3ᵈ 1814.

I HOPE that you have received my letter of 16ᵗʰ ultimate, by which you will have seen how very anxious I was about your health; fearing by the accounts I had found in the foreign papers, that you had, dear brother, a return of the inflammation on your chest which formerly occasioned us so much uneasiness. But now I understand that you are plagued by the gout which, though a suffering complaint, is, thank God, not so dangerous

1 The Duke of Clarence offered to marry her, but he met with no encouragement. According to Miss Knight (I, 282) the Grand Duchess complained of his assiduities, "of his vulgar familiarity, and of his want of delicacy".

2 William Carr Beresford, Viscount Beresford (1768–1854). He had reorganised the Portuguese Army, but since 1811 he had been serving under Wellington. He was a Marshal in the Portuguese army.

as an inflammatory illness. I hope that you will soon be free from all complaint and able to enjoy as usual air and exercise. I think the good news must do you good; and beg, dearest brother, that you will accept of my congratulations on the British troops having occupied Bourdeaux. God be praised for the great successes with which the English arms have been crowned. I doubly glory in being a Briton when I read Lord Wellingtons dispatches, they are written in so simple and plain a style they would have suited a Roman Consul; all must admire a General who performs such wonders without appearing to feel that he has done any thing extraordinary. These great events in the southern Provinces will certainly accelerate the march of the Allied armies, and I hope in a few days to have the happiness of writing you word that they are encamped near Paris. I do not wish them to enter the town as I dread its having the effect of Capua in days of yore on the army of Hanibal. Besides which I should fear concealed treason; it is a very serious thing to be quartered in a town where there are at least six hundred thousand inhabitants, all vain of their country and wishing to destroy those who have put an end to their imaginary superiority over the rest of Europe. These concealed enemies I dread more than open ones, as you are ever exposed when least aware to be attacked.—Our news from the Allied armies continues good on the 29th ultimate one of the corps entered Meaux. The King's eldest son has distinguished himself on every occasion and has gained the esteem of all who know him. He has equally acquired the good opinion of the Austrians and Russians; the Emperor of Austria has given him the Order of Marie Therese and the Emperor of Russia twice his military Order and now that of St Andrew.

I will now only add the King's compliments and remain with the sincerest affection [etc.].

420 THE PRINCE REGENT *to* QUEEN CHARLOTTE

Carlton House,
Saty. ¼ pt. one p.m. April 9th. 1814.

I TRUST that you will forgive me if I scribble but a line and that too I fear in a very trembling and hardly intelligible hand, but my heart is so overwhelm'd and overflows so with gratitude to the Almighty for all his Providential support and blessings innumerable, that I am really quite bereft of the means of expressing myself, or of giving vent to my feelings which surpass all discription, and indeed I may add and say, almost all comprehension.

I trust my dearest mother that you will think that I have fullfilled and done my duty at least, and perhaps I may be vain enough to hope that you may feel a little proud of *your son*.

I will not delay the servant a moment longer as he will be the bearer of such happy and glorious intelligence as I now enclose.[1] God for ever bless you my ever dearest mother, prays your ever and most affectionate and dutiful son.

P.S. Love to all the dear sisterhood.

421 THE DUKE OF CAMBRIDGE *to the* PRINCE REGENT

Hanover, April 11th 1814.

I CAN not let the mail go out without writing you just two lines to congratulate you on the glorious events which have occurred at Paris. We received the accounts here yesterday and I wish you could have seen the universal joy expressed on every countenance. The moment the guns fired the people began to cheer, and there was not one who did not participate in the joy which every honest and well thinking man must feel at the Bourbons being replaced on the throne of France. To think that you, my dearest brother, have contributed so much to this glorious event is a proud fact indeed to every Englishman, and when your health was drunk yesterday I assure you there was full as much enthusiasm shewn as there could be at a dinner in England. Some Prussian officers dined with me and they did justice to the toast.

From Harburg I have nothing new to mention; the French have in part marched back their troops to Hamburgh. They made another sortie from Harburg, but were driven back with great gallantry by one of the new batallions commanded by Colonel Beaulieu, the Grubenhagen sharpshooters.

General Bennigsen has not yet allowed General Lyon to move to Bremen; but I expect to hear that the troops are now on their march and I mean to go to Bremen next week to hurry the Regiments off to the Rhine.

I have seen this morning a very fine Brigade of Hanoverian Artillery which marches off tomorrow for Dusseldorf. On Friday the Luneburg &

1 The news of the entry of the Allies into Paris, and of the abdication of Napoleon. London was illuminated for three successive nights (11th to 13th).

Bremen & Verden Hussars begin their march. The first I have seen this morning & I am very well pleased with them.

I will now not detain you any longer than merely to add the assurance of my ever remaining [etc.].

422 SIR THOMAS TYRWHITT *to the* PRINCE REGENT

Stuttgard, April 12, 1814.

IN obedience to the commands of your Royal Highness, I dispatch the messenger Sylvester with this letter, as I last night found from Her Majesty, the "order of the day" was, she was too ill to undertake any journey at present.

I can, I believe thank God, safely assure you, there exists no cause on the score of health that can prevent the Queen of Würtemberg from seeing her family.

I arrived on Saturday and immediately waited upon Count Zeppelin with the letter which L.ᵈ Liverpool sent me, and which he had signed— the Count without delay transmitted this to the King, who sent word for answer, that the letter contained nothing which could entitle me to a private audience, but that I might be presented at Court as an English gentleman, in the usual way.

Private audience I had not requested, supposing such an interview flowed as of a consequence from the letter His Majesty had read. This notification to me, however unexpected, I was determined should not prevent my accepting the proposal of making my bow in another manner. Accordingly on Sunday, Monʳ de Zeppelin presented me at a full Court, and the very first moment my eyes met those of His Majesty, I plainly saw my mission was over.

Very few words passed, and those about the weather—At this time I had not seen the Queen, as I was well aware it would have been a cause of jealousy had I gone below stairs first.

At the usual hour on the same day, I waited upon Her Majesty, found her in the best spirits, much improved in looks, evidently capable of more activity than when I last saw her, seemed uncommonly happy to see me, & could not refrain from tears at the sight of the hand-writing of your Royal Highness—it does not appear that at this moment any instructions had been given from above, to plead illness; as our conversation was almost solely confined as to what manner we should place the subject of your Royal Highness's letter before the King, that was most likely to obtain its' object, and I am quite satisfied her heart was *then* with this object.

On paying however my duty yesterday to Her Majesty, I found a great alteration both of sentiment and of manner—She had evidently been ordered to plead her health, her cough was to be much worse, and things were in that state that I am persuaded your Royal Highness will not expect any further detail in writing, tho' I may have much to give de bouche.

But here, let me in justice to the Queen, and I do it with the most heartfelt satisfaction, assure your Royal Highness, that I am quite persuaded, her feelings, her love and affection for her family, and most particularly, Sir, towards yourself, remain the same as I believe in my conscience they ever have been—but alas! it is not her lot to be able to demonstrate them.

It was impossible for me in this interview, not to hint pretty broadly, but I trust, delicately, at the great alteration that had occurred in her sentiments since the last evening—that tho' not a medical man myself, I could not possibly trespass upon truth so far as to write home otherwise, than there was an evident improvement in her health. I complained of the raideur of the King towards me, which produced an expression from her that at once opened my eyes—she earnestly begged me to take as little notice of it as I consistently could, as, said she "I shall ultimately be the sufferer"—

I then assured her, her wishes were commands upon me and I took my leave.

I understand the King is shortly to write to Her Majesty at Windsor to say that in five or six months his Queen may be able to visit England.!!!

I reserve all other details till I have the happiness of seeing your Royal Highness and trust I shall find you in good health, (late events cannot but have added to the spirits of him who has had so great a share in producing them) so shall now only say, I am [etc.].

[P.S.] Yesterday was a great gala day here—I was at Court, at Church &c. At the Levée I had two sentences only—observations upon the news from France.

Thomˢ Golofkin, who is here as a FRIEND of the Emperor Alexander, and whom I knew very well at Töplitz, stood by me, and after the King had left us, whispered to me, "*Vous êtes vaincu par le corps de médecins, et j'en suis fâché*"—

The Minister named from hence to England, Monsʳ de Berolden,[1] set off last night for Paris, as I understand there to wait till a Minister is nominated by your Royal Highness to reside here.

1 The Count de Beroldingen. See Nos. 402, 406.

April 12th 1814.

THE delay of the vessels allows me to write again to you. By a former opportunity I wrote to you on a particular point; &, lest the letter should have failed, I will repeat now the tenor of what I then expressed.[1]

There were reasons which might make a certain person infer that a report of his having spoken unkindly of an absent individual might be transmitted. It is always better to meet a matter of that sort distinctly. In the first place I do not believe one word of a story so completely improbable. Secondly, were it sure, that individual must be dead to all just & honorable feeling did he not give the occurrence this natural construction; that a generous & unsuspecting spirit might by being practised upon slide into a momentary ebullition of dis-satisfaction with a certainty that the first hour of reflection would dispel the erroneous conception & bring back the original sentiment to it's true bearing. Could one believe this, & allow the most transient shade of vexation to pass over one's soul! The individual in question has not either doubts or jealousies, & is as unchangeable as he has been unchanged. Let there not, therefore, be a suspicion that such a rumor could have produced the slightest effect.

You have had such a flood of glories that poor despicable India has been necessarily erased from recollection. It is, however, of some importance to you still. The more & the nearer I contemplate it the greater is my wonder at the fabric. Never yet was there any other Government equally maintained by the general conviction of it's subjects with regard to it's justice & good faith. Perhaps I might say that in no other country was there ever such activity of Government kept up with such slight machinery. And this sway is not exercised over stupid, or uncultivated, or unenterprising races of men. On the contrary, these people are polished & acute, & daring & alive to military fame. The conclusion you would draw is, that all this requires most delicate management & in truth only exists upon the good conduct of those entrusted with the immediate guidance of affairs. Of course, we must be very cautious that the intercourse of such of our countrymen as are not under the strict control in which the Company's servants are held may not alarm the prejudices or excite the disgust of the multitude around us.

The weather is now excessively hot; yet I do not feel oppressed by it. A very heavy hail-storm the other day could not bring the thermometer below 83 in the house. By going out at the first dawn of day we get our

1 See No. 408.

exercise. After half past six the sun is too powerful to be faced without risk.

You would think that a sedentary amusement like the table would be much attended to here: but in nothing have I found my foresight more defective than in the not bringing out a good cook. The dinners are heaps of meat very ill dressed, & wines are in general far from good. Ten or eleven shillings a bottle for claret runs away with money when so much of that liquor is expended as must be the case at my table. By etiquette, we only dine with the Judges of the Supreme Court or the Members of Council, so that my table must be nearly constant.

I wrote to you relative to the probability of Madeira's being left to us on a final settlement with Portugal. Should it be so, do suggest Ld. Granard to the Prince as Governor.[1] The little that would be to be done there could be discharged by nobody better than by Ld G. accustomed as he is to reside among Catholics, & conversant with foreigners. Recollect how long his members in the Irish House of Commons were faithfully devoted. Adieu. Ly L[oudoun] & the children are well. Offer my best regards to Mrs. McMahon, & believe me [etc.].

424 *Memorandum.* [By SIR THOMAS TYRWHITT.]

Stuttgard, April 13, 1814.

THE QUEEN OF WÜRTEMBERG's commands reached me this morning towards nine o'clock whilst I was on a visit to Count Golowkin, to come to her apartments but without any notification that the King was there.

I lost no time in going to the Palace, where on entering the apartments, I found His Majesty seated by the side of the Queen.

I was desired to take a seat and the King immediately commenced a long history of himself, of his blameless conduct thro' life, (depuis ma naissance je ne rien fait [*sic*] que je devrais cacher!!!) his fault to have always used "trop de franchise"—his high opinion of honor, and his high opinion of what could in any degree wound that honor.

Then, adverting to the letter I had delivered to Count Zeppelin, he said it was nothing at all as far as my mission was concerned, that there were parts of it in contradiction to that from Lord Castlereagh—that as to the example I hear I am to follow, that of the King of Bavaria.

1 See Nos. 343, 352, 408.

I interrupted His Majesty but three times during the whole of his discourse, and here I had occasion to do it for the first time.

"I take the liberty of apprising your Majesty that the citation of the case of the King of Bavaria came from myself, and from no person in this place—it did not however arise as from my own knowledge, but was quoted to me at our Foreign Office that a letter of a similar nature as the one above alluded to was expected from your Majesty."

The King then continued without adverting to my observation in any other manner than merely saying "what the King of Bavaria does, [does] not impose upon me a necessity of imitating".

The next topic of His Majesty was that of the letter of His Royal Highness the Prince Regent to the Queen. "He had no scruple at the present moment in using that frankness for which he was so distinguished, and declaring that there was a want of politeness towards him. I am a husband, and ought to direct my wife—I ought to have been consulted, & the letter should have been addressed to me, and *possibly then much facility would have been given on my part to the object of His Royal Highness's letter*"—the Queen here, (I am persuaded by order) coughed a good deal—and then said the King, "Voyez Monsieur sa situation actuelle (more coughing) je doubte si elle pourra entreprendre le voyage même d'ici a Ludwisberg—selon ce que les médecins me disaient hier mais je vous avoue que j'ai attendu de la part de mon beau frère une autre conduite."

I here gave a second interruption and said, that if the cause of Her Majesty's not being able to visit her family arose from her Royal brother not having written to His Majesty, I had deeply to regret that I was not the bearer of such a letter, as I was certain her family loved her too sincerely to permit etiquette debarring them the pleasure they would have in once more seeing her.

"Monsieur, said the K. warmly, Je dois prendre les choses telles que sont"—His Majesty here worked himself into such a passion that nothing could have prevailed upon me to have heard him out, but the presence of the Queen—He said he could feel his own dignity as well as other Potentates—that he felt his sovereignty wounded—and as to the insinuation that had been copied from English Gazettes into those of Germany respecting himself and his beloved wife, (épouse) (here they shook hands and went thro' a scene worthy of the stage) and here I interrupted His Majesty for the last time—and told him, that since I had been in this town I had heard it insinuated that those paragraphs had come from me—that I should not condescend to regret such an insinuation in any other manner than by sending Her Majesty on my return home, the newspaper in which the whole idea was contradicted, and by myself.[1]

I here made my bow and retired [2]

425 THE QUEEN OF WURTEMBERG *to the* PRINCE REGENT

Stutgard, April 13th 1814.

I AM quite overcome by the very affectionate kind letter I had the happiness to receive from you. Words can never do justice to my feelings on the occasion. But the kindness with which you have ever treated me, my beloved brother, has imprinted the strongest gratitude on my heart which makes me hope I need not assure you of the sincere joy with which I should have accepted of your most affectionate invitation as the idea of having the blessing to see you again and enjoying for some time the society of my beloved family would have been a delight to my soul; but alas there are some untoward circumstances which too frequently destroy the best laid schemes for happiness. My health which has been far from good of late years and has gone on growing worse since the misfortunes which have befallen our family is a bar which it is impossible to remove at present. The physicians which were consulted two months ago and again on Monday have assured both the King and myself they thought at this moment a journey either by sea or land might be dangerous, as I suffer sadly from violent sickness's if I attempt either going in a shut carriage or quicker than a foot's pace; in addition to this since November a spasmodic cough and a variety of other little unpleasant complaints. This is the real state of the case and obliges me with the most heartfelt

1 See No. 412. The story must have been contradicted in the evening paper from which *The Times* copied it. I cannot find any contradiction in *The Times*. On 24 February, five days after the appearance of "that odious article", *The Times* reported that Sir Thomas Tyrwhitt was expected to leave town in a short time for the Continent in order to accompany the Queen of Wurtemberg to England.

2 Castlereagh wrote to Liverpool on 27 April: "Pray avoid, if possible, any interruption of intercourse with Wirtemberg, as their troops have fought well, and their Prince Royal is a very fine young man, and respected by the whole army. The King is a tyrant, both in his public and private character; but, if he did no more harm than refuse the Chevalier a private audience, *in form,* the Prince will not feel it necessary to resent this." (*Cast. Corr.* IX, 509.) It was believed in some quarters that the King of Wurtemberg poisoned his first wife, the Princess of Wales's sister. There are some very curious stories about her in *Bath Archives,* II, 410, and Lady Charlotte Campbell's *Memoirs,* I, 263–5. One of Castlereagh's correspondents reported to him in 1815 that the King was not much liked by his subjects, who accused him of being partial to the French, "having in his own apartments paintings representing battles where the French defeated the Germans". He added, "The Queen is much loved, and every apartment showed proofs of her industry." (*Cast. Corr.* XI, 95.) See also C. K. Webster's *Castlereagh,* I, 188.

sorrow to decline for the present accepting of the kindest and most affectionate of all invitations. The King desires me to express his gratitude for your message, my dear brother, with many compliments, and to add that as soon as the physical people think it safe for me to travel he will not fail to acquaint you with it and will then agree to my having the joy and comfort to visit the dearest and best of brothers. He has himself written to the Queen to explain the reasons concerning my health and to give her the same assurances. I hope, my dear brother, by this you will see how much we both regret the unfortunate difficulties which have arizen to prevent my having the delight to go to England; the spending some time with you would have made me the happiest of beings. But now I must seek to submit with resignation to this very severe disappointment; in the midst of my sorrow one only thought soothes my mind, which is your affection. This in every situation of life I look up to and know I can depend on it. God grant that the impediments which prevent my having the happiness to see you, my dear brother, may soon be removed and that in a short time I may have the happiness and comfort to find myself in the midst of my family. It would have delighted me to have assisted at the wedding of your dear daughter; most sincerely do I congratulate you on an event which I trust will be a source of happiness to her and of much satisfaction to you. The nation of old were ever anxious for an Alliance with Holland, therefore [I] am sure Princess Charlotte's being united to the heir of the United Provinces will diffuse universal joy.

I hope, my dearest brother, that the untoward circumstances which prevent my paying you a visit at present will soon be over and that they will neither diminish your affection for me nor alter the kind intentions you entertained in favour of the King's interests and mine. I am sure that I need not repeat this as your own good heart will lead you to diminish and not encrease the sorrow I feel at being for this moment deprived of the blessing of being united to my beloved relations and will not wish me to fret at the idea that my health should put a stop to your kindness, of which I stand every way in need of.

I am all gratitude, my beloved brother, for your considerate goodness in having had the odious article in the Times of February 22d contradicted.[1] You can have little idea of the trouble and anxiety it has occasioned here and in most parts of Europe where either the King or myself have any relations, most of them having either written to enquire into the truth of this report or had us spoken to on the subject, which is very unpleasant.

1 See No. 412. The date should be 19 February.

I trust, my dearest brother, that you will by this time be quite free from the gout, and able to go through all the fatigues which the Great Dutchess Catherine's being in England and after that the wedding will occasion. How happy would our dear father have been could he have seen this match. He always loved Charlotte very much and was very kind to the Prince of Orange's family. His situation is a drawback on every occasion and ever makes me melancholy. God grant that he may not always continue in this wretched state but recover sufficiently to enjoy at least his family. Sophia, I am sorry to hear, continues very weak, and the rest of the family pretty well, though my mother has undergone so much of late. My dear brother, having heard that poor old Monsieur de Salzas was fallen into bad circumstances, I did everything in my power to find him out, intending to assist him till I should have acquainted you with his unhappy situation; but after Count de Gollofkin, the Russian Minister, had taken much trouble on the subject, we heard he was dead. I take the liberty to send you a small note I have received concerning his affairs, as I think you will like to know what is become of his fortune.

May I beg of you, dear brother, to accept of the drawing which accompanies these lines. Its only merit is its being my work, which I hope will induce you to look on it with indulgence and perhaps to hang it up in one of the apartments at your country house, flattering myself it will sometimes put you in mind of a sister that loves you dearly.

Much do I regret that poor Sir Thomas has had this fatiguing journey for nothing and that you have out of kindness for me deprived yourself so long of one of your most attached servants. This is surely a great mark of affection which I feel deeply. Adieu, my dearest brother. Ever think of me with regard, and be convinced of my very sincere love and attachment. Your dear letter I shall never part with as long as I live, but put it into a pocket book with my dear father's which I have constantly in my writing box, and on which I have written that they are to be burnt in case of my death. God bless you, my beloved brother, and believe me far or near [etc.].

London, April 14th 1814.

I CANNOT refrain from congratulating your R.H. on the glorious &
happy events which have taken place & to which your own firmness has
so largely contributed. The gratitude of the French whom I have seen is
expressed in the warmest terms & by none more than by Lady
Ossulston.[2]

Permit me now my dear Sir to sollicit you once more to express your
kind interest about Captain Clifford,[3] & that as his dear father recieved
your R.H. assurance through me, that you would ever be his friend, so
that you will now express your wish that the application wch he made to
Lord Melville six weeks ago, to be employed, should be attended to.
Lord Melville recieved him with great civility & said that he hoped soon
to give him a ship, but the rapidity of events have been such that unless
you my dear Sir will express a wish about it, *this remnant* even of the
American War may end before he can again have an opportunity of distinguishing himself. He is very eager to go & I entreat of your R.H. to
protect his interests & his zealous ambition.

I do trust to you my dear Sir & am with unfeigned attachment your
respectfull hum^e servant.

427 THE QUEEN OF WURTEMBERG *to the* PRINCE REGENT

Stutgard, April 16th 1814.

HAVING just heard that Count de Beroldingen is to leave Paris to pay
his duty to you, I hasten to send him a few lines that he may have the
honour to present them and beg to recommend this gentleman to your
notice, who I hope will suit you as he has seen much of the world and a
great deal of actual service.

Allow me dear brother to offer you my warm congratulations on the
happy termination of the war, what heartfelt satisfaction must it be to
you to have brought about the great change which within this month has
overthrown the overgrown power of Napoleon which certainly would
have enslaved Europe if the Allies had failed in their great enterprize.

1 The fifth Duke of Devonshire (1748–1811) married, as his second wife, Lady Elizabeth
Foster, widow of John Thomas Foster, and daughter of the fourth Earl of Bristol. (d. 1824.)
2 The daughter of the Duc de Grammont. Her husband succeeded as fifth Earl of Tankerville
in 1822.
3 He and Caroline (Mlle St Jules), who married George Lamb in 1809, were the Duchess's
illegitimate children by the Duke, whom she married later. Clifford entered the Navy in
1800, became a captain in 1812, and ultimately an Admiral. He was knighted in 1830 and
created a Baronet in 1838. [1788–1877.]

Your generous heart, dear brother, must feel delighted to have assured the Crown of France to its ancient Sovereigns. I trust the Bourbons will never forget what you have done for them and that they will ever be grateful to England for the great things it has done in their favour.

I will now only add the King's compliments and remain [etc.].

428 THE QUEEN OF WURTEMBERG *to the* PRINCE REGENT

Stutgard, April 18th 1814.

BEING quite ashamed of the very short letter I wrote to you on 16th instant owing to my having been so hurried that I had not time to say half what I intended, I must trouble you again with a few lines to-day.

By this time I had flattered myself to have had it in my power to have congratulated you on the whole north of Germany being freed from French troops, but it appears that it is neither the intention of Marshal d'Avoust or of the Governor of Magdebourg to surrender these towns unless they are drove to it by superior force. Long have I sincerely wished that at least Harbourg should be retaken that you might dear brother have the satisfaction of knowing that our dear father's dominions were no longer exposed to the inroads of the enemy.

In the box which I have entrusted to Count de Beroldingen for my mother I have taken the liberty to put up a snuff box with a mosaic, which I hope dear brother you will do me the favour to accept of. I remember of old that you were partial to these pictures and have taken great pains to acquire some specimens of this work flattering myself they will serve to recall me sometimes to your thoughts.

It gave me sincere pleasure dear brother to hear that you were sufficiently recovered to attempt riding and hope that you will now be quite rid of all gouty twinges as the fine weather is coming on. In about ten days we shall attempt settling in the country which I hope will do me good as I am quite low and unhappy at having been obliged to decline for the present your very kind invitation, which however I flatter myself at a future period to accept of. We anxiously expect the account of Louis 18 arrival at Paris; all unite in saying the Count d'Artois[1] was received by the people with the greatest joy. Never in history has a revolution been mentioned which was brought about in so short a time; this must delight you dear brother who have ever shewed so much kindness to the House of Bourbon. The King desires me to present his best compliments and I remain with the sincerest affection [etc.].

1 He succeeded his brother Louis XVIII as King of France in 1824.

Berlin, April 20th 1814.

HALLELUJAH thank God you have succeeded now in *all* your endeavours, and you in England has gained the day, for she alone never did recognize that wretch,[1] and I think the baseness he has shewn at the end proves him to be baser than any man that ever has existed. France must feel itself humbled at having submitted so long to the despotism of such a man; had he fallen gloriously in battle, had he rushed when he saw he could do nothing to the cannon's mouth, one might have said he was *great* in his end, but to submit tamely & ask for his treasure proves a soul as mean in his misfortune as it was *cruel* in prosperity. God be praised that is now over & that you, who I ever must say was the first to rouse that spirit which has carried the day, have been happy enough to see your endeavours crowned with success. God grant you may live many many years to enjoy its advantages. I hear the two Sovereigns[2] either are gone or are going to pay you a visit; this they owed you & in return I hope to see you this Summer *here* on the Continent when I shall hasten to wherever you land to embrace you. I hope that the K. of Prussia will please you for he is a *great man* and his conduct has proved him so; his military talents after all I hear carried the day, and the Prussian military character has regained its antient splendour, and renoun. The levees are still going on famously; they have just made a fresh levy of 100,000 men. Four days ago one thousand Ersatz Maunschaft marched from here, for the Prussian foot guards are fine men as ever one saw. What a melancholy state poor Blücher is in. I understand his mind and health are so enfeebled that he was not able to march into Paris at the head of his conquerors.

I am dayly expecting letters from England & perhaps among them some commissions for you; the moment I receive them they shall be executed & I shall send over whatever you want by my A.D.C. Lieutenant Hawkins of my Regt. who is to go & join his Regt. I think you would like to have a pattern cuirassers helmet and perhaps you would adopt it for your cuirassers at Hannover. If I might be allowed to add a word it would be to have a complete cloathing of the Prussians put out for your inspection, which you might easily get by speaking to Jacobi Klout.[3]

I have not been able to see any thing since my arrival, for I met with an accident & very nearly broke my kneepan.

1 Napoleon.
2 The Tsar and Frederick William III; the Emperor of Austria declined the Prince Regent's invitation.
3 Baron von Jacobi-Kloest, the Prussian Minister in London.

I have a most famous good house, really magnificent. Now God bless you dearest brother & believe me [etc.].

P.S. His little honour's mama I see announced as *avec sa suite* at Francfort the *7th*.

430 THE HEREDITARY PRINCE OF ORANGE *to the* PRINCE
     REGENT

Hd Quarters, Rosendaal, Aprill 20th 1814.

I CAN not fail to congratulate your Royal Highness upon the happy and extraordinary events which have taken place in France, since I now consider your Royal Highness's great work as finished and the liberty of Europe consolidated, for nothing but the re-establishment of the Bourbons on the throne of France could have assured us a solid peace, and the happiness of the Continent. What a glorious event for your Royal Highness to whose firmness we owe all this and whom the whole of Europe is obliged to acknowledge as his deliverer. The kindness your Royal Highness has uniformly shewn towards me and my wish of conducting myself always with frankness towards you, encourages me to ask your Royal Highness to do me the favour to acquaint Mr. Fazel [*sic*] the Embassador, whether you do or do not approve of the letter I have written to Princess Charlotte's mother and which I have sent to him under flying seal to be submitted to your Royal Highness and which is or is not to be sent according to your opinion on the subject; for it seem'd to me right under the existing circumstances to direct this letter to the Princess, but I would not take this step without your Royal Highness being aware of it and having approved of it. I likewise take the liberty to enclose a letter for Princess Charlotte, and have the honor to subscribe myself with the most sincere respect and attachment [etc.].

431 THE QUEEN OF WURTEMBERG *to the* PRINCE REGENT

Stutgard, April 25th 1814.

THOUGH I have already written to you by Count de Beroldingen, having heard that the King has ordered him to leave Paris in some days for to begin his journey to London; I cannot deny myself the pleasure to send you a few lines, first to recommend this gentleman to your notice, who, being one of the King's Aide de Camps Generaux and Chamberlains, is constantly at Court, which I trust will give him some interest in your eyes as he will be able to give you a very exact account of me who he sees daily at Stutgard. His having been much on actual service and frequently at Paris and Vienna will perhaps make his conversation agreeable to you, and I beg that you will, dear brother, be convinced that I shall be very much pleased if I hear that the King's choice should suit your taste.

Secondly, my dear brother, you will I hope feel that this being a most interesting moment on the political horizon in which the situation of all Europe will of course be determined, it is natural I should have recourse to your affection, and entreat you to stand by us, and befriend us. My very unfortunate state of health not having allowed me to accept at present of your very kind invitation, which however can never be forgotten by a sister who is most sincerely attached to you, and looks forwards with impatience to the time when all circumstances may unite for to enable her to pay you a visit. Severe as this disappointment is to my heart I should feel doubly wretched could I imagine that my being prevented seeing you would be a reason for you, dear brother, to neglect or abandon the interests of those who are so nearly connected with you. I therefore think it a duty to the King and myself to recommend strongly our interests to you, being convinced that no body can do so much for us. A word from you, my dear brother, to the Russian Ambassador[1] and even to the Austrian[2] will certainly turn the balance in our favour. The King, who desires me to present his compliments to you, sets his whole confidence in the friendship you shewed him when he was in England, and much does he trust in the affection you have ever kindly professed for me. Be assured, dear brother, we wish for nothing but what is just, considering the great sacrifices this country has made to the Allies. Being convinced that your affection will lead you to do every thing for us in your power I think it needless to torment you longer on this subject and will now take my leave, remaining with the sincerest affection [etc.].

1 Count Lieven.   2 General Merveldt.

Frejus, April 27. 1814.

CONFORMABLE to the expectation which I had the honor of stating to your Lordship in my last dispatch, Napoleon, at the moment of quitting Roanne upon the morning of the 23d instant, requested me to proceed in advance to Aix, and from thence to transmit through Marshal Massena[2] commanding at Toulon, an application to the British Admiral off that harbour, requesting a British ship of war for his use and protection in going to the Island of Elba.

It was my wish to obtain this request in the form of a note, but it was not in my power, as he immediately went off in his carriage. Hearing at Aix that a British ship was at Marseilles, I proceeded there and found H.M. Ship "Undaunted", commanded by Captain Usher,[3] who took it upon himself immediately to comply with the application, and afterwards he obtained from Admiral King[4] an order to execute this service.

Napoleon arrived here this morning. His baggage is on board the "Undaunted", and he himself with the officers of his suite, the Austrian commissary and myself, will embark tomorrow morning.

I have reason to believe that his dislike to embarking in a French ship, arises from his fear of hearing unpleasant observations from the crew. The French frigate Duyad, a corvette which is to remain with Napoleon according to the Treaty, and a transport vessel, anchored here this morning; but he appears to be extremely dessatisfied with the manner in which this arrangement has been executed by the French Government. He has expressed himself to that effect this day, and in terms of thankfulness for the liberal treatment he has received from the Minister of His R.H. The Prince Regent, although formerly the avowed enemy of the British nation.

It is scarcely possible to describe adequately to your Lordship, the encreased violence in the enmity of the inhabitants towards Bonaparte as we travelled southwards. It was manifested equally in both sexes, in all ages, and in every class of the people, by cries of hatred, revenge and insult. At Avignon the carriages which preceded us by one day, were stopped and the eagles defaced. One of the servants who accompanied ourselves was threatened with instant death, if he would not cry out "Vive le Roi", and had Napoleon passed there the day before (Sunday) he would have been destroyed, as there was a collection of persons there resolved to attempt it.

1 General Sir Neil Campbell (1776–1827), afterwards Governor of Sierra Leone.
2 After Napoleon's abdication Masséna went over to the Bourbons. [1756–1817.]
3 Sir Thomas Ussher (1779–1848), who conveyed Napoleon to Elba. Knighted, 1831.
4 Sir Richard King, second Baronet (1774–1834). K.C.B., 1815.

At Orgon an effigy was prepared and brought before him during the change of horses dressed in uniform besmeared with blood—a label fixed upon it with the inscription—"voilà donc l'odieux tyran; tôt ou tard le crime est puni". The women and boys climbed upon the carriage, and he was only saved by the persuasion and the personal force of the commissaries and others who attended him, as there was no escort. Afterwards stones were thrown. It was unsafe to change horses in the villages even. Upon one occasion he rode off, (wearing a common hat with a white cockade) on horseback, accompanied by one of the couriers. Sometimes he changed parts of his dress with each of the commissaries and assumed the name of Colonel Campbell, and of Lord Burghersh.[1] All the party dined together without any marks of complement or deference and a mixed order of march was assumed.

Upon these occasions he shewed no small anxiety to preserve his existence by the finesse to which he had recourse for that purpose.

His spirits are not affected, and the reflections which might be expected to prey upon his mind, seem to be drowned by the occupation of the journey, and the disposition of his baggage.

His mother (Madame Mère) and Cardinal Fesch,[2] were at a Chateau near Roanne, but they had no communication with him that we heard of.

His sister (Princess Pauline) has been in this neighbourhood for some weeks past, and proposes to follow him soon to the Island of Elba. He stopped for some hours yesterday at her house.

433 JOSEPH FOX[3] *to* JOHN [*sic*] GRAY

Argyll Street, April 30, 1814.

IN laying before you an extract from the Minutes of a meeting of the Committee of the Institution for promoting the British system for the education of the labouring and manufacturing classes of society of every religious persuasion, held this day at Kensington Palace, His Royal Highness the Duke of Kent in the Chair, it is requisite for me to state that the conduct of Joseph Lancaster has led to an entire dissolution of the connexion which subsisted between him and the Institution,[4] and in consequence much difficulty is experienced in respect of subscriptions

1 Succeeded his father as eleventh Earl of Westmorland in 1841. (1784–1859.) In August 1814 he was appointed Envoy Extraordinary and Minister Plenipotentiary to Tuscany.
2 Cardinal Archbishop of Lyons; half-brother of Napoleon's mother. [1763–1839.]
3 The Secretary of the British and Foreign School Society; a dentist by profession.
4 See No. 355.

which happen to fall into his hands, as he persists in retaining them for his personal use unless they are forcibly withdrawn from him. This being the case with the subscription of His Royal Highness the Prince Regent which you were so good as to send last week, I have been directed to apply to you according to the following Minute, and I shall be much obliged to you for an answer for the information of the Committee.

[Extract from the Minutes]

"It having been stated to this meeting that Joseph Lancaster had received the annual subscription of the Prince Regent to the amount of £100 to the Royal Free Schools in the Borough Road and had not paid the same to the Treasurer of this Institution, resolved

That Mr. Fox be directed to apply to Mr. Gray requesting him to state whether the sum above-mentioned was intended for *the personal use* of Joseph Lancaster, or designed for the support of the British system conformably to the letter addressed to Mr. Whitbread by Colonel McMahon under date of 22nd. of December last."

I take this opportunity of presenting you with a copy of the last report of the Committee.

434 CAPTAIN HESSE *to* LORD KEITH

[*Copy.*]

Mérac, May 1st 1814.

THOUGH I had promised to write several weeks ago, we have had so much to do, with regard to military matters, that I could not find either time or a safe opportunity of getting a parcel conveyed; being not far from Bordeaux now, I shall send it to Lord Dalhousie[1] who I hope will take care of it, and get it conveyed to England.

I have told your Lordship once before, but like to repeat it "that *nothing* of what I have received from la *personne en question, in writing,* is still in existence. Those articles, which I have not with me out here, I shall deliver up after my arrival in England.

I have a favor to ask of you which is, to forward the enclosed parcel to its destination, without having it opened by any body but the person it is to go to. I trust my Lord the favor I ask will be granted & have the honor to be, [etc.].

1 George Ramsay, ninth Earl of Dalhousie (1770–1838), the father of the Governor-General of India. He commanded a division of the British Army in the Peninsula, 1812–14.

Tuesday [? 1814].

[*Copy.*]

MR. HESSE is extremely sorry he had not the honor of seeing Miss Mercer Elphinstone when he called this morn^g in Harley Street. Mr. H. told Ld Keith that the papers or rather letters that he had mentioned in his letter were not in existence.

I had given my word, that they were to be destroyed immediately after being read, and I have kept my word, for there is no vestige of them remaining.

With regard to the other articles which Mr. Hesse said he would send back on his return to England, he has not got them yet from the person who had taken care of them, but Mr. H expects to receive them every day, and he will then return them to Miss M: E. en personne.

Mr. Hesse is going out of town tomorrow morn^g to join his Regt. for a few days, but he will be back again before the end of the week—and thinks of staying in London four or five days previous to his going abroad for six months.

The day of his arrival in town he will do himself the honor of waiting upon Miss M. E.

436 PRINCESS CHARLOTTE *to* [CAPTAIN HESSE]

[? 1814.]

THE line of conduct you have thought proper to pursue is not what I mean to touch upon, for as this is a free country, every one may enjoy their own opinions & sentiments. But as this is the last letter you will probably ever receive from me, I think it highly necessary to explain the motives of my conduct.

The noble & generous temper of my father would not allow him to expose what had happened, nor would it have been known if you had not thought proper to make it publick yourself. Could I (after seeing no reguard whatever paid to my father's orders) could I, I say, do otherwise than resent such conduct. But not that only. Your reguard for me I fancy could not be very great when you endeavoured all in your power not only to deprive me of 2 people (I mean Lady de C[lifford] & Mrs. U[dney]¹) who next to my parents I love the best, also to injure their characters as much as possible in the eyes of the world.

1 Princess Charlotte's sub-governess, whom Miss Knight succeeded.

After that, I think it would have been not only extraordinary conduct in me but also the highth of ingratitude if I did not feel it in the strongest manner possible & to reguard it as a clear proof of your total disreguard of my father's wishes (not to say comands) & contempt for my feelings.

Having the approbation of my father, his love, & the advice of my two inestimable friends I neither can nor do wish for any thing more.

This long letter I have no doubt you will excuse as the subject required it.

437 PRINCESS CHARLOTTE *to the* PRINCE REGENT

[? 1814.]

ACCORDING to your desire I do not delay informing you that I went to my mother yesterday at 5 & returned *home* at seven to dinner, & that *I did not* (as was in the papers) dine with her. She is at Connaught Place & not at Kensington. The visit was very acceptable, & it went off very well. It only remains for me to express my thanks to you for having allowed me to go, & had I not thought you would be engaged last night, I should then have written to tell you, instead of now.

438 LADY ANNE BARNARD[1] *to* THOMAS LAWRENCE[2]

Berkly Sqr. May 2d 1814

YOUR very flattering note, and acceptable present of Genl. Stewart's print which *is the finest thing I ever beheld* and the strongest likeness, reached me this moment, and I thank you for both. Your note gives me much satisfaction—I had for some time been thinking of intruding a few words on your time, which words have remained unsaid, from my shyness of appearing presumptuous enough to suggest any thing to one whose genius and conceptions are so splendid.

But now that you have reassured my timidity, I will confess, that I should feel deeply sorry if such an occasion was lost in handing down to posterity by such a pencil as yours, the noblest events that the history of the world has to produce—No man possesses more *taste* or finer *ideas*

1 The daughter of James Lindsay, fifth Earl of Balcarres. She married Andrew Barnard, and, when he was appointed colonial secretary to Lord Macartney, Governor of the Cape of Good Hope, she accompanied him to Capetown, returning to England in 1807. [1750–1825.]
2 The portrait painter (1769–1830). He was knighted in 1815.

on an exalted scale than the Regent, and I make no doubt that he will propose to you what will meet yours.—I have as little doubt that from the moment you had reason to think the plan was in agitation, that you would give up your thoughts to the subject, and to the *inspirations* which can alone give energy to such works, but altho a far better idea may already have been suggested than any which has skimd across my fancy, yet its visions shall be laid before you, as in the multitude some little matter may present itself to be adopted.

In the first place it strikes me that *one* painting cannot properly contain our subject—two paintings of very considerable size, not inferior to that of West lately finished,[1] would be necessary, and companions to each other.

In the present day of wonders, is there any scene that *you* know of, that coud tell the tale more distinctly, or comprehend fact—feeling—and character, more favourably to an historical painting than that, where the King of France taking from his shoulders the order of the St. Esprit, threw it over the neck of the Regent—saying

"To you Sir I have owed my all!—even my sustenance—I have nothing to give but THIS—keep it to remind you of Louis the 18th"[2]— these strong, ingenuous, simple words, deserve I think to be engraved on the back of the painting, which woud descend to future ages, the testymony of the gratitude of a King of France, restored to his Throne by the firmness and liberality of an English Monarch (& no bad record of the virtues of this country who know not what national enmity is when misfortune is in the case)—The figure of the Dss D'Angoulême[3] connecting itself with her youth & past misfortunes woud add interest and charm to the groupe and the great heads of Administration most of whom were present at this affecting scene and who have aided the glorious cause deserve to be commemorated by your pencil also—

With respect to the other painting, you know better than I do, that

---

1 Probably his *Christ presented to the view of the people by Pilate.*

2 This Investiture took place in Grillon's Hotel in Albemarle Street on 20 April, when Louis XVIII drove to London in state from his retreat at Hartwell before returning to France. Lady Anne, however, was evidently drawing on her imagination: the King replied thus to the Prince Regent's congratulations: "Your Royal Highness will accept my most sincere and grateful thanks for your Royal Highness's congratulations—for the invariable kindness with which I have been treated by your Royal Highness and by every member of your illustrious House. It is to your Royal Highness's Councils, to this great country, and to the constancy of its people, that I shall always ascribe, under Providence, the restoration of our House to the throne of our ancestors, and that state of affairs which promises to heal the wounds, to calm the passions, and to restore the peace, tranquillity, and prosperity of all nations."

3 Marie Thérèse (1778–1851), Louis XVI's daughter. Her husband, Louis Antoine de Bourbon, Duc d'Angoulême (1775–1844), was the eldest son of Louis XVIII's brother, "Monsieur", afterwards Charles X.

the two Emperors, the King of Prussia and some of the greatest generals the world can boast are likely to be here soon to see our Regent and to visit this country—what a noble assemblage on such an occasion for your imagination to groupe! and in some befitting manner I think you coud obtain permission to introduce the figure of the Princess Charlotte to give the addition of female softness and beauty to this collection of heroes, forming a counterpart or rather companion to the other painting —One *stipulation* I must make with you, and no hint—I have two excellent precedents for what I propose. Sir Joshua Reynolds in the window at Oxford, where he represents himself as one of the shepherds;—and Titian in a picture of Our Lord's Supper, belonging to my brother Lord Balcarres.[1]—After having painted the Emperor Charlemain and all the monarchs of his own time as Apostles at the table of Our Saviour, he introduces himself as one of the attendants, bringing in a most excellent pye—Let me therefore see Mr. Lawrence introduced in some character into those national paintings—you will deserve your place.

I hope to see the Regent shortly, tho I know not when—I have been ill, but I am now quite recovered.—The moment is close at hand when the last mentioned painting shoud be thought of.—If the *present opportunity is lost*, its strength and force from collecting the countenances as they *now are*, will be lost to you for ever. I feel most zealous in the matter but from respect to the Regent have been silent to every human creature, one person excepted, of rank and of taste who is a safe person, on the part I have ventured to take in it.—And I shall from reasons that are but *just* to *you* be equaly silent on the letter I am now writing to you. —I hope a little time will see my wishes in train to be accomplished, meanwhile from my silence I have *no allys* to fight this cause along with me which is a pity—Pray let no false modesty prevent you from laying all your thoughts before His Royal Highness as they arise—I look on it as a duty you owe to the Regent and to your country, even more than to yourself, and if you neglect it now, you will repent it when the time is past—[etc.].

1 Alexander Lindsay, sixth Earl of Balcarres (1752–1825), one of the representative Peers of Scotland.

Hanover, May 2d 1814.

I HAVE at last the satisfaction of informing you that the garrison of Homburg has hoisted the white flag and sworn allegiance to Lewis the Eighteenth, and I enclose copies of General Bennigsen's letters which I received yesterday evening, and which I think will interest you.

I regret very much I was not present at your entry into London with the King of France.[1] It must have been indeed a proud moment for you, and a reward you so richly deserve from the firmness with which you have constantly acted to support the good cause and the family of the Bourbons. Thank God I shall soon have the pleasure of seeing you, & I am now making every arrangement to be off the moment I hear of the arrival of the frigate. I have been obliged to give up my journey to Gottingen on account of the number of things I have still to do, and I have ordered Colonels Best and Martin who are appointed to the command of the Landwehr Divisions, to inspect all those batallions which it has not been in my power to see. As the march of the troops has been stopped they will very likely be able to do this duty before the militia is sent home.

I have now nothing more to add than the assurance of my ever remaining [etc.].

440 THE DUKE OF CUMBERLAND *to the* PRINCE REGENT

Berlin, May 2d 1814.

A FULL year has now passed for it was last Thursday a 12 month that we shook hands for the last time in Carlton House. Great & prodigious have been the changes that have taken place in that period, and I am proud to think that the success is greatly if not solely owing to YOU. I am no flatterer, God knows, but I am convinced from what I hear that had you not remained *firm* and *decided* we should have made a disgraceful peace at Chatillon. Hallelujah that things are as they are, and you are the main spring of the whole, & that you may live many many happy years to witness the result is the wish of one of your sincerest friends, for by Heaven you know that I am devoted to you. I trust, dearest

1 On 20 April. "A most interesting and splendid scene", declared Lord Melville. "He was much gratified, as were his family and attendants, with their reception. It was everything they could possibly have desired." See the account in the *Annual Register*, 1814, *Chronicle*, pp. 32–4. He left London to embark on the *Royal Sovereign* yacht at Dover on the 23rd, the Duke of Clarence escorting him to Calais in his flagship, the *Jason* frigate.

brother, you received perfectly safe my letter written in which I took the liberty of calling your attention to the subject of the pays of *Münster &* *Paderborn* being added to Hannover. I make no apology for so doing for I have no more an interest to *that*, that I feel it a duty to call your attention to that, especially as it is generally reported *here* that Prussia is to have great additions to its possessions such as *Berg* and *Juliers, Lusas, Cologne*; certainly *charity* begins at home, and therefore as you have done so much for the great cause you ought to have some recompense. And the addition of Münster and Paderborn such as they were *under their Bishops* would be of great consequence to our House. It is also reported that Wittenberg & Torgau are to be given to Prussia, and South Prussia restored; it is said that Tauenzien's corps is to march immediately to take possession of it. The raising of troops is still going on with great energy here, and Lestorg[1] who dined with me the day before yesterday told me that as yet he had received no counterorders, aber alles bleibt bey den Alten. Here are nothing now but depots, the garrison is composed of the reserve battalions of the different regiments of footguards which are very fine, and of the cuirassiers of the Grand Duke Constantin (who has got a Prussian cuirassier regt), the Brandenburg Hussars, an Uhlan regt., & a dragoon regt. There is a squadron of each, in all about 1000 horse; the cuirassiers are very fine, and if I might presume to offer an opinion I would humbly recommend when you form your *new* troops for Hannover to adopt the uniform of the Prussian cuirassiers such as it is now, which is very handsome, & if you choose I will procure a correct statement of everything, but for THIS I must beg *your orders* directly from yourself. I know you hate writing at least, *never* having in the whole course of a year received a single line from you I must suppose so. Do let me entreat you, dearest brother, just to sacrifice to me five minutes while Dupaquet[2] is preparing your breakfast, just to put down to paper *what* I can send you. As I understand the Duke of Cambridge proposes leaving Hannover and returns to England[3] in the course of a fortnight, I shall send Morand on Wedy. the 4th. to Hannover with *letters* among which this will be one, and he shall carry the new military prints of the Prussian army as far as they are published, which are six numbers. Among them you will find a Garde du Corps whose uniform is beautiful and I should very much recommend a similar one for your Hannoverian Garde du Corps. The rest of the cuirassiers is similar, merely their cuffs & collars are of different colours and they have

1 Anton Wilhelm von L'Estocq, the Prussian General.
2 According to the *Court and City Register*, C. F. Du Pasquier was Groom of the Chambers, 1806–16; Mrs Du Pasquier was Housekeeper at Kew after 1820.   3 On leave.

no lace on theirs, & they have the eagle on the point of the helmet, whereas the Garde du Corps has the Star of the Order. The Prussians have 3 other cuirassier regts. besides the Garde du Corps, one with dark blue which are the Brandenburg cuirassiers, one with black which are the Silesian, & one with light blue, which are the East German or Constantine's. Their helmets are really beautiful and if you introduce the *silver & yellow*, such sash as I sent you, the Hannoverians will look beautiful, for that plain yellow sash is hideous, and as all the German services wear either silver or gold sashes, the Hannoverian look frightful. And a silver sash will last 10 years, & costs only 25 dollars or five pounds. I shall send you also what pattern *white and red* similar to what all the Prussian General Officers & cavalry officers wear in white and black. I think the King has spoilt some of his uniforms by introducing within the last two months epaulets of the most ugly shape. I understand they are raising new regts. and Krishe, the Mr. Hawkes of Berlin, told me he had now an order to complete for *1500* Uhlans near Münster, but here again they fail, for they do not wear the kapka which is a very handsome headdress for an Uhlan but they wear chakos. The Uhlans of the Guard alone here wear the kapka; all the Russian & Austrian Uhlans wear the kapka. I have no doubt that Merveldt has his with him, & in my opinion the Austrian Hussars & Uhlans are the best drest of any I have ever seen as yet. I cannot say as much of their cuirassiers.

The town of Magdeburg has made Tauenzien a present of a gold sword studded with diamonds, and a large turine of silver filled with 20,000 dollars, which sum of money he most nobly refused accepting; but at length accepted it on condition he might distribute it among his army. The King of Saxony[1] is still here & drives about in great parade, always with 3 carriages & a great suite of aide camps & chamberlains. I met the old man the evening before last riding to Charlottenburg in full galop with half a dozen officers round him, & a dozen grooms, the Queen & Princess Augusta driving in a coach & six close behind him. Berlin is very empty, I generally pass my evenings at Princess Radzivil's[2] where there is generally all the foreigners that are here. The stage is not good & I only go when they give operettas, but the singers are very so so, the orchestra however is capital. My house belongs to the Dss of Courland & is the identical house in which the precious Trenck[3] had a secret amour with *Princess Amelia* & was the original

1 Frederick Augustus I, King since 1806. (1750–1827.) He married, in 1769, Mary Amelia Augusta, sister of the Elector, afterwards King, of Bavaria. Their only child, Mary *Augusta*, was born in 1782.
2 The wife of the Polish Prince von Radzivil.
3 Friedrich, Baron Trenck (1726–1794), the son of a Prussian Major-General. It was in

cause of all his misfortunes, at least so I am told. Mr. de Hut left this yesterday morning in order to return to the Hague to accompany the Princesses to London. Now God bless you dearest brother & believe me [etc.].

441 ROBERT GRAY *to* JOSEPH FOX

Duchy of Cornwall, Somerset Place,
4th May 1814.

UNTIL the arrival of your letter[1] yesterday I supposed Mr. Joseph Lancaster to continue in the superintendance of the Free School in St. George's Fields, for the benefit and support of which I have been accustomed to pay to him His Royal Highness The Prince Regent's annual subscription; and it was for that purpose, and not for his own personal use, that the sum of one hundred pounds, paid by me to Mr. Lancaster on 25th of April last, was intended.

442 SIR THOMAS TYRWHITT *to the* PRINCE REGENT

Paris, May 4, 1814.

THE morning after I had dispatched my last letter to your Royal Highness, I obeyed Her Majesty's[2] commands in waiting upon her, and I herewith transmit the result of what passed in consequence in the shape of a memorandum which I drew up when expressions were alive in my ear, and for the accuracy of which, I think, I can say, I will be responsible.

I came here for the purpose of acquainting Lord Castlereagh with all that had passed—As he had written to the King from Troyes in consequence of Count Zeppelins notification, it does not appear that any letter from the King to your Royal Highness is, in point of form necessary; and therefore Count Beroldingen, is now on his way from this place to be presented to you, as the Minister from the Court of Stuttgard.

From all that I have collected of this gentleman's character, there cannot exist the smallest objection to him on any score whatever. He is well aware of the temper &c &c of the person he represents, and is very prudently silent upon all topics that regard him.

1744, two years after he entered the army, that he attempted an intrigue with the Princess Louisa Amelia, the daughter of the Duke of Brunswick-Wolfenbüttel, and the wife of Augustus William, son of Frederick William I of Prussia. He was later imprisoned by Frederick the Great, and was ultimately guillotined by Robespierre as an Austrian spy.

1 No. 433.   2 The Queen of Wurtemberg.

It was impossible to avoid paying my duty to His Imperial Majesty of Russia—I had a private audience of considerable duration—nothing can exceed the enthousiasm with which he speaks of his intended visit to *you*, for so he terms it—He says he is prepared to be hurraed two or three times but hopes to be allowed to ride out with your Royal Highness or go any where with you without drawing the observation of the populace—His sister, he told me, had written in the strongest possible terms of the satisfaction she had received by her reception in England.[1] She speaks most highly of the Princess Charlotte; and I could easily see the Emperor was delighted with her letter. A hope was expressed that the marriage might take place during his visit. Nothing could exceed his personal kindness to his unacknowledged Knight of St Anne.

I find the Duke of C[umberland] has left Strelitz about three weeks since, & has taken a tolerable good house at Berlin—I have seen a letter from him from thence of April 19. where there is no mention of any return to England. I am firmly of opinion his marriage will take place past all doubt.

In my audience with the Prince Hereditaire de Würtemberg, he spoke of your Royal Highness, in a manner that does him high honour—He also says, his visit to England is to *you*—He means to live very private —His talents as a soldier are spoken of here by the French Marshals as of first rate, and I think from the information I have received, nothing could prevent a popular commotion in his own country, but a persuation that his own principles were in direct opposition to those that are now there in force. His deportment is every way most unassuming, but has much of what is here termed the "Air noble".

I have been collecting here every thing I could find appertaining to the family of the exiled monster. I have also several other articles which I do not think expedient to permit to be rummaged by Dover gentlemen, I therefore return viâ Bruxelles which may make it a day or two later, than if I came by Calais, before I can say, I am, [etc.].

[P.S.] I cannot resist enclosing your Royal Highness a list of the company at Sr Charles Stewart's most magnificent Ball of last night.

---

1 She arrived at the end of March. "This was the lady", comments Miss Knight, "who had been so much talked of last spring for the Prince Regent, in case he could have got a divorce from the Princess." "She is a great favourite of Princess Charlotte", said Lady Charlotte Campbell, "and gives her (as it is supposed) excellent advice about her conduct." It is generally believed that her dislike of the Prince Regent, and her desire to prevent a closer union between Great Britain and Holland, prompted her to intrigue against the Orange marriage, and she helped to persuade Princess Charlotte that the Prince Regent wished her to reside in Holland so that he might be rid of her. See C. K. Webster's *Castlereagh*, I, 298–300.

Bristol, 7th May 1814.

I MUST beg leave to apologize to you for the liberty I take in requesting you (being a stranger) to do me the honor of laying the inclosed before His Royal Highness the Prince Regent.

I feel myself highly interested as an Englishman in the honor intended by the approaching visit of our most noble & illustrious Allies, the Emperor of Russia, the Emperor of Germany, the King of Prussia & others. A visit flattering to the Kingdom at large & to His Royal Highness the Regent in particular, unparallell'd in the page of history, & which (with the other great events in which they have borne so distinguished a part) tends to gild the setting sun of our beloved & aged Sovereign & the rising of that of his son with unexampled lustre.

As it will certainly be the desire of the Regent to afford these illustrious strangers with every personal attention, so I have no doubt he will wish to give them every specimen of our exalted national situation in arts, arms, architecture, & public benevolence and to afford for that purpose every encouragement to any and every subject (however humble) who might wish to come forward on such an illustrious occasion to render his mite to the national glory.

Amongst the many improvements in science I believe there have been none greater than in mechanics & in no branch of it more than in that noble, highly useful & most extensively applied machine the steam engine. This engine has been so generally applied that its novelty has almost subsided, except in its application to inland (& I have no doubt it may be also applied to marine) navigation.

The *steam boat* therefore I trust will not be deemed unworthy the notice of the Regent, nor thought by him a matter of small import to be introduced to his illustrious guests as an object not only of curiosity but real national utility.

About two years since I projected with another person (having heard of the steam boats in America where they are used with very great success[1]) to build a steam boat at Bristol to pass between this place and Bath, which was effected & which now plies between these two cities.

This boat the last autum I brought to London thro' the Kennett & Avon Canal & made use of it on the Thames for a short time, intending to have continued it as a passage boat from London to Richmond, but finding that (by Act of Parliament respecting the river) I could not use it for profit without being a free waterman, I hastily returned, fearing

1 At this time steamships were navigating the Mississippi, the Hudson and the St Lawrence; one carried passengers and cargo 2000 miles up the Mississippi from New Orleans in 21 days.

the approach of winter might otherwise have completely prevented my return. I assure you that the boat succeeded beyond my utmost expectation while on the river, it exceeded every thing in speed against wind, tide & stream, & would (I have no doubt) have been of great benefit to me & the neighbourhood could I have been suffered to retain the situation.

Since my return another steam boat has been nearly completed by my friend who projected the one before mentioned. This is infinitely superior in every respect to the former, & I have no doubt will go nearly double its speed, probably from 7 to 8 miles p. hour. It is very neatly fitted up, with two cabins fore & aft capable of taking from 25 to 30 persons & the engine is in the middle. The cabins have every comfort & have in each 4 sash windows, glass doors at the entrance, which may be all so opened as to make the cabins completely cool in the heat of summer & protect from cold in the winter. The boat has the appearance of a neat small yatch [*sic*] & will (I have no doubt) against wind, tide, & stream outstrip any vessel on the river.

From the above description I should hope this *self empelling boat* (as it may be well called) would afford novelty to, & excite some interest in His Royal Highness & his noble visitors; & with this view we beg to recommend it to his notice & patronage, & if considered worthy of them, & His Royal Highness should so far honor it as to command its being brought to the Thames for his inspection & use, every additional exertion will be used to complete it immediately & attend his order when & where to wait on him.

I trust you will yourself feel so much interested in this *steam boat* as not to consider your time mispent in reading this long letter, & also to present the inclosed to His Royal Highness for his inspection. If my address to him should not be sufficiently explicit, perhaps the additional explanation from this letter may not be unnecessary.

If my proposal be honor'd with approbation an early answer (for the reasons above stated) will confer a great obligation on [etc.].

444 THEODORE LAWRANCE *to the* PRINCE REGENT

Bristol, 7th May 1814.

I HUMBLY beg permission to congratulate your Royal Highness on the glorious & happy termination of the war, and the prospect of your being very shortly honor'd with a visit from those noble and illustrious personages who in conjunction with yourself have effected the same.

As your Royal Highness will wish to afford them every gratification in your power during their stay in England, and give them every specimen possible of our national improvement in science of every kind, tending either to utility or pleasure or both; I humbly beg (on my own behalf as of my friends) to request the honor of your Royal Highness' attention to that very useful, pleasurable and novel improvement in the science of inland (and which no doubt may be also applied to marine) navigation, the *steam boat*.

We have now a boat nearly finished at Bristol navigated by the power of a steam engine, surpassing in velocity every kind of vessel on navigable rivers against wind, tide and stream. It will run at the rate of seven or eight miles an hour and under some circumstances more. I tried a boat of this kind with great success on the Thames last autum, but this is on improved principles. It is capable of taking in its cabins from 25 to 30 persons, and would afford a most novel safe and agreable excursion to Windsor or elsewhere on that beautiful and picturesque river the Thames. It is neatly fitted up and may be more elegantly finished should your Royal Highness honor it with your patronage so far as to command us to bring it to London to attend your pleasure.

From your known taste and uniform desire to patronize science in every branch thereof, I humbly hope this proposal will not be thought intrusive.

I have written more at large to your Royal Highness' Secretary, wishing on this occasion to trouble you but as briefly as possible.

With every personal respect for your Royal Highness, & prayer for the prosperity of your illustrious house, I beg to subscribe myself, [etc.].

Foreign Office communication, dated 8 May 1814. [Abstract of Despatches from Lord William Bentinck in Italy. See *Annual Register*, 1814, Appendix to *Chronicle*, pp. 190–3.]

445 THE DUKE OF CUMBERLAND *to the* PRINCE REGENT

Berlin, May 10th 1814.

I HOPE you will excuse my writing you a few lines again, but as I know, at least I flatter myself that no change has taken place, that you are my friend I take up my pen to beg of you in case what I hear is true to think of me. I hear that Adolphus has asked leave to return to England, and it is said he does not like his situation there, but prefers returning to England which is more congenial to his liking. Should that *really* be the case I hope you will not pass me over again but at least give me an opportunity of serving you there, where I flatter myself I may be of *some use* at least if you give me your confidence. You may depend upon my zeal and anxiety to do my utmost to forward your wishes, and as naturally the Hanoverian army must *now* be nearly formed, I think I could lay before [you] a *plan* which I flatter myself might meet your approbation. You know I am the last man to push myself forward upon an improper occasion but surely you cannot take it amiss my so doing *now* in case Adolphus does not choose to return. I really & truly *love* the Continent· and mean to settle myself eventually here, therefore should prefer much to settle *there* where I might be of use I think to you, and you know I have served you and can be trusted in ticklish affairs. Tomorrow's event[1] that took place in *1812* will call to your recollection that *I* am worthy of trust and can be depended upon. Should I succeed in my wishes and get the appointment there, I trust you will allow me to give you my opinion upon the formation of the troops, and I think you should have a corps d'armes worthy of you & that would meet your approbation. Excuse this letter, but I know your friendship for me, and it is to *my friend* I write. You are the ONLY one of my brothers with whom I have any communication except Adolphus, and I trust you will never change towards me. I have, since I wrote to you, seen the Castle here; there are some magnificent apartments indeed, les grandes pièces are prodigiously fine and really when lighted up must be magnificent; the Ritter Saal and the room where the marriage ceremony is performed are prodigious fine apartments. I send you a small plan of the battle of Leipzig that only arrived *here* from the Fair yesterday; it is certainly the first copy that has reached England. I trust & hope you approve of what I have sent you. God bless you and believe me ever, [etc.].

446 LORD WILLIAM BENTINCK *to the* PRINCE REGENT

Genoa, May 10, 1814.

·IT will probably be known to your Royal Highness, that Marshall Murat has offered me a sword[2] which for reasons of a publick nature I did not feel myself authorized to refuse.

After the painful discussions which had taken place between us—after

1 The assassination of Perceval. The Duke and his friend the Lord Chancellor worked harder than any other individuals to keep the Tories in office.
2 For his achievement in capturing Genoa.

the very open manner in which I had arraigned his insincerity and perfidy, I must confess, that this offer, so much at variance from the cause that insulted honor would have taken, rather encreased than diminished my feelings of disrespect.

My first impulse of disdain engaged me to reject it. But directed to adopt a spirit of conciliation, and other circumstances rendering it desirable to lull any suspicion of hostile intention, I waved all private feeling for the benefit of your Royal Highness's service and accepted it.

To keep it, Sire, would deeply wound my honor—and I trust that your Royal Highness will graciously deign to grant me the satisfaction of laying it at your Royal Highness's feet. I shall then have the gratification of thinking that while to the best of my humble judgement I have done my duty, I am relieved from all personal obligation to Murat. I shall on the contrary have the real pleasure of feeling encreased the debt, which I am proud to owe, of gratitude for the many marks of goodness with which your Royal Highness has been pleased to honor me.

447 SIR WILLIAM MANNERS *to* COLONEL MCMAHON

Oxford Street, May 17, [1814].

THE PRINCE REGENT having created so many Peers, & intending, according to report, to create additional ones, allow me to remind you of His Royal Highness's written promise[1] to me, & to request, that you will have the goodness to inform me, when I may expect that promise to be fulfilled. Would there be any impropriety in an application to Lord Liverpool?

448 COLONEL MCMAHON *to* SIR WILLIAM MANNERS

Pall Mall, May 20th 1814.

I WAS not honor'd with your let^r of the 17th inst until last night when I return'd to town from an absence of three days, or I should not have omitted to sooner assure you, that I have no reason to believe there has been any intention whatever at present to extend the Peerage beyond those rewards for military services which have been almost just now confer'd.

1 No. 597.

Bruton Street, May 1814.

THE most respectful manner in which I could claim a seat in Parliament which was guaranteed to me during my life, by His Majesty's most gracious promise, I conceived was to address it to your Royal Highness through Lord Liverpool which I did so soon as I became again eligible to sit. The observations made upon my claim by Lord Liverpool I have clearly and incontrovertibly proved to be unfounded. The integrity of his Lordship's character imposed upon me the necessity of giving him every possible satisfaction upon the subject. The manner in which it has been so long suspended has originated feelings in my mind of too painful a nature not to occasion me more uneasiness than I think your Royal Highness would willingly subject me to even if it was not in my power to furnish the proofs which I have done both positive and presumptive of the truth of my statement, and which puts it beyond the possibility of doubt or contradiction.

I trust I do not presume too much when I feel confident that my character during a long life actively, honorably and confidentially employed in the service of my country; will screen me from any real, or apparent suspicion of attempting a fraud upon the son of my Sovereign.

If it is a fraud (and either it is or it is not) something stronger than vague surmise, erroneous conjecture, a mis-statement of facts, and a palpable misconception of the nature of my claim altogether, should be brought forward to invalidate the proofs I have advanced in support of it.

At His Majesty's request (in times very unlike the present) and to prevent a dangerous disturbance in the country, I sacrificed a popularity within my power to regain, and consented to remain in Parliament against the conviction of my own mind, against the general sense of the public, and contrary to the advice and influence of my own family, who were never afterwards reconciled to me. Such was the origin of His Majesty's promise—he never forgot it—he sanctioned it many years after, and Mr. Pitt did not hesitate to carry it into execution.

I challenge the severest investigation of my statement, and of the veracity of every part of it. I court the most minute enquiry into every circumstance connected with it. I shall rejoice to be cross-questioned on every part of it. I ask not to be treated with more ceremony or indulgence than would be given to any man (if any man there is,) who could be capable of attempting so stupid an imposition, and one in which he could be so easily detected.

Do me the justice Sir to believe I never ask'd any favor either of

1 See Nos. 304, 305, 321, 328, 329.

Mr. Pitt or Lord Liverpool; I applied to them only as they were the organ of communication between the Sovereign and the subject, considering neither of them competent to decide upon my claim. And therefore I hope it will not appear to your Royal Highness that I exceed the bounds of a reasonable expectation when I humbly request that your Royal Highness will be pleased to refer to the correspondence between Lord Liverpool and myself upon this subject, which I venture to hope will relieve me from the uneasiness of mind inseperable from the turn it has taken, and from that state of suspense and anxiety in which I have been kept for near *one entire year.*

450 VISCOUNT MELVILLE *to* COLONEL MCMAHON

Admiralty, 26 May 1814.

I UNDERSTAND that the Duke of Clarence has announced his intention of landing the Emperor & the King of Prussia at Deal. Unless the Prince Regent has given orders to that effect, it ought not to be sanctioned, because Dover is a much fitter place, & more convenient as well as much safer in landing. I do not know how carriages could possibly be landed in safety on the beach at Deal, & when the wind blows fresh, it is very unsafe for persons. The passage to Dover is also considerably shorter from Boulogne, & I understand that Lord Rosslyn is prepared to receive their Majesties at Dover.[1]

I have sent herewith a box containing a statement humbly submitted for the Prince Regent's consideration. I have not ventured to add what I have little doubt will immediately occur to His Royal Highness, viz. that the bare mention or surmise to any person of the possible disturbances therein contemplated, might without any other circumstance produce the effect which we are anxious to guard against.

I did not intend to be in town tomorrow, but I could easily come if necessary, & a messenger can come to me if you have any communication to make. I shall be at Wimbledon.

I think that I understood from the Prince Regent that it was His Royal Highness's pleasure that after accompanying their Majesties to Dover, H.R.H. the Duke of Clarence should strike his flag & come on shore.

1 The Tsar and the King of Prussia landed at Dover on 6 June, being brought over from Boulogne by the Duke of Clarence as Admiral of the Fleet. They were received on shore by Lord Yarmouth, Lord Charles Bentinck and the Earl of Rosslyn. Lord Rosslyn had been an A.D.C. to the King since 1795.

Russell Square, June the 5th 1814.

IN the confidence of your considerate delicacy and the strong impression of your friendliness of conduct towards me, I venture (after long interval of doubt and apprehension) to send to you the enclos'd letter;[1] the subject of which is too interesting to an artist (emulous undoubtedly of every fair distinction in his profession) to justify so long a silence, but from motives of propriety and that dread of being thought obtrusive and presumptuous, which ought *generally* to govern him in his professional conduct, but which here is still more binding on him from the distance of his situation, and his just and sincere feelings of reverence and duty.— The near approach however of these illustrious strangers, and the consideration that a moment may gain or lose the highest object that a life of exertion could possibly attain in painting a subject of such a nature, or the simplest portrait of either of these Monarchs whose cooperation with the Regent's views appears to have secur'd the happiness of Europe.— The greatest honor that I have ever receiv'd, after the gracious notice of His Majesty, is the having my picture of Lord Thurlow[2] placed in his Royal Highnesses collection; and *so* placed as to fill me with the liveliest gratitude for such generous distinction. Am I not justified in believing that another portrait recently painted by me is to have the same distinction? There indeed should be reward, sufficient for all reasonable ambition—but extraordinary events produce unusual feelings; and it is hardly possible that such a thought presented to the mind as is presented by the enclos'd letter, can leave it in repose.

To you, Sir, however I submit the whole—you will pass over the unmerited expressions which the courtesy of this lady has bestow'd on my suppos'd qualifications for tasks so arduous and not consider me deficient in knowledge of myself, for not withholding such a letter, because those compliments are in it.[3]

I beg you to believe me with much thankfulness, and the truest esteem, [etc.].

1 No. 438.

2 Edward Thurlow, first Baron Thurlow (1731–1806), the Lord Chancellor.

3 The portraits of the Prince Regent's royal visitors were painted at York House. "As these personages", says Sir Thomas Lawrence's biographer, "were absorbed in company, public affairs, and in visiting the institutions of the country, it required the utmost vigilance and importunity of Mr Lawrence to obtain even short and irregular sittings." (*Williams*, I, 342.)

Argyll Street, 9 June 1814.

NOTWITHSTANDING a copy of your letter[1] to me dated 4 May, was sent to Joseph Lancaster, accompanied with a letter by command, from the Duke of Kent, directing Joseph Lancaster to pay the £100 (being the annual subscription of His Royal Highness the Prince Regent to the Free Schools in the Borough Road) to Mr. Allen[2] the Treasurer, I am sorry to be under the necessity of informing you that he still refuses to give up the money. He alleges that the subscription was granted *to him*, by His Royal Highness, and not to the Institution; he has refused to acknowlege the authority under which you have written, and he declares that unless he receives a command from His Royal Highness, he will continue to retain it. I am exceedingly grieved to be called upon to communicate such information, concerning a man for whom so many efforts have been made, to maintain his credit and fame. It is certainly a most consoling reflection that the cause of education and the institution are preserved. I had some conversation with Mr. Adam on this subject a little while since and request you to be so good as to take an opportunity of consulting with Colonel McMahon, as the Colonel in his letter[3] to Mr. Whitbread, dated Dec. 22, stated that the subscription of His Royal Highness to the Institution would be continued as heretofore.

453 VISCOUNT WHITWORTH *to* [COLONEL MCMAHON]

Phoenix Park, 25th June 1814.

YOU some time ago gave me reason to expect a visit from the Earl of Granard, on the subject of the line of politics which his Lordship might in future be inclin'd to pursue. I have more than once had the pleasure of receiving his Lordship here, but without any such communication.

He call'd upon me however this morning, and requested to know how far I should be dispos'd to forward his views, or give effect to any recommendation which I might receive from home for his succeding to the office of Clerk of the Hanaper, on the death of the Earl of Westmeath.[4] His Lordship gave me distinctly reason to suppose that such recommendation would come from His Royal Highness the Prince Regent.

1 No. 441. 2 The Quaker philanthropist and scientist (1770–1843). 3 No. 375.
4 George Frederick Nugent, seventh Earl of Westmeath (1760–1814). He died on 30 December.

I should have observ'd that Lord Granard prefac'd this application with an assurance of his intention to give every support in his power to the present Administration upon all points, excepting the Catholic question, which, he said, he felt himself still bound to support, altho' from local motives rather than from conviction.

I endeavour'd to frame my answer in such a manner as might convey my respect for His Royal Highness's commands, or rather, as His Royal Highness is graciously pleas'd to term them, his wishes, and at the same time the anxiety which this Government would naturally feel to confer such a distinguished mark of favour upon a sure and steady friend.

Such he profess'd himself to be; and as such, I told him that I should not be dispos'd to throw any difficulties in his way, without however binding myself to any thing specifick.

I told his Lordship that I should communicate the purport of this conversation to you, for the information of His Royal Highness, which he appear'd to be very anxious that I should do.

I shall be extremely happy to hear that His Royal Highness has suffered no particular inconvenience from the very great fatigue which he must have undergone for some time past.

I confess I cannot help rejoycing that the visits are concluded.[1] The visitors must return impress'd with a deep sense of the amiableness of our Prince and of the greatness of the country; but they are always attended with great trouble & inconvenience, and sometimes worse.

454 THE DUKE OF CUMBERLAND *to the* PRINCE REGENT

Berlin, June 27th 1814.

KNOWING how much your time must have been taken up by all the fetes &c that have been going on during the stay of the Emperor and King of Prussia I did not choose to take up your time by any letter from me, but now that I must suppose things have returned into their old train I shall take up my pen & address myself to you upon my own wishes, knowing how *kind* and *friendly* you have ever been to me, & feeling conscious I have done nothing to lose your friendship and confidence, I therefore do it with the fullest persuasion *you will* do what *you can* to *forward them*.

I have written by this same opportunity, to Adolphus & have *mentioned* to him my having *written* to *you*, therefore he must see I have acted openly & fairly. I have been informed by credible persons from

1 The Continental Sovereigns did not leave Dover for Calais until the 27th.

Hannover & this has been confirmed to me in *letters* from England received this day, that Adolphus does *not* like his *situation* at *Hannover* & speaks with regret at the idea of his *returning* there; should *that really* be the case, it cannot be considered either as *indelicate* or *unbrotherly* in me if I address myself to you to say how *very very* happy I should feel myself to *succeed him there.* You may depend upon my exerting every nerve, for the trust reposed in me, & I flatter myself I could do it to your satisfaction. When you sent me Bloomfield last December to announce to me how *painful* it was to you, not to be able to leave me the command, you mentioned I knew it was an act of conscience on your part, as the King wished Adolphus to be there, you have therefore done your duty, but surely the King never could have wished to have left Adolphus *there* if he *disliked* it & therefore certainly if *that* is the case I do hope & trust you will confer on me that command; for I took the liberty of addressing you upon the subject the 10TH of May, & *then* I told you it was my intention to fix myself upon the Continent & therefore should be most happy to do so at Hannover where I believe I can say *I am known* & can be of *real service* to you provided you give me your confidence. Excuse my saying so much on this subject, but as *I have it so much at heart* the being fixed there I could not refrain from speaking most fully to you on the subject. Believe me that *wherever* I am and *whatever* situation I may be in I shall never cease to be [etc.].

455 THE QUEEN OF WURTEMBERG *to the* PRINCE REGENT

Louisbourg, June 27ᵗʰ 1814.

LONG have I waited with impatience for an opportunity to converse with you more openly than by the post, and am delighted to have it in my power to renew the assurances of my constant affection, and to write you a confidential letter.

My mind being taken up by the situation of the King my husband and my own I have often, dearest brother, troubled you with letters concerning the difficulties we have met with of late years; and mentioned how much the King's dominions have suffered from the necessary expences attending a war. Since the King concluded his Treaty with the Allied Powers, Wurttemberg has alone furnished to the amount of above fourteen millions of florins or near one million five hundred thousand pounds sterling to the Austrian and Russian troops, in various articles of commodities, and provisions, while they were either quartered in the country or on their marches, as also to the hospitals which have constantly remained in the Kingdom. Many magazines have been filled out of this country though they were in the dominions of other Sovereigns. These particulars and the King's having doubled his contingent, sending twenty four thousand five hundred men to the Great Army, instead of twelve thousand, who through their bravery and the military skill of the Prince Royal have on several occasions decided the battle in favour of the Allies; makes me hope that you will dearest brother grant the request which I venture to make trusting in your steady affection which I am convinced will lead you to do every thing in your power to contribute to my welfare and happiness—I therefore entreat you that you will be so very kind my dear brother to have an article inserted into the instructions which you will give to your Ambassador at the Congress of Vienna by which this Minister will be authorised to support the King of Wurttemberg interests: and that you will allow me to tell my husband that you are willing to assist him. He will in that case order Count Beroldingen to deliver to the Secretary of State for Foreign Affairs a memorial and instruct him to confer on these important subjects with Lord Castlereagh.—You will, my dear brother, feel how necessary and important your protection is to us at a moment on which depends our future welfare and doubly so as the natural ambition of our neighbours leads them to be as anxious as ourselves to aggrandize their dominions. Your supporting the cause of the King of Wurttemberg will not only be confering a great obligation on us and our family but serve to keep up the Protestant interest in Germany which would be lessened if the Catholics were to continue to extend their power. And if I may dear brother venture to add one word concerning Hanover I believe you will unite with me in thinking that it is for the future interest of the Electorate that a Sovereign in the South of Germany should be the Ally of that country and sufficiently powerful to be able to unite his troops to the Hanoverians in case they were attacked by their neighbours.

The King desires me to present his best compliments and express his gratitude for the very kind amiable manner in which you have treated his son, the Prince Royal, who I hope has had the happiness to please you. I will now take up no more of your time and remain with the sincerest affection [etc.].

[*Copy.*]

Bruton St., [28th June 1814.]

THE condescension of your Royal Highness when you were graciously pleased to assure me that you would peruse the statement which I felt it imperative on me to submit to the consideration of your Royal Highness, would have prevented me from obtruding myself again on your attention, if it was not essential to my honor and to the character I have so long supported that I should substantiate the claim which I had the honor to make.

I trust your Royal Highness will be of opinion that His Majesty's promise to me of a seat in Parliament during my life did but scantily recompence the services I had performed, and the injury I had sustain'd on the very trying occasion upon which it was given.

Amidst the crowd of more important matters necessarily pressing on the mind of your Royal Highness, I hope to be excused for a conjecture (suggested by anxiety, and the length of time that has elapsed, since I had the honor to wait upon you) that by accident the papers relative to my claim might have escap'd the notice of your Royal Highness: otherwise I should be more deficient in gratitude than I trust you will believe me to be, if I was insensible to the interest you were pleased to take in my claim, or unthankful for the patient hearing and gracious reception which your Royal Highness was pleased to give me on the subject of it.

457 THE QUEEN OF WURTEMBERG *to the* PRINCE REGENT

Louisbourg, June 30th, 1814.

HAVING yesterday been honoured by a very gracious letter from the Queen in which she most kindly acquaints me of Prince Paul's disrespectful behaviour to you at Carlton House, and since that of his very improper conduct at Ascot, I hasten to write and beg you will be convinced, dear brother, how wretched both the King and myself are that any person belonging to us could forget himself in such a shocking manner in your presence and the Queen's.[1] But at the same time I must take the liberty to remind you, dear brother, that I wrote in April as soon as we were apprized of Paul's intention to go to England, in the King's name and mine to warn you that neither of us could be answerable for this young man's behaviour, as he is so unhappy to have perverted all the talents and sense Providence has endowed him with to very bad

1 The Allied Sovereigns went to Ascot Races on 10 June.

purposes; and for thirteen years has done nothing but offend his father by the improprieties of his conduct. It is very painful to be obliged to make such a confession, but I think it a duty to state the truth that you may not blame the King for allowing Paul to go to London, as certainly he would have prevented it had it been in his power. I have explained these circumstances to our dear mother who I am sure will have the goodness to repeat them to you, dear brother; that I may not plague you with a volume. Nothing hurts me so much as Paul's having forgotten himself in your house and I shudder to think of his profligacy in drawing the amiable young Prince of Orange into a scrape in presence of Charlotte.[1] I intreat you, dear brother, to tell my neice how much I am affected on the subject but think it too delicate for me to mention it. Nothing but a parent can with propriety speak to a daughter on the errors a young Prince she is engaged to, has been drawn into. I will now only add the King's best compliments and express the sorrow he feels that one of his sons could be so very disrespectful towards you. We are therefore doubly grateful for your kindness to the Prince Royal, who is thank God very different from his brother, and who feels as he ought the notice you have taken of him.

I will now take my leave and remain with the sincerest love and friendship [etc.].

458 RICHARD BRINSLEY SHERIDAN *to* COLONEL MCMAHON

Saville Row,
Monday Evening, [Before July 1814].

I HAVE *decided* to stand for Westminster.[2] I have the Whig support made known to me thro' the Duke of Norfolk. This will enable me only to be a more powerful & efficient friend to the Prince. After what has

1 The Prince of Orange, it was said, returned from Ascot Races seated on the outside of a stage-coach, and in a highly excited state. (*Stockmar's Memoirs*, i, 10.) This letter helps to explain why she broke off her engagement. See No. 528 for Princess Charlotte's opinion of him.

Miss Knight copied the whole of the correspondence between Princess Charlotte on the one hand, the Prince Regent, the Duke of York, and the Hereditary Prince of Orange, on the other hand, and added a running commentary which forms the basis of this part of her *Memoirs*. I have not thought it necessary to reproduce these letters (the originals are missing): they throw no new light on the marriage negotiations, and the most important documents are quoted or discussed in Lady Rose Weigall's *Memoir of Princess Charlotte* and Miss Knight's *Memoirs*.

2 A by-election followed Lord Cochrane's expulsion (5 July) from the House of Commons. On grounds of expense the Treasury decided not to put forward a Tory but to support Sheridan. Having accepted the Radical programme of Reform Brougham came forward as the official

pass'd between me & Lord Sidmouth I cannot doubt the support of Government. Without a boast depend upon it no man can beat Brogham [*sic*] but myself, and against me I think he will yet shrink to stand. How hateful the ground of his mob popularity would be to the Prince, I need not state.[1]

459 SIR WILLIAM BEECHEY *to* [COLONEL MCMAHON]

Harley Street, Monday July 4th [1814].

M AY I beg the favour of you to communicate to His Royal Highness the Prince Regent the plan of a large equestrian picture, which I propose to execute on the principle of the one at Hampton Court. The subject of it —the late grand Review in Hyde Park,[2] rendered more peculiarly interesting than any other ever witnessed in this country, on account of the many illustrious personages who were present there, and the truly important circumstances under which they were assembled in London.

I own I feel myself impelled by an irresistable desire of conveying to posterity this commemoration of events equally glorious to His Royal Highness and the British nation, but as the Prince Regent will properly be the principle personage in the picture, I cannot satisfactorily commence my desire without His Royal Highness's gracious permission.

460 QUEEN CHARLOTTE *to the* PRINCE REGENT

Windsor Palace, the 4th July 1814.

I HAVE lost no time in attending to the wish which you expressed to me, and am now enabled to send you the replies in writing of the several individuals concerned, who have all acquiesced from a principle of duty in

---

Radical candidate and was backed by advanced Whigs such as Whitbread, Bennet and Creevey who distrusted Sheridan as a Carlton House man. On the other hand Major Cartwright, the veteran Radical Reformer, equally distrustful of Brougham's sincerity as a Reformer, threatened to split the Radical vote. But public feeling, which at first had been indifferent about Cochrane's fate, swung round in his favour; Brougham, Sheridan and Cartwright waived their pretensions and Cochrane alone was nominated on 11 July and therefore re-elected five days later. The House of Commons wisely made no attempt to prevent him from taking his seat.

1 Brougham was the Princess of Wales's legal adviser and had also advised Princess Charlotte on the question of her marriage. The letter cannot be accurately dated. As early as 10 March Byron said that Sheridan meant to stand for Westminster in the event of Cochrane's expulsion. On 11 June the Duke of Norfolk vainly tried to dissuade the Radical caucus from setting up a candidate, the Whigs being anxious to avoid a contest with the Reformers.

2 The Royal visitors attended the military review in the Park on 20 June.

the proposal made to them, at the same time that all have requested to
be permitted to annex to that acquiescence the condition that they shall
receive their instructions in writing signed by yourself,—which appears
to me reasonable and indispensible towards the effectual discharge of
their duties.

You will observe in the concluding part of the papers delivered by
Ladies Ilchester[1] and Rosslin[2] that they lay great stress upon, and indeed
state as inseparable from a compliance with your wish the circumstance
of the proposed experiment originating under your roof, in Carlton
House, and with the advantage of your direct and ostensible support;
as giving weight to their endeavors, as well as from the general influence upon public opinion.—Independently however of these grounds,
connected with the desired success of the measure, they are guided in
their opinions by a knowledge of the popular feeling, and of the sentiments which prevail in all circles of society, which their access to these
circles, as well as their habits of life give to them means of learning and
appreciating which I cannot possess—Upon these various grounds they
consider themselves bound, under the same principle of duty which for-
bids them to decline a most difficult and ungracious task, to represent
their conviction of the necessity of what they venture to propose, observing that an interpretation might otherwise be given to a measure of
national utility, which may create such a clamour as would probably
render it impossible for any persons to continue in the discharge of the
duty requested of them.

In communicating to you these their sentiments, I conceive that I owe
it to you, my dearest son, not only to state my entire concurrence in
them, but also earnestly to entreat you as you look to the general benefit
of what is now proposed, and as you value your own peace of mind and
your security from encreased trouble and embarassment, not to object to
receive Charlotte into Carlton House, were it only for a short period,
after which the removal to Cranbourne Lodge may take place upon the
plea of suggested change of air, at this season, or any other which shall
appear adviseable.—I am aware that you cannot admit this preliminary

1 The Dowager Countess of Ilchester (d. 1842), the second wife of the second Earl of
Ilchester.
2 The Dowager Countess of Rosslyn (d. 1826), the second wife of the first Earl of Rosslyn,
the Lord Chancellor. A fortnight earlier, Princess Charlotte had broken off her engagement
to the Hereditary Prince of Orange, and her father informed her that unless she could hold
out a hope that in a few months she might be induced to marry the Prince, arrangements by no
means agreeable to her inclinations would be made. Miss Knight and the rest of the Household
were dismissed, and Charlotte was told that she must forthwith reside at Cranbourne Lodge
and be under the superintendence of Ladies Ilchester and Rosslyn. Princess Charlotte then
ran away from Warwick House and drove in a hackney coach to her mother at Connaught
Place, but the Duke of York was sent after her and took her to Carlton House. See No. 465.

arrangement without putting yourself to great inconvenience, but the object, is one of such moment to yourself & to the country that I am certain you will not suffer this objection to weigh, and I do not scruple to say that, by the adoption of it alone, you can, in my view of the subject, save yourself from the effects of popular clamour which an impression that Charlotte is sent by you to a place of confinement may produce.

Nothing but my unalterable affection for you & my anxiety that you may not by any hasty step do that which might make you unpopular can make me press you upon a subject I know you are so much adverse to, but *nulle rose sans epine* & I yet hope that by adopting this plan you may enjoy the sweets of the rose without feeling the thorns.

461 VISCOUNT CASTLEREAGH *to the* PRINCE REGENT

St. James's Sq.,
Wednesday 2 a.m. [6th July 1814].

LORD CASTLEREAGH has the honor to acquaint your Royal Highness, that the Princess of Wales has written to the Speaker a letter, thanking the House of Commons for the intended provision of £50,000, and desired the grant may be limited to £35,000. Your Royal Highness will perceive from the enclosed note of this date to Lord C[astlereagh] that this is a change of determination probably press'd upon H:R:H: by her advisers.[1] The consideration of the Report stands for Friday.

Mr. Broadheads motion for the expulsion of Lord Cochrane was this night carried after a very long debate by 140 to 44. There was a previous division for delay, Ayes 74, Noes 142.

Lord Cochrane made a most libelous defence. Mr. Wilberforce and the Solicitor General made most useful speeches—as did Mr. Bathurst and Mr. Bankes.

1 In June the Government decided to increase the Princess's income from £22,000 to £50,000 a year so that she might maintain an establishment more suited to her station. Without consulting her advisers, Whitbread and Brougham, who would have urged her to reject the proposition, she wrote to Castlereagh accepting it. A few days later however Whitbread persuaded her to write to the Speaker, declaring her unwillingness to increase unnecessarily the taxpayer's burdens and to accept more than £35,000. (See *Parl. Deb.* XXVIII, 607.) The smaller sum was then voted, and a few weeks later, to the annoyance of her Whig friends, who wished to make political capital out of her wrongs, she left the country.

The Speakers were

Mr. Broadhead[1]
a — Mr. Browne[2]
Mr. Croker
Mr. Attorney Genl [Sir William Garrow]
a — Mr. Brand[3]
a — Mr. Barham
a — Mr. Ponsonby
Ld. Castlereagh
a — Mr. Wortley
Mr. Bankes
a — Mr. Whitbread

Mr. Bathurst[4]
a — Sir F. Burdet
Mr. W. Wynne
Solicitor General [Sir Samuel Shepherd][5]
a — Lord A. Hamilton[6]
Mr. Wilberforce[7]
a — Mr. Wrottesley
Lord Castlereagh
Mr. Lockart[8]
a — Mr. W. Smith[9]

Those marked a voted against expulsion.[10]

462 SIR WILLIAM BEECHEY *to* COLONEL MCMAHON

Harley Street,
Saturday morning [? 9 July 1814].

SIR WM. BEECHEY presents his compliments to Col! MacMahon, and begs leave to offer him his best thanks for his obliging attention.[11] He is under the necessity of trespassing still further upon the Colonel's kindness, in requesting him to make known to the Prince Regent the satisfaction he experiences, in the assurance of His Royal Highness's approbation of his intended plan, which he shall now proceed to put in execution immediately. At the same time he would feel obliged if Colonel MacMahon would ascertain His Royal Highness's pleasure with regard to the time it may be convenient to him to sit, as the groupe of which His Royal Highness will be the principal is the one he must first attend to, and will give the character to the rest of the work. Sir Wm. would be

1 Theodore Henry Broadhead, Tory M.P. for Wareham.
2 Anthony Browne, M.P. for Hedon.
3 Thomas Brand, Whig M.P. for Hertfordshire; succeeded as twentieth Baron Dacre, 1819.
4 Charles Bragge Bathurst, Tory M.P. for Bodmin, and related to Earl Bathurst. (d. 1831.)
5 Solicitor-General since December 1813; knighted, 1814. (1760–1840.)
6 Lord Archibald Hamilton, Whig M.P. for Lanarkshire (1770–1827); second son of the ninth Duke of Hamilton.
7 William Wilberforce, the philanthropist (1759–1833), M.P. for Bramber.
8 John Ingram Lockhart, M.P. for Oxford.
9 William Smith (1756–1835), M.P. for Norwich; belonged to Wilberforce's group, the "Saints".
10 The list of the minority printed in *Parl. Deb.* XXVIII, 606 omits Wrottesley; only forty-three names are there given. Castlereagh omits Colonel Vyse as a speaker.
11 See No. 459.

happy to avail himself of any incident which might have occurred, or be supposed to have occurred in the course of the Review, which the Prince Regent might be graciously pleased to point out, as well as of any directions which His Royal Highness might condescend to give with regard to the disposition of the groupes, as he is anxious that the commemoration he proposes of so remarkable a period in English history should be treated in the manner most proper for it, and most suitable to the importance of the subject.

Sir Wm. begs to apologise for the trouble he has occasioned Col. MacMahon, and trusts to the goodness which he has recently experienced to excuse the present intrusion.

463 PRINCE LEOPOLD OF SAXE-COBURG[1] *to the* PRINCE REGENT

Londres, ce 10 Juillet 1814.

LA bienveillance de Votre Altesse Royale m'est trop chère pour que je n'ose pas l'importuner en lui soumettant une justification qui lui prouvera, quand elle daignera la lire, que je ne suis pas aussi coupable envers elle, qu'elle paraît, à ce que je crains, le croire, et que mon intention était de régler mes actions de la sorte qu'elles puissent se flatter de l'aprobation de Votre Altesse Royale, et non pas de lui déplaire. Si Votre Altesse Royale, daigne lire avec indulgence le récit véridique, mais un peu long, des événémens qui ont eu lieu dernièrement, elle se convaincra de la verité de ce que j'avance, et elle verra qu'ils lui ont été mal interprêtés. Je suis venu dans ce pays, pour présenter mes hommages à Votre Altesse Royale, pour veiller aux interêts de nos affaires, l'arrangement definitive des affaires d'Allemagne devant se faire ici à ce que l'on disait à Paris, et puis pour voir un pays que depuis longtems j'avais eu le désir de connaître. Le tems passa si rapidement pendant le séjour des Souverains, que je n'eu pas la possibilité de m'occuper des affaires d'Allemagne. N'ayant pas une seule fois depuis les derniers jours de son séjour à Paris, pu parler en particulier à l'Empereur de Russie, et désirant lui recommander nos affaires d'Allemagne, et de lui dire que je désirais rester encore quelque tems ici, je dus saisir un moment favorable à cette belle fête du Lundi

1 Prince Leopold, who married Princess Charlotte in 1816, was at this time an officer in the Russian army. One of his sisters had married the Tsar's brother, the Grand Duke Constantine, and he was said to be a great favourite with Alexander, with whom he was now visiting England.

19[1] pour lui demander une audience avant son départ. Il me l'accorda pour mardi l'après-midi à 4 heures. Je m'y rendis exactement, mais comme c'était le dernier jour de sa présence il y avait[2] les Princes ses augustes frères, le Prince de Bavière,[3] le duc d'Orléans,[4] le Prince d'Orange sans compter les ministres, cette grande société fut la cause que je dus attendre fort longtems, d'autant plus que l'Empereur était, à ce qu'on disait, chez sa soeur à causer avec Son Altesse Royale la Princesse Charlotte, qui à mon arrivée avait déjà été chez la Grand-duchesse. Desoeuvré comme j'étais et las d'attendre, je me promenais dans la maison, et je remontais l'escalier venant du salon de service ou j'avais pris quelques renseignemens nécessaires pour le voyage, lorsque je vois descendre de chez la Grande duchesse la Princesse; elle daigna prendre mon bras pour la conduire à sa voiture, et me dit que je n'avais pas été poli du tout de ne pas avoir été une seule fois lui faire visite, et qu'elle espérait que si je ferai un plus long séjour ici, que je serais plus poli dans l'avenir. Je ne pus pas autrement que de lui assurer que certainement je n'y manquerais pas, mais en ajoutant qu'en vérité j'avais ignoré qu'il fut permis de lui faire des visites. A cause de la masse du peuple qui se trouvait devant la porte sa voiture tarda quelques minutes d'arriver, j'eu l'honneur de la conduire ensuite à sa voiture, après avoir attendu ces peu de momens au milieu d'une foule de curieux qui emplissait toute la maison. Quelque tems après j'eus enfin mon audience, on me donna la permission de rester ici aussi longtems que cela me serait agréable, en m'engageant seulement de venir au congrès de Vienne. A Portsmouth je ne pus que très furtivement prendre congé de l'Empereur,[5] n'ayant pas pu trouver de cheval pour aller à la revue je fus encore prendre congé de la Grande-Duchesse [*sic*], qui ne fut pas très tendre car je n'ai pas le bonheur d'être très fort en ses bonnes graces, à cause qu'elle avait dû épouser mon frère aîné,[6] ce qu'ensuite elle a changé pour rester en Russie, et cela a laissé un peu de froideur pour toute notre famille. De retour ici je balançais extrêmement si je devais suivre l'invitation de Son Altesse Royale Madame la Princesse Charlotte, ou non, enfin malheureusement on me dit que tous les autres

1 Monday the 20th. There was a Ball at Buckingham House.
2 The Tsar and his sister left for Coombe Wood, Lord Liverpool's seat, on Wednesday the 22nd.
3 Prince Lewis, who succeeded his father as King of Bavaria in 1825, and abdicated at the beginning of the 1848 Revolutions.
4 Louis-Philippe, afterwards (1830–48) King of France. [1773–1850.]
5 The Tsar and the King of Prussia visited the dockyards and reviewed the fleet at Portsmouth on 23 and 24 June.
6 Ernest, Duke of Saxe-Coburg-Gotha (1784–1844), married Louise, daughter of Augustus, Duke of Saxe-Coburg-Altenburg, and was the father of Albert, Prince-Consort of England.

princes avaient été. Le jour du concert Whitehall le 28 Juin, étant en grand uniforme et dans le costume nécessaire pour faire une visite de cérémonie, je quittais après le premier acte le concert à 4 heures, et je me fis annoncer. On me reçu dans la presénce de Madame la Duchesse de Leeds, après à peu près trois quarts heures où la conversation roulait sur les choses les plus indifférentes, comme le séjour de Portsmouth, la musique des fêtes qui se préparaient, voyant que la Princesse ne se portait pas bien et avait vraiment très mauvaise mine, ne sachant pas qui donnerait le signal du départ je me pris la liberté de me congédier moi-même.[1] J'avoue avec la franchisse que je dois à Votre Altesse Royale, que j'ai eu d'abord un remord de conscience, et que je regrettais déjà allors beaucoup de ne pas avoir demandé la permission de Votre Altesse Royale, mais j'avais crains d'un autre côté, que cette demande n'aye l'air d'être faite dans une autre intention, ce qui aurait été, si peu de jours après la rupture, tout à fait déplacé.[2] Je pris donc la ferme résolution d'agir avec la plus grande délicatesse, et de ne remettre le pied dans la maison de la Princesse sans la permission de Votre Altesse Royale. Cependant malgré ma bonne conduite je remarquais bientôt que Votre Altesse Royale était mécontente de moi, ce qui m'affligeait beaucoup, parceque excepté cette malheureuse visite je n'avais en aucune mannière démerité ses bonnes graces. Ayant de nouveau fait cette remarque affligeante dans l'audience qu'elle avait gracieusement daigné m'accorder, pour lui parler des affaires d'Allemagne, et qui pour jamais sera gravé dans ma memoire, pour le discours admirable qu'elle daigna faire sur la situation actuelle de l'Europe, et pour la sagesse profonde avec laquelle Votre Altesse Royale, un souverain aussi puissant, a su pénétrer dans le tissu de toutes ses relations les plus intimes, je pris la résolution de m'adresser à quelqu'un qui, jouissant de la confiance de Votre Altesse Royale, pourrait me justifier auprès d'elle, et s'informer sous main de ses augustes intentions, mon désir le plus ardent étant de les connaître afin de ne pas faire de nouveau quelque chose qui pourrait lui déplaire. Je m'adressais pour cet effet à cet excellent Comte de Munster. Aparament la faute est tout à fait à moi, je me souviens d'avoir été embarassé et de m' être mal expliqué, en lui ouvrant ma confiance, et que son amitié

---

1 Miss Knight thus refers to the visit to Warwick House: "He paid many compliments to Princess Charlotte, who was by no means partial to him, and only received him with civility." (I, 300.) The Princess however told Prince Leopold's friend and physician, Baron Stockmar, that she wished to become better acquainted with him, and that she had said the same to her aunt, the Duchess of York. But as she was allowed to attend only one dinner at Carlton House in honour of the royal guests, she had little opportunity of meeting him. The Dukes of York and Kent seem to have approved of him, and after his return to the Continent they enabled him occasionally to communicate with the Princess.

2 Princess Charlotte had broken off her engagement to the young Prince of Orange in June.

l'a porté à dire plus qu'il n'était bon de dire dans ce moment. Mon desir était de connaitre les intentions de Votre Altesse Royale, mais ce n'était pas le moment de dire aussi le plus petits mots de plus, si peu de tems après la rupture et des événémens véritablement désagréables; si cela avait été mon intention j'aurais bien osé moi-même en dire quelque chose à Votre Altesse Royale, ayant eu une si bonne occasion à l'audience qu'elle avait daigné m'accorder. Votre Altesse Royale qui connaît si parfaitement bien les hommes, et les juge avec tant de justesse, est trop bonne, pour condamner en moi, le désir, mais elle peut être sûre qu'avec un caractère aussi calme et peu extravagant que le mien je ne pouvais pas penser à faire dans le moment actuel des propositions. Connaissant à cet heure la volonté de Votre Altesse Royale je m'y conformerai scrupuleusement; si elle me permets je resterai jusqu'à jeudi où je prendrai congé de Sa Majesté la Reine et de la famille Royale, il me serait en tout cas à causes d'arrangemens de finances et de voyage difficile de partir avant ce tems, mais si Votre Altesse Royale désire allors que je parte je me soumets absolument à sa volonté suprême, quoique j'avoue qu'étant jeune je me serai beaucoup amusé a voir ces fêtes, mais je suis enchanté si je puis donner par ma résignation une preuve de plus de mon dévouement à Votre Altesse Royale. Elle ne daignera pas mal interpreter la sécurité dans laquelle elle m'a trouvé au bal chez Lady Howard, mais cela peut lui être un garant de plus de ma bonne conscience, et que je ne m'attendais pas à ce qui était arrivé. Votre Altesse Royale n'a pas d'idée de la peine que m'a déjà causé la disgrace dans laquelle je me trouve auprès d'elle, et je la supplie de grace de me rendre son ancienne bienveillance que je m'ai démerité que pour cette seule visite, quoique je puisse donner ma parole d'honneur à Votre Altesse Royale que malgré que la Princesse m'aye temoigné beaucoup de bienveillance dans le peu d'occasions ou j'ai eu l'honneur de la voir [1] que je ne lui ai pas dit un seul mot relativement à la possibilité d'un arrangement dans l'avenir, et que je me suis conduit dans cette occasion, en galant homme comme j'ai toujours coutume de faire. Je répète à Votre Altesse Royale ma très instante prière de ne pas me laisser partir sans me pardonner et de croire que je ne suis pas indigne de ses bonnes graces, auxquelles si même, comme il paraît, le sort devrait pour toujours m'éloigner de ces contrées, j'attacherai toujours le plus grand prix. Si Votre Altesse Royale daignait me donner connaissance de ses ordres et en même tems si elle m'a

---

1 Miss Knight says (I, 300), "When we drove in the Park he would ride near the carriage and endeavour to be noticed. There were reasons why this matter was by no means agreeable to Princess Charlotte. However he certainly made proposals to the Regent, and, though rejected, found means to get into his favour."

pardonné elle me rendrais bien heureux; en attendant je la supplie
d'agréer l'assurance du profond respect et dévouement sincère avec
lequel j'ai l'honneur d'être[1] [etc.].

464 THE QUEEN OF WURTEMBERG *to the* PRINCE REGENT

Louisbourg, July 11th 1814.

I TRUST you are too well convinced of my affection to doubt my being
sincerely interested in everything that regards you. These sentiments,
dearest brother, do not allow of my being silent, at a moment in which
I know you have been severely afflicted by the inconsiderate conduct of
your daughter. It grieves me to the soul to hear of the vexations you
have met with, and perfectly understand how much Charlotte's behaviour on this occasion must have displeased you. However I am too
well acquainted with your good heart and the affection you have for your
daughter not to flatter myself that, dear brother, you will even at this
very painful moment consider Charlotte's youth and be convinced she
could never have adopted so decided a line of conduct if she had not met
with some secret ill intentioned advisers who perhaps seek to create a
coldness between you and your daughter, which would have the most
melancholy consequences for Charlotte, as she would then most likely
give her whole confidence to those who only seek to make her a tool, and
destroy the harmony which for the good of all parties must reign in the
family. Can you, my dearest brother, after the improper manner in
which Charlotte has behaved both towards you and the Prince of Orange,
be so very good as to recollect that she has from a variety of circumstances met with many disadvantages in her education, and from not
being constantly under the eye of a parent, has from her infancy been a
little too much accustomed to act for herself; this will perhaps induce you
to have more indulgence for her errors. May I therefore, dear brother,
entreat you to forgive her, after you have made her feel the improprieties
she has been guilty of. Certainly you will soften her heart if you speak
to her with the affection of a father. Your unexpected kindness will prevent her falling into any fresh errors, and when she has her eyes sufficiently opened to know how the world criticises her having followed
her own fancies, she will feel the duty as well as necessity of having a

---

1 The Prince Regent remarked to Miss Knight next day that "this Prince was a most
honourable young man, and had written him a letter which perfectly justified himself".
(*Ibid.* I, 301.)

better guide, and will for the future rather trust to the good advice of a tender father, than to that of false interested friends. Forgive my dwelling on this unpleasant event, but I have your happiness as well as your daughter's too much at heart, not to think it a duty to offer my humble opinion on this important subject. Adieu my dearest brother and be convinced of the sincere love and affection with which I am [etc.].

·

465 HENRY BROUGHAM's *Minute of a conversation with* PRINCESS CHARLOTTE

Con[naugh]t House, July 12, 1814.

H.R.H. THE PRINCESS CHARLOTTE OF WALES said that she desired it might be distinctly noticed that she had of her own free will broken off the proposed match with the Hereditary Prince of Orange, and that she was firmly resolved it should never take place. She added that *this* was her voluntary avowal, and to be considered as such, whatever she might afterwards be represented to have said, she being now at liberty, and about to be taken back to Carlton House. Mr. Brougham asked H.R.H. if she made this statement advisedly and with the view of its being represented by herself and those who heard it as her final determination. H.R.H. was pleased to answer, "I do it in this sense & with this view, and desire you may take it accordingly, and I authorise Augustus to use it in this sense"—alluding to H.R.H. the D. of Sussex then present together with the others who sign this Minute.

"When I had made the note", says Brougham in his *Memoirs* (II, 231), "it was read distinctly and signed by all present, she signing first, and six copies were made and signed, and one given to each person present. Her positive injunction was that if ever we heard the match announced as being to proceed, we should make her declaration in the note public. What had passed was in substance known to the Regent, and put an end to all further attempts to bring about the marriage." This copy, in Brougham's handwriting, is not signed.

466 VISCOUNT CASTLEREAGH *to the* PRINCE REGENT

St. James's Sq., 13th July [1814].

LORD CASTLEREAGH has the honor to acquaint your Royal Highness that the Bill for the Preservation of the Publick Peace was read a second time tonight upon a division.[1] The *Ayes* were 131—*Noes* 16.

1 This Bill, designed to put an end to unrest in Ireland, empowered the Lord Lieutenant, when disturbances existed in a district, to proclaim it to be in a disturbed state, and to appoint

Mr. Whitbread, Sir F. Burdett, Mr. Brougham and Lord Althorpe[1] opposed the Bill.[2] The speakers in favor were Mr. Smith,[3] member for Cambridge; Mr. FitzGerald,[4] Mr. Grant junr, Mr. Frankland,[5] Mr Bankes, Mr. Bootle,[6] Mr. Stephen,[7] Mr. Lambe and Mr. Wilberforce.[8]

The support from other quarters was such, as to render it unnecessary for your Royal Highness's servants to take any part in the debate.

Mr. Grant the son of ye East India Director spoke for the first time, in a manner which promises a great deal.

The Bill it is hoped will be sent to the Lords on Friday.

467 VISCOUNT CASTLEREAGH *to the* PRINCE REGENT

St. James's Sq., Tuesday Night.
[19th July 1814].

LORD CASTLEREAGH has the honor to acquaint your Royal Highness that the Princess of Wales's Annuity Bill has pass'd through the Committee, after some debate. Lord C. thought it right to agree that the £35,000 should be nett independent of property tax. Nothing was said on the Princess Charlotte's subject.[9]

a sufficient number of special constables, at the expense of the district concerned, under the control of stipendiary magistrates who were to be responsible immediately to the Government. Clauses subsequently introduced authorised the Lord Lieutenant to enforce a curfew order in a proclaimed district and to dispense with trial by jury.

1 John Charles Spencer, Viscount Althorp, and (1834) third Earl Spencer (1782–1845), Leader of the Whig Party in the Commons, 1830–34, and Chancellor of the Exchequer in the Reform Ministry.

2 None of these speeches is in *Parl. Deb.*

3 John Henry Smyth, M.P. for Cambridge (University, not borough). This is possibly a mistake on Castlereagh's part, for Smyth was a member of the Whig Opposition who is never reported by Hansard as having voted against his party. There were eleven Smiths in Parliament at this time.

4 William Vesey Fitzgerald, later, Baron Fitzgerald and Vesey (1783–1843), Chancellor of the Irish Exchequer.

5 Colonel William Frankland, M.P. for Thirsk.

6 Edward Bootle-Wilbraham, Baron Skelmersdale (1771–1853), Tory M.P. for Clitheroe. His father assumed the name of Bootle on marrying the heiress of Lathom House; the son resumed the surname Wilbraham in 1814. Peerage, 1828.

7 James Stephen (1758–1832), Wilberforce's brother-in-law and an abolitionist. Father of Sir James Stephen, the Colonial Under-Secretary.

8 Of these pro-Government speeches only Fitzgerald's is in *Hansard*, where no indication of a division is given.

9 The subject of her flight from Warwick House and her subsequent treatment.

Lord Ebrington's[1] motion was withdrawn. The Attorney and Solicitor General made the most impressive speeches in support of the conviction and sentence, and carried the House completely with them. The remission of the pillory to all upon the ground of this being the first offence of the kind will sustain the Court of Kings Bench, & satisfy the publick repugnance to see this part of the sentence inflicted, whilst it leaves Lord Cochrane's guilt, as it ought to be, upon a level with the others.[2]

Mr. Bankes moved an Address against any reversion being granted till 6 weeks after the commencement of the ensuing Session.[3] Lord C. opposed this as unconstitutionally passing by the House of Lords. It was rejected by 58 to 34.

468 THE DUKE OF CUMBERLAND *to the* PRINCE REGENT

Berlin, 23d July 1814.

I HAVE seen my cousin Charles on his arrival at Potsdam the night before last where I went accompanied by his elder brother the Hereditary Prince;[4] after some conversation he said "I must excuse him but he must talk to me seriously upon a subject in which the character of a near relative of his was concerned, I replied immediately "if you mean your sister[5] I will save you the trouble for it is my intention to propose to her the moment she returns from M[e]ck[len]berg. Nothing had prevented my doing this before but the particular situation in which she had been placed the divorce having been thank God *prevented* by the death of the Prince." He then replied "he was charmed to hear what I said, for that the character of his sister required this as people talked already so much about us". I then said "my friend, *no time* shall be lost for I will directly write to her & the Duke, & shall at the same time deem it necessary to

1 Whig M.P. for Buckingham; succeeded his father as second Earl Fortescue in 1841. (1783–1861). He moved "That an Address be presented to the Prince Regent, praying that His Royal Highness would be graciously pleased to remit the ignominious punishment of the pillory included in the sentence passed upon Lord Cochrane, in consequence of the distinguished services of that noble Lord."

2 Sir Francis Burdett's determination to stand in the pillory with his fellow member for Westminster no doubt contributed to the Government's decision to remit this part of the sentence.

3 "That an humble Address be presented to His Royal Highness the Prince Regent, that he will be graciously pleased not to grant any office, place, employment or salary, in any part of his Majesty's dominions, in reversion, or for joint lives, with benefit of survivorship, until six weeks after the commencement of the next session of Parliament." The House of Lords had previously thrown out a Bill to make this practice illegal.

4 Of Mecklenburg-Strelitz.   5 Princess Solms.

inform my brother the Regent". He then delivered to me a very kind message "that you had asked him what was the state of things between the Pss and myself that every body talked of it, that both my honour & that of the Pss required either that I should propose to her, or see her no more, & that if I chose to marry her you had no objection, that I had only to put my confidence in you, that you should be happy to see us married, for as a *widow* you would have no objection to receive her into the family, whereas if she had been divorc'd there would have been some difficulty though as Elector of Hannover you could receive her there, you could not in England". But thank God she is *not divorced* but a WIDOW.[1]

My intention was, dearest brother, first to have known fully the sentiments of the Pss, which I had proposed doing on her return home, as *her mourning is now over*, and then I should have immediately written to you, for 'till now I have never out of decency spoke to her on the subject & therefore did not choose to talk to you on the subject till I knew her sentiments, and secondly I declare to you that till the night I spoke to the two brothers I have never opened my lips on the subject. I do not deny to you that I have loved her very long but after an acquaintance of more than a year when I have examined and watched her whole conduct, she appears to me *so perfect* that I have no doubt of being the happiest man with her, and I am certain her manners are such that they will captivate you & the rest of the family. I cannot find expressions to thank you for all the kind things you said of me to Charles & all your kindness to me on this occasion. It may be ten days before I receive the Princesses answer as she must naturally first mention it to the King of Prussia who is the head of *her* family. The moment I receive her answer I shall despatch a messenger over to you.

All arrangements I totally entrust to you, knowing it cannot be in better hands. In *none* of my letters do I say a word on the subject, and therefore must beg you will tell it my mother, who must be happy to receive her own brother's daughter as *her own*, and I know that both the Princess & the Duke lay great stress on her good opinion and friendship; have also the goodness to tell it to my friend the Chancellor and Charles Steward.[2] I have now placed my affairs into the hands of the best of brothers with full reliance on his affection & friendship. God bless you and believe me in no situation shall I ever cease to be [etc.].

1 It is sometimes wrongly stated that she was twice divorced: she would have been had Prince Solms lived longer.

2 Presumably Lord Stewart, the British Ambassador at Berlin, who accompanied the King of Prussia to England in June 1814.

Saville Row,
Wednesday, July 27th [1814].

I HAVE done exactly as you wish'd and seen Lord Liverpool as well as Lord Sidmouth—I said every thing to the former you advised, avowing your previous communication with me, and what I said was under the impression of very sincere gratitude.

I have grieved, & so I believe I express'd myself to you the other night at the Fete,[1] to learn from different quarters that the Prince was dissatisfied at my giving way on the Westminster election.[2]—Against Brogham I would have stood 'till I dropt, for that was a *personal assault* on the *Prince*—& meant to have produced the most mischievous effects —The other was a very different case, & one in which the Prince had no *personal* concern—Had I persever'd in being a candidate, look for a moment to what my situation would have been. I should have had to encounter a popular yell for three weeks, (for observe *during the contest* no *pardon of the pillory* could have been granted) which I would not do for any seat, and *that* while my best attentions were due to another tho' a domestic quarter—but how could I have maintain'd the conflict when I found my friend the Duke of Norfolk despairing of the supplies he hoped for, & feeling the cause unpopular, & desirous of beating a retreat. I was left myself personally in debt £1700 after the last Westminster election[3] which has press'd upon me grievously—what could I have done *now* when I found not a shilling subscribed to support me—I told both Lord Cholmondeley & Lord Yarmouth when I found the thing desperate, the line I meant to take—& I think I had their concurrance that it would be right to signify that I *would not have given way to Brogham*, which I think the last sentence of my advertisement very intelligibly intimates—I have no wish to be member for Westminster but as that seat would furnish me in these precarious days a more independent opportunity of being of service to the Prince, nor have a wish to be in Parliament at all but for

1 Held at Carlton House in honour of the Queen. Supper was served at 3 a.m. and Her Majesty had not retired two hours later. The card of invitation was as follows:

The Lord Chamberlain is commanded by

THE PRINCE REGENT
to invite‑‑‑‑‑‑‑‑‑‑‑‑‑‑
to a Dress Party on Thursday evening the
21st. of July at ten o'clock to
have the honour of meeting

HER MAJESTY THE QUEEN.

A Ball.

2 See No. 458.
3 I.e. in 1807, when he was defeated.

the same object.—Even in opposing Brogham it is lamentable to think that I now find that he would have been espoused & supported by the *leading Talents* against me. Grenville, Grey, & Whitbread &c. I cared not for, but it was a grief to my heart to find Tavistock,[1] with whom I had been living in such intimacy, & the name of Russell pledged to the same cause!—with others whom I will not name!! but Adam, who can only act in one line, and that is the line of perfect honor, can ascertain the fact to you, & perhaps deplored it more than I do.

It would be gross affectation in me if I did not confess that I write this letter with a sanguine confidence that you will communicate its contents to the Prince—I am sure he has only to glance his eye over it to be convinced, that those who have told him that in declining Westminster at this moment I have fail'd in duty to him or regard to the public, have not judged well.

Now my dear Mac, I must conclude this long letter—I shall do it with a short but sincere sentence—The Prince is an excellent critic in every thing and in nothing more than in his insight into political character—I believe he gives me credit for honourable and independent political principles and, I trust, for sincere personal attachment to him—but he places no confidence in my judgement to apply these well—& there, if I dare use the phrase, he is mistaken—but I yet feel confident that it would require a very strong effort to dislodge me from his good-will.

470 LORD ERSKINE *to* WILLIAM ADAM

Wednesday Morning [27 July 1814].

I ENCLOSE the paper I read to you yesterday. It was written in almost as little time as it occupied in the reading, but the more I consider *the principles it contains* the more I think it some how or other may be important.

Nothing could die a more natural death than the abortive motion in the House of Lords,[2] & nothing could be better than the manner it was received by Lord Liverpool & the Chancellor, but the abandonment of

1 The Marquis of Tavistock, Whig M.P. for Bedfordshire, succeeded his father as seventh Duke of Bedford in 1839. (1788–1861.)

2 On 25 July the Duke of Sussex withdrew his intended motion relative to Princess Charlotte, saying that as she had been allowed to ride in Windsor Great Park and to visit London for a few hours, he hoped she would be treated more leniently than she had been. Liverpool denied that she had been or was to be subject to any improper restraint, and Eldon said that Parliament had no right to interfere.

the motion tho desirable, & which could not be helped even if otherwise, precluded the opportunity of recording principles which some how or other should be made manifest & asserted.

To say the truth—the idea that run thro the paper arose in my mind from the Prince's own feelings so admirably expressed by himself when he did us the honor to speak to us in the great room at the fete last Thursday. The system of calumny is intolerable & with proper exertion may be extinguished.

I turned in my mind various ways in which the sentiments contained in the paper might be made useful but whether any use or no use can be made of it, it will at least shew the Prince that I am anxious to serve him.

P.S. The great object of the paper is to shew, which it unanswerably does, that nobody has any jurisdiction over Princess Charlotte but the Prince her father in his personal & not in his political capacity.

471 *[Enclosure]* LORD ERSKINE *to* PRINCESS CHARLOTTE

London, July 27th 1814.

WHEN I had lately the honor to see your Royal Highness at Carlton House after a long interval, I felt myself much obliged by the same gracious notice with which I had always been distinguished, and on that account I have been the more disturbed & concerned at seeing your Royal Highness brought forward to public view in a manner which in my view of it is equally dangerous to your present as to your future happiness. Nothing indeed can in my opinion be more destructive of both, than the imagination that your Royal Highness is under the protection of *Parliament*, and not the private paternal government of the Prince. If any person shall inculcate that idea, I beg most solemnly & sincerely to assure your Royal Highness that it proceeds from a total misunderstanding of the Constitution of this country; & that any application to the House of Lords of the kind lately promoted & abandoned has not only an obvious tendency to question the most undoubted authority of your father, but is an infringement of those prerogatives which it may hereafter be your Royal Highnesses most solemn duty to maintain inviolate.

The public appeal to *Ministers*, upon such a subject as the case of your Royal Highness, tho it carries the appearance of avoiding all insinuation against the Prince Regent (& may have been so intended) does not at all avoid it, & must be no less painful to the just feelings of a daughter, than it is injurious to the character of a father.

When any measures in the administration of the *political* Government are found to be inconvenient, or even in the highest degree disastrous, Ministers in *such cases* are undoubtedly alone responsible, & no diminution of just estimation attaches upon the King; because the presumption of Constitutional Law, & the presumption of fact are in obvious correspondence to impute all blame in such instances to those whom His Majesty has entrusted with the conduct of the State; but it is preposterous to apply this principle to any thing charged as oppressive or unjust in the exercise of the Sovereigns *parental authority in his family*. Such a charge or insinuation (whatever may be the intention with which they are made,) convey a manifest personal imputation; because in such a case the presumptions, neither of law nor of fact can ascribe such mismanagement to the *political* servants of the King.

It is absurd in the extreme to suppose that His Majesty consults his Ministers in the management of his children, or that without being consulted they ought to intrude their councils as in cases connected with the *political* Government.

But it may be said that the members of the Royal family, more especially those who are nearest in succession, are *public* persons, in whose safety & prosperity the nation is politically interested, & that they are therefore more immediately under the superintendence of Parliament. The *premises* are true—but the *conclusion* does not follow. The Law undoubtedly recognises all the members of the Royal family, as *public persons*, but after such recognition it gives the sole care & government over them *to the King*. It even takes away the ordinary parental dominion from all the Prince's of his House, & vests them wholly in himself; so that the Prince Regent at this moment has not only vested in him the ordinary authority of a father, which would otherwise have been in His Majesty, but also the sovereign *parental dominion*.

To this it may be answered, that the admission of these Royal prerogatives does not take away or diminish the constitutional controul of Parliament acting upon Ministers because the King is in all cases irresponsible. Undoubtedly it does *not*, in extreme cases which the imagination may conceive; but until these cases occur it is neither decent nor safe to suggest them. Parliament can have *no jurisdiction whatsoever*, to regulate or to animadvert upon the King's parental duty in any case where just & reasonable men could possibly differ as to the discreetest exercise of it, & could only fitly interfere upon the irreverend assumption that the Sovereign was lost to all the natural affections of a father; & if such an extreme case must be resorted to without any fact to stand on, to lay a foundation for jurisdiction over the King by the Parliament; imagination might equally suggest such a total neglect or dereliction of duty in *Parliament itself* as would justify the great body of the people in the overthrow of the whole frame of the Government for the preservation of those rights which God & nature have bestowed upon the whole family of man—but no person in his senses would ever resort in argument to such dangerous & indecent suppositions in either House of Parliament.

It is absurd therefore to argue the jurisdiction alluded to, without a case which applies or approaches in application, much less without any case at all. Poisons are administered to the human body for the expulsion of diseases; but they must be administered only upon rare occasions, by the most skilful hands; & that man's life would not be worth a week's purchase who should convert such medicines into diet.

It is the great vice of the times, Madam, which it is the office of wisdom & virtue to guard against, so to deal with the powerful & salutary remedies of Parliament in our Constitution; political quacks are constantly resorting to them, & bringing the most settled authorities into disrepute by the unjust or improvident application of them. In this manner individuals are frequently unjustly attacked & the general administration of justice disparaged & defamed.

Your Royal Highness has the deepest interest in the discouragement of such principles; they may destroy your private happiness & shake your public Government hereafter, if you should ever be placed upon the throne of these realms. The Sovereign is lifted up upon so high a pinnacle; charged too with duties which are obnoxious to so many, & those of the most dangerous description, that the Law is obliged to surround him with protections which apply to no other men. Even the *imagination* of his death is equal to the consummation of murder; yet of what avail is this unbounded anxiety to secure his *person*, if his *character* be not equally protected, without which his life can be of no value to the public. It is true that libelers & defamers may be punished, but that is of small value, if the estimation in which the Sovereign should be held to give strength & popularity to his Government is undermined by a system of calumny & misrepresentation which the tribunals of justice cannot reach.

Your Royal Highness should be informed how much reason the Prince your father has cause to complain of this injustice. Even in the very moment when the return of peace entitles him to superior gratifications in the affectionate expressions of the people, unprincipled attempts are constantly made to mix them with insolence & reproach. This, Madam, occurs *no where beyond the reach of systematic malice.* Wherever His Royal Highness has been, beyond the sphere of its influence, he has been received with that affection & respect which it is not only your Royal Highnesses duty but your deepest interest universally to promote. I was witness myself Madam, long before you were born, to the beginnings of the French revolution. In 1806 [*sic*, ? 1786] it was difficult with the best introductions to reach the Royal Palace of Versailles protected as it was with guards to an immense distance, and the King's person surrounded by all the great men who possessed the property & the influence that follows it throughout so vast a territory; but *opinion*, the root & foundation of all power was shaken by a systematic spirit of insolent and atrocious defamation, of which in a short time the Monarch & the nobles, but in the end, the whole body of the people, became the victims. Let me then conjure your Royal Highness to discourage by every possible means appeals to authorities which were intended only as ballances to the *political* authority of the Crown, & not as controuls to deprive the King of those *personal rights* which belong to the meanest of his subjects. Confide in His Royal Highnesses parental care—cultivate his affections, & depend *as you assuredly may* upon public respect & private happiness.

If your Royal Highness should be advised to consider this letter as presumptuous, I shall console myself in the affectionate motive which dictated it. I never can forget the graciousness & condescension with which your Royal Highness has at all times honored me—I have written under the sense of them & from the warm interest I must always take in whatever concerns your Royal Highness.

472 THE DOWAGER COUNTESS OF ILCHESTER *to the* PRINCE REGENT

Cranborne, August 4, 1814.

I AM requested by the Princess Charlotte to express her grateful thanks to your Royal Highness, for the kind indulgence allowed her, in the use of the phaeton, and ponies, and your Royal Highness may rely upon the Princess for adhering strictly to the command of never driving beyond the Park.

I have written by the Princess Charlotte's desire to Genl. Bloomfield on the subject of a horse of Her Royal Highnesses which will of course be submitted to your Royal Highness.

London, August 8th 1814.

MAY it please your Royal Highness to accept my affectionate acknowledgement of the gracious communication made to me this morning thro my friend Colonel McMahon by your Royal Highness's commands.

I can very sincerely say that the value to me of the honor which your Royal Highness is pleased so kindly to intend for me when the occasion shall offer by a vacancy, is that it proceeds from yourself, as a mark of that regard which for many years I have ever been anxious to cultivate & to deserve.[1]

I was distinguished by your Royal Highness before I was at all embarked in political life,[2] & nothing therefore belonging to it could honorably interfere *nor ever did*—nor *shall* with my personal attachment to your Royal Highness which remains as in former times, unaltered & unalterable.

474 AUGUSTUS CAVENDISH BRADSHAW *to* COLONEL MCMAHON

High Elms, August 11, 1814.

I CANNOT let you leave town without a few lines about myself. I have waited patiently in hopes something would have fallen that I could with propriety have asked for, but alas nothing has occured & I am distressed beyond measure by poverty brought on by annuities in raising money in the several contests I had at Honiton, all I trust in the cause I have most at heart the service of my Royal master.[3]

Would it be prudent? & would you with your usual kindness deliver a message to His R.H. to this effect & that I hope his R.H. still considers me his faithful servant & that to the end of my life I shall ever be so. That if H.R.H. would be graciously pleased to say one word to Lords Liverpool & Castlereagh or command you to speak to them, I am sure they would provide for me. Any little addition to what I receive from His Royal Hs favor at present would make us comfortable. Mrs. Bradshaw has not been used to poverty & is very unhappy which my imprudent elections have brought upon her & we both thought our expectations good. I will say no more—my heart is full!

1 He was made a Knight of the Thistle in January 1815, "the great object of his ambition", said Sir Robert Wilson. "His longing was a species of *craze.*"

2 The Prince of Wales appointed him his Attorney-General in November 1783.

3 He was M.P. for Honiton from March 1805 until the Dissolution of 1812, being re-elected in 1806 and 1807. For his earlier letters, see Nos. 175, 209, 253.

Tomorrow is His R.Hs birthday. All are happy & he must be so when he considers all he has done for his people since he became Regent of these Kingdoms! Perhaps an application on such a day might be propitious.

With your judgment I leave it & remain, [etc.].

475 THE EARL OF MOIRA *to the* PRINCE REGENT

On the Ganges, beyond Dinapore,[1]
August 17th 1814.

REMOTENESS or disconnection in other respects with the course of transactions never could make me a languid spectator of any scene in which your Royal Highness was concerned. I will not pretend to say that the wonderful occurrences of which we have recently had information do not touch any other string within me. A glowing sense of national pride has ever been to me a main impulse: and I do confess that I feel in a peculiar degree the comfort of being liberated from the consciousness that France had outstripped us in the race for sway & influence which must be the object of great nations. The overthrow of Bonaparte personally is not an ingredient in that self gratulation. He has shown himself so abject in mind that one can only wonder such an animal should have held pre-eminence so long. That France has been precluded from that insolent boast of victories which bade fair to gall perpetually every British ear, is noble & consolatory. One may like France, as I wish to do, reduced to a modest level. Strong as these sensations are, I can most truly say they were not the most prominent even at the moment when the news reached me. The share your Royal Highness has had in those splendid events, & the happiness you must have reaped from this glorious termination of your difficulties, was the first advertence of my heart & has continued to be my highest point of rejoicing. Congratulations from India must be so tardy that the objects to which they refer must be out of date. Still, I think, Sir, you will not be indifferent to the assurance of the exultation which my spirit felt in your satisfaction & renown; nor will I believe my knowledge of your Royal Highness to be so inaccurate as to apprehend you could disdain even so distant & so humble a participation in your triumphs as what I offer.

After the immense magnitude of such operations, this country can

1 Near Patna, in the Province of Bihar.

afford no intelligence interesting for your Royal Highness. Tho' I have experienced all that was predicted to me from the tediousness of the voyage & the heat in the boats, I would not for any consideration have omitted undertaking this expedition. I am now convinced that I shall be able to do much for the comfort of the natives at the same time that I materially promote the advantage of the Company. All this, however, will be the result of many little attentions & regulations, so that no credit will follow it; but it will be gratifying to have the internal conviction of not having discharged one's duties slothfully. In talking of the tranquillity of India one should always define the term & say that one speaks comparatively. This Government never ought to be deemed in a state of peace: for subjects of unexpected & unavoidable difference with the several Native Powers rise in such quick succession as to baffle all calculation. We are now forced to undertake movements against the Nipaulese. From our having resisted their encroachments on our territory, they surprised & murdered some of our police officers & atrociously endeavored to poison the wells of our frontier villages.[1] As this was done by their regular troops, & their Government shows no disposition to atone for the offense, we are forced to chastise the insult. Were we not to do so the forbearance would be imputed to inability; and the supposed reputation of power which would thence accrue to Nipaul would excite all sort of mischievous combinations with it against us. On that account we shall strike at it as soon as the floods of the rainy season have subsided. The mountainous frontier of Nipaul & its' dependencies is our principal difficulty. There is no road in its' whole extent. Simple & winding pathways over the woody heights are the only communications: therefore the impossibility of supplying any large body of men with provisions reduces us to the necessity of acting in moderate detachments. The discipline & courage of our troops must be relied upon for success against the superior numbers which will be opposed to them; tho' the Nipaulese have sepoy battalions formed on the model of ours. Our vigilance is requisite at the same time in another quarter. Scindeah[2] appears disposed to connect himself with the Pindarries[3] in a manner

1 The warlike Gurkhas had conquered the mountainous country of Nepal in the seventeen-seventies, and since their territory bordered on British India for a distance of seven hundred miles, frontier "incidents" and disputes were frequent and inevitable. In April 1814 Hastings sent a force to occupy the districts where the Gurkhas had made encroachments, but a few weeks later the incident occurred which he describes, and which led to the War of 1814–16. See No. 502.

2 Sindhia was the ruler of the State of Gwalior, and a member of the Maratha Confederacy.

3 Armed plunderers, numbering about 30,000, organised in bands of from one to four thousand men, who kept a large part of India in a perpetual unrest. They were under the protection of the Maratha Princes, whose armies they sometimes joined.

that would be equivalent to a declaration of hostility against us. Every effort is exerted by us to dissuade him from a step no less absurd in respect to his own interests than embarrassing for us: but these people act from such short-sighted speculations that the folly of a measure is no security against their undertaking it. This would be of little consequence were it not for the insufficiency of our troops in point of number & the great objection which exists against incurring the expense of collecting an adequate army. What we have of native force is in excellent order, & they are really fine troops. The cavalry is inferiorly mounted, for good horses are not now to be procured in India: And one should have wished them to have in that respect a superiority such as might have counterbalanced the numbers which the Mahrattas would oppose to us. I should blush to state to your Royal Highness these matters, so insignificant in calibre when contrasted with the politics which you have been triumphantly guiding, were it not that I am aware no circumstance belonging to any part of the Empire which you rule is too minute for your active contemplation.

With the most ardent prayers for every species of felicity to your Royal Highness, I remain, Sir, [etc.].

476 QUEEN CHARLOTTE *to the* PRINCE REGENT

Windsor, the 21st August 1814.

You will of course have received Dr. Baillie's[1] buletin to inform you of Charlotte's knee having increased very much since last week, attended with more pain in the night when the foot is stretched out, as also of an oppression upon her chest, for neither of which they can account, as she has abstained from both riding & walking & is very regular in her diet. The Dr therefore wishes that her journey to the sea side may be soon, as the month's of Septbr is the best for the Weymouth coast. If you would be so good as to write a line to Ldy Ilchester upon this subject she will still be able to go into Dorsetshire so as to be there if not the first, at least in the course of the first week in the next month. The Dr. hopes that the effect of the warm sea bathing may do much for her, for he & Keate[1] are seriously annoyd about the increase of a swelling without any possibility to give any reason for it.

I will not detain you any longer as I am sure you must be better employed than to read my scrawl, & will only add how unalterably I am [etc.].

1 Matthew Baillie (1761–1823), one of the Court physicians.
2 Robert Keate, the surgeon (1777–1857), and brother of John Keate, headmaster of Eton.

Brighton, Augt. 22d 1814.

BEFORE the post goes out, I take up my pen in the greatest haste, to thank you, my dearest mother, a thousand times for your most kind letter. Yesterday I sent Bloomfield over to Worthing to examine all the premises, & to see if it were possible to find a house that was at all suitable to contain Charlotte & her family; & his report is, that there is not any one there to be hired for love or money that is in the least calculated for that purpose. I therefore am reduc'd in consequence of what you have written to me, & of Dr. Baillie's report to me concerning her knee, to entreat that you will lend her for a month or six weeks the Lodge at Weymouth, as there are warm sea baths in the house itself, & that you will also have the goodness to signify the same to Lady Ilchester, & to take upon yourself to make all the arrangements with her Ladyship that may be necessary for this purpose, & to give all such directions & regulations, as to you may seem fittest & best, & upon all of which, I do most completely & entirely rely & depend upon you & you alone, as I feel quite secure that you will do all that is right, & if even I myself had been upon the spot, I should not & could not have done any thing in this business, without previously consulting with you, & taking your advice & pleasure. Therefore let me once more entreat of you, to put it all in train, without loss of time, & without any further reference to me, as I feel quite comfortable at the thoughts of its being all & entirely in your hands. Bloomfield also writes by this post, by my directions, to Lady Ilchester. I wish I had anything to tell you from this place, that could afford you the smallest interest or amusement, but there is alas! litterally nothing, a complete stagnation & dearth of every thing, no, not even one little scrap of scandal; in short we vegitate here, but in good air, a few male companions, my brother William at the head of them; we ride & walk in the morning, either on the Downs or in the Riding House, & in the evening about half a dozen ladies, Mme de Lieven[1] &c. &c. &c. come at nine o'clock, when we have a delightful concert, Mme de Lieven sometimes charming us for half an hour with her uncommon beautiful talent on the Piano Forte, & at half past eleven, or twelve at the latest, all is over, & we trip away to bed; pretty nearly what I must soon do, or else I shall be too late for the post, so now Addio for tonight my most beloved Madré, *goodnight*, instead of goodmorrow to your night cap as old Edwin used to say in his song, & beleive me, ever, [etc.].

P.S. Pray my best love to all the dear sisterhood.

1 The wife of Count Lieven, the Russian Ambassador.

Russell Square, August the 24th 1814.

You cannot escape additional trouble from me even at this distance—
Had you opportunity to speak to the Prince Regent for his permission
to let these pictures be engrav'd? All who see them express desire that
they should, and I am naturally anxious to extend my professional reputation by good prints from these works, which I consider as my best.

It would be dishonorable in me to conceal that they would be a source
of considerable profit either to me, or to a publisher; and you I know will
think that if emolument *is* to be gain'd from such a gratification to the
publick, the original artist may justly share in it.

Application has been made to me respecting them, particularly for this
portrait of Lord Wellington which is now very greatly improv'd; (and
I may fairly say admir'd) and as the plate would be executed by the first
engraver, and be under my immediate direction, I should close with the
offer, did I know myself justified in doing it by His Royal Highness
sanction and permission. The print would be dedicated to him, and the
distinction he mention'd of Lord W's sitting to me at H.R.H. desire.
Mr. Bowyer[1] is the applicant, who says he had the Prince Regent's permission to dedicate a print of Lord Wellington to him, tho' from what
picture he had not then determin'd.

In the case of Blucher and Count Platoff,[2] the publisher should be, a
very worthy man, Mr. Colnaghi[3] of Cockspur Street; if His Royal Highness and you thought had [*sic*] no objection.

I am more and more assur'd of my success in the Prince Regent's
portrait about which there has been *no* dissentient voice. This morning
Lady Liverpool[4] and her friends came to see it, and lik'd it equally with
the rest of my visitors. I am obeying His Royal Highness wishes in
proceeding with a copy of it which will be completed as far as the
original is by the time of his arrival in town; when he graciously
promis'd to sit to me for the figure.

I hope that Cheltenham does all for you that Mrs. McMahon and that
numerous circle who feel respect and friendship for you, wish—With an

1 Robert Bowyer, the painter and engraver (1758–1834).
2 Matvei Ivanovich, Count Platoff (1757–1818), Hetman of the Don Cossacks. He took
part in the campaigns against Napoleon. Lawrence's biographer remarks that it was a capital
portrait, and "represented him with his long, oval, Asiatic face, and with a considerable
expression of cunning, which was in fact his character". (*Williams*, I, 345.)
3 Paul Colnaghi (1751–1833), the print dealer. Born in Milan, he was a naturalised
Englishman.
4 The Prime Minister's first wife, who died in 1821. She was the daughter of the fourth
Earl of Bristol.

addition of peculiar thankfulness, I place myself amongst the number and desire to remain in it to my life's close; for believe me to be ever, [etc.].

PS. Your picture is in the hands of the engraver.

479 THE DUKE OF CUMBERLAND *to the* PRINCE REGENT

Strelitz, August [September][1] 3d 1814.

WHERE shall I find words sufficiently strong to express to you all the feelings of my heart for your very kind letter and all you have already done for me upon this occasion. No words no language can do that but believe me that it is not felt the less strong by me; all I can say is that I am bound to you for life, and am at all times ready to serve you in any way that you may think I may be of service to you. Your delicacy, your noble and handsome conduct to me on this occasion has exceeded every thing I could have expected, and you may rely upon one thing that the Princess[2] as well as myself are bound to you by the strongest ties of gratitude.

With respect to all future arrangements which you so kindly mention, I beg leave only to say that knowing your kind intention I leave it entirely to you to decide and shall in consequence of what you have written to me write to my friend the Chancellor[3] & thank him for all his trouble.

Many thanks I owe you for your dispatching Captain [illegible] so quick, he returned here last Tuesday evening the 23d having in all been only absent 18 days from Berlin. On the following morning the 24th I waited upon the King of Prussia who desired me to say every thing possible from him to you, he seems very happy at the match and has repeatedly spoken to me with tears in his eyes of his affection & friendship for the Princess. She will write to you herself upon this occasion to recommend herself to your future friendship. After having seen the King, who was to notify publickly that day the intended match, I saw Prince Hardenburg who promised to send me a copy of all the papers that took place on Frederic's marriage with the Dutchess,[4] as the King has

1 Obviously a slip. The 23rd of August was a Tuesday, and Queen Charlotte's letter to the Duke (for *copy*, see No. 480) is, no doubt, correctly dated. Also, the Duke would not have kept his letter open for more than a month.
2 The Princess of Solms.   3 Lord Eldon.
4 The Duke of York married Frederica, the eldest daughter of Frederick William II of Prussia, in 1791. The King's other children were the offspring of his second marriage.

always consider'd the Princess as belonging to his family; the moment
I receive all that is necessary I shall send over every thing by Morand.
I then paid my visit to all the members of the family and they dined that
day with me. That evening at eleven o'clock I left Berlin & arrived here
the next morning at eight o'clock when I was received most kindly by
my uncle[1] and the whole family. The next day the 26th the Duke assembled the Court and our fiancailles the exchange of rings was celebrated in the presence of the whole family & Court. Since my arrival
here I have written to Hardenberg to know from him what *his* opinion
and that of the *King* is respecting the time that the marriage ceremony
may take place according to the forms of *this* country, & then I shall
communicate that to you & shall beg of you to consult our friend the
Chancellor upon the same subject with respect to my own country, that
nothing may be wanting in form or decency to offend the most litigeous
person, and I trust, dearest brother, you will approve of this. The
moment I hear for certain that I may be married I shall, & then with your
permission shall hasten to return home and embrace the dearest friend
and brother I have.

I have received a very kind letter from my mother, but *entre nous* at the
end of her letter she gives me a long dose of difficulties &c, most [of]
which I shall touch upon in my letter to her, but that you may understand
what I mean I shall in confidence hand you a copy of her letter. Now in
one point she has chosen to misunderstand me, for I took special care to
explain to her that with respect to the children of Solms, that Princess
particularly states they will be of *no expence* to me, as they are already
provided for. And I myself have insisted on the Princesses making her
Will previous to our marriage by which she secures to *them* all she now
possesses, and thus puts it out of my power ever to injure them, nor could
I be such a villain to wish it. But of this naturally you will not take any
notice of to her, as I have no doubt she has meant all this in the kindest
way, at least I am determin'd to understand it so.

I really flatter myself, dearest brother, when I shall have the happiness
of presenting you the Princess you will like her, as she is amiable as
possible, & she feels the deepest gratitude to you for all your kindness on
this occasion the most important of our lives.

Your birthday the 12th was celebrated at Charlottenburgh by the
King who gave a great dinner of 80 persons, when your health was
drank with ecstacy by every Prussian, who, you may depend upon it, are
bound to you for life. It was also the birthday of the Hereditary Prince

1 The Duke of Mecklenburg-Strelitz.

of Mecklenburg whose name is also George.[1] The King and all the Princes came in the morning and paid me a visit to congratulate me on your birthday. I think there never existed a more honourable man than the King and I think you will do me the justice to say that I did not say *too much of him* in all my accounts of him, to see him with all his children is really charming, I have passed many pleasant days there. He is to set off the 15th of next month for Vienna, for which place the H. Prince leaves us the day after tomorrow. Alexander returns with him after the Congress to Berlin and the Empress meets him there, it is not yet decided whether Catherine is to be of the party, she is now at Dresden and goes to Vienna, but they say that she and the Empress are not well together. It is reported she is to marry the Prince Royal of Wirtemberg, who is just divorced from his present wife with whom he never was connected.[2] Blücher is gone to Silesia to see the new estates the King has given him; he has acted nobly by him, having settled upon this hero a salary of 12,000 dollars, 3,000 dollars for a house, forage for 16 horses, coals & candles, and an estate of 12,000 dollars, which altogether gives him near 30,000 dollars a year. He has settled upon Tauenzein, York,[3] Kleist and Buln (?) besides their other emoluments 6,000 dollars a year, so that all these Generals are very well off. The new arrangements for the army are not yet known, and it is supposed will not be made public till his return from Vienna. I do not choose to trouble you with all the idle reports that are current as they are probably only lies. Certainly one cannot see any thing more beautiful than the Division of Prussian Guards both cavalry infantry & artillery. These are quartered in Berlin and Potsdam. Their uniforms though grey are very handsome, and the cuirasses of the Horse Guards have a very military appearance, all the cuirassiers are cuirassed before & behind, just as the Russians are. As I have not yet received Hardenberg's answer I shall leave this open and add to it all that is necessary.

Septr. *8th 1814.*

It is but about an hour ago that I received Hardenberg's answer, and therefore my dearest brother must not attribute my not having sent off Morand sooner to any neglect on my part, but the real truth I believe is

---

1 The son of the reigning Duke of Mecklenburg-Strelitz. [1779–1860.] He succeeded his father as Grand Duke in 1816, and in August 1817 he married the daughter of the Landgrave of Hesse-Cassel. He was therefore the Princess Solms' brother and the King of Prussia's brother-in-law.

2 The marriage took place in January 1816.

3 Field-Marshal Count York von Wartenburg.

that Hardenberg has had too much to do all this Summer, and in order to be a little quiet he has been at his estate Templeberg, from whence he only return'd last Monday. I shall send you his *original* paper to see, & after you have perused it you will have the goodness to send it back to me. In his letter to the Princess a copy of which I shall also send you, you will see that according to the Laws of Germany a widow can marry again at the expiration of *nine* months sooner if a consense is granted, but neither the Princess nor myself would wish to do anything from sauter aux yeux of the public, and therefore I am most anxious to know for certain what the English Law allows, and therefore with your permission shall send a copy of the papers to our friend the Chancellor, and if *you* and he think at the expiration of *nine* months we may be married, I shall then do it. One thing is a fact that the Princess has been separated from her late husband since April *1813* therefore a year previous to his death which took place the 13th April *1814*. I am sure you will excuse me dearest brother of being so particular in all this, but as circumstances now are, it is a material thing for us that no flaw in any proceeding should take place, & it is for this reason that Hardenberg wishes an official document should be sent of your consent with an official letter signed by you to the King of Prussia. In case you are of opinion that at the expiration of the *nine months* I may marry the Princess, the marriage will be celebrated on *the 14th of Jany 1815*, and then I shall hurry over to England with the Princess to present her to *you* and the rest of the family. The King who is all kindness to his sister in law has settled one hundred and four thousand dollars on the children of Solms, & you will perceive by the direction of Prince Hardenberg the papers & letters are all directed A Son Altesse Royale Madame la Princesse Douairière *de Prusse* et de Solms, to prove that the King has always considered her as a branch of his family. The King has appointed Prince Hardenberg as his plenipotentiary to draw up the marriage articles; you will have the goodness to appoint *some* person who is to act in that capacity for *you* & myself, and the Duke[1] I believe will appoint one of his Ministers to act for him and his daughter. This I believe was the form used at the marriage of Frederic, at least Hardenberg told me he should examine all the papers that took place on that occasion & should suggest the same to be followed now. You will perceive that I had already given him a copy of the consent & memorandum as sent to me by you. I trust & hope dear brother I have been perfectly clear in all this business, & if I have been prolix at least I have tried to be clear.

One thing more I believe will be necessary that on our arrival in

1 The Duke of Mecklenburg-Strelitz.

England the ceremony of marriage must be performed again by an English Bishop; at least so it was with Frederic.

I take the liberty of sending you a *sabre* which is made at Berlin and I think does credit to the workman. Once more let me repeat to you my best my heartfelt thanks for all your kindness and gracious intentions for me & the Princess and believe me ever [etc.].

P.S. I send you also a copy of the *King's letter* to me. I have copied most correctly the Queen's letter to me.

480 QUEEN CHARLOTTE *to the* DUKE OF CUMBERLAND

Windsor, the 15th August 1814.

[*Enclosed in the above.*]

THO' the Prince Regent had informed me, that he had reason to expect a messenger from you, some time hence, I was not a little surprized to receive yesterday afternoon the 14th an account of Captain Poten's[1] arrival which your brother was so good to inform me of and to forward your letters imediately to me, the contents of which containing the notification of your intended marriage with my niece the Dow. Princess of Solms, I beg you will be assured that my earnest wishes for your happiness & wellfare are most fervent & sincere upon this occasion, and believe me tho' my congratulations may not be the most eloquent, they flow nevertheless from the heart.

You talk with much pleasure of the idea of introducing the Princess to your family; natural as this wish appears I hope that you will not think of taking such a step as to return to England without knowing first what additional income it is likely for you to obtain. Yr brother who is all goodness & ever ready to forward the happiness of his family, is not less ready upon this occasion to facilitate it as much as possible; but I think it a duty I owe to him and also to you, to tell you sincerely, that the difficulties will be considerable to succeed in the Prince's wishes. You are yourself too well acquainted with the Constitution as not to recollect that all money matters must be debated in Parliament, & how difficult it is to Ministers at all times even to obtain the most necessary pecuniary assistance and particularly so in the present times, when not only every action, but every trifling expence of the Royal family is criticised in both Houses to a more violent degree than in former times, which leads me to

1 The Duke's Equerry.

think, nay I am sure of it, that the Ministers will be hardly able to meet the Prince's wishes with success, & particularly so when it will be known that you have agreed to the Princesses children living with you, which they will always look upon as an additional burthen to you, particularly as their age requires an education which [will] probably be expensive. We will suppose for a moment that the Regent in case of failure to his proposal in Parliament that your income should be encreased, might be inclined to give you assistance from his Privy Purse. I am sure you are too generous to expect him with his encreasing expences, to distress himself on your account.

For my niece's own sake I will not deny that as the customs of the two countries are so different, it will appear *here* more respectable in her to remain in her own country till the year of her mourning is over, for though she could not esteem her husband, *this deecency of conduct will make a better impression in this country* where every *action of the great is liable to be criticised and unfortunately not always in a favourable light.* My affection for you as a mother has lead me to write a *coeur ouvert* and to put the pro & con of every thing I really think before your eyes, & I hope you will receive as I receive it with candour, if you enter into my feelings & judge as I do upon the subject (for I cannot think as a lover) & that all answers well, I beg you to remember that this was dictated from the heart of[1] [etc.].

481 DR MATTHEW BAILLIE *to the* PRINCE REGENT

Windsor Castle, Septr 3. 1814.

DR. BAILLIE has the honour of informing the Prince Regent most respectfully that Princess Charlotte's departure for Weymouth is now fixed for the 9th inst.

Dr. B. was surprised at this delay but he learnt upon enquiry that some circumstances in Her Royal Highness's periodical health render'd it adviseable that she should not undertake the journey immediately, and that if Her Royal Highness had been at Weymouth, she could not have made use of the tepid sea water bath for some days.

1 It is generally stated that Queen Charlotte refused to receive the Duchess of Cumberland (a refusal in which she persisted to the end of her life) on the ground that she had been a *divorcée*. The above letter shows that this view is untenable. It was only at a later date, after someone had said something (exactly what it was is unknown) to the Queen, that she decided not to receive the Duchess. In August 1814 she obviously knew of the contemplated divorce. It is worth noting that Queen Charlotte received Mrs Warren Hastings, the divorced wife of Baron Imhoff, at Court. (Lady Holland's *Memoirs*, II, 103.)

It does not appear necessary that Mr. Keate should reside constantly at Weymouth while Princess Charlotte remains there, but it would be adviseable that he should examine the knee occasionally. It would probably be enough that Mr. Keate should go to Weymouth once in ten days, and remain there about two days. He is ready to give a more constant attendance if the Prince Regent should wish it.

Dr. Baillie proposes to go to Gloucestershire the week after next, and after remaining there about eight or ten days he proposes to pay a visit to Princess Charlotte at Weymouth for one or two days, if this shall meet with the Prince Regent's approbation.

Dr. Baillie was exceedingly hurt to perceive that a copy of the medical opinion had found its way into the newspapers. He has made every enquiry into the channel by which it was communicated, but he has not yet obtained answers from two of the most important quarters. When he shall receive these answers he will immediately communicate them to Sir Henry Halford.

482 THE PRINCE REGENT *to* QUEEN CHARLOTTE

Ragley, Septr 6th 1814.

I HAVE a thousand thanks to return you for your most kind letter which I have this moment only receiv'd, & which I as instantly take up my pen to acknowledge, for our post here goes out at rather an inconvenient hour, & I was afraid that the delay of a day might possibly prevent your having the goodness to carry into execution respecting Charlotte, what you have so kindly suggested to me, & which does not for a moment even, admit the possibility of a question.

But I am afraid I can not myself forward to you at this peculiar instant the two hundred pounds that are requisite, for the reasons which I will assign. In the first place, I forgot very stupidly before I left town, to take any additional money with me but that which upon examination now, I find to be barely sufficient to frank me back to London; & as I only draw upon McMahon I do not wish at this particular moment as he is not in town, but at Cheltenham where he has been I am concern'd to state but with too much truth, at death's door, though now I trust in God, quite safe again, but still most dreadfully low & weak, I do not wish (nor indeed is he in a state to admit of it) I repeat to approach him with any thing like business, not even a draft which would require his writing & giving the order for payment to Mr. Coutts.[1] Will you therefore my dearest mother, have the goodness to add one more to all your other favours, by advancing temporarily yourself, giving to Charlotte in my name just as you have already yourself propos'd that it should be done, that sum, & which I will faithfully reimburse you immediately on my return to town. With regard to other points, principally her pocket money which you have alluded to, strange as it may appear to you, nevertheless it is most true, I have never in my life known what the sum or amount of that allowance was, as Lady De Clifford never but once hinted at the subject, & which I think was shortly after her appointment, when I told her Ladyship that she must know what the general sum was that was allowed by the King for the Establishment, that at all times I wish'd that Charlotte should be liberally supplied with money, & not stinted in the least, & that the allowance should be proportion'd to her years, increasing of course as she grew more advanced in her years; & that if hereafter the sum thus allow'd by the King was not sufficient for affording what was proper for Charlotte for her pocket, her ladyship should then apply to me, & I would endeavour to do all that was necessary as far as my means would admit. Since which short conversation I have never, as I told you before, heard a single word further upon the subject, I therefore concluded that there had always been ample means to supply Charlotte with all the money that was proper for her to have at command, & consequently never enquir'd farther into the matter.[2] And

1 Thomas Coutts, the banker (1735–1822).
2 Whilst Lady de Clifford was her Governess, Princess Charlotte was allowed £10 a month for pocket-money. "But though I spend it", she wrote, "I take care never to go further than my sum will allow." (Albemarle, *Fifty Years of My Life*, 1, 295.) Miss Knight, however, said that Lady de Clifford "was obliged to furnish her with money for her little charities out of the eight hundred pounds allotted for her wardrobe." (*Miss Knight*, 1, 234–5.) In 1814 Princess Charlotte, in the manner of her father, fell seriously into debt; her jewellery account alone exceeded £14,650, and she owed Colnaghi over £568 "for Prints". On 9 January 1815 she received a grant from the Treasury of £2925. "We ought to pay the debt in question", Lord Liverpool had written to Vansittart, two days earlier. "But there is no harm in her having a fright about it, and above all she ought to be urged to make a full disclosure of every difficulty of this sort in which she may have involved herself." (Add. MSS. 31231, fo. 214.) The Prime Minister must have been staggered by a letter he received from Mr Willis, her private secretary, some days later. "I have with great reluctance on the part of Her Royal Highness induced her to permit me to make a full inquiry into such debts as are exclusively confined to her person, and I am very sorry to add that the amount of them far exceeds the extent I had conceived of them, no less a sum to different jewellers and dressmakers than £20,000 and upwards.... According to the Establishment ordered by His Majesty in 1806, the money allowed to the Princess for her wardrobe and pocket expenses was limited to £750; it was subsequently increased to £1000. This sum was to furnish Her Royal Highness with every Article that had not a reference to the house and stable accounts. It is the custom among the ladies of the Royal Family to give and receive presents on their several birthdays. This was a constant source of heavy expense to Her Royal Highness, and far exceeding her scanty means. She has been on every occasion most anxious to attend to

even now, what perhaps will appear equally strange to you, I do not know correctly how her Establishment is, or is to be stipendiated, but I will take care to make myself master of all these different points on my return to London. Having already said so much, I am really quite ashamed to tresspass any longer upon you, but will you also have the goodness, to thank Dr. Baillie for his letter, & instruct either him, or Lady Ilchester, to give such orders to Mr. Keate for his occasional attendance at Weymouth upon Charlotte during her residence there as the Doctor himself has proposed. You are most gracious & kind, in thinking of us all here, so much; our weather has indeed been most propitious, we had the happiness of finding our good & kind hosts in perfect health, who wellcom'd us as indeed & in justice to them I must add, they do all their friends & visitors, with the warmest & kindest of receptions, the dear old Saint[1] followed me the next day after I came, & he is really all alive, & seems both delighted with the mansion & pleased with his society especially as he makes up his whist every evening, though I believe a sigh now & then escapes him for his Grande Patience, which he can not help missing & regretting. William is in one of his best styles, the Tulipanos[2] are also here; & the old Tulipans quite, quite, quite, the veritable Marquis in an Italian Buffo Opera. As to the rest they are not worth while mentioning, as they are but little known to you, & as I believe you can not care a groat about any one of them, except your humble servant, who is quite asham'd at the length of his epistle & who will therefore hasten to conclude, with imploring you to believe him, my dearest mother, [etc.].

P.S. I embrace most affectionately & with all my heart & soul, the whole of the dear sisterhood.

the call of liberality and clarity as became her rank and station—but the principal cause of the great increase of debt has been providing jewellery and other ornaments on the presumption of her marriage being solemnized, and her hope was that these debts would be paid out of the sum usually granted by Parliament on such an occasion. The expected event however not taking place, the inability of discharging these demands is constantly preying on her mind, and I have good reason for saying that her late indisposition originated in great measure from this circumstance. Her wish at present is to pay by instalments from any means she might have in her power, and her reason for preferring this mode is that she can adopt it without exciting the public attention. There are one or two other circumstances relative to this affair which I have scruples in committing to writing, but which, whenever you will condescend to honour me with five minutes audience I should prefer to communicate by word of mouth...." (Add. MSS. 38261, fo. 28.)

1 This must be Sir Thomas Tyrwhitt. The "Saint" had obviously been in the service of the Royal family for a long period (No. 723). So had Tyrwhitt (No. 44 n.). Princess Elizabeth had amplified the Prince Regent's joke by dubbing him Saint Thomas (Nos. 393–4). See also Nos. 484, 673, 718, 725.

2 The Hampdens. See No. 504.

Russell Square, Sept[br] the 9th 1814.

I HAVE but to give new thanks for new obligation, and attention the more kind, from its breaking in upon many important businesses which even in your retirement must press on your mind, whenever health permits you to turn to them. I did not hear of your illness till it was contradicted or rather known as pass'd and therefore my sincere sorrow for it was unattended with the apprehension I must otherwise have felt, in common with those many who (except from thankfulness) have more claim to express their solicitude to Mrs. McMahon, to whom I should then have address'd my letter—if you would give me one line with this only "I am still better"—it would very much oblige me.

Lord Stewart comes home today—he too is greatly your debtor for having gratified his laudable ambition by procuring from the Prince his consent to have his portrait at Vienna which (tho' a *minor* point, if at *all* felt by him) will doubtless add to his reception there.

Might I venture to say "dedicated by permission to His Royal Highness the Prince Regent"? This question is not however to lure you into the shortest letter unless moments of perfect health and leisure make it entirely convenient to you.

I beg my best respects to Mrs. McMahon and have the honor and pleasure to be [etc.].

484 QUEEN CHARLOTTE *to the* PRINCE REGENT

Windsor Palace, the 11th Septbr 1814.

I HAVE the pleasure to inform you that I delivered your present to Charlotte, which occasioned great satisfaction & I believe that before this can come to your hands she will have acknowledged your kindness by letter.

I had half an hours conversation with her on the 8th, to which she was very attentive, & after having left me expressed herself as pleased with what had passed between us both to Mary & Augusta. She had a visit from the Dutchess of York who assured me that she was extreamly reasonable in her conversation, particularly so when she talked upon the subject of the Grand Dutchess, declaring that she felt no partiality towards her, & that the last visits which passed between them were most disagreable & that she was a very intriguing woman. The Prince of Orange was of course not named but she assured the Dutchess of York that being convinced that you had the power over her person she was determined to submit entirely to your will. The same language she has held I believe to some of your sisters, which encourages me to believe her sincere in her professions.

I have had a letter from Stutgard announcing to me by the desire of the Prince Royal the divorce between him & the Princess Royal. She has left Stutgard & is at present with her aunt the Duchesse de Deux-pont. Yr. sister laments this event very much as nothing can be alledged against the Princess but her uglyness for she is a fine figure, mild in her disposition, talented & uncommonly well behaved, & with the Kgs leave & by Prince Royals desire your sister is to keep up a constant connection with her. No further particulars are mentioned, but I have the promise of having the whole communicated to me, to justify the Prince's conduct upon the occasion. If the report you mentioned when I last had the pleasure of seeing you is true, I think the Prince will not gain either more beauty nor perhaps so mild a disposition in his second choice as in the first, mais c'est son affaire.

The Saint is delighted with his party. He talks in raptures of the owners of the place, the place itself, & lastly of your kindness to every-body. I fear he will not like his return to Lord Chesterfield's[1] quite so well, for there is no company at all.

I beg to be remembered to William & that you will believe me [etc.].

485 DR JENNER[2] *to* COLONEL McMAHON

Cheltenham, Sept. 13 1814.

THE enclos'd manuscript, which your goodness allows me to send you for perusal, was written at the request of Count Orloff,[3] with the view of its being presented to the Emperor. The Count desired me to give a concise outline of the origin of vaccination, & then to state the pecuniary advantages I had derived from promulgating the discovery, as foreign nations conceived them to be immense; that is to say, that the British nation had rewarded me with unbounded generosity.

This brief memorial has not yet been sent to the Emperor. Count Orloff alter'd his mind on the subject and express'd a wish that it should

1 Philip Stanhope, fifth Earl of Chesterfield (1755–1815).
2 The discoverer of vaccination. [1749–1823.]
3 Count Orlov (1787–1862), a natural son of Count Theodore Orlov (1741–1796), fought against Napoleon and was afterwards Russian Ambassador at Constantinople.

first go to the Grand Duchess of Oldenburgh, & be presented by Her Imperial Highness to her illustrious brother. He urged as a reason, the uncertainty of its reaching the Emperor's hand, if sent thro' the channel of the Russian Ambassador. Hence the matter rests.

I should certainly without hesitation adopt the plan you kindly suggested, & proceed immediately to Vienna, were there not an insurmountable obstacle; the indisposition of my wife; which is of such a nature that I dare not go far from home.

Pray excuse the trouble I am giving you, & believe me, dear Sir, [etc.].

486 THE QUEEN *to the* PRINCE REGENT

Windsor, the 20th Septbr 1814.

I HAVE this morning received a letter from Lady Ilchester giving me an account of Charlotte which so far is pleasant, as it states that Keat[e] finds the appearance of her knee better, tho the size of it is not much diminished which he had flattered himself.

She also accompanied this letter with one from Ldy Jersey who is returned from Paris where she has made some purchases for Charlotte & desires to know where to send the parcel. Ldy Ilchester told yr daughter that her orders on the subject of Lady Jersey from you would not allow her to admit *of any parcel being sent without your leave or permission, and she took this opportunity of stating to her that Ldy Jersey's conduct towards you, justifyed you in disapproving of her as a friend for yr daughter.*

She did not take it in ill humour, but was rather discomposed, & it ended after a second proposal to have it first sent to Carlton House to await your orders upon the subject, that she desired Ldy Jersey would keep it for the present & thus it remains at present, as C. evidently is afraid of another conversation upon this subject. You know much better than I do the existing friendship between Ldy Jersey & Miss Mercer & that there is no controul about the correspondence between the latter & Charlotte, & how easy it is to convey any letter through her, or to hide it in a parcel. I thought it right to state this to you & mus[t] leave it to your better judgement of what is to be done.

I have received many letters from Strelitz & Berlin & shall prepare my answers, some will be difficult to answer but I trust I shall guide the sincerity of my mind by very great prudence. I am glad that the King of Prussia wishes that Princess Solms should be asked in form of him, his protection & friendship upon this occasion will make her reception in

England much more advantageous & favorable for herself & if you will not be offended at my sincerity I am still of oppinion that Ernest should not return to England untill you have been able to obtain a settlement from Parliament.

I was glad to see by the papers that you have passed a day at Hampton Court, the heat here is intolerable & what must you not have suffered in London if you had remained there.

& now I bid you adieu & with a sincere God bless you, I am & remain, [etc.].

[P.S.] Second thoughts are best & I inclose the two letters but beg them to be returned, as I keep every letter which relates to Charlotte. Pray let Bloomfield only inclose them to me.

487 THE PRINCE REGENT *to the* DUKE OF YORK

Carlton House, Septr 22d 1814.

I RETURN you a thousand thanks for the kind letter I received from you yesterday, & I rejoice most sincerely to learn from yourself that you have derived so much benefit from seabathing & from your residence at the Pavillion, where, I entreat that you will remain, & believe, that everything is entirely at your command, for quite as long as it may suit you & agree with you.

London is just as dull stupid & deserted as can be imagined, no event, not even the least spice of scandal stirring, & as to public news there is none but the American which to be sure is most excellent but upon which I shall say nothing further, as it must reach you at latest this evening & long before this hasty scrawl can find its way to your hands; I will not therefore tresspass any longer upon you than to assure you how truly I remain [etc.].

488 DR MATTHEW BAILLIE *to the* PRINCE REGENT

Weymouth, Septr 26, 1814.

DR. BAILLIE has the honour of informing the Prince Regent most respectfully, that he saw the Princess Charlotte yesterday. Her Royal Highness's knee is certainly better. The swelling is less, so that the limit of the knee pan is distinct to the eye, but there is still some swelling, a little under knee pan. Her Royal Highness also complains of less pain in it, than she did at Cranbourne Lodge.

Her Royal Highness looks better in the countenance, than she did a fortnight ago, and has gained a little flesh. Her pulse is still too frequent, for it was yesterday 84, but it is softer and more placid than it us'd to be. Her Royal Highness complains of distensions of the stomach from indigestion, but has much less of the feeling of constriction in her chest, than she had a few weeks ago.

It has been agreed upon with Mr. Robt Keate that the temperature of the bath should be considerably lower'd at the two next bathings, and if Her Royal Highness shall feel advantage from this change, it is propos'd that she shall go into the open sea.

Her Royal Highness is to be permitted to take a short walk daily, which Mr. Robt Keate thinks will now rather be useful to the knee.

Dr. Baillie is to see Princess Charlotte again this forenoon, and then immediately he leaves Weymouth.

489 THE EARL OF LIVERPOOL *to* COLONEL MCMAHON

Walmer Castle, Octr. 5, 1814.

I RETURN the draft of the answer to Lord Carhampton. I am aware that his object is a peerage, but the *engagement* to which he lays claim is a seat in the House of Commons, which he says the King promised him for his life. I see no objection however to the answer as amended by His Royal Highness the Prince Regent. If Lord Carhampton sends a *rejoinder* on the subject of a seat in the House of Commons, it may then be wise to inform him that the Prince has no power by the Constitution to secure it to any one.

I confess I wish the answer to be sent before the Prince receives another letter from him.

490 COLONEL MCMAHON *to the* EARL OF CARHAMPTON

Carlton House, 6 Octr. 1814.

COLONEL MCMAHON has received the Prince Regents commands to have the honor of acknowledging the receipt of Lord Carhampton's letter, and to inform him that the Prince Regent has attentively consider'd the case which his Lordship has laid before him.

Col. McMahon is commanded to add that His Royal Highness does not feel it necessary upon the present occasion to advert to any of the circumstances to which Lord Carhampton's letter refers, as His Royal Highness had no concern in the past transaction, [and] has not the power by the Constitution to secure to any one a seat in the House of Commons. And, with every respect and good disposition towards Lord Carhampton, His Royal Highness is not advised to confer the dignity of a peer of the United Kingdom.

491   THE DUKE OF CUMBERLAND *to the* PRINCE REGENT

Strelitz, October 6th 1814.

I AM induced to write to you this letter on account of my uncle the Duke [1] who has just received an express from his eldest son who is at Vienna. It appears that Castlereagh is very difficult to get to, but by the friendship of Tyrrwhit who has promised to introduce him to Castlereagh, he hopes soon to have an audience of him. However in the meantime he has learnt through Tyrrwhit a piece of news which gives him great uneasiness, & has been a dreadful blow to my uncle, namely that Castlereagh says he *has had no direction* from you to speak in favour of the Duke's claims, which he had flattered himself would have been the case as you expressed yourself so warmly on the subject to Charles [2] during his stay in London; the King of Prussia through Hardenberg has declared *his full concurrence and readiness to support with all his interest the just claims of the Duke.* My uncle very naturally fears that if it should appear that your Minister does not espouse his cause, that Prussia will feel less anxious about him. He therefore has begged of me to write to you on the subject without loss of time and to implore you will give Castlereagh instructions on this subject, especially as his claims for an indemnity are so just, & are acknowledged as such by the King of Prussia, and the Emperor of Austria at the interview he had with the Hereditary Prince admitted the same, and even on this occasion Alexander was very civil. As this moment of the Congress is of the greatest consequence to the Duke he does implore your assistance, and that you will give directions to Castlereagh to support his claims, which will be seconded most heartily by Hardenberg on the part of Prussia. Nothing can exceed the friendship of Hardenberg who has written by the King's direction to Charles to state

1 The Duke of Mecklenburg-Strelitz.
2 Prince Charles of Mecklenburg-Strelitz.

to him most unequivocally that the Duke's claims should be supported by him.

Charles arrived here the first, but to the universal regret of us all leaves us the 14ʰ and returns to Berlin where the King has had the kindness to appoint him to the chief command of *all* the Prussian Guards cavalry, infantry & artillery which it is supposed will be greatly encreased upon the King's return from Vienna. H.M. conferred this command in a most pointed manner having done for Charles a thing till now unknown in the Prussian army, for the Colonels of Regiments are no more to report in person to His Majesty, but all business is to pass solely through Charles hands; and he certainly could not have fixed upon a more distinguished General Officer, for his zeal is indefatigable.

As yet we learn little or nothing interesting from Vienna except accounts of the festivities, the Court est monté au possible; as a specimen there are one hundred sets of six horses each, & 400 sets of 4 horses besides others of pairs for the use of all the Sovereigns assembled. What a treat it would be for Bloomfield to be there. The Duke, the Princess & Charles desire their best respects & believe me [etc.].

[P.S.] I am expecting Morand's return with great impatience.

492 THE BISHOP OF SALISBURY [DR JOHN FISHER] *to* UNKNOWN CORRESPONDENT

Weymouth, Oct: 10, 1814.

YOUR ROYAL HIGHNESSES kind and gracious message of condolence upon the late melancholy event in my family, which I have been honored with thro' Princess Charlotte, demands my most grateful acknowledgements, and these I now beg leave to offer to your Royal Highness.

The sudden death of my brother[1] is indeed a source of great affliction to the whole of his family. He was a very valuable member of society both in his public & private capacity. I take the liberty of enclosing to your Royal Highness a character of him which has appeared in the Portsmouth Journal, written by an officer who had long served under him.

I will now address your Royal Highness upon a subject which I am persuaded will afford you much satisfaction.

I can assure your Royal Highness that every thing as far as my observation can reach is going on as well as possible.

1 Major-General Fisher.

Princess Charlotte's general health is very greatly improved, and considerable progress has been made in removing the complaint in the knee. Her spirits are uniformly good and her mind appears to be in a tranquil state. I am strongly inclined to think that she is really happy here. Her Royal Highness behaves with great kindness and attention to us all and makes our residence with her extremely pleasant. There is one circumstance which I have the greatest satisfaction in mentioning to your Royal Highness. The Princess Charlotte is highly pleased with the letters she receives from Windsor, & looks to the arrival of each day's post with great impatience. She speaks of your Royal Highness with great affection, but is particularly gratified by Her Majesty's letters.

I cannot omit this opportunity of speaking in the highest terms of the conduct of Lady Ilchester. She appears to me to be in every point most admirably calculated for the important situation in which she is placed, and I cannot but lament that Her Royal Highness had not been originally been [*sic*] placed in the hands of a person whose grand object is the care of the important charge entrusted to her.

As I have been honored with the Prince Regent's commands to communicate with your Royal Highness, I feel I need make no apology for troubling you [with] this letter, especially as I trust it will afford you some satisfaction.

I have the honor to subscribe myself with the highest esteem, [etc.].

493 THE QUEEN OF WURTEMBERG *to the* PRINCE REGENT

Stutgard, October 18th, 1814.

IT was my intention not to have let Sir Isaac Heard leave this town without troubling you with a few lines to recall to your remembrance a sister that is sincerely attached to you, and who ever thinks with gratitude of the marks of affection and friendship you have honoured her with. But since this morning I have a double reason to write, as the King most kindly sent me an express from Vienna to acquaint me, with the Hanoverian Ministers having informed him that our beloved father had taken the title of King of Hanover in addition to his other titles. I am sure, dear brother, you must feel very happy that by your exertions and wise politics you have brought about an event which would give our dear Sovereign such delight, could he know what was going forwards. This must secure to you the gratitude and love of all the family who see that by this means you have made a very handsome provision for the children of your younger brother and secured to the House of Brunswick never fading honours.

Though I have been two months without writing to you, I have been most anxious in my enquiries concerning Charlotte's behaviour, knowing how very essentially every thing regarding her affects your happiness. I rejoice to find that she grows reasonable; this I hope will be the first step towards her feeling her errors and being convinced she can never have a sincerer friend than her father, whose only object is her real happiness and the desire of her appearing well in the world.

I will now only add the King's compliments and remain with sincere affection [etc.].

494 VISCOUNT CASTLEREAGH *to the* PRINCE REGENT

Vienna, 20th Octr 1814.

I HAVE the honor to transmit to your Royal Highness a memorandum received from Cardinal Consalvi,[1] relative to some objects bequeathed to your Royal Highness by the late Cardinal of York[2]—If any further steps should remain to be taken I beg to be honor'd with your Royal Highness's commands.

I am sorry my official letters have not to report to your Royal Highness a more satisfactory progress—The whole arrangement stands still on the point of Poland, and as yet the Emperor has evinced no disposition to accommodate.[3]—We are also impeded by the succession of fetes and private Balls—they waste a great deal of valuable time, and prevent P[rince] Metternich from giving his mind to the subjects that ought to engross him. I hope on the return of the Sovereigns from Bude something decisive will take place.

The most interesting of the Fetes we have had was a military dinner given on the anniversary of the Battle of Leipsick to the garrison of Vienna. 20,000 men sat down to dinner in the great plain of the Prater, the Sovereigns and Court dining within view—The tables for the troops were very beautifully disposed, and every man had his plate, tumbler and a bottle of wine upon a clean table cloth, which gave the whole an

1 The Papal Secretary of State; represented the Pope at the Congress of Vienna. (1757–1824.)

2 The younger brother of Charles Edward, the "Young Pretender". (1725–1807.)

3 The Tsar was bent on annexing the Grand Duchy of Warsaw, the whole of which, except Posen and Thorn, he ultimately received as King of Poland.

appearance of comfort and hospitality that was highly gratifying to the soldiers, most of whom had fought on that memorable day.

I long most earnestly to return to your Royal Highness, but as yet I cannot much flatter myself that I am advancing towards my liberation. If Russia would bend I should be sanguine as to other interests being speedily adjusted.

495 THE DUKE OF CAMBRIDGE *to the* PRINCE REGENT

Hanover, Octr. 24th 1814.

I RECEIVED the account from Munster too late on Thursday last to be able to congratulate you on the new title which you have assumed for the Electorate of Hanover. The joy it has caused here is very great, and provided Munster succeeds in procuring sufficient addition of territory to the Electorate to make it worthy of the new title, no one will rejoice at it more than I shall. I am however fully convinced that under the present circumstances Munster could not act otherwise and therefore even if he should not be able to get all the additional territory he wishes, he deserves great credit for what he has done. We were for some days very uneasy about him, but thank God our last accounts were very satisfactory, & provided he will not overwork himself, I hope his health will not suffer materially from his late accident.

I have nothing new to write from hence. Everything is going on quietly and the officers are not quite so much overwhelmed with business as they were some months ago....

496 THE EARL OF CARHAMPTON *to* COLONEL MCMAHON

Bruton Street, 24th October 1814.

LORD CARHAMPTON presents his compliments to Colonel McMahon [and] will be much obligled [*sic*] to him if he will have the goodness to present for him in the most respectful manner the enclosed paper to His Royal Highness the Prince Regent.

Bruton Street, 24th October 1814.

To the letter[1] which you did me the honor to transmit through Colonel McMahon, I could not return an immediate answer, or venture to address your Royal Highness on a subject so nearly affecting my honor and my character until the feelings which it had excited had in some degree subsided, and until I could exercise upon it the cool and deliberate faculties of a collected mind. I do assure your Royal Highness that a seat in Parliament is in itself of no importance to me at my time of life, not so the refusal to carry His Majesty's promise into execution, and the implied accusation of an attempt on my part to urge your Royal Highness to a violation of the Constitution in order to obtain it.

It could not be unknown to me that your Royal Highness had no power by the Constitution to secure to any one a seat in the House of Commons; nor can I believe that His Majesty when he gave me that promise, or his Minister when he returned me to Parliament under it, either violated or intended to violate the Constitution by so doing. With respect to the peerage which your Royal Highness is not advised to confer, the answer is conclusive; 'tis natural enough for the Minister of the day so to advise, but I rejected it fourteen years ago, when it was offered to me on terms which did not accord with my notions of what it would be just and honorable for me to accept.

Permit me, Sir, to observe that my name will be found in the history of these countries connected at all times with the defence of His Majesty's Government, and of the Constitution. In Ireland, when both were nearly subverted and overthrown, my life was hourly sought after, and was perhaps less saved by the conviction and execution of those who conspired against it than by a total neglect of its preservation.

In England I cannot think them less meritorious because a faction hostile to both have attempted to brand them with obloquy: His Majesty and every loyal man in the country thought otherwise, but I am not claiming for those services; I never did; my whole life will acquit me of any charge either of troublesome importunity or presumptuous expectation. His Majesty's promise was not given to me in requital of any service I had perform'd; it was for the sacrifice which at his request I made by submitting to the odium and popular hatred which the cowardice of the Cabinet and of the Parliament brought upon me, when I might by pursuing the conduct which I felt I ought and intended to pursue, have become one of the most popular men in England. I call upon your Royal Highness to perform that promise, and to put me on a level with every

1 No. 490.

other man in the Kingdom, and until those who have advised you not to do so, shall be considered to have more virtue, purer principles, or to be more tenacious of trespassing on the Constitution than His Majesty and his Minister were, I cannot relinquish my right to the performance of it; and though the nature of the transaction precludes the possibility of an appeal to any other tribunal than the minds of honorable men, to their decision I shall be always ready to submit it with confidence.

Do me the justice, Sir, to believe that I am not in the habit of speaking of my services; what I have said has been extorted from me as much by the refusal of my claim, as by the reasons given for its refusal. And when I consider the deference your Royal Highness continues at all times to pay to His Majesty's intentions when made evident to you, and the good dispositions you have been pleased to express towards me, I can scarce persuade myself that you will not on a reconsideration of my claim, revoke a decision against which it is impossible for me not to remonstrate.

I am Sir with sentiments of zeal, duty and attachment, [etc.].

498 DR ROBERT KEATE *to the* PRINCE REGENT

London, Octr. 24th 1814.

MR. ROBT. KEATE has the honor to report for the information of His Royal Highness the Prince Regent that the complaint in the Princess Charlotte's knee, as well as the general state of Her Royal Highness's health, continues to improve.

The cold sea bathing has had a very beneficial effect and continues to agree with Her Royal Highness in every respect.

There is still a considerable degree of thickening below the joint of the knee. All the other surrounding parts have nearly resumed their natural size and form.

499 THE DUKE OF CUMBERLAND *to the* PRINCE REGENT

Strelitz, Novr. 4th 1814.

I SHOULD not have troubled you so soon again with a letter had I not been induced so to do at the request of my uncle the Duke who has a great favour to ask of you, & has commissioned me to do it in his name. His wish is to have the brevet rank of Field Marshall in the British service,

& thus be enabled to wear the English port épée & cordon, when he retired from the Hanoverian service. The King conferred on him the rank
of Hanoverian Field Marshall, and *all* he wishes is to have the same rank
in ours as 'tis merely a *title* and as there are now so many General Officers,
formerly Hanoverians, that have titular rank of General Officers, he is
most desirous to be allowed by you to enjoy the privilege of wearing our
feld zeichen as it is termed, being so very nearly related to us, and having
distinguished himself as one of the first German Sovereign Princes who
took up arms for the great cause, and having, to shew his zeal, sacrificed
all his private comforts, he feels that such a mark of favour & kindness
from you would be most highly grateful to his feelings & prove to the
world your approbation.

I seize this same opportunity of offering you my sincerest congratulations on *your* having been the person to have raised the rank of Hannover
to that of a Kingdom and may every earthly blessing attend you as their
present Ruler, and the nation that has the happiness of having such a
Sovereign. It is exactly a *twelve month this day* that I had the satisfaction
of entering at 11 o'clock a.m. the gates of that dear city & never shall I
forget my feelings on that occasion, or the enthusiasm with which I was
received there as the first member of the Brunswick family they had seen
since so many years, and it is on this same 4th Novr that I have again the
satisfaction of congratulating on your new dignity, a dignity you & your
steadiness and firmness have procured for OUR family. May you live
many many years to enjoy the same, is the sincerest and most anxious
wish of [etc.].

P.S. I just hear that Major General Gandi (?) is ordered to march with
a corps of Prussians to take possession of Saxony.[1] General Kleist is
appointed Military Governor, & Mr. de Reck (?) Minister for the Interior, and as the ex King of Saxony has not yet received any *official*
notice it is called *provisionally*. The King of Prussia has written to the
Prince Royal but does not mention his return to Berlin. The Princess
desires her best respects.

---

1 Prussia demanded the whole of Saxony as compensation for the loss of the greater part of
Polish Prussia, but a compromise was ultimately reached whereby Prussia annexed the northern
half of Saxony and Frederick Augustus, King of Saxony, who had adhered to Napoleon to the
last, recovered the remainder. On 4 November he issued an official protest against the
provisional occupation of his Kingdom by Prussian troops.

Strelitz, November 19th 1814.

THOUGH I can naturally have no great news for your information and naturally all great events are reported to you officially, therefore my letters can afford you very little amusing, however I must not allow too great a space to pass without giving some sign of life. Though I said above that you was informed of *all* the great events that took place at the Congress, still perhaps there may be often some much more trivial in appearance and yet that may lead to great consequences, and I will therefore relate the following are worthy of attention. Vous saurez ou ne saurez pas that Metternich is very much in love with the Dutchess of Sagan[1] (who was in England with the Schwacheldt) it appears that that a Prince Windegratz[2] a Bohemian nobleman, who it is said had been the son of the other sister's, fell in love with the Sagan but could not succeed as she was engaged to Metternich, but Alexander who hates Metternich like poison perceiving this attachment of Windergratz was determined to play a trick to Metternich. The Sagan who for some reason or other was *not well* with Alexander, who avoided her, seeing she wished to be reconciled to him, told her fairly the only manner she could be reconciled with him was by cutting Metternich and admitting Windergratz to her charms. This has actually taken place. Now at such a moment, that *A* can have acted so imprudently, not to say anything [else] is most weaksighted, and I fear he has done mischief by it. In short it is very much to be wished that the Monarchs had *not* staid so long together there, for as it happened at Paris, so I fear it will here, the people are grown tyred of *all* that is going on, and the consequence is pasquinades appearing. I own I am not at all pleased with the last letters I have read from Vienna. God grant all may end well, but it does not appear couleur de rose.

Believe me I never was more grateful than on reading the sentence of the C[ourt] M[artial] and now that it is over and we may give an opinion I must say I never read any proceedings which bear the appearance of *cabal* in them as these do, and to the military you have done an act which must raise you very very high in putting forth in so decisive a manner your opinion by the account of those officers.[3] Eliza has written to me in

1 The daughter of the Duchess of Courland. Writing from Vienna on 4 October, Lord Apsley said that she had emancipated three husbands from their ties, and in addition had frequently emancipated herself. "She is still very handsome and gives very good suppers. Her sister is married to Talleyrand's nephew." (b. 1781.)

2 Prince Windischgrätz (1787–1862), the Austrian Field-Marshal, who suppressed the 1848–49 revolution at Prague and Vienna.

3 For the Court Martial on Colonel Quentin, see No. 501.

[506]

extacy of her séjour at Brighton and I am happy to perceive that your
weather was so favourable, for here of late we have had most desperate
stormy weather. The Russian troops have at length begun to leave
Holstein, a column of 10,000 infantry pass through this Dutchy tomorrow. They will be five days in this country.

Last mail brought me a letter from George FitzErnest[1] who speaks
with gratitude for all your kindness to him, for which accept my sincerest
thanks.

I must send you a copy of one of the pasquinades found pasted against
the walls of the bourg.

> Le Roi de Danemarc *boit* pour *tous.*
> Le R de Wurtemberg *mange* pour *tous*
> Le R de Bavaria *parle* pour *tous*
> Le R de Prusse *pense* pour tous
> L'Empereur de Russie *aime* pour tous
> et
> Le Peuple *souffre* pour *tous.*

I think this shews more fun in the Vienna people than I expected from
them. Excuse all this trash but perhaps it may amuse you for five
minutes and, harrassed as you must be with business, this may be
acceptable.

501 COLONEL McMAHON *to the* PRINCE REGENT

Carlton House, Novr. 21st 1814.

ALTHOUGH the triumphant manner in which the question on Thursday
in the House of Commons was disposed of[2] & seemingly put at rest,
might occasion a doubt as to the policy or necessity of taking any public
notice of the very gross & abominable misrepresentations of Palmer &
Tierney; still, under all the circumstances of the case & of the times, it
was the clear opinion of both Wharton[3] & Street this morning, that the

1 Presumably the Duke's illegitimate son.
2 Twenty-four officers of the 10th Hussars (the Prince of Wales' Own Royal Regiment of
Light Dragoons) had accused their commanding officer, Colonel Quentin, of incompetence and
neglect of duty whilst on service in southern France at the beginning of 1814, and he was
court-martialled in October. At their request, Colonel Palmer (1777–1851), of the same
regiment, and Whig M.P. for Bath, acted as prosecutor. The charges were for the most part
dismissed; the Duke of York, as Commander-in-Chief, severely censured the conduct of the
officers in bringing forward unsubstantiated charges against their commanding officer, and
ordered them to be transferred to other Regiments. Colonel Palmer's motion, supported by
Tierney, was really an appeal to the House against the decision of the court-martial and the
Commander-in-Chief.
3 Richard Wharton.

three points, so shamefully perverted by them, should be distinctly stated & as distinctly refuted in the *Courier* of this evening, & therefore the paper which your Royal Highness will read in it, was accordingly prepared by Wharton, & embraced, as he conceived, all the most essential points of the instructions which Y.R.Hss had given him at Brighton. This statement studiously confines it's refutations to *positive* & *unanswerable* facts. It offers no comment, & strictly avoids every wanton provocation, & as it is declared to come "from authority" this course was unanimously thought to be the most fitting & dignified for such a communication. Neither does it leave to invite any further discussion, or to bring to life again the extinguish'd question.[1]

I saw the Duke of York, & Torrens[2] together this forenoon, who were both (as I think every honorable minded man *must* be) decidedly of opinion that Col. Palmer ought *not* to remain Aid de Camp, each differing only as to the mode of carrying the measure into effect, the former wishing nothing to be done for a fortnight or three weeks to come, in order to see whether Palmer should feel the propriety of resigning that honor, while the latter was for removing him *instanter*.

It is here necessary to acquaint Y.R.Hss that in *strict confidence*, I have learnt from G. Fitzclarence[3] that it is Palmer's fix'd intention *not* to quit the Army, & he has said, that he did not mean to resign his Aid de Campship, because "he fear'd it would be consider'd a personal offence to the P.R." & taking this determination for granted, I am induced to think with the D. of York, for if he was now dismiss'd, he would artfully say, he was just on the eve of giving in his resignation, which in a fortnight or three weeks hence (when his resolution to continue in the service would be obvious to every one) that tale would not hold water. In my superficial judgement I have no hesitation in feeling, that Y.R.Hss will be as strictly correct, as you will be strictly just, in not suffering him to remain your A.D.C., nor should Y.R.Hss's pleasure for dismissing him, be sent forth in the communication of it, as proceeding from his having been the prosecutor of Colonel Quintin. No, it has been for subsequent conduct, & what higher crime could a military man commit against his profession, than, *in such a case*, to avail himself of the adventitious circumstance of his being a member of Parliament, for the purpose of wresting

1 This article is too long to be reproduced and is of no great importance.

2 Major-General Sir Henry Torrens (1779–1828), Military Secretary to the Prince Regent, 1811; Adjutant-General of the Forces, 1820; K.C.B., 1815.

3 George Augustus Frederick Fitzclarence, first Earl of Munster (1794–1842), eldest son of William IV by Mrs Jordan, and a captain in the 10th Hussars. He was one of the twenty-four officers who signed the letter of 9 August to the Prince Regent, as Colonel of the Regiment, and in consequence was transferred to the 20th Light Dragoons. In January 1815 he went out to India as Lord Moira's A.D.C. Peerage, May 1831.

from the military jurisprudence their solemn determination, & to drag it before the very tribunal on earth that an army has the strongest right to be jealous & suspicious of. Besides, when sinking under personal kindnesses & obligations, to deliberately expose Y.R.Hss to the expected fury of a faction, & to all the vile filth of the rankest democracy. I have likewise seen Lord Liverpool this forenoon, who is also clearly of opinion that Palmer should be removed but concurs with the D. of York as to the time for doing it.

He told me that many of his best supporters in the H. of Commons are desirous that the rebuilding the Palace, should not be brought on until the question of the property tax shall pass the House, & this will be after the hollidays.[1]

502 THE EARL OF MOIRA *to the* PRINCE REGENT

Camp on the road to Bareilly,
Novr. 22d 1814.

SOME weeks ago, on receiving the first intelligence of the fortunate events by which the war in Europe was terminated, I took the liberty of expressing my humble congratulations on the share which the wise measures of your Royal Highness had in producing that glorious result. As letters from this country are subject to failure, I may be indulged with the permission to repeat those expressions of my joy at all that contributes to the honour of your Royal Highness. The general sense of Europe will establish how mainly this wonderful revolution in affairs is ascribable to your Royal Highness's influence. Long, very long, may you enjoy the consciousness of the inappreciable advantages which you have secured for your country.

All here must appear on so diminutive a scale after the gigantic contest just finished that I know not whether I ought to touch upon such inferior interests. The death of M[ajor] General Gillespie,[2] however, may excite more curiosity respecting our present warfare than would otherwise attend it. Not till after the year 1760 was the name of the Gorkhas known. They were an obscure tribe of mountaineers, numerous & bold, but of scanty resources. Emerging from their hills, they conquered the Kingdom of Nipaul (then in a state of civil war) more by perfidy than by

1 In 1815 there sprang up a tempestuous demand for the abolition of the income tax, which had always been regarded as a war tax, but the Government unexpectedly succeeded in carrying a Bill to renew it for one more year.

2 Sir Robert Rollo Gillespie (1766–1814). He was gazetted K.C.B. on 15 January 1815, the news of his death (31 October) reaching England only in the middle of May.

valor. This success gave them a treasury & an ampler command of men. They formed powerful armies; subdued a number of petty States in their neighbourhood; & at length made themselves masters of the Kingdoms of Kemaoon [Kumaon] & Sirinagur [Srinagar] with many adjoining territories. Their empire now extends eastwards almost as far as ours; & westward it has the same boundary—the River Sutledje, a branch of the Indus. Their encroaching spirit could not be satisfied with extension in that direction. They descended from the ridge of hills, their natural boundary, & occupied large tracts in the plain really belonging to us. By strange supineness, those aggressions were not timely checked; and they could plead a tacit admission on our part to justify their occupation of vast tracts thus appropriated. Recently, they established a new line of frontier in a particular district, including a very considerable portion of our possessions. Lord Minto remonstrated against the trespass. The Gorkhas insisted upon title: and his Lordship, reluctant to proceed to extremities proposed that commissioners should meet to determine the point. They met accordingly; but it was soon visible that the Gorkha commissioners had no purpose of substantiating any right, being in hopes that they should tire us by unmeaning disquisitions & that we should not ultimately prosecute the question. Ld Minto, however, indignant at being so trifled with, gave notice that if the matter were not settled by a specified time our troops should re-establish our Revenue Officers in the district. To this menace of the British Government I succeeded; &, having failed in another attempt to bring the Rajah of Nipaul to reason, felt the credit of our power staked upon our not making an idle threat. At the time fixed, our troops advanced. The Gorkha troops retired without contest, & it appeared that the procedure was quietly acquiesced in by the Nipaulese Government. When the season arrived in which fevers really pestilential reign in that tract, I was loth to expose our troops to the malady & I ordered them back to healthy positions. On this, the Gorkha troops attacked by surprise, & of course carried, our defenceless Revenue stations, murdering the prisoners in cold blood. Redress for this outrage, & for an atrocious attempt to poison the wells of our frontier villages, having been sought in vain from the Rajah of Nipaul, the chastisement of the aggressors was incumbent on us, and I was resolved it should be undertaken effectually. An army of the Gorkhas was on the banks of the Sutledje. Colonel Ochterlony[1] was directed to occupy it's attention, tho' there was little hope of being able to strike at it amid the mountains with which it is enveloped. M: General Gillespie was to penetrate with another Division in a direction which

1 Sir David Ochterlony (1758–1825), who conquered the Gurkhas. Created Baronet, 1815.

would facilitate Col: Ochterlony's movements, & was afterwards to secure the country of Kemaoon, by entering it on a side where it is open. M[ajor] General Wood was to advance from Garuckpore [Gorakhpur] to Palpah in the hope of raising those conquered districts against their savage taskmasters the Gorkhas & re-establishing the expelled Rajahs. The fourth & principal attack was to be conducted by M[ajor] General Marlay; & it's object was Catmanda [Khatmandu] the capital of Nipaul. Fearful of M: General Gillespie's impetuosity I gave him precise written instructions that no fortification of a description to require that cannon should be used against should be attacked in any other way. Colonel Mawbey of the 53d, second in command, reconnoitred the Fort of Kalunga [Kalanga]; &, in obedience to the instructions, declined assaulting it as he considered that nothing but artillery could reduce it. On this report reaching M: G: Gillespie, he hastened from his own column & immediately ordered the assault of the place. When the troops got to the foot of the rampart it was discovered that there was no possible mode of getting into the Fort. The walls were very high, there was no breach, no scaling ladders, in short no means whatever of gaining entrance. The troops of course retired with much loss. M: General Gillespie, probably frantic from sense of indiscretion, persisted in walking round the walls to look for some vulnerable place till he received a musket shot which killed him instantly. His heroic valor makes him a severe loss notwithstanding this error.

With no less devoted affection than respect, I remain, Sir, [etc.].

503 THE DUKE OF CAMBRIDGE *to the* PRINCE REGENT

Hanover, Novr. 24th 1814.

I SEIZE the earliest opportunity I have on my return from my journey to Gottingen and the Hartz to inform you that the reception I have met with everywhere has been most gratifying, and that the loyalty and the attachment of all ranks to you and the old established Government has been most marked in the strongest manner. On my way back I came through the country and town of Hildesheim, where I was received with nearly as much enthusiasm by the inhabitants as I was on my first arrival in the Electorate, and though I had wished that all the rejoicings should be put off till I made my publick entry into Hildesheim on the day of the Huldigung (or hommage) it was impossible to prevent the inhabitants from coming out to meet me. This clearly proves how delighted the people are at being your subjects, and I feel great satisfaction at being able to state this. I did not fail to mention that you had authorized me to say you looked upon the country of Hildesheim in the same light as your other possessions, and that they would be treated in the same way. You will easily believe, my dearest brother, that the manner in which I have been received everywhere in the country, and the expressions of loyalty and affection for you, must be most gratifying to me, and undoubtedly render my situation much pleasanter than it was last year. Your constant kindness to me and your delicacy in not pressing me to remain here I have deeply felt, and I have lately had a fresh proof of it in a conversation you have had with dearest Minny[1] which she has mentioned to me in her last letter. I therefore seize this opportunity of thanking you again and again for your kindness and of assuring you that I have of late repeatedly thought over my situation here. I clearly see that it will be a long time before I could conscientiously resign, and as I really believe that I am of some use, and knowing that your wishes that I should remain here are the same as those the King had, I feel it my duty to say that I am ready to stay here for some years at least, on certain conditions which I shall be ready to propose whenever I receive your commands.[2] In order that you may understand what I mean by conditions, I beg leave to add that there are three points which must be settled. The first concerns my civil situation, which must be defined, as at present I have nothing to do with the Government but in military concerns; and if I am really to do good I must have more power. The second point would be the permission to pass a part of the year in England whenever the affairs will permit me to leave Hanover. The third regards my allowance which of course must depend on your liberality.

With respect to the first I should propose that nothing should be settled till Count Munster comes to Hanover, as I should be very sorry that anything should be settled which *he* did not think right by you and the country. Indeed I feel very anxious that he should be consulted upon the other points. I have informed him by a messenger who is gone to-day to Vienna of the letter I have written to you.

Before I conclude I must add one line to say that an additional motive for my coming to this decision is the hope that it may relieve you, my dearest brother, from difficulties you might be placed in if you had not known my decision. And now God bless you, forgive this long letter and believe me far or near [etc.].

1 Princess Mary.
2 It is known that in accepting the governorship of Hanover the Duke made a considerable personal sacrifice, "giving up", as his brother, the Duke of York, remarks, "all his comforts to what he considers a public duty".

Pav^n, Br^n, Novr. 24th 1814.

I HAVE again, my dearest mother, to return you a thousand thanks for the kind letter which I receiv'd this morning, & I hope that the epistle which I inclose will in every point, meet your approbation & answer the desir'd purpose, if so, I will entreat of you to forward it to Lady Ilchester. Perhaps, there might be no harm, in giving a little private hint also to the Bishop[1] (to whom I have more than once spoken upon this subject) of the contents of my letter to Lady Ilchester, in consequence of which he should also speak his mind freely & fairly to Charlotte, for I am well acquainted with all the wickedness, perseverance, & trick, of that infernal Jezabel Lady Jersey, & of all her Jacobin[ic]al set of connexions, & that there is no one base, or infernal scheme, plot, or plan that they will stick at, to accomplish their views. Therefore we can not be too much upon our guard, or too much upon the alert, which I must implore of you to inculcate where it should & must be most attended to.[2]

Your other orders of yesterday have already been attended to, & I have had a letter written accordingly to Nash, which went off by the last night's post. In short I trust that you will perceive that not a moment has been lost in attending to your wishes on every head.

William thank God is much better in every respect, indeed I may add almost quite well, & no remains of complaint to be observ'd, but a little of feebleness & weakness, what one would rather call, pull'd down a little, & which it could not be expected should be otherwise after the sharpness rather than the severity of the attack. The truth is, it was fortunately taken just in time, & Dr. Tierney's[3] skill & good judgment, has done wonders for him.

The Hampden's,[4] that is to say the Marquise Tulipano, & his cara sposa came to us the day before yesterday, to pass a few days with us, & I have persuaded Mi Lordino Bijeux to prolong his visit also for a few days. One & all of us after dinner yesterday, could not help, after drinking your health, in a bumper, expressing how cordially we wish'd from the very bottom of our hearts, that we had the happiness of seeing you again at the head of the table here, as well as my dearest sisters, for you can not conceive the sensation your visit has made upon every one here, or of the regrets which your departure has occasion'd....

1 Dr Fisher, Bishop of Salisbury.

2 Lady Jersey had had a hand in the Whig intrigue against the Orange match in June 1814. It was she who supplied Lord Holland with a copy of Princess Charlotte's letter of 16 June to the Prince of Orange, in which she announced that their engagement was "totally and for ever at an end". (*Further Memoirs*, p. 200.)

3 Sir Matthew John Tierney (1776–1845), the Prince Regent's physician. Created Baronet, 1818.   4 ? Thomas Hampden-Trevor, second Viscount Hampden (1746–1824).

505 [? Sɪʀ Jᴏʜɴ Dᴏʏʟᴇ]¹ *to* Cᴏʟᴏɴᴇʟ McMᴀʜᴏɴ

Monday Evg. [1814].

Yᴏᴜʀ satisfactory intelligence was made doubly welcome by the kindness which prompted you so immediately to communicate it & for which
I beg you will accept my sincerest thanks.

I return you Ld Moira's letter.² The question of Popham's treatment
of him on the passage out is now gone by. It is clear that nothing ever
was more disgraceful than his table. As to Lord Moira's character of
him at the end, it is much too favorable. He has unquestionably some
resource but his acquirements are superficial & his judgement is far from
solid—he is much more likely to mislead those who wd trust to him, by
his plausibility, than to aid their views by any correct or useful information. This, at least, is the opinion which my observation of him (such as
it has been) has led me to form. I have received letters to-day from Ld
M. of the same date as yours in April.

506 Tʜᴇ Pʀɪɴᴄᴇ Rᴇɢᴇɴᴛ *to the* Pʀɪɴᴄᴇss Cʜᴀʀʟᴏᴛᴛᴇ

Carlton House, Decr. 26th 1814.

I ᴄᴀɴ not delay a single moment communicating to you the important
intelligence that has this moment reach'd me from the Continent, of
peace with America having been sign'd by our commissioners at Ghent.³
This opportunity of writing to you, my dear, I will not suffer to escape
me without just expressing to you the extreme satisfaction & happiness
I experienced at your conduct & at the candid communication you made
me yesterday, at the same time agonizing as my feelings as a parent were
during your recital & the different details you enter'd into. The hand of
Providence is strongly stamp'd in both events, Providence I trust will
ever be our best support & safeguard, for the hand of Providence alone,
I am sure, has & could alone have preserv'd you, my child.⁴

God bless you my dearest Charlotte.

1 Possibly Sir John Doyle (?1750–1834), Moira's lifelong friend. Private secretary to the
Prince of Wales, 1802–4; Lieutenant-Governor of Guernsey, 1804–15.
2 No. 405.
3 On 24 December. The British plenipotentiaries were Admiral Lord Gambier, Henry
Goulburn, and William Adams, D.C.L.
4 See Nos. 507–9.

Copy.

Decr the 26 [1814].

I HAVE many thanks to return you for your kind letter & I am not surprised after all that passed yesterday that you had a bad night, as I think I can judge by my own *feels* what yours *must have* BEEN who are so much more deeply concerned in what passed in my room from the situation of the parties than I am.[1] As far as regards myself nothing shall ever transpire from ME. Your letter however kind and flattering in wishing to have my *approbation* of *your conduct*, the purport of it is of so delicate a nature that all I can say is that if you feel *conscientiously you have told the whole truth*, leaving nothing *behind*, & that you felt yourself thrown into such a *situation* that it was *your duty* to reveal the *particulars* to your father without loss of time, then I feel confident you will be supported under this most heavy, most severe, & unexampled *trial*. I trust the Prince's kindness on the occasion will be so forcibly engraven on your mind as to lead you hence forward *never to* act with any concealment, & *now* that you are come to years of descretion you never will be drawn on to forget what is due to your rank & station in life as well as your duty towards your father & the country. And as you say you feel he is *now* nearly your chief & *only parent*, for God sake look up to him as your only *adviser* & *protector*; don't fancey for the future that people are to misrepresent you to him, let your *guide be truth* & apply to him upon every occasion, & that done you can have nothing to *fear*.

The Prince's delicacy of conduct towards you *on one subject* for many years passed ought to satisfy *you* that he will as far as he can *continue to consider your feelings as a child*. As no conversation can be more painful than what I witnessed yesterday I do not hesitate once more imploring you to consider well if there is any one thing, however trifling it may appear to you, left *unsaid*, as it will be wholly impossible for the P. to extricate you out of any *dificulty* should he not be apprized of every circumstance. It is impossible to say how much I have thought of you & do feel for you & share most truly & deeply in the awkward & distressing situation you are placed in, & I may venture to say one *circumstance brought out an other*; & Heaven grant, my poor dear Charlotte, it may all turn out for your future advantage & comfort. You have much to thank Providence for & I hope you are as sensible of this blessing as I am for yours.

1 See Nos. 508, 509.

Decr the 31, 1814.

I send you the paper you ordered me to *write,* which to the best of my recolection I have put together as far as passed between you & Charlotte but upon mature consideration & talking it over with the Queen & my sister we all agree that what passed in confidence between Charlotte & myself (though I have wrote it down) ought not to go out of my *own hands,* as I may be of more use if I can by degrees get her to tell it you herself. But you may depend upon my noteing down every thing that is necessary & keeping it for any future occasion should it be called for.

[*Enclosed*]

Princess Mary has obeyed the Prince Regent's commands, in submiting to paper, to the best of her recollection what passed between His Royal Highness & Princess Charlotte in Princess Mary's appartment on the 25 of December, & likewise what passed in an interview which took place at Cranborne on the 29th of December between the Prince Regent & Princess Charlotte, Princess Mary being witness to both these conversations by the desire of the Pss Charlotte and aprov'd by the Prince Regent.[1]

In consequence of a message the Prince Regent thought proper to send his daughter through Dr Short[2] to acquaint her of the conduct of the Princess of Wales towards the boy[3] who she took abroad with her, the Princess Charlotte wrote a letter to the Regent thanking him for the delicate manner in which he made this communication, & begged to know what steps she ought to take upon this subject. The Regent came down to Windsor Christmas Day, &, finding his daughter with the Queen, ordered her to go with him in to Princess Mary's appartment, & commanded Pss Mary to follow likewise, when the Regent said, it was not with the intention to do any thing, or with the idea that any thing could be done, that he sent her the message, it was only to prove to her, that her interest was his first object in life, that as long as he lived this boy could be of no sort of consequence, but that if he died then the boy might be a very serious misfortune to her, as well as to the country, & he hoped this would *now* make her see, upon what grounds he had acted for so many years past, & why the King & himself had so decidedly forbid

1 A second copy of this document reads simply "by order of the Prince Regent".
2 The Princess Charlotte's sub-preceptor. Miss Knight describes him as "a good sort of Devonshire man, with some classical knowledge, very little taste, an honest heart, but overcautious temper, fearful of offending". He "used to come every morning and read English to her Royal Highness from eleven to twelve".
3 William Austin.

her ever seeing that boy, for on two points of *view* he was an improper companion for his daughter. Princess Charlotte for answer said, the boy had always been greatly preferred before her, that she never had seen him in the drawing room from the time that order was given that she was not to keep company with him, but that the Princess often spoke of him with the greatest affection, that he was always in the house either at Black-Heath, Kensington or Connaught Place, that she had met him on the staircase, that he was a sickly looking child with fair hair and blue eyes—that to prove the love the Princess had for this boy, that he slept always in her room in the same bed with her untill he became too old, & then a small bed was placed in the Princess's own bed room for him. This lead to the society which Princess Charlotte used to meet at her mother's, & the Princess Charlotte having named Lord Henry Fitzgerald[1] amongst others—the Prince reminded her of an order made by the King (in consequence of some remarks she had let drop respecting that person after having hastily left her mother's room to Lady de Clifford) that she never should be allowed to see her mother alone. She not only admitted this, but stated that notwithstanding that order she generally saw her mother alone & had witnessed many things in her mother's room which she could not repeat. Some remarks were made at the same moment respecting a still further restriction in her intercourse with her mother in consequence of having met Sir William Drummond,[2] with whom an im-

1 The fourth son of the first Duke of Leinster, by Lady Amelia Mary Lennox, daughter of the second Duke of Richmond and Lennox. [1761–1829.]

2 The scholar and diplomatist (?1770–1828). In 1811 he printed for private circulation a book in which he attempted to prove that certain parts of the Old Testament were allegories, derived from astronomy. Cp. Farington's *Diary*, 3 August 1812: "Sir William has had access to the table of the Princess of Wales and once there talked to the Princess Charlotte in a way that she thought so improper as to cause her to rise, which being remarked, she said she had heard enough, and with a slight courtesy moved away." Lord Kenyon referred to Sir William Drummond's conversations with Princess Charlotte at her mother's table, in a Memorandum dated 5 February 1821, the Bishop of Salisbury being his authority. "Sir William Drummond told Princess Charlotte he understood she was reading history, and asked what history it was that most interested her; without waiting for her reply, he went on, and said that he had latterly been in the habit of reading Oriental history, as the most amusing, and added, as to what is called Scripture history, 'I can assure your Royal Highness there is nothing in it, it is all an allegory, and nothing more.' The next time of his being by Princess Charlotte, he brought forward several of Paine's objections against Christianity, which she met and confuted, and Lady E. [*sic*] Lindsay said she never saw any man in her life so completely thrown on his back. The third time of their meeting, Sir William Drummond was beginning again in the same style, by saying that the education of the nobility and of all ranks, even the highest in this country, was on a very bad plan, all in the hands of priests; and, addressing her Royal Highness, he said, 'you know that priests have always been the most corrupt and contemptible of mankind.' She replied, 'Sir William, you are now for the third time so good as to be giving me instruction in the same way; I do not know what your object can be; you seem to be an atheist, or at least a Deist, and I must beg to refrain from holding any more such conversation with you....'." (*Hist. MSS. Comm., Kenyon MSS.*, pp. 565–6.)

proper conversation took place on the subject of religion, & also Princess Charlotte having been present when the details of Mrs Clarke's[1] business where given by Mr. Littleton[2] to her mother. The King ordered she should never meet any society whatever there. This introduced Lady De Clifford's resignation, when the Prince hinted to a communication Lady de Clifford had made to him on the subject of Princess Charlotte's partiallity for Capt. Hesse, when Pss Charlotte took this opportunity of explaining that affair as follows—

She made acquaintance with him when out of [*sic*] riding at Windsor during the time the 18th of L[ight] D[ragoons] were quartered in that part of the world; that Lady de Clifford had allowed him to ride by the side of the open carriage morning & evening for six weeks before she reprimanded her for it. They then came to high words, & Lady de Clifford, finding she had no power over Princess Charlotte & had lost her confidence, resigned—And that after the regiment moved from Windsor & was quartered at Portsmouth & Lewes, the Pss Charlotte confessed to her father she always met him at her mother's at Kensington, & had private interviews with him (unknown to Lady de Clifford) but with the Princess of Wales's knowledge & connivance, as the Princess of Wales used to let him into her own appartment by a door that opens into Kensington Gardens, & then left them together in her own bed room, & turned the key upon them saying "*À present je vous laisse, amusez vous*". Upon the Prince being horror struck, she said "I can tell you what is more, that my mother carried on a correspondence for us, & all the letters backwards & forwards went through her hands untill I spoke to *one person*[3] who advised me to break off this correspondence, which I did just at the time of the Duchess of Brunswick's death,[4] & I will get that part of the correspondence for you". The Prince then asked her if any presents had been given mutually, & whether they were returned. She said all those he had given her as well as all his letters to her, she returned through her mother by mutual agreement, but which agreement had not been kept to on his side, as her letters & presents had never been returned, or did she think her mother had ever wished they should be returned. One article she had got back through the means of a friend, which was her picture which she herself had not given him; it had been painted for her mother, & missing it one day, enquired if she was out of favour, when her mother replyed she had sent it to *l'aimable sujet*, which was the name the Princess gave him. She told the Regent

1 Mary Anne Clarke, formerly the Duke of York's mistress. See No. 142.
2 Probably the Whig M.P., W. H. Lyttelton. See Nos. 67–9.
3 Presumably her friend Miss Mercer Elphinstone.   4 March 1813.

she felt she was in her mother's power, but that she had wrote her word, upon hearing that Captain Hesse had joined her abroad,[1] that if she did not get him to return all her letters & presents, she should throw herself upon her father's mercy & acknowledge the whole to him. She said "God knows what would have become of me if he had not behaved with so much respect to me["], to which the Prince answered "My dear child, it is Providence alone that has saved you". The Prince asked her if she had told this to the Duke of Brunswick;[2] she said "never", but he has often put me on my guard on the subject of my mother's conduct & told me he was sure that boy was her child. Princess Charlotte appeared to be perfectly acquainted with all her mother's favorites as she told the Prince unasked that she looked upon Mr. K. Craven[3] as the present lover; she told him that he had dismissed all her servants that went from England with her, barring Sicard,[4] at Lausanne; she added that she was acquainted with the preference the Pss had before she left England to young Sappio of the cottage she took near Kensington, where they used to meet, & which the Pss of Wales said was taken for Lady C. Campbell's[5] children. She herself never saw Sapio in the house, but knew he dined with the Pss every day; she saw his horse standing at her door in Connaught Place when she (Pss Charlotte) used to pass by in her carriage, & explained & told the Prince the door she (the Pss) used to let him in at. She appeared equally acquainted with the history of Capt. Manby[6] & told the Prince that at the house the Pss had near the sea side at that time there was an underway passage which communicated with the sea, & that a small place had been made that a boat might be moored in, & so he came in & went out, & that the shape of the boat was left in the place. She had heard of Sir W. Gell[7] being talked of as a

---

1 In August 1814. He returned to England in March 1815, to rejoin his Regiment after hearing of Napoleon's escape from Elba, and he was severely wounded at Waterloo.

2 He returned to Germany in 1814 to raise fresh troops for the Allies.

3 Richard Keppel Craven (1779–1851), the youngest son of the sixth Baron Craven. In 1814 he accompanied the Princess of Wales to the Continent as her Chamberlain, but resigned the appointment six months later. He was her Vice-Chamberlain in 1820.

4 See No. 766.

5 Lady Charlotte Susan Maria Bury (1775–1861), daughter of John Campbell, fifth Duke of Argyll. Her first husband, Colonel John Campbell, whom she married in 1796, died in 1809, whereupon she entered the service of the Princess of Wales as a Lady-in-Waiting. In 1818 she married the Rev. E. J. Bury, and in 1838 published, anonymously, a *Diary illustrative of the Times of George IV*. She had nine children by her first husband.

6 Thomas Manby (1769–1834). He had been presented to the Princess of Wales about 1802, and in 1806, when the charges against her were drawn up, she was accused of conducting herself towards him with excessive familiarity. Ill health compelled him to quit the navy in 1808, but he was promoted to the rank of Rear-Admiral in 1825.

7 The classical archaeologist (1777–1836). He accompanied the Princess to the Continent in 1814 as one of her Chamberlains, and though he soon quitted her service he gave evidence for the defence at her "Trial" in 1820.

former favorite but did not believe he was so now. And she ended by saying she never could make out whether Capt. Hesse was her lover or her mother's, & that she supposed the Pss's object was to draw her into this scrape to bring the boy forwards.

On the 29th of Decr the Regent came to Windsor where he took up Pss Mary & proceeded with her to Cranbourn in consequence of having received the promised letters named in the first part of this paper from Princess Charlotte, & as Pss Mary had been witness to the first interview, the Prince wished she should hear what passed. Nothing has transpired but a compleat repetition of all that passed on the 25, & strong assurances of the truth of what Pss Charlotte had stated in the former conversation, except that Miss Haman[1] had thought it her duty to apprize Pss Charlotte how much she dissaproved of the Pss of Wales's manner of going on with young Sapio, in consequence of which she intended to withdraw herself, which *she did*, & that Pss Charlotte declared she never had either in writing or by word of mouth ever given a promise of marriage to Capt. Hesse. The Prince represented the dreadful situation in which she had been placed, the necessity of concealing nothing, or he could not extricate her out of this difficulty, & that in her situation she was not only acting wrong by her father, & herself, but what was still worse by the country, & that his object must be to save her, not *now* to reproa[c]h her, but to prevent the possibility of such a thing ever happening again.

A true Copy signed MARY.

509 PRINCESS MARY's *Memorandum*

[1 January 1815.]

What has passed in private conversations between Pss Mary & Pss Charlotte.

ON the 25 of Decr Xmas evening after the conversation that Pss Mary was witness to between the Regent & his daughter in the morning & when the Regent had left Windsor, Pss Charlotte after dinner came into Pss Mary's room and said her mind was greately relieved since she had told *all* she had in her *mind* to her father. That she had been miserable & never had courage before this day to do so. Pss Mary asked Pss Charlotte if the Pss of Wales had any dislike to the idea of Pss Charlotte's *intended* marriage with the Prince of Orange, or any dislike to her *marriage at all*.

1 Miss Hayman was the Princess of Wales' Privy Purse.

Pss Charlotte replyed "*No*, my mother wants me to *marry*, she hates all the Orange family but rather than not have me married she made her mind up to this marriage & was furious when it was broke off", because my mother says no body marries but with the idea of *liberty* of gratifying one's own inclinations & pleasures & fathering them upon one's husband". Then added "that not having my ideas on this subject as I never will marry a man I can not *respect*—we could *not* AGREE. I asked her if she thought the Pss would return to England—she said "Never *without I marry*.

On the 29 when I went up to Cranborne with the Prince Regent & he left the room to speak to Miss Mercer "Pss Charlotte told the Pss Mary that Lady Charlotte Campbell had in the most delicate manner said to her just before she left England, that her own health & nerves could no longer stand the constant anxiety that attended the situation of Lady of the Bed Chamber to the Pss of Wales, but that she never should forget the Pss of Wales kindness to her. Pss Mary enquired how the Pss of Wales was informed of Pss Charlotte's acquaintance with Captn Hesse, upon which Pss Charlotte said that the first time she went to see the Pss at Kensington after Lady de Clifford had spoke to her on the subject of Captn Hesse & forbid his riding by the open carriage &c &c, they meet him in the road going to Kensington & Lady de Clifford *suspected* it was by *appointment* that he was *there*, & accused Pss Charlotte of having some private communication with him. This caused a violent dispute between them & when Pss Charlotte arrived at Kensington she was all in *tears*. The Pss of Wales asked what all this ment when Pss Charlotte told her mother what had passed in the carriage between herself & Lady de Clifford and named Captn Hesse. The Pss said "this will play the devil at Windsor but I will make amends for it"—and after that day Pss Charlotte met Captn Hesse every time she went to make the Pss of Wales a visit, untill Captn Hesse was ordered abroad with his regiment.

Talking of the Pss of Wales imprudence she said, I remember her sending me a letter once by mistake which I only read half of & upon finding it was not intended for me I returned it immediately to my mother assuring her I had not read it through. At first she would not tell me who it came from, but upon my pressing for the name she said Sir Francis Burdett, & it told to his credit for as far as she read, he blames her for the friendship for Lady Perceval & for all the last publications & declares he will have nothing to do with the business; & Pss Charlotte added "but I read enough to see he must have been a favourite in his time.

On the 1 of Janry Pss Mary went to Cranborne with the Queen, when

Pss Charlotte took Pss Mary on one side & said that the letter that was directed to her in the Pss of Wales's hand writing, & which Lord Liverpool sent down to her a day or two before the conversation she had with the Prince Regent the 29 of Decr, was intended for Mr. St. Ledger,[1] & Pss Charlottes's sent by mistake to Mr. St. Ledger & that Mr. St. Ledger had sent his *letter* & at the same time encloses Pss Charlotte's letter which had been miss-directed to him.

Pss Charlotte told Pss Mary that the Pss of Wales says in her letter "if she could be of any use to her daughter she would return to England but that she believes it more prudent for herself as well as daughter to remain for the present abroad. She sends her daughter views of all the places she has stoped at & calls them her drawings, but Pss Charlotte says she knows they are Mr K. Cravens drawings & the names of the places are in his hand writing, though the Pss of Wales has wrote over some of the names in her own hand writing. She said "I am sure the only thing for my mother is to keep abroad, & *should it ever come to her* being *ordered to* remain abroad I should hope then all intercourse between us will *entierly cease* & that no corespandance even will be allowed, for after what has passed the Prince never can let me see her again or do I *now* wish *it myself*. I asked her if when she put an end to the corespondance between herself & Captn Hesse if it was from any alarm she had had, or from the advice of *the friend* who told her she must put a stop to it. She said she had heard from authority she could not doubt, that the Pss of Wales had been imprudent enough to talk of her & Hesse, & that decided her to take the advice of a friend & to confess the scrape & fright she was in, & the *publications* in the newspapers coming out at the same time had alarmed her still more, & added "& now I see clearly my mother's object was to bring this boy forwards. Upon which I replyed, but as long as the Prince lives that child can be of no consequence—"So the Prince thinks but I am not so sure of that." Upon my saying I believe the Prince can prove he has not been for *many* years under the same roof with the Pss,—Pss Charlotte replyed "The Pss of Wales has been at Carlton House since she had Black Heath & though I was very young I am sure I remember seeing Captn Manby & Miss Manby his sister at Carlton House, & added, for Sir S. Smith you know was a favourite long before Capn. Manby & my idea is that Edwardina Kent[2] was his child".

1 Colonel Anthony Butler St Leger, Chamberlain to the Princess of Wales, 1808–19.

2 "The girl I took by a very romantic accident", the Princess told Lady Charlotte Campbell. "In the time of the disturbances in Ireland, a man and woman, apparently of the better class, left a female infant with a poor old peasant woman who lives at Blackheath, and with the infant, a sum of money sufficient to support it a certain time; but the time elapsed, the money was spent, and no one came to supply the old woman with means for the babe's future

I said what makes you think that she is his child: "because she is very like him & has [? hair] black as ink".

I then enquired why she thought Captn Manby was the father of the boy. "*I am sure of it*" was her reply. I asked her why the Pss called the girl *Edwardina Kent*. "By way of a good joke."

The Queen's carriage was called for & we ended our conversation.

Original Paper forwarded to me & receiv'd by me, on the 1st of Jany 1815. G. P.R.

510 THE DUKE OF BRUNSWICK *to* PRINCESS CHARLOTTE

Brunsvic, ce 1me Jan. 1815.

J'OSE saisir avec empressement l'occasion du jour pour vous réitérer mes sentiments sincères d'attachement et les vœux que je forme continuellement pour votre bonheur, veuillez aussi agréer ceux, pour votre jour de naissance et croyez chère Charlotte qu'il n'y a personne qui puisse prendre un plus vif intérêt à tout ce qui vous concerne, que je le fais. Le Ciel vous accordera toute satisfaction possible dans cette nouvelle année et je ne doute que vous en profiterez avec prudence.

Je n'ai pas eu le plaisir de reçevoir de vos nouvelles depuis six mois, cependant j'ai été informé par les gazettes de votre retour du bain de mer, mais point encore de votre arrivée en ville, voilà où en sont mes nouvelles. La Duchesse d' Oldenbourg m'a parlé de vous à plusieurs reprises et j'ai été étonné qu'elle était si bien instruite sur tout ce qui vous concerne: c'est une femme intriguante, elle tache de tirer profit de tout, et on la blâme beaucoup, d'avoir occasionner le divorce du Prince de Würtemberg, il a à son retour en Allemagne renvoyé de but en blanc sa femme, sans raison quelconque, et s'en est fait séparer, depuis cette affaire est arrangée à ce qu'on dit, et les gazettes en parlent ouvertement. Mes enfants sont auprès de ma belle mère, où je les avais amenés pour les présenter, mais le petit étant tombé malade et l'Impératrice de Russie désirant à les voir, j'ai dû consentir de les y laisser jusqu'à cet époque; depuis il a paru que les négociations du Congrès à Vienne ne finiraient point à l'amicale et de tout part il a paru qu'on se préparait à une nouvelle guerre, je crus sous ces circonstances de ne pouvoir mieux faire, qu'en demandant la permission au Prince votre père de permettre que mes

exigencies; so she came to me and told her story....At first I thought of putting the child to the parish, but somehow I could not bear that, so it ended in my taking charge of the infant entirely at my own expense...."

enfants, en ce cas osent retourner en Angleterre, cependant j'ai osé observer, qu'il n'était pas question d'être à charge au Gouvernement, pour leur subsistance, puisque je comptais de faire fournir à mes enfants les dépenses de leurs entertien, par mon banquier.

L'incertitude des évènements me met souvant dans un état assez désagréable, cependant j'ai tout préparé pour faire face à la force, le point de dispute roule sur l'indépendance de la Pologne, et que la Saxe doit être rendû à son maître, je suis de ceux avec l'Empereur d'Autriche et tous les Princes, pour la réstitution de ces Empires, la Russie et la Prusse sont contre ces demandes et on craint qu'une guerre s'en suivera, ce qui serait d'autant plus fâcheux, comme la France veut joindre les intérêts de ces Princes, mais guidée par son intérêt de regagner à cet occasion la rive gauche du Rhin.

Je crains de vous ennuyer avec tous ces détailles, qui ne peuvent être d'auqu'un intérêt pour vous. Le Duc de Cambridge est bien portant, i'ai été le voir, il me parait qu'il commence à se plaire et je suis bien aise de trouver en lui un sincère et bon cousin. Adieu, veuillez m'accorder la continuation de vos bonnes grâces et vous persuader que rien n'égale mes sentiments d'attachement inviolable, avec lequel je suis [etc.].

511 THE PRINCE REGENT *to* PRINCESS MARY

Brighton, Jan 2d. 1815.

A THOUSAND thanks, my beloved Mary, for your kind letter, with the papers contained in it, which I receiv'd yesterday in perfect safety; but which I had not a moment to acknowledge until now. The long paper I do, & mean to keep, unless you should wish me to return it to you, for you yourself to preserve, & in which case, should you desire me to do so, I will send it you back by return of post.

With respect to the remark you have made, of not having set down with the rest, what pass'd between you & Charlotte in your subsequent tête a tête conversation with her, it shall be exactly as you please, & I do not think it is any way very material (provided you make a separate note of that) whether it makes a paper of itself, or is embodied with the other conversations.

Though I have some little doubt, whether upon the footing upon which you & Charlotte & my self *now* stand, & the understanding which prevail'd between us through all these conversations, of their being perfectly frank, open & voluntary in their nature without any reserve or concealment in any of the parties, consequently that there is, & was no secret, nor anything that was to be kept back or behind; & as I also had a tête tête communication with Miss Mercer whilst you was left alone with Charlotte, & the whole of which conversation *I* stated *verbatim* to *you & Charlotte* when I return'd to you both in the room where I had left you. I repeat that I entertain therefore some little doubt whether upon this statement, & with this consideration, it would not be more desireable & preferable to keep the whole in one Paper together than that Charlotte should have room to fancy or suppose it possible that either I have, after you being so principal a person in our first interview, any reserve or concealment upon this particular subject, or in whatever relates to it, from *you*, or that you on the other hand can or ought to have any such mistaken notion or feeling towards me. But, after having now first suggested this to you, my beloved Mary, I shall not trouble you further upon it at present, but let you turn it over in your mind at your leisure, & then decide upon it as you think upon further consideration is best & most eligible, & with which decision whichever way that may be on your part, I shall be most perfectly satisfied, as no one can entertain a higher opinion than I do of the solidity, accuracy & integrity, of your good sense, judgment & understanding in all occurrences of life, as I have had so many proofs of them, which have long made me make up my mind completely upon these heads. And now adieu my dear angel for as I have been too short a time here to have any thing either of novelty or interest to tell you from hence, I shall not tresspass any longer upon you, but conclude with every assurance of how truly & sincerely I am [etc.].

P.S. My best duty & love where you know I wish them to be presented.

CAMBRIDGE: PRINTED BY
W. LEWIS, M.A.
AT THE UNIVERSITY PRESS